MW01703201

COMMUNICATION

MAKING CONNECTIONS

CUSTOM EDITION FOR BERGEN COMMUNITY COLLEGE

TAKEN FROM:

COMMUNICATION: MAKING CONNECTIONS, SIXTH EDITION
BY WILLIAM J. SEILER AND MELISSA L. BEALL

THE INTERPERSONAL COMMUNICATION BOOK, TENTH EDITION
BY JOSEPH A. DEVITO

PEARSON
Custom Publishing

PEARSON
A and B

Cover Art: *Coral Panorama,* by Alisa Harding Stein.

Taken from:

Communication: Making Connections, Sixth Edition
by William J. Seiler and Melissa L. Beall

Published by Allyn and Bacon, Inc.
Boston, Massachusetts 02116

The Interpersonal Communication Book, Tenth Edition
by Joseph A. Devito

Published by Allyn and Bacon, Inc.

This special edition published in cooperation with Pearson Custom Publishing.

Printed in the United States of America

10 9 8 7 6 5 4 3

ISBN 0-536-83110-6

2004560021

AP

Please visit our web site at *www.pearsoncustom.com*

PEARSON CUSTOM PUBLISHING
75 Arlington Street, Suite 300, Boston, MA 02116
A Pearson Education Company

Contents

CHAPTER 2 Connecting Perceptions and Communication 28

CHAPTER 3 Connecting Self and Communication 54

CHAPTER 4 Connecting through Verbal Communication 78

PART TWO
Connecting in the Public Context

CHAPTER 11 Informative Speaking 286

CHAPTER 12 Persuasive Speaking 316

PART THREE

Connecting in Relational Contexts

CHAPTER 13 Interpersonal Communication 348

CHAPTER 13A Culture in Interpersonal Communication 13A

CHAPTER 14 Developing Relationships 376

CHAPTER 15 Group and Team Communication 410

CHAPTER 16 Participating in Groups and Teams 436

CHAPTER 17 Connecting to Mediated and Mass Communication

available online at www.ablongman.com/seiler6e

CHAPTER 18 Connecting in the Organizational Context

available online at www.ablongman.com/seiler6e

APPENDIX Employment Interviewing: Preparing for Your Future 463

Index 485

Preface

Communication: Making Connections is about communication and the way it connects us to others in our everyday lives. As authors, we made our first communication connection at the University of Nebraska in Lincoln a good number of years ago. We grew up in different states, had very different family backgrounds, and took our first courses in communication studies at very different universities. Yet we both had the same thoughts related to this experience: "Wow! This field is not only interesting, it's useful—something that we can use in our lives."

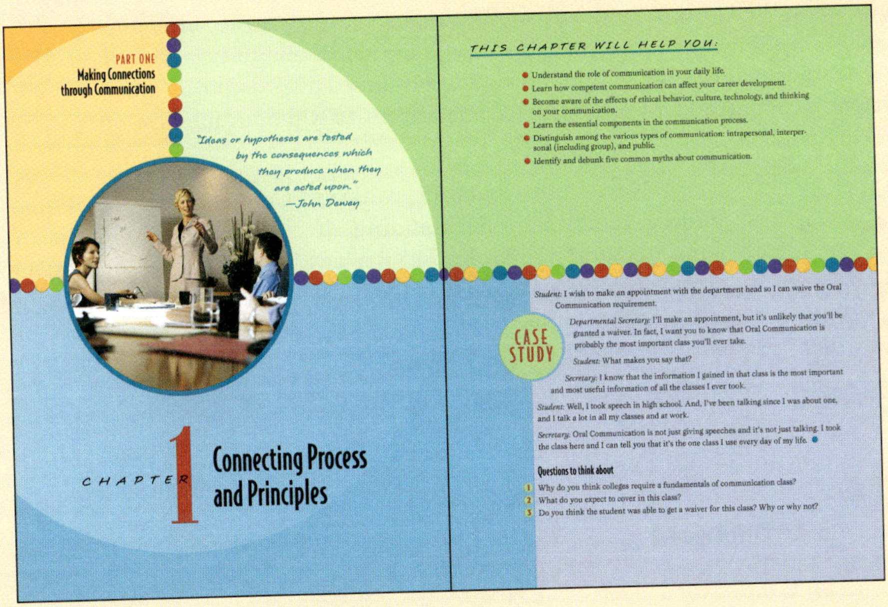

Several decades have passed since we first had those thoughts, but we are more convinced of them today than ever. We came together to write this book because we both love the introductory communication course. Our overall theme in this edition, as in the previous editions, remains "helping students make connections between communication and their daily lives."

Our Goals for the Sixth Edition

Because we want this book to help students become more competent communicators in a variety of contexts, we emphasize theory and up-to-date research as it relates to practical application and concrete communicative skills. Our purpose is to help students learn communication principles, as well as practical public speaking, interpersonal communication, and group communication skills, that they can use in the years ahead.

Our goal was to write an enjoyable, yet comprehensive, practical, readable, and intellectually sound book. We have also made every effort in this edition, as in previous editions, to provide very practical connections between theory, research, and skills, so the reader is challenged but not overwhelmed. How have we tried to accomplish this goal? Primarily by fine-tuning the features that have worked well in previous editions, by adding several new ones to the book, and by updating content throughout with new research and examples.

Changes in the Sixth Edition

The sixth edition, like its predecessors, represents input from many talented and helpful individuals. We listened not only to those who reviewed our text and draft chapters but also to the many students and instructors who have used our text. We want to assure you that the changes, although substantial, did not take away from the strengths that so many have said they enjoyed in our previous editions—and for that we are very grateful. Here are some of the most obvious changes that we made:

- **Many new quotations and case studies at the beginning of each chapter help to make the content come alive.** We expanded the scenario concept to become a case study with questions, all of which are action oriented and relevant to what is happening in students' lives. In addition, the questions posed after each case study relate to the chapter's content and invite students to analyze critically the communication scenario before they read the chapter.

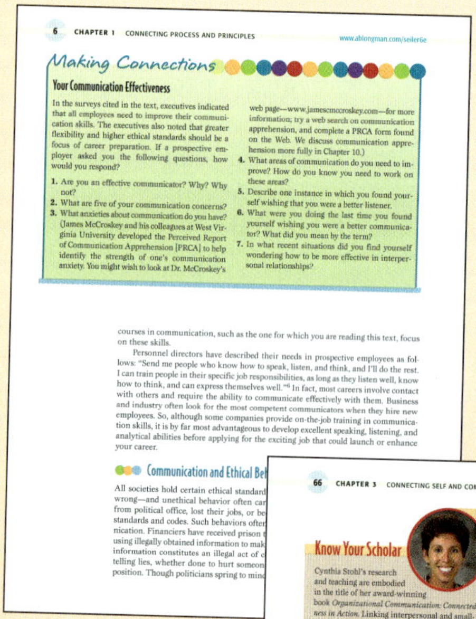

6 CHAPTER 1 CONNECTING PROCESS AND PRINCIPLES www.ablongman.com/seiler6e

Making Connections

Your Communication Effectiveness

In the surveys cited in the text, executives indicated that all employees need to improve their communication skills. The executives also noted that greater flexibility and higher ethical standards should be a focus of career preparation. If a prospective employer asked you the following questions, how would you respond?

1. Are you an effective communicator? Why? Why not?
2. What are five of your communication concerns?
3. What anxieties about communication do you have? (James McCroskey and his colleagues at West Virginia University developed the Perceived Report of Communication Apprehension [PRCA] to help identify the strength of one's communication anxiety. You might wish to look at Dr. McCroskey's web page—www.jamescmccroskey.com—for more information; try a web search on communication apprehension, and complete a PRCA form found on the Web. We discuss communication apprehension more fully in Chapter 10.)
4. What areas of communication do you need to improve? How do you know you need to work on these areas?
5. Describe one instance in which you found yourself wishing that you were a better listener.
6. What were you doing the last time you found yourself wishing you were a better communicator? What did you mean by the term?
7. In what recent situations did you find yourself wondering how to be more effective in interpersonal relationships?

courses in communication, such as the one for which you are reading this text, focus on these skills.

Personnel directors have described their needs in prospective employees as follows: "Send me people who know how to speak, listen, and think, and I'll do the rest. I can train people in their specific job responsibilities, as long as they listen well, know how to think, and can express themselves well."[6] In fact, most careers involve contact with others and require the ability to communicate effectively with them. Business and industry often look for the most competent communicators when they hire new employees. So, although some companies provide on-the-job training in communication skills, it is by far most advantageous to develop excellent speaking, listening, and analytical abilities before applying for the exciting job that could launch or enhance your career.

Communication and Ethical Be

All societies hold certain ethical standard wrong—and unethical behavior often car from political office, lost their jobs, or be standards and codes. Such behaviors ofter nication. Financiers have received prison using illegally obtained information to mak information constitutes an illegal act of c telling lies, whether done to hurt someon position. Though politicians spring to min

- **New and updated Making Connections boxes enhance students' understanding of communication theories, concepts, and principles.** We reviewed each Making Connections box for its relevance and for how it would aid students in becoming more critical thinkers as well as competent communicators. The boxes have been arranged on the page near the related discussion, but in a way that does not interrupt the flow of the text.

66 CHAPTER 3 CONNECTING SELF AND COMMUNICATION www.ablongman.com/seiler6e

Know Your Scholar

Cynthia Stohl *University of California, Santa Barbara*

Cynthia Stohl's research and teaching are embodied in the title of her award-winning book *Organizational Communication: Connectedness in Action.* Linking interpersonal and small-group communication processes to larger structural and cultural systems, Professor Stohl develops a global perspective on organizational communication. Building on her early work on the development of communicative competence and young children's social networks in daycare centers, Dr. Stohl's research explores the ways in which interpersonal, group, and organizational communication processes are embedded in overlapping networks of relationships that transcend personal and organizational boundaries.

In 1995, Dr. Stohl wrote, "It is through communication we evolve our culture, our social structure, our world views and shape our perceptions of what is and what could be. . . . To conceive of the world in terms of our communicative connections produces exciting possibilities and great responsibilities." Throughout her work, Dr. Stohl reminds us of the ethical dimensions of communication structures and practices.

Dr. Stohl is a Professor of Communication at the University of California, Santa Barbara. Before moving to Santa Barbara, she was the Margaret Church Distinguished Professor of Communication at Purdue University. She is the recipient of several teaching and research awards, including the 1998 National Communication Association's Organizational Communication Division "Best Article" award for "Democracy, Participation, and Communication at Work," an article she co-authored with Dr. George Cheney.

Self-Fulfilling Prophecy and Impression Management

In addition to values, attitudes, and beliefs, expectations determine how we behave, who we eventually become, and what we communicate to others and ourselves. Our own expectations and those of others influence our perceptions and behavior. Thus our self-concept is affected by our past experiences, our interactions with others, the expectations others have of us, and how we present ourselves to create an image.

Self-Fulfilling Prophecy

Expectations we have of ourselves or that others have of us help to create conditions that lead us to act in predictable ways. The expectation becomes a **self-fulfilling prophecy.**[7] The expectations that are placed on us by ourselves or others can be a powerful force for shaping our self-concept. A research study asked college students who were either characteristically optimistic or generally pessimistic to describe their future selves.[8] According to the research, both types of students could imagine a positive future, but the optimistic students had higher expectations about actually attaining a positive possible self than did those who were pessimistic. Thus we are more likely to succeed if we believe that we have the potential for success. By the same token, we are more likely to fail if we believe ourselves to be failures.

Self-esteem can have effects on the prophecies people make about themselves. It is a matter of attribution: People with positive high self-esteem confidently attribute their success to past successes; therefore they expect to succeed in the future. People with low self-esteem, however, attribute any success they might have had to luck and

self-fulfilling prophecy Expectations we have of ourselves or that others have of us that help to create the conditions that lead us to act in predictable ways.

- **A new feature, Know Your Scholar, brings research to life.** We have highlighted the research of some of the most prolific and influential scholars in the communication discipline. We tried to balance our selection of scholars in order to provide a variety of those who have contributed research and knowledge to our discipline. The purpose of this feature, which is found in several chapters, is to introduce undergraduates to several influential communication researchers and to put a human face on communication scholarship. We believe it is important for students to know that what they are reading is based on research and that the research was done by communication scholars. We are convinced that if instructors promote the Know Your Scholar feature and if students take the time to learn about the scholars, they will have a greater understanding of the people in our discipline and the role communication research plays in what they are learning.

- **Learning Connections questions, new to this edition, ask students to think about what they have read.** These ques-

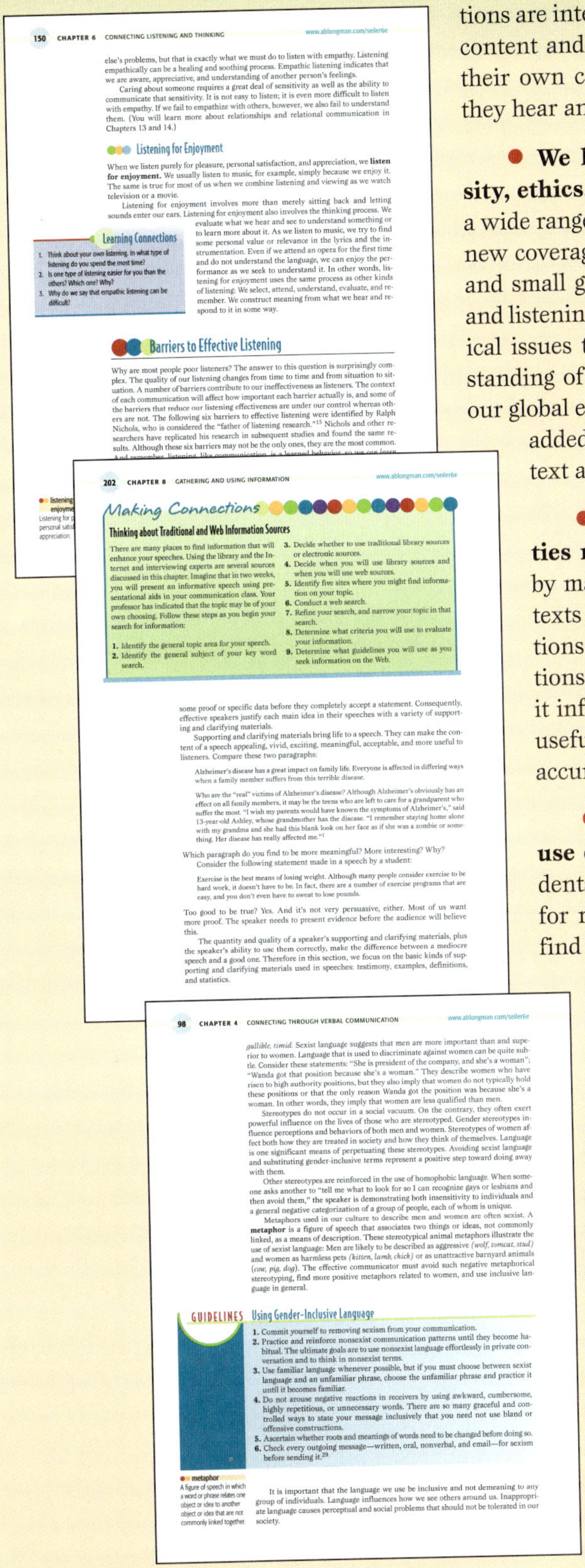

tions are intended to get students to think more specifically about the content and how they can make the connections that will improve their own communication as well as their understanding of what they hear and read.

- **We have expanded coverage of gender, cultural diversity, ethics, and critical thinking.** We added examples relevant to a wide range of students, including nontraditional students. There is new coverage of gender differences in interpersonal, presentational, and small group communication; new coverage of critical thinking and listening; and a much more balanced coverage of cultural and ethical issues throughout the text in order to provide a better understanding of the communication competencies needed to succeed in our global environment. We expanded critical thinking exercises and added many new thought-provoking questions throughout the text and in new end-of-chapter discussion questions.

- **We have integrated more information and activities related to technology.** Our last edition was considered by many to be a leader and a model for other communication texts in the area of technology.We have added even more sections exclusively related to technology and its practical applications in order to help students learn about technology and how it influences communication in their lives. We included many useful Internet sites, which we thoroughly checked to ensure accuracy and accessibility.

- **We updated and expanded coverage of the proper use of the Internet for research in Chapter 8.** Many students, for better or worse, use the Internet as a default option for researching their speeches. This section explains how to find information by using a search engine. Instructors who want to give even greater attention to the Internet can do so with the *Allyn & Bacon Research Navigator Guide for Speech Communication,* which is available as a supplement to *Communication: Making Connections.* Used together, these resources provide the most up-to-date, thorough, and helpful coverage of the Internet available with any introductory textbook.

- **Coverage of online discussion is included in the small group chapters.** We discuss the research relevant to online discussions and how they can be used, as well as their advantages and disadvantages. This information instructs students on how they can make the most of online discussions.

- **Guidelines boxes help students become competent communicators.** The Guidelines feature offers examples and raises questions about what it takes to be a competent communicator. Students are asked more frequently in this edition to assess their communication competence by responding to questions or measures that evaluate their communication competencies and to follow guidelines on what they can do to improve.

- **We have revised the section on public communication.** New examples and explanations are provided in each chapter. The focus is on the listener and demonstrates how the speaker needs to "think like a listener" in order to be an effective public communicator.

- **Updates include the most recent research and examples.** When appropriate, actual research studies and the names of important researchers have been added to help students understand the relationship between content and the research that supports it.

- **The updated appendix, "Interviewing: Preparing for Your Future," includes more information on online job searches, preparation for the employment interview, and many other aspects of the employment interview.** It contains information specifically written for first- or second-year students to help prepare them for their futures. Nevertheless, the information in the appendix is useful to all students because it addresses many of the important issues involved in preparing for and participating in the employment interview. It also has one of the best sections on using the Internet for job searches and résumé development of any introductory communication textbook.

- **Discussion Starters provide springboards for class discussion.** Almost all of the discussion starters at the end of each chapter have been revised so that they build on the Learning Connection boxes included in each chapter. The goal of the discussion starters is to provide another vehicle to get students to actively discuss and apply what they have read in each chapter.

- **A new design makes the text even more appealing and readable.** A colorful and appealing new design visually conveys the making connections theme while being readable and student friendly.

- **Many new photos and updated contemporary examples of communication situations were added to bolster existing examples and to make the content relevant to all students.** Captions link the images to the chapter content so that photos become important examples of communication concepts and principles to help the students learn.

Content Changes in the Sixth Edition

Part I: Making Connections through Communication (Chapters 1 through 6)

- We increased the focus on communication competence and how communication helps students make connections between what they are learning and their lives during and after college. Chapter 1 provides the initial focus on communication competence and on how communication helps students make connections between this course and the other courses in their academic careers. Communication examples and features draw from a diverse variety of contemporary situations and issues that allow students to use concepts and principles and apply them to their own lives.

- We added a new section on understanding perception, which includes awareness and verbal communication influences on perception. Additional coverage includes discussions on cultural background and its influence on perception, a new section on cultural myopia, additional research on gender and perception differences, and a new section on the impact of the Internet on perception. Finally, in order to help students understand the significant role perception plays in their everyday communication, we expanded the section on perception checking and on being a competent communicator.

- We expanded the discussion on understanding self-concept and its influence on our communications. New and expanded sections on impression management, culture and self-concept, new models to help explain the eight components of self-concept, and a further expansion and update of relevant research related to gender and self-concept have been included.

- A revised section on the power of language adds the concept of everyday talk, revises the section on how language affects thought, adds muted group theory related to power and affect of language, revises the section on words, and updates the section on slang.

- A new section offers reasons why we should study nonverbal communication, including a revised section on facial expressions and the impact they have on our communication, a new discussion on silence and cultural differences related to silence, and a new section on smell communication.

- A revised section on stages of effective listening includes the HURIER model. Two new Guidelines boxes, one for short-term memory and another for long-term memory strategies, plus a new section on intercultural listening and additional job/career life examples, help illustrate the importance of effective listening.

Part II: Connecting in the Public Context (Chapters 7 through 12)

- We added more emphasis on the value and incidence of the principles of public speaking to all areas of life. Our coverage of the use of web-based sources and electronic databases has been expanded, and we now have more emphasis on thinking about what the listener wants and needs to hear.

- We expanded our emphasis on the numerous sources for one's speech. The section on finding and recording information is updated with current examples from recent events.

- We integrated new sample classroom speeches into the chapters, complete with teaching annotations. All new explanations about organizational strategies are presented as well as new guidelines for outlining and for organizing the speech.

- We provided numerous new visuals and new examples of the various types of presentational aids. Text descriptions and examples of line drawings, tables, graphs, and computer-generated visual aids are offered.

- We updated and refreshed the informative and persuasive chapters to include up-to-date examples and more applications of these two types of speeches to everyday life. In addition, persuasion is now integrated throughout the text.

Part III: Connecting in Relational Contexts (Chapters 13 through 16 and the Appendix)

- We revised the section on interpersonal communication and relationships, added new guidelines for more effective small talk, completely revised the section on online relationships, revised and updated the section on why we self-disclose, and added a new section on when we should not self-disclose too much.

- We revised the section on culture and attraction, added a new section on managing relational tensions, expanded the section on what causes interpersonal conflict, added a new section on whether conflict has to be destructive and when conflict is beneficial. We also revised the section on strategies for managing and resolving interpersonal conflict and revised the section on improving interpersonal communication competence in relationships.

- We added a new section on types and purposes of small group communication, which is more relevant to students. We added more on ethical group behavior, which includes guidelines for students to follow. We also expanded the discussion of the disadvantages of small groups, added a new section on goal setting in groups, and updated the coverage of leadership styles and behavior, including leadership and gender differences. Finally, we added a new section on reaching consensus in groups.

Features

Effectiveness in speech communication is an acquired skill. Although natural speaking ability is an asset, any person's capabilities in communication can be improved through (1) an understanding of communicative theories and principles, (2) training in its basic principles, (3) practice, and (4) improving communication competence. This edition meets students' needs in all four areas by providing:

- Actively stated and specific learning objectives at the beginning of each chapter that will help students focus on what they will learn.
- Case studies that allow students to think critically about communication and its effects on their lives.
- Thorough and systematic explanations of basic principles.
- Thought-provoking Making Connections boxes that encourage students' active involvement throughout each chapter.
- Clear, concrete, student-oriented examples, photos, cartoons, and other visual materials that support and expand on key concepts.
- Learning Connections boxes that ask students to critically think about, synthesize, and apply what they have read.
- Lists of down-to-earth hints and guidelines that help students transform theory into practice.
- End-of-chapter summaries that review key concepts.
- Discussion starter questions that engage students to think critically and apply what they have learned.
- Key terms defined in the margins.

Organization

As in all previous editions, the chapters are arranged to provide a practical and workable approach to teaching the fundamentals of communication. Part One, "Making Connections through Communication," provides the necessary background and basic principles for all communication. Part Two, "Connecting in the Public Context," helps students develop their speaking skills as they learn to select a topic, analyze an audience, gather and use supporting and clarifying materials, organize and outline speech material, deliver a speech with confidence, and inform and persuade an audience effectively. Part Three, "Connecting in Relational Contexts," describes communication in relationships and in small groups and teams. Two bonus chapters, Chapter 17, "Connecting to Mediated and Mass Communication," and Chapter 18, "Connecting in the Organizational Context," are available in electronic format on the Companion Website, www.ablongman.com/seiler6e.

Foundations are presented first. Then public communication skills are discussed, followed by interpersonal and group communication. We discuss public communication skills before interpersonal communication because we believe that they are fundamental to all communication. All communication is goal-oriented. Therefore, in order to communicate effectively throughout life—whether socially, on the job, in one-to-one situations, in small groups, or before an audience—a person must be able to communicate with confidence, support and clarify his or her thoughts, organize information, analyze those with whom he or she is communicating, and inform and persuade effectively. This sequence of presentation is also based on the recognition that, although students in an introductory communication course must master a great deal of basic information before they give a speech, because of time constraints they need to begin preparing and presenting speeches as early in the term as possible. Introducing public speaking skills first provides a more even balance between speech presentations and other activities and alleviates the tendency to focus on speechmaking exclusively at the end of the term.

Considerable demands are placed on the introductory communication course, and as a result, there are a wide variety of ways to teach the course—by emphasizing interpersonal communication, emphasizing public speaking, or by placing equal emphasis on all types of communication. To meet these differing needs, each chapter is completely self-contained so that an instructor can easily arrange the emphasis and sequence to meet the demands of his or her specific teaching situation.

Supplements for the Instructor

Print Resources

- ***Instructor's Resource Manual*** by Melissa Beall and Marilyn Shaw. This provides nut-and-bolts information about designing and developing an introductory communication course and methods for aiding instruction. Included in the manual are suggestions for managing and organizing the course; classroom as well as outside-classroom exercises and assignments; resources for instruction, including additional readings, games, simulations, and films; a section on evaluating speeches; a section on training and working with part-time instructors and graduate teaching assistants; and finally, a section on the Personalized System of Instruction, which is an efficient and effective method for teaching the introductory course.

- ***Test Bank*** by Paul Schrodt, University of Texas at Arlington. Completely revised, the test bank contains multiple-choice, true/false, and short answer questions for each chapter. All questions are referenced by text chapter and page number and include an indicator of difficulty.

- ***A Guide for New Teachers of Introduction to Communication*, Second Edition,** by Susanna G. Porter, Kennesaw State University. This guide helps new teachers teach the introductory course effectively. It covers topics such as preparing for the term, planning and structuring your course, evaluating speeches, utilizing the textbook, integrating technology into the classroom, dealing with challenges, and much more. A resource matrix at the end of the guide outlines how best to utilize the guide with *Communication: Making Connections,* Sixth Edition.

- ***Blockbuster Approach: A Guide to Teaching Interpersonal Communication with Video,* Third Edition,** by Thomas Jewell, Bergen Community College. This guide provides lists and descriptions of commercial videos that can be used in the classroom to illustrate interpersonal concepts and complex interpersonal relationships. Sample activities are also included.

- ***ESL Guide to Public Speaking,*** by Debra Gonsher Vinik, Bronx Community College of the City University of New York. This guide provides strategies and resources for instructors teaching in bilingual or multilingual classrooms. It also includes suggestions for further reading and a listing of related websites.

- ***Great Ideas for Teaching Speech (GIFTS),* Third Edition,** by Raymond Zeuschner, California Polytechnic State University. This book provides descriptions of and guidelines for assignments successfully used by experienced public speaking instructors in their classrooms.

- ***Allyn & Bacon Public Speaking Transparency Package.*** This package, which contains 100 public speaking transparencies created with PowerPoint™ software, is available to provide visual support for classroom lectures and discussion on a full range of course topics. An expanded version is available at www.ablongman.com/suppscentral.

Electronic Resources

- ***Computerized Test Bank.*** The printed test questions are also available electronically through our computerized testing system, TestGen EQ. The fully networkable test generating software is now available on a multiplatform CD-ROM. The user-friendly interface enables instructors to view, edit, and add questions; transfer questions to tests; and print tests in a variety of fonts. Search and sort features allow instructors to locate questions quickly and arrange them in a preferred order.

- ***PowerPoint™ Package,*** prepared by Paul Lakey, Abilene Christian University. This text-specific package consists of a collection of lecture outlines and graphic images keyed to every chapter in the text. Available on our website at www.ablongman.com/suppscentral.

- ***VideoWorkshop for Introduction to Communication: A Course-Tailored Video Learning System*** (www.ablongman.com/videoworkshop), by Edward Lee Lamoureux, Bradley University. *VideoWorkshop for Introduction to Communication* is a new way to bring video into your course for maximized learning. This total teaching and learning system includes quality video footage on an easy-to-use CD-ROM, plus a Student Learning Guide and an Instructor's Teaching Guide—both with textbook-specific correlation grids. The result? A program that brings textbook concepts to life with ease and that helps your students understand, analyze, and apply the objectives of the course. *VideoWorkshop* is available for your students as a value-pack option with this textbook.

- ***Allyn & Bacon Communication Studies Digital Media Archive, Version 2.0,*** available on CD-ROM, offers more than 200 still images, video excerpts, and PowerPoint™ slides that can be used to enliven classroom presentations.

- ***CourseCompass for Introduction to Communication.*** CourseCompass, powered by Blackboard and hosted nationally, is Allyn & Bacon's own course management system. CourseCompass helps you manage all aspects of teaching your course. The Introduction to Communication course features preloaded content such as quiz questions, video clips, instructor's manuals, PowerPoint™ presentations, still images, course preparation and instruction materials, *VideoWorkshop for Introduction to Communication,* weblinks, and much more. CourseCompass provides an abundance of resources to help you teach and manage your class effectively in the CourseCompass environment. Go to www.coursecompass.com for more information.

Video Materials

Allyn & Bacon has an extensive collection of video materials available for use in teaching the Introduction to Communication course. Some restrictions apply. See your sales representative for details.

- ***Allyn & Bacon Student Speeches Video Library.*** This video library includes three two-hour American Forensic Association videos composed of award-winning student speeches and three videos containing a range of student speeches delivered in the classroom.
- ***Allyn & Bacon Public Speaking Video.*** This video includes excerpts of classic and contemporary speeches as well as student speeches that illustrate aspects of the public speaking process.
- ***Allyn & Bacon Public Speaking Key Topics Video Library.*** This library contains three videos that address core topics covered in the classroom: Critiquing Student Speeches, Speaker Apprehension, and Addressing Your Audience.
- ***Allyn & Bacon Communication Video Library.*** This video library contains a collection of communication videos produced by Film for the Humanities and Sciences.
- ***Allyn & Bacon Interpersonal Communication Video, Volume Two.*** This thirty-minute video presents a variety of different scenarios that portray interpersonal concepts and relationships. A user's guide accompanies the video and contains scripts, discussion questions, and exercises for each scenario.
- ***Allyn & Bacon Interpersonal Communication Video.*** This video features three scenarios that illustrate concepts in interpersonal communication. A user's guide provides a script and discussion questions.
- ***Allyn & Bacon Video: Interpersonal Communication.*** Eight interpersonal scenarios examine a wide range of interpersonal issues. An extensive guidebook provides a script, class discussion questions, and exercises for each of the episodes.

Student Supplements

Print Resources

- ***Research Navigator Guide for Speech Communication,*** by Terrence Doyle, Northern Virginia Community College, and Linda R. Barr, University of the Virgin Islands. This free reference guide includes tips, resources, activities, and URLs to help students. Part 1 introduces students to the basics of the Internet. Part 2 includes over thirty Net activities that tie into the content of the text. Part 3 lists hundreds of Internet resources for speech communication. The guide also includes information on how to cite research correctly and a guide to building an online glossary. In addition, the Research Navigator booklet contains a student access code for the Research Navigator database, offering students free, unlimited access to a collection of 25,000 discipline-specific articles from top-tier academic publications and peer-reviewed journals, as well as popular news publications and the *New York Times.* This is available free when packaged with any Allyn & Bacon text. (Some restrictions apply.)

- ***Speech Preparation Workbook,*** by Jennifer Dreyer and Gregory H. Patton, San Diego State University. This workbook takes students through the various stages of speech creation—from audience analysis to writing the speech—and provides guidelines, tips, and easy-to-fill-in pages. This product is available for student purchase or is available free when value-packed with any Allyn & Bacon text. (Some restrictions apply.)

- ***Preparing Visual Aids for Presentations,* Second Edition,** by Dan Cavanaugh. This thirty-two-page booklet provides a host of ideas for using today's multimedia tools to improve presentations. It includes suggestions for how to plan a presentation, guidelines for designing visual aids and storyboarding, and a walkthrough that shows how to prepare a visual display using PowerPoint™. This product is available for student purchase or is available free when value-packed with any Allyn & Bacon text. (Some restrictions apply.)

- ***Public Speaking in the Multicultural Environment,* Second Edition,** by Deborah A. Lieberman, Portland State University. This product includes activities to help students think about the effects that the diverse backgrounds of audience members can have, not only on how speeches are prepared and delivered but also on how those speeches are perceived. It is available for student purchase or is available free when value-packed with any Allyn & Bacon text. (Some restrictions apply.)

- ***Outlining Workbook,*** by Reese Hanson and Sharon Condon, Haskell Indian Nations University. This workbook includes activities, exercises, and answers to help students develop and master the critical skill of outlining. This product is available for student purchase or is available free when value-packed with any Allyn & Bacon text. (Some restrictions apply.)

- ***Personalized System of Instruction (PSI) Study Guide Manual.*** This manual provides students with questions and exercises to aid them in studying. The manual is designed for use at the University of Nebraska–Lincoln, but could be modified or changed to meet different uses. For a sample manual, contact Bill Seiler, Department of Communication Studies, University of Nebraska–Lincoln, Lincoln, Nebraska 68588-0329, or call (402) 472-2069 or e-mail bseiler@unl.edu.

Electronic Resources

- ***Companion Website with Online Practice Tests.*** This text-specific site provides Web links for the Internet resources in the Making Connections boxes, online learning objectives, flashcards, and a fully expanded set of practice tests for each chapter. Two additional electronic chapters, Chapter 17, "Connecting to Mediated and Mass Communication," and Chapter 18, "Connecting in the Organizational Context," are available for download, as well as the complete text of "What Every College Student Should Know to Prepare for the Job Interview." This site can be accessed at www.ablongman.com/seiler6e.

- ***Allyn & Bacon Communication Studies Web Site,*** by Terrence Doyle, Northern Virginia Community College, and Tim Borchers, Moorehead State University. This site includes modules on interpersonal communication, small group communication, and public speaking. It includes web links, enrichment materials, and interactive activities to enhance students' understanding of key concepts. Access this site at www.ablongman.com/commstudies.

- ***Interactive Speechwriter Software, Version 1.1,*** by Martin R. Cox. Allyn & Bacon's Interactive Speechwriter Software contains sample speeches, tutorials, self-test questions on key concepts, and templates for writing informative, persuasive, and motivated sequence speeches. This product is available for student purchase or is available free when value-packed with any Allyn & Bacon text. (Some restrictions apply.)

- ***Speech Writer's Workshop CD-ROM, Version 2.0.*** This exciting public speaking software includes a *Speech Handbook* with tips for researching and preparing speeches; a *Speech Workshop,* which guides students step-by-step through the speech writing process; a *Topics Dictionary,* which gives students hundreds of ideas for speeches; and the *Documentor* citation database, which helps students format bibliographic entries in either MLA or APA style. This product is available for student purchase or is available free when value-packed with any Allyn & Bacon text. (Some restrictions apply.)

- ***VideoWorkshop for Introduction to Communication: A Course-Tailored Video Learning System*** (www.ablongman.com/videoworkshop), by Edward Lee Lamoureux, Bradley University. *VideoWorkshop for Introduction to Communication* includes quality video footage on an easy-to-use CD-ROM, plus a Student Learning Guide with textbook-specific correlation grids. The result? A program that brings textbook concepts to life with ease and that helps you understand, analyze, and apply the objectives of the course. This product is available free when value-packed with any Allyn & Bacon text. (Some restrictions apply.)

- ***Communication Tutor Center.*** (Access Code Required.) Our Tutor Center provides free, one-on-one tutoring for students who purchase a new copy of participating Allyn & Bacon textbooks. Qualified instructors tutor students on all material covered in the texts. The approach is highly interactive, providing both knowledge of the academic discipline and methods for study of that discipline. Tutoring assistance is offered by phone, fax, Internet, and email during Tutor Center hours. For more details and ordering information, please contact your Allyn & Bacon publisher's representative.

Acknowledgments

Numerous people have contributed to the previous editions as well as this edition of the book. First and foremost are the students who have shared their time and learning experiences with us, the instructors who patiently taught us about communication and life, the colleagues who have shared their expertise with us, the many graduate students who have worked in our basic speech courses over the years, and the hundreds of undergraduate assistants and assistant supervisory instructors who have assisted in the University of Nebraska's Personalized System of Instruction basic communication course during the past twenty-five years.

As with any project of this proportion, there are many people who helped make this edition possible. We extend our appreciation to Dr. Larry Routh, the Director of Career

Planning and Placement at the University of Nebraska–Lincoln, for his review and guidance in the writing of the Employment Interview appendix.

Special thanks go to Marilyn Shaw, instructor of the Introductory Communication course at the University of Northern Iowa, for assisting in writing the *Instructor's Resource Manual.* We would also like to thank Paul Schrodt, University of Texas at Arlington, for his help in revising the *Test Bank.* In addition to Marilyn and Paul, there have been many other faculty and graduate students—especially Diane Badzinski, Karla Bergen, Mary Bort, Chuck Braithwaite, Dawn Braithwaite, Ann Burnett, John Caughlin, Jeff Cook, Susan Cusmano-Reans, Linda Dickmeyer, Karen Durst, Gus Friedrich, Bobbi Harry, Adam Jones, Jack Kay, Karen Lee, Ronald Lee, Drew McGukin, Carol Morgan, Rob Patterson, Jack Sargent, Shawn Wahl, and Nicole Zumbach—who have helped us by providing ideas and suggestions too numerous to mention here. Finally, thanks go to all of the undergraduate and graduate students, as well as the students at University of Nebraska–Lincoln and the University of Northern Iowa, who provided resources and examples.

We are also grateful to Carol Alper, Senior Development Editor at Allyn and Bacon, for her guidance and her editing and developmental skills. It is Carol who puts her editorial skills to our manuscript to make it come alive as a textbook. We would also like to thank all those at Allyn and Bacon who had a hand in getting our manuscript into book form. We also thank Karon Bowers, Executive Editor (even though she is a huge Texas football fan), and Brian Wheel, Series Editor, for their continued support of our book.

The publishing of any book requires people dedicated to quality, and this book is no exception. We thank all those who participated in the review process of the first five editions of the book:

Philip M. Backlund, Central Washington University
William Patrick Barlow, Madison Area Technical College
Barbara L. Breaclen, Lane Community College
Scott Britten, Tiffin University
Allan R. Broadhurst, Cape Cod Community College
Michael Bruner, University of North Texas
Diane O. Casagrande, West Chester University
Patricia Comeaux, University of North Carolina at Wilmington
Juanita E. Dailey, University of Rio Grande
Carley H. Dodd, Abilene Christian University
Terrence Doyle, Northern Virginia Community College
Skip Eno, University of Texas at San Antonio
Jeanine Fassl, University of Wisconsin at Whitewater
Julia Fennell, Community College of Allegheny County, South Campus
Mary C. Forestieri, Lane Community College
Robert E. Frank, Morehead State University
Anne Grissom, Mountain View College
Kelby K. Halone, Clemson University
Ted Hindermarsh, Brigham Young University
Colleen Hogan-Taylor, University of Washington
David D. Hudson, Golden West College
Mary Lee Hummert, University of Kansas
Stephen K. Hunt, Illinois State University
Karla Kay Jensen, Nebraska Wesleyan University
Kathryn C. Jones, Northern Virginia Community College, Annandale Campus
Charles J. Korn, Northern Virginia Community College
Donald L. Loeffler, Western Carolina University

Mary Y. Mandeville, Oklahoma State University
Sharry Messer, Hawkeye Community College
Kay E. Neal, University of Wisconsin, Oshkosh
Nan Peck, Northern Virginia Community College
Sandra E. Presar, West Virginia Wesleyan College
Marlene M. Preston, Virginia Tech University
Richard G. Rea, University of Arkansas
Marc E. Routhier, Frostburg State College
Thomas E. Ruddick, Edison Community College
Marilyn M. Shaw, University of Northern Iowa
Cheri J. Simonds, Illinois State University
Beth Waggenspack, Virginia Polytechnic Institute and State University
Catherine Egley Waggoner, Ohio State University
Gretchen Aggertt Weber, Horry—Georgetown Technical College
Kathie A. Webster, Northwest Missouri State University
Larry A. Weiss, University of Wisconsin, Oshkosh
Cherie C. While, Muskingum Area Technical College

Finally, thanks to those who provided analysis of the fifth edition, suggested changes, and reviewed the sixth edition:

Marty Birkholt, Creighton University
Linda Y. Devenish, Ithaca College
Sean M. Dunn, Bridgewater College
Richard C. Emanuel, University of Montevallo
Thomas J. Knutson, California State University at Sacramento
Louis A. Lucca, La Guardia Community College (CUNY)
Corinne E. Morris, Northeast Community College
Nan Peck, Northern Virginia Community College
Donald B. Simmons, Asbury College
Mary Anne Trasciatti, Hofstra University
David W. Worley, Indiana State University

Some Concluding Comments, and a Request for Your Thoughts

It is time to ask for *your* help again. As we have in previous editions, we have spared no effort to make this new edition the best ever. While we are always looking for perfection, we realize that there is always room for improvement. In this respect, we sincerely request your comments. If there is something you feel can be improved, please let us know. Write, call, fax, or email us at the addresses below. We will listen, and we will respond to your comments as quickly as possible. Thanks in advance for your help.

Bill Seiler
Department of Communication Studies
University of Nebraska–Lincoln,
Lincoln, Nebraska 68588-0329
(402) 472-2197
bseiler@unl.edu

Melissa Beall
Department of Communication Studies
University of Northern Iowa
Cedar Falls, Iowa 50614-0357
(319) 273-2992
melissa.beall@uni.edu

About the Authors

Bill Seiler is currently Professor and Chair of the Department of Communication Studies at the University of Nebraska–Lincoln, where he has taught since 1972. He is an avid golfer who plays every chance he gets, which unfortunately is never enough (his excuse for not playing well). He loves his Nebraska Huskers and will travel to one or two "away" games each year. He has been married to his college sweetheart, Kathi, for over thity-five years. They live on a small acreage outside of Lincoln with their cat Jordan. Their two daughters, Dana and Dionne, no longer live at home.

Dr. Seiler received his bachelor's of education from the University of Wisconsin at Whitewater and his master's from Kansas State University. He received his doctorate from Purdue University and has an adjunct appointment in Teachers College as a professor of Curriculum and Instruction. He is an experienced educator, consultant, researcher, and author and has published numerous monographs, articles, and educational materials in the area of communication.

In addition, he has presented lectures and speeches throughout the Midwest. He has published two other textbooks, *Communication in Business and Professional Organizations* and *Communication for the Contemporary Classroom*. He has also served on editorial boards for several of his discipline's major research journals and has held a variety of offices in his discipline's professional associations.

Dr. Seiler has been honored as an Outstanding Educator of America, an Outstanding University and College Teacher by the Nebraska Communication Association, has received the Outstanding Young Alumni and Distinguished Alumni Awards from the University of Wisconsin at Whitewater (the only person to receive both awards in the university's history), has received the 2003 Boss of the Year Award at the university, and is listed in the *International Who's Who in Education*.

Dr. Seiler has been directing the introductory course at the University of Nebraska for over thirty years. He was one of the first people in the nation to use a Personalized System of Instruction (PSI) in a large, multiple-section basic communication course. Currently, the University of Nebraska–Lincoln teaches over a thousand students per year using the PSI method in the basic communication course.

Melissa Beall is a professor in the Communication Studies Department at the University of Northern Iowa. She came to UNI in 1990 as the Basic Course Director and is also a member of the teacher education faculty. Dr. Beall received all three of her degrees from the University of Nebraska–Lincoln and appreciates the fact that she has two home states, Iowa and Nebraska. Her expertise includes listening, communication education, communication and technology, and communication theory. She has taught at all levels, pre-kindergarten through adult education, and loves to teach. When she was a high school teacher in Nebraska, she taught English, theatre, speech, and debate; directed plays; and coached the speech and debate teams. In her spare time, she taught classes at the University of Nebraska–Lincoln and Doane College–Lincoln. At UNI, she teaches Oral Communication and other courses such as Listening; Public Speaking; Critical Thinking in Communication; Organizational Communication; Ethics; Communication Education: College Teaching; Communication and Technology; Language and Communication; and Communication Theory.

Dr. Beall was selected as a Scottish Rite Distinguished Educator; an Outstanding Young High School Teacher by the Nebraska Speech Communication and Theatre Association; the National Communication Association's Marcella E. Oberle Outstanding K–12 Teacher; and Master Teacher by the National Communication Association, the Central States Communication Association, and the Western States Communication Association. She has served on numerous editorial boards and has presented over 600 papers, programs, or workshops for professional organizations. She presents technology, listening, and critical thinking workshops for schools, departments, and business organizations. Dr. Beall is president of the International Listening Association, a past president of the Central States Communication Association, a former National Communication Association Administrative Committee member, and a past Chair of the Educational Policies Board. She also serves on the Executive Boards of both the International Association for Health-Communication Sciences and the World Communication Association.

Communication

PART ONE
Making Connections through Communication

"Ideas or hypotheses are tested by the consequences which they produce when they are acted upon."
—John Dewey

CHAPTER 1 Connecting Process and Principles

THIS CHAPTER WILL HELP YOU:

- Understand the role of communication in your daily life.
- Learn how competent communication can affect your career development.
- Become aware of the effects of ethical behavior, culture, technology, and thinking on your communication.
- Learn the essential components in the communication process.
- Distinguish among the various types of communication: intrapersonal, interpersonal (including group), and public.
- Identify and debunk five common myths about communication.

CASE STUDY

Student: I wish to make an appointment with the department head so I can waive the Oral Communication requirement.

Departmental Secretary: I'll make an appointment, but it's unlikely that you'll be granted a waiver. In fact, I want you to know that Oral Communication is probably the most important class you'll ever take.

Student: What makes you say that?

Secretary: I know that the information I gained in that class is the most important and most useful information of all the classes I ever took.

Student: Well, I took speech in high school. And, I've been talking since I was about one, and I talk a lot in all my classes and at work.

Secretary: Oral Communication is not just giving speeches and it's not just talking. I took the class here and I can tell you that it's the one class I use every day of my life.

Questions to think about

1. Why do you think colleges require a fundamentals of communication class?
2. What do you expect to cover in this class?
3. Do you think the student was able to get a waiver for this class? Why or why not?

You, too, might feel that you've been talking for a long time and know how to do it fairly well. You may also have enrolled in a high school speech class. But as the secretary in the scenario indicated, the fundamentals of communication course you're enrolled in is more than talking, more than public speaking, even more than interacting with people individually or in groups. Our goal for this textbook and a likely goal for your communication course is to help you become a more *competent communicator*. Competence means many things to many people. For our purposes, **communication competence** is the ability to take part in effective communication that is characterized by skills and understandings that enable communication partners to exchange messages and meanings successfully.

Communication in the Workplace

communication competence
The ability to take part in effective communication that is characterized by skills and understandings that enable communication partners to exchange messages successfully.

Most businesses identify communication skills as critical for all employees. Academic advisers in many areas tell us that they require communication courses. A former undergraduate advisor at the University of Northern Iowa says, "Speaking, listening, and thinking are definite skills our graduates must have. I recommend that our majors take Oral Communication and at least one other communication class. I tell them that one cannot do well in the workplace without communication skills and listening is essential."[1]

Look at the top ten list in Table 1.1, and then compare that list to the topics covered in your class syllabus and this textbook. Among the suggestions employers offer students are that they take writing and public speaking courses, use mock interviews at college career services, participate in campus organizations, and find student

Employers want workers who can speak effectively, listen carefully and efficiently, and think critically.

internships.[2] Employers also suggest that students use college experiences to demonstrate transferable characteristics and skills. Some day, a prospective employer might ask you for evidence of your communication skills. If you tape the speeches you present in this class and save the tape and the outlines, you will have excellent materials for your personal or professional portfolio, provided, of course, that you carefully heed the instructions your instructors give you!

Communication helps us to make connections with each other and with the world. We must all communicate with a variety of people in a variety of situations each day. No matter what your cultural background, no matter what your learning style, you'll find that your communication proficiency can mean a better job, better relationships, and greater satisfaction in your life. In this text, we provide a variety of ideas and approaches to help you learn more about the exciting ways in which people *make connections* through communication. This chapter presents the concepts and processes of effective communication in everyday life. In particular, we examine the essential components and principles, the types and contexts, and the myths about communication. You will have the opportunity to think about the role of communication in an increasingly multicultural and technological world. We provide some hands-on activities and some reflective questions to apply to your personal life and to use communication to *make connections* in all areas of your life.

Making Connections

Communication and the Workforce

We have suggested that communication skills are essential in the workplace. Employers advise that communication skills are critical to finding and holding jobs and meeting the requirements of many careers. Table 1.1 identifies the top ten qualities and skills employers seek. Peruse the Help Wanted section in your local newspaper.

1. What kinds of skills are identified?
2. How many of the ads specify speaking, listening, thinking, and group or people skills?
3. What are some of the other requirements?

TABLE 1.1

Top Ten Qualities and Skills Employers Seek

1. Communication skills (verbal and written)
2. Honesty/integrity (ethics)
3. Teamwork skills (see Chapters 15 and 16)
4. Interpersonal skills (see Chapters 13 and 14)
5. Motivation/initiative
6. Strong work ethic
7. Analytical skills (see Chapters 6, 9, 10, 11, 12, 15, and 16)
8. Flexibility/adaptability (see Chapter 10)
9. Computer skills
10. Organizational skills (see Chapters 9, 15, and 16)

Sources: National Association of Colleges & Employers, *Job Outlook 2003;* 21st Century Workforce Commission, *A Nation of Opportunity: Strategies for Building Tomorrow's 21st Century Workforce* (Washington, D.C.: U.S. Department of Labor, 2003).

What Is Communication?

What is communication? And what do we mean when we say that communication occurs? How do we know when we have communicated effectively? How do we use communication to *make connections* in our lives? The answers to these questions require an understanding of the principles and process of communication as well as some guidelines for achieving success.

We define **communication** as the simultaneous sharing and creating of meaning through human symbolic interaction. (The terms in this definition will be explained in more detail throughout the book.) It might seem obvious but bears repeating: Communication is complex. If it were simple, people would have few difficulties with

communication
The simultaneous sharing and creating of meaning through human symbolic action.

Making Connections

What Is Communication?

Effective communicators are aware of the concepts and practices related to communication. Now that we have provided a definition, you should stop and think for a moment about the communication process. Respond to each of the following statements with either "true" or "false." Explain and justify your answers on a separate sheet of paper. Then compare your responses with those of a classmate or the class as a whole, or ask a co-worker to complete the exercise and compare notes.

1. Communication can solve all of our problems.
2. The more we communicate, the better.
3. Meanings are in words.
4. Communication is a natural ability.
5. Communication is reversible.

Discuss your answers and explanations for each statement with others. The answers for this exercise can be found on page 27. Be sure to discuss any questions you may have with your instructor.

it, and we would not need to study it! But this complex and challenging process is critical to making connections in all our relationships, from the professional to the romantic and everything in between.

As a discipline, communication has existed for thousands of years. Scholars since the ancient Greeks and Romans have recognized communication as a powerful means of influence. Classical rhetoricians studied the principles of the effective composition and delivery of persuasive speeches. In the Middle Ages in Western Europe, religious leaders developed written and spoken means of communication such as letter writing and preaching in order to spread the Christian faith. In the Western world, public speaking, storytelling, and debating have been important means of urging political action and swaying public opinion. Eastern cultures, too, have long emphasized the importance of effective communication. According to Samovar and Porter, "the Buddha advised his disciples to avoid 'harsh speech.'"[3] Colleagues in Japan and Malaysia confirm that the study of communication is an ancient and valued tradition. Well-known practitioners of this art include Madeline Albright, Maya Angelou, Susan B. Anthony, Fidel Castro, Winston Churchill, Mohandas Gandhi, Barbara Jordan, Martin Luther King, Jr., Abraham Lincoln, Colin Powell, Margaret Thatcher, Mother Teresa, Mao Tse-tung, and Oprah Winfrey.

Communication refers to the process by which we create and share meanings. **Communications,** however, is the word generally used to denote the delivery systems for mediated and mass communication. People often confuse the two words, but they are quite different. Communication is what you and your friend do when you discuss the next speech assignment. Communications involve ways of disseminating information, as in "The Internet is a vital communications link for students and office workers."

communications Denotes the delivery systems for mediated and mass communication.

According to this definition, speech communication involves a range of behaviors and occurs in a variety of situations: public and private, business and social, home and school, formal and informal. The diverse situations are all connected by one common thread—*human symbolic interaction,* or people using a symbol system (language) to share thoughts, feelings, beliefs, attitudes, customs, and ideas. As you read this text, you will learn about human symbolic interaction as it occurs within and among individuals, groups, organizations, cultures, and co-cultures. You will learn more about the nature of the communication *process:* listening, thinking, speaking in public settings, speaking in small-group settings, and speaking with one, two, or a small number of people in your interpersonal relationships. Your ability to communicate by using speech will be one of the determining factors in your success in the classroom, in the workplace, and in your personal life. Being an effective communicator saves time, makes life more enjoyable, allows people to establish and maintain relationships successfully, and facilitates accomplishing personal goals. The humorist James Thurber may have said it best: "Precision of communication is important, more important than ever, in our era of hair-trigger balances, when a false, or misunderstood word may create as much disaster as a sudden thoughtless act."[4]

Why Should We Study Communication?

Although you have communicated for many years, you probably have not had the opportunity to learn about communication competence. The ability to communicate might seem natural because unless there are disabilities, most of us readily develop speaking skills. But the ability to *communicate* (not simply to utter words) is learned, and learning to be a competent communicator is a difficult, lifelong project. You can make progress quickly, however, if you work hard to learn the principles and concepts and then apply them in practice situations. Think about your life experiences, then connect the chapter material, class applications, and discussions to your life. These skills will enable you to reap benefits in career development, ethical behavior, and the promotion of positive relationships among people of diverse cultural backgrounds. We live in a time of rapid technological change. Put simply, effective communication is critical to living successfully in today's society.

Communication and Career Development

Most of us aspire to succeed in our chosen careers. We enter college to better ourselves and to prepare for satisfying jobs. Communication plays an important role in career success. Leaders in education, business, and industry have identified several critical life skills that are necessary to function successfully in the workforce, and communication is one of the most valued areas of expertise. For example, several recent studies[5] reinforce what previous research had already demonstrated: Employers want workers at all levels who know how to communicate. The specific recommendations are as follows:

- Speak effectively.
- Listen carefully and efficiently.
- Think critically.
- Get along well with others.
- Be aware of and sensitive to differences in cultural perspectives.
- Make good decisions, individually and in groups.

In other words, effective workplace communicators can explain ideas clearly and give good directions. Effective communicators are good listeners who work well with others and represent their companies well in small- and large-group settings. Too often, employers believe that these skills are lacking in their employees. Introductory

Making Connections

Your Communication Effectiveness

In the surveys cited in the text, executives indicated that all employees need to improve their communication skills. The executives also noted that greater flexibility and higher ethical standards should be a focus of career preparation. If a prospective employer asked you the following questions, how would you respond?

1. Are you an effective communicator? Why? Why not?
2. What are five of your communication concerns?
3. What anxieties about communication do you have? (James McCroskey and his colleagues at West Virginia University developed the Perceived Report of Communication Apprehension [PRCA] to help identify the strength of one's communication anxiety. You might wish to look at Dr. McCroskey's web page—www.jamescmccroskey.com—for more information; try a web search on communication apprehension, and complete a PRCA form found on the Web. We discuss communication apprehension more fully in Chapter 10.)
4. What areas of communication do you need to improve? How do you know you need to work on these areas?
5. Describe one instance in which you found yourself wishing that you were a better listener.
6. What were you doing the last time you found yourself wishing you were a better communicator? What did you mean by the term?
7. In what recent situations did you find yourself wondering how to be more effective in interpersonal relationships?

courses in communication, such as the one for which you are reading this text, focus on these skills.

Personnel directors have described their needs in prospective employees as follows: "Send me people who know how to speak, listen, and think, and I'll do the rest. I can train people in their specific job responsibilities, as long as they listen well, know how to think, and can express themselves well."[6] In fact, most careers involve contact with others and require the ability to communicate effectively with them. Business and industry often look for the most competent communicators when they hire new employees. So, although some companies provide on-the-job training in communication skills, it is by far most advantageous to develop excellent speaking, listening, and analytical abilities before applying for the exciting job that could launch or enhance your career.

Communication and Ethical Behavior

All societies hold certain ethical standards—ideals about what is right and what is wrong—and unethical behavior often carries a penalty. People have been removed from political office, lost their jobs, or been publicly chastised for violating ethical standards and codes. Such behaviors often involve unethical acts related to communication. Financiers have received prison terms for participating in insider trading—using illegally obtained information to make money on the stock market. Sharing such information constitutes an illegal act of communication. Another such behavior is telling lies, whether done to hurt someone else or to protect or enhance one's own position. Though politicians spring to mind as typical offenders in this category, other examples show that the problem is more widespread, for example, enhancing one's résumé to increase the chances of being hired or "borrowing" a friend's old term paper or speech to pass a course.

A colleague of ours received an email from an instructor in another state. The message was something like the following: "I appreciate the sample speeches and outlines on your website. Apparently, so do my students. One of them took the exact speech on your website and presented it in class. Fortunately, I, too, use the Internet, and it didn't take long to find the real source of the speech." (The colleague decided to create a password function so that only students enrolled in her classes could access the examples.)

The Internet has made plagiarism a much greater possibility because of the ease with which people can access information. There are so many sites with so much information that people often believe they can access sites, take what they want, and never be caught. Plagiarism, in whatever form and however accessible, is still unethical, and it can result in students failing courses and even being removed from their colleges and universities. In the workplace, plagiarism and other unethical behaviors can result in the loss of one's job or a demotion. In recent years, newspaper reporters have been in the news for fabricating stories and losing their jobs. Ethics and plagiarism are discussed throughout the text and are defined here. **Ethics** refers to an individual's system of moral principles. **Plagiarism** is the use of another person's information, language, or ideas without citing the originator and making it appear that the user is the originator.

Ethical communicators speak responsibly and give credit to any sources that contribute to the message being conveyed. An ethical communicator does not plagiarize and does not equivocate. Aristotle, a Greek rhetorician (384–322 B.C.), suggested that communication was most powerful when the speaker's character, or *ethos* (ethical appeal), was engaged in presenting the truth.[7] (Chapter 10 further develops this concept.) Quintilian (A.D. ca. 35–ca. 100), another rhetorician, stated (before the days of inclusive language) that communication needed to be presented by "a good man speaking well."[8]

An important distinction to make here is that unethical communication may, in fact, constitute effective communication. If one person persuades another to do something morally wrong, the communication has been effective, but it is not virtuous. Unethical communication should never be condoned, even when it has appeared to succeed. A good deal of critical thinking is needed as we attempt to be effective *and* ethical communicators and as we evaluate others' communication to determine its ethical content.

Learning Connections

1. Where do we get our view of ethics?
2. What are your own views about ethical behaviors?
3. What behaviors violate your ethical code to the point that you would have to confront someone if he or she acted in a certain way?

Today, many colleges and universities offer or even require ethics classes to encourage students to take ethical responsibilities seriously and to remind them that the need for responsible, ethical behavior pervades all aspects of life. Throughout this text, examples of ethical dilemmas and perspectives will help you become aware of the need for ethical communication behaviors.

ethics
An individual's system of moral principles.

plagiarism
The use of another person's information, language, or ideas without citing the originator and making it appear that the user is the originator.

Communication and Our Multicultural Society

Job transfers, changes in economic and political conditions, and numerous other factors cause people to move from place to place, often leaving their country of birth

Making Connections

Ethics in Research

Read this account and answer the questions that follow.

Ethan works at two part-time jobs and is supporting a wife and baby. He needs to maintain at least a 2.5 GPA to keep his scholarships and student loans. This week, he has to give a speech in his communication class, and both of his bosses insist that he work additional hours because other employees are on sick leave. He feels that he cannot afford to say no to his employers, but that means he won't be able to spend as much time at the library researching his speech. While surfing the Net, Ethan found a complete speech on an aspect of the topic he had already begun to research. He decides that this one time he will use this information in his speech and hope that his communication instructor will not realize that he hasn't done original research. He wishes he had found more time earlier and vows that he'll start the next assignment as soon as he knows exactly what to include.

1. Is it wrong for Ethan to "borrow" information from the speech on the Web?
2. What would you do if this happened to you?
3. What do you think will happen to Ethan if his instructor thinks there's something strange about Ethan's speech?
4. Check the plagiarism and ethics policy of your institution. (This usually can be found on the college website as well as in the course and program handbook of most institutions.) Does Ethan's behavior constitute plagiarism or a breach of ethics in your school? What are the penalties?

to put down roots elsewhere. Many countries are experiencing an increase in this trend. In the United States, for example, what was once a population with a white majority of northern European roots is now a diverse mosaic of people of different ethnic and cultural backgrounds. In this environment, we can all grow to appreciate the distinctions that make each culture unique as well as the interconnectedness shared by all, sometimes described as the "global village." But a great deal of knowledge, flexibility, and sensitivity are necessary if people of diverse cultural backgrounds are to communicate successfully and live well together.

Current demographic trends and projections in the United States make it not an option, but a necessity, to interact successfully with people of all racial, ethnic, cultural, and religious heritage. The U.S. Census Bureau reports the following demographic breakdown by race (all ages) in 2000:

Hispanic Origin (any race)	32,832,000
White, Not Hispanic	196,929,000
Black, Not Hispanic	33,619,000
American Indian, Eskimo, and Aleut, Not Hispanic	2,059,000
Asian and Pacific Islander, Not Hispanic[9]	10,620,000

This translates to roughly the following percentages: 75 percent of the population is White; 12.5 percent, Hispanic; 13 percent, Black; 3.6 percent, Asian and Pacific Islander; and 1 percent, American Indian. Projections suggest a significant increase in

Hispanic, Black, and Asian numbers in the near future, with a decline or stable percentage for Whites. The changes in "how we look" are already occurring in elementary schools and high schools, as well as college and university classrooms. Language differences complicate communication within many schools. Some kindergarten through twelfth-grade schools on the East and West Coasts and in such populous areas as Chicago, Cincinnati, Dallas, and St. Louis have students representing fifty to one hundred or more different native languages. College and university classrooms, too, have increasing numbers of students whose first language is not English, and each one's cultural and ethnic background affects the way these students communicate in the classroom, the residence hall, the supermarket, and the workplace.

Language structure itself influences and is influenced by culture. Nonverbal communication behaviors, such as physical stance, eye contact, style of speaking, and so on, are also largely determined by cultural background. It takes a great deal of patience, understanding, and respect to learn to communicate effectively in situations involving different language backgrounds and different social and conversational customs. Thus, it is important to learn all we can about the backgrounds of the people with whom we relate at work or in the community, to consider how our own customs might seem unusual to a person of a different heritage, and to cultivate an open mind and a good sense of humor. These attitudes will facilitate communication and will also enrich our lives.

Making Connections

Communication and Culture

One of the ways in which any society or culture ensures the transmission of cultural traditions and values is in its stories. Many of the stories we read as young children contain life lessons. The stories of Dr. Seuss, for example, always have a moral: *Green Eggs and Ham* teaches us the value of repeatedly presenting ideas in slightly different forms in order to convince others, and *The Lorax* provides reasons we should value our natural resources. Even common folk stories such as "The Three Little Pigs" may demonstrate the value of a work ethic. Other stories provide examples of specific cultural values. Most immigrants to the United States bring their cultures' stories with them. Paul Fleischman's small book *Seedfolks* describes how a neighborhood of people from many different countries of origin learn how to become a community.

1. What are some of the stories you learned, read, or were told as you grew up?
2. What values did the stories convey or emphasize?
3. What stories will you or have you shared with your own children or relatives? Why?

Communication and Our Technological Society

The world seems to be getting smaller, because so many people travel and because the mass media bring the world to our living rooms, residence hall rooms, offices, and even our automobiles. Only a few years ago it took a day or so to get news from one part of the world to another. Now advancements in technology often make it possible for us to experience historic events not only moments after they occur, but sometimes even *while* they occur. We can communicate with people in almost any part of the world; we can send messages via email, fax, and telephone. We can use digital cameras at our computers and visit face to face with people around the world. We can turn on the television and see and hear what is happening anywhere in the world or even in space. Interviews with world leaders, celebrities, and ordinary people are broadcast on television and radio every day. If you happen to be in the right place at the right time, witnessing a news event or simply crossing the path of a reporter looking for a story, your image, words, or voice may be instantaneously transmitted to your community, the nation, or the world.

Advancements in technology, such as the satellite communication used here, often make it possible for us to make immediate contact. Messages by way of email, fax, or telephone can be sent to almost any part of the world.

The way technology has sped the pace of communication adds to the challenge of both presenting and receiving meaningful messages. Flashing images and sound bites can be hard to interpret. The sheer volume of communication presented through electronic media can seem overwhelming. Yet technological developments are exciting in that they increase the avenues through which communication can occur and make the process quick and easy. Those who take time to learn and practice the principles of sound communication will be able to use to the best advantage these technological means of sending and receiving messages. (See Chapter 17, available on the

Making Connections

Communication and Technology

The Internet is a potent force in our lives. We use the Internet in the classroom, in the workplace, and in our homes. Some people are concerned that people will forget how to relate to others because so much of our time is spent at the computer. Think about your own Internet or intranet use and answer these questions.

1. Have you (or do you know someone who has) experienced a cyber relationship?
2. How did the relationship develop?
3. What rules did you or your friend follow in establishing this relationship?
4. What concerns do you have about this type of relationship? Why?
5. How is your cyber communication easier or more difficult than face-to-face communication with your friends or family?

Discuss these questions and your answers with (1) others who do not use the Internet very often and (2) those who spend a great deal of time on the Internet. What are the similarities in and differences between the answers of the two groups?

Internet at www.ablongman.com/seiler6e, for more information on mediated and mass communication.)

Principles of Communication

To appreciate the true nature of communication, it is important to understand four fundamental principles:

1. Communication is a process.
2. Communication is a system.
3. Communication is both interactional and transactional.
4. Communication can be intentional or unintentional.

These principles are readily applicable to life beyond the classroom (and they improve interactions within the classroom as well). No doubt, situations from your personal life—work experiences, family relationships, or your participation in sports teams, music groups, social clubs, or political or community action organizations—will come to mind as we discuss the dynamics of communication. An understanding of these principles should make a difference in your life, building greater understanding and cooperation into relationships at any level.

Communication Is a Process

Communication is considered a **process,** because it involves a series of actions that has no beginning or end and is constantly changing.[10] It is not an object that you can hold to examine or dissect. It is like the weather, which changes constantly.[11] Sometimes the weather is warm, sunny, and dry; at other times, it is cool, cloudy, and wet. The weather is a result of complex interrelationships among variables, such as high and low pressure systems, the position of the earth, and ocean currents, that can never be exactly duplicated. Similarly, communication is an ongoing, constantly changing process.

Communication also involves variables that can never be duplicated. The interrelationships among people, environments, skills, attitudes, status, experiences, and feelings all determine communication at any given moment. Think about a relationship you developed with someone recently. How did it occur? It may have happened by chance (striking up a conversation with someone you met while walking to class), or it may have been a prearranged meeting (a business meeting with a prospective client). No two relationships are developed in the same way. And like the weather, some relationships are warm and others are cool.

Communication is both ever-changing and capable of effecting change. Saying something that you wish you hadn't said is an excellent example of this principle. No matter how hard you try to take back your comment, you cannot. It has made its impact and has, in all likelihood, affected your relationship with another person in some way. The change might not be immediate or significant, but it does take place as a result of your communication.

Furthermore, the communication and the changes it produces might not have a clearly identifiable beginning or end. Certain events led up to it, and as we noted,

process
Series of actions that has no beginning or end and is constantly changing.

results of the communication will follow in its wake. Communication generally is not characterized by abrupt endings and beginnings; rather, it takes place within a flow. If you were to stop in mid-conversation and walk away, that conversation would still have an effect on you; it would not end. You would carry away some new information or at least a general impression, whether positive or negative. If you understand that communication is a process, you will be able to see how events and relationships constantly change and yet also have continuity.

Communication Is a System

Simply stated, a **system** is a combination of parts interdependently acting to form a whole. The human body is an excellent example of a system. All parts of the body are interdependent and work together to form one complex system. If something is not functioning correctly, some response usually occurs either to correct what has gone wrong or to warn that something is going wrong. When you have a headache, it affects not only your head but also the rest of your body, including the thinking process and emotions. You may find that you have trouble seeing and even walking. You may not wish to eat, because your head pain seems to have taken over your body. If you have a severe headache, you may have trouble thinking clearly because of the pounding in your head. You may also have difficulty explaining something to your co-workers or friends. Because each part of the system is connected, your ability to think clearly, speak clearly, or listen effectively leads to ineffective communication.

Systems also exist in the workplace, in the family, and in the classroom. If your supervisor had a fight at home, that event may affect the supervisor's relationship with the workers; the supervisor may be irritable and snap at you and others. Although you don't know what has caused the irritability, it does affect all who must deal with it. In other words, the supervisor's domestic squabble has an impact not only on the home system but also on the system at work. In a similar sense, the communication process is a system and occurs only when the necessary components interact. If components of communication malfunction or are absent, communication is prevented or ineffective.

Communication Is Both Interactional and Transactional

The interactional and transactional aspects of communication are closely related and should be considered together. **Interaction** is an exchange of communication in which people take turns sending and receiving messages. It is similar to playing catch. Someone throws a ball. Another person catches it and throws it back. Each throw and each catch is a separate action. It is, however, necessary for the ball to get to the other person before it can be thrown back. Figure 1.1 illustrates this interaction. In interaction, there is a distinct time delay between each message being sent. An example of communication as an interaction is a phone conversation between two people. Person A speaks and Person B listens, then Person B speaks and Person A listens, and so on. Each message is a separate action. Even though there is a reaction to each message being sent, the reaction and message are not simultaneous.

Most face-to-face communication does not occur as a series of distinctly separate actions. Thus, the term **transaction** is used to extend the concept of interaction to include simultaneous actions. Persons involved in transaction engage in sending (encoding) and receiving (decoding) messages at the same time (see Figure 1.2). For

system
Combination of parts interdependently acting to form a whole.

interaction
Exchange of communication in which communicators take turns sending and receiving messages.

transaction
Exchange of communication in which the communicators act simultaneously, that is, encoding and decoding occur at the same time.

FIGURE 1.1

Communication as Interaction Interaction is a series of distinctly separate actions, or turn taking. That is, Person A communicates (message 1) to Person B, then B communicates (message 2) to A, then A communicates to B, and so on.

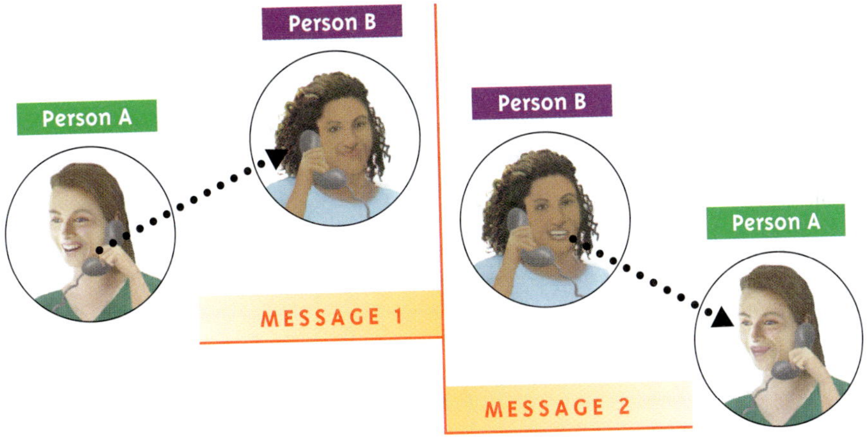

example, when teachers communicate to their students or supervisors to their employees, they not only send information but also receive information at the same time. The teacher and students and supervisor and employees are sending and receiving messages simultaneously. This does not necessarily mean that they are talking at the same time; it does mean, however, that two-way communication is taking place. Your handshake communicates a message that another person interprets at the same time that you are receiving and interpreting the message in the handshake that you are receiving. In addition, you both are simultaneously receiving feedback about the message your own handshake is sending.

Without simultaneous actions, face-to-face communication would be impossible or extremely limited, like sending a letter to someone and then having to wait a week or two for a response. In face-to-face communication, each person affects the other and shares in the process simultaneously. Thus, communication transaction can be seen as the simultaneous exchange by which we share our reality with others. The principle of transaction is more fully depicted in the figure on page 15.

FIGURE 1.2

Communication as Transaction In a transaction, each person communicates simultaneously. That is, both Person A and Person B are communicating at the same time. This does not mean that they are both speaking at once. Instead, each is aware of and reacting to the other. The sender is also a receiver, and the receiver is also a sender. Each is actively involved in what is happening.

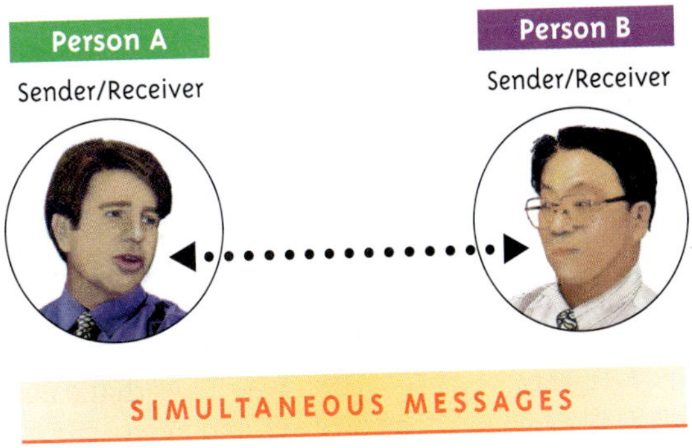

Communication Can Be Intentional or Unintentional

When one person communicates with another, he or she intends that specific messages with specific purposes and meanings be received.

FIGURE 1.3

Types of Intentional and Unintentional Communication Communication occurs both intentionally and unintentionally. Thus, we must be aware that even when we do not intend it, communication can occur. Can you recall any instances in which you unintentionally communicated to another person?

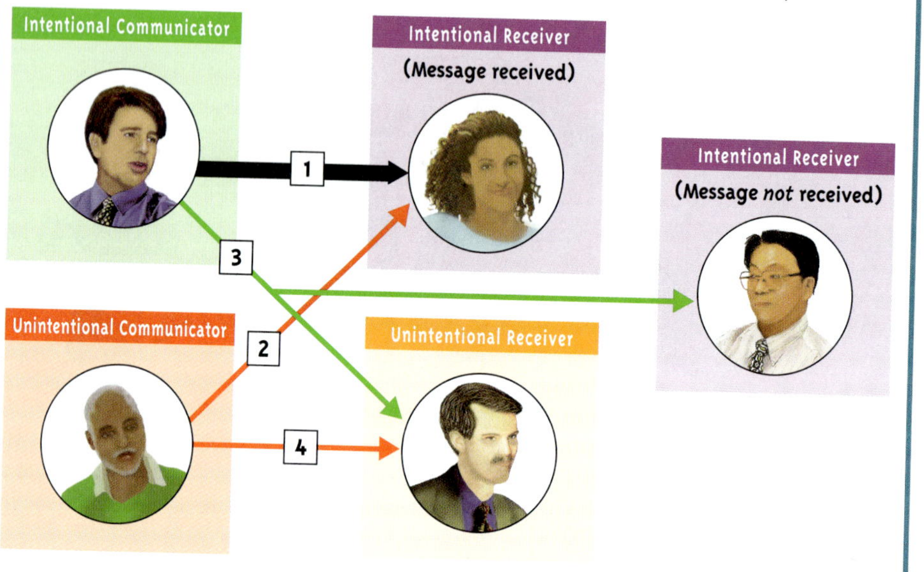

Communication can occur, however, regardless of whether it is intended. **Intentional communication** is a message that is purposely sent to a specific receiver. **Unintentional communication** is a message that is not intended to be sent or was not intended for the individual who received it. On the basis of intent or lack of intent, four possible communication situations can occur, as shown in Figure 1.3. This is shown by Arrow 1 and is generally the way communication takes place. Arrow 2 indicates a situation in which a person unintentionally communicates something to someone who is intentionally trying to receive a message or messages. This situation occurs every time someone reads more into a communication act than was intended by the source. For example, when a student in a quiet classroom gets up to sharpen a pencil, the eyes of other students immediately focus on the moving student, who might have no specific intention of communicating anything. The movement, however, provides an opportunity for observers to attribute varying meanings to the message. For instance, one person might believe that the moving student is trying to flirt with her, another might think he is trying to call attention to himself, and the instructor might think he is trying to disrupt the classroom. Despite the student's lack of intention to communicate anything, others have read meaning into his behavior, and he may have to deal with their interpretations.

intentional communication
A message that is purposely sent to a specific receiver.

unintentional communication
A message that is not intended to be sent or is not intended for the person who receives it.

Arrow 3 illustrates the opposite situation. Here the source intends to send a message, but the person for whom the message is intended is not consciously or intentionally receiving it. Such a situation happens in the classroom when students daydream while the instructor is lecturing.

Arrow 4 shows that communication can be unintentional for both the source and the receiver and can occur without anyone intentionally sending or receiving a message. Communication that is not intended or that is at least not consciously sent and received is usually nonverbal. Nonverbal communication is any information that is expressed without words. For example, the clothing a person wears might not be worn to communicate any specific message, and persons observing the clothing might not intentionally or consciously receive any message through it, but they do see it. Thus, communication occurs even though neither the person nor the observer has any intention of communicating.

Learning Connections

1. What's the difference between an interaction and a transaction?
2. Why should we be concerned with interactions and transactions?
3. Think of a time when you received a message that was not intended for you and you were upset by your interpretation. Why were you upset?

Essential Components of Communication

Although there is no exhaustive list of the myriad components of communication, eight of the most basic elements are worth examining in detail:

1. Source
2. Message
3. Interference
4. Channel
5. Receiver
6. Feedback
7. Environment
8. Context

Figure 1.4 illustrates how these components interact when two people are communicating, yet it depicts each element's movement and interdependence on the other

FIGURE 1.4

Schematic Model of the Essential Components of Communication The essential components of the transactional communication process are constantly changing, ongoing, and dynamic, and they affect one another.

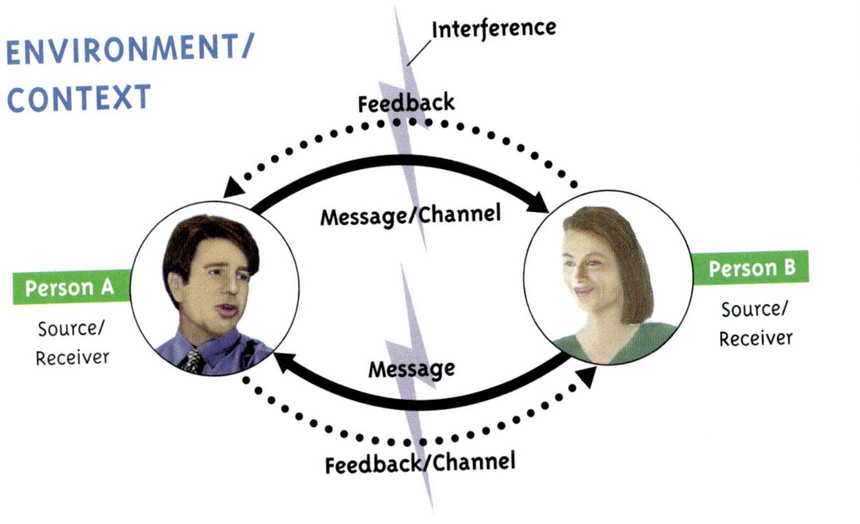

Making Connections

Communication in the Workplace

Manuel and Travis work full time in the auto service department of the local Farm and Fleet. Both take one class at the community college and one class at the university as they pay their own way toward a college degree. Neither plans to work at his current job for the rest of his life, but each sees the value of the job as "an honest way to make a living" as he moves toward his goal of a college education. Manuel and Travis have also learned the value of effective communication through their interactions with customers. In fact, the service manager encouraged them to take a communication class because he found that his own class helped him immensely in his roles as supervisor and customer service representative. One of their assignments in Oral Communication is to make a five-minute speech on a communication concept that is important outside the classroom or in the workplace. Travis is uncertain about a good topic.

1. What would you recommend?
2. Focus on a workplace experience of your own. What communication concept would you talk about? Why?
3. How do the principles of communication identified in this chapter relate to your own work role?
4. Which of the four principles of communication are involved in your communication roles outside the classroom?
5. In what ways have the explanation and examples of communication helped you make connections between this class and other areas of your life?

elements only in a limited way. During actual communication, these components are constantly in flux as the communicators react to each other. The model also shows that communication is a process, that the components work together as a system, that interaction and transaction are both possible modes of communication, and that intentional and unintentional communication can occur—thus illustrating the principles of communication that we have already discussed.

Now that you can see how these elements relate during communication, we will discuss each one separately.

Source

The **source** is the creator of the message. Because communication usually involves more than one person, more than one source of communication can exist at one time. In the model in Figure 1.4, both persons function as a source. Likewise, both the teacher and the students in a classroom can function as sources, sending messages simultaneously to one another—teacher to students, students to teacher, and students to students.

The communication source performs four roles: He or she determines the meaning of what is to be communicated, encodes the meaning into a message, sends the message, and perceives and reacts to a listener's response to the message. Person A, when acting as source, also brings into play the communicative skills, knowledge, attitudes, and sociocultural background that make him or her a unique individual. No two communicators are identical in their abilities to communicate, nor do they see others, events, or situations in exactly the same way. The greater the differences between Person A and Person B, the more effort and skill it will take for Person A to effectively communicate with Person B. Respecting another person's views,

source
The creator of messages.

even when they differ from one's own, is the first step to communicating well in such situations.

Determining Meanings. A source has many decisions to make in creating a message. The meaning of some communication messages is relatively simple, but others can be extremely complex and difficult. For example, telling someone about a high grade you received on a recent speech entails making a decision about the meaning you wish to convey. Do you want the other person to know that this is the highest grade you have ever received on a speech or merely that you got a high grade? Do you want the person to know what you did to get the high grade?

Encoding. Once a source has chosen a meaning, she or he **encodes** it. In other words, a source translates the thoughts or feelings into words, sounds, and physical expressions, which make up the actual message that is to be sent. According to symbolic interactionism, a theory created by George Mead and his students, the most human and humanizing activity people engage in is talking with one another. It is our conversations with others, our participation in the communication process in social settings, that allow us to construct meaning. According to social interactionism, the meaning we attribute in those interactions is determined by our language choices. Furthermore, symbolic interactionism also explains that we talk to ourselves (intrapersonal communication) as we sort through difficult circumstances, solve problems, and make decisions.

Sending. The source then sends the message, which involves the source's ability to communicate overtly, that is, to use voice and body to express the intended meaning accurately. For example, if your internal meaning is to tell the other person how pleased you are to receive a high grade on your speech, then you must use words and actions to illustrate what you are feeling and thinking.

Reacting. Finally, a source must interpret the receiver's response to the message. A source's perception of a receiver's response in most communication situations is simultaneous with the response. For example, the person you are telling about the high grade will be sending you messages (smiles, nods of the head, eye contact) as you speak in reaction to what you are saying. If you interpret that response as positive, you will probably continue to tell more about your high grade.

Message

A **message** is the stimulus produced by the source. It comprises words, grammar, organization of thoughts, physical appearance, body movement, voice, aspects of the person's personality and self-concept, and personal style. Environment and noise can also shape the message. Any stimulus that affects a receiver is a message from the source, regardless of whether the source intended to send it. Hence, if a teacher tells a student that everything appears to be fine while frowning, he or she might be communicating more to the student than was intended, even if the teacher's facial expression has nothing to do with the student.

Remember, each message is unique. Even if the same message were to be created over and over again, it would differ in each instance because messages cannot be repeated or received in exactly the same way or in the same context. To illustrate this, imagine reading the headline "The World Has Been Invaded by Small Green People!"

encoding
Process by which the source translates thoughts or feelings in words, sounds, and physical expressions, which together make up the actual message that is to be sent.

message
The stimulus that is produced by the source.

in a comic book and then in your local newspaper. Although the words might be the same, the messages conveyed would be quite different.

Interference

Anything that changes the meaning of an intended message is called **interference.** It is included in our model because it is present, to one degree or another, in every communication environment.

Interference can be external and physical, such as noise caused by the slamming of a door or the blasting of a stereo. Other examples of external interference include an unpleasant environment, such as a smoke-filled room or a room that is too cool or too hot; an odor, such as that of overly strong perfume; or distracting characteristics of the speaker, such as too much makeup, a speech impediment, talk that is too fast or too slow, mumbling pronunciation, or weird clothing.

Interference can also be internal and psychological. For example, thoughts going through a person's mind can interfere with the reception or creation of a message. A person who speaks in a loud voice to get someone's attention may create both physical and psychological interference. If the receiver perceives the loudness as anger, the loud voice creates not only a distraction from attending but also a distortion of interpretation. If the receiver responds accordingly, the sender may be quite surprised. Essentially, interference is anything that reduces or distorts the clarity, accuracy, meaning, understanding, or retention of a message.

Channel

A **channel** is the route by which messages flow between sources and receivers. The usual communication channels are light waves and sound waves, which allow us to see and hear one another. The medium through which the light and sound waves travel, however, may differ. For example, when two people are talking face to face, light and sound waves in the air serve as the channels. If a letter is sent from one person to another, light waves serve as the channel, but the paper and the writing itself serve as the means by which the message is conveyed. Books, films, videotapes, television sets, computers, radios, magazines, newspapers, and pictures are media through which messages may be conveyed.

We also receive communication by smelling, touching, and tasting. We sometimes take these senses for granted, but imagine walking into a bakery and not being able to smell the aroma or taste the flavors. All you have to do is hug someone you care about to recognize how important touch is as a means of communicating. All five senses, therefore, contribute to communication.

Receiver

Both persons function as receivers in the model depicted in Figure 1.4. A **receiver** analyzes and interprets messages, in effect translating them into meaning. This process is called **decoding.** *You are simultaneously a receiver and a source.* As you listen to another person's message, you react with body movements and facial expressions, and the person sending the message receives the information conveyed by your physical reactions. Like the source, a receiver has several roles: to receive (hear, see, touch, smell, or taste) the message; to attend to the message; to interpret and analyze the message; to store and recall the message; and to respond to the source, message, channel, environment, and noise. In addition, Person B also has communication skills,

interference
Anything that changes the meaning of an intended message.

channel
The route (such as sound waves or light waves) by which messages flow between sources and receivers.

receiver
The individual who analyzes and interprets the message.

decoding
The process of translating a message into the thoughts or feelings that were communicated.

knowledge, attitudes, and a sociocultural background that differ from those of Person A. The greater the differences between Person A and Person B, the more effort Person B must make to be a competent receiver.

Feedback

Another component in the communication process is **feedback,** the response to a message that a receiver sends back to a source. Feedback enables a sender to determine whether the communication has been received and understood as intended. To share meaning accurately, the sender must correct faulty messages and misconceptions, repeat missed meanings, and correct responses as necessary.

Feedback is a natural extension of effective receiving. Receivers have the responsibility of attending to, decoding, and determining a message's intended meaning. The next logical step is to provide responses (feedback) that let the sender know that the message was received and understood. It is then up to the sender to decide whether the feedback provides enough information to judge whether the receiver accurately interpreted the message. Thus, feedback serves as a kind of control mechanism in the communication process. Unfortunately, we too often fail to monitor our own communication and, more important, others' reactions to it, so we are often not heard or are misunderstood. To imagine the consequences, consider what would happen to the temperature in a room if the heater and the thermostat acted independently of each other.

Feedback is an essential component of the communication process, because it is not only a corrective device but also a means by which we learn about ourselves. It helps us adjust to others and assess ourselves. Giving feedback to others is just as important as receiving it, making the communication truly a shared process.

Feedback offers other advantages. A classic study found that when feedback is increased, reception of information is enhanced.[12] The experiment required four groups of students to construct geometric patterns that were described by a teacher under conditions that differed for each group: (1) zero feedback—the teacher's back was turned to the students, and students were not allowed to ask questions or make noise; (2) visible audience feedback—the students could see the teacher's face but could not ask questions; (3) limited verbal feedback—the students were allowed to ask the teacher questions, but the teacher could respond only with yes or no; (4) free feedback—all channels of communication were open, with no limits placed on the type of questions asked of the teacher or the depth of response the teacher could provide. Students provided with no opportunity to receive feedback from the teacher fared poorly, whereas each increasing level of feedback produced better results. This study resulted in two important findings: (1) As the amount of feedback increases, so does the accuracy of communication and (2) as the amount of feedback increases, so does the recipient's confidence in performance.

Environment

The **environment,** or atmosphere, refers to the psychological and physical surroundings in which communication occurs. The environment encompasses the attitudes, feelings, perceptions, and relationships of the communicators as well as the characteristics of the location in which communication takes place, for example, the size, color, arrangement, decoration, and temperature of the room.

The environment affects the nature and quality of the communication. For example, it is much easier to carry on an intimate conversation in a private, quiet, and comfortable setting than in a public, noisy, and uncomfortable setting. Most of us find

feedback
The response to a message that the receiver sends to the source.

environment
The psychological and physical surroundings in which communication occurs.

it easier to communicate with someone we know than with someone we do not know. Some environments appear to foster communication, whereas others seem to inhibit it. Consider these contrasting environments:

> The room is clean, painted light blue, and has quiet music playing in the background. Two people, seated in soft, comfortable chairs, are facing each other, smiling, and one is gently touching the other. They show genuine concern for each other. Their communication is open and caring.
>
> The room is dirty, painted dark brown, and has loud music playing in the background. Two people, seated ten feet apart on folding chairs, are staring at each other. They show little respect or concern for each other. Their communication is guarded.

How does the appearance of the room ultimately affect the negative communication? Both effective and ineffective communication are, in part, products of their environments. Effective communication can occur anywhere and under most circumstances, but pleasing, comfortable environments (along with open, trusting relationships) are more likely to produce positive exchanges.

Context

The broad circumstances or situation in which communication occurs is called the **context.** Communication does not occur in a vacuum. It takes place in informal and formal settings such as between two friends, among five colleagues in a business meeting, or between a rabbi, priest, or minister and a congregation. The number of people, the type of communication, and the situation in which the communication occurs all lend themselves to the context. Each context affects what we say and how we say it. Contexts also influence environment and vice versa. They also help to determine the type of communication that would be used.

GUIDELINES Understanding Yourself and the Communication Process

1. Remember that competent communicators do everything they can to help their listeners understand the communication in the way it is intended.
2. Recognize that interference from both external and internal sources may make the communication act difficult to interpret the way you, the sender, intend it.
3. Although you cannot control environmental factors (heat or lack of it, outside noise, dim or too bright lighting), you can control your own speech rate, volume, use of pauses, use of gestures and correct pronunciations, and these factors can help you be more effective.
4. If you carefully choose your words and the way you present your message (encoding), your listeners have a better chance of understanding you.
5. If you observe your listeners (receivers), you will learn how to read their feedback and be able to adapt your message to them.

Types of Communication

context
Circumstances or situation in which communication occurs.

Type of communication is usually distinguished by the number of people involved, by the purpose of the communication, and by the degree of formality in which it occurs. Each type of communication involves appropriate verbal and nonverbal behaviors.

Five types of communication are discussed in this text: intrapersonal, interpersonal, small group, team, and public. We also refer to elements of mass, or mediated, communication here and throughout the text.

Intrapersonal Communication

To communicate with others, we must first understand how we communicate with ourselves. This process of understanding information within oneself is called **intrapersonal communication.** As we mature, we learn a lot about ourselves and our surroundings. Much of what we learn is gained from our own experiences. Even though there are many things we are taught by others, there are many things we must learn through our own experiences and can learn no other way. For example, the first time you experience the sensation of warmth coming over your chilled body is a form of intrapersonal communication. If the warmth is coming from a fire, the fire is the source of heat, but that heat is not really known to you until it is felt by your body and is eventually registered in your brain. Your skin senses the heated air and transmits the sensation through your central nervous system to your brain, which records it as warmth. In this sense you are communicating within yourself.

Intrapersonal communication also occurs anytime we evaluate or attempt to understand the interaction that occurs between us and anything that communicates a message to us. We are involved in intrapersonal communication as we receive, attend to, interpret and analyze, store and recall, or respond in some fashion to any message. Thus, communication between two individuals is far more complex than it appears on the surface.

Intrapersonal communication includes diverse internal activities such as thinking, problem solving, conflict resolution, planning, emotion, stress, evaluation, and relationship development. All messages that we create first occur within us. This makes communication a personal event, because we can never divorce ourselves from our interaction with others, no matter how neutral or empathic we may think we are. We say, "I understand your feelings," to someone, but we understand another's feelings only after they are filtered through our own feelings and perceptions. Ultimately, all communication takes place within each of us as we react to communication cues. Intrapersonal communication may occur without the presence of any other type of communication, but all other types of communication cannot occur without it. In fact, intrapersonal communication is occurring almost always, and yet we don't often think about it as a type of communication.

intrapersonal communication
The process of understanding information within oneself.

Interpersonal Communication

The informal exchange of information between two or more people is referred to as **interpersonal communication.** It is similar to intrapersonal communication in that it helps us share information, solve problems, resolve conflicts, understand our perception of self and of others, and establish relationships with others. (In Chapters 13 and 14, interpersonal relationships and our relationships with friends and family members are discussed in more detail.)

A subcomponent of interpersonal communication is dyadic communication. **Dyadic communication** is simply defined as an exchange of information between two people. It includes informal conversations, such as talks with a parent, spouse, child, friend, acquaintance, or stranger, as well as more formal conversations, such as

interpersonal communication
The informal exchange of information between two or more people.

dyadic communication
An exchange of information between two people.

interviews. An **interview** is a carefully planned and executed question-and-answer session designed to exchange desired information between two parties. (Chapter 8 and the Appendix discuss, respectively, information and employment interviews.)

Another subcomponent of interpersonal communication is **small-group communication,** an exchange of information among a relatively small number of persons, ideally five to seven, who share a common purpose, such as doing a task, solving a problem, making a decision, or sharing information. (Chapters 15 and 16 discuss the purposes, characteristics, leadership, participation, decision making, problem solving, and evaluation of communication in small groups.)

Public Communication

In **public communication,** a message is transmitted from one person who speaks to a number of individuals who listen. The most widely used form of public communication is the public speech. We find ourselves on the listening end of a public speech in lecture classes, political rallies, group meetings, convocations, and religious services.

Although there are many similarities between public speaking and other types of communication, there are also some differences. Public speaking almost always is more highly structured than the other types. If it is to be done well, it demands much detailed planning and preparation by the speaker. Unlike participants in other types of communication, listeners do not regularly interrupt the speaker with questions or comments. It is the responsibility of the public speaker to anticipate questions that listeners may have and to attempt to answer them.

Public speaking almost always requires a more formal use of language and a more formal delivery style than the other types. The use of jargon, poor grammar, or slang is usually not accepted or tolerated in public speeches. The public speaker must use language precisely and must speak clearly in order to be heard throughout the audience. This may require that the speaker eliminate distracting vocal and physical mannerisms that might be tolerated in other types of communication.

Public speeches are often presented for three purposes: to inform, to persuade, and to entertain. They are also presented to introduce, to pay tribute, to accept, and to welcome. (Chapters 7 through 12 consider public speaking in detail.)

Mass and Mediated Communication

Mediated communication is any communication that is transmitted by some kind of mechanistic means, such as radio, television, telephone, or the Internet; it may be one-on-one communication. **Mass communication**, on the other hand, generally means that someone is communicating with or to a large number of people. Radio, television, newspapers, magazines, books, the World Wide Web, movies, recordings, CD-ROM, and DVD are types of mass communication. They are the means by which messages of some type are directed to a large group (mass) of people. It becomes confusing when we use some form of media to communicate with large numbers or masses of people; and despite the popularity of mass communication, there is very little interaction between the sender and the receiver of the communication.

Technology has advanced so quickly and is so popular that we can purchase relatively inexpensive hardware and software and have global "face-to-face conversations." Digital cameras allow us to share pictures of ourselves, our families, and special events with friends all over the world. Email messages have even become a part of the international space program. The seven astronauts on the ill-fated *Columbia* sent numerous email messages to their families and friends during their

interview
A carefully planned and executed question-and-answer session designed to exchange desired information between two parties.

small-group communication
An exchange of information among a relatively small number of persons, ideally five to seven, who share a common purpose, such as doing a task, solving a problem, making a decision, or sharing information.

public communication
Transmission of a message from one person who speaks to a number of individuals who listen.

mediated communication
Any communication transmitted by some kind of mechanistic means, such as radio, television, telephone, or the Internet; it may be one-on-one communication.

mass communication
Communicating with or to a large number of people.

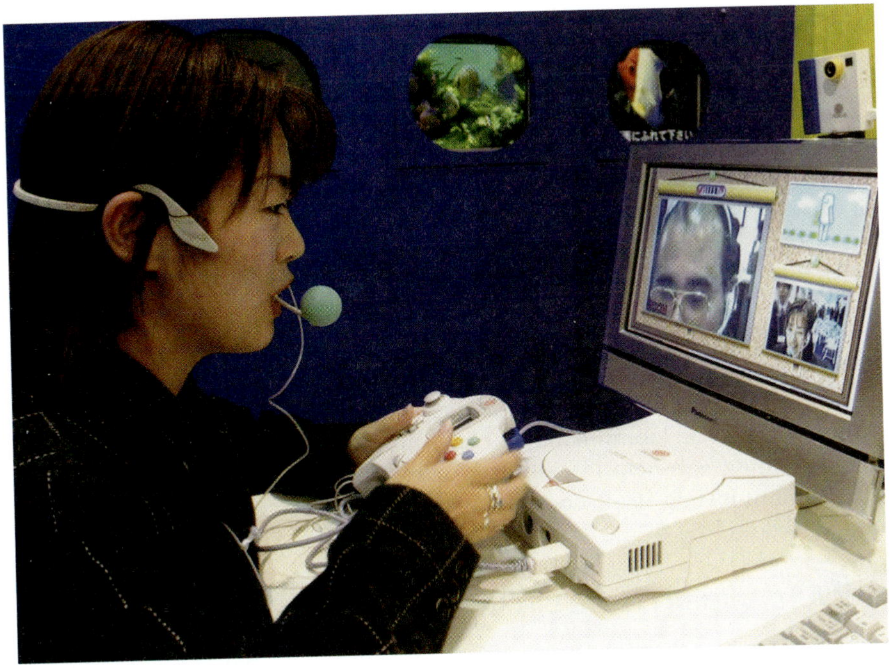

Technology allows us to make connections with each other and with the world. Technology is indeed changing our way of communicating and how we relate with others.

shuttle mission. In fact, emails were sent early on the morning of February 1, 2003, just before the shuttle's reentry into the earth's atmosphere. Family members were quoted as saying that they found comfort in the knowledge that their loved ones sent emails describing their love of their work. (For a comprehensive view of the Internet, its technologies, and usage, check this website: http://livinginternet.com.) As technology continues to develop and change, one thing remains consistent: Communication is the process that helps us *make connections*. Communication is a learned tool that helps us in our personal and family lives, our social and work lives, and in our roles as citizens of the world. Although it is a necessary skill, people often overlook the significance of effective communication. Technology plays an important and powerful role in our lives. Its effects transcend geographical boundaries. It has an impact on the ways we communicate, the ways we learn, and the ways we listen. It can enhance or disrupt our interpersonal relationships. Many people are concerned that the way we interact with each other on a one-to-one basis will be negatively affected because of technology. Therefore, it becomes increasingly important to search for ways to use it positively.

Misconceptions about Communication

Several misconceptions keep many of us from examining *our* own communication more closely. Notice the emphasis on *our* own! Most of us who have problems communicating tend to look for the fault in places other than ourselves. Becoming aware that these misconceptions exist and that many people accept them as truths should help us to understand why the study of communication is necessary. Here are some of the most common myths that interfere with people's improving their own communication skills.

Myth 1: Communication Is a Cure-All

The first misconception is the notion that communication has the magical power to solve all of our problems. The act of communicating with others does not carry any guarantees. Obviously, without communication, we cannot solve our problems, but sometimes communication can create more problems than it solves.

You can probably provide several personal experiences that prove this point. Let one of us provide one of our own. Our neighbor is a realtor. She created a flyer for distribution in the neighborhood and asked me to read it and tell her what I thought about it. She had obviously spent a great deal of time on the project. When I looked it over, I told her that I thought the message would not reach what she said was her intended audience. She became quite agitated and said that I was the only one who had anything negative to say. I had taken her message literally, when she really wanted affirmation that she had done a good job. How might I have prevented making her angry?

Communication can help to eliminate or reduce our problems, but it is not a panacea. Communicating itself does not make the difference; the message that is communicated does.

Myth 2: Quantity Means Quality

Most of us assume that the more we communicate, the better. People who communicate a great deal are often perceived to be more friendly, competent, and powerful and to have more leadership potential than those who do not. However, quantity of communication is not the same as quality. I had a discussion with a colleague about the colleague's view of graduate student theses and the process of defending the proposed thesis. He explained his view, and I explained mine. Because the views were different, he thought I was criticizing him and became defensive. The more I explained, the more frustrated he became. He got red in the face, and his voice kept getting louder and louder. Hence, as in the case of the first myth, it isn't the act or the amount of communication, but the content of communication that makes the difference.

Myth 3: Meaning Is in the Words We Use

If your sister tells you that she doesn't feel well, what would that mean to you? That she is sick? That she has a cold? That she has an upset stomach? That her feelings have been hurt? It could mean any number of things, for, without context and more information, the statement is not clear. If she tells you that she has a cold and doesn't feel well, is that message clear? Well, at least it would narrow the choices a little. Confusion may arise because the statement "I don't feel well" is relative; that is, it might not mean the same thing to you that it does to her. Some people use the statement to refer to a minor discomfort, whereas others mean they are more seriously ill. The words themselves could refer to many degrees or types of conditions. Thus, *meanings are in people and not in the words they use.*

The notion that words contain meanings is probably the most serious misconception of all. Words have meaning only when we give them meanings. *No two people share the same meanings for all words, because no two people completely share the same background and experiences.* Thus, the meaning of a word cannot be separated from the person using it.

Myth 4: We Have a Natural Ability to Communicate

Many people believe that because we are born with the physical and mental equipment needed to communicate, communication must be a natural ability. This simply is not true. The ability to communicate, like almost everything we do, is learned. Most of us possess the physical ability to tie our shoes, but we still have to learn how the strings go together. Similarly, most of us are born with the ability to see, but that does not make us able to read. Reading requires knowledge of the alphabet, the acquisition of vocabulary, and practice. The ability to communicate requires not only that we be capable but also that we understand how human communication works and that we have an opportunity to use that knowledge.

Myth 5: Communication Is Reversible

All of us sometimes make a blunder in communication. We might think that we can take something back, but that is impossible. Once something is said, it is out there; the listener will have to deal with that message, and the speaker will have to try to explain and compensate for what was said. For example, in a moment of anger, we say something that we regret and later ask the other person to "forget that I even said that." Although the other person may forgive us for speaking in anger, it is not likely that he or she will forget what was said. When we communicate through writing, we can take things back until we let someone else see what we've written. When we send oral messages, others can hear and will respond to what we say, even if we don't really mean to say things the way they come out. It is important, therefore, to carefully organize our thoughts and choose our words before we utter them to others. As you study this textbook and the communication process in class, you will learn more about communication competence.

The successful career woman, in addition to other qualifications, has developed a broad communication repertoire—a wide range of communication behaviors from which to choose. Competent communicators are able to coordinate several communication tasks simultaneously.

Improving Communication Competence

To be competent communicators, we must understand the role of communication in our lives and be aware of the complexity of the communication process and different types of communication. We also need to realize that myths about communication may hinder our ability to develop effective communication.

Throughout this chapter we have referred to the concept of communication competence. We will discuss it throughout the text, provide examples of such competence, and ask you to evaluate your ability to communicate effectively in a variety of situations. Earlier in the text, we described communication competence as the ability to engage in effective communication. Communication competence, however, is a concept that various authors have defined in various ways. One noteworthy definition is provided by Dan O'Hair, Gustav Friedrich, John Wiemann, and Mary Wiemann, who state that "communication competencies are skills and understandings that enable communication partners to exchange messages appropriately and effectively."[13] This chapter has only introduced the types of skills and understandings necessary to successful communication. One such skill is the ability to select and implement the most appropriate communication behavior for a particular situation. Good communicators have developed a broad communication **repertoire,** a range of communication behaviors from which to choose.[14] Another hallmark of communication competence is the ability to evaluate the effectiveness of a given communication after the fact.[15]

repertoire
Wide range of communication behaviors from which effective communicators make choices.

Competence is also characterized by the ability to coordinate several communication tasks simultaneously. For example, a competent communicator will, at the same time, choose a way of conveying a message, consider what the receiver's various responses might be, and plan a way to restate the message if the first attempt is not effective.

Consider the last time you asked a question or responded to another student or your professor in a classroom. What did you think about before you raised your hand or before you spoke? How did the reactions of your professor or classmates as you spoke affect the way you presented your ideas? What would you do differently the next time? Reflecting on your answers to these questions can help you find ways to become a better communicator.

Learning Connections

1. What is your definition of communication competence?
2. How do you know whether someone understands a message the way you intended it?
3. What are some specific behaviors you will cultivate to enhance your communication competence?

Through practice and study, you will become comfortable with communicating in a variety of situations. Background knowledge about communication, practical experience, and feedback given in the classroom will help you think on your feet and make better decisions as you communicate. You will also gain confidence and the ability to evaluate your skills as your work in this course progresses.

Summary

Competent communication is essential in all aspects of our everyday lives. Effective communication enhances our personal, social, and career relationships and allows us to make connections with people from other cultures. The communication process is one that is learned; therefore, we can improve our effectiveness as communicators by applying the guidelines and principles identified in this chapter.

In this course, you will be involved in practical and applied situations involving the various types of communication. Intrapersonal communication occurs when we communicate with ourselves (thinking, making choices, making decisions). Interpersonal communication involves creating and sharing messages with one or more other people. When we work in small groups in the classroom or the workplace, we need to know more about group and team communication. When you give a speech in front of your class, you are a public communicator who considers all aspects of the communication process in order to effectively present your messages to your classmates. Technology is important to most of us, and mediated communication and mass communication demonstrate the role of technology in our lives.

We sometimes mistakenly believe that communication can solve all problems. It cannot, but learning how to be an effective communicator can go a long way toward helping us get along better with the people around us. Merely increasing the amount of communication might lead to more confusion and misunderstanding. Problems stem from communicators, not from the act of communication. Communication is a tool we need to learn to use as effectively as we can. We should strive for *communication competence* if we wish to *make connections* with others.

DISCUSSION STARTERS

1. Why is communication regarded as difficult and complex?
2. Whom do you identify as an effective communicator? Why?
3. What is the difference between effective and ineffective communication?
4. Why should you study communication?
5. What is the role of communication in our lives?

6. Explain what it means when we say that communication is a process.
7. How does a system differ from a process?
8. What would happen if there were no feedback?
9. How can feedback motivate you to be more effective?
10. How can feedback deter you from effective communication?
11. What can you do to improve your own communication with people from another culture?
12. How will the Internet change the way we communicate?

ANSWERS AND EXPLANATIONS

Making Connections: What Is Communication?

1. **F** Communication can help solve our problems, but it is not a cure-all. In fact, sometimes more communication can create more problems than it can solve.
2. **F** Quantity does not equate with quality. Thus, it is not the amount of communication but the content that is communicated.
3. **F** Meanings are in people—the words we use are symbols but do not contain meaning until we give them meaning.
4. **F** Many people believe that communication is a natural ability, because there are some individuals for whom it appears to be so easy. However, like most everything we do, it is learned.
5. **F** Once something is said, it is said and it cannot be taken back. That does not mean that you cannot say you're sorry or make a correction to what you have said. It does, however, mean that no matter what you say, you cannot change the fact that you said it.

NOTES

1. Mindy Berkland, former undergraduate advising coordinator, Information Technology, University of Northern Iowa, personal conversation, June 2002. Although not a communication scholar, Ms. Berkland interviewed employers who hire Industrial Technology (IT) graduates. In that role she has determined what proficiencies IT employers seek.
2. National Association of Colleges & Employers, *Job Outlook 2003*; 21st Century Workforce Commission, *A Nation of Opportunity: Strategies for Building Tomorrow's 21st Century Workforce* (Washington, D.C.: U.S. Department of Labor, 2000).
3. L. A. Samovar and R. E. Porter, *Communication between Cultures* (5th ed). Belmont, Calif.: Wadsworth Publishing Co., 2004), 146.
4. J. Thurber, "Friends, Romans, Countrymen, Lend Me Your Ear Muffs," in *Lanterns and Lances* (New York: Harper & Row, 1960), 40.
5. *Spanning the Chasm: Corporate and Academic Cooperation to Improve Work-Force Preparation* (Washington, D.C.: American Council on Education, 1997). Also, "Survey by the National Association of Colleges and Employers," in Work Week, *Wall Street Journal*, February 8, 2000; and the 21st Century Workforce Commission Report, June 2000.
6. Personal conversations with business executives, personnel managers, and recruiters, May 2000 and January 2003.
7. Aristotle, *The Rhetoric and Poetics of Aristotle*, trans. W. R. Roberts and I. Bywater (New York: The Modern Library, 1954), 24–25.
8. W. M. Smail, *Quintilian on Education*, Book XII, Chapter 1 (Oxford: Clarendon Press, 1938), 108.
9. U.S. Census Bureau, "Resident Population Estimates of the United States by Sex, Race, and Hispanic Origin: April 1, 1990 to July 1, 1999, with Short-Term Projection to November 1, 2000," www.census.gov/population. Internet release date: January 2, 2001; accessed April 30, 2003.
10. D. K. Berlo, *The Process of Communication* (New York: Holt, Rinehart and Winston, 1960), 23.
11. J. T. Masterson, S. A. Beebe, and N. H. Watson, *Speech Communication Theory and Practice* (New York: Holt, Rinehart and Winston, 1983), 6–7.
12. H. J. Leavitt and R. Mueller, "Some Effects of Feedback on Communication," *Human Relations* 4 (1951): 401–10.
13. D. O'Hair, G. W. Friedrich, J. M. Wiemann, and M. O. Wiemann, *Competent Communication*, 2nd ed. (New York: St. Martin's Press, 1997), 21.
14. B. S. Wood, ed., *Development of Functional Communication Competencies: Grades 7–12* (Urbana, Ill.: ERIC Clearinghouse on Reading and Communication Skills and Speech Communication Association, 1977), 5.
15. Ibid., 5–6.

"Resemblances are the shadows of differences. Different people see different similarities and similar differences."

—Vladimir Nabokov

CHAPTER 2 Connecting Perceptions and Communication

THIS CHAPTER WILL HELP YOU:

- Make the connection between perception and communication competence.
- Know what perception is and its affects on our communication.
- Understand why perceptions differ from one person to another.
- Interpret perceptions as well as improve your communication competence.

CASE STUDY

Jason's brother sees him as a guy who is not going to be pushed around. When he describes Jason to others, he will begin his description by saying that he's six-four, 280 pounds, very intelligent, doesn't say much, and someone you don't want to argue with.

Jason's girlfriend describes him as sweet, tall, muscular, smart, good looking, and very athletic. She also says that he is very quiet in large groups.

Jason's best friend describes him as hardworking, easy to get along with, average looking, an okay student, fun, not very talkative, and a team player.

Jason's mother describes him as shy, thoughtful, and her little boy.

Jason's father describes him as tough, big, lazy, and difficult to talk with.

Jason's coach describes him as a big kid with a real desire to win, a fearless competitor, a leader, quiet, smart, and a real team player.

Questions to think about

1. Not having met Jason, which description do you think best represents him? Why?
2. How do you think the above descriptors (i.e., tall, don't want to mess with him when he's mad, sweet, muscular, good looking, lazy, shy, team player, fearless, difficult to talk with) would influence your communication should you talk to Jason on the phone or meet him in person?
3. Is your perception of Jason affected by who is doing the describing?
4. What lessons can we learn from this scenario about perception and communication?
5. How do you think a competent communicator would respond to the above statements?

Perceptions do influence our reactions and our communication. It is virtually impossible for our feelings about things to be the same as others'. We perceive feelings based on communication.

Perception and Communication

Perception involves selecting, organizing, and interpreting information in order to give personal meaning to the communication we receive. What we perceive about ourselves, others, objects, and events gives meanings to our experiences, and it is these meanings, based on our perception, that we communicate to others. The meanings we give to our experiences almost always originate in us and do not reflect a totally objective account of the experiences themselves. No two people have internalized identical meanings for the same words, messages, or experiences. Communication is indeed personal! In this chapter, we discuss perception and how it is connected to communication. In Chapter 3, we focus on self-concept.

Perception is at the heart of all communication. It can also be argued that without communication, perceptions could not exist. Thus, the statement that communication is at the heart of all perceptions is equally true. Robert L. Scott, a communication scholar, writes, "Nothing is clear in and of itself but in some context for some persons."[1] A difference between two people's perceptions, for example, does not necessarily make the perception of one person more correct or accurate than that of the other. It does, however, mean that communication between individuals who see things differently may require more understanding, negotiation, persuasion, and tolerance of those differences.

Perception, like communication, is a complex phenomenon. To receive stimuli from our surroundings and to form perceptions requires that we utilize at least one of our five senses: hearing, touching, smelling, seeing, and tasting.

perception
The process of selecting, organizing, and interpreting information in order to give personal meaning to the communication we receive.

It is impossible to form perceptions without communication and vice versa. Because perception is a part of everything we do, it is very easy to dismiss it as unimportant—after all, it is something that happens automatically, and it seems as if we have little control over it. However, as was stated earlier, perception is an integral part of our communication. Perception does influence our reactions as indicated in the opening scenario where each description of Jason would influence our communication and behavior toward him. We also know that perceptions are relative. There is no

The 2000 presidential election demonstrations illustrated a controversial issue in which perception was at the heart of communication. When different people view the outcome of a situation in different ways, such as in this election, we need to stress understanding, negotiation, persuasion, and tolerance of our differences.

way to view people, situations, events, or objects objectively. For example, when someone says to another person, "I understand your feelings," the statement is based on perceptions of those feelings—not an identical experiencing of them. It is virtually impossible for one person to actually feel what another person feels; we perceive those feelings based on communication. Thus, it is extremely important to understand how perception influences our communication.

Know Your Scholar

Robert L. Scott *University of Minnesota*

Robert L. Scott is best known for his assertion that "rhetoric is epistemic," which means that in the process of communicating with others, people construct new knowledge. In other words, when we talk with others, we say things in certain ways that create a social meaning. The social meaning that is created relates to his statement: "Nothing is clear in and of itself but in some context for some persons." Thus, when different individuals see things differently it does require more understanding, negotiation, persuasion, and tolerance on everyone's part.

In 1976, Dr. Scott, wrote an article in which he reasserts the ethical character of rhetoric (persuasive discourse). In the article he attempts to answer three questions that seem to come up often: (1) "Is there one way of knowing or many?" (2) "What sort of knowing does rhetoric strive to achieve?" and (3) "Is rhetorical criticism vicious?" Scott concludes that rhetoric may be the art of persuasion but is also a means to understanding the human condition.

Dr. Scott is an emeritus faculty member at the University of Minnesota. He has published numerous research articles and books and was named a Distinguished Scholar by the National Communication Association—one of the first ten people in the communication discipline to be given this honor.

Understanding Perception

Perception as defined previously involves selecting, organizing, and interpreting, which are related to our cognitive abilities and how we internalize and process information. Perceiving in and of itself sounds and appears simple enough. After all, we do it every day, and it seems so natural that we hardly give our perceptions a thought. We just do it, think little about it, and move on. But perception is a very complex cognitive process that, if not understood, could lead to a variety of problems, some of which could be quite costly. To perceive our surroundings, we must first be aware of them. Second, we must cognitively analyze them, and then, finally, we must verbally communicate our perceptions.

Awareness

Imagine walking into the student union on your campus for the first time. What do you notice? More than likely your senses are fully engaged and you observe people moving in all directions. You see the food courts, the ATM, the beautiful carvings in the entrance, the signs that lead to various sections of the building, the bookstore, and so on. Being aware of your surroundings and taking in the sights, sounds, smells, and so on is basically paying attention to what's going on, absorbing each detail as if it were something at which to marvel. It is especially true when the situation is new or novel. However, we are creatures of habit, and when others behave in routine ways or when something is very predictable, we are more likely to gloss over the details of the other person or situation and become unaware or mindless.

Cognitive Process

Our cognitive processes have a profound effect on how we perceive others, how we talk with them, and how they respond to us. The way we process our experiences and the type of knowledge schemata that we use to organize and interpret those experiences differ for each of us. The level of our **cognitive complexity** is measured by the number of mental structures we use, how abstract they are, and how elaborately they interact to shape perceptions. For example, most children have simple cognitive systems in which to classify what they experience. When children see another person, they are likely to focus on concrete aspects, such as a person's height (tall or short), attractiveness (pretty or not pretty), or race (the same or different), rather than on abstract psychological aspects, such as sincerity, honesty, and so on. In addition, children often do not perceive relationships among multiple perceptions, such as how sincerity may relate to honesty or vice versa. For example, if a child sees an animal with four legs for the first time and is told that it is a dog (doggie), because of the child's low level of cognitive complexity, he or she will call every animal with four legs a dog (doggie) until taught otherwise. Young children cannot cognitively distinguish among four-legged animals until they are taught to make those distinctions.

cognitive complexity
The number of mental structures we use, how abstract they are, and how elaborately they interact to shape our perceptions.

Of course, as we mature and become adults, we learn to distinguish between and among different experiences, all of which help to develop our cognitive abilities. The more cognitively complex we are, the more sophisticated our level of perception. You might notice that a person talks a lot, dresses well, tells good jokes, and is attractive in appearance. At an abstract, psychological level you might infer that the behaviors you observe reflect an extroverted, sincere, secure, and self-confident personality. This level of assessment is a sophisticated explanation, because it involves perceptions of why the person acts as he or she does, and it is not based solely on concrete observations.

People who have high levels of cognitive complexity are likely to be flexible in interpreting complicated events and situations and are able to integrate new information into their perceptions. Also, people who are cognitively complex are likely to use "person-centered" messages when communicating with others. These individuals are likely to take multiple considerations into their perspective when communicating with others. For example, those with high degrees of cognitive complexity are able to take into account others' values, beliefs, and emotional needs and incorporate them into their messages. Being able to do this allows those with high levels of cognitive complexity to be effective communicators, because they are able to understand and process multiple perspectives at one time. Individuals who have less complex cognitive abilities, however, are unable to process multiple perspectives and, thus, often ignore information that does not fit their past experiences. They may even throw out their old perceptions completely and replace them with new ones.

Verbal Communication

Perceptions are usually associated with visual images, but we also form images of others based on their verbal communication. For example, how we use grammar, the words we choose, the way we pronounce words, or how we sound when we speak can lead to perceptions about a person's age, competency, intelligence, cultural or ethnic background, gender, and so on. Words, grammar, pronunciation, and sounds spoken create images, which can influence our communication and behaviors. Therefore, the connection between our perceptions and how we communicate and behave cannot be ignored.

The opening scenario of this chapter illustrates that what people say and how they say it can influence our perception of others. For example, the words used by those describing Jason depict extremely different ideas or pictures about who Jason is and what he is like. The image you form of Jason, however, depends on whose description you hear, his or her credibility, his or her ability to communicate perceptions of him to you, and the image you form on the basis of your understanding of the words used to describe him. Thus, your image of Jason is created through words and not through any action or behavior of Jason's that you have experienced.

Let's assume that you recently visited with Jason's girlfriend, and she told you how much she loved him but said that he was difficult to understand. You then meet a friend of Jason's girlfriend, who informs you that Jason is abusive to his girlfriend. How would this information affect your perception of Jason? More important, how would it influence your communication should you encounter Jason in person? Perceptions do change; it is not unusual for initial impressions we form about someone to change or become disconfirmed after subsequent interactions. We often set expectations for what we think someone is like based on what we have heard, but after time and additional interaction, we either find our initial perceptions to be accurate, modify our perceptions, or change them completely.

The Nature of Perception

Our lack of awareness of how perception operates can lead us to misunderstand and misjudge others' ideas and behavior. Many people imagine the brain to be similar in

TABLE 2.1

The Perception Process

TERM	DEFINITION	EXAMPLE
Selection	Sorting one stimulus from another	Selective exposure Selective attention Selective retention
Organization	Sorting, organizing, or categorizing	Closure Proximity Similarity
Interpretation	Assigning meaning to stimuli	Based on past experience Based on new situations Based on opinions of others

operation to a camera or tape recorder; information enters through the eyes or ears and is stored in the brain. Actually, far too much information exists for the brain to absorb at once, so the brain ignores much of it. It accepts a certain amount of information and organizes it into meaningful patterns. It discards a tremendous amount of information. Much of what we know about the way we perceive events, objects, and people seems to involve how we select, organize, and interpret information (see Table 2.1). All of these connections happen in milliseconds. Selecting must always occur first; however, organizing and interpreting do not always occur in exactly the same sequence. For example, it is possible to perceive information, interpret it, and then organize it or to organize it and then interpret it.

Selection

Because it is impossible to attend to, sense, perceive, retain, and give meaning to every stimulus we encounter, we narrow our focus. A **stimulus** incites or quickens action, feeling, or thought. Although we are exposed to millions of bits of stimuli, or data, at one time, the mind can process only a small fraction of them. On both the unconscious level of the nervous system and the conscious level of directing attention, **selection** occurs as the brain sorts one stimulus from another, based on criteria formed by our previous experiences. There are three kinds of selection: selective exposure, selective attention, and selective retention.

stimulus Something that incites or quickens action, feeling, or thought.

selection Sorting of one stimulus from another.

selective exposure The deliberate choices we make to experience or to avoid particular stimuli.

selective attention Focusing on specific stimuli while ignoring or downplaying other stimuli.

Selective Exposure. The deliberate choices we make to experience or to avoid experiencing particular stimuli are referred to as **selective exposure.** For example, you might dislike violent and sexist lyrics in the music you listen to, so you avoid purchasing CDs by certain individuals or groups known for such lyrics. When we choose to communicate with certain individuals instead of others, we are also using selective exposure.

Selective Attention. Focusing on specific stimuli while ignoring or downplaying other stimuli is called **selective attention.** That is, you concentrate on the data you wish to attend to, in order to eliminate or reduce the effects of all extraneous stimuli. This task is often easier said than done. Paying attention to something usually requires decisive effort, but even the best attempts to concentrate can be interrupted by

Making Connections

Not Seeing What Is Really Going On or Simply Bad Timing?

Nate has received his final grade back from his instructor, and he believes that he was treated unfairly. He decides to go the department chair to register his complaint about the instructor's unfair grade and the treatment he received from the instructor, which he thought was rude and insensitive.

Nate has heard from other students that the chair is autocratic, extremely busy, and difficult to talk with. The chair's office door is open. Nate walks in unannounced while she is at her computer. She looks over at him. Her facial and body expressions suggest that she doesn't want to be bothered.

Nate immediately tells her in no uncertain terms how upset he is about the grade he received and how rude the instructor was to him.

From what she has heard from instructors who have had him in class, the chair immediately recognizes Nate as a student who complains and believes that he has been treated unfairly.

Nate interprets the chair's reaction to him as uninterested and that she is more concerned with what she is doing on the computer than his complaint. This makes him even more upset.

1. Describe how perceptions affected the interaction in the above scenario?
2. On what are the chair's perceptions based? Are they fair and accurate?
3. If you were Nate, what would you have done differently?
4. If you were the chair, what would you have done differently?

distractions. For example, a book dropped in a quiet classroom, a loud sneeze, background talking, a siren, a baby's cry, a call for help, an odor, or a movement can avert our attention from the task in which we are involved. Continuing to attend to the original task may require extra effort. Similarly, when we converse with someone in a crowded lounge with loud music playing in the background, we focus on each other's words more attentively and ignore the other sounds. This blocking out of all extraneous stimuli to concentrate on the other person is an instance of selective attention. To make sense out of the multitude of stimuli that surrounds us, we learn to focus our senses on a few stimuli at a time.

Selective Retention. Because we cannot possibly remember all the stimuli we encounter, we also select the information we will retain. **Selective retention** occurs when we process, store, and retrieve information that we have already selected, organized, and interpreted. We are more likely to remember information that agrees with our views and to selectively forget information that does not. Also, after perceiving and selecting certain stimuli, we may retain only a portion of them. For example, how many times have you listened to someone tell you how to do something, and later, after thinking that you had completed the task, found that you had done only a portion of it? Chances are that you retained the pleasant parts of the task and forgot the not-so-pleasant parts. Selection plays an important role in what, why, and how we communicate.

selective retention Processing, storing, and retrieving of information that we have already selected, organized, and interpreted.

Organization

To help you understand how we organize stimuli and its effect on communication, consider what happens when you enter a room filled with people. When you first walk in, you begin to sort and organize people into groups or categories. Chances are

FIGURE 2.1

Closure: Cow or Incomplete Drawing? The partial outlines of this shape lead us to fill in the missing lines so that we can make sense of it. This organizing of the visual data allows us to give meaning to the drawing.

The Perception of Illusory Controls, Susan Petry and Glen E. Meyer, Eds., Figure 29.5, p. 266. New York: Springer-Verlag, 1987.

you will first begin to look for people whom you know; by doing so you are categorizing the people in the room according to those you know and those you don't know. People whom you know and who happen to be nearest to you are those whom you will likely visit first. It is also likely that you will spend more time with those whom you perceive to be like you than with those who are not.

In the crowd, a woman spots a man she has been interested in but whom she has met only briefly at another gathering. As she moves through the crowd toward him, another woman moves next to the man and places her arm around him. He also places his arm around her, and they engage in what seems to be intimate conversation. The first woman quickly moves back into the crowd so as not to be noticed by him and begins talking with another friend, but her mind is still concentrating on the image of the man and the other woman. Her thoughts of him drift off as she tries to involve herself in conversation with her friend. From this example, it is clear that the way we organize the stimuli around us affects our choices concerning with whom we communicate, what we communicate, how we communicate, and why we communicate with others.

We categorize stimuli in our environment in order to make sense of them. This **organization** of data plays an important role in how we perceive and communicate about events, objects, and people.

Closure. Another way to organize the stimuli around us is through **closure.** We tend to fill in missing pieces and to extend lines in order to finish or complete figures. This completion process is called closure. In Figure 2.1, we see a figure—a cow—that doesn't really exist in the printed material. This occurs because we are always trying to make meaningless material meaningful. We perceive the image of the cow by mentally connecting the white spaces. Interestingly, such illusory figures often seem to stand out in front of the disconnected shapes that suggest them, thus appearing to be closer to the viewer than the paper on which they are printed.

Filling in the blank spaces or missing information helps us categorize, label, and make sense of the things we see and hear. We sometimes do the same thing as we try to understand people. For example, if we don't know someone or the person is from a different ethnic or cultural background, we sometimes fill in unknown information in order to make sense of the person. Unfortunately, what we fill in may be based on biases and ignorance. When supplying missing information, we must remain aware of what we are doing and remember to distinguish between what we know and what we don't. Otherwise we increase our chances of forming a wrong or at least inaccurate perception of who the person really is. Our inaccurate perceptions about others can adversely affect communication, and that can be costly.

organization
Categorizing of stimuli in our environment in order to make sense of them.

closure
Filling in of details so that a partially perceived entity appears to be complete.

Making Connections

The Internet and Perception

Open your college or university's home page and randomly select three or four department home pages. Briefly examine the department websites by opening at least several of their links, for example, faculty, majors, course offerings, and so on. Answer the following questions:

1. What impressions did you form about the department based on what you saw on its home page?
2. Does the department's website give you the perception that it is friendly or unfriendly? Organized or unorganized? High or low quality? Professional or unprofessional? Personal or impersonal?
3. On the basis of your impressions (regardless of your major), would you want to visit the department to learn more about it? Why or why not?
4. If you met the department chair after seeing the website, would your interaction with him or her be affected? If so, how?
5. What did you learn about perception and communication from this Making Connections exercise?

Proximity. **Proximity** is the grouping of two or more stimuli that are close to one another, based on the assumption that because objects or people appear together, they are basically the same. This, of course, is not always true. For example, people who live close to each other do not necessarily behave in the same way, and for us to assume that they do would be inaccurate.

Similarity. Organization based on **similarity** involves the grouping of stimuli that resemble one another in size, shape, color, or other traits. For example, Shelly, who likes baseball, might believe that others who enjoy baseball resemble her in other ways as well. Thus, if Shelly likes both baseball and opera, she might assume that others who like baseball will also like opera. Of course, this may be wishful thinking on her part; just because two people are similar in one attribute doesn't automatically mean they will be similar in another. We sometimes make perceptual assumptions, such as Shelly's, when we see people from different cultures. We tend to assume that because people are similar in appearance, they must behave similarly as well.

Interpretation

Interpretation of what we see, hear, taste, touch, and smell is an integral part of how our perceptions influence our communication. **Interpretation** is the assigning of meaning to stimuli. We use our experiences, both past and present, as well as the opinions of others to aid us in interpreting the meaning of stimuli.

Interpretation Based on Past Experience. Our interpretations of stimuli depend on our past experiences. The more familiar you are with objects, events, and people, the less ambiguous your interpretations of them will be. For example, when you first arrived on campus, you probably either asked for help or consulted a map to locate various buildings and classrooms. Your perception of the campus layout was a bit unclear. With each passing day, however, you probably found it much easier to get around and probably even discovered shortcuts from one place to another. In similar ways, all of our experiences provide contexts that help us make sense of the world around us.

proximity
The grouping of two or more stimuli that are close to one another.

similarity
The grouping of stimuli that resemble one another in size, shape, color, or other traits.

interpretation
Assigning of meaning to stimuli.

FIGURE 2.2

Interpreting Perception: Young Woman or Old Woman? There is a distinct relationship between our perceptions and communication. This figure points out the importance of validating our perceptions and the experiences in which our perceptions are based before we communicate them to someone else. There may be more than one way to look at something and thus more than one interpretation of it.

(a) (b) (c)

Figure 2.2 demonstrates the connection between communication and perception. The figure also illustrates how our perceptions guide our interpretations of what we believe to be reality and how we communicate that reality. Look at part (a), and describe what you see. Do you see a person? If so, of what sex is the person? How old is the person? What is the person wearing? How easy would it be to communicate with the person you see? Did you see a young woman in the picture? An old woman? Or both? If you saw only one woman, look again until you see both the young woman (b) and the old woman (c) in part (a).

Although part (a) is designed to create an illusion, it does point out how easy it is for us to misinterpret what we see and to assume that we see the full picture. If you were shown only part (b) or only part (c) before you saw part (a), you would probably see the image you were first exposed to as you looked at ambiguous part (a). Try a little experiment by showing some of your friends part (b) first and some of your friends part (c) first. Then ask them to look at part (a). Do they see only the image to which they were first exposed? Tell them there is a second image and what it is. Can they find the second image? What does this tell you about how perception is connected to communication?

Interpretation Based on New Situations. Good communicators understand that others may not always agree with their view. They know that almost every issue has many sides and that if they don't want to be misunderstood, they must be careful to examine an issue from as many angles as possible before they try to pass on their views about it to others. They also know that jumping to conclusions can be a useless exercise, especially if those conclusions are not based on fact.

Although past experiences become a basis for our interpretations of stimuli, we must be careful not to let these experiences keep us from finding fresh meanings in new situations or events. For example, having an experience with an incompatible roommate does not automatically mean that your next roommate experience will be the same. Sometimes past experiences can act as blinders and thus produce inaccurate perceptions.

Each of us perceives the world through our own set of lenses or filters. We can never see precisely the same river, tree, mountain, person, or event, or hear the same message in exactly the same way that others do. We are different from one another.

Often people think that information by itself constitutes communication. It is not unusual to hear people say, "The truth doesn't lie," "Seeing is believing," or "The facts speak for themselves." This approach to communication is unfounded. Any information, regardless of the form in which it is received, must always be interpreted to be meaningful. Because interpretation is based on the experiences of the person who is receiving the information, often different people who receive exactly the same information will disagree about what it means, what it entails, or what conclusions can be drawn from it.

Each of us perceives the world through our own set of "lenses" or "filters." We can never see precisely the same river, tree, mountain, person, or event or hear the same message in exactly the same way that others do. We are different from one another. The scenario at the beginning of this chapter illustrates this quite clearly. One interpretation about Jason is not necessarily more accurate than another, but it is important to recognize the differences and how these differences affect communication.

Interpretations Based on Others' Opinions. Our perceptions are often altered or influenced by how and what others communicate to us. Much of what we learn about our world comes from magazines, newspapers, and television. Through these media, many of our perceptions of reality are formed. Often the world we know is shaped and created for us by the perceptions others have formed.

A few years ago, Washington D.C., had several major snowstorms. One day the headlines in two different newspapers read "Blizzard Paralyzes Capital" and "Snow Gives 300,000 Day Off in D.C." Both headlines were factually correct, but as you can see, they gave quite different interpretations of the same event. If you read the first headline, you would get one impression of the storm; if you read the second, you would get an entirely different message. Thus

Learning Connections

1. Explain the perception process in your own words.
2. What does one need to know to understand the perception process and its influence on communication?
3. Why is it that you can't always accept what you see and hear as being reality?

the perceptions and experiences of the authors of the headlines would shape your understanding of the snowstorm's effects on the city.

Perceptual Differences

Because communication takes place within each of us and because each of us is different, our perceptions of incoming messages may differ from what others perceive. Sometimes those differences are small and have no appreciable effect on the meaning of a specific message. In some situations, however, the differences between individuals and the circumstances in which they receive a message can actually reverse the communication's intended meaning or seriously distort it.

Our past experiences, our physical makeup, our cultural background, and our current psychological state determine what we perceive; how we interpret, evaluate, and organize our perceptions; and what actions we might take in response to them. The following sections discuss how our perceptions are influenced by these factors.

Perceptual Set

When we ignore new information and instead rely solely on past experiences—fixed, previously determined views of events, objects, and people—to interpret information, we are using a **perceptual set.**[2] A perceptual set allows our past experiences to control or focus our perceptions so that we ignore information that is different or has changed about an event, object, or person. It is a form of stereotyping. **Stereotyping** refers to the categorizing of events, objects, and people without regard to unique individual characteristics and qualities. Stereotyping, for example, exists in nearly every intercultural situation. Stereotyping is pervasive because of the human psychological need to categorize and classify information. Through stereotyping, we categorize or profile people. This tendency may hamper our communication, because it may cause us to overlook individual characteristics.

Also, stereotypes often oversimplify, overgeneralize, or exaggerate traits or qualities and thus are based on half-truths, distortions, and false premises—hardly fertile ground for successful communication. Finally, stereotypes repeat and reinforce beliefs until they come to be taken as the truth. Stereotypes ultimately perpetuate inaccuracies about people and thus impede communication. Although many stereotypes are negative, there are positive stereotypes as well. For example, to stereotype men as decisive or women as sensitive projects positive images that should be equally applicable to both genders.

Perceptual sets and stereotypes both involve selective attention and selective retention. The difference between a stereotype and a perceptual set is that a stereotype uses categories and perceptual set does not. To illustrate perceptual set, quickly read the statements inside the triangles in Figure 2.3. Look again. Did you notice two *as* and two *thes* in the statements the first time you read them? If you didn't, you are not alone. Most people don't notice these extra words for several reasons: (1) The statements are familiar and common, (2) most of us have learned to read groups of words rather than each individual word, (3) the words are placed in an unusual setting and in an unusual arrangement, and (4) we have been conditioned to ignore certain types of errors to achieve speed and efficiency in processing information. But perceptual set can interfere with communication. For example, some parents communicate with their offspring as if they were still children, even though they are adults. Their per-

perceptual set
A fixed, previously determined view of events, objects, or people.

stereotyping
The categorizing of events, objects, and people without regard to unique individual characteristics and qualities.

FIGURE 2.3

Perceptual Set Sometimes we see only what we want to see. Once we are familiar with something, we tend not to look closely to see if it differs from our expectations. How does this figure reveal how perceptual set affects us?

ceptual set may be the belief that "they are our children, and they will always be our children." Therefore, the parents are unwilling to communicate with them as adults.

Perceptual set may prevent us from seeing things that differ from what we expect to see and from noticing changes in things. Massimo Piattelli-Palmarini, in his book *Inevitable Illusions: How Mistakes of Reason Rule Our Minds,* uses the example of the St. Louis arch to illustrate the point that "the eye sees what it sees, even when we know what we know."[3] He points out that the arch is as wide as it is tall, yet it appears to be taller than it is wide. According to Piattelli-Palmarini, this inability to see the similarity between the arch's height and width demonstrates that our minds are unable to adjust their perceptions even when we know the facts. He says these errors, or cognitive illusions, usually occur without our being aware of them. Perceptual sets operate in a similar manner. Differences between what we do, what happens to us, and what is innate within us create bias, something that all of us have.[4] Our brain's ability to process information therefore is based on our experiences. Thus we should always make sure, or at least try to make sure, that what we see or hear or both see and hear represents reality rather than assumptions that may be false. A nineteenth-century humorist, Artemus Ward, put it this way: "It ain't the things we don't know that hurt us. It's the things we do know that ain't so." We are all at times victims of unconsciously making fallacious assumptions that can insidiously affect our encoding and decoding of messages.

Perceptual sets, like stereotypes, do not always limit or hinder us. Sometimes they help us to make decisions more efficiently. We could not make sense of the world without perceptual sets. They provide us with expectations of how things, events, or people should be, and they enable us to compare our expectations with the reality of the moment and to respond accordingly. The key is to avoid the assumption that perceptual sets will always be accurate. Many communication scholars believe that *the greatest single problem with human communication is the assumption that our perceptions are always correct.*[5] The fact is, people do not always act in prescribed ways in similar situations. Thus it is necessary for us to adapt to each individual circumstance.

Attribution Error

It is human nature to attribute, or assign, causes to people's behavior. **Attribution** is the complex process through which we attempt to understand the reasons behind

attribution
The complex process through which we attempt to understand the reasons behind others' behaviors.

others' behaviors. There are two sets of reasons that allow us to assign attributions about our own and others' behavior: the *situation* (environment) and the *disposition* (traits of the person). We are always trying to explain why people behave the way they do, and to do this, we must make assumptions. For example, imagine that you witness the following scene. A man arrives at a meeting one hour late. On entering, he drops his notes on the floor. While he is trying to pick them up, his glasses fall out of his coat pocket and break. Later, he spills coffee all over his tie. How would you explain these events? The chances are good that you would reach conclusions such as "This person is disorganized and clumsy." Are such attributions accurate? Perhaps. But it is also possible that the man was late because of unavoidable delays at the airport, dropped his notes because the paper was slick, and spilled his coffee because the cup was too hot to hold. Research shows that we are more likely to overestimate dispositional causes and underestimate situational causes of others' actions. This bias is referred to as the fundamental attribution error.[6] **Attribution error** occurs when we perceive others as acting as they do because they are "that kind of person" rather than because of any external factors that may have influenced their behavior.

Suppose, as actually happened during 1997 and 1998, a woman accuses the president of the United States of sexual harassment—for example, of making unwanted sexual advances toward her. Why would she do this? One possible reason is that she was very upset at the time and believed that it was her duty to call this inappropriate (and illegal) behavior by the president to public attention. But now suppose that soon after she made her claim, a reporter discovers that the woman had an affair with the president and was upset about being dumped by him. So another possible explanation for her action is revenge—perhaps she wanted retribution for what she perceived as mistreatment. After learning of this second potential cause, how would you view the first cause (her desire to do her duty and warn other women)? The chances are good that you will view it as a less likely or less important cause. Our tendency is to attribute dispositional causes to others' behaviors (she did it for revenge) and to attribute situational causes to our own behavior (I did it because I wanted to warn other women).

Now, in contrast, imagine the same situation involving the president with one difference: The woman makes her claim of sexual harassment even though she strongly supported the president and worked vigorously for his election in the past. What will you conclude about her claim now? You will probably believe that it is true and that it is motivated by the woman's desire to warn the public about the president's behavior. The difference in our perception of the woman depends on what we already know about the woman and what we attribute to her behavior.

Physical Characteristics

A person's weight, height, body shape, health, strength, and ability to use his or her five senses account for the way he or she takes in perceptual differences. For example, a person who is visually impaired experiences the world in ways that a sighted person finds difficult to comprehend or even imagine. Sighted people might not automatically take such differences into account, thus making communication more difficult.

Short people and tall people sometimes perceive events differently. Consider this situation: Two young boys were walking to a neighborhood store when two older boys threatened them with a knife and demanded their money. Afterward, the police asked the victims to describe their assailants. One boy gave the robbers' heights as about five feet six inches and five feet ten inches and estimated their ages to be about sixteen and

attribution error Perceiving others as acting as they do because they are "that kind of person" rather than because of any external factors that may have influenced their behavior.

twenty. The other boy described them as about five feet ten inches and six feet two inches and guessed their ages to be about twenty and twenty-seven. The first boy was nine years old and just over five feet tall; the other was six years old and four feet tall. Of course, the smaller boy perceived the robbers as much taller and older.[7]

The age and physical height differences between the son and the father clearly affect their perception of the snow depth. However, the father has not taken this difference into account in his communication.

Reprinted by permission of Jerry Marcus.

Psychological State

Another factor that can influence or alter our perceptions of people, events, and things is our state of mind. All information that we receive goes through various filters and screens that sort and color what we receive and how we perceive it. Obviously, when everything is going well and we are in a positive frame of mind, we view things, events, and people much more positively than when our mind-set is negative. When we are under a great deal of stress or if we have a poor self-image, these conditions will influence how we perceive the world around us. Sometimes this distortion is small and temporary and has no appreciable effect on communication. At other times, our state of mind can actually reverse meaning or alter a message, changing how we select, organize, and interpret it. It is undeniable that psychological disposition can color or alter perceptions and, ultimately, communication. Think about how you feel when you are upset, angry, or frustrated with someone or something and when you are not. How does your disposition affect your perception of that person or event? Our perceptions depend on our state of mind and how we see ourselves. In the next chapter, the connections between self-concept and perception are discussed in more detail.

Cultural Background

Cultural background can also affect the way in which people perceive other people, events, and things. To many people, culture can be explained as a status issue concerning manners, music, art, and types of food. Some historians, sociologists, archaeologists, and anthropologists use the term *culture* to describe particular early civilizations characterized by certain artifacts or

Making Connections

What Does This Mean to You?

Think about the two examples of interpretation that are described in the text: Two boys are accosted on their way to a neighborhood store and give contrasting descriptions of the assailants. A father and son depicted in the cartoon perceive the same physical conditions, the deep snow, in very different ways.

Now identify a set of physical characteristics in your own life that might be interpreted differently by you than by someone else.

1. How likely are your different interpretations of the same physical characteristics to influence your interaction with others?
2. Are some of the characteristics that you identified more likely to influence men's communication than women's, or vice versa? Why do you think so?
3. Ask students in your class who come from various cultural backgrounds to discuss their responses to questions 1 and 2. What were the differences, if any? Why are there differences?

Making Connections

Perceptions of Groups

Create a list of groups, such as Korean Americans, Midwesterners, Catholics, homosexuals, Muslims, ranchers, Protestants, and so on. You can use these groups if you wish, but you should try to add at least three to five of your own groups. Now select several of the groups, and list the traits most characteristic of each.

Would you find this a difficult task? Probably not. You likely will be able to construct a list of traits or characteristics of each group; moreover, you can do so even for those groups with whom you have had limited or no personal contact.

1. Why?
2. How do the characteristics you listed affect your perceptions?
3. In what ways would the list of characteristics you developed influence how you communicated about and with individuals in these groups?
4. Given the list you constructed and given what you have read about perception and communication, how would the list influence your communication with individuals from these groups?

practices. There are well over a hundred different definitions of culture, each taking a different perspective. For our purposes, **culture** may be best defined as learned behaviors that are communicated from one generation to another to promote individual and social survival.[8] A culture evolves through communication, beliefs, artifacts, and a style of living that is shared among people. A group's culture usually includes similarities in religion, language, thinking, social rules, laws, perceptions, communicative style, and attitudes, all of which contribute to a group's identity as being different from other groups.

Take a moment and reflect about the cultural beliefs that you hold that influence how you perceive the world and interact in it. Your views on work, education, freedom, age, competitiveness, personal space, cleanliness and hygiene, gender, loyalty, death and mourning, etiquette, health, status differentiation, bodily adornment, courtship, family, art, music, technology, and the like all play a role in your cultural identity.

Cultural identity has little or nothing to do with physical features such as skin color, shape of eyes, or sex because these characteristics are passed on genetically and not by communication. Because people of a particular race or country are often taught similar beliefs, values, and attitudes, those similarities have created such labels as "African American," "Hispanic American," "Native American," or "European American." Each of these labels by definition suggests that there are cultural differences among these groups, but the labels do not suggest that there may also be differences within the groups as well. Most of us have been conditioned to believe that people who are similar in race or nationality think and behave in the same way. This way of thinking, however, is likely to lead to misunderstandings and perceptual errors. For example, two European American business owners, one in New York City and the other in rural Nebraska, while labeled "European Americans," are likely to have different values, beliefs, and lifestyles because of where they live. Yet both are labeled European Americans. Therefore, to assume that they think and act alike because of how they are labeled or because of their physical features is likely to be wrong. The competent communicator does not rely on physical characteristics to make assumptions about people's values, attitudes, beliefs, or behaviors. The competent communicator does, however, learn about others through communication and observations of others' behaviors.

culture
Learned behaviors that are communicated from one generation to another to promote individual and social survival.

Culture is an integral part of each of us and determines many of our individual characteristics. Culture identifies us as members of a particular group and shapes our values and biases. Much cultural influence occurs without our realizing it; typically, we are not conscious of the fact that much of our behavior is conditioned by our culture. The way we greet others, the way we use language, our opinions about what and when to eat, and many of our personal preferences are all culturally conditioned.[9]

Ethnocentrism is a learned belief that one's own culture is superior to all others. This can affect how we look at others who are different from us and how we believe they should behave.

The connection between culture and communication is crucial to understanding communication. In fact, it is through the influence of culture that we learn to communicate at all according to Porter and Samovar. For example, a Korean, an Egyptian, or an American learns to communicate like other Koreans, Egyptians, or Americans. Each knows that certain behaviors convey certain meanings, because they are learned and shared in their respective cultures.[10] Just as they behave in a certain way, people also perceive and organize their thoughts, observations, and values according to the dictates of their culture. For example, in a purely scientific sense, the moon is a rocky sphere; yet when they look at the moon, many Americans see the "man in the moon." Some Native Americans view this same image as a rabbit, the Chinese interpret it as a lady fleeing her husband, and Samoans see in it the shape of a woman weaving.[11] These particular differences might not seem significant, but they point to the way that people from different cultures can view the same phenomenon quite differently. When cultural differences are apparent, it requires sensitivity, patience, and tolerance to avoid or reduce misunderstandings that can create barriers to effective communication and to relationship development.

Effective communication between people of diverse backgrounds can be limited or impossible if either party is unwilling to recognize that there is more than one correct viewpoint. Those who understand that they hold only one of many possible views are more likely to be tolerant and understanding when they encounter differences. Communicators must be willing to make appropriate adjustments when communicating with people from different cultures.

Those who cannot appreciate ideas, customs, or beliefs that differ from those of their own cultural background and who automatically assume that their own view is superior to that of any other culture are ethnocentric. **Ethnocentric** individuals go beyond pride in their heritage or background to the conviction that they know more and are better than those of other cultures. Those who lack interaction or contact with

ethnocentric
A person whose pride in his or her heritage or background leads to the conviction that he or she knows more and is better than those of other countries.

other cultures may find it hard to understand that other cultures and their practices may be as acceptable as our own. Even if we know of weaknesses in our own culture (too competitive, too materialistic, too informal, and so on), we are unlikely to criticize our culture when comparing it to others.

Ethnocentrism is a learned belief that our own culture is superior to all others. This is not necessarily a bad thing, but it does alter our perceptions and often colors how we look at others who are different from us. We learn to behave through our culture, and the way we behave, most of us believe, is the way everyone else should behave. We use our culture and our cultural behaviors as a yardstick by which we judge all other cultures and people who are different from us. The difference between a person's own culture and other cultures is often judged on a superiority–inferiority scale. People often view cultures that are different from their own as inferior. The greater the differences, the more people perceive other cultures to be inferior to their own.

A form of ethnocentrism is **cultural myopia,** which not only refers to perceiving one's own culture as superior to other cultures but also means a very narrow or shortsighted view of other cultures. Like ethnocentrism, cultural myopia is not usually a conscious act; it is usually learned at the unconscious level. For example, most American schools teach American history, geography, literature, and government, which indirectly is teaching cultural myopia and ethnocentrism. Of course, this kind of myopia and ethnocentrism also occurs in other cultures.

The way to avoid cultural myopia and ethnocentrism is cultural sensitivity training, which is training that makes each of us more sensitive to different cultures. Cultural sensitivity is not intended to change cultural behaviors, but it is intended to move people from a narrow view of the world to a broader worldview. Cultural sensitivity is understanding that being different doesn't mean being inferior. When people take on a broader worldview and open their minds to different cultures as merely being different and not judging them as inferior because they are different, they are accepting the philosophy of **cultural relativism.** People who have a cultural relativistic attitude strive to understand differences rather than to judge them so that intercultural relations can develop. Cultural relativism is "we-oriented," whereas ethnocentrism is "me-oriented." Cultural relativists are willing to put themselves in the place of others who have a different culture in order to understand it without making judgments about it. Understanding differences, however, does not require accepting those differences or even condoning them. Of course, anything or anyone who violates the basic human rights of others should not be supported or defended.

cultural myopia
Perceiving one's own culture as superior and having a very narrow or shortsighted view of cultures other than your own.

cultural relativism
Taking on a broader worldview and opening our minds to different cultures as merely being different and not judging them as inferior because they are different.

gender
A social construct related to masculine and feminine behaviors that are learned.

Gender

Another factor that colors the way we perceive the world is gender. Unlike biological sex, **gender** is a social construct related to masculine and feminine behaviors that are learned. Some theorists believe that women and men learn to perceive the world around them differently, resulting in different ways of communicating.

It has been shown, in groups containing both females and males, that males tend to talk for longer periods of time, take more turns at speaking, exert more control over the topic of conversation, and interrupt females more frequently than females interrupt males. Also, what males say appears to be taken more seriously than what females say.[12] These communication differences may occur because of how females and males perceive their roles and how the roles are defined by culture.

An interesting study on voice usage and perceived affection in initial interactions by Kory Floyd and George B. Bay, two communication scholars, found that men whose voices were higher-pitched were seen as weak or effeminate and would therefore not be seen by women as being a good relational fit.[13] However, with women, the opposite was found to be true. Women with higher-pitched voices were perceived to be more affectionate than women with lower-pitched voices. The researchers' conclusion is that men's voices are perceived to be friendlier and less dominant or aggressive when they are lower in pitch, whereas women's voices are perceived to be friendlier and less dominant when they are higher in pitch.[14]

There remains a great deal of uncertainty about what causes the differences in the roles of men and women in our society. We are told about "the gender gap" and that men and women don't understand each other or speak the same language. Men are often confused when women want to continue to talk about something that they think has been settled; women often find themselves frustrated when men don't seem to listen or respond to what they say. The perceptions that men and women have of each other and of themselves is not always clear, especially in this time of transition in which the roles of men and women are changing. Men are no longer the sole breadwinners, nor are women solely responsible for taking care of the home, as was once the traditional arrangement. Most of us today believe that there is no reason why both men and women cannot pursue careers or cannot be involved in homemaking and child care. Americans, as a group, have to some extent enlarged their perspectives on the roles and abilities of both men and women.

Media

Sometimes other people influence our perceptions deliberately. Advertisers, government leaders, political advocates, and many others attempt to shape our views. Advertisers have mastered techniques to encourage us to think and behave in ways that will benefit their clients.

Have you ever wondered how much the media influence our perceptions? In recent elections, candidates have hired people often referred to as "handlers" or "spin doctors." Their job is to create a positive image of the candidates and to protect them from any exposure that might create a negative image.

What about the shows we watch on television? Do they create or alter our perceptions? Although family sitcoms, for example, present families that are generally atypical, regardless of race or ethnic background, they still influence our image of families. Network news shows select events from all the reports they receive and present them to us in a half-hour broadcast, which, when the commercials are removed, amounts to approximately 24 minutes of actual news. The information we see is not only limited but also selected and edited for our consumption, affecting our perceptions of the world.

The influence of the media on our perceptions was no more evident than in the coverage of Operation Iraqi Freedom by the world's media. The media, whether supporting the Iraqi forces or supporting the allied forces, can create differing perceptions of who is winning or losing the war via what they say or what they show to their audiences. For example, Iraqi television showed captured and dead American soldiers to show that they were defeating the Americans. At the same time, American television, radio, and print media, while showing some of these same pictures, also showed thousands of Iraqi soldiers who had been captured or who had surrendered. The information sent by the media as to what was happening in the war depended greatly on what the media could and wanted to show its audiences.

These examples show that the media mold our perceptions in powerful ways. You might believe that there is nothing wrong with this, but think about how we depend on the media for information and how literally so many people accept what is presented to them. There can be a great deal of difference between reality and what is presented to us.

Making Connections

Media and Ethics

Bob, a photographer, was hired to create a positive image for a motel in a large city. His job is to take photographs that will make the motel appear attractive in a brochure. Bob discovers quickly that the motel is located in an undesirable part of town, parking is difficult, and there are few attractions nearby. Therefore, he does not take any shots that show the motel's surroundings. He photographs a model dressed to look like a distinguished businessperson approaching the newly remodeled entrance. He takes photos of a few attractive models in the pool. He takes a shot of one of the rooms using a wide-angle lens to give the illusion of spaciousness. Thus, Bob creates the impression that the motel attracts businesspeople, its customers are attractive, and its rooms are spacious. Bob's brochure is successful in influencing our perceptions of the motel.

1. Did Bob capture a sense of the real motel?
2. Can we assume that because "pictures don't lie," we should accept Bob's interpretation of what the motel is?
3. If Bob had taken his photographs without the attractive models, shown more of the surrounding area, and not used a wide-angle lens, would we have the same image of the motel? Would the brochure have been printed?
4. Are advertisers obligated to present their products in a completely truthful way?

Internet

As we come to depend more and more on the Internet for our information, it too has a tremendous influence on our perceptions of the world around us. Like the print and broadcast media, the Internet can be a valuable source of information that can provide both accurate and inaccurate perceptions. People who want to distort information or mislead us can easily do so via the Internet or in their email messages. Many who use email believe that their messages do not create perceptions or that, if they do, the perceptions are not interpretable. However, like anything that we communicate, our emails do create perceptions that are very interpretable. As senders of emails, we should always be aware that the messages we send are open to inferences and interpretations by those who receive them. Therefore, we need to be careful in what we write and how we write it. Those who receive our emails form impressions and make inferences based on the language we use, spelling accuracy, and the tone in which we write our messages.

We must also keep in mind that the information we receive via the Internet and email messages is only as good or as reliable as the sources of the websites or messages. What you see, hear, or read on the Internet or in your emails does affect your perceptions and ultimately your view of the world. The Internet is a powerful tool like the media, and like the media, the Internet cannot be assumed to be reliable information in and of itself. Competent communicators check the information they receive, especially when the source is unknown to them, to determine its truthfulness and accuracy.

Learning Connections

1. To what can we attribute perceptual differences?
2. Can you provide examples of perceptual mind-sets that occur in our society?
3. What is an attribution? Give an example.
4. How does ethnocentrism influence perceptions and ultimately communication?
5. Explain how perceptions influence how men and women are treated and how perceptions influence communication between men and women?
6. In what ways do the popular media influence how we see the world around us? Is this influence good or bad? Explain.

Improving Perception Competencies and Perception Checking

For us to be competent communicators, we must understand the impact that perceptions have on us, how we communicate with others, and what we accept as reality through the communication we receive. We tend to take the validity of our perceptions for granted and fail to look beneath the surface. But if we analyze specific personal experiences, we can begin to recognize and identify misperceptions that create communication problems for us. In this section, we first discuss ways to improve our competencies as perceivers of information, and then we discuss ways for us to check our perceptions for accuracy so that we can become more competent communicators (see Table 2.2).

Become an Active Perceiver

First, we must be active as perceivers. We must be willing to seek out as much information as possible about a given person, subject, event, or situation. The more information we obtain, the deeper our understanding and the more accurate our perceptions will be.

TABLE 2.2
The Perception Process

COMPETENCIES	ACTION/OUTCOMES
Be an active perceiver.	Seek out as much information as possible. Be ready to receive messages and attend to what is being communicated. Question your perceptions and the interpretations you give them to ensure that they are accurate.
Recognize that each person's frame of reference is unique.	Our view is only one of many possible views. Ask yourself whether there are multiple ways in which the message could be intepreted; if so, make sure that you ask questions to ensure that the correct message has been received.
Distinguish fact from inferences.	Know the difference between what is factual and what is being inferred—label inferences. For example, you might say, "I didn't see what actually happened, but this is what I believe happened."
Become aware of the role perceptions play in communication.	Avoid the tendency to assume too much about what you perceive before you test your perceptions for accuracy. Ask yourself whether there are other possible interpretations for the message received and how reliable is the message. Ask yourself whether it is possible that you are jumping to a conclusion too quickly.
Keep an open mind.	Always remind yourself that your perceptions might not be complete or accurate. You should ask yourself whether you are making judgments too quickly and whether you have considered all the information. This should be done especially when messages are coming from unknown or culturally different sources, to ensure that you are interpreting the messages correctly.

We must question our perceptions to determine how accurate they are. By considering the possibility that we may misinterpret information, we prompt ourselves to confirm facts and impressions before we draw conclusions. Taking the time to gather more information and to recheck the accuracy of our perceptions is well worth the effort.

Recognize That Each Person's Frame of Reference Is Unique

Second, we must recognize the uniqueness of our own frame of reference. We must remember that our view of things may be only one of many views. Each of us has a unique window to the world, as well as a unique system of understanding and storing data. Some of us make judgments about people based on appearance, whereas others base their judgments on ability, income, education, gender, ethnicity, or other factors. This variety of approaches shows that all of us operate on different perceptual systems, and it is wrong to assume that one system is better than another.

Distinguish Facts from Inferences

A third way to improve our perceptions and interpretations is to distinguish facts from inferences or assumptions. A fact is something put forth as objectively real that can be verified (proved), for example, which building is the world's tallest, that Gina has been late to class five times this semester, or that person *X* received more votes than person *Y*. An inference is an interpretation that goes beyond what we know to be factual. For example, Bonnie is always late to group meetings, she always stares off into space, and generally does not give her opinion. The members of the group see her as lazy, unprepared, and rude. Saying that she is lazy, unprepared, and rude goes beyond the facts; she might be late because of other commitments, she might stare off into space because she feels unwanted in the group, and she might not give her opinion because she is extremely shy.

Because facts and inferences are often extremely difficult to distinguish, it is very easy to confuse them. We sometimes treat inferences as if they are facts. A statement such as "Bonnie is lazy" sounds factual, and we tend to accept those types of statements as truth rather than communicating to find out what is fact and what is inference. We need to label our statements as our inferences when we communicate them. For example, saying "Bonnie seems to be lazy" is much more tentative and is not stated as a fact or certainty.

Become Aware of the Role Perceptions Play in Communication

A fourth way to improve our perceptions and interpretations is to be aware of the role that perceptions play in communication, take others' perceptions into account, and avoid the tendency to assume too much about what we perceive. To make the most of the information that we receive, we must first evaluate it. We should check the source of the information and the context in which the information was acquired. We should make sure we are not reading too much into the information. To help ensure that our perceptions are accurate, we should ask questions and obtain feedback whenever possible. We cannot determine whether our perceptions are accurate without testing them.

Keep an Open Mind

A fifth way to improve our perceptions and interpretations is to keep an open mind and remind ourselves that our perceptions may not be complete or totally accurate. Thus we must continue to make observations, seek out additional information, be willing to describe what we observe mentally and out loud, state what a given observation means to us, and put our perceptions into words to test their logic and soundness.

Making Connections

Checking Your Perceptions

From what you have read and studied in this chapter, are you convinced that our perceptions play a significant role in our communication? Below are two examples of situations in which the accuracy of perception is important to the outcome and future communication.

> Sue runs into the room crying. She can barely speak, but there is anger written all over her face. Sam, her boyfriend, knows from past experience that when Sue behaves in this way, he should leave her alone.
>
> Bob's eyes begin to drift over to Joan's paper. He begins to appear self-conscious and a little shifty in his behavior. The teacher observes Bob and begins to question Bob's honesty.

In both situations, the observer's initial perception might be wrong. To verify the accuracy of such perceptions, it is counterproductive to rush to judgment or to assume the worst. Discuss in class the following issues:

1. What questions might Sam ask of Sue to check his perceptions of her behavior?
2. What questions might the teacher ask Bob to confirm or to counter initial perceptions of Bob's behavior?
3. Write a brief paper describing a situation in which you have been involved where your initial perception of someone's behavior was incorrect. Also describe how the misperception was brought to your attention and what you did to correct the situation.

Perception Checking: Being a Competent Communicator

To improve the accuracy of our perceptions and their interpretations, we must learn to check our perceptions. There are so many variables and possibilities for misunderstanding that when it comes to interpreting perceptions, we must understand that it is very easy to jump to conclusions without knowing all of the information. For example, a friend of mine and I exchange emails periodically, but if I don't respond within a day or so of receiving his email, he assumes that I am upset with him. I am not upset with him, but that is what he perceives when I don't email him almost immediately after receiving his message. Think about this example, and think of how many times others have jumped to inaccurate conclusions about your thoughts, feelings, or motives.

Developing the skill of perception checking should help to prevent jumping to the wrong conclusions about others' thoughts, feelings, or motives. For example, a teacher who you think likes you walks by, you say, "Hi" and smile, but the teacher does not even acknowledge your presence, though you believe she looked directly at you. It would be very easy to assume that the teacher ignored you because she doesn't like you or that you are simply unimportant to her. A competent communicator would employ perception-checking skills, which would include the following:

1. Describe the teacher's behavior, which was that she ignored your presence.
2. Provide at least two interpretations of the teacher's behavior. Did she ignore you because she doesn't think you are important enough or because her mind was preoccupied and she didn't hear or see you?

Learning Connections

1. What is the most important lesson you learned from this chapter about perceptions and being a competent communicator?
2. Why do we so easily fall victim to drawing the wrong conclusions from perceptions?
3. Explain why perceptions play such an important role in our communication.

3. Finally, to verify your interpretation, you should ask the teacher, "Why didn't you say hello to me when we passed in the hall?" This will allow an opportunity to clear up any misunderstandings.

When you use perception checking as a means of verifying your perceptions, you are less likely to assume that your first interpretation is the only one or the correct one. To prevent misunderstandings or misinterpretation of perceptions requires cooperation and willingness to communicate and to leave your mind open to the communication received.

GUIDELINES Check Your Perceptions: Competent Communicators Do!

1. Learn to separate facts from assumptions.
2. Do not evaluate until you have ample information.
3. Remember that perceptions, especially first impressions, are not always accurate.
4. Learn to recognize your personal biases.
5. Recognize that people from different cultural backgrounds do not always attach the same meanings to events, objects, and people.
6. Remember that perceptions are a function of the perceiver, the perceived, and the situation in which the perception occurs.
7. Don't be afraid to communicate to verify your perceptions. If you don't ask, you leave yourself open to misinterpretations and misunderstandings.
8. Be willing to change your misperceptions.

Summary

Perception is the process of selecting, organizing, and interpreting information in order to give it personal meaning. It lies at the heart of the communication process. It is a part of everything we do; therefore, it is important to understand how it influences our communication. For us to be perceptive about our surroundings, we must first be aware of them, cognitively process them, and finally classify them via our language.

Perception involves selecting, or deliberately choosing to experience or to avoid particular stimuli; to focus on some stimuli and ignore or downplay other stimuli; and to retrieve information that we have already selected, organized, and interpreted. Organization is the categorizing of stimuli so that we can make sense of them and interpretation is the assigning of meaning to stimuli. A common phenomenon that can distort our perception of reality is a perceptual set, a fixed, previously determined view of people, things, or events. Perception set is a form of stereotyping. Stereotyping and our desire to attribute causes to people's behavior can also lead to inaccuracies in our perception and ultimately our communication.

When the sender and receiver have different cultural backgrounds, their communication can become more complicated. People whose pride in their heritage or background leads to the conviction that they know more and are better than those who differ are ethnocentric. A form of ethnocentrism is cultural myopia, which is a very narrow or shortsighted view of cultures other than your own. The opposite of ethnocentrism is cultural relativism, which is when people take a broader worldview and open their minds to different cultures as merely being different and not judging them as inferior because of differences.

Communication between men and women is also shaped by culture. Because our communication is grounded in our experiences and because our experiences exist within a culture, people who come from different cultural backgrounds bring a variety of perspectives and worldviews to their interactions with others.

To improve our communication, we should constantly remember that perceptions are not always the same for everyone and that our perceptions are only one view of many that may be possible. It is always wise to check your perceptions, especially when you might not have all of the information or if you are uncertain of its accuracy.

DISCUSSION STARTERS

1. Describe a person who is perceptively competent.
2. Explain the connection between perception and communication.
3. What effect does cognitive complexity have on our perception of the world around us?
4. Provide a personal experience that illustrates attribution error. How did the error affect communication?
5. Compare and contrast perceptual set with ethnocentrism.
6. What does it mean to take a position of cultural relativism?
7. Explain the role the Hollywood media have on our perceptions and ultimately how we perceive the world around us.
8. How do we form perceptions of people over the telephone and the decisions we make about them?
9. Are we more or less likely to make inferences about people if they send us an email message than if we see the individual in person?

NOTES

1. R. L. Scott, "On Viewing Rhetoric as Epistemic: Ten Years Later," *The Central States Speech Journal* (Winter 1976): 261.
2. W. V. Haney, *Communication and Organizational Behavior: Text and Cases,* 3rd ed. (Homewood, Ill.: Irwin, 1973), 289–408. The term "perceptual set" is similar to what W. V. Haney refers to as "programming" or "frozen evaluation" in his book *Communication and Interpersonal Relations: Text and Cases,* 5th ed. (Homewood, Ill., Irwin, 1986), 205–206, 408–38.
3. M. Piattelli-Palmarini, *Inevitable Illusions: How Mistakes of Reason Rule Our Minds* (New York: Wiley, 1994), 17.
4. Ibid., 18–19.
5. C. Stewart and W. Cash, *Interviewing: Principles and Practices,* 10th ed. (New York: McGraw-Hill, 2003), 31.
6. S. Kassin, *Psychology* (Upper Saddle River, N.J.: Prentice Hall, 1998); D. T. Gilbert and P. S. Malone, "The Correspondence Bias," *Psychological Bulletin* 117 (1995): 21–28; F. Van Overwalle, "Dispositional Attributions Require the Joint Application of the Methods of Difference and Agreement," *Personality and Social Psychology Bulletin* 23 (1997): 974–80; and E. E. Jones, "The Rocky Road from Acts to Dispositions," *American Psychologist* 34 (1979): 107–17.
7. J. Pearson and P. Nelson, *Understanding and Sharing: An Introduction to Speech Communication,* 3rd ed. (Dubuque, Iowa: Brown, 1985), 27.
8. The definition is based on the work found in L. A. Samovar and R. E. Porter, *Communication between Cultures,* 4th ed. (Belmont, Calif.: Wadsworth, 2001), 32–49, and 3rd ed. (Belmont, Calif.: Wadsworth, 1998), 36, and L. A. Samovar and R. E. Porter, "Understanding Intercultural Communication: An Introduction and Overview," in *Intercultural Communication: A Reader,* 10th ed., eds. L. A. Samovar and R. E. Porter (Belmont, Calif.: Wadsworth, 2003), 6–28.
9. N. L. Gage and D. C. Berliner, *Educational Psychology,* 6th ed. (Boston: Houghton Mifflin, 1998), 152–53.
10. R. E. Porter and L. A. Samovar, "An Introduction to Intercultural Communication," in *Intercultural Communication: A Reader,* 8th ed., eds. L. A. Samovar and R. E. Porter (Belmont, Calif.: Wadsworth, 1997), 20.
11. N. Dresser, *Multicultural Manners* (New York: Wiley, 1996), 89–90.
12. L. P. Stewart, P. J. Cooper, A. D. Stewart, and S. A. Friedley, *Communication and Gender,* 4th ed. (Boston: Allyn and Bacon, 2003), 44–45.
13. K. L. Floyd and G. B. Bay, "Mapping the Affectionate Voice: Vocalic Predictors of Perceived Affection in Initial Interactions," *Western Journal of Communication* 67 (Winter 2003): 56–73.
14. Ibid., 68.

"There's only one corner of the universe you can be certain of improving, and that's your own self."
—Aldous Huxley

CHAPTER 3 Connecting Self and Communication

THIS CHAPTER WILL HELP YOU:

- Make the connection between self-concept and perception.
- Understand how your self-concept is developed.
- See how self-concept is connected to communication.
- Understand how culture and gender affect self-concept.
- Improve your self-concept.

CASE STUDY

According to social and political commentator Andrew Sullivan's October 14, 2002 *Time* magazine essay "Lacking in Self-Esteem? Good for You!," Senator Robert Torricelli of New Jersey used the word *I* ninety-nine times in his speech bowing out of the New Jersey Senate race. The following are excerpts of what Torricelli said in his speech:

> *I* want to live life again . . . *I* want to notice the passing of the seasons . . . *I* even want to notice the aging of my friends and family . . . it is time for me to reclaim my life . . . *I* have done my duty to my country . . . Somewhere today in one of several hospitals in New Jersey, some woman's life is going to be changed because of mammography centers *I've* created for thousands of women . . . Somewhere all over New Jersey some senior citizen who doesn't know my name lives in a senior center that *I* helped build . . . that's my life. Don't feel badly for me. *I* changed people's lives.

What we tell others about ourselves says a lot about who we think we are and the images we want others to believe about us. From Senator Torricelli's comments, one could easily conclude that he has a lot of regard for himself and the accomplishments he attributes to himself. What his comments don't tell you, according to Sullivan, is that Torricelli's withdrawal from the Senate race was because his colleagues in the Senate and House had admonished him for unethical behavior and his poll numbers were plummeting.

Sullivan writes, "Such details were obscured by the blinding brightness of the man's self-love."

Questions to think about

1. What lesson or lessons can we learn about self-esteem from the above scenario?
2. How can the scenario and the lessons you have learned from it help us better understand how self-esteem and self-concept affect our communication?

CASE STUDY *(continued)*

3. Why have self-esteem, self-image, and self-concept become so important, especially to people in American culture?
4. Describe the role that self-concept has in your communication with others?
5. What are the differences—if any—among self-concept, self-esteem, and self-image?
6. How can the above scenario help you to become a more competent communicator?

The question that most of us have asked at one time or another about ourselves is "Who is the real me?" We know from Chapter 2 that our perceptions of things and others are subjective as well as open to interpretation. We also learned that the accuracy of our perceptions is always questionable because what we perceive about objects or others may not be the same as others perceive them. In this chapter, we provide possible answers to the above question—a question that each of us asks about ourselves but for which we seldom find a complete, entirely accurate, or satisfying answer.

Each of us is an extremely complex person. Very early in our lives, we begin learning who we are—or at least who we think we are. We develop a social identity, or self-definition, that includes how we conceptualize ourselves and how we evaluate ourselves. For each of us, this identity includes our sex, relationships, vocation or avocation, political or ideological affiliation, and other aspects of the self, such as religion, race, or ethnic background.

To become competent communicators, we must understand that our image of self plays a significant role in how we communicate with others and how others communicate with us. Therefore we must understand what self-concept is and how it connects to our communication with others.

Many psychologists believe there are many selves: a social self, a psychological self, a physical self, and so on. Each of these aspects of self contributes to a larger general view of self, which is in essence our identity. Each aspect is discussed in more detail in this chapter.

Who then are you? Describe yourself. (For a Personal Inventory questionnaire, go to www.ablongman.com/seiler6e.) It's not easy for most of us to describe ourselves, but we are often asked in interviews or personal conversations to do just that. Therefore, it is important to be able to respond with a thoughtful description that includes strengths and weaknesses. The next question that arises is "What makes you think your description actually describes you?"

Understanding Self-Concept

self-concept
A person's perceived self, which consists of an organized collection of beliefs and attitudes about self.

Our **self-concept** or self-identity is our perceived self, which consists of an organized collection of beliefs and attitudes about self. Who we perceive ourselves to be is determined by our experiences and communication with others, the roles and values we

FIGURE 3.1

The Self-Concept Self-concept is determined by our experiences and communication with others, the roles and values we have selected for ourselves, our perception of how others see us, and how we evaluate ourselves.

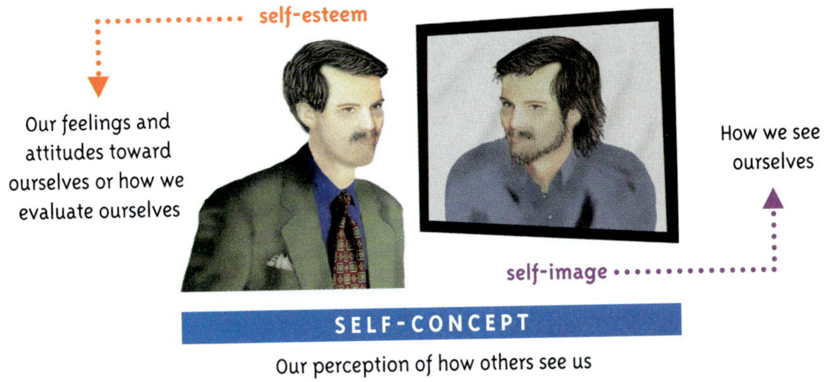

have selected for ourselves, and how we believe others see us (see Figure 3.1). Self-concept consists of two subcomponents: **self-image,** how we see ourselves or our mental picture of self (for example, I see myself as being a person, an athlete, student, worker, female, daughter, and mother), and **self-esteem,** our feelings and attitudes toward ourselves or how we evaluate ourselves (for example, I feel that I am an okay person, an average athlete, a good student, a hard worker, sexy, loving daughter, and an average mother). Both self-image and self-esteem make up our self-concept.

Self-concept and perception are very closely related, so it is difficult to separate them. They constantly interact. For example, what you think about yourself shapes, and in many ways determines, what you do and say. What you think about yourself is influenced by the information you receive from others, which helps you create an image of who you are. If you think of yourself as a good piano player, you would take positive comments made about your piano playing as affirmation of your ability and skill. If someone made a disparaging comment, however, you probably would dismiss it as not reflecting your notion of how well you play the piano. In fact, you might interpret the comment as a sign of jealousy or humor or simply feel that the person who made the comment doesn't know you.

The messages that we communicate, intentionally or unintentionally, relate directly to how we feel about and view ourselves. Who and what we perceive ourselves to be influence how we present ourselves to others. What and how we communicate with others and the reactions of others toward us help develop our self-image and self-esteem, both of which ultimately make up our self-concept. Each of us has a unique identity and a special sense of who we are.

Why is it important for us to understand the connection between communication and self-concept? Think about this, and read on to find an answer to the question.

self-image
A person's mental picture of himself or herself.

self-esteem
A person's feelings and attitudes toward himself or herself.

Self-Concept as a Process

Communication is a dynamic process because it has no beginning or end and is constantly changing. In the same sense, self-concept is also a process. Self-perceptions and

Making Connections

Discovering Your Self-Esteem Level on the Internet

Go to www.queendom.com/tests/personality/self_esteem_r_access.html. On this website you will find a test that is designed to evaluate your general level of self-esteem. Follow the instructions, and you will get a score and a brief interpretation of what the score means.

1. How would you explain the score you received?
2. What factors or events in your life do you think contributed most to your self-esteem?
3. What are the things that you would change about yourself if you could?
4. How can taking a test such as this one help you to better understand the role your self-esteem has in your communication with others?
5. Using an Internet search engine, search using the word *self-concept, self-identity, self-esteem,* or *self-image.* What do you find?

the perceptions others have of us differ from time to time, from situation to situation, and from person to person. For example, your view of yourself may vary somewhat according to how you feel about yourself at a given time. If you receive a high grade in a difficult class, you might feel good about yourself or at least about your effectiveness as a student. Your view of yourself might differ if you receive a low grade. In addition, the perception you have of yourself as a student is probably different from the one you have of yourself as a worker or a family member.

In the opening scenario, we get a glimpse of Senator Torricelli's perception of himself and some indication of the perceptions of those who want him out of the Senate, but do we know the real Senator Torricelli? The perceptions, however, whether accurate or inaccurate, become Senator Torricelli as seen by others and himself. His self-concept consists of his and others' perceptions and is determined by the beliefs he holds about those perceptions. Although the perceptions held by others might not be accurate or completely known to the Senator, nevertheless, these perceptions affect him, and he must deal with them. If Torricelli knows what his colleagues and constituents think of him, how will it affect his communication with them?

The perceptions we believe others have of us affect how we receive their communication and influence our responses and vice versa. Equally, our view of ourselves influences how we communicate with others. Communication and self-concept are inseparable and both involve process—continuous change with no beginning or end.

Making Connections

Journaling Online: The Internet Offers the Opportunity

A July 14, 2002, lead article in the Life Trends, People, Issues section of the *Lincoln Journal Star* newspaper by Crystal K. Wiebe entitled "Making Connections" describes how people use the Internet to create their identity with others through online journaling. If you are interested in journaling online, go to www.livejournal.com. Please read all the information on the website to ensure that you understand how the site operates.

Caution: The Web is open to the public, and there is no certainty of privacy. This website does allow users several privacy settings, however, depending on how much you want to limit others' access to your writing.

Development of Self-Concept

When we were children, our first communication involved sensing our environment—all the sights, sounds, tastes, and smells that surrounded us. We learned about ourselves as others touched us and spoke to us. Their responses to us helped to determine how we view ourselves. Parental communication, both verbal and nonverbal, generally has an extremely strong impact on the initial development of self-concept. For example, the clothes and toys that they provided and what and how they communicated to us affected who we have become in some way. As we age and expand our environment and relationships, the communication of others

In Papua New Guinea, two Huli children see themselves in an instant photograph. We see ourselves based on how we think we look and on how we think others see us. Our self-image and self-esteem are often based on these interactions.

may reinforce or alter our perceptions of self. In her book *Old Is Not a Four-Letter Word: A Midlife Guide,* Anne Gerike writes that there are advantages to aging. For example, she says that aging brings increased self-confidence, a more reliable inner voice or "gut feeling," an acceptance of not being perfect, a sense of perspective that difficult situations get worked out, an acceptance that life isn't fair, and a willingness to accept responsibility instead of directing the blame elsewhere.[1] Assuming that Gerike's observations are correct, why do you think such developments occur with age?

Making Connections

What Others Say Can Influence Who We Are

You're pathetic. You can't do anything right!

Get outta here! I'm sick of looking at your face.

You're more trouble than you are worth. I wish you'd never been born.

You're so talented. You do everything so well!

I enjoy having you around! Your smile makes me feel good!

You're so helpful and easy to love. I am glad you are here.

People often believe what others tell them. Stop and listen to what you are saying. You might be surprised at some of the messages you've been sending to people for whom you care or should care.

1. In what way does our communication help to form others' concepts of themselves?
2. In what way does our communication reflect who we are?
3. Why is it that putting other people down seems to be so fashionable in our society?

"Gordon's got very low self esteem. Haven't you? You bald headed four eyed twit."

We sometimes make insulting comments to be funny—especially at the expense of those we supposedly care about—not realizing the negative impact those comments may have on them.

www.CartoonStock.com

Social psychologist Daryl J. Bem believes that sometimes we don't know our own attitudes, feelings, or emotions directly. We therefore focus on others to obtain such information.[2] Bem does, however, indicate that we learn a great deal about ourselves by observing our own behaviors. He suggests that what we do or how we act is a guide to what is happening inside us and how we feel about ourselves. Further, according to Bem, we draw inferences about ourselves in the same manner that we do about others. Thus the process through which we come to know ourselves is very similar to the process through which we come to know others.

Our self-concept, which develops through an extremely complex process, usually consists of many images that we place on a continuum, ranging from negative to positive. There is no way to predict which image will dominate because our view of ourselves is a composite of all the self-images, which is ever in a state of flux. Self-concept is affected not only by how we perceive ourselves, but also by how we perceive others, how others perceive us, and how we think others perceive us, as the cartoon on this page suggests. Self-concept is based on both past and present experiences, which affect how we will perceive ourselves in the future. Our self-concept is further determined by the values, attitudes, and beliefs we possess; how we attribute these qualities to others; and how they connect them to us.

Values. General, relatively long-lasting ideals that guide our behavior are called **values.** Values can be classified into broad categories, such as aesthetic, religious, humanitarian, intellectual, and material. Each category determines our behavior as well as our communication and is reflected in our self-concept. For example, if material objects are important to us, we tend to judge ourselves by what we do or do not possess. A desire to have the finer things in life is not unusual, at least in our society, but the strength of the desire can greatly affect our behavior. Possessions can become so important to some people that they ignore other concerns. They may pursue high income at the expense of job satisfaction, family life, leisure time, and personal health. Thus values can have both positive and negative influences on how we behave and communicate.

value
A general, relatively long-lasting ideal that guides behavior.

attitude
An evaluative disposition, feeling, or position about oneself, others, events, ideas, or objects.

Attitudes. Evaluative dispositions, feelings, or positions about oneself, others, events, ideas, or objects are called **attitudes.** Attitudes help determine self-concept, but unlike values, they are more narrowly defined. The relationship between values and attitudes is close because values are reflected in attitudes. For example, your attitude might be that the university is spending too much money on athletics, especially at the expense of undergraduate academic programs. Your attitude says something about your value system; in other words, you value academics over athletics.

Making Connections

Values, Attitudes, and Beliefs about People with Disabilities

Be honest: Have you ever felt uneasy in the presence of a person with a physical disability? Words and phrases such as "Handicapped person confined to a wheelchair . . ." or "Young women stricken with cerebral palsy . . ." can shape incorrect perceptions of people with disabilities. The stigma or negative attitudes are often the greatest barrier that those with disabilities must overcome. People with disabilities are more similar to people without disabilities than most of us think. Most people with disabilities don't see their disability as a liability or limitation but see it as who they are. The problem for most of us is that we are strongly influenced by the visible characteristics and appearance of others. We might not be conscious of these reactions until they are pointed out. However, our actions, whether or not they are conscious, communicate our values and attitudes and ultimately affect our beliefs as well.

1. Why do phrases like those above form our values, attitudes, and beliefs about people with disabilities?
2. What are some of the values, attitudes, and beliefs that many people hold that make them see the disability first rather than the person first?
3. How might we use what we have learned here to help ensure that we communicate with sensitivity? Develop your own suggestions first, and then do an Internet search using the key words *interacting with people with disabilities* to see whether there are suggestions that you haven't thought about.
4. Provide a written example of a value, attitude, or belief of your own to share with your classmates.

An excellent resource on communicating with people with disabilities is the *Handbook of Communication and People with Disabilities Research and Application,* edited by Dawn O. Braithwaite and Teresa L. Thompson, New Jersey: Lawrence Erlbaum Associates. For a fascinating perspective regarding self-esteem, see an interview with Lucy Grealy, author of *Autobiography of a Face,* at www.findarticles.com/cf_0/m1285/n2_v26/18082720/p1/article.jhtml.

Making Connections

The Excuse?

Suppose that you are meeting a friend, and this person is late. In fact, after forty minutes, you begin to suspect that your friend will never arrive. Finally, your friend appears on the scene and says, "Sorry, our meeting just slipped my mind!" How would you react?

Imagine that your friend instead says, "I am really sorry for being late. There was a terrific accident, and there was a huge backup of traffic for miles." Now how would you react?

If this is the first time your friend has been late for an appointment or your friend has never used this type of an excuse before, you may accept the explanation as true.

Now suppose that your friend is always late and has used similar excuses before. You might well be suspicious about whether this explanation is true.

1. On what will your reaction to this situation depend?
2. On what will your judgment regarding the real reason for your friend's lateness depend?
3. How will your communication be affected by the values, attitudes, and beliefs you hold regarding your friend?

TABLE 3.1

Values, Attitudes, and Beliefs

	DEFINITION	EXAMPLE	YOUR EXAMPLES
Values	Broad-based ideals that are relatively long-lasting	Everyone should have an education.	
Attitudes	Evaluative dispositions, feelings, or positions about ourselves, other persons, events, ideas, or objects	Our educational system, as it operates today, is too costly.	
Beliefs	Convictions or confidence in the truth of something that lacks absolute proof	Even though it has its faults, our educational system is the best in the world.	

Beliefs. Closely related to attitudes are beliefs. A **belief** is a conviction or confidence in the truth of something that is not based on absolute proof. We have, for example, beliefs about history, religion, schools, events, people, and ourselves. We say, "Space exploration is helpful to humanity," "God is good to us," "Speech class is important," "We will win the homecoming game," "I know Sally loves me," or "I am going to get a high grade on my next speech." These statements and hundreds of similar statements that we make daily could begin with "I believe . . . " or "There is evidence that . . . ."

Our beliefs, like our attitudes and values, have a hierarchy of importance. That is, some are much more important to us than others. Our most important beliefs, such as those about religion, education, and family life, do not change easily, but our less important beliefs, such as those about today's weather or the outcome of a sports event, are only momentary in duration.

Making clear and absolute distinctions among values, attitudes, and beliefs is difficult because they are interrelated. Consider, for example, the close relationship among the following three statements:

Value (ideal): People should love one another.

Attitude (feeling or position): Love is good.

Belief (conviction): Love is important in our lives.

Attitudes differ from beliefs in that attitudes include an evaluation of whether someone or something is good or bad. Beliefs, in turn, reflect the perception of whether something is true or false. Your attitudes and beliefs about love may change as a result of your experiences, but the value you place on love endures. Table 3.1 provides definitions and examples of values, attitudes, and beliefs, with space for you to add your own examples.

belief
A conviction or confidence in the truth of something that is not based on absolute proof.

The Hierarchy of Self-Concept

Like the beliefs we hold, the components of our self-concept may be organized into a hierarchy, as shown in Figure 3.2. At the highest level is our general self-concept, a set

FIGURE 3.2

Hierarchy of Self-Concept Our self-concept is made up of many different levels of beliefs, images, feelings, and characteristics that help determine who we are.

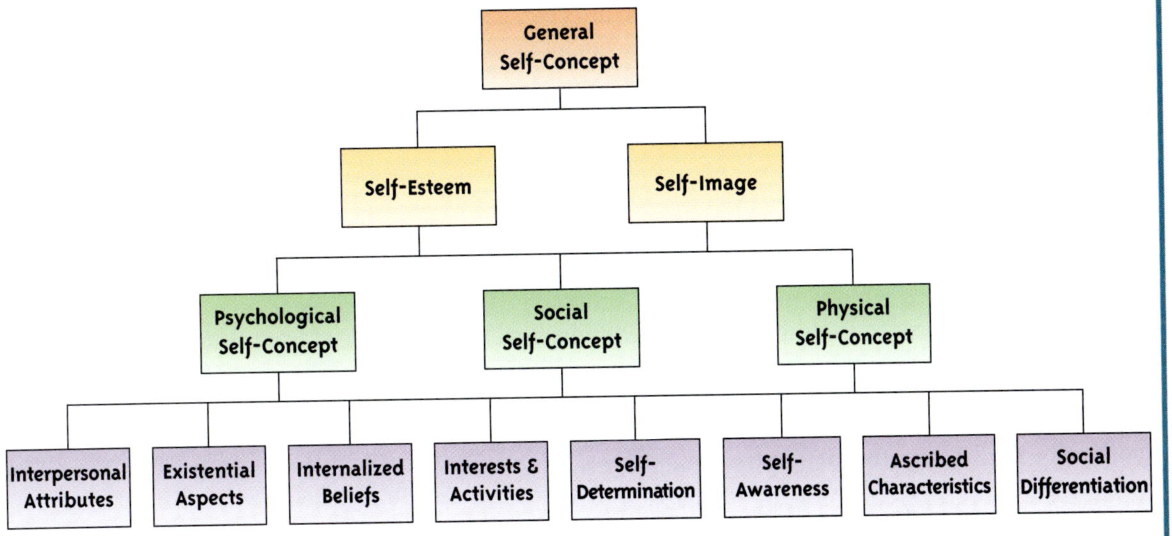

of beliefs we hold about ourselves. These beliefs are well established and relatively difficult to modify. At the second level are the principal components of self-concept: self-esteem and self-image.

The next level consists of the elements that form our self-esteem and self-image: psychological self-concept, social self-concept, and physical self-concept. On the lowest level are self-concepts related to specific characteristics, such as interpersonal attributes, existential aspects, internalized beliefs, interests and activities, self-determination, self-awareness, ascribed characteristics, and social differentiation.

The farther we travel down the hierarchy, the more specific and the more susceptible to change the elements become. On the lowest level, the elements not only are susceptible to change, but also often vary from situation to situation, develop over time, and affect our self-concept in positive or negative ways. For example, during high school, the academic self-concept of one of the author's daughters was heavily based on her grades and the teacher feedback she received about her work and attitude. Her athletic self-concept was heavily dependent on her play during a given game; on how the coach, teammates, and her friends reacted to that play; and on her perceptions of her own play. During the past several years, her self-concept regarding her academic ability has changed dramatically from modestly positive to extremely positive since she has graduated from college. Yet her perceptions of her intelligence and academic ability seem to vary somewhat from one day to the next, depending on how successful she perceives herself to be. However, her success in athletics as a high school student brought her self-confidence and respect from her peers and coaches. Her athletic self-concept has been quite positive and remains that way even though she is no longer involved in formal athletics.

Learning Connections

1. How is self-concept formed?
2. Why is it important to understand self-concept and its influence on our communication?
3. What, if anything, do our attitudes, beliefs, and values have to do with our self-image?
4. Explain why it is important to know that our self-concept forms a hierarchy.

Communication and Self-Concept

A reciprocal connection seems to exist between self-concept and the way we communicate: Communication affects the self-concept, and self-concept affects how and what we communicate. A model developed by social psychologist John W. Kinch[3] demonstrates this relationship (see Figure 3.3). Our perceptions of how others respond to us (P) affect our self-concept (S). Our self-concept affects how we behave (B). Our behavior is directly related to how others react to our behavior (A). The actual responses of others relate to our perceptions of others' responses (P), and so we have come full circle.

According to William W. Wilmot, a leading communication scholar, "each person's view of himself affects his as well as his partner's behavior."[4] This view of self is referred to as our *social self-concept.* It in turn consists of two components: one derived from interpersonal relationships and one derived from belonging to larger, less personal groupings such as race, ethnicity, or culture. This means that our self-concept is influenced by our interaction with others. How we perceive the communication that we receive from others has a direct impact on our self-concept and our subsequent communication.

Personality theorists such as the late Carl Rogers believe that our self-concept is the single most important aspect of our personality. Our image of self determines our personality, which in turn determines our style of communication. When interactions are considered with respect to self, it becomes necessary to take the context and the person or people with whom you are communicating into account. It is generally

FIGURE 3.3

Kinch's Model of the Connection between Self-Concept and Communication Kinch illustrates the relationship between self-concept and communication. Our self-concept is based on our communication with others.

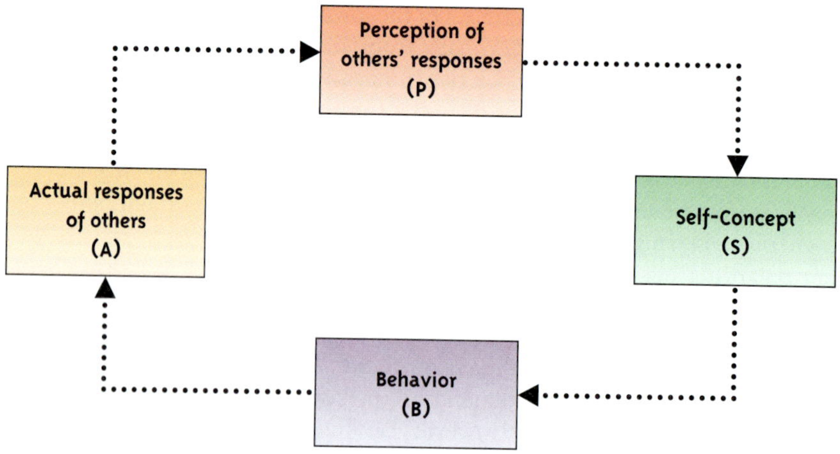

Source: J. Kinch, "A Formalized Theory of the Self-Concept," *American Journal of Sociology* 68 (January 1963): 481–86. University of Chicago Press. Reprinted by permission.

agreed that people with high social self-concepts function better in interpersonal situations than do those with low social self-concepts. The question here is not so much "Who are you?" but "Who are you when you are with your best friend, your mother, your father, both your mother and father, people you don't know, and so on?" In other words, our image of self determines our communication style as seen by others and internalized by us, which in turn affects how we communicate with others.

There is some evidence that how others see us relates to our style of communication, which in turn is a reflection of our self-concept. A study by Cynthia Stohl, a communication scholar, examining the connection between preschool children's style of communication and their physical attractiveness as perceived by their teachers and peers found that the higher children were rated on communication style, the more attractive they were to others. Those who were rated as less attractive were seen as having lower "communicator image," that is, were less "open, dramatic, contentious, animated, or impression leaving."[5]

There is a connection between self-concept and the way we communicate—our communication affects our self-concept, and self-concept affects how and what we communicate. The way we perceive the communication we receive from others has a direct impact on our self-concept and our subsequent communication.

Also relevant to style of communication is the notion of communication apprehension, which also relates directly to self-concept. **Communication apprehension** is "an anxiety syndrome associated with either real or anticipated communication with another person or persons."[6] Fear of communicating with others is a learned behavior that is usually based on how we think others will respond to our communication and to us. Communication apprehension can involve a fear not only of public speaking, but also of any form of communication. Some highly apprehensive people avoid talking, but others talk incessantly or inappropriately because of their nervousness. The fear of communicating with others also forms a part of self-concept, and thus communication apprehension affects how we interact with others and how they interact with us. Those who have a high level of anxiety are often perceived as unwilling to communicate, shy, withdrawn, less intelligent, less social, less attractive, less competitive, lower in self-esteem, lower in credibility, and so forth. These perceptions may not reflect reality. This problem can also reinforce itself over time. If we expect ourselves to be anxious in a particular situation, we are likely to be anxious. For those who have little communication apprehension, the opposite would likely be true. For more on communication apprehension, see Chapter 10. If you are interested, you can do a quick analysis of your level of communication apprehension by going to www.rollins.edu/communication/wschmidt/apprehension.htm.

communication apprehension
Anxiety associated with real or anticipated communication with another person or persons.

Expectations that others have of us play an important role in determining our self-concept because others often behave and communicate with us on the basis of their expectations. Thus our self-concept is formed to a large extent by the communication we receive from others.

Know Your Scholar

Cynthia Stohl *University of California, Santa Barbara*

Cynthia Stohl's research and teaching are embodied in the title of her award-winning book *Organizational Communication: Connectedness in Action.* Linking interpersonal and small-group communication processes to larger structural and cultural systems, Professor Stohl develops a global perspective on organizational communication. Building on her early work on the development of communicative competence and young children's social networks in daycare centers, Dr. Stohl's research explores the ways in which interpersonal, group, and organizational communication processes are embedded in overlapping networks of relationships that transcend personal and organizational boundaries.

In 1995, Dr. Stohl wrote, "It is through communication we evolve our culture, our social structure, our world views and shape our perceptions of what is and what could be. . . . To conceive of the world in terms of our communicative connections produces exciting possibilities and great responsibilities." Throughout her work, Dr. Stohl reminds us of the ethical dimensions of communication structures and practices.

Dr. Stohl is a Professor of Communication at the University of California, Santa Barbara. Before moving to Santa Barbara, she was the Margaret Church Distinguished Professor of Communication at Purdue University. She is the recipient of several teaching and research awards, including the 1998 National Communication Association's Organizational Communication Division "Best Article" award for "Democracy, Participation, and Communication at Work," an article she co-authored with Dr. George Cheney.

Self-Fulfilling Prophecy and Impression Management

In addition to values, attitudes, and beliefs, expectations determine how we behave, who we eventually become, and what we communicate to others and ourselves. Our own expectations and those of others influence our perceptions and behavior. Thus our self-concept is affected by our past experiences, our interactions with others, the expectations others have of us, and how we present ourselves to create an image.

Self-Fulfilling Prophecy

Expectations we have of ourselves or that others have of us help to create conditions that lead us to act in predictable ways. The expectation becomes a **self-fulfilling prophecy.**[7] The expectations that are placed on us by ourselves or others can be a powerful force for shaping our self-concept. A research study asked college students who were either characteristically optimistic or generally pessimistic to describe their future selves.[8] According to the research, both types of students could imagine a positive future, but the optimistic students had higher expectations about actually attaining a positive possible self than did those who were pessimistic. Thus we are more likely to succeed if we believe that we have the potential for success. By the same token, we are more likely to fail if we believe ourselves to be failures.

self-fulfilling prophecy
Expectations we have of ourselves or that others have of us that help to create the conditions that lead us to act in predictable ways.

Self-esteem can have effects on the prophecies people make about themselves. It is a matter of attribution: People with positive high self-esteem confidently attribute their success to past successes; therefore they expect to succeed in the future. People with low self-esteem, however, attribute any success they might have had to luck and so predict that they will not necessarily succeed again unless they are lucky. How we describe ourselves is a powerful influence on our expectations. Our expectations therefore are a powerful force for shaping our self-concept.

Self-fulfilling prophecies occur all the time, even though we might not label them as such. Here are a couple of examples: You predict that you are going to be nervous when you give an oral report in class, and you are. A good friend tells you that a teacher she had and one that you are about to have is a fantastic teacher, and she is. Another example is when parents tell a child over time that she can't do anything right. Ultimately, the child will incorporate the parents' prediction into her self-concept, and she will likely fail at many or most of the tasks she attempts. The opposite prediction could result in positive outcomes. The self-fulfilling prophecy is a communicative force that does influence self-concept; however, it cannot explain all outcomes.

It is important that we communicate high expectations for others rather than place unnecessary limitations on them, but the expectations that we do communicate should be realistic and obtainable. According to Andrew Sullivan, the author mentioned in the case study at the beginning of this chapter, we might have pushed self-esteem too far for many children because from birth we tell them that they can do no wrong. This places unrealistic expectations on them that can result in an inflated self-image, which is likely to lead to an inflated self-worth, which may be totally unrelated to objective truth.[9] What do you think about Sullivan's statements?

You can probably think of many times when the expectations you had for a certain outcome didn't come to pass. Thus the more we understand about the role that self-fulfilling prophecy plays in our lives and recognize its influence on our self-concept, the better we will be able to set realistic expectations not only for others, but for ourselves as well. How can knowing about the effects of self-fulfilling prophecies help us to communicate more effectively?

Impression Management

The creation of a positive image of oneself in order to influence the perceptions of others is referred to as **impression management.** As your own experiences have probably suggested, impression management can take many forms. Most fall into two major categories: self-enhancement (efforts to boost your own image) and other-enhancement (efforts to make a target person feel good in your presence).

To better understand impression management, we have to know more about "self." Our *perceived self* is a reflection of our self-concept. This self is the person that we believe ourselves to be at any given moment of self-examination. There are many aspects of our perceived self that we keep private because we don't wish to tell others; for example, regarding appearance, we might see ourselves as being too fat even though everyone else tells us we are too thin, we might see ourselves as inept in social settings with people we don't know well, or we might see ourselves as smarter than everyone else.

Our *presenting self* is the public image or the way we want to appear to others. Most of us seek to create an image that is socially acceptable, that is, nice person, good student, articulate, hardworking, friendly, wild, ambitious, truthful, loyal friend, funny, competent, highly motivated, likeable, and so on. A research study asked college students to self-select fifteen adjectives from a list of 108 possible adjectives describing their perceived self and presenting selves.

impression management
Creating a positive image of oneself in order to influence the perceptions of others.

> Males and females described themselves similarly in 12 of 15 choices, differing in only three. Both males and females were most likely to select active, attractive, busy, capable, curious,

faithful, friendly, generous, happy, independent, polite and responsible. Males also selected able, funny, and smart, whereas females also selected careful, sensible, and special.[10]

When describing their most commonly presented characteristics males and females were similar in the following characteristics: able, active, proud, and responsible. Males listed wild, strong, smart, brave, capable, and rough, whereas females more commonly presented the qualities of bright, funny, independent, sensible, and warm. How would you describe your presenting self?

Specific tactics when presenting self to others is referred to as facework. **Facework** is a term that was first used by Erving Goffman, a sociologist, to describe the verbal and nonverbal ways we act to maintain our own presenting image and the images of others.[11] Goffman says that each of us creates various roles or characters that we want others to believe about us. He suggests that we maintain face by putting on a front when we wish to impress others. The front consists of our choice of behaviors and what we communicate when we are around others that we want to impress. Think about the notion of facework for a moment and what you do differently when you are by yourself and when you are with others. How do you behave and communicate differently when at school, at home, at the library, at work, out on a first date, a job interview, and so on when you want to impress someone? How do facework behaviors reflect a person's self-concept?

We also use facework enhancements to induce moods and reactions in others. Among the most commonly used and most important of these is the use of flattery. Flattery is a way of building another person's self-concept, but it is also a way to help promote a positive image for us. Flattery may involve heaping praise on other people even if they don't deserve it, expressing agreement with their views, showing a high degree of interest in them (hanging on their every word), doing small favors for them, asking for their advice and feedback,[12] and expressing liking for them, either verbally or nonverbally.[13] All of these types of behaviors appear to work, at least to a degree. They do cause the other person to experience, in almost all situations, positive reactions to us. Thus through impression management, we can attempt to build a positive self-image and thereby strengthen our self-concept.

Making Connections

Self-Respect, Ethics, and Self-Image

We express our values and image in a thousand ways—when we submit our tax returns, when we vote, when we return money to the clerk who has made a mistake or a wallet to the stranger who lost it on the street, when we teach our children, and when we help our friends and families. Most of us try to "do the right thing" because we care about how others perceive us. This is especially true when it comes to our family, friends, fellow students, teachers, and co-workers.

1. What does it mean to have personal integrity? To be ethical?
2. How does personal integrity affect self-image and how others see us?
3. What image does an ethical person create and how does that image affect his or her communication with others?
4. In what ways does our culture or media influence our personal integrity?
5. How can we create an image or reputation of being a person of high integrity?

facework
A term that is used to describe the verbal and nonverbal ways we act to maintain our own presenting image and the images of others.

Culture and Self-Concept

Culture has a broad, all-encompassing effect on each of us. Self-concept involves our perception of self, what we believe others perceive of us, our culture, our perception of our culture, and others' perception of our culture. The development of self-concept varies from one culture to another and is determined by a specific combination of cultural norms and behaviors.

Because our self-concept develops in a cultural context, one would expect differences across cultures. There are specific cultural factors that can influence the development of self-concept. For example, young Palestinians living in Jordanian refugee camps often have a low positive self-concept because they are raised in an autocratic setting of traditional Arab families and schools, giving them little independence and responsibility. However, among Chinese secondary school students, a cohesive, achieving family environment is found to be associated with a more positive self-concept and less depression.[14]

Much of the research related to cultural differences has focused on the effects of individualism versus collectivism on the self-concept. If you hold an **individualistic orientation,** you would tend to stress self or personal goals and achievements over group goals and "I" consciousness and a tendency to focus on individual accomplishments. Somewhat unique to the Western world are cultures that stress individualism with the norm of prescribing that self-interest is and ought to be a central determinant of one's behavior.[15] Individualist cultures have an "I" consciousness and a tendency to focus on individual accomplishments. This might help to explain Senator Torricelli's remarks in the case study at the beginning of the chapter and why self-esteem has become so important to Americans.

If you hold a **collectivistic orientation,** you are more likely to put aside your individual goals for the well-being of the group. Researchers have examined the influence of specific situational arrangements in which the participants were asked to describe themselves: in a group, with a faculty member, with a peer, and alone.[16] The investigators found self-concept variations as a function of culture, of the situation, and of the interaction of the two. The Japanese students were not only more self-critical, but also more affected by the situation than the American students were. American students were more likely than Japanese students to provide self-descriptions in terms of abstract, internal attributes, and they were more likely to make references to friends and family, for example, "I love my family." Japanese students tend to describe themselves in terms of physical attributes and appearance, activities, the immediate situation, and possessions, for example, "I am the youngest child in my family." Americans overall tended to generate more positive self-descriptions than did the Japanese. Why do you think Americans are more likely to give themselves positive self-descriptions?

Within a culture, social, institutional, and personal norms and beliefs related to self-concept are considered universal and not bound to a particular culture. This view is reinforced when two people from the same culture communicate within the context of their own culture. For instance, a white Anglo-Saxon Protestant in American society or a Japanese in Japanese society would have a stable self-concept with relatively few problems.

But when individuals are taken out of the context of their own culture and placed in a totally different society and culture, problems can arise. One's long-standing views and expectations no longer fit in the new culture. For example, if two people with different cultural backgrounds are communicating, each will have different expectations of the other. This situation can create a cultural conflict and may eventually lead to a redefining of self-concept, which then allows the person to function more comfortably in the new culture. Being able to communicate with individuals from different cultural backgrounds requires an understanding both of their culture and of culture's influence on self-concept and the ability to adapt communication to accommodate differences.

individualistic orientation
Tendency to stress self or personal goals and achievements over group goals and achievements.

collectivistic orientation
Tendency to put aside your individual goals for the well-being of the group.

Making Connections

It's Me, Me, All Me!

In North American culture, the individual occupies a very important place. If you listen to how people who were raised in North America communicate, you will hear the word *I* fairly often. Other cultures do not necessarily share this perception of the self as being at the center of the universe.

1. How often do you and those with whom you communicate use *I* in conversations? Keep a log over a one- or two-day period, and note the number of times you and others use this word in your conversations. Are your findings consistent with the statement that North Americans use *I* fairly often?
2. Talk to people from cultures different from your own to discover how much value they place on self.
3. In your discussions with people from other cultures, use the saying "the squeaky wheel gets the grease" (explain its meaning if you have to), and ask them whether this statement would hold true in their culture. Report your findings to the class.

To conclude this exercise, discuss in class what adjustments, if any, you should make when interacting with people from cultures that do not place such emphasis on the self.

To succeed in such communication requires developing a way to sense when messages have been successfully conveyed. It might also require overcoming fear. One African American woman stated one reason why such communication is difficult: "If people don't share the same life experiences, they can't be expected to understand each other. If whites haven't been exposed to blacks, there will be a 'fear of the unknown.' "[17] This same fear or potential for misunderstanding can happen whenever people from different backgrounds or experiences come together. Interestingly, in today's global village, our self-concept is in part established through social interaction with others both inside and outside of our culture. This ongoing trend may bode well for the future because it familiarizes us with those whose ways differ from our own. Contact with other cultures in the early development of self-concept might help us to avoid some of the communication problems that occur when people of different backgrounds get together.

Gender and Self-Concept

It seems that the most pervasive element of our personal identity is the aspect of social identity that is referred to as gender. That is, you might or might not pay much attention to your social class or ethnic identity, but it would be extremely rare for you to be unaware and unconcerned about being male or being female. In hundreds of ways, we are reminded each day of our gender by how we dress, how we act, and how others respond to us.

Sex and Gender

sex
The anatomical and physiological differences between males and females that are genetically determined.

The terms *sex* and *gender* are often used interchangeably. We defined gender in Chapter 2 as a social construct related to learned masculine and feminine behaviors. **Sex** is defined in biological terms as the anatomical and physiological differences between males and females that are genetically determined.[18] Note, however, that these definitions are not universally accepted.

The origin of gender differences is sometimes a matter of dispute, but we are willing to assume that most gender attributes are based entirely on what one learns (such as an association between hairstyle and femininity), whereas other attributes may be based entirely on biological determinants (such as the presence of facial hair). Each of us has a gender identity: A key part of our self-concept is the label of "male" or "female." For the vast majority of people, biological sex and gender identity coincide, though there is a relatively small proportion of the population in which gender identity differs from sex.

Some male and female differences may be explained by biological differences in brain structure and development. According to Julia T. Wood, a well-known communication scholar, research indicates that although both men and women use both lobes of the brain, each tends to specialize in one. Wood says that men generally exhibit greater development of the left lobe of the brain (the locus of mathematical abilities, analytical thought, and sequential information processing), whereas women manifest greater development of the right lobe of the brain (the locus of intuitive thought, imaginative and artistic activity, and some visual and spatial tasks). To support this theory, she states that research reported in 1995 suggests that women are more likely to use both sides of the brain to do language tasks, whereas men are more likely to depend on the left side of the brain. Women's brains, according to Wood, work less hard than men's to understand emotions.[19]

Gender identity occurs when gender becomes a part of one's self-concept. We develop a sense of self that includes maleness and femaleness,[20] and somewhere between the ages of four and seven, the concept of gender consistency (the sense that one is permanently male or female) develops. We begin to accept the principle that gender is a basic attribute of ourselves. As soon as these attributes become known to us and are firmly in place, our perceptions of self are affected by what we believe about gender.

From the moment of birth, no other characteristic of the self slants the treatment we receive more directly than our biological sex. Children's behavior begins to be shaped by their very first pink or blue blanket. It appears that these initial influences placed on children lead to gender stereotypes and expectations that strongly influence a person's self-concept.

Gender Stereotypes

A research study found that when children (ages five to nine) and adolescents (age fifteen to college age) are shown videotapes of four nine-month-old infants, both age groups agree that the babies identified as female (named Karen or Sue) appear to be smaller, more beautiful, nicer, and softer than those identified as male (named William or Matthew).[21] Actually, the experimenters had assigned a male or female name to infants of both sexes. For example, each male baby was identified correctly as a boy for half the participants and incorrectly as a girl for the other half; similarly, each female baby was identified for half the participants as a girl and as a boy for the other half. The findings illustrate that gender stereotypes determined how the infants were perceived.

Even though our society has taken great strides to reduce stereotypical thinking about males and females, stereotypes and narrowly defined role expectations are still accepted by many in our culture and even more so in certain other cultures. These stereotypes affect communication behavior. There are many similarities in the communication behaviors of men and women. For example, there are soft-spoken men and verbally aggressive women; many men discuss their families and friends, and many women discuss sports and investments. It is, however, commonly accepted in our society that men and women communicate differently and prefer to discuss certain subjects. In addition, in some situations, men and women are expected to communicate differently because of imposed cultural norms.

Females have often been the objects of stronger and more persistent stereotypes than males. That is not to say that there are no stereotypes assigned to males; they, too, are perceived as being "all alike" in possessing certain traits. Female stereotypes, however, are often more negative in content than those applied to males. The positive stereotypes of feminine behaviors include characteristics such as nurturance, sensitivity, and personal warmth. These traits are believed by some to be less desirable and less suited for the valued roles of leadership and authority than are the gender stereotypes for males.[22]

Are the stereotypes about males and females accurate? Are the traits assigned to feminine behaviors less desirable than those assigned to masculine behaviors? Do men and women really differ in the ways that stereotypes suggest? The answers to these questions are complex, for such differences between males and females, even if observed, may be based more on the perceived stereotype itself than actual differences between men and women. Research does seem to imply that when differences are observed between sexes, those differences tend to be overstated. Overall, the magnitude of such differences is far less than prevailing stereotypes imply.

Gender Expectations

An overwhelming body of evidence demonstrates that sex differences in communication are the result of gender expectations. According to psycholinguist Deborah Tannen, men and women do see themselves as different, and as a result, they communicate differently. She says, "In this world [the man's] conversations are negotiations in which people try to achieve and maintain the upper hand if they can and protect themselves from others' attempts to put them down and push them around. Life, then, is a contest, a struggle to preserve independence and avoid failure." The

When compared to men, women are much more likely to be concerned about body image and about physical appearance in general. One explanation may be that from infancy on, other people place more emphasis on the appearance of females than of males.

man's world is a hierarchical social order in which people are either one-up or one-down. In the women's world, according to Tannen, "conversations are negotiations for closeness in which people try to seek and give confirmation and support and to reach consensus. They try to protect themselves from others' attempts to push them away. Life, then, is a community, a struggle to preserve intimacy and avoid isolation." The women's world is also hierarchical, but the order is related more to friendship than to power and accomplishment.[23] Are we really different?

According to one researcher's perspective, "the two sexes are essentially similar and . . . the differences linked to sexual functions are not related to psychological traits or social roles."[24] He further believes that most gender differences are relatively superficial and that differences that are perceived to exist are socially constructed in one's cultural upbringing. The differences between males and females, therefore, are more or less learned in and reinforced by culture.

When asked to describe themselves, males and females differ in their descriptions. Males tend to mention qualities such as ambition, energy, power, initiative, and control. They are likely to discuss their success in sports and with females. Females, however, typically list qualities such as generosity, sensitivity, consideration, and concern for others.[25] Males, it seems, are expected to be powerful and authoritative, whereas females are expected to be concerned with relationships and expressiveness.

When compared to men, women are much more likely to be concerned about body image and physical appearance in general. Furthermore, the male–female differences in body image satisfaction have increased from the pre-1970s era to the 1990s.[26] In an article in the *Miami Herald* (January 30, 1998) entitled "Beauty and the Beast," columnist and humorist Dave Barry describes the gender differences as follows: Men think of themselves as average-looking, and average is fine; in contrast, women evaluate their appearance as "not good enough." Why is it that our society places so much emphasis on appearance?

Despite some strides toward equality of the sexes, our society still has a cultural bias toward masculinity. But because communication behaviors are learned and are culturally defined, they can be unlearned and changed over time. To some extent, this has happened and continues to happen. For a long time in our society, women expected and were expected by others to stay home and rear children, whereas men were expected to be breadwinners. According to the U.S. Department of Labor Women's Bureau website (www.dol.gov/wb) and Secretary of Labor Elaine L. Chao, 26 percent of all privately held firms are owned by women. The number of businesses owned by women is almost 5.5 million, and they employ over 7.1 million paid workers and generate $818.7 billion annually in sales and receipts. The website also reported that Hispanic women own 337,708 businesses, black women own 312,884, Asian and Pacific Islander women own 247,966, and American Indian and

Making Connections

Public and Private Selves: Our Image

A headline in the *Lincoln Journal Star* read, "DYING TO BE THIN." The newspaper ran a three-day series on the pressures of being thin in American culture. It is clear that there is a constant focus on weight and body image. The image of being thin is portrayed in our media, magazines, and store catalogues. Probably the most famous are Victoria's Secret swim summer catalogue or the *Sports Illustrated* Swimsuit issue.

1. Being physically attractive is important, but has it become too important?
2. Conduct an Internet search using the key words *self-concept and body image* or *self-esteem and body image.* Visit several of the sites that you locate to see whether they provide more insight or other answers related to question 1. Share what you learned with your class.

Alaska Native women own 53,593. These data illustrate not only that more and more women are changing the expectations of what women can do, but also that women from different ethnic groups are taking part in this change. The expectations and accomplishment of women in the business world as in many other areas, such as education, athletics, and careers, have influenced how women see themselves.

If men and women are to break the stereotypes and expectations attributed to them, we must avoid categorizing behaviors as exclusively male or female. Psychologists indicate that women and men who are **androgynous**—who have both male and female traits—are more likely to be successful in their interactions and careers than are people who are totally masculine or feminine in their behaviors. For example, as you move from interactions with co-workers to interactions with your family, you might move from more "masculine" behaviors to more "feminine" behaviors. If you are a manager or owner of a business, you are expected to be assertive or task oriented; but when you spend time taking care of your children, you are expected to be patient and loving.

Learning Connections

1. What is the relationship between self-concept and communication?
2. Why do you think so many people have communication apprehension? What do you think can be done to reduce it?
3. What does impression management mean? Are there ethical considerations to consider when presenting yourself to others?
4. How does culture influence our self-concept?
5. Do men and women really differ in how they think about self-image? If so, how?
6. What is the best advice you can give to help others improve their self-concept?

Enhancing Self-Concept

Throughout this chapter, we have been discussing what self-concept is, how it is developed, and how it connects to communication. Building on what you have learned about self-concept, we next explore guidelines for enhancing your self-concept and growth as a communicator.

androgynous
Having both male and female traits.

GUIDELINES Improving Your Self-Concept

1. *Decide what you would like to change about yourself.* To begin the process of improvement, you must know what needs to be changed. Describe, as accurately and specifically as you can, what you would like to change about yourself. If you are unhappy about something or you don't like something about yourself, identify exactly what it is and state it, for example, "I want to be a more effective communicator," "I want to be thinner," or "I want to be better organized." To help you with a self-analysis you might go to www.webheights.net/lovethyself/home.htm. This site provides links to self-analysis tests, self-improvement magazines and books, and other resources.
2. *Make a commitment to improving yourself.* Changing one's self-concept is not easy. It usually begins with a concentrated effort and a strong commitment to want to change and a belief that you can change. For example, if you say that you want to be more outgoing, lose weight, or be a better listener that is the first step. But just thinking about change or improvement won't make it happen; you must take action. Any time you act, you run the risk of failure, but successful people learn that without risk, nothing can be accomplished. It is when you understand your short-

comings, learn how to deal with them, believe and commit yourself to making changes, and believe that you can succeed, that you will begin to see yourself accomplish your goals. It is important to realize that to change self-concept not only requires commitment, but also takes time.

3. *Describe why you feel the way you do about yourself.* Is your problem brought on by yourself or by others? Many students, for example, do not really want to be in college. They are there because their parents or their friends put pressure on them. Although they would rather be doing something else, they are afraid to take a stand. Before they can begin to feel better about themselves, they must recognize why they are unhappy and who is contributing to their problem. You might think that you are not capable of earning good grades in a certain subject or that you are too shy to make friends easily. Ask yourself why you feel that way. Are you living out a self-fulfilling prophecy?
4. *Decide that you are going to do something to change your feelings about yourself.* If you can describe your problem, you can almost always find a solution—that is, if you want to find one. If you are unhappy about your appearance, make plans to change it. If you feel inadequate about meeting people, plan some ways to build your confidence. Nothing will ever change unless you want it to change.
5. *Set reasonable goals for yourself.* You must be reasonable in setting your goals. You may be able to change some things overnight, but other things may require a long-term effort. For example, you might decide that you are going to improve your grades by studying for several hours every night. You can begin your new study schedule immediately, but actually raising your grades could take much longer.

   Sometimes a problem becomes more manageable if it is solved step by step. For example, you might feel hesitant to visit your professor in his or her office. Why not start by speaking briefly with your professor before or after class? You might begin by asking a question about your progress. Once you begin to feel comfortable, ask for an appointment or stop in to visit during office hours. If you continue such visits, you will gradually gain more confidence in yourself.
6. *Associate with people who will support and help you.* Try to surround yourself with people you like and trust. That will make it much easier to discuss your problems and ask for support. When others know what you are trying to do and how you need help, they can provide support to make your behavioral changes easier.

Summary

Our self-concept, or self-identity, is our mental picture and evaluation of our physical, social, and psychological attributes. Like communication, self-concept is a process that has no beginning or end and is constantly changing. Competent communicators understand that our self-perception and other people's perceptions of us change from time to time, from situation to situation, and from person to person. Our self-concept is also based on our values, attitudes, and beliefs, which all play a significant role in who we are and how we communicate. The components that make up our self-concept are organized into a hierarchy. The lower in the hierarchy a particular component is, the easier it is to change.

Part of our self-concept has to do with how we see ourselves as communicators. Competent communicators know that there is always some anxiety in communicating with others and therefore see it as a natural part of the communication process. Some people are overly anxious when confronted with real or anticipated communication with another person or people; this feeling is referred to as communication apprehension. This type of expectation can become self-fulfilling and ultimately determine how we behave, who we eventually become, and what we communicate to others and ourselves. The competent communicator knows how to use self-enhancement or other enhancement techniques to bolster his or her image in order to create a positive outcome in his or her communication with others.

Our cultural background and gender affect our development of our self-concept and how we communicate. Competent communicators know that communicating with people from different cultural backgrounds requires understanding of other cultures and an ability to adapt to them. They also know how gender stereotyping can affect the communication behavior of both males and females. People who understand gender roles are more likely to be successful in their interactions and careers than are those who do not.

Although it is not easy to alter self-concept, we can achieve progress through hard work, a desire to improve, and the belief that we are and will be successful. The following steps were discussed to help improve our self-concept: (1) decide what we want to change, (2) describe why we feel the way we do, (3) decide that we are going to take action, (4) set reasonable goals, and (5) surround ourselves with supportive people.

DISCUSSION STARTERS

1. What steps can you take to help others improve their self-concept?
2. Why is it important to understand the influence of self-concept on communication competency?
3. In what ways does your self-concept affect your communication effectiveness?
4. What do you need to know about self-concept and gender to become a more effective communicator?
5. Discuss the influence culture has on a person's self-concept?
6. What is the connection between self-concept and communication competency?
7. Discuss situations in which you use impression management techniques to improve your chance of reaching a goal.
8. What is the most useful information that you obtained in this chapter to aid you in becoming a more competent communicator?

NOTES

1. A. Gerike, *Old Is Not a Four-Letter Word: A Midlife Guide* (Watsonville, Calif.: Papier Mâché Press, 1997).
2. D. J. Bem, "Self-Perception Theory," in *Advances in Experimental Social Psychology*, vol. 6, ed. L. Berkowitz (New York: Academic Press, 1972).
3. J. W. Kinch, "A Formalized Theory of Self-Concept," *American Journal of Sociology* 68 (January 1963): 481–86.
4. W. W. Wilmot, *Dyadic Communication*, 3rd ed. (New York: Random House, 1987), 61.
5. C. Stohl, "Perceptions of Social Attractiveness and Communicator Style: A Developmental Study of Preschool Children," *Communication Education* 30 (1981): 367–76.
6. J. C. McCroskey, "Classroom Consequences of Communication Apprehension," *Communication Education* 26 (1977): 27–28.

7. R. Rosenthal and L. Jacobson, *Pygmalion in the Classroom: Teacher Expectation and Pupils' Intellectual Development* (New York: Holt, Rinehart & Winston, 1968) vii; T. Good and J. Brophy, *Looking in Classrooms,* 4th ed. (New York: Harper & Row, 1987).
8. C. S. Carver, L. A. Kus, and M. F. Scheier, "Effects of Good Versus Bad Mood and Optimistic versus Pessimistic Outlook on Social Acceptance versus Rejection," *Journal of Social and Clinical Psychology* 13 (1994): 138–51.
9. A. Sullivan, "Lacking in Self-Esteem? Good for You!," *Time* (October 12, 2002): 102.
10. C. M. Shaw and R. Edwards, "Self-Concepts and Self-Presentations of Males and Females: Similarities and Differences," *Communication Reports* 10 (1997): 55–62.
11. E. Goffman, *The Presentation of Self in Everyday Life* (Garden City, NY: Doubleday, 1959).
12. E. W. Morrison and R. J. Bies, "Impression Management in the Feedback-Seeking Process: A Literature Review and Research Agenda," *Academy of Management Review* 16 (1991): 322–41.
13. S. J. Wayne and G. R. Ferris, "Influence, Tactics, and Exchange Quality in Supervisor–Subordinate Interactions: A Laboratory Experiment and Field Study," *Journal of Applied Psychology* 75 (1990): 487–99.
14. S. Lau and L. K. Kwok, "Relationships of Family Environment to Adolescent's Depression and Self-Concept," *Social Behavior and Personality* 27 (2000): 41–50.
15. D. T. Miller, "The Norm of Self-Interest," *American Psychologist* 54 (1999): 1053–60.
16. C. Kanagawa, S. E. Cross, and H. R. Markus, "Who Am I? The Cultural Psychology of the Conceptual Self," *Journal of Personality and Social Psychology Bulletin* 27 (2001): 90–103.
17. S. A. Ribeau, J. R. Baldwin, and M. L. Hecht, "An African-American Communication Perspective," in *Intercultural Communication: A Reader,* ed. L. A. Samovar and R. E. Porter (Belmont,Calif.: Wadsworth, 1994), 143. J. R. Baldwin and M. Hecht, "Unpacking Group-Based Intolerance: A Holographic Look at Identity and Intolerance," in *Intercultural Communication: A Reader,* 10th ed., eds. L. A. Samovar and R. E. Porter (Belmont, Calif.: Wadsworth, 2003), 358.
18. J. B. Beckwith, "Terminology and Social Relevance in Psychological Research on Gender," *Social Behavior and Personality* 22 (1994): 329–36.
19. J. T. Wood, *Gendered Lives: Communication, Gender and Culture,* 5th ed. (Belmont, Calif.: Wadsworth, 2003), 40.
20. N. Grieve, "Beyond Sexual Stereotypes. Androgyny: A Model or an Ideal?" in *Australian Women: Feminist Perspectives,* eds. N. Grieve and P. Grimshaw (Melbourne, Australia: Oxford University Press, 1980), 247–57.
21. D. A. Vogel, M. A. Lake, S. Evans, and K. H. Karraker, "Children's and Adults Sex-Stereotyped Perceptions of Infants," *Sex Roles* 24 (1991): 601–16.
22. M. E. Heilman, R. F. Martell, and M. C. Simon, "The Vagaries of Sex Bias: Conditions Regulating the Underevaluation, Equivaluation, and Overevaluation of Female Job Applicants," *Organizational Behavior and Human Decision Processes* 41 (1988): 98–110.
23. D. Tannen, *You Just Don't Understand: Women and Men in Conversation* (New York: Morrow, 1990), 24–25.
24. C. E. Epstein, *Deceptive Distinctions: Sex, Gender, and the Social Order* (New Haven, Conn.: Yale University Press, 1988), 25.
25. M. R. Gunnar-Von Gnechten, "Changing a Frightening Toy into a Pleasant Toy by Allowing the Infant to Control Its Actions," *Developmental Psychology* 14 (1978): 157–62; J. H. Block, "Differential Premises Arising from Differential Socialization of the Sexes: Some Conjectures," *Child Development* 54 (1983): 1335–54; J. T. Spence and R. L. Helmreich, *Masculinity and Femininity: Their Psychological Dimension and Antecedents* (Austin: University of Texas Press, 1978).
26. P. Pliner, S. Chaiken, and G. L. Flett, "Gender Differences in Concern with Body Weight and Physical Appearance over Life Span," *Personality and Social Psychology Bulletin* 16 (1990): 263–73.

"Ideas never lack for words. It is words that lack ideas."
—Joseph Joubert

CHAPTER 4 Connecting through Verbal Communication

THIS CHAPTER WILL HELP YOU:

- Explain the role of language in the communication process.
- Identify examples of the power of language in communication events.
- Provide examples of language as a set of symbols in a system.
- Demonstrate that words and meaning depend on many variables.
- Explain how language is personal and how we all use language in unique ways.
- Identify the ways in which language influences perceptions, thought, culture, and views of reality.
- Explain the four elements of language.
- Describe language-based barriers to communication and suggest how they can be overcome.
- Explain how language choices can improve a speaker's effectiveness.

CASE STUDY

Anya, a student from Russia, speaks English fluently. Her mother teaches English in Russia, Anya spent time in England studying the language, and many courses in her Russian schools were taught in English with responses required in English. Despite this immersion in the English language, Anya worries about what others will think of her and her use of the language when she answers questions in class and especially when she has a presentation to make. Anya approaches all of her instructors with the same message: "I don't know your language as well as I should. I'm nervous about responding in class."

Anya is fluent in English but has concerns about her use of English, her second language. Anya is not alone. A graduate student recently completed a thesis on the topic of international students in U.S. classrooms. In her interviews with international students, Ms. Xiaofan Liao learned that most international students shared Anya's concern about responding in class. Furthermore, the international students in Ms. Liao's study indicated that they felt they had little opportunity to share either their knowledge or their culture with their classmates. They also felt that their "foreign" status often precluded their U.S. classmates from even trying to interact with them.[1] Interestingly, the students who express this kind of concern are usually more knowledgeable about the English language than are U.S. students. We often find that international students who contribute to class discussion have similar concerns, but their need to be a part of the discussions allows them to make contributions. We also know that in some cultures students are taught to listen and not talk.

CASE STUDY *(continued)*

Questions to think about

1. Have you ever found yourself in a situation in which you were reluctant to respond?
2. What concerns do you have about your responses in class, whether in the full group or with an individual classmate?
3. What do you think you could do to help Anya feel more comfortable about her use of the English language?

According to the Educational Testing Service, college campuses will become increasingly diverse in the twenty-first century. During the next fifteen years, enrollment is projected to increase by 19 percent to sixteen million students enrolled in U.S. colleges and universities. Minority students are expected to account for 80 percent of the growth, with the proportion of African or African American students rising from 12.8 to 13.2 percent by 2015; the proportion of Hispanic students increasing from 10 to about 15 percent; and the proportion of Asian students increasing from 5.4 to 8.4 percent. The proportion of white students who attend college is expected to decline from about 71 percent to about 62 percent.[2]

English is increasingly *the* language of higher education around the world. This trend is enhanced by the spread of technology because much of the available computer software is written in English and because of the growth of the Internet where the English language prevails.[3] As technology grows, the world seems to shrink, and our careful use of language will become even more important than it was previously. As effective communicators, we must make appropriate language choices so that diverse groups of people can understand us.

Mark Twain once said, "The difference between the right word and the almost right word is the difference between lightning and the lightning bug." This quotation certainly illustrates this point: Word choice does make a difference. Because the language we use is a message in itself, our use of language can convey a positive image of us, or it can damage and degrade us as well as others. The United States is primarily an English-speaking culture, and even though there are many co-cultures within our society, educated people need to know which forms of English are expected and appropriate for different settings. In many college classrooms and in many business meetings and other workplace settings, standard English use is dominant and expected, whereas different forms of language might be more suitable in more informal settings. Competent communicators must determine which form of language is appropriate for a particular situation and which is not.

Language is critically important to the communication process. In this chapter, we examine what language is, some common barriers to effective language use, the use of inclusive language, and the avoidance of stereotypes. We also provide suggestions about effective language use.

Making Connections

Words Can Be Harmful

Too often, language is viewed as neutral and innocent. But it can get you into trouble. A supervisor overheard two employees discussing some customers who had just entered the store. One made a comment about that "really old guy" and wondered why he would even come into the store. The second responded, "Yeah, but what's even more interesting is that the old guy's companion is clearly a flaming gay."

The supervisor took the two workers aside and made it clear that the company would not tolerate disrespectful language about anyone, further cautioning the workers to think carefully about what they say and how they say it. The supervisor reminded the workers that company policy demanded that each customer be treated with respect. Talking about customers, even quietly or out of earshot, was rude. Future violations of this policy, he said, would result in termination.

1. Search a local newspaper, contemporary magazines, or the Internet or simply listen to people's choices of words to locate other examples of language that could be considered degrading, hurtful, or disrespectful. Share what you find with your classmates and discuss why this type of communication occurs.
2. Discuss what you can do to help stop rude, insensitive, and degrading messages.
3. List words or phrases that offend you when they are used in your presence. Describe why they offend you—after all, they are only words.
4. Identify ten positive words, and explain the difference in your feelings as you compare their meanings with the meanings of negative words.
5. Discuss the following question with your classmates: How can we balance our right to free speech with our obligation to avoid language that is disrespectful or harmful to others?
6. Continue the discussion by responding to the following: Have we become too sensitive and too politically correct in our use of language? Explain.

The Importance of Language

Language is a structured system of signs, sounds, gestures, or marks that is used and understood to express ideas and feelings among people within a community, nation, geographic area, or cultural tradition. In this chapter, we concentrate on spoken language; in the next chapter, we consider nonverbal communication. Without language, there would be little or no human communication as we now know it. Language allows us to encounter our world in meaningful ways because it allows us to share meaning with others. Can you imagine what it would be like to be unable to tell someone what you know or think or feel? Language is a powerful tool! But it is only as effective and efficient as the people using it. Although we often believe that language is neutral, in actuality, it communicates much about what we are and what we think and therefore must be carefully used.

language
A structured system of signs, sounds, gestures, and marks that is used and understood to express ideas and feelings among people within a community, nation, geographic area, or cultural tradition.

Language Is Powerful

How many times have you walked through a crowd of strangers and momentarily paused when you thought you heard someone call your name? Why? Our names are not *just* names or words. Our names define who we are. "If any one thing is universal, it is a name. At every place and at every time, everyone has received a name. Names brand us with distinctive marks that separate us from the rest of the herd and,

Making Connections

How Powerful Is Language?

Language is so powerful that it has toppled kingdoms, changed political careers, and started and ended international conflicts and wars. How powerful is language? Ask Trent Lott, the latest in a long line of politicians whose political careers changed because their use of language led to a political gaffe. In December 2002, Lott was the designated incoming U.S. Senate majority leader. Lott made comments at a birthday and retirement celebration for Senator Strom Thurmond that suggested sympathy with one-time segregationist policies. A furor arose, and Lott was forced to remove himself from the position. Language must be carefully chosen to effectively communicate who we are and what we mean.[4]

1. Can you recall a time when you used the "wrong words"? What was the result?
2. What did you learn from that unfortunate use of words?
3. What can you do to remind yourself of the power of words?
4. How will you share with others the message, "Language is powerful"?

at the same time, make us a part of it."[5] Names are so important, for example, that people legally change them. In many cases, people change their names when the change better fits them or when their given names do not truly demonstrate their perceptions of themselves. Communication scholar Victoria De Francisco, for example, changed her paternal surname for her mother's surname. De Francisco and other feminist scholars suggest that naming has been a male-dominated power. They suggest that males do the naming and use "male" terms and that the world is viewed through a male perspective, leaving women in subordinate roles.[6] Name-calling can also affect

Politicians need to be careful about word choice when they speak and they must constantly assess how others might interpret their words. They know that failure to do so may place them in an awkward position, cost them an election, or even jeopardize national security.

individuals. If you have ever been told you were "really dumb" or been called "fatso" or "faggot," you know how name-calling can hurt.

Feminists raise issues about perspectives on language because they want an inclusive world. In a recent CRTNET (Communication Research and Theory Network) posting on the National Communication Association email list, communication scholar Anita Taylor pointed out how even Internet sources use language and images to perpetuate male perspectives.[7] What's wrong with that, you ask? If you are a woman who hears a speech about heart disease, and the speaker always uses the word "he" when describing effects and symptoms, you might think "heart disease only affects men" and not concern yourself with the message when, in fact, heart disease is a major killer for both men and women.

Language Affects Thought

The misuse of language involves more than misuse of words. Misused language affects our ability to think. Thought and language are inseparable. Most scholars agree that words help us to form thoughts. How many times have you found yourself struggling to find *the* word and without it, you could not express what you really meant. When you take the time to think a minute, however, the word usually appears. It is important to carefully consider language choices before we speak. We cannot erase what we said. We can correct or retract a statement and apologize for it, but as Trent Lott learned, we cannot eliminate the fact that we said it.[8]

Those whose career success is profoundly affected by the ability to communicate expend great effort on evaluating the potential effects of using certain words. Musicians, for example, often search a long time for just the right word for their lyrics. Chuck D., co-founder of Public Enemy, in a speech on the campus of the University of Northern Iowa said, "Vocabulary is critical. It's critical to success in the world and it's critical to lyrics. Only those who know and use the language well will succeed."[9] The Dixie Chicks, too, learned the power of language. When lead singer Natalie Maines told a London audience, "We're ashamed the president of the United States is from Texas,"[10] the backlash in the United States was significant. Some radio stations stopped playing the group's songs, there was public outrage resulting in condemnation and the burning of their CDs, and those who were most offended offered to buy concert tickets so that no one would attend. Fans at the Academy of Country Music Awards even booed when the Chicks' name was mentioned. These two examples should reinforce what communication and language scholars have long maintained: Language is powerful, and what you say can either help you or hurt you. Communication scholar Cheris Kramerae suggests that people who do not have the power of "correct or appropriate" language have little voice in their worlds. Her **muted group theory** suggests that status and power are clearly linked.[11] Kramerae says that muted groups are often women and ethnic minorities or out-groups (people with disabilities, the elderly, and the poor). Communication scholar Marsha Houston reports that African American women **style-switch,** or move between dominant culture language and the language of their own co-culture, to successfully operate in both the dominant society and their own co-culture.[12]

muted group theory A theory suggesting that status and power are clearly linked and that women, ethnic minorities, and out-groups have little voice and people do not pay attention to them because they lack the power of appropriate language.

style-switch The process of moving between the language of one's own co-culture and the language of the dominant culture to successfully operate in both.

When we communicate, we first form thoughts and then decide how we're going to express them. Competent communicators begin with clear thinking, followed by careful language choices that reflect an understanding of what language is, how it is used, and what effects it might have on listeners.

The Elements of Language

Language, talk, speech, and communication are four different but related phenomena. *Language,* as we noted earlier, is a structured system of signs, sounds, gestures, or marks (in other words, *symbols*) that allows people to express ideas and feelings to others; *talk* is what we do every day; *speech* is one vehicle used to transmit language; and *communication* involves the exchange of meanings. Language is one means by which we communicate, and speech is one way in which we use language. The fact that we process language does not automatically mean that we communicate well, but we cannot verbally communicate without language, and language would be useless if it did not help us convey meanings. Of course, as you will see in Chapter 5, nonverbal communication also allows us to express ourselves. What is the relationship between language, speech, communication, and talk? Communication scholar Karen Tracy says,

> Language has always been part of the study of communication, but language only partly overlaps with talk. Language is an abstract code; talk is a, if not the, focal activity of ordinary life. Talking is how we express who we are and who we want to be; it is how we make relationships as well as relational problems; it is the instrument that creates, exacerbates, and—not quite as often as we'd like—solves problems.[13]

Tracy provides these distinctions: "**everyday talk** [includes] the ordinary kinds of communicating people do [in their lives from school to the workplace, and in relationships]. Who people are is what communication theorists call *identity***.** Identity includes the most personal aspects of people . . . character, personality, [and] fixed characteristics."[14] In other words, we use language to create talk, to create ourselves, and to share ourselves and our views with others. Talking is what we do in our everyday lives, and communication is the process we engage in to be able to make sense of it all.

To more clearly differentiate these concepts, consider the fact that you can indicate an affirmative response to a question by nodding your head, thus using a gesture to communicate without speech. You can indicate the same response by writing the word *yes,* thus using writing instead of speech as the vehicle to transmit language. If you were traveling in a foreign country and said "yes," you might use language and speech without communicating.

The goal is to coordinate language and speech to produce effective communication, which is the transfer of meaning as intended. You can learn more about language by examining four of its key elements: sounds, words, grammar, and meaning.

Sounds

Most of us learn to speak language before we learn to write it, and most of us are born with the physical mechanisms that enable us to make speech sounds. However, we do not all learn to produce the sounds in exactly the same way. Though using the same language, people of certain geographic regions or cultural groups may speak quite differently. Dialects and other speech patterns can complicate communication between people who speak the same language.

everyday talk The ordinary kind of communicating people do in their lives.

word A symbol that stands for the object or concept that it names.

Words

Words are symbols that stand for objects and concepts. A word can represent an object or an abstract concept: The word *desk* represents an actual piece of furniture, an object, while the word *love* represents a whole range of emotions associated with our feelings for those closest to us.

Words have meanings because communities and cultures give them meaning. People agree that certain sound combinations mean certain things to them. One of the intriguing things about languages is the **idioms,** or words whose meanings cannot be understood by the ordinary usage. I spent several months in Sweden and learned many words in Swedish so that I could better communicate with my colleagues. Despite a Swedish–American English dictionary, I am still confused by the use of some terms. For example, we visited a KultureHus (Culture House) in one place, and I read about the KultureHuset (also culture house) in another community. There is an agreed-upon meaning for the Swedes that my dictionary does not explain. But for understanding to occur, all parties in the communication event must agree on meanings.

Grammar

Just as language has rules that govern how sounds may be joined into words, it also has rules that govern how words may be joined into phrases and sentences. This set of rules is called **grammar.** For example, the English grammar system requires that singular nouns take singular verb forms and plural nouns take plural verb forms (table *is;* tables *are*).

As we join sounds together to form words and join words together to form phrases, sentences, and paragraphs, we use language's sound and grammar systems simultaneously. The ability to use sounds and grammar correctly is crucial to competent communication. Grammar enables us to make complete sentences and to understand the sentences made by others.

Despite the many rules that govern language, there is virtually no limit to the number of different messages that can be created. It has been estimated that in the English language, it is possible to create ten quintillion twenty-word sentences.[15] This does not include sentences either shorter or longer than twenty words. Thus the number of possible sentences and messages is nearly infinite.

Learning Connections

1. Why do you think language is important?
2. What events in your life made an impression on you because of the use of language?
3. From what you have read so far, why do you think a whole chapter of this book is devoted to language?

Meaning

The study of meaning, or the association of words with ideas, feelings, and contexts, is called **semantics.** If language did not have meaning, it would serve little or no purpose. Because words and word patterns can be used to exchange meanings between people and even between generations, language is a useful tool for communication.

Do Words Contain Meaning? We tend to associate language symbols (words) with specific meanings and to take that relationship for granted. But it is important to understand that, in fact, language by itself has no meaning.

This notion might seem to contradict our entire discussion so far. You might wonder how language can be a system involving rules and meanings, yet still have no meaning itself. Actually, it is entirely arbitrary that the word *cat* represents those four-legged felines that some of us love and some of us hate. There is nothing about the letters *c, a,* and *t* that is essentially related to the being of a cat. When we see or hear the symbol, we fill in the meaning.

idioms
Words whose meanings cannot be understood by the ordinary usage.

grammar
Rules that govern how words are put together to form phrases and sentences.

semantics
The study of meaning, or the association of words with ideas, feelings, and contexts.

Words are symbols that represent people, objects, concepts, and events; the word is not actually the person, object, concept, or event. For example, *animal, blue, house, lawn mower, liberty,* and *tyranny* are only words, not the entities they symbolize. It is easy to miss this distinction. Even though words are symbols, try screaming "Spider!" in front of someone who dislikes spiders, and you will quickly see how words cause reactions—as if they were the actual thing!

The belief that words have meaning in themselves is widespread. During the past several years, we have asked students in beginning communication classes whether words have meaning. The data, though not scientifically collected, suggest that more than 75 percent of the students believe words do have meaning. But the simple fact is that words do *not* contain meanings by themselves. Words only acquire meaning through the context in which they are used and the fact that those who use them give them meaning. Figure 4.1 shows how two different people attach different meanings to the word *house.*

The following scene from Lewis Carroll's *Through the Looking Glass* illustrates this notion. Humpty Dumpty and Alice become involved in an argument about language and meaning:

> "I don't know what you mean by 'glory,' " Alice said.
>
> Humpty Dumpty smiled contemptuously. "Of course you don't—till I tell you. I meant there's a nice knock-down argument for you!"
>
> "But 'glory' doesn't mean 'a nice knock-down argument,' " Alice objected.
>
> "When I use a word," Humpty Dumpty said, in a rather scornful tone, "it means just what I choose it to mean—neither more nor less."
>
> "The question is," said Alice, "whether you can make words mean so many different things."
>
> "The question is," said Humpty Dumpty, "which is to be master—that's all."[16]

Who determines meaning? The answer is *you.* You control which words you use, the meaning you wish to give them, and, if you have mastered the art of communication, how people react to them. Although everyone has the ability to impart meaning to words, not everyone does so in the same way. Thus, a sender might intend one mean-

FIGURE 4.1

Meanings Are Not in Words but in People We cannot assume that using words that we consider appropriate and adequate to convey a particular message will succeed with every listener. As this figure illustrates, different people associate different meanings with even the simplest words. This is because words are symbols only—people fill in the meaning.

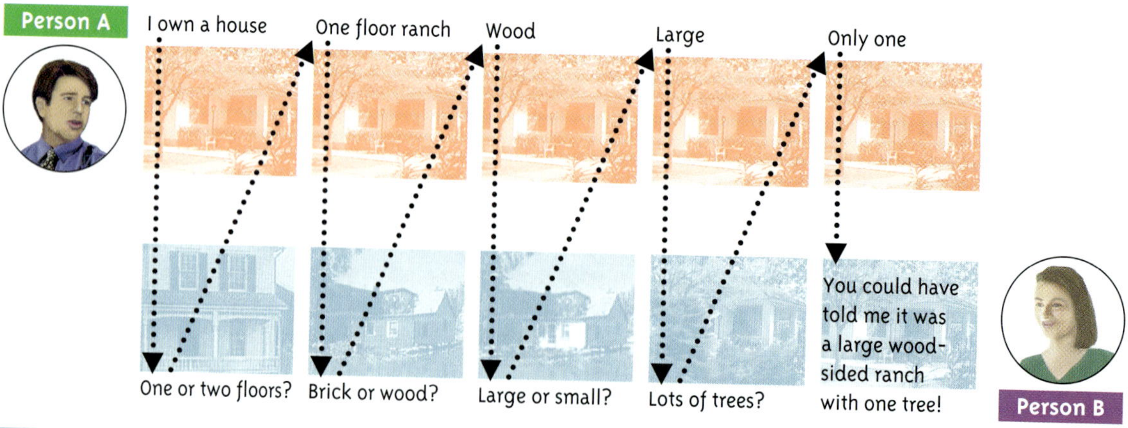

ing for a message, but the receiver might either intentionally or unintentionally give the message a different meaning. Disparity between the meaning sent and the meaning received can be a greater problem when the sender and receiver have different cultural backgrounds or even different experiences and knowledge. For example, people who keep up with computers and technology often use specialized language that is unfamiliar to someone who doesn't have much knowledge about computers. Care in choosing words is especially important in such situations.

Words Have Denotative and Connotative Meanings. **Denotation** is the core meaning associated with a word—its standard dictionary definition. Denotative meanings are usually readily understood. Many people use words as if they had only a denotative or specific meaning, but this is not the case. Although commonly understood dictionary definitions (denotative meanings) do exist, when we communicate we usually use words connotatively.

Connotation is the subjective meaning of a word, what a word suggests because of feelings or associations it evokes. The connotative meaning is based on the context in which the word is used, how the meaning is expressed nonverbally (tone of voice, facial expression of the speaker, and so on), and the understanding of the person who is receiving it. The competent communicator can differentiate between denotative and connotative meanings and understands which is being used in a given situation. Connotative meanings may be generally accepted by most of the people who use the language, by people within a particular group, or by an individual. For example, to one city person, the word *farm* might mean a place where crops are grown and animals are kept, but to a particular rural person, *farm* might represent a livelihood, a workplace, or a home.

Words Can Be Concrete or Abstract. **Concrete words** are symbols for specific things that can be pointed to or physically experienced (seen, tasted, smelled, heard, or touched). For example, words such as *car, book, keys,* and *dog* are concrete words. They represent specific, tangible objects, and therefore their meanings are usually quite clear. We can be even more specific with *Buick, the Bible, my house keys,* and *cocker spaniel.* Consequently, communication based on concrete words leaves little room for misunderstanding, and any disagreement can typically be resolved by referring to the objects themselves.

Abstract words, however, are symbols for ideas, qualities, and relationships. Because they represent things that cannot be experienced through the senses, their meanings depend on the experiences and intentions of the persons using them. For instance, words such as *right, freedom, truth,* and *trust* stand for ideas that mean different things to different people. Thus the use of abstract words can easily lead to misunderstandings and result in ineffective communication, as illustrated by the following conversation:

Student: Your tests are unfair.

Instructor: Why do you say that?

Student: They're unfair, and it's impossible to get a high grade on them.

Instructor: Do they include material that wasn't covered in class or in our readings?

Student: No.

Instructor: Do you mean the wording is too ambiguous for you to understand?

Student: No.

Instructor: What's unfair about them?

denotation
The objective meaning of a word; the standard dictionary definition.

connotation
The subjective meaning of a word; what a word suggests because of feelings or associations it evokes.

concrete word
A symbol for a specific thing that can be pointed to or physically experienced.

abstract word
The symbol for an idea, quality, or relationship.

Making Connections

Language and Meaning

"When people talk to each other, the actual meanings of the words stated convey a very small part of the meaning of the conversation."

—Deborah Tannen, psychologist and author

In small groups, discuss the following:

1. What is Dr. Tannen saying about spoken language?
2. Create and present a conversation in which meanings of words themselves are not the main carriers of meaning. Role-play the conversation to the class to see whether others outside of your group can determine your intended meaning.
3. What did you discover about communication from participating in this exercise?

This conversation is problematic because the student expects the instructor to understand what the student meant by the word *unfair.* But because *unfair* is an abstract word, its meaning can vary greatly from person to person and from situation to situation. To clarify what he or she means by *unfair,* the student needs to use more concrete language, for instance, "Your tests are unfair because they contain too many items to complete in the time allotted." It is always a good idea to define or illustrate any abstract word that may be misunderstood in a conversation.

Figure 4.2 represents the "ladder of abstraction" first described by Alfred Korzybski in 1933 and expanded on by S. I. Hayakawa in 1964.[17] Figure 4.2 illustrates the varying degrees of concreteness among related words. *Cynthia* is the most tangible word because it refers to a specific individual named Cynthia. You can see that as the words move from concrete to abstract, they become less specific.

Meaning Depends on Commonalities. The more communicators have in common in terms of background, experience, and attitudes, the more likely they are to hold

FIGURE 4.2

The Ladder of Abstraction Word meanings become more concrete when they refer to a specific person, place, or thing. Concrete language helps to reduce the number of interpretations for that which is intended by the sender, leaving less chance for misunderstanding.

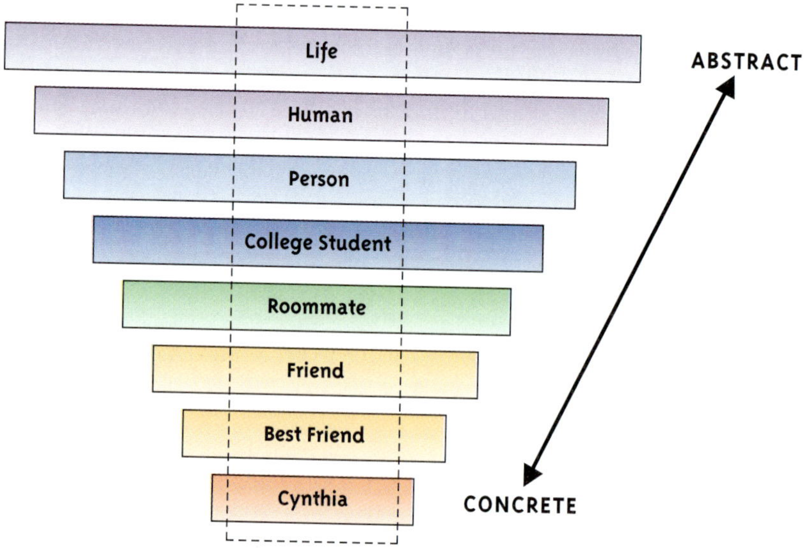

similar meanings for the words they exchange. However, competent communicators should not assume too much about how others will interpret their messages; they should continuously refine messages based on the feedback they receive. Individuals' personally held connotations can skew their interpretations of messages that are made up of words that seem straightforward and concrete. Consider the following situation:

> Deirdre and Karina are roommates. They have trouble budgeting for household expenses. Karina wants to buy the economy sizes of dish and laundry soap because they can save money over the semester. Deirdre becomes upset because she doesn't want to spend her entire budget the first week of the month. *Economy, budget,* and *careful spending* mean different things to the two, and stating those words usually causes a major conflict.

Instead of talking things through, each person goes her own way and spends the joint budget in ways she thinks best. The problem is that the roommates have never taken the time to try to understand the other's position. Their own backgrounds and experiences make a big difference in the way they choose and use language and meaning, and unless they can talk about it, they will not achieve a common understanding.

Language Can Obscure Meanings. Word meanings vary from person to person on the basis of each one's experience and the direct relationship of those experiences to particular words. For example, the term *myocardial infarction* has limited meaning for most people, whereas the term *heart attack* is understood by almost everyone to denote a serious health crisis related to the heart. However, a doctor, a patient, a relative of a patient, and a statistician in a hospital will understand the term quite differently. The doctor thinks of procedures that will help the patient. The patient thinks, "Will I live or die?" The family members ask, "What can I do?" The statistician sees a probability related to life and death. The medical doctor knows that using the term

Making Connections

Using Language in Your Role as Student

Imagine that you have been assigned to write a brief research paper and then to use that same topic for an informative speech three weeks later. Because language use should vary according to the time, the place, the situation, and the mode of communication, think about the similarities and differences between the language used in written reports and oral presentations.

1. List the characteristics of language appropriate to writing a paper.
2. List the characteristics of language appropriate to making an oral presentation on the same topic.
3. Together with a classmate, compare and contrast the two lists. What differences do you note between language suited to writing and to speaking?

Now consider different audiences:

4. You are speaking to a group of high school students. How will that affect your use of words? List the characteristics of language appropriate to this audience.
5. How will your language use change if you are speaking to a group of people over the age of sixty-five? List the characteristics of language appropriate to this audience.
6. Together with a classmate, compare and contrast the two lists. Why should language use vary according to context?

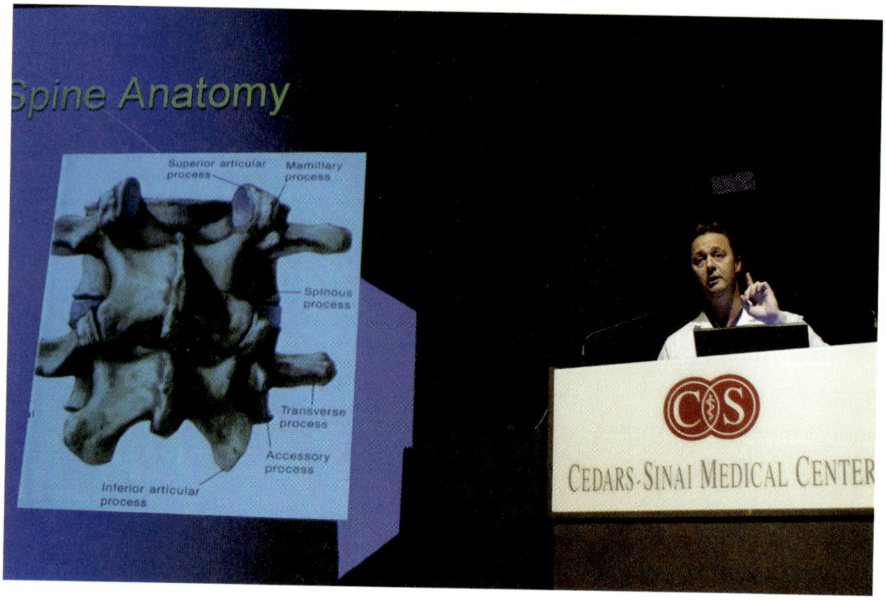

Language, or jargon, used by a particular group or discipline may be too specialized or technical to be understood by the general public. In such a situation, one would need specific knowledge about the subject to understand what is being said.

myocardial infarction might confuse the patient and family members, so the more common term *heart attack* must be used. Employing the wrong language in such a sensitive situation can lead to misunderstanding and confusion.

Also, the meanings of words, like words themselves, change from time to time and from place to place. It is easy to forget that the meaning we have for a word might not match the meaning held by others. For example, ask a person over age sixty the meanings of these words: *grass, geek, speed, pot, joint, gay, high,* or *stoned.* What words do we use now that might change in meaning over the next twenty years? We constantly add words to our language, especially those related to new technologies. Consider *emoticons, email, snail mail, fax, CD-ROM, compact disc, cell phone, ATM, spamming, surfing the Web, netiquette, download, upload,* and so on.

Word meanings also vary from region to region. For example, in some regions of the United States, if you ask for pop at a store, the clerk will not understand you until you rephrase your question and ask for soda or a Coke. In Nebraska and Iowa, people get a drink of water from the drinking fountain, but in Wisconsin, people use a bubbler. Regional word use can lead to misunderstandings, and we must be sensitive to such potential differences. Also, cultures and co-cultures hold differing meanings for certain words. For example, for most Americans *very dear* means something that is highly valued or loved, whereas in Ireland *very dear* means very expensive and has nothing to do with value or love.

jargon
Language used by certain groups or specific disciplines that may be technical or too specialized to be understood by the general population.

slang
Language used by groups to keep the meaning of the communication within the group. Slang words change frequently and are specific to specific regions or groups.

Co-cultures within a language community sometimes use words or phrases in ways that are unique to their group. Scientists, engineers, and health care providers use language that might be too specialized to be understood by the general public. This unique language use is referred to as **jargon.** Other co-cultures, such as students, might use **slang** or words to communicate only with those who know the words, and the words and meanings change quickly. A car salesperson might use a slang term such as *flea* to identify a person looking for a bargain. Prisoners refer to a knife or to stab with a knife as *shank,* and a real estate agent might use the term *handyperson's special* to refer to a house in need of repair.[18] Professor Judi Sanders and her students in the Department of Communication at California State Polytechnic University in Pomona have a College Slang Project.[19] For the past thirteen years, Sanders and her students have collected slang terms from colleges and universities across the country. The top twenty terms include some that my own students provided in an assignment on slang and how it affects communication. Included in the top twenty 2003 college slang terms were the following:

> *Sick:* excellent, great, cool, unique, nice, awesome (number 20)
>
> *Bling-bling:* jewelry, money, expensive items (number 15)
>
> *Dope:* nice, cool, interesting, tight, awesome, appealing (number 10)
>
> *Trip:* (verb) to become upset, angry, or agitated (number 5)
>
> *Tight:* great, good, cool, interesting, nice, extraordinary (number 1 for the third consecutive year)

Are these terms still commonly used? Have new slang words replaced them? Such words are constantly being discarded and new ones invented—sometimes just to make sure that people outside a particular group will not catch on to their meanings. All kinds of groups, including members of a given profession, college students, ethnic groups, and gangs, develop and use slang terms.[20]

Language is used to share meaning, but it also can be used to obscure, distort, or hide meaning. One way to obscure meaning is to use a euphemism. A **euphemism** is an inoffensive or mild expression given in place of one that may offend, cause embarrassment, or suggest something unpleasant. Our society also uses euphemisms to avoid taboo subjects or words that can trigger negative reactions. Employing euphemisms can defuse the emotional charge associated with controversial or difficult concepts. For example, when a person has died, we often use a euphemism such as "passed away" instead of blunter words. The phrase "passed away" seems to make a difficult, complex situation more approachable.

Euphemisms can also be used to enhance something, to make it seem a little more glamorous than it actually is. In our society, we have become so concerned with labels that we have renamed many things to give them a more positive connotation. For example, we rarely use the term *salesman* because, apart from being sexist, it also conjures up a negative image that is not exactly characterized by scrupulous business ethics. This unfavorable connotation has been fostered by the media and sometimes by personal experience. Thus referring to a person who sells merchandise as a sales associate, sales consultant, or sales representative sounds more positive. Sometimes the term *trash collector* or *garbage man* is recast as *sanitation engineer,* which makes the job seem more attractive.

Language can also be used to create deliberately ambiguous messages. William Lutz, a professor at Rutgers University, says that he can live with ordinary euphemisms, but his teeth are set on edge when a worker is told he has been "dehired" because the firm is experiencing "negative employee retention." Actually, the employee has been fired in a layoff. But no one is willing to say so, laments Lutz, who wrote *Doublespeak,* a book denouncing the use of words to conceal meaning. **Doublespeak** is the deliberate misuse of language to distort meaning.

"It is going just too far," says Lutz, when the Pentagon refers to bombs that accidentally kill civilians as "incontinent ordinance" or when lawyers write off a plane

euphemism
The use of an inoffensive or mild expression in place of one that might offend, cause embarrassment, or suggest something unpleasant.

doublespeak
The deliberate misuse of language to distort meaning.

crash as "the involuntary conversion of a 727." That, he says, is language "designed to distort reality and corrupt thought."[21] Lutz thinks the practice is disgraceful, dangerous to democracy, perverse, and pervasive. It's hard work, too. Doublespeak isn't just the natural work product of the bureaucratic mind; it is invented painstakingly by committees laboring to cloak meaning. Doublespeak is not a slip of the tongue or language used improperly because of ignorance. It is a tool that the powerful use to achieve their ends without clearly communicating with those who may be affected by their actions or who may foot the bill for them. According to Lutz and other scholars, doublespeak is particularly harmful when it makes something inappropriate or negative appear to be appropriate or positive.

As you can see, language and meaning are inseparable parts of communication. They mesh smoothly in successful communication. Unfortunately, a type of communication also occurs when a message is misunderstood.

Language-Based Barriers to Communication

Although it takes little physical effort to say something to someone, it does take mental effort to ensure that what we say conveys our intended meaning. Even if we create what we *think* is the perfect message, the possibility always exists that the receiver will misinterpret the message or find it ambiguous. Therefore the receiver must also make an effort to receive the intended message.

"There are over 300 different languages in everyday use in the United States. This number includes more than 200 Native American languages, the languages of the colonizers (English, French, and Spanish), languages of immigrants—both old and new—and a variety of dialects spoken in various regions of the country."[22] We must recognize that communication is a symbolic interaction rich in subtlety. It will never be strictly concrete or objective and thus always carries the potential for misunderstanding. Misunderstandings occur for numerous physical, mental, and cultural reasons. Ineffective use of language is one reason. Among the most common language-based barriers to effective communication are bypassing, indiscrimination, and polarization.[23]

Meanings Can Be Misunderstood

What is *meant* by a speaker and what is *heard* and *understood* by the listener often differ. Such misunderstanding between a sender and a receiver is called **bypassing.** How many times have we said to someone, "But that's not what I meant"? Here is an illustration of bypassing:

> The radio commercials ring out, "Everything's on sale! Visit the store now for the greatest bargains ever!" Of course everything is on sale! People open businesses to sell something. If they have products, they offer them for sale. The commercials and window signs can be misleading, however. If you enter the store believing that every single item is marked down, you might well be wrong. "Everything's on sale" is correct, but that does not mean that everything is being sold at a reduced price.

bypassing
A misunderstanding that occurs between a sender and a receiver because of the symbolic nature of language.

Bypassing occurs in similar situations every day.

Making Connections

Dictionary.com

Web searches on different language topics can provide interesting and exciting information. Some sites help you learn more about words, their usage, and their definitions. Dictionary.com is one such site. When you key in a word, seeking a definition, the search engine provides several definitions from different dictionaries so that you can compare meanings. The site features "Dr. Dictionary" so that you can ask questions relating to words and grammar and will translate anything from a phrase to an entire web page from one major European language, including English, to another.

1. Access Dictionary.com by going to www.dictionary.com.
2. Seek the definition of a word of your choice. (Try to find a word with which you are relatively unfamiliar that you recently read or one you heard from someone else.) If you can't think of a word, try one of these: *etymology, homophily, multiculturalism, panacea,* or *volition.*
3. Compare the definitions returned. How are they similar? How are they different? How would you know which was the "best" definition?
4. Go to Dr. Dictionary in Dictionary.com and ask a question about a word or phrase (e.g., "What is the word meaning 'to throw out of a window'?").
5. Share what you've learned with other students.

Bypassing usually results from the false belief that each word has only one meaning and that words have meaning in themselves. But a glimpse at our everyday language quickly illustrates that most words have multiple uses and meanings. For example, the *Random House Dictionary of the English Language* provides sixty different definitions for the word *call,* thirty for *fast,* twenty-two for *seat,* twenty-nine for *see,* and ninety-six for *turn.* Words acquire many meanings because they change over time, are used and understood differently in various cultures and regions, and often reflect the knowledge and situation of the user. Therefore it is crucial that all of us as communicators, both senders and receivers, stay alert to the fact that words can be interpreted differently by different people.

The interpretation of words becomes even more complex when people from different cultures exchange everyday communication. The problem is magnified when someone uses common phrases that are unfamiliar to non-native speakers of English. For example, consider this sentence: "Won't you have some tea?" The non-native speaker of English listens to the literal meaning of the question and would answer no if he or she did in fact want tea. Because they use this wording so frequently, native English speakers forget that it contains a double negative. But a non-native speaker might not know that, in practice, "Won't you have some tea?" and "Will you have some tea?" mean the same thing. In this situation, bypassing occurred because of cultural differences between the two speakers.[24]

Some speakers deliberately invite bypassing by using euphemisms or doublespeak to soften or distort meanings. It is important to be aware of this. Politicians and advertisers sometimes will say one thing in order to get people to believe or accept something else. Listeners should critically examine what is being said. Both speaking and listening involve ethical considerations. Issues of conscience—what is right or wrong and what is beneficial or harmful—are everyone's responsibility.

GUIDELINES Reducing Bypassing[25]

1. *Be person-minded, not word-minded.* Think about words and their meanings, but also consider the persons using the words and the meanings they might give to them. Constantly question your own interpretation: "This is what the word means to me, but what does it mean to the others?"
2. *Query and paraphrase.* Ask questions and paraphrase your message or the meaning you've derived from others' messages, whenever there is a potential for misunderstanding. Differences in background, age, gender, occupation, culture, attitudes, knowledge, and perceptions may affect communication. If you are uncertain, ask others to explain. Restating a message in your own words gives you and the sender a chance to check that you received a similar message to what was sent. As the importance and complexity of a message increase, so do the need to ask questions and paraphrase.
3. *Be approachable.* Encourage open and free communication. The most frequent barrier to effective communication is an unwillingness to listen to others. Allow others to question and paraphrase your messages, and show respect for what they say. Being receptive is not always easy, but the effort will ensure a clear exchange of information.
4. *Be sensitive to contexts.* Consider the verbal and situational contexts in which communication occurs. The meaning of a word can be more precisely interpreted by considering the words, sentences, and paragraphs that precede and follow it and the setting in which communication takes place.

Language Can Shape Our Attitudes

Indiscrimination is the neglect of individual differences and the overemphasis of similarities. Indiscrimination is a form of perceptual set (see Chapter 2) in which a person chooses to ignore differences and changes in events, things, and people. Language plays a significant role in our tendency to see similarities between things, even when they don't exist. Nouns that categorize people *(teenager, divorcé, student, professor, African American, southerner, liberal, friend, government official, politician, salesperson)* encourage us to focus on similarities. Statements such as "Politicians are crooks" and "Students cheat in school" may be interpreted to include all politicians and all students, instead of some politicians and some students. They fail to distinguish between individuals. Such categorization often results in stereotyping.

A stereotype, as defined in Chapter 2, is a categorizing of events, objects, and people without regard to unique individual characteristics and qualities. Stereotypes are often negative, but they may also be positive, for example, "All liberals are hardworking," "All conservatives want peace," "All teachers are dedicated professionals," "All environmentalists are concerned citizens." Whether the stereotype is negative or positive, the problem is the same: Individual qualities are ignored. Stereotyping is quick and easy to do because it does not require analysis, investigation, or thought. By precluding distinctions, stereotypes give us neat, oversimplified categories that facilitate our evaluation of people, situations, and events.

indiscrimination The neglect of individual differences and overemphasis of similarities.

indexing A technique to reduce indiscrimination by identifying the specific persons, ideas, events, or objects a statement refers to.

There are ways to reduce indiscrimination in our communication. **Indexing** points up differences that distinguish various members of a group and thus reduces indiscrimination. Indexing identifies the specific person, idea, event, or object to which a statement refers. When you hear someone say, "Politicians are corrupt," "College men are oversexed," "Homosexuals have perverted values," "Athletes are dumb," or any statement that lumps people, ideas, events, or objects into a single category, immediately ask, "Which ones are you talking about?" No matter what people might think, not all politicians are corrupt. Politician A is different from politician B, and politician B is different from politician C. The same is true of college men, homosexuals, and athletes. They might belong to a class or group that has an identity and whose members have similarities, but the group is composed of individuals, each different from the other.

Dating, another technique for reducing indiscrimination, is a form of indexing that sorts people, ideas, events, and objects according to time. By telling when something occurred, we acknowledge that things change over time and add specificity to a statement. As an example of how important dating is, indicate the year in which you think each of the following news bulletins was probably made:

> **Pope Condemns Use of New "Horror" Weapons**
>
> Vatican City—Prompted by widespread fears that new weapons of mass destruction might wipe out Western civilization, the Pope today issued a bulletin forbidding the use of these weapons by any Christian state against another, whatever the provocation.
>
> **Moral Rot Endangers Land, Warns General**
>
> Boston—The head of the country's armed forces declared here today that if he had known the depth of America's moral decay, he would never have accepted his command. "Such a dearth of public spirit," he asserted, "and want of virtue, and fertility in all the low arts to obtain advantages of one kind or another, I never saw before and hope I may never be witness to again."[26]

The thoughts expressed in these two paragraphs could easily apply to what is happening today, but, in fact, the first paragraph pertains to a statement made by Pope Innocent II in 1139, and the second is a comment made by George Washington in 1775.

Did you think that these news bulletins referred to recent events? If so, you fell victim to indiscrimination. Why do such errors occur? How can we avoid or prevent them? The contexts of the statements in these news bulletins could be greatly clarified merely by adding dates: Vatican City, 1139, and Boston, 1775. Dating gives listeners valuable information that can increase their understanding of the intended message.

dating
A form of indexing that sorts people, events, ideas, and objects according to time.

Language Can Cause Polarization

Polarization is the tendency to view things in terms of extremes—rich or poor, beautiful or ugly, large or small, high or low, good or bad, intelligent or stupid—even though most things exist somewhere in between. This either–or, black-or-white way of thinking is aggravated by aspects of language.

polarization
The tendency to view things in terms of extremes.

Polarization can be destructive, escalating conflict to the point at which two parties simply cannot communicate. This escalation is referred to as the **pendulum effect.** The pendulum represents a person's perception of reality, which includes feelings, attitudes, opinions, and value judgments about the world. When the pendulum is hanging in the center, a person's perception is considered to be realistic, virtuous, intelligent, sane, honest, and honorable. Of course, most of us believe that our pendulums are at or near the center most of the time. When two individuals disagree in their

pendulum effect
Escalating conflict between two individuals or groups that results from their use of polar terms to describe and defend their perceptions of reality.

Polarization is the tendency to view things in terms of extremes—rich or poor, beautiful or ugly, large or small, high or low, good or bad, intelligent or stupid—even though most things exist somewhere in between. This either–or, black-or-white way of thinking is aggravated by aspects of language.

perceptions of reality, their pendulums begin to move in opposite directions. The distance the pendulum swings represents their differences in opinion or conviction. As the conversation intensifies, each remark provokes a stronger reaction from the party to whom it is directed until both parties are driven to positions at opposite extremes. For example, when two roommates argue over whose turn it is to clean, one might begin by saying, "It's your turn. I did it the last time." The other is likely to respond, "No, I did it the last time. Now it's your turn." If the disagreement continues and no solution is found, both will become more entrenched in their positions, and their comments may turn into personal attacks: "You're always so messy and lazy." "And you're always so picky and critical." The situation can degenerate to the point at which one or the other threatens to move out. Such an extreme outcome is typical of a discussion driven by the pendulum effect. Emotions can eventually run so high that the differences between the parties seem insurmountable and a mutually agreeable settlement seems unattainable.

Speakers can avoid the dangers of polarization by recognizing the potential for misunderstanding and by making statements that do not represent unnuanced extremes. For example, a noncontroversial statement such as "Nebraska is hot in the summer" is not as meaningful as it could be because the word *hot* represents a generalized extreme. Further information will prevent misunderstanding: What is the basis of comparison (Florida or Minnesota)? Are Nebraska summers all the same, or do they vary from year to year? Is a Nebraska summer the same in all parts of the state, or does it vary from north to south? What is the average summer temperature? The problem of making an incorrectly overgeneralized and extreme statement is avoided here: "Nebraska summers can be hot. The average temperature is 85 degrees Fahrenheit, with lows around 74 degrees and highs around 105 degrees." Such clarification is especially important when the topic at hand is likely to provoke emotional, defensive, or unpredictable reactions.

Language Can Be Sexist

There is a difference in how men and women may use language and converse with one another (as indicated in Chapter 3). Deborah Tannen, for example, suggests that men tend to use language to assert status, whereas women use language to establish and maintain social relationships.[27] Tannen says that, rather than using language to dominate another, women tend to employ it to establish closeness and support. Men, by contrast, use language to dominate or compete. The result, according to Tannen, is that the game of communication for men and women is the same, but the rules are dif-

Making Connections

Grumpy Martha's Guide to Grammar and Usage

Want to learn more about language and grammar and how to use the correct word at the appropriate time and in the appropriate manner? Check out Grumpy Martha's Guide to Grammar and Usage on the web at http://encarta.msn.com/column/grammarmain.asp.

Here's a brief look at what she says:

You may think, "Grammar, schmammar. Usage, schmusage," but when you use words incorrectly, you sound as funny as someone wearing underwear for a hat looks.

I'd like to spare you from this fate. You can sound smarter in just ten minutes with "Grumpy Martha's Guide to Grammar and Usage." This list isn't comprehensive, but it covers most of the frequent mistakes I hear. Plus, I give you a fat list of links you can use to get more information and have a little more fun.

1. Go to Grumpy Martha's website.
2. Check the explanations for "my, myself, and I."
3. Create a correct sentence for each term.
4. Then check "Be effective, not affected."
5. Create a sentence using each word correctly.
6. Check the remainder of Grumpy Martha's website for suggestions about correct grammar and usage.
7. Go to the Encarta World English Dictionary from the link in Grumpy Martha's web page, and look for the definitions of the word *language.* What is the core meaning of the word? From where does the word come?

ferent. When men and women communicate with each other, there is the potential for clash and conflict because of different language use. The problem is magnified when sexist language is used either consciously or unconsciously. Our goal should be to use **gender-inclusive language**—language that does not discriminate against males or females.

Unfortunately, the English language is structured with an inherent bias in favor of men. There are, for example, no singular gender-neutral pronouns in the English language. Therefore, traditionally, the masculine pronouns *(he, him, his)* have been used to refer to people in general, even if the referent could be a male or female. Use of the masculine pronoun is not incorrect grammatically, but its use in generic situations is a social issue. Language sets expectations that at times discriminate against and stereotype women. According to traditional usage, the omnipresence of *he* and *him* and the general absence of *she* and *her* subtly but powerfully give the impression that men hold important roles but women do not. Thus our language creates the expectation that males are active and have important roles, whereas females are inactive and do not hold important roles. Furthermore, sexist language can be misleading. If a speaker were to talk about skin cancer and use only *he* or *she* when describing the symptoms, the effects, the reasons, and the treatment, the group that was not included in the discussion might believe that it is a "male disease" or a "female disease" and does not pertain to them. If that happens, half or more of the audience members will not pay attention to the speech and thus might not heed the precautions and expose themselves to greater danger.

Sexual stereotypes and the assumption that the male gender is superior to the female gender characterize **sexist language.**[28] In our society sexist language involves an attitude as much as the use of specific words. Words with a positive connotation are used to describe males—*independent, logical, strong, confident, aggressive;* females are associated with words having negative connotations—*dependent, illogical, weak,*

gender-inclusive language
Language that does not discriminate against males or females.

sexist language
Language that creates sexual stereotypes or implies that one gender is superior to another.

gullible, timid. Sexist language suggests that men are more important than and superior to women. Language that is used to discriminate against women can be quite subtle. Consider these statements: "She is president of the company, and she's a woman"; "Wanda got that position because she's a woman." They describe women who have risen to high authority positions, but they also imply that women do not typically hold these positions or that the only reason Wanda got the position was because she's a woman. In other words, they imply that women are less qualified than men.

Stereotypes do not occur in a social vacuum. On the contrary, they often exert powerful influence on the lives of those who are stereotyped. Gender stereotypes influence perceptions and behaviors of both men and women. Stereotypes of women affect both how they are treated in society and how they think of themselves. Language is one significant means of perpetuating these stereotypes. Avoiding sexist language and substituting gender-inclusive terms represent a positive step toward doing away with them.

Other stereotypes are reinforced in the use of homophobic language. When someone asks another to "tell me what to look for so I can recognize gays or lesbians and then avoid them," the speaker is demonstrating both insensitivity to individuals and a general negative categorization of a group of people, each of whom is unique.

Metaphors used in our culture to describe men and women are often sexist. A **metaphor** is a figure of speech that associates two things or ideas, not commonly linked, as a means of description. These stereotypical animal metaphors illustrate the use of sexist language: Men are likely to be described as aggressive *(wolf, tomcat, stud)* and women as harmless pets *(kitten, lamb, chick)* or as unattractive barnyard animals (*cow, pig, dog*). The effective communicator must avoid such negative metaphorical stereotyping, find more positive metaphors related to women, and use inclusive language in general.

GUIDELINES Using Gender-Inclusive Language

1. Commit yourself to removing sexism from your communication.
2. Practice and reinforce nonsexist communication patterns until they become habitual. The ultimate goals are to use nonsexist language effortlessly in private conversation and to think in nonsexist terms.
3. Use familiar language whenever possible, but if you must choose between sexist language and an unfamiliar phrase, choose the unfamiliar phrase and practice it until it becomes familiar.
4. Do not arouse negative reactions in receivers by using awkward, cumbersome, highly repetitious, or unnecessary words. There are so many graceful and controlled ways to state your message inclusively that you need not use bland or offensive constructions.
5. Ascertain whether roots and meanings of words need to be changed before doing so.
6. Check every outgoing message—written, oral, nonverbal, and email—for sexism before sending it.[29]

metaphor
A figure of speech in which a word or phrase relates one object or idea to another object or idea that are not commonly linked together.

It is important that the language we use be inclusive and not demeaning to any group of individuals. Language influences how we see others around us. Inappropriate language causes perceptual and social problems that should not be tolerated in our society.

Culture Affects Language Use

Just as there are differences in the ways in which men and women use language, there are also cultural differences in the use of language. As we saw in the opening case study, people visiting from other nations often are reluctant to speak in front of groups in classrooms, social gatherings, and the workplace because they worry that they will not use the "correct" words and might embarrass themselves by communicating ineffectively. According to the **Sapir-Whorf hypothesis,** our perception of reality is determined by our thoughts, and our language influences our thought processes. According to Sarah Trenholm, this hypothesis involves two theories: **linguistic determinism** (the theory that language determines thought) and **linguistic relativity** (the theory that people from different language communities perceive the world differently).[30] Together they suggest that culture helps create variations in communication. In other words, according to the Sapir-Whorf hypothesis, language is more than simply attaching labels to the world around us. Language shapes our reality. We "know" the world only in terms of the language we have at our command, and that language determines our cultural reality. If we don't have the words to explain something, we don't really know it, and it doesn't exist. When we can use words to explain the concept, event, or idea, it takes on meaning that can be shared. Judith Martin and Thomas Nakayama suggest that the relationship between communication and culture can be viewed in three complementary ways: (1) Culture influences communication, (2) culture is enacted through communication, and (3) communication is a way of contesting and resisting the dominant culture.[31]

Further, anthropologist Edward T. Hall suggests that for some cultures the situation in which a particular communication occurs tells us a great deal about its meaning.[32] In a **high-context culture** the meaning of the communication act is inferred from the situation or location. In Japan (a high-context culture), for example, businesspeople do not conduct business in a social setting, although they might refer to their business interests. If one visits Japan on business and is invited out to dinner, there is no hidden agenda—the objective for the evening is to eat a meal together, not to conduct business. Business is saved for the office or the meeting place. Also, in a high-context culture, language is indirect, nonspecific, and not very assertive. In a **low-context culture** the meaning of the communication act is inferred from the messages being sent and not the location where the communication occurs. According to Hall, the United States is a low-context culture in which businesspeople are as likely to conduct business on the golf course, in a restaurant, or at a reception as they are in the workplace. People in a low-context culture typically are more assertive and more direct. They get immediately to the point. Because understanding such distinctions is essential to sending and receiving messages successfully, the competent communicator will learn as much about language and cultural differences as possible.

You should also be aware that there are cultures that have greater or lesser expectations for an individual's involvement in communication events. Students in Japan, Korea, China, Finland, and Thailand, for example, are expected to listen to their professors and not ask questions during class unless the professor gives them permission to become involved. These cultures seem to prefer low involvement on the part of the students. In Russia and the United States, however, students are expected to have high involvement in the learning process and are encouraged to ask questions and otherwise participate.

Neil Postman, in *Technopoly,* says that technology redefines culture through its control over and elevation of information. "The uncontrolled growth of technology

Sapir-Whorf hypothesis
An explanation of how thought influences our reality and how our thought process is influenced by our language.

linguistic determinism
The theory that language determines thought.

linguistic relativity
The theory that suggests that people from different language communities perceive the world differently.

high-context culture
A culture in which the meaning of the communication act is inferred from the situation or location.

low-context culture
A culture in which the meaning of the communication act is inferred from the messages being sent and not the location where the communication occurs.

Making Connections

Understanding the Difference between High- and Low-Context Cultures

Aleta is from China (a high-context culture). Her neighbor, Jennifer, is from the United States (a low-context culture). Jennifer's daughter is learning to play the piano and practices early in the morning, after school, and in the evening before bedtime.

One night at 9 P.M., Aleta knocked on Jennifer's door and said, "You must be so proud of your daughter. She practices the piano so much. You must plan to have her become a concert pianist."

"Why, no." Jennifer responded, "She's just beginning to play the piano."

"You must be proud that she practices early in the morning, after school, and into the night. She is certainly a dedicated student. She plays the piano so many hours." With that, Aleta turned around and went into her own apartment.

1. What is the difference between the language use in high- and low-context cultures?
2. What was the real message here?
3. Did Jennifer get the message?
4. If the neighbor had been another person from the United States, what do you suppose would have been said?

Learning Connections

1. How does language shape our thinking?
2. How can language be misused?
3. How can we avoid sexist or racist language?

destroys the vital sources of our humanity."[33] Given the rapid growth of technology, it is likely that some changes will occur simply because of the technological advances. Language, however, will still influence thought, and Martin and Nakayama's third point (communication is a way of contesting and resisting the dominant culture) might well be more needed than ever before.

How to Use Language Effectively

People of all ages, cultures, and educational levels use language every day. Nevertheless, the ability to use language efficiently and effectively requires years of practice and study. Although many variables influence the effectiveness of language use, five aspects of language merit special attention. They are accuracy, vividness, immediacy, appropriateness, and metaphor.

Use Accurate Language

Using accurate language is as critical to a speaker as giving accurate navigational directions is to an air traffic controller. Choosing a wrong word can distort your intended message, misguide your receiver, and undermine your credibility. When you speak, your goal should be precision. Don't leave room for misinterpretation. You should constantly ask yourself, "What do I want to say?" and "What do I mean?" When necessary, consult a dictionary to be sure you have chosen the correct word to express your message.

The more words you can use accurately, the more likely it is that you will find the one you need to make your meaning clear. You must expand your vocabulary. Two of

Making Connections

Using Language Effectively

Compare the following two messages. The first was made by President Franklin D. Roosevelt. The second expresses a similar thought, though in a different way.

I see one-third of a nation ill-housed, ill-clad, ill-nourished.

*It is evident that a substantial number of persons within the continental boundaries of the United States have inadequate financial resources with which to purchase the products of agricultural communities and industrial establishments. It would appear that, for a considerable segment of the population, perhaps as much as 33.333 percent of the total, there are inadequate housing facilities, and an equally significant proportion is deprived of the proper types of clothing and nourishment.**

1. How would you describe the word choice in each message?
2. How does each message affect your emotions?
3. What impression do you have of each speaker?

*Excerpt from "Gobbledygook" in *Power of Words*, copyright 1954, 1953 and renewed 1982, 1981 by Stuart Chase, reprinted by permission of Harcourt, Inc.

the best ways to do this are through listening to others and reading. Pay attention to words that you don't understand. Whenever you come across an unfamiliar word, determine the context in which it is used, and consult a dictionary to find its meaning. Once you have learned a new word, try to put it to use. Words that are not used are typically forgotten. Expanding your vocabulary takes effort and time, but with practice, it can become part of your daily routine.

One word of warning: As you develop your vocabulary, avoid the temptation to use long or little-known words when short or common words serve the purpose. Also be sure you know the shades of meaning and connotations of new words before you use them, and remember that words may have different meanings for different people.

Sometimes a message is unclear because it was not structured effectively. Poor sentence structure and word usage can wreak havoc on a statement's clarity. For example, classified ads in newspapers frequently are so condensed that their intended meaning becomes distorted or obscured. The result might be "1999 Cadillac hearse for sale—body in good condition" and "Wanted to rent—four-room apartment by careful couple; no children." Obviously, these advertisers knew what they intended to communicate, but their failure to phrase their messages accurately interfered with conveying their intended meaning.

When conversing, we can easily clear up misunderstandings caused by scrambled sentence structure or poor word choice. But to do so, we must first be aware of listeners' reactions to what we are saying. If they appear confused or ask a question, we should rephrase the message more clearly.

Effective speakers do not assume that what is clear to them will necessarily be clear to listeners. They are especially aware of this potential problem in situations such as public speeches, during which listeners might not be able to ask questions. To ensure comprehension, such speakers strive to make their meaning clear by, among other things, using familiar and concrete rather than abstract language and by being aware of the connotations associated with particular words.

To narrate this ceremony in a Vietnamese temple, the language should vividly and animatedly highlight the event, what people are wearing, the background ornamentation, and so forth. People tend to listen more completely when language is alive and remember more accurately when they are able to recall mental images.

Use Vivid Language

To communicate effectively, make your message animated and interesting. Direct, fresh language given in the active voice can bring a sense of excitement, urgency, and forcefulness to what you say. Such **vividness** tells your audience that they had better listen because what you have to say is important.

For example, suppose an organization is trying to raise money for homeless people. It could take one of two approaches in seeking a donation from you: (1) present statistics to illustrate the number of people who are believed to be homeless in our society or (2) present cases of actual individuals who are homeless, including children and their families. The first approach is rational, informative, abstract, and emotionally distant. The second approach is emotional, urgent, concrete, and forceful. The vividness of the second approach is likely at least to get your attention and perhaps influence you to contribute.

According to social psychologists, vivid language affects us in several ways. It is more persuasive than a flat, pallid presentation of information, because it is more memorable and has an emotional impact. Vivid messages are more likely to create readily retained and recalled mental images. Finally, people tend to listen more attentively to vivid messages than to uninspiring or uninteresting messages.[34]

To increase a message's vividness, fill in details and use interesting, but not obscure, words. Use active verbs, and vary the sentence structures. The sentence "They had realized their most cherished dream; they discovered the ancient tomb of the Egyptian king they had sought for so long" shows action and conveys a sense of excitement. Note how much more animated and energetic it is than this dry and passive statement: "The old tomb was found by the explorers."

vividness Active, direct, and fresh language that brings a sense of excitement, urgency, and forcefulness to a message.

You should also avoid using clichés such as "happy as a lark," "blind as a bat," and "fit as a fiddle." Such overused, unimaginative phrases lack impact. You are more likely to hold your audience's attention by using fresh language to present your ideas in a new and exciting way.

Making Connections

Technology and Language Use

The language we use is important in initiating web searches. The way you use words to search and the specific search engine you use will affect the results of your search. You need to know whether to ask a question (such as on Ask Jeeves, www.ask.com), put quotation marks around each separate word, or put *and*, *or*, or other joining words with the concepts for which you're searching. Here are some general guidelines to help you quickly find the information you are seeking.

1. The search entry form usually consists of an empty space or rectangular box in which you type in search criteria, either words or phrases, or both.
2. The "Search," "Submit," or "Go" button activates the search.
3. Click on the "Help," "Options," or "Tips" icon to learn how to put your words and punctuation marks together for the most effective search.
4. Some search engines use plus (+) when you require the words and minus (–) when you prohibit words.
5. When you use AltaVista (www.altavista.com), use quotation marks to separate words in the topic. This search engine considers each word independently unless you identify a group of words as a phrase within quotation marks. If you're looking for information on *lesson plans for health and nutrition*, you should enter the words as follows: + health + "lesson plans" + nutrition (or + nutri*, which tells the search engine that you will accept any form of the word that begins with the five letters *nutri*).
6. When you use Yahoo! (www.yahoo.com), you should set your options before you begin the search. The Yahoo! search engine gives you the option of restricting how far into the past you wish to search. To use this option you must make a selection from a drop-down menu from three years to one day. You can tell Yahoo! to handle the text you type into the search entry form as a group of single words or as a phrase. This is accomplished by using *or* or *and* as your connecting words.
7. If you use Google (www.google.com) type in a few descriptive words and hit the enter key (or click on the Google Search button for a list of relevant web pages). Google only returns web pages that contain all the words in your query. You should, therefore, refine or narrow your search. You can do this by adding more words to the search items you have already entered. Choose your key words carefully in order to get better results.
8. You can save yourself a great deal of time by checking the specific search engine to learn how to use words most effectively to search the Web.
9. If one word or term does not provide results, think of synonyms, key in those words, and search again. There is much information on the Web. You must choose your words carefully to get the most from your search.

Use Immediate Language

Verbal immediacy identifies and projects the speaker's feelings and makes the message more relevant to the listener. Verbal immediacy draws listeners in and involves them in the subject at hand. The following statements illustrate different levels of verbal immediacy. The first sentence displays a high immediacy level, and the last displays a low immediacy level:

1. We certainly will enjoy the baseball game.
2. You and I will enjoy the baseball game.
3. I think you and I may enjoy baseball.
4. People often enjoy baseball games.

verbal immediacy
Identifies and projects the speaker's feelings and makes the message more relevant to the listener.

The first statement is directly related to the speaker, the listener, and the situation. It is assertive, and the speaker makes a connection with the listener by using the word *we.* In each successive statement, the speaker decreases the intensity of this association with the listener and the event. The language becomes less immediate, more distant in tone.

Verbal immediacy also makes the speaker appear relaxed, confident, competent, and effective. Also, receivers tend to view messages characterized by immediacy as similar to their own beliefs more readily than those cast in language unrelated to the speaker, topic, or receiver.[35]

Use Appropriate Language

Each time you speak, your listeners have specific expectations about the kind of language you will use. Different kinds of language are appropriate to different situations. For example, the language you would use in addressing the president of your college or university would be much more formal than the language you would use when chatting with friends. You would be unlikely to call the president by a nickname, and you would be equally unlikely to call a friend Dr. or Mr. or Ms., except in jest.

Using language that is inappropriate for a given situation damages your credibility, and your message might be misinterpreted or disregarded. It is therefore crucial to assess each speaking situation and adjust your language accordingly. In public situations, profanity, improper grammar, and slang are always inappropriate.

Use Metaphorical Language

According to some language scholars, our way of looking at the world around us is fundamentally metaphorical. Metaphors help us to structure what we think, how we perceive things, and what we do. Metaphorical language pervades our everyday language and our thoughts. A metaphor is a figure of speech in which a word or phrase relates one object or idea to another that is not commonly linked to it. A successful metaphor makes an object or idea more clear and vivid. Anna Levina used the following examples of metaphorical language in a presentation about her thesis:

> Twenty years ago, Postville, Iowa was the epitome of the "melting pot" of United States culture. Postville, located in Northeast Iowa, was for nearly 150 years an all-white, all-Christian farming community of 1000 residents, mostly of German and Norwegian ancestry. Stephanie Simon, Los Angeles *Times,* 1999, described "the used-to-be" Postville as an "everyone-knows, live-and-die-here kind of town run by farmers of German and Norwegian stock."
>
> In 1987 a Russian-born Jew, Aaron Rubashkin, a butcher from Brooklyn and a member of the ultra-orthodox Lubavitcher sect, bought a bankrupt slaughterhouse. He converted it to a kosher meat-packing plant and created new jobs. Three dozen rabbis and their families came to Postville. The plant brought jobs filled by people from Mexico, Guatemala, the Ukraine, Nigeria, Bosnia, the Czech Republic, Russia, and other places. Postville today is home to 20 different ethnicities. The packing plant is now the largest kosher plant in the world and Postville's population has increased by more than 54%.
>
> Postville is no longer a melting pot. It is a tossed salad. The cultures have not melted together. Each new culture is unique, distinct, and retains its own traditions, dress, religious customs, and behaviors. And, the people seemingly get along quite well in this new milieu. When you visit the kosher deli, *Jacob's Table,* your eyes will be drawn to the row of brightly colored flags representing the native lands of Postville's residents. And, there's an

Making Connections

Making Meaning with Metaphorical Language

Suzanne McCorkle, a communication scholar at Boise State University, has used metaphors to examine managing interpersonal conflict and to teach critical thinking and the ethical implications of language use.* She asks students to think about metaphorical language as a tool. In this activity, think about common terms and find new ways to explain them using metaphorical language. Complete the following:

1. College is . . . (fill in your metaphor) because . . . (give an explanation).
2. Communication is like the game of . . . because. . . .
3. Discuss your metaphorical choices with your classmates, family members, or friends.
4. Defend your choices.
5. What other metaphors or analogies might you have chosen?
6. Why did you choose these instead of the other ones?
7. Listen for others' use of analogies and metaphors. Write them down and bring them to class with you so that the whole group can discuss metaphorical ways of looking at things.

*S. M. McCorkle, "Metaphor in the Classroom: A Patchwork of Inconsistency," *Speech Communication Teacher* (Annandale, Va.: National Communication Association, summer 1999), 9–10.

array of wall clocks showing the time in places from Istanbul to Los Angeles. The "tossed salad" metaphor best describes this small town that has become a microcosm of the global society in which we live.[36]

Metaphorical language is culture bound, and most metaphors have meaning only within a specific language community. If your receivers cannot identify with a particular metaphor you use, it will be meaningless to them. Also, as we pointed out earlier in the chapter, avoid metaphors that negatively or unfairly categorize a specific person or group of people.

Know Your Scholar

Karen Tracy *University of Colorado, Boulder*

Karen Tracy is Professor of Communication at the University of Colorado, Boulder. She teaches classes in language and social interaction, conversational discourse, and discourse analysis, and she studies everyday talk. She published a popular textbook, *Everyday Talk, Building and Reflecting Identities,* in 2002. (We use her definitions of everyday talk and identity in the text.) She believes that people create themselves through their talk and that identity, or how we view ourselves, comes through our interactions (talk) with others in everyday life.

Tracy studies interactional dilemmas in institutional settings with a focus on educational and justice-linked institutions. Her past work focused on academic colloquia and on exchanges between citizens and 911 call-takers. In a current project, she is investigating the difficulties of enacting democracy in the ordinary public meetings of school boards. Tracy is especially interested in institutional sites where participants hold conflicting beliefs about good conduct.

As a student, you probably can think of many metaphors that describe your college experiences. For example, some students have said that college life is like a roller-coaster ride. There are many ups and downs, as well as turns. What are some other metaphors that vividly express your college experience?

Summary

Learning how to use language is important for effective communication in any situation. The ability to use language determines our success, makes communication personal, and allows us to translate our thoughts, feelings, and experiences into messages.

The misuse of language is more than simply a matter of misusing words; it also affects our ability to think. According to most scholars, thought and language are inseparable. When we cannot find the words to express a thought, perhaps our thinking is not clear. If our thoughts are not expressed clearly and accurately, misunderstanding is inevitable.

The elements of language help us to fashion our messages so that most people will be able to understand our meanings. Thus the ability to carefully choose the elements of language to construct and share messages effectively and efficiently helps us to become competent communicators.

The goal of communication is to exchange meanings. If language did not convey meaning, it would serve little or no purpose. We tend to associate specific words with specific meanings and to take that relationship for granted, but in reality, words have been arbitrarily paired with meanings. Words are not actual objects or ideas but symbols that represent objects or ideas. Meanings therefore are not in words but in people. As such, language can obscure, distort, or hide meaning and create barriers. The competent communicator will find ways to understand and be understood.

Language, culture, and thought are bound together. Effective communicators are aware of how to interact with people from other cultures. Competent communicators avoid unfamiliar words, seek to be sensitive toward another's culture and command of the language, and exercise patient effort to create and share understanding. The words and manner of speaking we choose to use can make our ideas clearer and more meaningful. Effective use of language requires practice and study.

DISCUSSION STARTERS

1. Can you provide personal examples of the power of language?
2. How are language and thought related?
3. Why are language, communication, talk, and speech defined separately and not considered synonymous?
4. We say that language has rules, but we also say that language is arbitrary. Is that a contradiction in terms?
5. Why should we recognize and defend against the use of inappropriate language?
6. Why is "meanings are in people" an important concept?
7. Which of the language barriers discussed in this chapter is most likely to occur in your interactions?
8. How do indexing and dating affect communication efforts?
9. What words are common in your conversations that are the result of advances in technology?

NOTES

1. X. Liao, "Effective Communication in Multicultural Classrooms: An Exploratory Study," unpublished Master of Arts thesis, University of Northern Iowa, May 2003.
2. Educational Testing Service Study on College Enrollment. Reported in *The Chronicle of Higher Education,* May 26, 2000: A35–A37.
3. *The Chronicle of Higher Education,* September 8, 2000.
4. T. Raum, "Political Careers Marred by Foot-in-Mouth Disease," Associated Press, in *Lincoln/Journal Star,* Dec. 20, 2002, p. 1A.
5. P. Le Rousic, *The Name Book* (Fairfield, Iowa: Sunstar, 1994).
6. V. De Francisco, personal conversations, March 24, 2003, and June 3, 2003. De Francisco writes about feminist perspectives on communication and wrote an article on the concept of naming.
7. A. Taylor, CRTNET postings, National Communication Association email list, June 3 and June 4, 2003.
8. Ibid.
9. Chuck D., co-founder of rap group Public Enemy, Hearst Lecture Series speech, University of Northern Iowa, January 2003.
10. "Country Music Fans Boo Dixie Chicks at Awards," *Waterloo/Cedar Falls Courier,* May 22, 2003, p. A10.
11. C. Kramerae, *Women and Men Speaking (*Rowley, Mass.: Newbury, 1981).
12. M. Houston, "Multiple Perspectives: African American Women Conceive Their Talk," *Women and Language* 23 (2002): 11–23.
13. K. Tracy, *Everyday Talk Building and Reflecting Identities* (New York: Guilford Press, 2002), viii.
14. Ibid., pp. 8–9.
15. G. A. Miller, *The Psychology of Communication* (Baltimore: Penguin, 1967).
16. L. Carroll, *Alice's Adventures in Wonderland, Through the Looking Glass, and The Hunting of the Smark* (New York: Modern Library, 1925), 246–47.
17. A. Korzybski, *Science and Sanity: An Introduction to Non-Aristotelian Systems and General Semantics* (Lancaster, Pa.: Science Press Printing, 1933).
18. P. Dickson, *Slang!* (New York: Pocket Books, 1990).
19. J. Sanders, "College Slang Page," from the College Slang Research Project, Department of Communication, California State Polytechnic University, Pomona, www.csupomona.edu/ ~ jasanders/slang. Professor Sanders may be contacted at jasanders@csupomona.edu (last retrieved May 13, 2003)
20. P. Dickson, *Slang!* (New York: Pocket Books, 1990).
21. W. Lutz, *Doublespeak: From "Revenue Enhancement" to "Terminal Living": How Government, Business, Advertisers, and Others Use Language to Deceive You.* (New York: Harper & Row, 1987), 3–4.
22. K. Cushner, A. McClelland, and P. Safford, *Human Diversity in Education: An Integrative Approach* (New York: McGraw-Hill, 1992), 159.
23. Adapted from W. V. Haney, *Communication and Organizational Behavior,* 3rd ed. (Homewood, Ill.: Irwin, 1973), 211–330; and *Communication and Interpersonal Relations,* 5th ed. (Homewood, Ill.: Irwin, 1986), 213–405.
24. L. M. Barna, "Stumbling Blocks in Intercultural Communication," in *Intercultural Communication: A Reader,* 7th ed., eds. L. A. Samovar and R. E. Porter (Belmont, Calif.: Wadsworth Publishing, 1994), 340.
25. Adapted from Haney, 232–33.
26. News bulletins from W. R. Espy, "Say When," *This Week,* 13 July 1952, quoted in W. V. Haney, *Communication and Organizational Behavior,* 396.
27. D. Tannen, *You Just Don't Understand* (New York: Morrow, 1990).
28. C. Miller and K. Swift, *The Handbook on Nonsexist Writing,* 2nd ed. (New York: Harper & Row, 1988).
29. Adapted from B. D. Sorrels, *Nonsexist Communicator: Solving the Problem of Gender and Awkwardness in Modern English* (Englewood Cliffs, N.J.: Prentice-Hall, 1983), 17.
30. S. Trenholm, *Thinking through Communication* (Boston: Allyn and Bacon, 2000), 87.
31. J. N. Martin and T. K. Nakayama, *Intercultural Communication in Contexts* (Mountain View, Calif.: Mayfield Publishing Co., 1997), 59.
32. E. T. Hall, *The Hidden Dimension* (Garden City, N.Y.: Doubleday, 1966).
33. N. Postman, *Technopoly* (New York: Alfred A. Knopf, 1992), 4.
34. S. T. Fiske and S. E. Taylor, *Social Cognition* (Reading, Mass.: Addison-Wesley, 1984), 190–94.
35. J. J. Bradac, J. W. Bowers, and J. A. Courtright, "Three Language Variables in Communication Research: Intensity, Immediacy, and Diversity," *Human Communication Research* 5 (1979): 257–69.
36. Adapted from remarks made in an oral defense of an unpublished thesis by Anna Levina, entitled, "Recent Jewish Immigrants' Communication in Postville, Iowa: A Case Study," University of Northern Iowa, June 3, 2003.

"There is no such thing as an empty space or an empty time. There is always something to see, something to hear. In fact, try as we may to make a silence, we cannot."
—John Cage

CHAPTER 5 Connecting through Nonverbal Communication

THIS CHAPTER WILL HELP YOU:

- Explain what nonverbal communication is.
- Tell why six key characteristics of nonverbal communication are crucial to using and interpreting it.
- Know the five common functions of nonverbal communication.
- Describe different types of nonverbal communication and their connection to cultural and gender uses.
- Explain why nonverbal communication is difficult to interpret and understand.
- Improve your interpretation of, and be a more competent user of, nonverbal communication.

CASE STUDY

"Hi, did you see the game last night? I'm done—it's your turn to speak."

"No, but I did go to a movie with Lee. Your turn—I am done."

"Thanks, the game was really great. Dana was really hot. She must have made . . . "

"Do you mind? I'd like to say something."

"Oh! You want to talk about the movie some more—sure, go ahead."

Unusual conversation you say, but is it?

Questions to think about

1. What would communication be like without unspoken cues?
2. How does nonverbal communication make communication easier? More difficult?
3. Explain the role nonverbal communication has in our everyday communication.

What Is Nonverbal Communication?

Nonverbal communication includes all behaviors, attributes, or objects (except words) that communicate messages that have social meaning. Nonverbal communication includes tone of voice, facial expressions, posture, gestures, and appearance, all of which are used to communicate messages. Nonverbal communication supplements words, such as when tone of voice, volume, or facial expression adds emphasis to the meaning of a word. Unfortunately, nonverbal communication can also change the intended meaning of a message or make it confusing and unclear. Nonverbal communication can be intentional or unintentional, serving a variety of functions. Nonverbal communication does not, however, include gestures that represent words, such as American Sign Language (ASL), written words, or words transmitted electronically. To hearing persons, sign language is often seen as nonverbal communication. However, to persons who are hearing impaired, sign language is mostly verbal because the signs, body language, and facial expressions are signals for words, phrases, and emphasis.

The inclusion of nonverbal behavior in the study of communication is relatively recent. We tend to take nonverbal communication for granted because it is so basic, but its importance is unmistakable, and its connection to communication is undeniable. Research indicates that in most situations, we spend more of our time communicating nonverbally than verbally and that our nonverbal messages carry more meaning than our verbal messages. Studies have estimated, for example, that the average person speaks for only ten to eleven minutes per day and that the average spoken sentence spans about 2.5 seconds. In a normal two-person conversation, 60 to 93 percent of communicative meaning is transmitted through nonverbal behaviors.[1]

Although the percentages that verbal and nonverbal messages contribute to the meaning of a communication can vary dramatically, they are indicators of the role each plays in our everyday conversations. Even if we assume the lowest percentage of meaning at 60 percent, nonverbal communication plays an important role in our communication with others. People do indeed reveal much about their current moods, preferences, and emotions through nonverbal communication; however, the process of reading and deciphering such information is far more complex and subtle than it appears on the surface.[2]

A review by Mark Knapp and Judith Hall of nonverbal research concluded that some people depend more heavily on verbal messages, whereas others seem to rely more on nonverbal messages.[3] Another research study found that nonverbal behaviors were twelve to thirteen times more powerful in impact compared to the accompanying verbal message.[4] These findings indicate the importance and impact of nonverbal behaviors. Our communication must be viewed as a whole and not simply as verbal or nonverbal messages.

Without realizing it, we often use nonverbal communication as the basis for many daily decisions. Can you think of recent decisions you have made on the basis of the nonverbal communication of another person? For example, your professor's facial expression suggests that she is in a really good mood, so you decide that now is a good time to ask her whether you can miss next week's class to attend a friend's wedding.

Even though our culture is verbally oriented, more and more scholars and teachers are recognizing the significant connection of nonverbal behavior to the communication process.

nonverbal communication
Behaviors, attributes, or objects (except words) that communicate messages that have social meaning.

Know Your Scholar

Mark Knapp *University of Texas*

Mark L. Knapp received his B.S. and M.A. from the University of Kansas and his Ph.D. from Penn State University. He is a former Chair of the Department of Communication Studies at the University of Texas. He is a member of the University of Texas Academy of Distinguished Teachers. He is a Fellow of the International Communication Association and served as its President. He received the Distinguished Scholar Award from the National Communication Association and also served as President of that association. He is the author of many books, including *Interpersonal Communication and Human Relationships* (with A. Vangelisti), *Nonverbal Communication in Human Interaction* (with J. Hall), and *The Handbook of Interpersonal Communication* (with J. A. Daly). Dr. Knapp has published research on nonverbal behavior that humans use to manage their interactions such as greeting and goodbye rituals and turn-taking processes. Other publications have examined the nonverbal behavior manifested by liars and truth-tellers and the changing nature of nonverbal behavior during the process of developing a close relationship. He has also written about theoretical and methodological issues bearing on the study of nonverbal communication and the interconnections between verbal and nonverbal behavior. To learn more about Dr. Knapp, go to www.utexas.edu/coc/speech/faculty/MLKnapp.

Characteristics of Nonverbal Communication

A question that students often ask is "Why is it important that we study nonverbal communication?" There are many reasons for studying nonverbal communication, the primary one being its pervasive effects on what and how we communicate; we are always communicating something nonverbally, whether we intend to or not. Besides occurring constantly, nonverbal communication depends on context, is more believable than verbal communication, is a primary means of expression, is related to culture, and is ambiguous or easily misunderstood.

Nonverbal Communication Occurs Constantly

When another person is present, you have to communicate. Whether you make eye contact, smile, frown, or try to totally ignore the other person, you are communicating something. Sometimes, what is said is less important than what is not said. For example, not attending a meeting at which you were expected, coming late to an employment interview, wearing jeans when you were expected to dress formally, wearing a suit when jeans were expected, talking about a sad situation with a smirk on your face, and speaking to someone but never looking him or her in the eye all convey strong messages. We all believe we can tell a great deal about people on the basis of their facial expression, appearance (sex, race, physique), clothing, willingness to make eye contact, body movements, and posture.

To illustrate that we are always communicating, whether intentionally or unintentionally, consider these two students: Jack is always perfectly groomed and smells of expensive aftershave lotion. George has shoulder-length hair, has tattoos on both arms, wears stud earrings in his left earlobe, and always wears sweatshirts and jeans.

By simply looking at them, we cannot really tell what the two men actually intend to communicate. Jack might simply be neat and use aftershave lotion because it feels good, or he might really want to communicate that designer clothes and expensive aftershave lotion are important to him. Similarly, George might simply like to dress comfortably, or he may be attempting to communicate that he disdains society's seeming obsession with outward appearances. Ultimately, it's not so much what Jack and George intend to communicate as what others perceive. Both students, whether they want to, are communicating something about themselves through appearance.

Nonverbal Communication Depends on Context

The context in which nonverbal communication occurs plays a crucial role in its interpretation. Pounding on a table to make a point during a speech means something entirely different from pounding on the table in response to someone's calling you a liar. Direct eye contact with a stranger can mean something entirely different from direct eye contact with a close friend.

When you communicate, your nonverbal and verbal cues usually supplement and support each other. Your appearance, tone of voice, eye movement, posture, and facial expression provide cues about the communication relationship. For example, when you talk to a friend, your relaxed tone of voice, eye contact, and posture reveal much about your friendship. Your nonverbal cues can tell your friends how much you value them, how comfortable you feel, and how intimate your relationships have become. Such nonverbal communication is interpreted within the context of your friendships and is complemented by casual and personal conversations.

Without understanding the context in which communication occurs, it is almost impossible to tell what a specific nonverbal behavior may mean. In fact, misunderstandings can occur even when the context is fully understood. That is why we must think twice about our interpretation of others' nonverbal behavior and their possible interpretations of ours. When you see and hear nonverbal communication without a complete understanding of the context, you might not get the message that was intended. When you assume too much about a nonverbal message, further miscommunication and misunderstanding can result.

Nonverbal Communication Is More Believable than Verbal Communication

Most of us tend to believe nonverbal communication, even when it contradicts the accompanying verbal message. Consider this conversation between a mother and her daughter regarding the daughter's husband:

> "What's wrong? Are you upset with Chad?" asks Jess's mother.
>
> (Stare and frown) "Whatever, I'm not upset, why should I be?" responds Jess.
>
> "You seem to be in a funk, and you are avoiding talking to me. So what's wrong? Did you and Chad have a fight?" asks Jess's mother.
>
> "I SAID NOTHING IS WRONG! LEAVE ME ALONE! EVERYTHING IS FINE!"

Throughout the conversation, Jess seems upset, snappy in tone, and to be sending a signal to her mother that she isn't telling the whole story. It seems clear from the interaction and the mother's intuition that Jess is hiding something, hence the second inquiry. Indeed, the real story is that Jess and her husband have not been getting along lately. They have been fighting over money, and the mother could sense that something was on Jess's mind. Nonverbal messages are much more difficult to control than

Making Connections

Emotion and Emphasis via Electronic Communication

The messages we communicate are given more meaning and emphasis through our nonverbal communication. But how can you use nonverbal expressions to illustrate emotions if you are communicating mainly via email with someone? When we write to others, we can put certain words in all capitals to emphasize their importance or to convey a strong meaning, such as frustration or anger. For instance, "CALL ME SOON!" illustrates a stronger message than simply "call me soon."

To emphasize that we are happy or sad about something, we sometimes use visual images, such as a happy, smiling face or an unhappy, sad face, on a letter or message to the make the point that we are pleased or displeased with something. Some symbols that convey a variety of emotions, which can be used when sending email messages, have become popular. The most common emotions are conveyed by combining a colon, dash, and other symbols to relay nonverbal messages (they are referred to as *emoticons*). Here are some common ones.

:-(Depressed or upset by a remark
:-| Straight face
:-o Surprise

1. Locate or illustrate other symbols that convey emotions or feelings that might also be used when communicating electronically. Do a web search using the terms "electronic emotional expressions." Here are two sites to get you started: www.disabilitytravel.com/behavior/emoticon.htm and www.pb.org/emoticon.html.
2. What did you learn from your Internet search and investigation of nonverbal communication?
3. Do you accept these symbols as nonverbal communication? Why or why not?

verbal messages because nonverbal cues are more representative of our emotions, which are more difficult to control.

Is the nonverbal or the verbal communication more likely to be truer? Verbal communication is more conscious; it involves more processing of thoughts and impulses into words. Although nonverbal messages can be conscious and deliberate, they often, as we have suggested, are unintentional and subconsciously generated. It is almost always easy to determine what you are going to say, but it is very difficult for most of us to control our voices, facial expressions, and other body movements when we are upset, hurt, or angry. Jess's mother interpreted her daughter's nonverbal communication as a more accurate reflection of Jess's feelings than her verbal communication.

Nonverbal Communication Is a Primary Means of Expression

We can often detect other people's feelings of frustration, anger, sadness, resentment, or anxiety without their actually saying anything. We can detect others' emotions because nonverbal communication is so powerful. Almost all of our feelings and attitudes are expressed through our nonverbal behavior. For example, at a graduation party attended by many young children, one little girl entered with her parents and spotted a neighbor. She turned up her nose and walked away. Her mother, running after her, asked why she had suddenly left, to which the girl replied, "I don't like that girl over there." The nonverbal communication really didn't need much explanation; it was obvious what the little girl was saying through her actions, whether intentionally or unintentionally.

Nonverbal Communication Is Related to Culture

Culture contributes significantly to differences in nonverbal behavior. Norms and rules that govern the management of behavior differ from culture to culture. Yet because human beings around the world share common biological and social functions, it should not be too surprising to also find areas of similarity in nonverbal communication. For example, studies comparing facial expressions have found that certain universal expressions, such as those indicating sadness and fear, are easily understood across varying cultures. Although much outward behavior is innate (such as smiling, touching, eye contact, moving), we are not born knowing what meanings such nonverbal messages communicate. Most scholars would agree that cultures formulate display rules that dictate when, how, and with what consequences nonverbal expressions are exhibited. For instance, all of us are born with the capacity to cry, yet what makes us cry and who is allowed to see us cry need to be learned within cultural boundaries.

Nonverbal Communication Is Ambiguous

Because nonverbal messages are always present, we must recognize their importance or impact yet also be very careful when interpreting them. Like verbal communication, nonverbal behavior can be ambiguous, abstract, and arbitrary. We can not assume that nonverbal messages have only one meaning. For example, does crying always signify grief or sadness, or could it also express joy or pain? Interpreting nonverbal behavior requires understanding the context in which it takes place and the cultural norms governing it. Yet even when a person understands these dynamics, it is still very easy to misperceive nonverbal behaviors. For example, does a fellow student's yawn signal boredom or fatigue? Does a speaker tremble because of nervousness or excitement? Most nonverbal behaviors have a multitude of possible meanings, and to automatically assume that you have grasped the only possible meaning could lead to a serious misunderstanding. There are no consistent rules for using nonverbal communication.

There are many reasons why you should study nonverbal communication. The following are some of the more important reasons. Nonverbal communication:

- carries most of the meaning of a message, particularly feelings and attitudes toward others.
- is a frequent source of misunderstandings.
- is not governed by a set of universal rules.
- is not a language.
- is multichanneled, complicated, and ever-changing.
- is context- and culture-bound.
- is more likely than verbal communication to be spontaneous and unintentional.
- is powerful and is more believable than verbal communication.
- is learned (not always consciously).
- is critical in relationship initiation, development, and termination.

Learning Connections

1. What do you think is the most important aspect of nonverbal communication that every competent communicator should know?
2. Explain why nonverbal communication is more believable than verbal communication.
3. What is the relationship between nonverbal communication and ethics?
4. Besides the reasons given to study nonverbal communication, are there others that you would add to the list?

TABLE 5.1
Functions of Nonverbal Communication

CATEGORY	CHARACTERISTICS	EXAMPLES
Complementing	Completes, describes, or accents a verbal message	A person needs help immediately, so he yells as loudly as he can.
Repeating	Expresses a message identical to the verbal one	A person says yes and nods her head up and down.
Regulating	Controls flow of communication	A person shakes his head up and down as a way of communicating "I am interested in what you are saying," implying "tell me more."
Substituting	Replaces a verbal message with nonverbal signals to exchange thoughts	Two people use hand signals to communicate, because it is too loud to hear each other's voices.
Deceiving	Nonverbal cues that purposely disguise or mislead to create a false impression	A doctor examining a patient discovers a serious problem, but the doctor's facial expressions remain neutral so as not to alarm the patient.

Functions of Nonverbal Communication

Nonverbal communication adds life to our exchanges by complementing, repeating, regulating, and substituting for our words. Sometimes we even use it to deceive others (see Table 5.1).

Complementing Verbal Behavior

Nonverbal cues can be used to complete, describe, or accent verbal cues. This use is called **complementing.** For example, after shooting a chip shot from about seventy-five yards, a golfer tells her partner that she missed the cup by inches and uses her thumb and index finger to show the distance. When saying hello to a friend, you show your genuine interest by displaying a warm smile, maintaining steady eye contact, and holding the friend's hand.

We use complementary nonverbal cues to accent verbal behavior by emphasizing or punctuating our spoken words. For example, a mother trying to get her children to quiet down might say quietly, "Will you please keep it down." If that doesn't work and the noise is really bothering her, she might raise her voice to indicate that she wants quiet immediately.

People who are excited or enthusiastic are more likely to use nonverbal cues for accenting their messages than are people who are restrained, having a difficult time expressing themselves, not paying attention, or not understanding what is being said. If used correctly in a public speech, that is, if accenting gestures and changes in tone of voice appear natural and flow smoothly with the message, they can be especially effective ways of making a point clearer to an audience.

complementing The use of nonverbal cues to complete, describe, or accent verbal cues.

Repeating Verbal Behavior

Whereas complementing behaviors help to modify or elaborate verbal messages, repeating behavior expresses a message identical to the verbal one. For example, a father attempting to keep his child quiet at an adult gathering might place his index finger to his lips while saying, "Shush!" A speaker stating that she has two points to make might hold up two fingers. The actions of the father and the speaker are called **repeating** because they convey the same meaning as the verbal message.

Such repetition is especially common in sports. For instance, a referee on a basketball court shouts, "Traveling!" while rolling her arms in a circular motion, or a baseball umpire cries, "Strike," while raising his right arm. These repeating nonverbal signals are deliberately planned so that all players and spectators will know the official's call. But most repeating messages are sent without much thought. They are simply a natural part of our communicative behavior.

Regulating Verbal Behavior

Nonverbal cues can also be used for controlling the flow of communication, a behavior known as **regulating.** For example, we frequently use nonverbal signals to indicate that we want to talk, to stop another person from interrupting us when we are talking, or to show that we are finished talking and that the other person may take a turn. When we are listening, we might nod our head rapidly to suggest that the speaker hurry up and finish, or we might nod slowly to show that we want to hear more.

Senders might not even realize that they are sending regulating cues, but receivers are usually aware of such signals. In class, for example, a professor receives a clear message when students put on their coats or close their notebooks to indicate that class is over. Although the students are merely recognizing that it is time for them to leave, the message the professor receives might be quite different.

repeating
The use of nonverbal cues to convey the same meaning as the verbal message.

regulating
The use of nonverbal cues to control the flow of communication.

substituting
The use of nonverbal cues in place of verbal messages when speaking is impossible, undesirable, or inappropriate.

deceiving
Purposely misleading others by using nonverbal cues to create false impressions or to convey incorrect information.

Substituting for Verbal Behavior

Using nonverbal messages in place of verbal messages is known as **substituting.** It is common when speaking is impossible, undesirable, or inappropriate. For example, ramp controllers at airports use hand signals to guide planes to their unloading positions, because the noise level is too high for spoken communication; friends often exchange knowing looks when they want to communicate something behind another person's back; some people with hearing impairments use a sophisticated formal sign language in place of the spoken word, as discussed on page 110.

Deceiving

When we purposely mislead others by using nonverbal cues to create false impressions or to convey incorrect information, we are **deceiving.** Among the most common of such *deceiving* nonverbal behaviors is the poker face that some use when playing cards. Masking is a form of deceiving. We might try to appear calm when we are really nervous or upset, and we often act surprised, alert, or happy when in fact we are feeling quite the opposite. In addition, we consciously try to manage our nonverbal behavior when we give a speech or attend a job interview in order to disguise our true purpose and emotions.

Nonverbal messages can substitute when verbal ones are impossible. This man is signaling to the pilot, with batons that are used by day or night, where and when to bring the plane to a complete stop.

Deception research has identified a set of nonverbal cues that people display when they are not telling the truth. In one study, it was found that people who lie make fewer hand movements and tend to look away from a person when they are not telling the truth. The research further found that liars' voices can also be a telling sign; there is a tendency to hesitate and to shift their pitch more often than those telling the truth.[5] Another study found that liars often try to control their voices, which often leads to sounding overcontrolled or undercontrolled, indicating anxiety or deception.[6] In spite of what we know about people's nonverbal behaviors when they are not telling the truth, very few of us are able to detect or interpret these behaviors as signs of deception. People who can detect untruthfulness usually consider more than one nonverbal cue to determine whether someone is telling the truth. There is a very fine line between the nonverbal behaviors of someone who is legitimately anxious and someone who is

Making Connections

Telling the Truth: It's Not What You Say, It's How You Behave

There is a lot of guessing when it comes to people's honesty in relation to their nonverbal communication—are they telling the truth? Often, we make assumptions about the truthfulness of people based on the inconsistencies of their nonverbal and verbal messages.

1. Why is or isn't it ethical to make assumptions about others' truthfulness based on their nonverbal messages?
2. What can we do to prevent premature judgment about the truthfulness of others' nonverbal messages?
3. Why is it that we assume we know when people are lying or being deceptive from their nonverbal messages?

Nonverbal messages unrelated to the verbal message are sometimes helpful in identifying deception.

Used by permission of Mell Lazarus and of Creators Syndicate, Inc.

not being truthful. Therefore there are no sure ways to confirm lying using nonverbal behaviors alone.

Types of Nonverbal Communication

When you dress in a suit for a meeting, smile at someone, sit in a specific seat in class, use your hands while talking, play with a pen or pencil while listening, dim the lights to create a romantic atmosphere, play music loudly, look someone directly in the eyes, or burn incense to create a pleasant odor, you are communicating nonverbally. Every day, we perform a wide range of nonverbal behaviors without even thinking about them, yet such behaviors can convey definite messages to others. Because nonverbal communication is so diverse, complex, common, and informative, we need to be sensitive to its many manifestations. In the following pages, we examine some of the more significant forms of nonverbal communication, such as kinesics (body movements, including gestures, facial expressions, and eye behavior), physical characteristics, haptics (touch), proxemics (space), chronemics (time), vocalics/paralanguage (use of voice), silence, olfactics (odors), artifacts, and environment.

Facial Expressions and Body Movements

We use body movements—gestures, facial expressions, and eye behavior—to create an infinite number of nonverbal messages. For our purposes, we define **kinesics,** which is sometimes referred to as *body language,* as any movement of the face or body that communicates a message. Two particularly significant categories of kinesics are eye behavior and facial expressions. **Eye behavior** is a subcategory of facial expressions that includes any movement or behavior of the eyes and is also referred to as **oculesics,** which is the study of eye movement or eye behavior. The eyes, through eye contact with others, have the primary function of establishing relationships. **Facial expressions** include configurations of the face that can reflect, augment, contradict, or appear unrelated to a speaker's spoken message.

kinesics
Sometimes referred to as "body language"; any movement of the face or body that communicates a message.

eye behavior
A category of kinesics and a subcategory of facial expressions that includes any movement or behavior of the eyes.

oculesics
Study of eye movement or eye behavior.

facial expression
Configuration of the face that can reflect, augment, contradict, or be unrelated to a speaker's vocal delivery.

Eye Behavior or Oculesics. According to some researchers, eye behavior is the first and primary characteristic people notice. The researchers found that during interactions, people spend about 45 percent of the time looking at each other's eyes.[7] Through eye behavior, we establish relationships with others. Eyes also convey a variety of other important messages. We notice a speaker's eye contact, share mutual glances with friends, and feel uncomfortable when others stare at us. Eye behavior, according to Dale Leathers, a communication scholar, can serve one of six important communicative functions: (1) influence attitude change and persuasion; (2) indicate degree of attentiveness, interest, and arousal; (3) express emotions; (4) regulate interaction; (5) indicate power and status; and (6) form impressions in others.[8]

Eye gaze at the interpersonal level communicates sincerity, trustworthiness, and friendliness. Romantic partners are more likely to gaze into each other's eyes for prolonged periods when expressing their affection for one another.[9] Members of groups or teams use eye contact to build their relationships and to show unity or a sense of belonging to the group or team. In Chapter 10, we discuss the importance of eye contact between a speaker and an audience. In general, effective speakers use more frequent eye contact with their audiences than less effective speakers do. Eye contact is also important for those of us who are listeners, because looking at the speaker indicates our interest in what is being said and is a sign of respect for the speaker.

Making Connections

The Eyes Have It

Try the following experiment. Get on an elevator—the more people on it, the better—and try to be the last person on it. Then, instead of facing the door, face the people and look at each of them directly. Do not talk; look directly at the people. After fifteen or twenty seconds, look down slightly, but still try to observe the people's reactions to you.

1. What did you notice about people's behavior when you looked directly at them?
2. Describe any changes in the people's behavior when you looked down.
3. How did you feel during the experiment?
4. What does this experiment tell you about oculesics (eye movement)?

Have you ever had a conversation with someone who was wearing dark glasses? If you have, you know that it is a bit uncomfortable because you can't completely see how the other person is reacting to you. We do learn much about others' feelings and emotions from their eyes. For example, we associate a high level of gaze or indirect eye contact from another as a sign of liking or friendliness.[10] In contrast, if others avoid making eye contact with us, we are likely to conclude that they are unfriendly, don't like us, or are simply shy.[11] Although a high level of eye contact can be interpreted as positive, there are some exceptions to this rule. If people look at us continuously and maintain the eye contact regardless of actions we take, they are said to be staring. When confronted by unwanted staring, most of us tend to withdraw from the situation.[12] Generally, people find being stared at an unpleasant experience; it makes most of us nervous and tense.[13] This is especially true of what is referred to as a "cold stare," because it is a form of intimidation, and unwanted stares are often interpreted in our society as a sign of hostility and anger.[14] This is one reason experts on road rage—highly aggressive driving by motorists, sometimes followed by actual assaults—recommend that drivers avoid eye contact with people who are disobeying traffic laws and rules of the road.

Facial Expressions. Facial expressions are windows to our emotions. They provide clues about our and others' emotional states, which at times can be very complex and difficult to interpret accurately. Alan Robinson of the Associated Press wrote, "If any NFL coach fits the description of a mad scientist, it's the unmistakable Bill Cowher (pictured), with his jutting jaw and angry eyes, his irrepressible intensity and spittle-flying sideline rages."[15] Coach Cowher's nickname is "Face," not only because he is an in-your-face coach but also because his distinctive facial expressions seem to tell his mood.

Our facial expressions typically display our emotions, but because of their complexity, these emotions can be difficult to interpret. Researchers have identified more than a thousand different expressions of the human face.

More than two thousand years ago, the Roman orator Cicero stated, "The face is the image of the soul." By this, he meant that human feelings and emotions are often reflected in our faces. Modern research suggests that Cicero and others who observed human behavior were correct: It is possible to learn much about others' current moods and feelings from their facial expressions. Researchers have found that our faces depict six different basic emotions clearly and from a rather early age: anger, fear, happiness, sadness, surprise, and disgust.[16] Other research suggests that contempt as an emotion may also be quite basic.[17] However, agreement on what specific facial expression represents contempt is less consistent than in the case of the other six emotions just mentioned.

It is important to realize that the relatively small number of basic facial expressions in no way implies that human beings can show only a small number of facial expressions. The human face is said to produce more than a thousand different expressions. Emotions often occur in many combinations (for example, joy tinged with sorrow, surprise combined with fear), and each of these reactions can vary greatly in emphasis. Thus, while there might be only a small number of basic themes in facial expressions, the number of variations on these themes is immense.

Facial expressions have an extremely powerful role in communication and relationships. Of all the body motions, facial expressions convey the most information. Researchers have examined the judgments we make regarding the facial expressions of others and have found that not only do we judge emotions but we also make judgments about personality, such as the tendency to be friendly or unfriendly, harsh or kind, based on facial expressions.[18] We perceive people who have relaxed facial expressions as having more power and being more in control than people whose facial expressions seem nervous.[19]

Although observers are able to determine the specific emotional content of certain expressions with high accuracy, the meanings associated with other facial expressions differ from culture to culture. For example, expressions of happiness or sadness but not other facial expressions can be interpreted quite accurately as to intensity and meaning by observers from differing cultural backgrounds.[20] Interpretation of emotions is learned and usually conforms to specific cultural expectations. When observing the facial expressions of members of other cultures, we must remember that there are cultural differ-

Making Connections

Learning on the Internet

Learn about nonverbal communication at http://zzyx.ucsc.edu/~archer/intro.html. See how good you are at identifying emotions displayed on the faces in the photos at the site. How well did you identify emotions on those faces that were from different cultural backgrounds than your own? What did you learn?

TABLE 5.2

Facial Management Techniques

TECHNIQUE	DEFINITION	EXAMPLE
Intensifying	Exaggerating an expression to meet others' expectations	You receive a gift and try to look completely surprised, excited, and delighted.
Neutralizing	Understating reaction to meet others' expectations	You receive an A on a speech, and a friend receives a C. You tone down your elation, just in case your friend feels bad about receiving a lower grade.
Deintensifying	Avoidance of any emotional expression in a situation—"poker face" showing no emotion	You show no fear or sadness when fear or sadness might be justified but you don't want to show your emotions.
Masking	Replacing of one expression with another that is considered more appropriate for the situation	You smile when a friend wins a scholarship and you don't, even though you think you deserved it.

ences in the circumstances that produce an emotion, the effect of the emotion, and the rules that govern the use of a particular facial expression in a specific social situation.

Overall, then, it seems safest to conclude that although facial expressions are not completely universal—cultural and contextual differences do exist with respect to their precise meaning—they generally need very little translation, compared to spoken language. However, despite cultural rules, our faces often communicate feelings and emotions spontaneously in reaction to a situation. For example, if you open the door to your house and a group of your friends hiding in the dark turn on the lights and yell, "Congratulations!" your face will probably automatically and unconsciously express surprise. If you open the door and they yell, "Boo!" your face will probably show fear or anxiety.

Although many facial expressions are unconscious, involuntary reactions to certain stimuli, researchers have found that facial cues may be only partially reliable in terms of what they express. Michael Motley, a communication researcher, in a study confirms that facial expressions are often ambiguous and may be only relevant and interpretable as they relate to the particular conversation and context in which they occur.[21] In addition, people learn to conceal their real feelings.[22] They learn to control their facial muscles to hide inappropriate or unacceptable responses. Such controlling behaviors are referred to as **facial management techniques.** Facial management techniques may be used to intensify, deintensify, neutralize, or mask a felt emotion.[23] (See Table 5.2.)

Body Movements. To make sense of thousands of different body movements, Paul Ekman and Wallace Friesen, two psychologists, have devised a classification system based on the origins, functions, and coding of nonverbal behavior.[24] Their system divides body motions into five categories: emblems, illustrators, regulators, affect displays, and adaptors (see Table 5.3). Because there are so many body motions, many of which are interdependent, it is important to understand that the categories are not mutually exclusive. Some body motions may be classified under more than one category.

facial-management techniques
Control of facial muscles to conceal inappropriate or unacceptable responses.

TABLE 5.3

Categories of Body Movements and Facial Expressions

CATEGORY	CHARACTERISTICS	EXAMPLES
Emblems	Translate directly into words and are used for specific words or phrases. Meanings of are like those of words—arbitrary, changeable with time, learned, and culturally determined	A hitchhiker's extended thumb, the thumb and circle sign for "OK," the peace sign
Illustrators	Accent, reinforce, or emphasize a verbal message	A child holding up his hands to indicate how tall he is while saying, "I'm a big boy," an instructor underlining a word on a poster to emphasize it
Regulators	Control, monitor, or maintain interaction between or among speakers and listeners. Cues that tell us when to stop, continue, hurry, elaborate, make things more interesting, or let someone else speak. The case study at the beginning of the chapter is a good example of the need for regulators.	Eye contact, shift in posture, nod of the head, looking at a clock or wristwatch
Affect displays	Body movements that express emotions. Though your face is the primary means of displaying affect, your body may also be used.	Sad face, slouching, jumping up and down
Adaptors	Help one feel at ease in communication situations. Are difficult to interpret and require the most speculation.	Scratching, smoothing hair, playing with coins, smoking, hands in front of the face, moving closer to someone

Making Connections

Body Language and Facial Expressions: It's All about Culture and Meaning

Examine the three photos and interpret what the gestures mean to you. Each gesture has a specific meaning in the United States and most other Western cultures.

1. What do the gestures mean?
2. Show photos to people from other cultures (especially non-Western cultures) to determine whether they interpret the gestures as you do.
3. What advice would you give to someone about nonverbal communication and traveling to different cultures?

Finally, body movements and posture can reveal much about our physical states (vigor, age) and perhaps the extent to which we possess certain traits.[25] Evidence from several research studies supports these conclusions. For example, one study investigating males and females in four age groups (five to seven, thirteen to fourteen, twenty-six to twenty-eight, and seventy-five to eighty years old) had the participants walk back and forth at a pace they felt was comfortable.[26] The walkers were videotaped and then shown to others who rated the walkers on various dimensions, such as gait, traits, age, and sex. By using adjustments and lighting techniques, the researchers were able to disguise the walkers so that the subjects saw only their gait.

The subjects made judgments about the walkers two different times. The first time, they rated the walkers' gait in terms of revealing certain traits (submissive or dominating, physically weak or physically strong, timid or bold, sad or happy, unsexy or sexy). The second time, they rated the walkers' gait in terms of several other characteristics (amount of hip sway, knee bending, forward or backward lean, slow or fast pace, stiff or loose jointed gait, short or long strides). In addition, the subjects were asked to estimate each walker's age and guess whether each was female or male.

The study's results were very interesting and clearly indicate that people's gaits provide important nonverbal cues about them. For example, as predicted, ratings of traits and gaits did vary according to age. Ratings of sexiness increased from children to adolescents and young adults but decreased for older adults. Further analysis revealed that possession of a youthful gait (one characterized by hip sway, knee bending, arm swing, loose-jointedness, and more steps per second) was strongly related to ratings of the walkers' happiness and power. Thus, persons with a youthful gait—regardless of their actual age—were rated more positively along several dimensions than persons with an older gait.

Making Connections

Walk the Walk, Talk the Talk

Consider the research studies about how gait influences perceptions. Then answer the following questions, and discuss your responses with a classmate.

1. Think of situations in which a person's gait influenced your perception of him or her. In what ways did the gait influence you?
2. Can you think of cultural or gender influences that have affected your perception of others, based on their gait?

Physical Characteristics

Whereas body movements and facial expressions change quickly and can be controlled to some extent, physical characteristics, such as body type, attractiveness, height, weight, and skin tone are fairly constant and more difficult to control, especially in the course of a single interaction. Physical appearance in our culture plays a significant role in communication and relationships. In recent years, segments of our society have become obsessed with physical appearance and general health, spending billions of dollars each year on modifying, preserving, and decorating their bodies. We might say that "beauty is only skin deep," but we are likely to respond positively to those who are attractive and negatively to those who are unattractive.[27]

Physical attractiveness has an extremely powerful influence on everyday communication. It appears that both males and females are strongly influenced by attractiveness, though males seem to be more responsive to appearance than are females.[28] Overall, though, an appealing physical appearance is perceived as a positive characteristic that influences interpersonal attraction (see Chapter 14 for more on interpersonal

Making Connections

Physical Attractiveness and Stereotypes

Look at the people in this photograph and think about what they might be like.

1. Make a list of the physical characteristics that you think might best describe each person. For example, how would you describe each person's sociability, intelligence, poise, independence, masculinity or femininity, popularity, vanity, potential for success, integrity, concern for others, temperament, sexuality, and other qualities?
2. When you have finished, return to the text to see whether your answers correspond to what others think and to what research has determined.
3. Do you agree with the text? Why or why not?

attraction) and interpersonal preferences. Numerous stereotypes are consistently associated with physical appearance, and it would not be surprising if you hold some of them yourself. Before continuing, take a look at the photo in the Making Connections box and follow the instructions.

Numerous research studies have indicated that attractive people, when compared to unattractive people, are perceived to be more popular, successful, sociable, persuasive, sensual, and happy. One research study found that attractive students receive more interaction from their teachers,[29] unattractive defendants are less likely to be found innocent than attractive defendants in a court of law,[30] and attractiveness plays a predominant role in dating behaviors.[31] Attractiveness affects credibility and a person's ability to persuade others, to get a job, and to gain a higher salary. Handsome males are likely to be perceived as more masculine, whereas beautiful females are seen as more feminine, in comparison with those who are perceived as less attractive.[32]

In a few situations, attractiveness can be a disadvantage. Although attractiveness was found to be an asset for men throughout their executive careers, one research study found that being attractive could be a liability for women managers. Even when such women had reached top executive levels, their success was attributed to their looks rather than to their abilities, and they were consistently judged less capable than unattractive women managers.[33] Attractive females, in comparison to other women, are judged by some to be more vain, more materialistic, and less faithful to their husbands.[34] For both males and females, attractiveness is often considered the reason for their success, rather than their ability or hard work.[35]

We know that our society places a great deal of value on physical appearance, but do attractive individuals differ in behavior from others who are less attractive? The answer is no. In fact, attractive people do *not* seem to fit the stereotypes associated with them.[36] Surprisingly, self-esteem is not consistently high among those who are considered the most attractive. This could be because they believe that they are re-

Making Connections

Whom Do You Touch?

A schoolteacher in Lincoln, Nebraska, loses her job for touching a student; a worker in Canton, Ohio, sues an employer for "improper" touching behavior; a person talks on the radio about touching behavior between male coaches and female athletes. Touching has many different meanings. When is it inappropriate, and when isn't it? Here are some situations to consider:

1. Does it mean the same thing when the boss places an arm around the secretary and when the secretary places an arm around the boss?
2. Does it mean the same thing when a teacher places a hand on a student's shoulder and when a student places a hand on a teacher's shoulder?
3. Does it mean the same thing when a doctor touches a patient and when a patient touches a doctor?
4. When is touch appropriate, and when isn't it?
5. How does the gender of the people affect your answer to these questions?

warded not for what they have done, but for how they look, thus diminishing their sense of self-worth.[37]

Touch

Touching is referred to as either tactile communication or **haptics.** Haptics is one of the most basic forms of communication. "Reach out and touch someone" is a slogan once used by a national phone company. Although the company's advertisement suggests touching in an abstract sense, the idea behind the advertisement is that touch is a personal and powerful means of communication. As one of our most primitive and yet sensitive ways of relating to others, touch is a critical aspect of communication. It plays a significant role in giving encouragement, expressing tenderness, and showing emotional support, and it can be more powerful than words. For example, when you have just received some bad news, a pat on the shoulder from a friend can be far more reassuring than any number of understanding words.

The kind and amount of touching that are appropriate vary according to the individuals, their relationship, and the situation. Some researchers have set up categories to describe these variations in touch. The categories are functional–professional, social–polite, friendship–warmth, love–intimacy, and sexual arousal.[38] Definitions and examples are given in Table 5.4.

The meaning of a particular touch depends on the type of touch, the situation in which the touch occurs, who is doing the touching, and the cultural background of those involved. Some cultures are more prone to touching behavior than others. Research has found that people in the United States are less touch-oriented when compared to persons in other cultures. For example, a study examining touching behavior during a one-hour period in a coffeeshop found that people in San Juan, Puerto Rico, touched 180 times in an hour; those in Paris, France, touched 110 times; and those in Gainesville, Florida, touched only 2 times.[39]

haptics
Tactile, or touch, communication; one of the most basic forms of communication.

Gender differences in touching behavior are also interesting to note. Men tend to touch more than women do, women tend to be touched more often than men, and women seem to value touch more than men do. Gender differences in touching behavior may be partially attributed to men's sexual aggressiveness in our culture

TABLE 5.4

Touch/Haptics

CATEGORIES OF TOUCH	DEFINITION/EXPLANATION	EXAMPLE
Functional–professional	Unsympathetic, impersonal, cold, or businesslike touch.	A doctor touches a patient during a physical examination or a tailor touches a customer while measuring.
Social–polite	Acknowledges another person according to the norms or rules of a society.	Two people shake hands in our culture or kiss in other cultures to greet one another.
Friendship–warmth	Expresses an appreciation of the special attributes of another. Expresses warm feelings for another. The most misinterpreted type of touching behavior.	Two men or two women meet in an airport, hug, and walk off with their arms around each other. Athletes touch a shoulder or pat each other on their buttocks.
Love–intimacy	Occurs in romantic relationships between lovers and spouses. Highly communicative and usually requires consent between both parties even though one party might not reciprocate.	Two people hug, caress, embrace, kiss, and so on.
Sexual arousal	The most intimate level of personal contact with another. Expresses physical attraction between two consenting individuals.	Sexual touch behavior including foreplay and intercourse.

Making Connections

It's All in the Hands: How Much Information Does a Handshake Convey?

Handshaking is a common form of greeting in many cultures around the world. We can learn a lot about others by the way they shake our hand. Do an Internet search using the following key terms: handshake, proper handshake, proper handshake for women, handshake differences.

1. What can you learn about a person through his or her handshake?
2. What does it mean to give a proper handshake?
3. What advice would you give to another person about the importance of the handshake and what it communicates to others?

and their expression of power and dominance. According to Nancy Henley (see http://henley.socialpsychology.org), men have access to women's bodies, but women do not have the same access to men's bodies. This, according to the research, may be a man's way of exerting power because touch represents an invasion of another's personal space.[40]

FIGURE 5.1
Edward T. Hall's Four Distance Zones

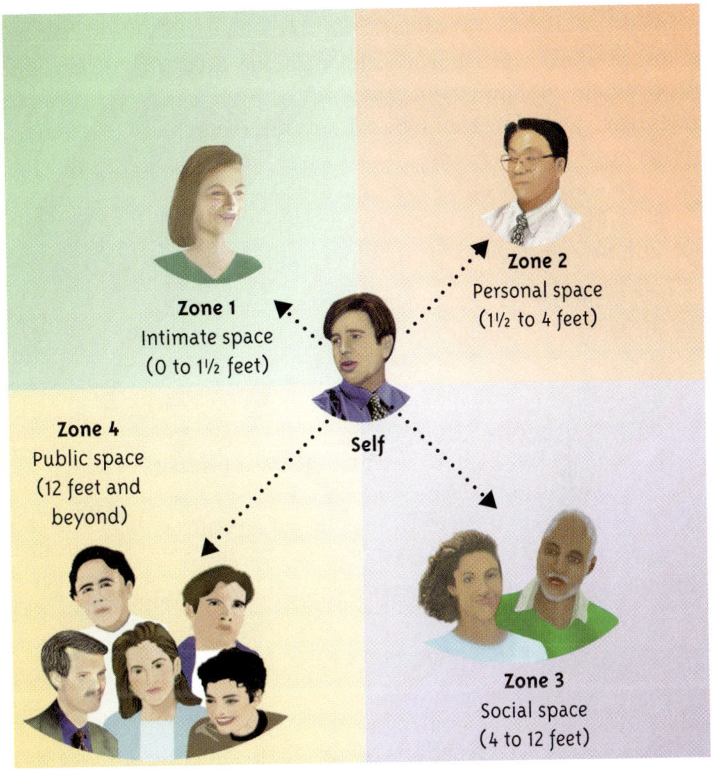

Space

Statements such as "Give me some room to operate," signs that say "Keep Out," and the bumper sticker that reads "Keep Off My" followed by a picture of a donkey all are attempts to regulate the distance between people. Such behaviors are of special interest to researchers in **proxemics,** the study of how we use space and the distance we place between others and ourselves when communicating. Edward T. Hall, anthropologist and author of two classic books, *The Silent Language* and *The Hidden Dimension,* coined the term *proxemics.*[41] Hall was a pioneer in helping to explain how space is used in North American culture. In his study of proxemics, Hall identified four zones, which are illustrated in Figure 5.1. *Intimate space* is defined as the distance from no space between people to one-and-a-half feet between people. This zone is the most personal, and it is usually open only to those with whom we are well acquainted, unless such closeness is physically forced on us, such as in a crowded train or elevator.

The second zone is referred to as *personal space* and ranges from distances of one-and-a-half feet to four feet between people. It is not unusual for us to carry on conversations or other activities with close friends and relatives in this zone. If someone we don't know enters this zone, we are likely to feel uncomfortable or violated. The third zone is called *social space.* It ranges from four to twelve feet and is where most professional conversations occur, as well as group interactions, such as meetings. *Public space,* the fourth zone, includes twelve feet or more. This distance is not unusual for public speaking situations or other formal presentations. The actual distance or zone might be determined by the context and relationship of those involved in the interaction. To read about Edward T. Hall, go to www.csiss.org/classics/content/13.

The need for us to identify certain amounts of space as our own is an aspect of proxemics called **territoriality.** We often position markers such as books, coats, pencils, papers, and other objects to declare our space. Some students become upset when someone else sits in a seat they usually occupy, even though seating is not assigned. This uneasiness stems from a strong desire to stake out and protect territory. Similar

proxemics
The study of the use of space and of distance between individuals when they are communicating.

territoriality
The need to identify certain areas of space as one's own.

Making Connections

Space: Who Needs It?

Edward Hall, a renowned scholar in the area of nonverbal communication, devised a system of identifying spatial zones based on interpersonal relationships. For example, he suggests that in professional–business or educational situations in the United States, the appropriate distance between communicators should be from four to twelve feet.

1. Go to the library, the student union, or some other place with a number of tables. Find a person sitting alone (someone of the other sex), and sit right next to the person. Notice the reaction and how the person looks at you. After a while—before the person leaves—tell him or her that you were doing an experiment for your communication class. Then ask what the person thought when you sat down close by and how he or she felt.
2. Now do the same thing with someone of your own sex. What happened? How did you feel?
3. If you feel uncomfortable doing the experiments in items 1 and 2, try this: When sitting with a friend or friends at a table where there are salt and pepper shakers or other items, slowly but surely start pushing the items toward a friend. Move them very slowly, and move as many items as you can—not all at once, but one at a time. Notice what happens. Discuss what the person was thinking as you kept moving items in his or her direction.
4. What do the results of these experiments tell you about how people treat space and its importance to them? Do men and women react to space considerations differently?
5. Do the results of your experiments match the findings of Hall? If not, why do you think your results were different?

reactions occur when someone enters a room without knocking or tailgates when driving; it seems like an invasion of our territory.

We usually give little conscious attention to the role of space in our communication, yet the way in which others use space gives strong clues to what they are thinking and how they are reacting to us. There are many variables that influence our use of space when communicating; status, sex, culture, and context are but a few.

Status affects the distance that is maintained between communicators. Research shows that people of different status levels tend to stay farther apart than do individuals of equal status. Furthermore, people of higher status tend to close the distance between themselves and people of lower status, but seldom do people of lower status move to close the distance between themselves and a person of higher status.

Men and women tend to differ in their proxemic patterns, but the differences in part hinge on whether the interaction is with someone of the same or opposite sex. In same-sex situations, men prefer, expect, and usually establish greater conversational distance than women do. Opposite-sex distancing depends on how intimate the relationship is.

Culture creates a wealth of differences in the way individuals use distance for communication. For example, people from the United States tend to stand farther apart during conversations than do people from many European and Middle Eastern cultures. Arabs, for example, consider it polite to stand close to the person with whom they are communicating. There are as many culture-based differences as there are cultures, and it is not unusual for one group to be perceived as cold and unfriendly and another as pushy and forward as a result of their use of space. The important thing is to recognize that not all cultures view distance in the same way.

Context also influences the space that is maintained between individuals. For example, people in line at an automated teller machine usually stand back far enough to give the person who is using the machine the feeling that a transaction is not being observed. But passengers waiting to board a bus ordinarily stand close together to avoid losing their places.

Time

Chronemics is the study of how people perceive, structure, and use time as communication.[42] People in our society are preoccupied with time. Everything seems to have a starting time and an ending time. We worry about how long we have to wait for something and how long it takes to do something. We even go so far as to say that time is money. Because we place such a high value on time, it plays a significant role in our nonverbal communication. We are particularly sensitive to people and events that waste our time or make exceptional demands on it. Consider your reaction, for instance, when your date keeps you waiting, when an instructor continues to lecture after the bell has signaled the end of class, or when you are given only one day's notice of an upcoming test. Your feelings might range from confusion to indignation to outrage, but you will almost certainly not be neutral. To some extent, your reaction will depend on who the other person is. You will probably be more tolerant if the offending party is a friend or someone who has great power over you. For example, if a blind date keeps you waiting too long, you might decide to leave, but if your professor is late for an office appointment, you will probably suffer in silence and continue to wait for his or her arrival.

We tend to have many expectations about how time should be used, and we often judge people by their use of time. For example, students are expected to be on time for class. Therefore, students who are punctual are more likely to create a positive impression, whereas those who are consistently late may be perceived as irresponsible, lazy, or uninterested. We must be constantly aware of the messages we send through our use (and misuse) of time.

Individuals can differ in their approaches to time. For example, some people are always looking to the future, others long for the past, and still others live for the moment. Each approach communicates something about people and the ways they use time to communicate who they are. Each culture teaches its members about time expectations, and these expectations vary. In some cultures, being punctual is expected; in others, being punctual is not important, and in fact it is expected that people will be late. In U.S. culture, for example, you are expected to be on time for a dinner party, but being up to twenty minutes late is socially accepted and still considered on time. In some European countries, arriving late for a dinner party is considered an insult. Our use of time communicates messages about us, and it is important that we adhere to the time-related norms of the culture in which we are communicating.

Paralanguage/Vocalics

Paralanguage/vocalics is the way we vocalize, or say, the words we speak. Paralanguage includes not only speech sounds, but also speech rate, accents, articulation, pronunciation, and silence. Sounds such as groans, yawns, coughs, laughter, crying, and yelping, which are nonsymbolic but can communicate very specific messages, are also included. Expressions such as "um," "uh-huh," "ya know," "like," and "OK" are referred to as vocal fillers and are considered paralanguage. Vocal fillers are often sprinkled throughout conversations without forethought or a set order. They might reflect nervousness, speech patterns of a particular subculture, or a personal habit. In any case, the use of vocal fillers can influence our image positively or damage and degrade others and us.

chronemics
The study of how people perceive, structure, and use time as communication.

paralanguage/vocalics
The way we vocalize, or say, the words we speak.

Making Connections

It's Not What You Say, But How You Say It!

"My teacher is wonderful."

Read the preceding statement aloud in four different ways: (1) with no expression at all, (2) as if your teacher is really wonderful, (3) as if you actually think your teacher is anything but wonderful, and (4) as if you are really trying to convince someone that your teacher is wonderful. Note how you can change your meaning without changing the words.

1. What do you actually do with your voice to change the sentence's meaning?
2. What else do you notice about your behavior each time you try to create a different meaning?

From this exercise, you should see the importance of vocal expression and its impact on the meaning of the message.

The content of words is verbal communication, whereas the sound quality or volume that creates the words is a form of nonverbal communication. We rely more often on paralanguage than on the words themselves when interpreting another person's message. Note how the meaning of a sentence can vary according to the word that is emphasized:

1. *Jane's* taking Tom out for pizza tonight. (not Hilary or Dana)
2. Jane's taking *Tom* out for pizza tonight. (not Bill or Dave)
3. Jane's taking Tom *out* for pizza tonight. (not staying home)
4. Jane's taking Tom out for *pizza* tonight. (not seafood or hamburgers)
5. Jane's taking Tom out for pizza *tonight.* (not tomorrow or next weekend)[43]

Even though the words in each sentence are identical, each creates an entirely different message solely because of the emphasis placed on specific words.

Paralanguage includes pitch (how high or low the voice is), vocal force (intensity or loudness of the voice), rate (speed), quality (overall impression of the voice), and pauses or silence. The way we vary our voices conveys different meanings to receivers. For example, a person who speaks quickly may communicate a message that is different from a person who speaks slowly. Even when the words are the same, if the rate, force, pitch, and quality differ, the receiver's interpretations will differ. Researchers estimate that approximately 38 percent of the meaning of oral communication is affected by our use of voice, by *the way* in which something is said rather than by *what* is said.[44]

On the basis of paralanguage, we make many judgments about what is being said, the person saying it, the speaking and listening roles, and the credibility of the message. Of course, judgments about people based on paralanguage can be just as unreliable as judgments based on body type. We must therefore recognize the effect that paralanguage has on our communication and adjust our use of it accordingly.

Silence

The sound of silence is a contradiction in terms; as hard as you try, it is almost impossible to have complete and absolute silence. Silence or vocal pauses are very communicative, very powerful messages that often say volumes, whether intended or not. **Vocal pauses** or hesitations are usually short in duration, whereas **silence** generally refers to extended periods of time without sound. Vocal pauses can be used to emphasize a word or thought or to make a point to get others' attention. For example, a speaker stands in front of an audience and gazes at the audience in the hope of gaining the audience's attention so that they will listen. A teacher pauses during a lecture to get students' attention. Sometimes, people use vocal pauses to gather their thoughts or to allow others time to think. Vocal pauses or prolonged periods of silence can

vocal pause
A hesitation, usually short in duration.

silence
An extended period of time without sound.

create the perception that you are unsure of yourself, unprepared, or nervous. Regardless of why vocal pauses occur, they do send messages.

Silence sometimes seems very awkward in a conversation, especially when you are talking to someone whom you do not know well and who might be of higher status than you. Most of us in this situation feel or sense the pressure to say something to get the conversation going again. Silence can also be used to disconfirm or create discomfort in others. Have you ever said "hello" to someone you admire or respect and he or she didn't reply or acknowledge you? You likely felt slighted or less than important. It is not unusual to use silence to prevent communication with others. Silence can be used to prevent certain topics from surfacing or to prevent someone from saying something that he or she might later regret.

Silence is expected in certain contexts, for example, during a funeral or while listening to a speech presentation, or it can be self-imposed as a way of thinking or doing nothing at all. Silence has many possible meanings, none of which is easily interpreted. The next time a good friend says "Hi," try pausing for five to ten seconds before reacting. You will quickly learn the effect silence can have as a message. There are also cultural differences related to silence. What are some negative perceptions conveyed in our culture by silence at a business meeting or social gathering? In many cultures, silence is seen more positively. In Japan, for example, silence is considered more appropriate than speech in many situations.[45] The intercultural implications of silence are as diverse as those of other nonverbal cues.

Smell

Smell communication, or **olfactics,** which is the study of smell or odors, is extremely important in our society. Billions of dollars are spent on perfumes, colognes, aftershave lotions, scented candles, deodorant, scented air sprays, soap, and other such products to enhance our surroundings and us. It is likely that when smells are pleasant, we feel better about ourselves.

Smell communicates very powerful messages, which can create a multitude of interpretations. In most developed parts of the world, people use an array of cosmetics to eliminate body odor or to replace it with other smells. Americans have the most smell-aversive culture in the world, according to Peter Andersen, a communication scholar.[46] We base many of our perceptions on smell; for example, when food smells good to us, we assume that it will taste good as well, and we are more attracted to others who have pleasant smells than those who do not. Many cultures consider natural odors to be normal; in fact, in some cultures, a person's smell is an extension of that person. As with all types of nonverbal communication, not knowing cultural variations in attitude toward smells can create misunderstandings and misperceptions, which ultimately can lead to incorrect assumptions.

Artifacts

Artifacts are personal adornments or possessions that communicate information about us. Such things as automobiles, eyeglasses, briefcases, grooming, clothing, hair color, body piercing, tattoos, makeup, and the many hundreds of other material perceptions that we create to communicate our age, gender, status, role, class, importance, group membership, personality, and relationship to others. For example, what are you telling people by the type and color of vehicle you drive? A silver SUV conveys a different message from a green sedan, a red car conveys a different message from a white car, a sports car conveys a much different message from a minivan, and a Cadillac

olfactics
Study of smell or odors.

artifact
A personal ornament or possession that communicates information about a person.

Making Connections

Impression Management: It's All in the Clothes You Wear—Or Is It?

We are told to dress to impress! There is nothing wrong with dressing nicely, but can there be potential ethical problems?

1. Think of an occasion when someone you know wore clothing that created a misperception of status or personal attributes. Describe the situation. What were the consequences?
2. Think of an occasion when you used clothing to create a positive or favorable image even though it was not accurate. Describe the situation. What were the consequences of this misleading impression that you created?
3. What are the ethical implications of this type of impression management?

Escalade conveys a different message from a Ford Escape. The number of cars you own also conveys messages about you.[47]

How do you react to people who have body piercing and tattoos? It depends, but what does it depend on? Effective communicators learn to adapt their use of artifacts to a specific situation and not to judge others by appearance alone. It is important that we use artifacts that are consistent with and reinforce our intended messages. If the messages that are conveyed are inconsistent, contradictory, and not reinforcing, it might be time to do a reality check on the messages others are receiving from the artifacts we use.

Environment

Environment, as discussed in Chapter 1, is the psychological and physical surroundings in which communication occurs, including the furniture, architectural design, lighting conditions, temperature, smells, colors, and sounds of the location and the attitudes, feelings, perceptions, and relationships of the participants. The impact of the environment has a lot to do with the individuals, their backgrounds, and their perception of what is important to them at the time of the interaction. The best environment allows a speaker's intended message to be delivered accurately. Thus soft background music, dim lights, a log burning in a fireplace, a tray of hors d'oeuvres, and two candles would create the perfect environment for a romantic encounter but would fail to create the proper atmosphere for a pregame pep rally.

Learning Connections

1. On the basis of what you have read so far, what would you tell a friend that he or she should know about nonverbal communication that would help the friend become a more competent communicator?
2. What have you learned in this section that you could use to make you a more competent public speaker?
3. How can the information on space, touch, smell, and eye contact help you when communicating in different cultures than your own?
4. Suppose you are about to interview for a job. What role will your nonverbal communication have in helping you get the job?
5. When can silence be a more powerful message than saying something?

Interpreting and Improving Nonverbal Communication

If nonverbal communication is so credible and powerful and if we can define, categorize, describe, and observe it, why do we still have difficulty interpreting it? There are at least three good reasons:

1. *Nonverbal cues have multiple meanings.* Nonverbal communication is difficult to understand because a single behavior can have many potential meanings. For example, a frown might indicate unhappiness, sadness, anger, pain, thought, aggressiveness, disapproval, dejection, fear, fatigue, discouragement, disapproval, or a combination of some of these. Unlike words, nonverbal cues lack dictionary definitions.

Interpretations are unreliable because they depend so heavily on perceptions. Suppose, for example, that you have just walked out of a sad movie when you see a friend with tears in her eyes, talking to her sister. She might be reacting to the movie, or her crying could stem from breaking up with her boyfriend, hurting herself, or hearing about a death in the family. Her tears could even result from laughing hard at something that occurred after the movie. Of course, some nonverbal behaviors, such as nodding the head for yes and shaking it for no (in U.S. society), are consistent in both their meaning and their interpretation. Unfortunately, such consistency is the exception rather than the rule.

2. *Nonverbal cues are interdependent.* The meaning of one nonverbal cue often depends on the correct interpretation of several other simultaneously occurring cues. For example, when we see someone enter a room, we begin to select certain cues about that person, such as gender, physical traits, facial expressions, voice characteristics, and clothing. Each cue intermeshes with the others and adds to the total picture. This interdependence of nonverbal behaviors and our inability to perceive all aspects of any one nonverbal communication make interpretation risky.

Looking for meaning by using more than one nonverbal message at a time is called the **functional approach.** The functional approach examines nonverbal behavior not by isolating nonverbal cues, but by seeing how each cue interacts and works with the others to perform various communicative functions.

3. *Nonverbal cues are subtle.* Many nonverbal behaviors are subtle and difficult to observe. A cue that one person notices immediately might be overlooked by another person; thus multiple interpretations may be made in the same situation. For example, a friend tells you that a person whom you are interested in getting to know has been looking at you, but you haven't noticed the glances or you see the eye contact as more accidental than a deliberate message of interest in you.

Improving Our Interpretation of Nonverbal Communication

Nonverbal communication is complex, but there are some things that you can do to interpret it better. First, be observant of and sensitive to the nonverbal messages that you receive. Second, verify nonverbal messages that you are not sure of or that are inconsistent with other cues. Assume, for example, that a friend who used to visit regularly hasn't come over in several weeks. It might seem logical to conclude that she doesn't want to see you anymore, but then again, she might have become wrapped up in her studies, taken a part-time job, or fallen ill. To accurately interpret her behavior, consider all the possibilities and avoid jumping to conclusions. Because it is so tempting to make inferences based on nonverbal behavior, it is important to remember not to go beyond actual observations.

One method to help verify the meaning of a nonverbal message is to use **descriptive feedback,** which is the stating of the interpretation of the message received back to the sender. The other person can then clarify an intended meaning. Descriptive feedback is not always necessary, but when a message seems inconsistent with the situation or other behaviors or when you're not sure you have accurately interpreted an important message, you should verify your perceptions with the other person. When

functional approach
Using more than one nonverbal message at a time to look for meaning.

descriptive feedback
The stating of the interpretation of the message received back to the sender.

using descriptive feedback, do not express agreement or disagreement or draw conclusions; simply describe the message you believe was communicated. For example, if you think someone's behavior seems to indicate that he is uncomfortable around you, but you're not sure, don't ask, "Why are you so nervous when I'm around?" Rather, describe the situation nonjudgmentally: "Jim, I get the impression that you may not be comfortable around me. Is that the case?" This allows the other person to explain without feeling defensive, and it enables you to avoid inaccurate interpretations.

Improving the Nonverbal Communication We Send

We must be aware of the nonverbal messages we send to others. Fortunately, most of us do a good job of communicating nonverbally and thus do not need to make dramatic changes in the way we behave. Nonetheless, we cannot afford to ignore the effects of our nonverbal behavior or to allow the nonverbal messages that we send to go unexamined. If you find that others often misunderstand your intended meaning, you might want to consider how you communicate nonverbally. When you take action to show that you care about how others perceive your behavior, you are engaging in self-monitoring. **Self-monitoring** involves the willingness to change behavior to fit a given situation, an awareness of how we affect others, and the ability to regulate nonverbal cues and other factors to influence others' impressions. In Chapter 3, we discussed impression management techniques that can enhance a person's image. Self-monitoring is similar, but it goes beyond impression management. It entails both concern with projecting the desired image and the ability to assess the effects of it.

GUIDELINES Monitor Your Nonverbal Communication

1. *Be aware of how people react to you.* If you notice that people react to you differently than you anticipate, you may be giving nonverbal messages that differ from your intentions.
2. *Ask friends or colleagues for their help.* It is very difficult to know whether you are sending nonverbal messages that are being misunderstood unless you seek feedback.
3. *Videotape yourself to see how you appear to others.* Then review the videotape by yourself, with a friend, or with your teacher to analyze your nonverbal behaviors.
4. *Adapt to the context or situation in which you find yourself.* As you carry out different roles or find yourself in different communicative contexts, your nonverbal behavior should conform, when appropriate, to the expectations and norms associated with the role or the context. To learn about expectations related to various contexts, observe how others behave in them. For example, if everyone is always on time for a meeting and you are always late, chances are you are violating an established norm. Thus you must make an effort to conform, or you will find that your nonverbal behaviors will be perceived in ways that you might not want them to be.

self-monitoring
The willingness to change behavior to fit situations, awareness of effects on others, and the ability to regulate nonverbal cues and other factors to influence others' impressions.

Our nonverbal messages greatly influence how others perceive us and our communication. For example, an extremely bright and talented student was constantly being turned down for jobs that he should have been getting. When I asked why he thought this was happening, he replied that he had no idea. To find out, friends videotaped a mock interview in which he was interviewed by another student. When he reviewed the tape, he immediately noticed that he never looked at the interviewer. Instead, his gaze wandered about the room. The lack of direct eye contact by the student gave the impression that he lacked confidence and that he might not be totally candid in what he was saying. Once he knew why he was being rejected, he could try to change his behavior. To help him practice, his friends videotaped another interview session. This time, he was reminded to look at the interviewer each time his gaze wandered. After several such sessions, he grew relaxed about looking at the interviewer and consequently appeared more confident and truthful in his communication.

Although changing your nonverbal behavior is not simple, it can be done with a little effort and desire. The key is to examine conscientiously how your nonverbal cues may be undermining your intended message. If you realize that you have distracting mannerisms, such as smirking, playing with coins, twisting your hair, shuffling your feet, or saying "you know" or "OK" too much, you can ask others to call your attention to these things. Then you can make a conscious effort to change.

Learning Connections

1. Explain how a competent communicator interprets nonverbal messages.
2. You hear someone say something, but the person's nonverbal communication contradicts what he or she said. What message are you going to accept?
3. Does a nonverbal message or a verbal message have the strongest influence on how people perceive us? Explain.
4. What is the most important thing you learned about nonverbal communication from this chapter that will help you become a more competent communicator?

Summary

Nonverbal communication encompasses everything that we communicate to others without using words. It is not what we say, but how we say it with our tone of voice, body movements, appearance, use of space, touch, and time, all of which competent communicators understand.

We are always communicating something through our nonverbal behavior, regardless of whether we intend to. The interpretation of nonverbal cues depends on context. Nonverbal communication is more believable than verbal communication. It is our primary way of expressing our feelings and attitudes toward others, is related to culture, and is often ambiguous.

Nonverbal communication adds life to our exchanges by complementing, repeating, regulating, and substituting for what we have to say. It can also be used to deceive others. There are at least ten types of nonverbal communication, including kinesics or body language, physical characteristics, haptics or touch, proxemics or space, chronemics or time, paralanguage/vocalics or voice, silence, olfactics or smell, artifacts, and environment. All are interdependent and, together with verbal communication, contribute to the total communication process.

Competent communicators know that their nonverbal behavior may be interpreted differently by different people, because each cue has multiple meanings, the meaning of nonverbal cues often depends on the correct interpretation of several other simultaneous cues, and some nonverbal cues are so subtle that they might be difficult to detect. To avoid misinterpretation, competent communicators are observant of and sensitive to the nonverbal messages they receive, consider all their possible meanings, and avoid jumping to conclusions. They use descriptive feedback whenever possible to ensure that the message they received is the one that was intended.

Competent communicators are also aware of the nonverbal messages that they send to others. They can change their behavior to fit different situations, are aware of what they communicate nonverbally, and are able to regulate their nonverbal cues and other factors to influence others' impressions of them. They know that their nonverbal messages influence how others perceive them. They also are not afraid to ask others for help in changing any distracting nonverbal behaviors that they might have.

DISCUSSION STARTERS

1. Why do you think people don't take their nonverbal communication seriously?
2. In developing relationships with others, what role does nonverbal communication play?
3. Why is it important that we take our nonverbal communication seriously?
4. "You cannot not communicate." Describe situations in which you thought you weren't communicating anything but later you found out that you did.
5. Which nonverbal function do you think contributes the most to your understanding of a message? Why?
6. Explain what paralanguage is.
7. In what ways do we use vocal cues to make judgments about others?
8. Explain why you think nonverbal communication is more believable than verbal communication.
9. What is the most important lesson you learned about nonverbal communication from this chapter?

NOTES

1. M. L. Hickson III and D. W. Stacks, *Nonverbal Communication: Studies and Applications,* 3rd ed. (Dubuque, Iowa: Brown & Benchmark, 1993), 4; A. Mehrabian, *Silent Messages: Implicit Communication of Emotions and Attitudes,* 2nd ed. (Belmont, Calif.: Wadsworth, 1981), 77; R. L. Birdwhistell, *Kinesics and Context: Essays on Body Motion* (Philadelphia: University of Pennsylvania Press, 1970), 158; R. L. Birdwhistell, "Background to Kinesics," *ETC* 13 (1955): 10–18; A. Mehrabian and S. R. Ferris, "Inference of Attitudes from Nonverbal Communication in Two Channels," *Journal of Consulting Psychology* 31 (1967): 24–252.
2. B. M. De Paulo, J. L. Stone, and G. D. Lassiter, "Deceiving and Detecting Deceit," in *The Self and Social Life,* ed. B. R. Schlenker (New York: McGraw-Hill, 1985), 323–70.
3. M. L. Knapp and J. Hall, *Nonverbal Communication in Human Interaction,* 4th ed. (New York: Harcourt Brace, 1997), 24.
4. M. Argyle, F. Alkema, and R. Gilmour, "The Communication of Friendly and Hostile Attitudes by Verbal and Nonverbal Signals," *European Journal of Social Psychology* 1 (1971): 385–402.
5. T. H. Feeley and M. A. Turck, "The Behavioral Correlates of Sanctioned and Unsanctioned Deceptive Communication," *Journal of Nonverbal Behavior* 22 (1998): 189–204; and A. Vrij, L. Akehurst, and P. Morris, "Individual Differences in Hand Movemens During Deception," *Journal of Nonverbal Behavior* 21 (1997): 87–102.
6. L. Anolli and R. Ciceri, "The Voice of Deception: Vocal Strategies of Naïve and Able Liars," *Journal of Nonverbal Behavior* 21 (1997): 259–85.
7. S. W. Janik, A. R. Wellens, J. L. Goldberg, and L. F. Dell'osso, "Eyes as the Center of Focus in the Visual Examination of Human Faces," *Perceptual and Motor Skills* 4 (1978): 857–58.
8. D. Leathers, *Successful Nonverbal Communication: Principles and Applications* (New York: Macmillan, 1986).
9. P. Andersen, *Nonverbal Communication: Forms and Functions* (Mountain View, Calif.: Mayfield, 1999).
10. C. L. Kleinke, "Gaze and Eye Contact: A Research Review," *Psychological Review* 100 (1986): 78–100.
11. P. G. Zimbardo, *Shyness: What It Is, What to Do about It* (Reading, Mass.: Addison-Wesley, 1977).
12. P. Greenbaum and H. W. Rosenfield, "Patterns of Avoidance in Responses to Interpersonal Staring and Proximity: Effects of Bystanders on Drivers at a Traffic Intersection," *Journal of Personality and Social Psychology* 36 (1978): 575–87.
13. P. C. Ellsworth and J. M. Carlsmith, "Eye Contact and Gaze Aversion in Aggressive Encounter," *Journal of Personality and Social Psychology* 33 (1973): 117–22.
14 Ibid.
15. A. Robinson, "57 Varieties of a Coach," *Lincoln Journal Star,* September 8, 2002, 3D.
16. C. Izard, *The Psychology of Emotions* (New York: Plenum, 1991); and P. Rozin, L. Lowery, and R. Ebert, "Varieties of Disgust Faces and the Structure of Disgust," *Journal of Personality and Social Psychology* 66 (1994): 870–81.
17. P. Ekman and K. Heider, "The Universality of a Contempt Expression: A Replication," *Motivation and Emotion* 12 (1988): 303–308 and P. Ekman, "Are There Basic Emotions?" *Psychology Review* 99 (1992): 550–53.
18. B. Knutson, "Facial Expression of Emotions Influence Interpersonal Trait Inferences," *Journal of Nonverbal Behavior* 20 (1996): 165–82.

19. H. Aguinis, M. Simonsen, and C. Pierce, "Effects of Nonverbal Behavior on Perceptions of Power Bases," *Journal of Social Psychology* 138 (1998): 455–70.
20. P. Ekman and H. Oster, "Review and Prospect," in *Emotion in the Human Face,* 2nd ed., ed. P. Ekman (Cambridge, England: Cambridge University Press, 1982), 148.
21. M. T. Motley, "Facial Affect and Verbal Context in Conversation: Facial Expression as Interjection," *Human Communication Research* 20 (1993): 3–40.
22. M. Zukerman, D. T. Larrance, N. H. Spiegel, and R. Klorman, "Controlling Nonverbal Displays: Facial Expressions and Tone of Voice," *Journal of Experimental Social Psychology* 17 (1981): 506–24.
23. P. Ekman, W. V. Friesen, and P. Ellsworth, "Methodological Decisions," in *Emotion in the Human Face,* 2nd ed., ed. P. Ekman (Cambridge: Cambridge University Press, 1982), 7–21.
24. P. Ekman and W. V. Friesen, "The Repertoire of Nonverbal Behavior: Categories, Origins, Usage, and Coding," *Semiotica* 1 (1969): 49–98.
25. D. S. Berry and L. Zebrowitz-McAuthur, "Perceiving Character in Faces: The Impact of Age-Related Craniofacial Changes on Social Perception," *Psychological Bulletin* 100 (1986): 3–18.
26. J. M. Montepare and L. Zebrowitz-McAuthur, "Impressions of People Created by Age-Related Qualities of Their Gaits," *Journal of Personality and Social Psychology* 54 (1988): 547–56.
27. W. Wells and B. Siegel, "Stereotyped Somatypes," *Psychological Reports* 8 (1961): 77–78.
28. M. A. Collins and L. A. Zebrowitz, "The Contribution of Appearance to Occupational Outcomes in Civilian and Military Settings," *Journal of Applied Social Psychology* 71 (1995): 129–63.
29. V. P. Richmond, J. C. McCroskey, and S. K. Payne, *Nonverbal Behavior in Interpersonal Relations* (Englewood Cliffs, N.J.: Prentice-Hall, 1991).
30. M. G. Efran, "The Effect of Physical Appearance on the Judgment of Guilt, Interpersonal Attraction, and Severity of Recommended Punishment in a Simulated Jury Task," *Journal of Research in Personality* 8 (1974): 45–54.
31. E. H. Walster, E. Aronson, D. Abrahams, and L. Rohmann, "Importance of Physical Attractiveness in Dating Behavior," *Journal of Personality and Social Psychology* 4 (1966): 508–16.
32. B. Gillen, "Physical Attractiveness: A Determinant of Two Types of Goodness," *Personality and Social Psychology Bulletin* 7 (1981): 277–81.
33. "When Beauty Can Be Beastly," *Chicago Tribune,* 21 October 1986, 26a.
34. T. F. Cash and N. C. Duncan, "Physical Attractiveness Stereotyping among Black College Students," *Journal of Social Psychology* 122 (1984): 71–77.
35. S. M. Kalick, "Physical Attractiveness as a Status Cue," *Journal of Experimental Social Psychology* 24 (1988): 469–89.
36. A. Feingold, "Gender Differences in Effects of Physical Attractiveness on Romantic Attraction: A Comparison across Five Research Paradigms," *Journal of Personality and Social Psychology* 59 (1990): 981–93.
37. G. Maruyama and N. Miller, "Physical Attractiveness and Personality," in *Advances in Experimental Research in Personality,* ed. B. Maher (New York: Academic Press, 1981); B. Major, P. I. Carrington, and P. J. D. Carnevale, "Physical Attractiveness and Self-Esteem: Attributions for Praise from an Other-Sex Evaluator," *Personality and Social Psychology Bulletin* 10 (1984): 43–50.
38. R. Heslin and T. Alper, "Touch: A Bonding Gesture," in *Nonverbal Interaction,* eds. J. M. Wiemann and R. P. Harrison (Beverly Hills, Calif.: Sage, 1983), 47–75.
39. S. M. Jourard, *Disclosing Man to Himself* (Princeton, N.J.: Van Nostrand, 1968).
40. N. Henley, "Power, Sex, and Noverbal Communication," *Berkeley Journal of Sociology* 18 (1973–1974): 10–11.
41. E. T. Hall, *The Silent Language* (Greenwich, Conn.: Fawcett, 1959) and *The Hidden Dimension* (Garden City, N.Y.: Doubleday, 1969).
42. J. K. Burgoon, D. B. Buller, and W. G. Woodall, *Nonverbal Communication: The Unspoken Dialogue,* 2nd ed. (New York: Harper & Row, 1996), 122.
43. B. E. Gronbeck, R. E. McKerrow, D. Ehringer, and A. H. Monroe, *Principles and Types of Speech Communication,* 11th ed. (Glenview, Ill.: Scott Foresman, 1990), 325.
44. M. L. Knapp, *Essentials of Nonverbal Communication* (New York: Holt, Rinehart and Winston, 1980), 7; M. L. Knapp and J. Hall, *Nonverbal Communication in Human Interaction,* 4th ed. (New York: Harcourt Brace, 1997), 10–11.
45. E. R. McDaniel, "Japanese Nonverbal Communication: A Reflection of Cultural Themes," in *Intercultral Communication: A Reader* 10th ed., ed. L. A. Samovar and R. E. Porter (Belmont, Calif.: Wadsworth/Thomson, 2003), 257.
46. P. A. Andersen, "The Cognitive Valence Theory of Intimate Communication," in *Progress in Communication Sciences, Volume XIV: Mutual Influence in Interpersonal Communication: Theory and Research Cognition, Affect, and Behavior,* eds. M. T. Palmer and G. A. Barnett, (Stamford, Conn.: Ablex, 1998), 39–72.
47. "You Are What You Drive: A Silver SUV Broadcasts a Very Different Message from a Green Sedan," *USA Weekend,* October, 2002, 20–1.

"All thought is a feat of association: having what's in front of you bring up something in your mind that you almost didn't know you knew."

—Robert Frost

CHAPTER 6 Connecting Listening and Thinking in the Communication Process

THIS CHAPTER WILL HELP YOU:

- Recognize the importance of listening so that you understand why you need to be a good listener.
- Recognize the prevalence of high expectations of employees' listening abilities by employers and their clients or customers.
- Distinguish between hearing and listening.
- Outline and explain the six stages of the HURIER model and the listening process.
- Explain the role of feedback on communicators' ability to be effective.
- Identify and explain the functions of listening.
- Identify specific attitudes and behaviors to help you overcome the barriers to listening.
- Identify instances in which you must be a critical listener.
- Create your own guidelines for listening improvement.
- Use technology to take better notes and organize your work.

CASE STUDY

The following conversation takes place in a for-profit art gallery:

Badreya (gallery owner): We really need to change the opening display. The artist demands that we showcase her art in a more realistic setting. How do you think we ought to make that happen?

Shefali: It seems to me we ought to make the area look like someone's living room. I heard the artist say she wanted to place her art in living rooms around the world. What if we were to create a typical east Indian living room to begin with, and then a typical German or French room, and finally, an American living room?

Karina: What a great idea! Just this morning I heard some of the people browsing through the exhibit question how any of those pieces would work in a home. Their unique sizes and shapes, they said, would not lend themselves to just any room in any home.

Badreya: Perfect! Why didn't I think of that?

Most of us have probably not worked in an art gallery and have not tried to set up displays that would meet the demands of the artist and the buying public, but we have been in situations in which our listening or failure to listen could have serious significance on the situation.

CASE STUDY *(continued)*

Questions to think about

1. What evidence do you find that the three women at the art gallery were listening to their clients and customers?
2. Why would artists, art gallery managers, and art gallery or museum workers need to listen?
3. Think of a job task or a class assignment in which your failure to listen meant more work, embarrassment, or even a lower grade. What factors led you not to listen as well as you could have?
4. What did you learn from that negative experience?
5. Now think of a situation in which your good listening made a difference. How did that make you feel? Why were you a better listener in that situation?

Learners bring a variety of learning styles into the classroom; auditory, kinesthetic, and visual are among the most commonly known. Some of us are visual learners. We need to be able to see what is being discussed. Overheads, chalkboard text and drawings, or PowerPoint presentations help the visual learner. The kinesthetic learner experiences things. She or he needs to move around, touch things, watch things work, and take things apart or put them back together. The auditory learner, by contrast, listens to messages and processes information. This kind of learner doesn't need models or hands-on experiences as much as he or she needs to listen to and process information. **Listening** is defined as the active process of receiving, constructing meaning from, and responding to spoken or nonverbal messages. What kind of learner are you? What is the role of listening in your learning? How do you know? What kinds of activities help you learn? What kinds of activities help you listen?

Skills in listening, analyzing, processing, and recording information are often neglected during formal education. Have you ever had any formal training in listening? If you are a typical college student, you have completed course work in reading, writing, and speaking, but few students have ever enrolled in a listening course. Not only are there few opportunities for formal listening instruction, but informal listening training is not generally provided either. Yet as students, you are expected to listen approximately 50 percent of the time—listening is proportionately the most used language skill.[1] In Chapter 1, we discussed surveys from business executives who suggested that graduates need more work on communication skills; *listening* was high on all lists.[2] Listening scholars Andrew Wolvin and Carolyn Coakley surveyed Fortune 500 companies to determine the status of listening training. They learned that more than 50 percent, including Boeing, ITT, and Qwest, consider listening so essential that they provide special employee listening training.[3] Inefficient listening is a prevalent (and expensive) problem in our lives, in terms of time wasted, poor customer relations, and the need to redo many tasks. The International Listening Association (ILA) is a professional organization comprising members dedicated to the study, application, and improvement of listening in all contexts. Visit the ILA website at www.listen.org for listening resources.

listening
The process of receiving, constructing meaning from, and responding to spoken or nonverbal messages.

Know Your Scholar

Andrew Wolvin *University of Maryland*

Dr. Andrew D. Wolvin has had a distinguished educational career as a Professor of Communication at the University of Maryland. A Lilly Teaching fellow and one of the most popular teachers on campus, he developed and teaches a senior-level course in listening behavior that enrolls a wide range of students. Dr. Wolvin's web page begins with the word *Listening,* and he writes, "In today's oral society, speaking and listening skills are paramount. Since listening behavior is the focus of my research agenda, I center much of what I do in the classroom on listening. This focus engages for its uniqueness and its significance, and it establishes an important communication expectation of [the student's] engagement with me in the learning process."

Dr. Wolvin enjoys an international reputation as a leading researcher and theorist in the area of listening behavior. His work in listening is used by scholars in many fields around the world. Scholars come to the International Listening Association (he is a past president) conventions to interact with him and to share research ideas and questions. His research interests center on issues dealing with listening behavior in the basic communication course, listening in the parent–teen relationship, and effective listening across the life-span. He is the author or co-author of many articles and five books, including *Listening in the Quality Organization, Listening,* and *The Public Speaker/The Public Listener.* You can visit his website at www.wam.umd.edu/ ~ awolvin.

This chapter will help you become an effective listener and, as a result, an effective respondent. To enhance your listening competence, you will need to understand the importance of effective listening, the elements of listening, the functions of listening and the most common barriers to listening. You need to analyze and evaluate what you listen to and make the connection between listening and thinking, which are separate but related processes. We will provide specific ideas to improve your listening.

The Importance of Effective Listening

Most misunderstandings that arise in our daily lives occur because of poor listening habits. Poor listening skills can create serious personal, professional, and financial problems. For students, poor listening can result in missed appointments, misunderstood directions, lower grades, and lost job opportunities.

It might surprise you to realize how much of your waking day you spend listening; when you are not talking or reading, you are probably listening to something or someone. Communication scholar Larry Barker and several colleagues found that college students spend nearly half of their communication time listening, almost one-third of it speaking, and less than one-third of it reading and writing (see Figure 6.1).[4] In a more recent study, communication researchers Owen Hargie, Christine Saunders, and David Dickson found similar results.[5] If, as is noted in Figure 6.1, the average person spends less than one-third of the communication day in speaking, you can see just how much time is left for listening to others, to television, to radio, to music, and to thousands of other sounds. If so much of our time is spent listening, why is it such a problem?

From the time we get up in the morning until we end the day, we are constantly listening to something. Yet most of us give little thought to the role that listening plays

FIGURE 6.1

Proportional Time Spent by College Students in Communication Activities The graph indicates how typical college students spend their waking time. The proportions given in this graph are averages and, of course, can vary dramatically from person to person and situation to situation.

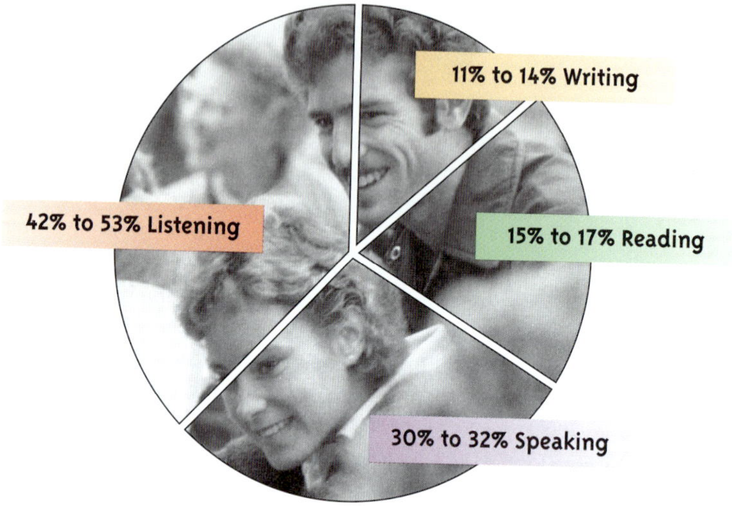

"An Investigation of Proportional Time Spent in Various Communicating Activities by College Students," L. Barker, R. Edwards, C. Gaines, et al., *Journal of Applied Communication Research 8* (1980): 101–109. Copyright by the National Communication Association. 1980. Reproduced by permission of the publisher.

in our everyday experiences. Parents and children both complain, "They don't listen to me." A similar refrain may be heard from relationship partners, workers and bosses, teachers and students. You might even have heard a friend say to you, "You

Effective listening is important to our success in all aspects of our lives. It may surprise you to realize how much of your waking day you spend listening, but when you are not talking or reading, you are probably listening to something or someone.

really ought to listen to yourself." As simple as listening appears to be, many of us are not efficient listeners.

According to a survey of executives by Office Team, a leading staffing service in Menlo Park, California, 14 percent of each work week is wasted because of poor communication between staff and managers—amounting to seven weeks per year.[6] Jim Presley, vice president of professional services at SeeCommerce (www.seecommerce.com), a company that develops applications allowing customers to visualize supply chains and form collaborative groups, says that effective listening can improve sales by 30 to 40 percent.[7] Students, too, seem to have trouble as listeners. Informal surveys of our colleagues reveal that the instructors believe the "failure to listen" is one of the major problems in their students. There is little doubt that communicating, and in particular, listening, plays a significant role in society. Because we spend so much time as *consumers* of communication, we need to learn as much as we can about effective listening. In the global community in which we live and work, listening carefully to the messages conveyed by people of other cultures and backgrounds is a skill required to succeed in many areas of life.

Listening scholar Andrew D. Wolvin, author of *Listening in the Quality Organization* (1999), suggests that the individuals who make up organizations must be effective listeners. His book identifies the role of listening in the communication process and provides suggestions for how people can be more effective listeners. He concludes, "Quality listening, then is a benchmark for the quality organization of the twenty-first century. Some organizations have gotten there, while others are yet to develop a listening culture. . . . The challenge to get there is significant, but the rewards are tremendous. Indeed, our very economic, technological, political, and social lives depend on quality listening."[8]

Making Connections

Your View of Effective Listening

Think about someone whom you believe to be a good listener.

1. What behaviors does this person exhibit that make you think she or he is a good listener?
2. How do the things good listeners do and say make you aware of their effective listening?
3. How do you compare your own listening behaviors with those of the person whom you identified as a good listener?
4. How might you improve your own listening behaviors?

Learning Connections

1. How are hearing and listening different?
2. Can a person with a hearing loss be a good listener? Why or why not?
3. How can you improve your own listening behaviors?

Listening and Hearing: Is There a Difference?

Because most of us take listening for granted, we tend to think of it as a simple task. However, listening is actually quite complex. Scholars agree that listening, like communication in general, is a process and that it is closely linked to the thinking process. Wolvin and Coakley suggest that listening is a distinct behavior that is separate from other intellectual activities. They acknowledge, however, that much of the research closely links listening with reasoning, comprehension, and memory.[9] Listening scholars and teachers agree that hearing and listening are not the same. It is impossible to listen to sounds without first hearing them, but it is possible to hear sounds without listening to them. What distinguishes listening from hearing?

Communication scholars suggest that the major difference between listening and hearing is the difference between active and passive processes. Hearing is passive. If you have normal hearing, your ears receive sounds.[10] You don't have to work at hearing; it just happens. People can have excellent hearing and be terrible listeners. Listening, on the other hand, is active and requires energy and desire. The ILA defines listening as "the process of receiving, constructing meaning from, and responding to spoken or nonverbal messages."[11] This definition is best illustrated in the six stages of the **HURIER model** developed by listening scholar Judi Brownell.

The Stages of Effective Listening

Brownell's HURIER model involves six stages: hearing, understanding, remembering, interpreting, evaluating, and responding (see Figure 6.2).

Hearing

Hearing is the passive physiological process in which sound is received by the ear. Brownell suggests that accurate reception of sounds requires the listener to focus attention on the speaker, discriminate among sounds, and concentrate.[12] Given our discussion of the difference between hearing and listening, answer this question: When you play music while you study, do you *hear* the music or do you really *listen* to it? The sounds provide background that you hear; your hearing becomes listening only when you also carry out the remaining stages of the listening process.

HURIER model
A six-stage model of the listening process involving hearing, understanding, remembering, interpreting, evaluating, and responding.

hearing
A passive physiological process in which sound is received by the ear.

FIGURE 6.2

Stages of the Listening Process Listening is a very complex process that involves more than simply hearing sounds. It also requires selecting, attending, understanding, evaluating, remembering, and responding to the message of the sender.

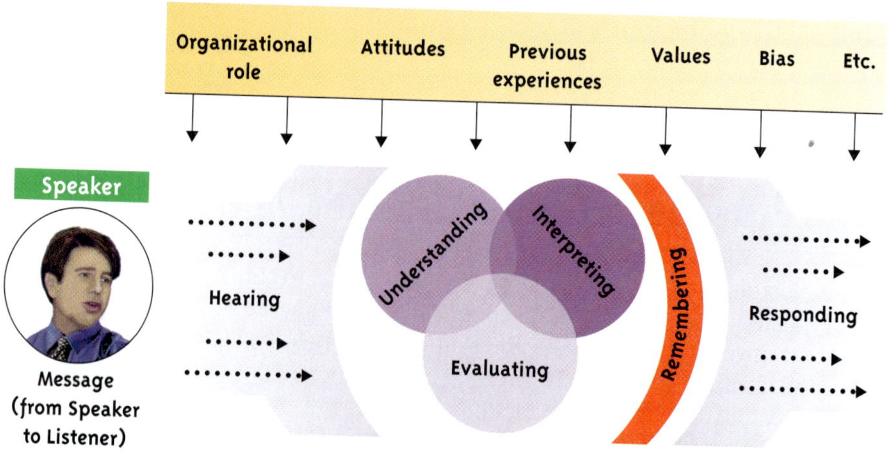

Brownell, Judi. *Listening Attitudes, Principles, and Skills*, 2nd ed. (Boston: Allyn and Bacon, 2004), 14.

Understanding

Understanding might also be labeled *comprehension* and simply means that you assign meaning to the stimuli that you hear or otherwise perceive. Understanding involves the processing of information. The ability to accurately follow directions is one of the ways in which we can measure whether or not we understand what we hear. Students are often in situations in which understanding is critical. Another difference between hearing and listening is understanding. Although there is no commonly accepted explanation of how understanding occurs, we know that past experience plays an important role and that you relate and compare new sounds and ideas to those you have previously heard. To learn statistics, for example, you must first learn algebra and other mathematical principles. However, if you are unprepared when you walk into your statistics class, you can attend to what the teacher is saying, but because you are unable to interpret the professor's message, you will not understand the material presented. This inability to understand reduces your listening effectiveness.

Remembering

As a student, you are very likely aware of the importance of **remembering,** or recalling something from stored memory. Most of your professors expect you to recall and apply what you have heard in lectures, discussions, assignments, and activities. Researchers suggest that working memory and long-term memory are both essential processes and that different aspects are required for different situations. Researchers found that 25 percent of what most people listen to can be recalled. Of that 25 percent, 80 percent is distorted or not accurately received; this leaves only 5 percent of the total message accurately received.[13] As you'll recall from Chapter 2, the process of perception (selective perception and selective attention) can also account for the loss of information. We tend to remember only information that supports our own views. Other information is forgotten. Remembering helps you complete class assignments. Memory will also be very important in your work responsibilities when an employer expects you to acquire and apply knowledge on the job. To find strategies to enhance your working (short-term) memory as well as the information you've stored in long-term memory, check out the Guidelines boxes on pages 147 and 148 for specific strategies.

Interpreting

In the interpreting stage, the listener simply tries to make sense of the information received. Brownell says that there are two parts to the **interpreting** process: "[Y]ou take into account the total communication context so that you are better able to understand the meaning of what is said from the speaker's point of view,"[14] and you let the speaker know that you understand the message. This is where the nonverbal aspects of communication come into play. An effective listener knows that facial expressions, posture, eye contact (or the lack of it), silence, and even paralanguage affect messages. Good listeners will work to develop greater sensitivity to these dimensions of communication.

Evaluating

In the **evaluating** stage, the listener analyzes evidence, sorts fact from opinion, determines the intent of the speaker, judges the accuracy of the speaker's statements and conclusions, and judges the accuracy of personal conclusions. Once we begin to assess the message we

understanding
Assigning meaning to the stimuli that have been selected and attended to.

remembering
Recalling something from stored memory; thinking of something again.

interpreting
The process of understanding the meaning of the message from the speaker's point of view and letting the speaker know that you understand.

evaluating
The listener analyzes evidence, sorts fact from opinion, determines the intent of the speaker, judges the accuracy of the speaker's statements and conclusions, and judges the accuracy of his or her own decisions.

The main difference between hearing and listening is understanding. Once we have heard, selected, and attended to sounds, we must assign meaning to them for listening to be complete. We can enhance our listening by being open and receptive to what the speaker has to say.

received and understood, we might no longer hear and attend to other incoming messages. Later in the chapter, we discuss further analyzing and evaluating messages.

responding
Overt verbal and nonverbal behavior by the listener indicating to the speaker what has and has not been received.

Responding: Sending Feedback

A receiver who has listened to a message can connect with the sender by verbally or nonverbally verifying the message's reception or indicating a lack of reception. This verification is referred to as responding or feedback. **Responding** is the listener's overt behavior that indicates to the speaker what has and has not been received. Examples of such behaviors are total silence (didn't hear the message, ignored the message, or was angry about what the message said), smiling or frowning (agreeing or disagreeing with the message), and asking for clarification of what was received.

Giving feedback is an important part of being an effective listener. Feedback was defined in Chapter 1 as the response to a message that a receiver sends back to a source. Feedback helps to ensure understanding and also helps speakers determine whether they have been successful in communicating. Feedback should be appropriate to the situation, deliberate, thoughtful, and clear. When it is important that you grasp every detail of a message, you should paraphrase or repeat the information for the sender to verify your reception, understanding, and recall of it. This also indicates to the sender

Making Connections

Listening Behaviors

A simple experiment illustrates what people tend to remember and for how long. For two or three minutes, read a newspaper or magazine article to a friend, and then ask the friend to repeat the key information. Do the same with several other friends. Most people will be able to report only about 50 percent of what they've heard. Then wait twenty-four hours and ask each person to repeat the information again.

1. Discuss with your friends what you learned from the exercise.
2. Did some people do better than others? If so, why do you think they did?

Tell someone what you learned about listening from doing this exercise.

that you are actively listening and are committed to receiving the intended message.

Students provide their instructors with feedback, both consciously and unconsciously. Some students, however, might not always be completely honest in their responses. For example, even though they might be totally confused, they might indicate through verbal and nonverbal cues that they are listening to, understanding, and agreeing with everything being said—even if the communication has made little sense to them. This behavior, unfortunately, can lead to more unclear messages and further confusion. When those who are confused admit their confusion, their instructors are more likely to improve their presentations. Active listeners always try to get the most out of the message by making sure that they have received it accurately and completely.

Listening is more than merely paying attention. Listening is an active, complex process. The HURIER model suggests that six interdependent stages are necessary for effective listening. A good listener knows that effective listening includes hearing, understanding, remembering, interpreting, evaluating, and responding.

Making Connections

Thinking about the Stages of Listening

The six stages of the listening process are critical to effective listening in every situation. Think about a recent situation in which you were not a good listener.

1. Identify the situation. Did it play a role in your poor listening? Why?
2. Why were you not an effective listener?
3. At what stage of the listening process did effective listening end?
4. Did the stage make a difference in your listening? Why or why not?

Working Memory

GUIDELINES

Brownell and others suggest approaches to enhance your working memory. The following strategies will help you retain information long enough to use it.

1. *Repetition.* This is a strategy in which you repeat things to keep them in mind. When you have to go to the bookstore to get school supplies without a written list, you might constantly repeat your needs as you walk over: "PDA, stapler, staples, index cards, special pen for art class, zip disks, book for listening class." Any kind of interference, however, can make you forget some or most of your list.
2. *Chunking.* When you have many things to remember, you might group them into categories so that you have fewer details to remember. Have you ever thought about why telephone numbers are created as they are? Researchers suggest that we can remember up to seven individual pieces of information. If you use chunking, you will keep your groupings in seven or fewer categories to retain information long enough to use it immediately, or help move it to long-term memory.
3. *Identification of logical patterns.* If you can identify patterns or themes in the information you hear, it is usually easier to remember, at least for a short time. Numbers in a sequence, or acronyms ("gee, I'm a tree" for remembering how to spell geometry or "every good boy does fine" and "face" for remembering the notes on the treble clef musical scale) are logical patterns that some of your earlier teachers may have provided to help you remember their subjects.

Source: Judi Brownell, *Listening: Attitudes, Principles, and Skills,* 2e. Published by Allyn and Bacon, Boston, MA. Copyright © 2002 by Pearson Education. Reprinted by permission of the publisher.

GUIDELINES Long-Term Memory

If you want to keep the information in working memory for the future, you have to find other strategies to process and put it in your long-term memory (see the previous guidelines box on page 147). Brownell suggests five techniques to help us store things in memory for later use.

1. *Association.* Relating something you have heard to something you already knew is a good way to help you retain information. The situation can often provide the stimulus for association. If you remember that you met Connie in Chicago, that she always orders cafe latte, and that she now lives in Columbus, you have a number of cues that can help you remember who Connie is and what she does.
2. *Categorization.* When you organize information into categories, you can often remember better and longer. You might plan your grocery shopping according to the aisles where things are located. Remembering what categories to study for exams, what divisions to include in reports, and what tasks need to be accomplished can increase your work efficiency because the logical order facilitates retrievable storage in your memory.
3. *Mediation.* Unrelated pieces of data are harder to remember. Meaningful information is much easier to retrieve. Brownell suggests three techniques to make mediation work: (a) Form a meaningful word out of foreign words or meaningless syllables. If you want to remember Ms. Churchill, think of "church-on-the hill." (b) Words can also be made out of the initial letters of the items presented. For example, SADD, or Students Against Destructive Decisions, is one way to make sense of data. Creating these "words" can enhance your recall of information.
4. *Imagery.* According to Brownell, most information is processed into your memory through one of two channels: the visual or the auditory. To use imagery, you need to create visual/mental pictures from the information presented. If you want to remember something, you create vivid mental images of that information in order to later recall and apply it.
5. *Mnemonics.* With this strategy, you create ways to make sense of the information presented and use visual imagery to make the impression vivid. By combining meaningful words and vivid images, you can recall information more quickly and accurately.

Note: Memory is one aspect of the thinking process. The more we are able to remember, the better we will be able to analyze, evaluate, and apply concepts to the information we listen to; thus, we can use memory and thinking to be better consumers of information.

Source: Brownell, Judi, *Listening Attitudes, Principles, and Skills,* 2nd ed. Boston: Allyn and Bacon, 2002, 152–54.

The Functions of Listening

You wake in the morning to the sound of an alarm clock, the noise your roommate makes moving around in the next room, or the ring of a telephone. While you dress, students talk outside your door, and a fire engine wails in the street. You turn on your radio. At breakfast, you join in a heated discussion about the proposed destruction of a historic building on your campus. Then you rush off to the last lecture before an upcoming exam. In the evening, you go to a concert. After the concert, you meet a good friend who is really upset over receiving a low grade on a test.

Throughout the day, you listened to many different people and things for a variety of purposes. You listened to the alarm clock to get up at the right time; you listened to your friends' opinions to evaluate the proposed removal of the oldest building on campus; you listened to your professor to get information about a subject; you listened to the concert for enjoyment; you listened to your troubled friend to understand his feelings. In each case, listening served a different function and involved different skills. Let's look at each of these functions in greater detail and the listening skills that each requires.

Empathic listening occurs when we listen to what someone else is experiencing and seek to understand that person's thoughts and feelings. When we empathize, we try to put ourselves in the other person's place to understand what is happening to him or her.

Listening to Obtain Information

You probably spend great amounts of time **listening for information,** that is, listening to gain comprehension. You listen as your teacher discusses process, perception, nonverbal and verbal communication, famous speakers, and similar topics in order to learn about speech skills. Each day, you listen for information such as news, weather forecasts, sports scores, directions, orders, assignments, names, numbers, and locations.

Listening to Evaluate

Evaluative listening is listening to judge or to analyze information. A car owner who hears a squeak coming from the front end rolls down the window and does some evaluative listening. The owner tries to pinpoint the exact location and cause of the bothersome noise. A teacher listens to students' speeches to discriminate between good and poor presentations and to assign grades. In most situations we all should listen critically. We should constantly judge evidence, arguments, facts, and values. We need to ask questions to be effective listeners. We are bombarded by messages asking us to believe, accept, or buy things. For our own protection, we must evaluate everything to which we listen. (Later in this chapter, specific guidelines are presented for evaluating what we hear.)

Listening with Empathy

Empathic listening occurs when you listen to what someone else is experiencing and seek to understand that person's thoughts and feelings. It is not sympathy, which means that you feel sorry for the other person. Empathy means that you try to put yourself in another person's place to try to understand what is happening to that person. We might find it difficult to avoid making judgments when we listen to someone

listening for information
Listening to gain comprehension.

evaluative listening
Listening to judge or analyze information.

empathic listening
Listening to understand what another person is thinking and feeling.

else's problems, but that is exactly what we must do to listen with empathy. Listening empathically can be a healing and soothing process. Empathic listening indicates that we are aware, appreciative, and understanding of another person's feelings.

Caring about someone requires a great deal of sensitivity as well as the ability to communicate that sensitivity. It is not easy to listen; it is even more difficult to listen with empathy. If we fail to empathize with others, however, we also fail to understand them. (You will learn more about relationships and relational communication in Chapters 13 and 14.)

Listening for Enjoyment

When we listen purely for pleasure, personal satisfaction, and appreciation, we **listen for enjoyment.** We usually listen to music, for example, simply because we enjoy it. The same is true for most of us when we combine listening and viewing as we watch television or a movie.

Listening for enjoyment involves more than merely sitting back and letting sounds enter our ears. Listening for enjoyment also involves the thinking process. We evaluate what we hear and see to understand something or to learn more about it. As we listen to music, we try to find some personal value or relevance in the lyrics and the instrumentation. Even if we attend an opera for the first time and do not understand the language, we can enjoy the performance as we seek to understand it. In other words, listening for enjoyment uses the same process as other kinds of listening: We select, attend, understand, evaluate, and remember. We construct meaning from what we hear and respond to it in some way.

Learning Connections

1. Think about your own listening. In what type of listening do you spend the most time?
2. Is one type of listening easier for you than the others? Which one? Why?
3. Why do we say that empathic listening can be difficult?

Barriers to Effective Listening

Why are most people poor listeners? The answer to this question is surprisingly complex. The quality of our listening changes from time to time and from situation to situation. A number of barriers contribute to our ineffectiveness as listeners. The context of each communication will affect how important each barrier actually is, and some of the barriers that reduce our listening effectiveness are under our control whereas others are not. The following six barriers to effective listening were identified by Ralph Nichols, who is considered the "father of listening research."[15] Nichols and other researchers have replicated his research in subsequent studies and found the same results. Although these six barriers may not be the only ones, they are the most common. And remember, listening, like communication, is a learned behavior, so we *can learn* to overcome the obstacles that interfere with our listening effectiveness.

Considering the Topic or Speaker Uninteresting

The level of interest and the amount of importance we place on a subject or a speaker usually govern how much effort we put into listening. Deciding that a subject or person is uninteresting or boring often leads us to the conclusion that the information being presented is not important. However, this is not necessarily true. What appears to

listening for enjoyment
Listening for pleasure, personal satisfaction, or appreciation.

be dull or insignificant might very well be vital for passing an exam, doing an assignment correctly, learning something, following your supervisor's instructions, making a sale, or learning a new way of doing something on the job. In other words, a competent listener keeps an open mind.

Criticizing the Speaker Instead of the Message

How many times have you judged a speech by the number of "ahs" and "ums" the speaker used? How many times has a speaker's volume, mispronunciations, or accent influenced your opinion? Have you ever missed a message because you were focusing on a mismatched shirt and tie, bizarre earrings, or the speaker's facial expressions or nervous behaviors?

Of course, when possible, speakers should do everything in their power to eliminate personal quirks that may distract attention from their message, but listeners must also share responsibility for receiving the message. An effective listener must be able to overlook the superficial elements of a person's delivery style or appearance to concentrate on the substance of the presentation. In short, the listener must stay involved in the message, not the speaker or the speaker's attire or behaviors.

Concentrating on Details, Not Main Ideas

Many of us listen for specific facts such as dates, names, definitions, figures, and locations, assuming that they are the important things to know. But are they? Specific facts are needed in some situations, but we often focus too much on details. As a result, we walk away with disjointed details and no idea how they relate to each other and to the total picture.

Competent listeners focus on the main or most important ideas, not on every single word. All stages of the listening process are affected adversely when we forget that general ideas can be more significant than the details that surround them. Listen carefully to your professors or your supervisors for clues to what is most important and note when they ask you to carefully select what to write in your notes, or include in your work tasks.

Avoiding Difficult Listening Situations

Most of us find it difficult to keep up with the vast amount and increasing technical complexity of the information that confronts us each day. At times, we might deal with complex listening situations by giving up and ignoring what is being presented.

Concentration and energy are needed to overcome the temptation to ignore or avoid what might seem difficult and confusing. When you are faced with a difficult listening situation, the best approach is usually to ask questions. For example, physicians often use complex medical terminology when talking to patients, but patients can take the responsibility for gaining understanding. They can ask the physician to explain terms, to review procedures, and to supply missing information. The same principles apply to the classroom or to the workplace. You should never hesitate to ask about something when you don't understand it, because without understanding, you cannot learn.

Sometimes, you might not listen to new and difficult information because you lack motivation, but once again, the responsibility falls on you to make the effort to listen. Try consciously and continually to listen to such communication. Each time you are successful at staying tuned in, you will acquire not only some information, but also improved confidence and ability.

Tolerating or Failing to Adjust to Distractions

Distractions constantly disrupt our concentration. As listeners, we have the responsibility to adjust to, compensate for, or eliminate distractions and to focus on speakers and their messages.

We can control some distractions. If noise from another room competes with a speaker, for example, the listener can close the door, ask the person who is creating the noise to be quiet, move closer to the speaker, or ask the speaker to talk louder.

Some distractions must be overcome through mental rather than physical effort. A noise in the background can become a major distraction, or we can reduce it to a minor nuisance by forcing ourselves to listen more intently to the speaker. When distractions occur, we must consciously focus on selecting the appropriate messages and attending to them. We must take advantage of our ability to filter out extraneous noise and distractions and concentrate on the sounds that are important to us. If we cannot modify external noise, we must alter our internal listening behavior in order to understand the speaker's message.

Faking Attention

At one time or another, everyone pretends to pay attention to something or someone. You appear to listen intently, but your mind is somewhere else. You might even smile in agreement when all you are really doing is maintaining eye contact. In class, you might pretend to take notes, although your mind might not be following what is being said.

Pretending to pay attention can become a habit. Without even realizing what you are doing, you might automatically tune out a speaker and let your mind wander. If, after a speech, you cannot recall the main purpose or the essential points presented by the speaker, you were probably faking attention. Although it might seem harmless, such deceptive behavior can lead to misunderstandings and cause people to question your credibility and sincerity.

Table 6.1 summarizes the differences between ineffective and effective listening habits.

TABLE 6.1

Ineffective and Effective Listening Habits

BAD LISTENER	GOOD LISTENER
Thinks that topic or speaker is of no interest	Finds areas of interest—keeps an open mind
Focuses on the speaker's appearance and delivery	Concentrates on the content of the presentation and overlooks speaker characteristics—stays involved
Listens only for details	Listens for ideas
Avoids difficult material	Exercises the mind—prepares to listen
Is easily distracted	Resists distractions
Fakes attention	Pays attention

Effective Listening

GUIDELINES

1. Effective listeners check their attention periodically. They ask themselves, "Am I paying attention?" When listeners realize that they are distracted, they should make an effort to pay attention. Good listeners recognize when they are not listening well and do whatever it takes to return their attention to the speaker.
2. Effective listeners adopt behaviors that support listening effectiveness. They demonstrate active nonverbal behaviors, such as maintaining eye contact and leaning forward toward the speaker. They mentally prepare themselves to receive the message. Effective listeners demonstrate attitudes, behaviors, and thinking that allow them to focus on others. They know that listening is an active process, requiring energy and effort on their part.

Critical Listening and Critical Thinking: Analyzing and Evaluating Messages

As listeners, our goal is more than simply understanding a message; we also try to become critical listeners. Practicing **critical listening** involves analyzing and assessing the accuracy of the information presented, determining the reasonableness of its conclusions, and evaluating its presenter. In other words, we must ask ourselves questions about the message: Is the message true? Is it based on solid evidence? Is it complete? Is it logical? What motivates the speaker to present the message?

We are constantly confronted with choices and decisions. For example, we are exposed to numerous commercial messages each day in addition to the interpersonal messages we receive at school, home, work, and in recreational situations. We also live in an increasingly technological world. Web searches to find information for our college papers and presentations; to enhance a presentation at work; or even to learn more about a city, country, or company provide an infinite number of resources very quickly. (We discuss web searches for speeches in greater detail in Chapter 8.) Because we are limited in the amount of experience we can acquire on our own, we must depend on others to provide information and advice. Thus we must evaluate and assess that information in order to judge its value and utility. We do this through critical thinking. Critical thinking is integrally linked to critical listening, because they are both a part of the process of gaining an understanding of our world. There are many definitions of critical thinking. One definition of **critical thinking** suggests that critical thinkers ask and answer the right questions to determine the appropriate responses to problems and issues.[16] In an earlier work, Ennis defined critical thinking as the ability to analyze and assess information.[17] From these two definitions alone, you should be able to make the connection between listening and thinking. You must listen carefully and construct meaning from ideas, messages, and so forth if you are to make sense of the world around you. Critical thinking has become so important to academic institutions and to employers that more and more colleges and universities include courses or units in critical thinking in their curricula; some even provide a web page devoted to the

critical listening Listening that judges the accuracy of the information presented, determines the reasonableness of its conclusions, and evaluates its presenter.

critical thinking The ability to analyze and assess information.

Making Connections

Listening Self-Assessment

Do you want to learn more about your own listening? HighGain, Inc. is a training organization that specializes in listening and other communication skills. The company provides an interactive Listening Self-Assessment that you can use to check your own listening skills and even provides an analysis. For these, go to www.highgain.com/SELF/index.php3. The company also has a free newsletter, found at www.highgain.com/newsletter/hg-enews-current.html.

characteristics of the critical thinker.[18] Bellevue Community College's web page identifies nine characteristics of a critical thinker and two implications and six aspects of critical thinking. Basically, you need to remember that the link between critical thinking and critical listening is that critical thinkers have specific attitudes and mental habits. They are intellectually curious, flexible, objective, persistent, systematic, honest, and decisive. They use their critical listening abilities to assess information and choose the best options from among those available. Critical thinkers are aware of the ways they learn best and capitalize on opportunities to expand their learning abilities. One goal of a liberal arts education is to encourage students to think critically. We hope that this text helps you develop habits of mind to enable you to become effective thinkers, listeners, and communicators.

Critical thinking and critical listening are closely linked. The critical thinker knows how to analyze and assess information. The critical listener knows how to make connections between messages and issues. The critical listener also uses the ability to analyze and evaluate messages to determine whether ideas are logically presented and whether the speaker is well informed and exhibits clear thinking. Critical listeners must be critical thinkers. Critical thinking and critical listening are closely related parts of a very complex process. Listening with a critical ear involves two phases: (1) assessing the speaker's values and intent and (2) judging the accuracy of the speaker's conclusions.[19]

Assessing the Speaker's Motivation

Assessing a speaker's motivation generally involves three stages of information processing: (1) making a judgment about the speaker's beliefs, (2) comparing our standards and those of the speaker, and (3) evaluating the worth of the message being presented.

Values are strongly held beliefs central to the communication process and to each individual's perceptual system. They affect our perception and interpretation of both the messages we send and the messages we receive. (Values are discussed further in Chapter 12.) The first consideration in listening, therefore, is to examine the message to determine the speaker's values: We critically think about what the speaker is saying and how it compares to our own value system. Of course, we should not automatically dismiss a message merely because the speaker's values conflict with our own. However, any time we are confronted with a message that differs from our own views—one that asks us to do something, buy something, or behave in a certain way—we should be aware of the purpose behind it.

The second consideration is to determine whether the message urges us to conform to or go against our principles or standards. Finally, we consider how to evaluate and respond to the messages. We use our critical thinking skills to recognize and understand the motivation behind the messages we receive.

In order to be an effective listener you must know what to do and how to do it. With a desire to learn and with practice you can improve your listening.

Judging the Accuracy of the Speaker's Conclusions

To make accurate judgments and to think critically about important messages, ask the following questions:

- Is the speaker qualified to draw the conclusion?
- Has the speaker actually observed the concept or issue about which he or she is talking?
- Does the speaker have a vested interest in the message?
- Is there adequate evidence presented to support the conclusion?
- Is the evidence relevant to the conclusion?
- Does contrary evidence exist that refutes what has been presented?
- Does the message contain invalid or inadequate reasoning?

Improving Listening Competence

With appropriate knowledge and practice, all of us can become better listeners (refer to the cartoon). First, we must recognize the importance of listening effectively. Second, we must think of listening as an *active* behavior that requires conscious participation. Third, we must recognize that a willingness to work and a desire to improve are essential to increasing listening effectiveness.

Making Connections

How Do Others Rate You as a Listener?

How do you think the following people would rate you as a listener? Use a scale of 0 to 100, with 100 being the highest rating.

1. Your best friend
2. Your boss or a teacher
3. Your roommate or a co-worker
4. Your parents

After you rated yourself, go to each person and ask him or her to rate you (without disclosing your rating, of course). Compare the ratings. Were they the same? If not, why?

In some situations, we need not listen with full attention. For example, if we listen to a CD while conversing with a friend, we're not likely to create problems by attending closely to the friend and partially to the music. However, each listener must be able to identify when total energy and involvement in the listening process are crucial. Effective listening often requires both energy and concentration; listeners need to constantly remind themselves that listening is vital to communication. People call on different listening skills, depending on whether their goal is to comprehend information, critique and evaluate messages, show empathy for others, or appreciate a performance. According to the National Communication Association, competent listeners demonstrate (1) knowledge and understanding of the listening process, (2) the ability to use appropriate and effective listening skills for a given communication situation and setting, and (3) the ability to identify and manage barriers to listening, all of which we have covered in this chapter.

Competent listeners work at listening (see the Guidelines for Competent Listeners). They are prepared to listen and know what they wish to gain from their listening experiences. Competent listeners also engage in appropriate listening behaviors. They realize that being a good listener is an active and complex process. They know that they must pay attention if they are to listen well. They do not interrupt others, they look at the speaker, they listen to ideas, and they concentrate on what is being said.

GUIDELINES Competent Listeners

1. Be prepared to listen. Learn to control internal and external distractions.
2. Behave like a good listener. Stop talking, and let others have their say. Do not interrupt. Concentrate on what is being said, not on who is saying it or what the speaker is doing. Good listeners maintain eye contact with speakers, ask questions at appropriate times, and maintain flexibility as they carefully listen to the speaker's views.
3. Take good notes. Listen for main ideas, and write down the most significant, most important points; don't attempt to write down every word. Good note taking helps listeners remember better and longer and provides a written indication of ideas to remember. Brevity is usually best so that you can carefully listen to the speaker and the speaker's intent. Write clearly to facilitate the review of your notes later. Review your notes as soon as possible after the event as possible to help you recall them later. Finally, reorganize or rearrange your notes if necessary for clarity before filing them for future reference. Do not get so involved in note taking that effective listening is lost. Note taking should be used as an aid to listening, not as a replacement for it. All six stages of the listening process are brought into play when we listen effectively. Never concentrate so hard on writing everything down that you fail to think about what is said.
4. Ask questions to clarify information. Make sure you know what your supervisor or teacher requires.

Listening and Technology

Just as some people think that computers and technology will destroy families and relationships, some believe that computers, email, and the Internet will harm listening

Making Connections

Thinking and Listening

A student in a lecture class approaches you as you both go into the lecture hall and says, "I do not understand what's going on in this class. It's so hard to take notes. The instructor always has so much stuff on that computer screen, and then she says, 'Listen to the examples, because that's where the exam questions will come from.' I can't listen to those examples. It's all I can do to listen and look at what's on the screen and get those ideas down. What do you do? Do you have any suggestions for me?"

1. On the basis of what we've discussed in this chapter, what kind of advice could you give to your classmate?
2. What would you tell that person about listening?
3. What suggestions would you give about taking notes in the class where the computer-projected images *and* the teacher's examples and explanations are important?

in all areas of our lives. What we and other communication scholars have found in our communication classrooms, however, is that technology can be used to students' advantage if it is used as a tool. We suggested that taking notes helps us become better listeners, and appropriate technology as a delivery tool can also serve that function. Recent studies reported at ILA conventions indicate an increasing use of computer-enhanced presentations (such as PowerPoint) and an expanding student ability to take better notes help students perform better on exams when technology and note-taking instruction are provided early and reinforced throughout the semester.[20] Listeners must remember to think independently. The words on the screen cannot eliminate individual choices. It is too easy to let the screen images take priority. But, as we have pointed out in this chapter, listeners must listen with their eyes, their

Technology can be used to the listener's advantage if it helps the listener focus on the central point in a presentation.

Email conversations are similar to other communication, especially one-to-one interactions. Interactants should carefully "listen" to each other for meaning, and "eavesdroppers" are not appreciated!

minds, their bodies, and their ears. Students need to listen to determine where the instructor's emphases are and take notes accordingly.

Our students interviewed employers about their expectations of listening behaviors for employees. Many of the employers said that listening is more critical than ever and that electronic messages are harder to "listen to" because the nonverbal elements are missing. Interviewees suggested that technology and listening requires people to ask clarifying questions.

Intercultural Listening

Research in intercultural listening is fairly new, so there is not a great deal of information available. What we do know, however, is that people in all cultures are required to listen. We also know that some cultures value listening much more than we do in the United States. Interviews with international students suggest that people in Asia, Mexico, and Venezuela especially value listening. In contrast, Northern European students report that listening is "just something we do" and "something that is expected of us. We aren't really taught to listen." Interviews with teachers in Europe indicate that they would like to know how to get their students to be better listeners.[21]

When asked how listening is taught in Eastern cultures, interviewees state that children are taught to listen to others in a respectful way. Much of the teaching in schools is done through examples and specific statements of expectations to be courteous and to attend to what others are saying. Students in Asia and in Mexico are taught to listen first and ask questions later. The Chinese symbol for the term *to listen* is made up of symbols for eyes, ears, and heart and corresponds with the Chinese view that people must listen with their entire beings: their eyes, their ears, and, most especially, their hearts (see Figure 6.3). The Chinese believe that listening is very important and that when one listens, nothing else should occur because listening should take one's entire attention and energy.[22]

Although we don't have the answers to the similarities and differences in listening in every culture in the world, we do know that communicators need to be aware of both. In the United States, we think nothing of interrupting a speaker in conversation. According to the responses gained in interviews, in places such as Hong Kong, China, Taiwan, Japan, China, Mexico, and Venezuela if you interrupt, you will be branded as a discourteous person, and the local residents will avoid speaking with you. The best advice for communicating with people from other cultures is to (1) respectfully ask questions and (2) be aware of cultural differences. The guidelines for competent listeners (p. 156) apply equally to intercultural listening and domestic listening experiences. Listening requires energy and commitment with whomever we communicate.

FIGURE 6.3

The Chinese character for the term *to listen* The elements of this character incorporate a person's entire being.

Summary

The listening process is often taken for granted because people think that it "just happens." However, listening actually is a complex process crucial to effective communication. Hearing and listening are two different but related things; hearing is the first stage in the listening process. Unless you can accurately receive (hear) the sounds and messages that are sent, you will not be able to understand, remember, interpret, evaluate, or respond. The six stages of the HURIER model demonstrate the complexity of listening.

Students spend a great deal of time listening, and the function of that listening is often to gain information for future use. You also need to learn and apply thinking skills to evaluate the messages you receive. If you want to enhance your relationships, you will listen empathically to understand your family, friends, or partners. Most of us spend large amounts of time in pleasurable listening pursuits. All in all, you spend the majority of your waking hours in some kind of listening behavior. It is therefore important to understand the process and functions of listening.

To be competent, you must work at listening. I tell my students that the listener is 51 percent responsible for effective communication. This does not take away the responsibilities of the speaker; it merely emphasizes the importance of listening in the communication process. You can learn to be a better listener, overcome bad listening habits, and develop effective attitudes, behaviors, and mind-sets. The benefits might well be that you take better notes, follow assignments better, get higher grades, perform more effectively on the job, and receive pay raises and promotions because you took the time to learn effective listening behaviors. Technology should be used as a tool to enhance listening. In Asian cultures, listening is a very important skill. The Chinese symbol for the term *to listen* suggests that true listening comes from using the eyes, the ears, and the heart.

DISCUSSION STARTERS

1. Why do we take listening for granted?
2. Why do you think listening is important?
3. What are the characteristics of effective listening?
4. Why is listening more complex than hearing?
5. What is the role of memory in the listening process?
6. How are listening and thinking connected?
7. How can you improve your memory?
8. Why is it important to understand the different functions of listening?
9. What does it mean to listen with empathy?
10. How can effective listening help you take better notes?
11. On the basis of what you read in this chapter, how can technology help you take better notes?

NOTES

1. R. Bohlken, "Substantiating the Fact That Listening Is Proportionately Most Used Language Skill," *The Listening Post* 70 (1999): 5.
2. National Association of Colleges and Employers, Work Week, *Wall Street Journal,* February 8, 2000. Also, American Council on Education, *Spanning the Chasm: Corporate and Academic Cooperation to Improve Work-Force Preparation* (Washington, D.C.: American Council on Education, 1997).
3. A. D. Wolvin and C. G. Coakley, "A Survey of the Status of Listening Training in Some Fortune 500 Corporations," *Communication Education* 40 (1991): 152–64.
4. P. Rankin, "Listening Ability," *Proceedings of the Ohio State Educational Conference's Ninth Annual Session,* 1929; L. Barker, R. Edwards, C. Gaines, et al., "An Investigation of Proportional Time Spent in Various Communication Activities by College Students," *Journal of Applied Communication Research 8* (1980): 101–109
5. O. Hargie, C. Saunders, and D. Dickson, *Social Skills in Interpersonal Communication,* 3rd ed. (New York: Routledge, 1994).
6. Office Team Survey, 2000, cited in *Sssh! Listen Up!* HighGain, Inc. Newsletter (June 2000): 4.
7. J. Presley, "Putting It into Practice," cited in *Sssh! Listen Up!* HighGain, Inc. Newsletter (June 2000): 3.
8. A. D. Wolvin, *Listening in the Quality Organization* (Ithaca, N.Y.: Finger Lakes Press, 1999), 54.
9. A. Wolvin and C. Coakley, *Listening,* 5th ed. (Dubuque, Iowa: William C. Brown, 1998), 70.
10. E. C. Glenn, "A Content Analysis of Fifty Definitions of Listening," *Journal of the International Listening Association* 3, (1989): 21–31.
11. International Listening Association Definition, 1994, in A. Wolvin, "On Competent Listening," *Listening Post* 54 (July 1995), 1.
12. Brownell, Judi, *Listening Attitudes, Principles, and Skills,* 2nd ed. (Boston: Allyn & Bacon, 2002), p. 14.
13. S. S. Benoit and J. W. Lee, "Listening: It Can Be Taught," *Journal of Education for Business* 63 (1986): 229–32.
14. Ibid., p. 15
15. R. Nichols, "Factors Accounting for Differences in Comprehension of Material Presented Orally in the Classroom" (Ph.D. diss., University of Iowa, 1948); R. O. Hirsch, *Listening: A Way to Process Information Aurally* (Dubuque, Iowa: Gorsuch Scarisbrick, 1979), 36–41.
16. V. R. Rugierro, *Beyond Feelings: Critical Thinking,* 6th ed. (Belmont, Calif.: Mayfield Publishing, 2000).
17. R. H. Ennis, "A Concept of Critical Thinking," *Harvard Educational Review* 32 (1962): 83–84.

18. Bellevue Community College, http://ir.bcc.ctc.edu/library/ilac/critdef.htm. Accessed on February 15, 2001.
19. E. D'Angelo, *The Teaching of Critical Thinking* (Amsterdam, The Netherlands: B. R. Gruner, 1971), 7; R. H. Ennis, "A Taxonomy of Critical Thinking Dispositions and Abilities," in *Teaching Thinking Skills: Theory and Practice,* eds. J. Baron and R. Sternberg (New York: Freeman, 1987).
20. P. E. Emmert and V. Emmert, ILA Convention Papers, 1997, 1998; M. L. Beall, ILA Convention Papers, 1997, 1998, 2001.
21. Beall, Melissa L., "Perspectives on Intercultural Listening," an unpublished paper presented at the National Communication Association convention, New Orleans, Louisiana, November 2002.
22. Beall, Melissa L., "Asian Perspectives on Intercultural Listening," an unpublished paper presented at the World Communication Association Summer Conference, Lincoln, Nebraska, August 2002.

PART TWO

Connecting in the Public Context

"Imagination will often carry us to worlds that never were. But without it, we go nowhere."
—Carl Sagan

CHAPTER 7

Selecting a Topic and Relating to the Audience

THIS CHAPTER WILL HELP YOU:

- Explain the requirements for choosing a topic.
- Describe the options for choosing a topic.
- Assess the appropriateness of a topic for speaker, audience, and occasion.
- Formulate general purpose statements.
- Create specific purpose statements.
- Formulate thesis statements for a variety of speeches.
- Explain the process of audience analysis used for topic selection.
- Apply the data you gain from your audience analysis to a specific speaking situation.
- Evaluate the suitability of the topic for the audience.

CASE STUDY

Soon you'll go to your communication class, and your professor will say something such as "Today we will begin our discussion of the public communication process. In about one month, you will present an informative speech to your classmates. Before that, we will cover everything you need to know to apply to your own situation. In the next few weeks, you will experience the entire range of activities for giving a public speech: selecting a topic and relating to the audience, gathering and using information, organizing and outlining your speech, informative and persuasive speaking. Your assignment for the week of October 19th is an informative speech on a topic of your own choosing. Generally, we present informative speeches in order to share information that is relevant and potentially useful for the listeners in every aspect of our lives."

When your professor makes a presentation like the one in this scenario, you need to begin thinking about the assignment. It is never too early to start thinking about the speech situation, your topic, and how it will serve the needs of informative speeches for your listeners. Most of us are concerned that we don't have anything worthwhile to share. It is your task to make sure that you choose a topic your listeners can relate to and one that you'll enjoy learning more about and sharing with your classmates.

Questions to think about

1. How many speeches have you previously presented?
2. What were your concerns?
3. How did you overcome your reservations before?
4. How do you think you will you go about choosing a topic?
5. What things about your listeners will you keep in mind?

Students often tell us they plan to give very few speeches in their lives and they've been talking for 18 or so years, so they really don't need to have additional information about the public communication context. As we have suggested throughout this text, talking and communication are hardly the same thing. And although we don't want people to make cookie-cutter speeches, there are principles and guidelines of public communication that have been established to help people prepare for the numerous times they will give speeches. Although you might never be a public speaker, you can expect to give speeches on the job, in social organizations, in your place of worship, in the courtroom, or classroom. At some time, almost all of us are called on to "make a speech."

Surveys of people from all walks of life over the last thirty years suggest that officers in both for-profit and not-for-profit organizations want employees who know how to make effective presentations. In a national survey of 1,000 human resource managers, oral communication skills were identified as valuable for both obtaining employment and successful job performance.[1] Fortune 500 company executives have indicated that college students need better communication skills, as well as the ability to work in teams and with people from diverse backgrounds.[2] College faculty members, too, identify communication skills as critical to students' success.[3] An economics professor asserts that "we are living in a communications revolution comparable to the invention of printing. . . . In an age of increasing talk, it's *wiser* [emphasis added] talk we need most."[4] Although public speaking is only one of the oral communication skills required for careers, it is necessary for those who wish to achieve success. Judith Trent has conducted research about the role of communication in our lives. She believes that communication will continue to play an important role in everything we do.[5]

Know Your Scholar

Judith S. Trent *University of Cincinnati*

Judith S. Trent is a Professor of Communication at the University of Cincinnati where she directs the departmental graduate program and teaches undergraduate and graduate courses in presidential campaigns, women in politics, and rhetorical criticism. Dr. Trent's research is related to the campaign communication of women who run for elective office at local, state, and national levels, and to the early stages of presidential campaigns (the surfacing and primary periods). Since 1988 she and her colleagues have conducted field research in New Hampshire during the primary campaign, focusing on the image of presidential hopefuls, media bias, and voter characteristics for a series of journal articles that discuss "the ideal candidate."

The author or editor of textbooks, book chapters, and academic journal articles, Dr. Trent is perhaps best known for the book *Political Campaign Communication: Principles and Practices* which is coauthored with Robert Friedenberg and is now in its fifth edition. *Political Campaign Communication* was the first book-length study of election campaigns that utilized the principles and practices of speech communication to examine elective politics. This book has been characterized as a "classic" and as a "seminal work in the field."

Dr. Trent has served as the president of the Central States Communication Association and the National Communication Association.

Here are some examples of class projects typical students have in addition to their presentations for this class.

- Roman has to make a ten-minute report on advertising strategies for a new product he has created for his marketing class.
- Jackie has a service project for her personal wellness class. She will speak to students at the local middle school about the importance of eating right and getting enough exercise for a healthy lifestyle.
- Demetrious is a member of the campus International Club. He has been asked to speak to the local Kiwanis Club about his recent trip to Malaysia.
- Lora is a Campus Ambassador. She shares college information with potential students and their parents at least twice a week each semester for new student orientation.

In U.S. culture, the ability to communicate effectively is one of the most important skills a person can possess. In formal public speaking, in which the speaker is the central focus of an audience's attention, the presentation of a speech is usually prepared in advance.

These students are preparing for public speaking events, even though each event is labeled as a project or assignment. The ability to give effective presentations in classes, campus organizations, residence hall meetings, sports team meetings, student government campaigns, political demonstrations, or other events on campus is critical. **Public speaking** is the presentation of a speech, usually prepared in advance. In such instances, the speaker is the central focus of an audience's attention. In Chapter 1, we stated that the ability to communicate is one of the most important skills a person can possess. Public speaking and listening are two vital and significant forms of communication. Beginning public speakers frequently express two concerns: fear of not having anything worthwhile to say and fear of speaking in front of others. Both of these concerns will be discussed in detail in this part of the text.

What you learn and apply about making effective presentations will help you in your role as a student and the rest of your life. The speech-making process will help you develop researching, organizing, listening, and thinking skills for both oral and written communication. In addition, these skills will also help you gain self-confidence.

Selecting a Speech Topic

Selecting a topic is the first step in preparing a speech. In these chapters on public communication, you will read about topics that were presented in a variety of classroom, business, and professional situations. The choice of topics is often prompted by the situation itself, the needs of others, and the position and qualifications of the speaker. Selecting a good topic for you and the speaking situation requires thought and a systematic approach.

public speaking Presentation of a speech, usually prepared in advance, during which the speaker is the central focus of an audience's attention.

Making Connections

Thinking about Public Speaking

At some point in this course, you will research, organize, prepare, practice, and present one or more speeches in front of your instructor and classmates. Think about your own listening to speech experiences.

1. What speeches or presentations have you heard that you particularly enjoyed?
2. What do you remember about the content of the speech or presentation?
3. What specific ideas do you remember?
4. What did the presenter do to make the speech or presentation enjoyable?
5. Were there particular words (language choices) that were memorable?
6. What strategies did the speaker employ to keep listeners involved?

Selecting an Appropriate Topic

Many factors contribute to an effective speech presentation, including research, organization, wording, and delivery, but none is more important than selecting an appropriate topic. The topic and your interest and motivation in developing and presenting it are vital to your success as a speaker. The best topic for your audience, the assignment, and you isn't always easy to determine.

Some beginning speakers worry that they might not be able to think of something about which to talk. This concern is simply unwarranted. For example, if you read a newspaper or magazine or watch television, you will be exposed to a variety of stimulating and interesting topics ranging from military involvement in foreign lands to health care. When a topic isn't assigned by the instructor, the trick is to identify a topic that matches *your* interests and qualifications, the interests and existing knowledge of your audience, and the requirements of the situation in which the speech is to

Many factors contribute to an effective speech presentation, including research, organization, wording, and delivery, but none is more important than selecting an appropriate topic. The topic and your interest and motivation in developing and presenting it are vital to your success as a speaker.

be presented. If you are vitally concerned about the topic and have enthusiasm for sharing it with others, your concerns can be drastically reduced.

Selecting an Appropriate Topic

GUIDELINES

1. *Choose a topic that is meaningful to you.* The more meaningful a topic, the more likely you are to put the necessary time and effort into researching and developing your speech. The stronger your commitment to a topic, the more enthusiastically you will present it. A speaker's commitment to a topic usually transfers to the audience members and gets them involved. The audience involvement in a topic can be an effective gauge of your success as a speaker. After all, the reason for giving a speech, besides completing the assignment, is to gain your listeners' attention, and this is more easily accomplished if you consider the topic to be important.
2. *Choose a topic that will allow you to convey an important thought to your audience.* The thought does not have to be a matter of extreme urgency, but it should at least be relevant to your audience's interests, have some direct effect on them, or be something that you believe the audience should know. Ask yourself the following questions:

   Will the audience want to learn more about the topic?

   Will the audience believe the topic is relevant?

   Will the audience be affected in some way by the topic, either now or in the future?

   Will the audience benefit from listening to a presentation on the topic?

   Will the audience believe you are a credible speaker on the topic?

   If you can answer yes to each of these questions about your topic, you are on your way to selecting an appropriate one.
3. *Choose a topic that is familiar and interesting to you.* This will make the development and delivery of your speech easier. It would be easier to begin your research and development of a talk on DVD technology if you had some knowledge of DVD and the principles on which it is based. Researching and developing a speech will be more enjoyable if you are interested in the topic. You may find it enjoyable to select a topic in which you are interested but about which you know little. For example, you are intrigued by the idea of in vitro fertilization (fertilization of an egg by a sperm in a test tube) but do not know the exact procedure or issues surrounding it. Choosing a topic that interests you can increase the likelihood of audience interest and speaker credibility. (We discuss speaker credibility in Chapter 12.)
4. *Think like a listener.* Evaluate your topic as if you will be the listener. If it seems to be a topic you would enjoy listening to, it probably will be more interesting for you to prepare and more interesting for your listeners. Focus your attention on what the audience will like and want to hear about this topic you know and enjoy, and you are well on your way to choosing an interesting, informative, relevant, and potentially useful topic.

Techniques for Finding a Topic

If you have difficulty thinking of interesting subjects, there are some techniques that might help you: self-inventory; brainstorming; reviewing current magazines, newspapers, and television news programs; and conducting an Internet search. All four techniques will generate a wide range of possible topics from which you can then select the most appropriate.

Self-Inventory. A **self-inventory** is a list of subjects that you know about and find interesting. The list might include books and newspaper articles you've read; television shows you watch; hobbies you enjoy; sports you participate in; and community, state, regional, national, or international issues that concern you. Here are some sources of topics that might spark your interest:

Books and Articles

"Internet Puts Last-Minute Trips Just a Click Away"

"The American Empire: Is the United States Trying to Shape the World?"

"How Your Mind Can Heal Your Body"

Harry Potter and the Order of the Phoenix

The Book Against God

Living Longer Depression Free

Living History

The Art of War

Television

Law and Order

The Discovery Channel

Survivor

Friends

Community Issues

Tax Incentives and Municipal Growth

Violence and Female Students

Building Community

Economic Recovery

Saving our Marshlands

Education Issues

Regional Issues

The Aging Population

Wind Energy

Tax Cuts and the Economy

Organ Donor Deficits

Hobbies

Gardening

Antiquing

Quilting

Sports

Supplements and Athlete Fitness

Playoffs for Football?

The Popularity of Soccer in the United States

National Issues

Tax Cuts

The Views on U.S. Military

Changing the SATs

International Issues

Recovering Iraq's Antiquities

New Hope for World Peace

Global Terrorism

Another self-inventory technique involves listing things and ideas as broad categories and then narrowing them down to specific areas. For example

Healthy living

Personal wellness

Exercise and personal wellness

Effects of exercise in personal wellness

Exercise as a means of promoting personal wellness

self-inventory
A list of subjects that you know about and find interesting.

Making Connections

A Self-Inventory

We suggested that a self-inventory is one of four useful tools for choosing an appropriate topic for a presentation. Complete the following self-inventory by supplying as many items as you can for each category. Then examine each item to determine whether it could be an appropriate topic for a speech.

Books and Newspapers

____

____

Television

____

____

Hobbies

____

____

State Issues

____

____

International Issues

____

____

People

____

____

Problems

____

____

Sports

____

____

Regional Issues

____

____

Community Issues

____

____

National Issues

____

____

Places

____

____

Values

____

____

Activities

____

____

1. Are there any patterns in the kinds of topics you chose?
2. What specific characteristics made you discard certain topics?
3. What specific characteristics made you decide to keep certain topics?

Discuss in class what you learned from this inventory exercise.

The category *healthy living* was narrowed to a specific area, exercise as a means of promoting personal wellness. This is specific enough to be a possible speech topic.

brainstorming
A technique used to generate as many ideas as possible within a limited amount of time, which can be used during any phase of the group discussion process to produce topics, information, or solutions to problems.

Brainstorming. Another topic selection technique that you might find useful is brainstorming. **Brainstorming** is a technique used to generate as many ideas as possible within a limited amount of time. Set aside a short period of time (four to six minutes) for intensive concentration, and list all the ideas that come to mind as topics. To keep things simple, write key words or phrases only. Don't stop to think about

Making Connections

Brainstorming

Brainstorming involves simply thinking about topics. It is an effective tool to help you find an appropriate topic for your speeches.

Use brainstorming to generate topics you might use for your next informative speech. Take five minutes, and write down whatever ideas come to mind, without stopping to evaluate them. At the end of five minutes, look over your list and select terms that appeal to you. Then brainstorm for another five minutes, listing topics related to them. Now look at your list and answer the following questions:

1. What criteria would you use to determine the *best* topic for your presentation?
2. Apply those criteria to the topics you've generated.
3. Using the criteria you have established, determine which topic you will use.

Compare and contrast the criteria you listed for selecting the best topic to the criteria provided in the chapter.

whether the ideas are good or bad. The goal of brainstorming is to generate a lot of ideas, so every word or phrase is appropriate.

After listing as many thoughts as you can, select those that appeal to you. Then have a brainstorming session to list more ideas related to them. For example, the term *education* could serve as the springboard for an entirely new list:

Distance education
Meeting affirmative action quotas
Ethics in the classroom
Liberal arts core classes
Tuition increases
Online exams
Public education
Funding concerns
Online courses
PowerPoint for presentations
Assessment and technology
Classroom evaluation
College education and the job search
Experiential learning
Private schools
Education trends
Entrance exams
Research projects
Evaluating teachers
Use of textbooks
Online texts
Service learning
Home schooling

With a little effort, brainstorming will help you generate a number of potential topics in a short time. And the process can be repeated over and over until a suitable topic is found.

reviewing the current media A technique for developing a list of possible topics by looking at current publications, television, movies, and other forms of public communication.

Reviewing the Current Media. A third way to generate topic ideas involves the popular media. The media are channels or means of communicating messages to the public, such as through newspapers, books, magazines, television, and movies. **Reviewing the current media** is an excellent way of developing a list of potential topics. *The Readers' Guide to Periodical Literature* is a source of hundreds of up-to-date topics. For example, you will find listings of articles on education, government, finance, marketing, terrorism, crime, air safety, health, television violence, technology, and entertainment. Specialized indexes, such as those in the fields of agriculture and natural resources, business, economics and statistics, biology and life sciences, computers, education, and history, can provide thousands of suggestions. You can scan the headlines, the articles, and even the advertisements in any magazine or newspaper—*Time, Newsweek, Sports Illustrated, Consumer Reports, Money, Business Week, Wall Street Journal, USA Today,* or your local newspaper. A wealth of current topics are presented in television documentaries, news specials, and regular programs.

One caution should be noted about using the current media to generate speech topics. Some beginning speakers have a tendency to rely on one media source for the entire speech. A summary of an interesting article or movie is not acceptable for most classroom speaking assignments. The media are an excellent source for potential topics, but they are only a starting point from which to build. The content must be adapted to suit you and your specific audience, and most classroom assignments require a variety of sources. You should always bring something new to your topic, for example, a fresh insight or an application that is suitable to the speaking situation.

Surfing the Web. The rapid development of technology, the ever-increasing number of websites, and the amount of new information on the Web provide unique opportunities for students in a speech communication class. Using one or more of the many search engines available can provide unique topics and sources of information on the topic for the careful student.[6] Because information is often not reviewed and accepted by experts or authorities on the subject before it is placed on a web page, and because anyone who knows how to put a web page together can put it online, students need to carefully evaluate both the information presented and its source. How do you evaluate a web source? Use the same process you use when evaluating other sources and information, asking questions like these:

1. Who is the author or producer? What are the author's credentials?
2. How reliable is the source? What is the authority or expertise of the individual or group that created this site?
3. Is the writer or producer biased? (For example, if you find information that cites a study conducted to determine whether a specific product is carcinogenic and learn that the company that commissioned the study is the top producer and marketer of that product and the study results indicate a safe product, think twice before accepting its report as a scientific study.)
4. How complete and accurate is the information?
5. For whom is the information intended?
6. Is the web page up to date?
7. Does the writing on the page follow basic rules of grammar, spelling, and usage? Is the language used appropriately?
8. Is the webmaster identified? Or is contact information for the author or producer provided so that you can seek additional information?
9. Check these websites for more information: "Evaluating Information Found on the Internet" at www.library.jhu.edu/elp/useit/evaluate/index.html and "Thinking Critically about World Wide Web Resources" at www.library.ucla.edu/libraries/college/help/critical/index.htm.

We discuss Internet research further in Chapter 8.

Making Connections

Research on the Web

Surfing the Web to find all kinds of information has become a habit for many of us. When you plan trips, you can access Travelocity.com or individual airlines to find the least expensive fares. Or if travel times and dates are flexible and you are willing to wait, you might be able to find some really good airfares, car rentals, and hotels on Priceline.com. If you are driving to some new place, you can get door-to-door directions from sites such as MapQuest. If you're interested in genealogy, there are numerous sites to help you locate your ancestors, determine exactly when they entered the United States, and even on what specific ship.

"Okay," you say, "so what's your point?" We can use the Web not only to find information but also to help us choose topics for our presentations. Try the following exercise.

1. Take about a minute to brainstorm five to ten topics in which you have some interest, already know something about, or want to learn something more about.
2. Choose four or five items that seem most interesting to you.
3. Access a search engine that you have not used before or one that is relatively unfamiliar.
4. Click on the help area or the icon that will help you understand how to do the most effective search.
5. Key in the words of your first topic.
6. How many hits did you get? What does this number tell you?
7. Check the first ten hits by scrolling through the list and reading the responses.
8. Pick the one that seems most interesting to you. Carefully read and evaluate that site.
9. Does this topic seem like a good one? If so, pursue it further. If not, go back to the next most interesting topic and repeat the process.

This combination of personal brainstorming and web surfing can help you find topics with adequate information. This process uses the Web to help you choose a topic that your web research reveals has information that you can appreciate.

How you find your topic is not the critical issue, but it is important that you begin looking as soon as possible. Over the years of talking with students who have succeeded in selecting appropriate topics, one common factor emerges: They start looking for a topic immediately on receiving the assignment. Students who delay almost always have more difficulty finding an appropriate topic. Whenever you come across something that you think might be a good idea, write it down. The more ideas you can accumulate, the easier your job of selecting a good topic will be. Also, the earlier you choose your topic, the more time you will have to research, prepare, and practice your speech.

Assessing the Appropriateness of a Topic

Once you have identified a possible topic, the next step is to determine whether it is appropriate for you, your assignment, and your audience. Ask yourself these questions:

1. Does the topic merit the audience's attention?
2. Will the audience see a relationship between you and the topic and between the topic and themselves?
3. Will the topic meet the objectives of the assignment?
4. Does the audience have sufficient knowledge and background to understand the topic?

5. Can you make the topic understandable to everyone in the audience?
6. Is the topic of sufficient interest to you that you will be motivated to present it effectively?
7. Do you have adequate knowledge of the topic?
8. If you are not already familiar with the topic, will you be able to learn enough about it to give an informed speech?
9. Is the topic appropriate for the situation in which you will present it?

Narrowing the Topic

Once you have determined that your topic is appropriate to your audience and yourself, the next step is to decide whether it is narrow enough to fit the time limit and accomplish the goal of the assignment. This step can save you much time and trouble because a topic that is well focused is much easier to research than one that is too general. For example, you could work for years on a speech called "The Problems with American Education" and still not cover all the information exhaustively. If you restrict the scope to problems with education in the United States during the past five years, you begin to focus your search for information. You could narrow the topic even further by choosing a single issue with U.S. education during the past five years. Each time you narrow your topic, you increase its potential depth.

The more abstract the topic, the more important it is to narrow it to meet the constraints of the speech situation. Let's say that you have an assignment for a ten-minute speech on a concept about something you wish to gain more information about for yourself and your listeners. You think the Muslim religion would be a good topic. Obviously, you cannot talk about everything in the religion in ten minutes. So you narrow the topic to "the teachings and practices of the Muslim religion." There is still an abundance of information, far too much to cover. You decide to focus on the principles of the Muslim religion in Indonesia, the single nation with the largest Muslim population. This continual narrowing of the topic allows you to focus your research and content development on a more clearly defined area of the topic. This will be helpful to you, the speaker, as well as to your listeners because you will have more substance on an important concept. Speakers can narrow the scope of a subject according to time limits, function, goals, location, and the requirements of a specific topic. Narrowing the topic is a skill critical to your success as a communicator not only in the classroom but also in the workplace and in the organizations of which you are a member and for which you may be called on to make a presentation.

Learning Connections

Selecting and Narrowing Topics

1. What are the techniques one can use for choosing a topic?
2. Have you used any of these techniques in the past?
3. Which do you like best? Why?
4. How does the strategy affect your thinking about the topic?

Determining the General Purpose, Specific Purpose, and Thesis of a Speech

Once you have chosen and narrowed your topic, you need to begin thinking about how the final presentation will be structured. Speakers should begin their preparation

This speaker on drug and alcohol abuse has a specific purpose in his talk to high school students in upper New York state. He uses his ambulatory mike to make his points, to demonstrate face to face his concern and his message. The audience's reaction suggests he is being successful.

with a clear idea of the general purpose, the specific purpose, and a specific thesis statement. In this section we briefly discuss each of these concepts. Chapter 11 provides in-depth coverage of informative speaking, and Chapter 12 is devoted to persuasive speaking.

The General Purpose

The **general purpose,** or overall goal, of a speech is usually to perform one of three overlapping functions: to inform, to persuade, or to entertain. A speech rarely serves only one function. Even though most classroom speech assignments are intended to emphasize a single function, the speeches themselves may contain aspects of all three functions. For example, a speech about rappelling is meant to inform, but this does not mean that the speech cannot contain some persuasive and entertaining elements as well. If you are assigned an informative speech, however, you need to think carefully about how to organize and present those ideas to your listeners. If the general purpose is to inform your audience, your emphasis should be on presenting information about a new, interesting, and potentially useful and relevant topic.

general purpose
The overall goal of a speech, usually one of three overlapping functions: to inform, to persuade, or to entertain.

For classroom speaking assignments, your general purpose is usually specified by the instructor, but for speeches outside the classroom, the occasion, what the audience knows or doesn't know about your topic, and how you want the audience to respond will determine whether you speak primarily to inform, to persuade, or to entertain.

The speaking goal is usually designed to affect the listeners in some purposeful way. The reaction of the listeners determines whether your speech has accomplished its purpose successfully.

informative speech
A speech that enhances an audience's knowledge and understanding by explaining what something means, how something works, or how something is done.

Speeches That Inform. When the general purpose of your speech is to inform, you are expected to convey your knowledge of a particular subject. An **informative speech** enhances an audience's knowledge and understanding by explaining what something means, how something works, or how something is done. Communication scholar David Zarefsky suggests that informative speeches do not specifically ask listeners to believe or do any particular thing.[7] The goal is to share information clearly and accurately while making the learning experience as enjoyable as possible for the audience. If you are assigned an informative speech, you need to think carefully about how to organize and present those ideas to your listeners. If the general purpose is to inform your audience, your emphasis should be on presenting information about a new, interesting, and potentially useful and relevant topic.

Whether you describe how to protect yourself during an assault, discuss a proposed apartment complex development in a rundown neighborhood, explain the important uses of an electromagnetic field, report how the university uses its parking fees, or explain how the electoral college works, you should assume that most of your audience does not already know all the information you plan to present. The content of the speech depends heavily on what you think the audience knows and on how much you know or are able to learn about the topic. Your task as a speaker is to provide more information than the audience would normally get from reading a short article or listening to the news.

When a topic is controversial, for example, "homosexual religious leaders," speakers whose general purpose is to inform should not take sides; instead, they might provide background on the various religious views on homosexuality and statistics or facts about how different religions and denominations view homosexuality, alternative interpretations, and so on. The speaker presents the information and allows audience members to draw their own conclusions.

Making Connections

Informative Speaking

The speech to inform is meant to provide new ideas or perspectives on topics. People often give informative speeches in a variety of settings. Reflect about times in the past year when you have heard someone give a speech or presentation in which the speaker's purpose was to provide information that would be "potentially useful," either now or in the future.

Discuss in class the following either in groups with four or five students or with the class as a whole:

1. Identify the situation—organization, school, meeting, guest speaker in class, and so on—when you heard informative speeches.
2. Identify the topics of the messages.
3. Explain how you knew the messages were informative.
4. What did speakers do to keep listeners interested?

In your discussion with your classmates, determine what makes an informative topic interesting to listeners.

Speeches That Persuade. A **persuasive speech** attempts to change listeners' beliefs, attitudes, or behaviors by advocating or trying to gain acceptance of an idea or point of view. When speakers try to convince a\udience members to eat breakfast, to endorse the building of a new athletic complex, to change the way we elect U.S. presidents, to become a volunteer, to ensure a safe campus or neighborhood, or to believe that ethical behavior in the United States is on the decline, they are attempting to persuade. Speakers must present evidence and arguments to justify their positions in order to win their audience over to their point of view.

The difference between informing and persuading is not always clear. You have a persuasive action goal when you try to persuade your parents to loan you money for a car. Your message contains the following: informing about the circumstances and need for a car and convincing them that you need the car and the money. They may accept your reasons and agree that you need the car but still might not loan you the money. In this example, the persuasive purpose is not only to inform and convince your parents that you need a car and the money to buy it but also for them to take

persuasive speech A speech that attempts to change listeners' attitudes or behaviors by advocating or trying to gain acceptance of the speaker's point of view.

action—to actually give you the money you need. Providing information is a necessary part of a persuasive speech, but its ultimate goal is action. Once your parents give you the money, you have achieved your purpose.

Whereas the focus of an informative speech is to convey information and understanding by explaining, reporting, or demonstrating your point of view, the purpose of a persuasive speech is to change beliefs or attitudes or motivate listeners to act in a specific manner. The action might be to think, to respond, or to behave in a certain way. The purpose might be to eat a healthy breakfast, to place greater personal and societal emphasis on ethics, to approve a proposal, or to join a group.

The important and necessary ingredient that makes persuasion different from information is the action (to think, to respond, to behave) taken by the listener as a result of the message presented. The informative speech provides more knowledge about a topic, whereas the persuasive speech provides information and a direction or course of action the listener is to take.

Speeches That Entertain. An **entertainment speech** provides enjoyment and amusement. Speeches that entertain may be dramatic or humorous in nature and often occur on special occasions, such as after a dinner or a "roast." A speech to entertain generally has three key qualities: It is light, original, and appropriate to the situation. An appropriate speech does not offend the sensibilities of the audience. The speaker may use humor but not at the expense of the audience's sense of values or ethics. Effective speakers do not use offensive language or potentially offensive jokes or situations. Audience members, unlike television viewers, are a captive audience and cannot click the remote to switch off offensive words or ideas. The speaker must use tasteful examples and stories that will not hurt anyone's feelings or violate their ethical principles.

In using humor, the speaker may create imaginative illustrations and figures of speech, twist meanings, tell amusing stories, create amusing character sketches, or tell jokes—all with the willing participation of the audience and in the spirit of the occasion. This does not mean, however, that an entertaining speech cannot be both informative and persuasive or that informative and persuasive speeches cannot be entertaining. What distinguishes these three kinds of speeches is the function (informing, persuading, or entertaining) on which the speaker places the most emphasis. The entertaining speech should, therefore, leave the audience members feeling entertained or amused.

The Specific Purpose

The general purpose of a speech provides direction for its content. In the classroom, the general purpose is usually specified in the assignment. Outside the classroom, it may or may not be specified. When the general purpose is not identified, you must determine it for yourself. To be a successful speaker, you must know exactly what you plan to accomplish by speaking.

Once you have determined your general purpose (to inform, to persuade, or to entertain), you are ready to determine your specific purpose. A **specific purpose** is a single phrase that defines precisely what you intend to accomplish in your speech. Anneke chose videogames as her topic. Her specific purpose was "to inform my listeners about the three major effects of videogames on children." The clear and concise statement tells exactly what the speaker intends to do and what she wants her audience to know.

entertainment speech
A speech that provides enjoyment and amusement.

specific purpose
Single phrase that defines precisely what is to be accomplished in a speech.

An effective specific purpose identifies (1) the general purpose of the speech, (2) the audience, and (3) the exact topic to be covered. These three pieces of information significantly help the speaker develop and deliver the speech. Note that in the videogames example, the speaker's specific purpose cites the general purpose of the speech, which is to inform. The specific purpose also identifies the audience, which is important, because different audiences may require different information. For example, if a speech is to be presented to children only, to adults only, or to both children and adults, the content will have to be adjusted to fit the group. Thus, even though the general and specific purposes are the same, the content of the speech will vary depending on the listeners' backgrounds, knowledge, and attitudes toward the topic.

The careful writing of a specific purpose is important to all aspects of planning and developing a successful speech. The following guidelines should help you write an effective specific purpose.

GUIDELINES

Specific Purpose

1. The specific purpose should include a verb form that describes the general purpose of the speech. The inclusion of the verb form clarifies the action the speaker hopes to accomplish.

   Ineffective: Media violence and children
   Effective: To inform my audience of the three effects of media violence on children aged five to ten

2. The specific purpose should be limited to one distinct thought or idea. The following ineffective statement is too long and contains more than one subject. An entire speech could be developed around either area. It is best to select only one idea and refine it as the purpose for the speech.

   Ineffective: To inform the audience of the three effects of drugs and the four best ways to prevent binge drinking by college students
   Effective: To inform the audience about the three most dangerous effects of drugs on college students
   or
   To inform the audience about the four best ways to prevent binge drinking by college students

3. The specific purpose should not be a question. Although a question may indicate the topic, it fails to specify the general purpose of the speech.

   Ineffective: How does volunteerism create a sense of community?
   Effective: To persuade the audience that increased rates of volunteerism have a positive effect on community building

4. The specific purpose should be concise and carefully worded. The ineffective statement given here tries to cover too much material, is too general, and does not state clearly what is to be achieved by the speech.

   Ineffective: The effects of a permissive society can be extremely harmful to children and can also create a society that eventually becomes desensitized to reality
   Effective: To persuade the audience that a permissive society limits children's views of reality

Making Connections

Identifying Specific Speech Purposes

Let's practice creating specific speech purposes. The following sentences do not meet the criteria for expressing the specific purpose of a speech.

What is wrong with each of them? Improve each one, further narrowing the topics as necessary.

1. Linguistic relativity is important.
2. To inform my audience about rappelling.
3. To persuade my listeners that a need exists for a quality education in U.S. society.
4. Biomedical advances can protect us.

What did you learn from this exercise about writing specific purpose statements?

Formulating your general and specific purposes makes it easier to develop your speech. They will guide your thinking and planning. You should be ready to reconsider your specific purpose, however, throughout the development stages of the speech. As you research a topic, you might find information that leads you to revise your thinking. Or you might learn something about your audience members that will make you want to adjust your specific purpose to their needs.

The Thesis

The specific purpose of your speech states what you wish to accomplish or what effect you wish to have on your audience. It also serves as the foundation for the thesis of the speech. The **thesis** is a sentence that states specifically what is going to be discussed in a speech. For example, the specific purpose "to explain to my audience the four advantages of using computer-aided instruction" tells what the speaker wants to do but does not describe the content of the speech. A thesis concisely states the content: "Computer-aided instruction saves time, allows for self-pacing, provides practice, and is enjoyable." This clearly worded statement tells exactly what the four advantages of computer-aided instruction are.

If the specific purpose is "to persuade the audience to contribute to the performing arts center," the thesis might be "The new performing arts center will help the university attract Broadway shows, will generate increased ticket sales and thus more money for the university, and will create a renewed sense of community pride in our university." The thesis gives the three main ideas the speaker will discuss (1) why the new performing arts center will attract Broadway shows, (2) why it will generate more money through ticket sales, and (3) why it will renew a sense of community pride in the university. The thesis should be expressed as a full sentence, should not be in the form of a question, and should be clearly and concisely worded.

Here are two examples to show the relationship of the topic to the general purpose, specific purpose, and thesis:

Topic: Inexpensive, renewable energy

General purpose: To inform

Specific purpose: To inform my audience about wind as an energy source

Thesis: Wind is an inexpensive, easily accessible, renewable energy source

Topic: Biological research

General purpose: To inform

thesis
A sentence that states specifically what is going to be discussed in a speech.

Specific purpose: To inform my audience about the development and implications of biological research

Thesis: I will examine biological research by looking at the history of biological research, the research conducted, and the advances influencing future biological research

You can easily see in these examples how a broad topic area is narrowed as the speaker moves from the specific purpose to the thesis. This narrowing procedure is a crucial step in preparing a speech.

Learning Connections
Purpose and Thesis Statements

1. Define a general purpose statement.
2. Define specific purpose, and explain the difference between general and specific purposes in speeches.
3. How does the thesis differ from the specific purpose statement?
4. How do purpose statements and the thesis help the speaker? The audience?

Relating to the Audience

Selecting a topic, narrowing it, choosing a specific purpose, and creating a clear thesis statement so that you can relate your speech to the specific listeners in your audience require careful thinking as well as knowledge and understanding of your audience. The development of ideas requires similar understanding and knowledge. Therefore the speaker needs specific information about the listeners. You have now spent several weeks with the people in your communication class. It is likely that you have each had a chance to respond to the activities and class discussions. What people say, how they act, and their nonverbal communication have all helped you to form impressions of your classmates. Those impressions are important, but you might need to get further information to do a good job of reaching your audience. Because this is so critical to a speaker's success, the remainder of this chapter examines the audience's point of view, kinds of audience members, key information to gain about audiences, methods for researching audiences, and adapting your speech to an audience.

An audience is the collection of individuals who have come together to watch or listen to a speech. The more you know about your audience's past experiences, knowledge of the subject, relation to the subject, and reason for being there, the easier it will be for you to develop a speech that is meaningful to them.

Audience analysis is the collection and interpretation of data about characteristics, attitudes, values, and beliefs of an audience. Analyzing the audience is an essential step in developing and delivering a speech. An audience becomes actively involved in a speech and reacts to the speaker, to the subject, to what is said, to how it is said, to other audience members, and to the situation. The more speakers know about the audience, the better they can adapt their speeches to them.

Understanding the Audience's Point of View

For our purposes, the **audience** refers to the collection of individuals who have come together to watch or listen to a speech. The individuals may become part of the audience for many different reasons. Each individual may have several reasons for being present, and the audience members may come from many different backgrounds. Students, for example, come to class to listen to lectures because attendance is required to obtain a passing grade.

The reason individuals come together to form an audience is an important point that every speaker should consider when planning a speech. If people join an audience because they wish to listen to a speech, it is reasonable to assume that they also want to hear something that is meaningful to them. Most individuals ask the same basic questions about their involvement in an audience. What's in this for me?

This question suggests that your audience will judge what they hear on the basis of their past experiences and the relevance of the information presented. The more you know about your audience's past experiences, knowledge of the subject, relationship to the subject, and reason for being there, the easier it will be for you to develop a speech that is meaningful to them. For example, imagine that you are an expert on reading and have been asked to give a speech entitled "How to Teach Children to Be More Effective Readers." You have spent many hours getting ready for the speech and are now prepared to present it. But are you really prepared? Have you thought about the members of your audience? Who are they? What do they know about reading? What is their attitude toward reading? Would you present the same information to professionals who teach reading, to parents who want their children to become better readers, to children who are indifferent about reading, or to a combination of all three groups? What results would you expect if you used the same approach for all three audiences? What results would you expect if you varied your approaches? Asking these questions and finding answers to them are essential preparation for an effective and successful presentation.

audience analysis
The collection and interpretation of data about characteristics, attitudes, values, and beliefs of an audience.

audience
The collection of individuals who have come together to watch or listen to someone or something, such as to listen to a speech.

captive participant
A person who is required to hear a particular speech.

Captive versus Voluntary Participants

Many kinds of people attend speeches for many reasons, but all are either captive or voluntary participants. Audience members required to listen to a particular speech are called **captive participants.** They may happen to want to hear the speech, but they have no choice but to attend. Some people may resist participation more than others.

Even though few circumstances force a person to be part of an audience, some situations demand attendance to avoid a penalty. For example, a teacher requires attendance during speech presentations, an employer requires employees to attend new product demonstrations, or a military leader orders troops to attend lectures on military maneuvers. In such situations, audience members cannot be absent and cannot leave without being noticed or penalized for doing so. To be effective, a speaker must recognize when he or she is dealing with captive participants.

In contrast to captive participants, **voluntary participants** choose to hear a particular speech because of interest or need. True volunteers attend only because of what they expect to hear. There is no other motivation or force behind their presence.

Key Audience Information

You should gather two kinds of information about your prospective audience: demographic and psychological. The more you know about your audience members, the better able you will be to adjust to them and relate your topic to them.

Demographic Analysis. **Demographic analysis** is the collection and interpretation of basic information such as age, gender, cultural or ethnic background, education, occupation, religion, socioeconomic status, geographic location, political affiliation, voting habits, family relationships, marital and parental status, and group memberships. The more similar the demographic characteristics of members of an audience, the easier it is for a speaker to adapt to their needs and interests.

Age. Knowing that members of the audience differ in age can help the speaker select a range of appropriate examples and evidence. An age difference between the speaker and the audience can also alter what messages are presented and how they are expressed. For example, if an audience consists of only eighteen and nineteen year olds, the speaker has only one age group with which to deal. If audience members range from fifteen to sixty-five years of age, the speaker will have to take into account several age groups and make language and content choices on the basis of that wide range of listener ages.

Gender. Gender is an important demographic characteristic and can present challenges. The speaker should consider the attitudes of each sex toward the other as well as the attitudes of each sex toward itself. As we indicated in several places in this text, gender-based biases should be avoided. Speakers should be sensitive to potential gender-based biases, for example, referring to women as "passive" or providing examples of women only in certain careers, such as nursing or teaching. Although some topics may still be more appropriate for one sex than the other, clear-cut distinctions are becoming increasingly rare.

Cultural or Ethnic Background. Cultural or ethnic background is often not considered as thoroughly as it should be, even though a tremendous diversity of backgrounds exists in our society. Speakers should be sensitive to the different groups that may be present. The following communication variables are culturally determined and influence interactions between and among members of different ethnic and racial backgrounds.

- Attitudes
- Social status within the group
- Thought patterns
- Expected behaviors
- Use of language
- Values
- Respect for age
- Use of spatial relationships
- Meanings of words
- Time
- Nonverbal expressions
- Beliefs
- Cooperation versus competition
- Collectivism versus individualism

voluntary participant
A person who chooses to listen to a particular speech.

demographic analysis
The collection and interpretation of characteristics (age, gender, religion, occupation, and so on) of individuals, excluding values, attitudes, and beliefs.

Making Connections

Culture and the Public Speaker

Pajaree and Dawn are discussing their upcoming assignment: a ten-minute informative speech on a topic demonstrating ethical principles. Pajaree says she wants to talk about the concept of "saving face," but Dawn does not understand what this expression means and how it is appropriate for the assignment. Pajaree explains that saving face is a concept in her native culture that means a person does not purposely do anything to make another lose credibility or status. Pajaree says that she often does not ask the other students questions because she is aware that the questions could cause people to lose face in their own minds or in the minds of others. According to Thai beliefs, ethical speakers and ethical listeners will not willingly cause another to lose face, nor will they willingly lose face by making a mistake. Dawn is fascinated and asks more questions to learn about Pajaree's culture.

Each of us should be aware of cultural perspectives and how they may affect speakers and listeners in a speaking situation. Think about the cultures (or co-cultures) represented in your communication class, and then answer these questions:

1. What values do these other cultures promote?
2. How do the cultural values affect the way a person might respond to certain topics? Give some examples.
3. How can you increase your sensitivity and awareness of cultural perspectives?
4. What can you, as a speaker, do to adjust to different cultural values in your communication class?

Each of these variables determines and regulates how an individual creates and interprets messages. Although the list is not exhaustive, it points out some of the important cultural and ethnic factors to consider as you plan a speech. Culture is dynamic and extremely important; culture helps define who individuals are in relationship to the world around them. Speakers who do not take culture into account may embarrass and insult an audience, and ultimately, themselves. Speech content should not offend values, customs, or beliefs held by members of the audience.

Education. Although it may be impossible to find out exactly what an audience knows and understands about a specific topic, it is often possible to ascertain their general education level. Knowing whether most listeners have completed high school, college, or graduate school can help you to gauge their intellectual level and experience and to adapt your speech accordingly.

Occupation. Knowledge about audience members' occupations can also tell you something about possible interest in and familiarity with some subjects. For example, lawyers might be interested in topics related to the law or in legal aspects of some topics.

Religion. Speakers must be as sensitive to religion as they are to ethnicity. That is, they must recognize issues that touch on religious beliefs and treat them carefully. If you plan to speak on an issue that may have religious ramifications, you should evaluate how your message will affect audience members. Otherwise, you run a risk of offending or losing the attention of some or all of your audience. For example, choosing a quotation to support your viewpoint might be more appropriately taken from the Koran than from the Bible if your audience is of the Islamic faith.

Geographic Origins. Knowing your audience's geographic origins can help you adapt your speech to them. For example, people from rural communities are more likely to know and care more about agricultural topics than are people from large urban areas. People from the South might not be interested in information related to heating their homes in winter, but if they live in an oil-producing state, they might be interested in the price of a barrel of oil.

Group Membership. A **group** is a collection of individuals who have joined together for some common cause or purpose that may be social, professional, recreational, or charitable. Recognizing that individuals in your audience come from groups with special interests can help you relate your speech directly to their needs and concerns. Of course, it isn't always possible to reach every group in your audience, but by appealing to the largest group, you can create strong attention and interest. For example, a student who belonged to a sorority decided to inform her audience about sorority and fraternity functions other than social activities. Three-quarters of her student audience was not affiliated with a Greek group. Knowing this, she began her speech by talking about her thoughts on Greek organizations before she became a member. By first pointing out her reservations about such groups, she created a common understanding between herself and her listeners. Had her audience been three-quarters sorority and fraternity members, that kind of introduction would have been unnecessary.

Other Demographic Factors. We earlier identified marital status, family makeup, and socioeconomic status as other possible elements of demographic analysis. Knowledge of the listeners' marriage and family status provides information about their priorities and interests. An awareness of socioeconomic status will also provide information about the interests and abilities of audience members to grasp the ideas presented. All in all, more information about who the listeners are and what characteristics they share with us and with others will promote a better understanding of how to prepare the speech for the specific audience.

Psychological Analysis. **Psychological analysis** is the collection of data on audience members' values, attitudes, and beliefs. A psychological analysis seeks to determine how the audience will react to the speaker, the speaker's topic, and the surroundings in which the speech is presented. In addition to the items related to demographic analysis, a psychological analysis helps the speaker become aware of what motivates listeners to attend to the message of a particular speech. The size of the audience; the physical setting for the presentation; the knowledge level of the audience; and the attitude of the audience toward the speaker, the topic, and the situation all play vital roles in the planning, development, and delivery of a speech.

Size of Audience. The number of audience members has a considerable psychological effect on a speaking situation and strongly influences how a speech should be delivered. The larger the audience, the more difficult it is to use an informal, conversational speaking style. Size also affects the speaker's use of language, gestures, and visual aids. There is a difference between speaking to ten or thirty people, as in a typical classroom speech assignment, and speaking to several hundred people in an auditorium.

The size of an audience can also affect the psychological disposition of the audience members and their relationship to each other and the speaker. For example, each

group
Collection of individuals who have joined together for some common cause or purpose that may be social, professional, recreational, or charitable.

psychological analysis
The collection and interpretation of data about audience members' values, attitudes, and beliefs.

member of a small audience is aware of himself or herself as a unique member of the audience, and each feels a close, intimate relationship to the speaker. As the size of the audience increases, members lose their sense of identity as unique individuals and feel more distanced from the speaker. Effective speakers know this and plan their presentations to meet the requirements of each situation.

Physical Setting. In evaluating the physical setting, consider factors such as room size, ventilation, seating arrangement, lighting, speaker's platform, and potential for using visual aids. Some professional speakers require specific settings and will refuse to give presentations if their conditions can't be met. Unfortunately, you do not have that choice in a classroom assignment. You can, however, assess the physical setting and take full advantage of what is available to you.

The seating arrangement of your audience is often predetermined, as it is in classroom settings, but sometimes a slight modification can make your presentation more effective. For example, a speech professor was asked to address a group of thirty police officers. He purposely arrived early so that he could see the room and assess the speaking conditions. The seats were arranged classroom-style: The chairs were placed in uniform rows directly in front of a raised speaker's podium, on which stood a large wooden lectern with a microphone. The professor believed that the setting was too formal and would inhibit his presentation, so he quickly rearranged the room by placing the chairs in a semicircle and moving the speaker's podium off to one side. These simple changes gave his presentation a more casual feeling and encouraged audience involvement.

The physical setting can also affect audience members' psychological disposition toward one another as well as toward the speaker. The more relaxed the physical setting, for example, the more open and comfortable audience members will feel in relation to one another and to the speaker. The proximity of audience members to one another can also have an effect. If, for example, the audience members are scattered throughout a large meeting room, they will not have the sense of inclusion that occurs in a physical setting in which the members are densely packed together. The close proximity of other people may create a feeling of belonging to the group and help the speaker reach the audience.

Knowledge Level. The extent of an audience's knowledge about a topic has a tremendous effect on the outcome of a speech. If an audience has little or no background on a topic and the speaker does not realize this, both the audience and the speaker can become frustrated. When an audience isn't ready to receive information or when the information is too technical for them to understand, the speaker must present the material in terms everyone can understand.

A speaker must also adjust a presentation to reach a knowledgeable audience. A physician addressing a medical conference would not explain familiar medical terms. Even though people are apt to be more interested in subjects they know something about, an audience does not want a rehash of familiar information; they want to hear a new twist and add to their existing knowledge. For example, a student decided to present a five-minute informative speech about the lead pencil. After interviewing his classmates, the speaker noted that they all had a similar response: "What can you say about a lead pencil other than that it is made of lead and wood and is used for writing?" On the basis of his analysis, the student developed a creative, fascinating speech. Using a casual and entertaining style, he provided detailed information about the history of the lead pencil and its affect on society. The speech was a great success.

Relationship to the Speaker. The audience's knowledge of the speaker strongly influences how a speech should be developed and delivered. Two professors arrived late to a workshop they were offering on effective communication. Anxious to start, the professors said little about themselves and quickly launched into their main topic. Fifteen minutes into the presentation, they noticed that most of the participants were not paying attention and appeared confused. Finally, an audience member asked, "Who are you?" When the speakers replied that they were speech communication professors and listed their credentials and qualifications, the audience settled down and became attentive. As this example illustrates, an audience's attitude toward a speaker can make the difference between success and failure. Audience members always formulate some attitude toward a speaker.

This example also demonstrates how character (*ethos*, or ethical traits, discussed as an aspect of credibility more fully in Chapter 12) is derived from what the audience members know and believe about the speaker as well as their perceived view of the speaker's use of reasoning. Because effective speakers recognize that character, logic, and emotional appeals can affect the listeners' views of the speaker and the speech, they can adjust their presentations accordingly.

Attitudes and Values Related to the Topic. The audience's attitude and values as they relate to the topic are as significant as their knowledge of the speaker. If audience members do not relate to a topic, the speaker will have a difficult time getting them to listen. For instance, a student chose to speak on individual retirement accounts for his persuasive speech. He researched the subject thoroughly, practiced his delivery, and presented the speech in an enthusiastic manner. His audience remained cool and uninvolved. The speaker had failed to consider the value the audience placed on the topic; the age of its members should have tipped off the speaker. Saving for retirement is not a high priority for most college students. The speaker could have made the speech more relevant by discussing young people's indifference to retirement saving and convincing them that they should become concerned now.

Attitudes Related to the Situation. The speaker must also examine the audience's relationship to the overall situation in which the speech is presented. Why has the audience gathered? Audience members' expectations influence their attitude toward the situation, which in turn reflects on the speaker and the topic. A speaker who talks about the need to further fund social security to a group of seventeen- to twenty-four-year-olds has chosen the wrong topic for an audience who cares little about retirement and social security, which is decades away for them. Listeners who believe a topic is not relevant to their own situations are less likely to listen to the speaker.

Ways to Learn about the Audience

The three most common ways of gathering information about an audience are observation, survey interviews, and questionnaires.

Observation. Probably the easiest method of audience analysis is through observation. The speaker draws on accumulated experience with a particular audience and with similar groups. Through **observation,** the speaker watches audience members and notes their behaviors and characteristics. Although this approach relies strictly on the speaker's subjective impression, it can be useful.

observation
A method of collecting information about an audience in which the speaker watches audience members and notes their behaviors and characteristics.

No doubt you have already learned a great deal about your audience from classroom assignments. You already know the number of students, the number of males and females, and their approximate ages. Through introductions, general conversations, and other interactions, you have learned about their majors, group memberships, jobs, whether they commute or live on campus, and their interests. You have learned about your classmates' attitudes, interests, values, and knowledge. You know your instructor's views and expectations for your classroom performance. You also know the size of the classroom, the location of the lectern (if there is one), the seating arrangement, the availability of audiovisual equipment, and other physical features of the environment. You have obtained all of this information by observation.

Survey Interviews. A **survey interview** is a carefully planned and executed person-to-person, question-and-answer session during which the speaker tries to discover specific information that will help in the preparation of a speech. Such interviews can be done in person or over the phone. The purpose of the survey is to establish a solid base of fact from which to draw conclusions, make interpretations, and determine future courses of action. This method of audience research can be highly productive. To be most useful, however, surveys require a great deal of planning and organization, which take time and energy. (Specific interviewing skills are discussed in more detail in the next chapter.)

Questionnaires. A **questionnaire** is a set of written questions distributed to respondents to gather desired information. The same questioning techniques used in survey interviews are also used in questionnaires. In some cases, questionnaires are more practical and take less time than interviews. They can be administered to relatively large groups of people at the same time. One advantage is that the respondents can remain anonymous, which often leads to greater honesty and openness in answering questions. Although learning to develop good questionnaires takes time and practice, here are some simple guidelines to help you get started:

1. Decide exactly what information you want to gather.
2. Decide on the best method for making multiple copies of your questionnaire.
3. Decide when, where, and how to distribute the questionnaire.
4. Plan the introduction to the questionnaire. Will the respondent need specific instructions on how to answer it?
5. Make sure your questions are clear and understandable.
6. Limit the number of possible responses to each question.
7. Keep the questionnaire as brief as possible.

Figure 7.1 shows a typical questionnaire. Note that it provides simple instructions, it is brief, the questions are clear, and the number of possible responses is limited.

Choosing the Best Information-Gathering Technique. The easiest way to find out about your audience is through observation. Your success with this method depends on the amount of experience you have with your audience and your ability to make accurate inferences. In most classroom situations, observation will yield adequate information for planning a speech, but if you seek more specific data, you may want to use a survey. A survey interview takes planning and time and is not very efficient, but it does provide an opportunity to get information in person and to probe for more data

survey interview A carefully planned and executed person-to-person, question-and-answer session during which the speaker tries to discover specific information that will help in the preparation of a speech.

questionnaire A set of written questions that is distributed to respondents to gather desired information.

FIGURE 7.1

Sample Questionnaire Questionnaires contain a set of written questions and are an excellent way of gathering information from large groups of people quickly. If done effectively, they can be practical, take less time than interviews, and provide for the anonymity of the respondent.

Check one: _____ Male _____ Female

Directions: Check the response that best indicates how strongly you agree or disagree with each statement.

1. Student rage is a serious problem.

______ Strongly agree

______ Slightly agree

______ Undecided

______ Slightly disagree

______ Strongly disagree

2. People who are very angry know that they are.

______ Strongly agree

______ Slightly agree

______ Undecided

______ Slightly disagree

______ Strongly disagree

3. More explanation and instruction on anger management are needed.

______ Strongly agree

______ Slightly agree

______ Undecided

______ Slightly disagree

______ Strongly disagree

4. The students, faculty, and administrators must do more to provide a safe campus environment for all students.

______ Strongly agree

______ Slightly agree

______ Undecided

______ Slightly disagree

______ Strongly disagree

when necessary. If you are dealing with a large group of people, you may decide to gather information by using a questionnaire. Although good questionnaires take time to write, they can be administered more quickly than survey interviews and often yield more candid responses, especially to sensitive topics.

Relating and Adapting to the Audience. The goal of observing, survey interviewing, and administering questionnaires is to gather information so that you can relate and adapt your speech to those who make up your audience. Can you discern any patterns in the information you have gathered? What conclusions can you draw? How certain can you be of them? How can you use what you have learned to improve your speech? For example, if you surveyed twenty-five female and twenty-five male students on your campus using the questionnaire in Figure 7.1 and found that 75 percent of the women thought student rage was a serious problem but only 30 percent of the men thought so, how could that information help you prepare a speech to convince your audience that student rage is a serious problem on your campus?

To give the best results, a questionnaire must be completed by a group of people who represent a sample of the entire population. You also need to make sure you have enough responses to make reliable generalizations about the group you are surveying. If your analysis is thorough and correct, you should have a fairly good picture of your audience—their relevant demographics; interests; knowledge levels; and attitudes toward the topic, the speaker, and the general situation. Although your findings will

Making Connections

Planning a Persuasive Speech

Persuasive speeches require the speaker to try to convince listeners to think about something, accept a perspective as valid, or actually do something. In small groups, discuss how a speech with the specific purpose of persuading students that a higher student fee is needed to purchase more computers for student use should be developed. A survey of the student body indicates that 30 percent favor the increase, 50 percent are moderately opposed, 10 percent are strongly opposed, and 10 percent don't care one way or the other. Discuss the following issues:

1. How can you use a survey to help plan the speech?
2. What information contained in the survey, if any, should you give the most consideration?
3. In developing the speech are there certain types of information that you should include to make the speech as persuasive as possible? Provide some examples.
4. How can a survey help you relate your speech to your listeners?

Discuss what you learned from this exercise, and how it should help you in developing other speeches that relate to your specific audience members.

rarely be uniform, you should be able to reach some general conclusions. For example, you may find that 70 percent of your audience members strongly disagree that capital punishment should be used in U.S. society, 15 percent have no opinion, and 15 percent strongly agree. If your purpose is to persuade them that capital punishment should be used in U.S. society, you will need to adjust your speech to this audience. How will you get those who oppose you to listen to what you have to say? What can you say to draw in those who have no opinion or who already strongly agree with you?

Although it is never easy to win over people who oppose your views, you can try to do so by discussing their views first and then discussing your views. You should also make use of credible, unbiased sources—people are more likely to accept information from them. In addition, you should acknowledge that your listeners' views have as much merit as yours but assert that your views will lead to a better outcome.

If your research indicates that your audience has little or no opinion about the information you are presenting, you need to provoke their interest. Begin by telling why they should listen to what you have to say and by showing how the topic relates to them personally. Focus on helping them recognize the benefits and importance of your topic, and remember that clearly communicating your own enthusiasm can help generate interest. Tell your listeners a memorable story using the information you gained.

Finally, when you are dealing with an audience that agrees with you and what you have to say or knows a lot about your topic, you need to acknowledge what you share with them. For example, if you and your audience agree that a new auditorium should be built, note your shared agreement and then go on to talk about what can be done to get the new facility built. In the process, you might try to strengthen their beliefs about the need for the auditorium.

No matter what your audience's position on your topic may be, your research will enable you to identify it in advance. You can use this information to pursue your specific purpose and to adjust your presentation to your audience. Of course, the more information you have, the better your ability to adapt your speech to your audience.

Learning Connections

Audience Analysis

1. Why should you learn more about your listeners?
2. How will this help you?
3. What specific information should you gather? Why?

Summary

One of the most important aspects of public speaking is choosing a topic. If a speaker has interest in and some degree of passion for the concept, the topic is more likely to be an excellent choice. In addition, speakers should choose topics that are interesting, relevant, and potentially useful to the listeners. Therefore the speaker should focus on the listener. "What's in it for me?" is a phrase I tell my students to remember as they choose topics, prepare, and present their speeches. Selecting a topic for class speeches need not be a difficult task. You can use personal inventories, brainstorming, web searches, or some combination of techniques to help you find an appropriate topic for you, your listeners, the situation, and the course requirements.

You need to narrow your topic so that it fits the assignment and time limits and still allows you to provide adequate information for your listeners. In addition, you need to think about the general and specific purposes and decide exactly what you want your listeners to walk away from the speech knowing or able to do.

Effective speakers have a focus on the listener. They realize that listeners vary in their interests, knowledge, motivation to listen, and ability to attend to messages. As a result, they will carefully analyze who the listeners are and what strategies might best allow the speaker to keep listeners interested. They will gather additional information about their listeners to help them develop a speech that will make listeners aware that the speaker really *is* interested in sharing something with the listeners and answers the question "What's in this for me?"

DISCUSSION STARTERS

1. What is the role of public communication in society?
2. How can effective public speaking influence your life?
3. Identify the criteria you would use to determine whether a topic is appropriate for this class.
4. Why should you formulate both a general purpose statement and a specific purpose statement?
5. Why do speakers need a thesis statement?
6. How can demographic analysis help you develop and deliver a speech?
7. How can a speaker reach a captive audience?
8. Why should you be concerned with your audience's attitudes toward you and your topic?
9. What web sources have you found useful in choosing topics?

NOTES

1. J. L. Winsor, D. B. Curtis, and R. D. Stephens, "National Preferences in Business and Communication Education: A Survey Update," *Journal of the Association for Communication Administrators* 3 (1997): 170–179.
2. "Graduates Are Not Prepared to Work in Business," *Association Trends* (June 1997): 4.
3. R. Diamond, "Curriculum Reform Needed if Students Are to Master Core Skills," *The Chronicle of Higher Education* (August 1997): B7.
4. D. McCloskey, "The Neglected Economics of Talk," *Planning for Higher Education* 22 (1993): 11–16.
5. Judith S. Trent, Keynote address, Central States Communication Association Convention, Omaha, Nebraska, April 2003.
6. Speakers may also wish to check this Hilton College (South Africa) "Speech Topics" site that I found when surfing the Web: http://library.hilton.kzn.school.za/English/speech.htm.
7. D. Zarefsky, *Public Speaking Strategies for Success* (Boston: Allyn and Bacon, 2002), 343.

"In all things, success depends upon previous preparation, and without such preparation there is sure to be failure."
—Confucius

CHAPTER 8 Gathering and Using Information

THIS CHAPTER WILL HELP YOU:

- Identify four principal sources of information for your speech topic.
- Explain how each source of information contributes to the research process.
- Identify appropriate sources for specific kinds of information.
- Use the library, electronic databases, and the World Wide Web to gather information.
- Explain how to evaluate information from various sources.
- Cite at least five guidelines that can make the research process more efficient.
- Explain how the various types of sources can be used to support and clarify a speaker's message and enhance the impact of a speech.
- Describe why a variety of sources is better.

CASE STUDY

Your professor reminds you that the informative speeches will be presented in class in just over two weeks. You have selected your topic but are not really sure where to go next. Your professor says you have to do research, but you're not sure what kind of research you need to do to really create a superb speech. This chapter will help you make those decisions. In the meantime, think about and respond to the following questions.

Questions to think about

1. Think about a really good presentation you've heard. What made it good?
2. Why do you remember it?
3. What, specifically, do you remember about it?
4. Now think about a really poor presentation. What made it bad?
5. What differences can you identify between the memorable speech and the poor one?
6. What did the kind of information that was presented have to do with your evaluation of the speech?

What impresses listeners? Professors, supervisors, colleagues, and audience members will have similar responses. Listeners are impressed with worthwhile, current information that is carefully constructed to tell a story. If you find an adequate amount of good, relevant, up-to-date information, you can create an impressive speech. Gathering information can be exciting and fun as well as a great learning experience. The information you gather becomes the backbone of the speech, which is only as good as your information. In this chapter, we focus on the research process and how to use the information you gather to support and clarify your message.

Gathering Information

College professors and professional speakers have said that every ten minutes of speaking time requires at least ten hours of research and preparation time. Each topic and speaking occasion will require a different amount of information, but there is no question that the more information you have, the better equipped you will be to design and develop your presentation and adapt it to your audience. Of course, quality of information matters more than quantity, especially when your time is limited. That is why it is important to develop your research skills. The more skilled you become at doing research, the better use you will make of your time.

Using Yourself as a Source of Information

If you want to make the best use of your time and gather the best information, where should you begin? Most often, with yourself. You are one of the most valuable sources of information available.

Your own experiences and knowledge can contribute to the content of your speech and give you authority to speak on a subject. Kent, for example, works in the Wellness and Recreation Center. In addition, he is a rock climber who spends every break rappelling and climbing. When Kent had to prepare a speech, he naturally thought first of his own personal passions and experiences. He knew he had lots of good information to share with his audience, and he also knew that there were sources of information that would enhance his own knowledge. Think about the effect of Kent's experiences as he related them in his informative speech:

> During spring break, three friends and I went to Colorado to climb mountains. We were pretty sure we could make it halfway to the top of Pike's Peak in one day. We learned a lesson in good equipment care when one of our climber's ropes broke and he fell a short distance. Luckily, he was not badly hurt, but his equipment failure and fall were good lessons for us. Today I'd like to explain a rock climber's equipment and its functions. I'll also explain how to care for that equipment so no one will have an accident similar to Tom's.

How does Kent's personal experience enhance the speech? What is added that would not be there if Kent were merely talking about something he had read?

Paulina, an international student, used her own experiences of growing up in Venezuela in her informative speech. She talked about her people and their music, clothing, and dances. She explained some of the unique differences between her country and the United States. You also have experiences that can be valuable sources for your speeches.

Probing your own knowledge of a subject can help you to organize your thoughts, develop a research plan and eventually move you more quickly through the research process.

The Interview as a Source of Information

Of course, for most topics your firsthand experience and knowledge will not be sufficient. The interview can be a valuable tool for gathering **expert opinion** (ideas, testimony, conclusions, or judgments of witnesses or recognized authorities) and the most up-to-date information. A good interviewer can often discover information that could never be obtained through any other sources.

An interview is a carefully planned, person-to-person, question-and-answer session aimed at gathering information. An interview requires a constant exchange of questions and answers between two individuals. Both people speak and listen, as in a social conversation. In fact, social conversations constitute the most frequent interview situation because they are frequently a series of questions and answers. Let's look at the steps involved and some questions you need to ask in the interview process.

Of course, for most topics your firsthand experience and knowledge alone will not be sufficient to develop an effective speech. The interview resource can be valuable for gathering expert opinion and the most up-to-date information.

Steps in the Interview Process

1. *Establish the purpose of the interview.* What do you want to know? What information will be most helpful? How can you learn what you need to know about the topic?
2. *Choose the interviewee.* From whom will you get the best, most up-to-date information? What are that person's credentials? Is the interviewee willing to openly and honestly provide that information? Is the interviewee accessible? How many people should be interviewed to get complete and accurate information?
3. *Conduct research prior to the interview.* You need to learn as much as you can before the interview on both the interviewee and your topic so that you can ask intelligent questions to gain the best, most important information.
4. *Record the interview.* You should either take notes or audiotape the interview in order to accurately recall information later. Choose the method that best allows good interaction. Use the note-taking guidelines on page 194.
5. *Prepare questions.* Carefully prepare questions in advance. Be flexible enough to ask additional questions to get more information, to probe further, or to follow an unexpected opportunity the interviewee might provide.
6. *Organize the interview.* An interview, like a speech, usually has three identifiable segments: an opening, a body, and a closing. Organize your interview, and provide a template for the interviewee's responses.
7. *Other considerations.* Appropriate dress, punctuality, and attentive listening contribute to a successful interview. Always give the interviewee your complete, undivided attention during the interview. After you check your notes or listen to the tape, if anything is unclear, contact the interviewee for clarification as soon as possible after the interview.

expert opinion
Ideas, testimony, conclusions, or judgments of witnesses or recognized authorities.

Making Connections

Connecting Speaking and Thinking

Interviews often provide speakers or researchers with the most up-to-date information available. Consider the following topics, and then identify some people you might interview to get expert opinions on the topic. The first item has been completed.

Subject	**Interviewee**
International travel guidelines	Travel agency, international travel agent, tour guide, member of a foreign embassy, seasoned travelers
Highway safety	______
Municipal government reform	______
The benefits of organic foods	______
The role of computers in the classroom	______
Growing orchids for pleasure and profit	______

1. For each subject, identify two individuals who would give you unbiased information.
2. Whom would you interview first? Why?

GUIDELINES Preparing for an Interview: A Review

1. Determine the kind of information you are seeking.
2. Formulate a clear and concise general objective.
3. Research the topic and the person before the interview.
4. Prepare questions and possible probes.
5. Organize the interview: opening, body, and closing.
6. Dress appropriately.
7. Be on time.
8. Give the interviewee your undivided attention.

GUIDELINES Recording Interviews

1. Ask permission to take notes or to tape the interview, and let interviewees know that they will have the opportunity to check the notes or that you will send a copy of the transcribed notes.
2. If you are using a tape recorder, be sure it is in good working order and test it prior to the interview. Make sure that you know how long your tape is and how the machine operates. Set the volume before you begin. The tape recorder should be positioned as inconspicuously as possible during the interview.
3. Maintain eye contact as much as possible.
4. Take notes throughout the interview.

5. Agree to follow any ground rules the interviewee establishes and offer the interviewee the opportunity to review the script of your speech prior to your presentation.
6. Review your notes or tape recording as soon after the interview as possible.
7. Remember to be courteous throughout the interview and to thank the interviewee for taking the time to speak with you.

The Library as a Source of Information

Making use of the library requires some effort, but once you understand how the system works—and most libraries use essentially the same system—you will find that the library is a useful and beneficial resource for speech preparation. Libraries are very user friendly. Many libraries have invested great sums of money to install computerized systems to help researchers find materials quickly and easily.

If you do not know how to locate material, now is the time to learn. A little time invested now will save you a great deal of time later, and you will find that the library is a convenient and pleasant place to locate information. If you do not use the library, you will be at a disadvantage not only in your speech class but also in your other classes.

Start by attending one of the tours or orientation sessions that many libraries offer. Some also provide educational packages or Web-based tours with instructions on how to use the library. After your introduction to the system, you need to practice using the library. Principal sources of information in the library include: the librarian, library computer-assisted search programs, the computerized catalogues, and the reference department.

The Library Computer Search. Most libraries have computer-assisted research systems. Each year these systems improve and become easier to use.

Many universities and colleges have network systems that allow you to enter the library indexes through home or campus computers. Once you learn the appropriate log-on procedures to access the library computer, menus guide you through the steps to find what you want. You will learn where the materials are located and whether they are available at your library.

The Reference Department. Most library research begins in the reference department. Here you will find sources for specific subject areas such as dictionaries, almanacs, biographical aids, encyclopedias, yearbooks, atlases, bibliographies, indexes, and guides to periodical literature. If you are uncertain what to use or how to use them, ask the librarian.

There are specialized indexes for particular subjects, such as agriculture and natural resources, business and economics, statistics, biology and life sciences, computers, education, and history. An index widely used by beginning speech students is the *Readers' Guide to Periodical Literature.* This index lists articles from popular periodicals. Issues of the guide, published semimonthly or monthly, are bound separately for the latest publications and compiled in volumes for publications that are a year or more old.

Because magazines, research journals, and newspapers have the most recently available information on a subject, they are the most often used resources for speech

Web searches can provide a wealth of information quickly and easily. Web information comes from a variety of sources. Some are reliable and credible, and others are not very useful, credible, relevant, or reliable. It is important that you check out your sources to ensure they are reliable and accurate.

writing. If you want to know the latest opinions and trends on almost any social, political, or economic issue, weekly magazines and newspapers will probably be your best resources. If you are looking for specific scientific research, research journals might be your best alternative.

Magazine and newspaper articles are usually brief and written for a general audience, so they are rich sources of basic information for speeches. Given their brevity, you can read several articles in order to gather different points of view. In addition, libraries not only have local and state newspapers but they also usually subscribe to major newspapers from all over the world. They provide you with an even broader perspective.

If you do not know what your library has to offer, take time to learn about it. The search for knowledge is never easy, but thought and preparation will enable you to find ample information about almost any speech topic.

Electronic Information Sources

Many libraries have access to an online database of current periodicals: newspapers, magazines, newsletters, transcripts, and wire information. Some libraries have access to services such as Lexis-Nexis, an electronic source of newspapers from around the world. Lexis-Nexis provides the most current information available. In some cases, you can access Lexis-Nexis at midnight your time and read the next morning's news from another part of the world. Many libraries have an ERIC (Educational Research Information Clearinghouse) database as well. ERIC provides access to reviewed convention papers, a source of the most up-to-date research findings as well as opinion pieces by experts in their fields. When searching an electronic database, you need to determine keywords and phrases to use in your search before you begin so you can maximize your time and effort. Check the options for each, but, generally, the word *and* is used as a connector between keywords. This allows the database to search the available materials for the information you need. Complete directions for carrying out searches are provided by your library or may be found on the screen where your search begins. Electronic databases are a valuable source of information.

Most colleges and universities have access to the **World Wide Web (WWW),** a global information system that allows users to access Internet information. Web searches can provide a great wealth of information quickly and easily. Remember that web information does not go through a review process, nor is it necessarily fact-checked in any way, so material on a web page is more suspect than that gathered from traditional sources. Critically weigh and verify the information you find, because much of it is unreliable. In Chapter 7, we reviewed ideas for evaluating web sources; review that section as you consider the information and the qualifications of the authors of your web sources.

To find information on the Web, conduct a search using one of the many available search engines. There are topic-based searches and site-based searches. The most common Internet search is the topic-based search. When you identify a general topic (computers, health issues, communication), you can access information about all aspects of that topic. You may, however, receive too many responses to your query and need to narrow your topic to find responses you can easily peruse to find information for your speech. Each search engine has a tutorial to help you get started. Among the more readily accessible are these:

Lycos (www.lycos.com)	Infoseek (www2.infoseek.com)
AltaVista (www.altavista.com)	Google (www.google.com)
Yahoo! (www.yahoo.com)	Excite (www.excite.com)

When you find information on the Web, be sure to write down the specific bibliographic information (the URL [uniform resource locator or address], date accessed, page number, and author or producer), print the information, save it on a floppy disk, or bookmark it. If you're using Netscape, for example, pull down the File menu to Page Setup. Click on each of the boxes so that a check mark appears in front of Document Title, Document Location, Page Number, Page Total, and Date Printed. If you create a bookmark, you will also need to save it on the hard drive or on a floppy disk. Many campus computer labs do not allow users to save information, or it may be saved only for a short period of time. In many cases, you will not be able to save the URL, so be sure to print at least the first page with the URL or write it down so you can find it later.

Surfing the Web: The Internet as a Source of Information

Searching the Web can be interesting, entertaining, frustrating, addicting, and educational, and the Web facilitates access to a wealth of information in a relatively short period of time. Web information comes from a variety of sources. Some are reliable and credible, and others are neither useful, credible, relevant, nor reliable. Websites are not subject to the same evaluation and review as print sources are, so it is important that you assess not only the information on a website but also the people, or organizations responsible for the site. It is no accident that when you key in the words *critical thinking,* many responses will be suggestions for evaluating web sources. Several of the scores of critical thinking websites were actually titled "Thinking Critically about Web Sources." Three of our favorite guides for evaluating web sources (because of their thoroughness and because they are from respected university libraries) are

World Wide Web (WWW)
A global information system that allows users to access information from the Internet.

provided by Esther Grassian at the UCLA library, Elizabeth Kirk of the Milton S. Eisenhower Library of the Johns Hopkins University, and Cornell University. Each is different, yet all contain similarities. Each asks the surfer to consider specific questions about websites being accessed for information or research purposes.

Kirk (www.library.jhu.edu/elp/useit/evaluate/index.html), for example, offers four basic evaluative criteria:

1. *Author.* Who wrote the material? How do you know this person is qualified to write about this subject? Can you contact the author if you have questions?
2. *Publishing body.* Who "publishes" or sponsors the website? When you look at the web page, do you see a header or footer that shows a connection to a larger website? Is there a link on the page that takes you to the home page of the website? What can you learn from the Internet address (the URL)? Check the letters just to the left of the first backslash (/). Following are some abbreviations that provide some insight to a web source, which are used with URLs:

.edu	Refers to a college or university
.cc(state)us	Refers to a community college
.k12(state)us	Refers to a school for kindergarten through twelfth grade
.com	Refers to a business or other commercial enterprise
.org	Refers to a nonprofit organization or trade association
.mil	Refers to a military site
.gov	Refers to a government agency, official, or organization
.net	Refers to a network administration organization

   Look beyond the backslash. If you see a tilde (~) or if the URL includes terms such as "/users/" or "/people/," you may be looking at an individual's personal page within the official pages of a larger website. If it is a personal page, you have no way of knowing whether the information on the page represents the organization. However, if you know the author's identity and qualifications (say, a librarian at an educational site), you will be able to ascertain the credibility of the personal page.
3. *Currency.* How recently was the website published, created, or updated? This information should be at the bottom of the web page or home page of the website. Does the document contain data that must be recent? Is there a date connected to that information? (When the population of Hispanics in the United States is given with a 1990 date, for example, the information is not current.) Does the website have links to other sites that no longer work?
4. *Purpose.* Can you determine why the information is on the Web? Does the site provide information, give explanations, persuade, publicize, sell products, or entertain? Sometimes the URL will give you a clue. Part of the URL contains a function indicator, such as *gov* or *com,* that indicates the purpose of a website:

.edu or .gov	Provides factual information and explanations
.com	Promotes and sells products, or provides current news and information
.org	Influences public opinion and advocates for particular issues
.net or .com	Entertains

Making Connections

Checking and Evaluating Websites

Most college libraries identify criteria so that you can check the accuracy and validity of websites. Check and compare the criteria established by the following sites.

Evaluating Web Sites: Criteria and Tools, Michael Engle, Cornell University Library (especially note the Webliography provided on this page): www.library.cornell.edu/okuref/research/webeval.html

UCLA College Library: Thinking Critically about WWW Resources (Esther Grassian): www.library.ucla.edu/libraries/college/help/critical

1. How are the criteria similar?
2. How are they different?
3. How do they compare to the information in the text from Elizabeth Kirk at the Johns Hopkins University libraries?

.info	Especially used to provide truly global general information; most current registrations are in the United States
.biz	Specifically for businesses
.name	Indicates the site is for individuals
.pro	Indicates professionals; attorneys, dentists, or medical doctors, for example, register their sites for easy access. (For example, Janedoe.law.pro identifies a site belonging to attorney Jane Doe.)
.museums	Accredited museums worldwide
.aero	Globally recognized suffix for airlines, airports, computer reservation systems, and related industries
.coop	Identifies business cooperatives, such as credit unions and rural electric co-ops worldwide

Finally, consider one more question: How does web information compare with other available resources? If there are discrepancies among sources, do some further checking to find the best sources of information you can. Remember, too, that websites change quickly. You might search a specific topic and find 15,050 hits and then return an hour later and find 16,589 hits. Websites are added rapidly and changed often. Also, a search engine may sample more or fewer individual sites at different times. The library websites in the Making Connections box above may have changed from the initial writing to the time this book is published. Sometimes you will automatically be redirected to another site. At other times, you will need to search further or find another source. This is another good reason for writing down URLs and bookmarking websites: You can go back to the exact site to get further information or direct others to a specific site.

Learning Connections

1. How do you know whether a web source is reliable?
2. Why should you have a variety of sources?
3. What electronic resources have you used and found helpful?

Suggestions for Doing Research

There are no shortcuts to good research, but there are ways to make research more enjoyable and easier no matter what sources you choose to use. Here are several suggestions:

1. *State a clear purpose before starting your research.* Knowing what you want to find makes the job of searching easier. If the purpose of your speech is to persuade your audience that breakfast is the most important meal of the day, the key word would be *breakfast.* You will begin your search with that term but might also want to look at *health, nutrition,* or *healthy lifestyles.* You need to consider all possible areas of research in advance to keep your research productive and efficient.

2. *Begin your research early.* Because finding appropriate materials takes time, you should start your research as soon as possible. If you wait until the last minute, you might discover that the materials you need are unavailable or that it takes longer to find them than you anticipated.

3. *Use computer searches when possible.* The computer is one of the simplest means of obtaining lists of sources on any topic. If you are unfamiliar with your library's computer system, ask for help. Librarians will gladly help you find what you need.

4. *Maintain a bibliography of sources.* As you find sources on the computer, in the card catalogues, and in periodical guides, copy them in the same form onto a sheet of paper or index cards (3 × 5 inch or 4 × 6 inch). The advantage of index cards is that you can sort them quickly, either alphabetically or by importance to your speech. List each item separately and make notes about its importance to your speech presentation. Although this may seem tedious, it is essential that you keep track of the materials you find. Keying this information into computer files can also help you stay organized.

5. *Take notes.* Efficient and accurate note taking is a must. Once you have located information, either record it by hand or photocopy it for later use. Whether you quote a statement verbatim, summarize it, or paraphrase it, record the original information accurately and completely. Take plenty of notes, and always make sure that the source is fully and accurately indicated, as in the sample note cards in Figure 8.1. Nothing is more frustrating than having information you cannot use because you don't know the source and cannot return to it for additional information. The more information you record, the better. You should always have more than you need to write your speech.

Using Research to Support and Clarify Ideas

More than 2,000 years ago, Aristotle, a famous Greek scholar, wrote that there are essentially two parts to every speech: a statement and its proof. Aristotle's description is still valid today. How a speaker clarifies and supports ideas determines the quality of the speech. For example, consider the following statement:

> Today's students are much smarter than students of every earlier generation. The reason? Students have access to computer technology that gives them more available information than ever before.

FIGURE 8.1

Sample Note Cards Note taking, if done accurately and completely, can save you a great deal of time and effort. It is always best to take plenty of notes and to record the sources of the notes correctly.

Urban Legends and Folklore — Subject heading

David Emery
"Foiled Abduction at Sam's Club"
http:urbanlegends.about.com/library/weekly/aaaa082599.htm — Reference

Many stories on the web are hoaxes, rumors, or urban legends

This particular story is at least twenty years old and is very popular and believable but cannot be substantiated.

There are at least three current versions of the child abduction story. — Specific Information

The SARS Scare — Subject heading

Michael D. Lemonick and Alice Park
"The Truth about SARS"
Time, May 5, 2003. pp. 48–53. — Reference

Facts about SARS:

1. What: a respiratory illness that primarily affects the lungs but may also affect digestive tract.
2. Symptoms: fever of 100.4 degrees F or more with chills, headache, muscle aches, developing into a dry cough and difficulty breathing.
3. Cause: coronavirus family, spread by microbes
4. How it spreads: person-to-person contact
5. No known cure, yet.

— Specific information

On the surface, this statement might seem valid, but is it accurate, and will an audience accept it at face value? Does the statement offer any data to help you accept the first sentence as true? What proof is provided that students who have access to computer technology have advanced more quickly than those who do not? Careful analysis shows that we need to think carefully before we accept the statement as true.

Audiences generally accept information because of the perceived believability of the speaker or the information itself. Thus the statement would likely be more acceptable to audiences if it were made by a well-known educator and researcher than if it were made by a student. But regardless of the source, most listeners require

Making Connections

Thinking about Traditional and Web Information Sources

There are many places to find information that will enhance your speeches. Using the library and the Internet and interviewing experts are several sources discussed in this chapter. Imagine that in two weeks, you will present an informative speech using presentational aids in your communication class. Your professor has indicated that the topic may be of your own choosing. Follow these steps as you begin your search for information:

1. Identify the general topic area for your speech.
2. Identify the general subject of your key word search.
3. Decide whether to use traditional library sources or electronic sources.
4. Decide when you will use library sources and when you will use web sources.
5. Identify five sites where you might find information on your topic.
6. Conduct a web search.
7. Refine your search, and narrow your topic in that search.
8. Determine what criteria you will use to evaluate your information.
9. Determine what guidelines you will use as you seek information on the Web.

some proof or specific data before they completely accept a statement. Consequently, effective speakers justify each main idea in their speeches with a variety of supporting and clarifying materials.

Supporting and clarifying materials bring life to a speech. They can make the content of a speech appealing, vivid, exciting, meaningful, acceptable, and more useful to listeners. Compare these two paragraphs:

> Alzheimer's disease has a great impact on family life. Everyone is affected in differing ways when a family member suffers from this terrible disease.

> Who are the "real" victims of Alzheimer's disease? Although Alzheimer's obviously has an effect on all family members, it may be the teens who are left to care for a grandparent who suffer the most. "I wish my parents would have known the symptoms of Alzheimer's," said 13-year-old Ashley, whose grandmother has the disease. "I remember staying home alone with my grandma and she had this blank look on her face as if she was a zombie or something. Her disease has really affected me."[1]

Which paragraph do you find to be more meaningful? More interesting? Why?

Consider the following statement made in a speech by a student:

> Exercise is the best means of losing weight. Although many people consider exercise to be hard work, it doesn't have to be. In fact, there are a number of exercise programs that are easy, and you don't even have to sweat to lose pounds.

Too good to be true? Yes. And it's not very persuasive, either. Most of us want more proof. The speaker needs to present evidence before the audience will believe this.

The quantity and quality of a speaker's supporting and clarifying materials, plus the speaker's ability to use them correctly, make the difference between a mediocre speech and a good one. Therefore in this section, we focus on the basic kinds of supporting and clarifying materials used in speeches: testimony, examples, definitions, and statistics.

Making Connections

Hear the Words That Changed the World

Have you ever thought about the great ideas of the world? The History Channel has a website with great information. The URL is www.historychannel.com/speeches/index.html. Once there, click on the "Speech Archive" to access audio clips of speeches, including Neil Armstrong's Walks on the Moon, Lou Gehrig's farewell to baseball, and eyewitness accounts of a variety of historical events. To listen to the actual voices, you must have RealPlayer installed. The site allows you to download a free copy of RealPlayer.

Whether your interests are in music, art, political science, history, education, sports, or the sciences, there is a speech to interest you. Try it out. Go to the History Channel speech archive site. Click on "F-L" and scroll down to Mohandas Gandhi, then "On his religious beliefs." Listen to the clip, and answer the following questions:

1. Is Gandhi's voice what you expected?
2. On what aspect of his religious beliefs does Gandhi speak?
3. Why is Gandhi's speech included in the list, "Hear the Words That Changed the World?"

Testimony

The opinions or conclusions of witnesses or recognized authorities are referred to as **testimony.** Speakers use testimony to support or reinforce points they want their audiences to accept. The value of the testimony is related both to the listeners' opinion of its acceptability and to the speaker who presents it. Consider this opening of a student's speech:

> What do you think when you see a person who has Down syndrome? If you're like most people, you feel pity. I'm here to tell you that you need not feel pity, because people with Down syndrome are some of the most loving, caring people in the world! Why do I say that? Because my son is a Down syndrome child, and he gives us more love and caring than I ever imagined anyone could possess.[2]

The young mother who gave this speech immediately captured our interest and attention. She expressed her own emotions and shared the wonderful things that had happened to her family because of her son. Her story moved every member of the audience.

The use of testimony usually adds trustworthiness to what a speaker says—a necessity for all speakers who are not yet established as experts on their chosen speech topic. The speaker's own experience can be an excellent form of testimony as in the previous example. When the speaker's reputation and experience are insufficient, the use of a recognized and trusted authority can be invaluable in gaining listeners' acceptance.

Testimony can either support or clarify material or both. Here is an example of testimony that does both:

> The Malignant Hyperthermia Association of the United States (MHAUS) says that all surgical patients and their families should be screened for Malignant Hyperthermia, or MH. MH is an uncommon disorder that may cause a life-threatening crisis triggered by anesthetics.[3]

testimony
Opinions or conclusions of witnesses or recognized authorities.

The value of testimony is related both to the listener's opinion of the acceptability of the message and to the credibility of the speaker who presents it. Tennis star Venus Williams is a credible spokesperson for Reebok, but she might not be a qualified authority on other subjects.

The speaker uses testimony from MHAUS to support and clarify the nature of a serious disorder.

Testimony can be either quoted directly or paraphrased. Paraphrasing is an effective method of condensing a long text or clarifying a technical passage. Sometimes audience members tune out speakers who use long and complex quotations. Restating long quotations in your own words helps to make the source's words fit the tone of your speech. If you paraphrase, do not violate the meaning of the original statement.

Certain statements are so well phrased that they cannot be stated any better. An example is the forceful and unforgettable statement made by John F. Kennedy in his 1961 presidential inaugural address: "Ask not what your country can do for you; ask what you can do for your country." Always quote such statements word for word. Misquoting someone can be embarrassing, but even worse, it can destroy your believability. Double-check every quotation for accuracy and source, and never use a quotation out of context.

Testimony should meet two essential tests: The person whose words are cited must be qualified by virtue of skills, training, expertise, recognition, and reputation; and the expert's opinion must be acceptable and believable to your listeners.

The person you quote should be a qualified authority on the subject. For example, an athlete's endorsement of tennis shoes and a movie star's endorsement of cosmetics are fairly believable because they use such products in their work. But when celebrities advertise products completely unrelated to their area of expertise, their opinions becomes less believable. Avoid using names solely because someone is well known. The best testimony comes from a person whose knowledge and experience are related to the topic and who is recognized by your listeners.

For maximum believability, testimony should also come from objective sources. The objectivity and neutrality of authorities is particularly important when your subject is controversial. For example, in trying to persuade an audience that today's automobiles are safer than those of a decade ago, it is more convincing to quote the American Automobile Association or the National Safety Council than the president of an automotive company. Listeners tend to be suspicious of opinions from a biased or self-interested source.

Using Testimony: Some Tips

GUIDELINES

1. Use testimony or expert opinion when you need additional supporting or clarifying information.
2. Cite sources completely and accurately.
3. Paraphrase long and difficult quotations in your own words.
4. Keep quotations short, accurate, and relevant to what you are saying.
5. Use recognized, qualified, unbiased, and trusted authorities.

Examples

An **example** is a simple, representative incident or model that clarifies a point. Examples are useful when you are presenting complex information to listeners who are unfamiliar with a topic and when your purpose is to inform or instruct. Brief examples, illustrations, and analogies are three kinds of examples that help make things clear for an audience.

Brief Examples. A **brief example** is a specific instance used to introduce a topic, drive home a point, or create a desired impression. The following brief example was used to introduce a subtopic related to the main topic of computer-assisted presentations.

> Presentational computer software programs have made it possible for speakers to enhance their business presentations.

A series of brief examples can also be used to create a desired impression:

> Presentational computer software programs have made it possible for speakers to enhance their business presentations. In fact, many businesses now have a hiring requirement that future employees have specific experience in PowerPoint or similar presentation aids. Some companies provide mandatory PowerPoint workshops for their employees. Because computer technology is so prevalent in the workplace, both employers and customers rely on computer presentations to make a positive impact on clients and the general public. Knowledge of presentational programs can greatly increase the professional look of business and professional presentations, so it is in your best interest to be aware of effective strategies for incorporating this technology. Edward R. Tufte, considered the "guru of visual explanations," quoted in the February 6, 2000, edition of the *New York Times,* offers caveats about graphic presentations. He suggests that presentational aids such as PowerPoint presentations are overused, have too many flashy elements, and do not contain enough information. Dr. Tufte said, "The task is not to have 'high-impact presentations,' or 'point, click, wow' or 'power pitches.' The point is to explain something." Tufte also suggests "that the goals of presentational aids should be to exchange information and demonstrate clear reasoning and problem-solving."[4] These examples of the use of computer-assisted presentations

example
A simple, representative incident or model that clarifies a point.

brief example
A specific instance that is used to introduce a topic, drive home a point, or create a desired response.

Dr. Martin Luther King Jr., Nobel prize winner and leader of the Civil Rights movement, was a brilliant and mesmerizing speaker. In 1963, he gave his famous "I Have a Dream" speech to a crowd of thousands in Washington, D.C. His rhythmic repetition of the phrase "I have a dream" pinpointed his message and captivated the audience.

illustrate the importance of including some media or visual presentations in our personal portfolios.

Illustrations. An **illustration**, or extended example, is a narrative, case history, or anecdote that is striking and memorable. Illustrations often exemplify concepts, conditions, or circumstances, or they demonstrate findings. If an example refers to a single item or event, it is an illustration. Because illustrations go into more detail than brief examples, they are useful in establishing proof.

An illustration lends depth and explanation to the point a speaker is trying to make. It also gives the information more meaning. An illustration may be either factual or hypothetical. A **factual illustration** tells what has actually happened; a **hypothetical illustration** tells what could happen, given a specific set of circumstances.

A hypothetical illustration, because it is speculative, asks listeners to use their imaginations. Such examples are often short stories that relate to a general principle or concept. One instructor used the following hypothetical example to help her students envision how to use their voices when delivering an emotional speech:

> Imagine that an angry mob has accused your friend of a crime—a serious crime—and that they are going to hang him because they believe he is guilty, even though you know he isn't. Your only chance to save your friend is to persuade the unruly mob that he is innocent.

This hypothetical illustration demonstrates that people who are involved in serious situations must use their voices to make their point. The speech to the mob would have to be vivid, forceful, convincing, and highly emotional.

The use of a hypothetical illustration can be particularly effective when it involves the listeners. The illustration should create a vivid picture in the listeners' minds. The more realistic the situation, the more likely it is that the listeners will become involved. A speaker should always specify whether an illustration is factual or hypothetical.

Analogies. An **analogy** is a comparison of two things that are similar in certain essential characteristics. Analogies explain or prove the unknown by comparing it to the known.

There are two kinds of analogies. A **figurative analogy** draws comparisons between things in different categories. For example, in her description of the immigration experience in Postville, Iowa (previously cited in Chapter 4), Anna said that in the past, Postville was a "melting pot" where the primarily German and Norwegian

illustration
An extended example, narrative, case history, or anecdote that is striking and memorable.

factual illustration
A report of something that exists or actually happened.

hypothetical illustration
A report of something that could happen, given a specific set of circumstances.

analogy
A comparison of two things that are similar in certain essential characteristics.

figurative analogy
A comparison of things in different categories.

cultures had blended and melted together. The recent immigration experience, however, was a "tossed salad" in which the newcomers kept their own cultural practices and did not try to blend to become more like each other.[5] A **literal analogy** is a comparison of members of the same category and makes a simple comparison, for example, two majors (art and music), two search engines (Yahoo and Google), or two genres of literature (drama and poetry).

Most topics offer opportunities to use analogies. Figurative analogies make ideas vivid and clear, whereas literal analogies supply evidence to support points. Analogies are effective, efficient, and creative means of supporting and clarifying information.

Restatements. Speakers can and should use a variety of strategies to make their speeches memorable. Effective speakers have often used both restatement and repetition to support and clarify their ideas. A **restatement** is the expression of the same idea using different words. It may take the form of a summary, synonym, or rephrasing.

Restatement does not provide evidence, but it often has a persuasive effect. A well-planned use of restatement can add clarity, meaning, and dramatic rhythm to a message. Martin Luther King Jr., in his famous "I Have a Dream" speech, used both repetition and restatement to make his point:

> I say to you today, my friends, so even though we face the difficulties of today and tomorrow, I still have a dream. It is a dream deeply rooted in the American dream.
>
> I have a dream that one day this nation will rise up and live out the true meaning of its creed, "We hold these truths to be self-evident, that all men are created equal."
>
> I have a dream that one day on the red hills of Georgia the sons of former slaves and sons of former slave owners will be able to sit down together at the table of brotherhood.[6]

Using Examples: Some Tips

GUIDELINES

1. Use factual examples to add authenticity to your presentation. Factual examples build on the basic information presented and add believability to both you and your speech.
2. Use realistic examples that relate directly to your discussion. If you try to generalize from unusual or rare situations, you risk undermining believability.
3. Use authentic, accurate, and verifiable examples. Always give credit to the source so your listeners can verify it.

Definitions

You must define all unfamiliar words and concepts, especially technical terms, if you want your listeners to understand and accept your speech. Nothing is more bothersome to listeners than a speaker who uses terminology they do not understand. In most cases, it is better to offer too much explanation than too little. However, do not patronize your audience by explaining the obvious. You can use several different kinds of definitions to keep your audience's attention. For example, "Calculus is defined as a system of calculation in advanced mathematics, especially a system using algebraic

literal analogy
A comparison of members of the same category.

restatement
The expression of the same idea using different words.

symbols to solve problems dealing with changing quantities."[7] The definition tells us what calculus is and separates it from other forms of mathematics.

A **logical definition**, the most common form used by speakers, usually contains two parts: a term's dictionary definition and the characteristics that distinguish the term from other items in the same category.

An **operational definition** explains how an object or concept works, gives the steps that make up a process, or states how conceptual terms are measured. Here are some examples:

> People who have communication apprehension are those who score a 90 or higher on the Personal Report of Communciation Apprehension (PRCA) test.
>
> For our purposes, an A will be awarded to those who correctly identify 94 or more items in the exam.
>
> The average of the grades received in this class is the sum of all scores divided by the number of students in the class.

logical definition A definition consisting of a term's dictionary definition and the characteristics that distinguish the term from other members of the same category.

A **definition by example** clarifies a term not by describing it or giving its meaning but by mentioning or showing an example of it.

> When I talk about sexist language, I mean any words that do not include everyone in the room. If you say, "I think you guys ought to know this," you are using sexist language because usually at least half of the people in the class are female.

GUIDELINES Using Definitions: Some Tips

1. Define a term or concept whenever you suspect your audience might not understand what you mean or that multiple interpretations are possible.
2. Keep definitions short and to the point. Do not make your explanation more complex than necessary.
3. Use clear and concise language your audience can easily understand. Make your definitions come alive for your audience by providing examples.

operational definition A definition that explains how an object or concept works, or lists the steps that make up a process.

definition by example Clarifying a term, not by describing it or giving its meaning, but by mentioning or showing an example of it.

statistics Numerical data that show relationships or summarize or interpret many instances.

Statistics

We read that the earth's population is more than six billion, that there are more than 1.3 billion people in China alone, and that India has a population of more than one billion. Although statistics can be interesting or even compelling, they can also be confusing and difficult to interpret. Numerical data that show relationships or summarize or interpret many instances are known as **statistics.** Every day we are confronted with numerical analyses.

Statistics enable speakers to summarize a large amount of data rapidly, to analyze specific occurrences or instances, to isolate trends, and to calculate probabilities of future events. They are used to clarify and support a speaker's position. For example, consider these two statements.

> Wind is an increasingly important source of energy.

> According to the June 5, 2003, *New York Times,* wind energy now accounts for less than 1 percent of all electricity produced in the United States. But the American Wind

> Energy Association, the industry's trade group, predicts it will grow to 6 percent in 2020.

The first statement is broad and possibly misleading. The second cites specific numbers and predictions and gives listeners a clearer view of how much wind energy contributes to U.S. usage. The second statement also uses a current source to add credence to the data. Statistics can also be used to emphasize the magnitude of a problem as seen in the following example:

> Interestingly, a study of nearly 3,000 victims of Augusto Pinochet's violent 17-year regime in Chile showed that it was the lingering memories of torture that did the greatest psychological damage.[8]

Statistics can also be informative:

> Lung cancer is among the least curable cancers. For people diagnosed with the disease, the average five-year survival rate is only about 14 percent.[9]

Making the Most of Statistics. Following five simple guidelines will help you make the most of the statistics you've gathered.

1. *Make sure that the statistics you present in your speech are from reliable and neutral sources.* The motives of the source of any statistics must be carefully assessed. For example, if you heard two sets of data on fuel economy per gallon of gasoline—one prepared by the DaimlerChrysler Corporation and the other by the Environmental Protection Agency—which would you expect to be more reliable? Although DaimlerChrysler's data may be perfectly accurate, listeners would tend to believe that their data are biased. It would be to a speaker's advantage, therefore, to use the more neutral source, in this case, the Environmental Protection Agency.

It can often be difficult to identify the most neutral source. For example, whose statistics would you use if you wished to inform your audience about the U.S. strength in nuclear weapons: the Department of Defense or the Americans for Peace? Here the choice is debatable unless you intend to take a position on the issue. Remember, statistics can be used in many different ways and can thus influence interpretations and outcomes.

2. *Take time to explain the statistics you are using.* Interpret and relate your statistics to your listeners. Consider the following use of statistics:

> The sun's radius (distance from its center to its surface) is about 432,000 miles (695,500 kilometers), approximately 109 times Earth's radius. The following example may help you picture the relative sizes of the sun and Earth and the distance between them: Suppose the radius of Earth were the width of an ordinary paper clip. The radius of the sun would be roughly the height of a desk, and the sun would be about 100 paces from Earth.[10]

This explanation makes use of analogy and provides meaningful statistics by clearly comparing the size of the sun to commonplace objects.

When using data that listeners may have difficulty understanding or visualizing, try to provide appropriate comparisons in order to make the data more meaningful.

3. *Use statistics sparingly.* Statistics are difficult to comprehend. If you use too many, you run a risk of boring or confusing your audience. Use statistics only when necessary, and make sure they are easy to understand. The following example would be difficult for even the most attentive listener to comprehend:

> If my new proposal is accepted, we will have at least a 20 percent increase in production efficiency and at least a 50 cent per unit cost reduction, according to our 2005 projections. This, I might add, means a 10 percent, or a minimum of 35 cents per unit, cost reduction over the next five to six years. What this all adds up to is a 15 percent increase over this time period and an eventual profit of $110,000 per year. That will also give us a 6 percent depreciation allowance.

It would be much easier to understand if the data were presented as follows:

> The new proposal, if accepted, will increase production efficiency by 20 percent or 50 cents per unit according to our 2005 projections. This would provide a minimum cost reduction of 35 cents per unit over the next five to six years and a $110,000 per year profit for a 15 percent increase over the time period.

4. *Round off large numbers when possible.* Listeners understand and remember uncomplicated figures better. For example, it is easier to remember nearly one billion than 999,999,900. And although you can say that the Washington Monument rises 555 feet, 5⅛ inches high or 169.29 meters high,[11] listeners will more easily remember 555 feet or 169 meters. Unless exact measurements are required (when people actually create something as you talk), round off most statistics to the nearest whole number.

5. *Use visual aids to present statistical information, if appropriate and possible.* Using visual aids saves explanation time and also makes statistics easier to understand. Compare the following paragraph with Table 8.1. Note how everything in the paragraph is quickly summarized in a simple four-column display.

> The first quarter brought $30,000 in donations and $5,000 in interest income. The second quarter saw an increase in donations to $35,000 and a slight drop in interest income due to the volatile economy. From July through September, there was a drop in donation income to $31,000 but a slight rise in interest income at $4,500. The fourth quarter brought an increase in donation income up to $50,000, with only $3,500 interest added to capital funds. Balance this against the budgeted expenses of $100,000. What we have

TABLE 8.1

A Simplified Way of Presenting Statistics: ABC Charitable Causes Financial Summary, 2003

	DONATION INCOME	INTEREST INCOME	BUDGETED EXPENSES
January–March	$ 30,000	$ 5,000	$ 25,000
April–June	35,000	4,250	25,000
July–September	31,000	4,500	25,000
October–December	50,000	3,500	25,000
Total	$144,000	$17,250	$100,000

FIGURE 8.2

Visualizing Statistical Data Viewing statistical data can help summarize complex data and make it come alive to interest your audience.

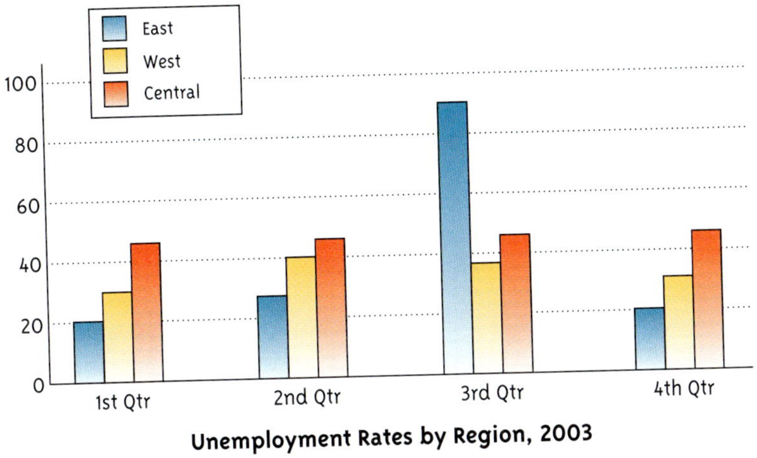

for ABC Charitable Causes for 2003 are the usual expenses in the amount of $100,000, $144,000 in donation income, and $17,250 in interest income. We took in just over $61,000 more than we spent for the year and are healthy!

Figure 8.2 represents another example of how complex data can be summarized and presented in an interesting way. Note how the graphics make it easier to understand the statistics presented. (Chapter 10 discusses presentational aids in greater detail.)

Learning Connections

1. What kinds of materials can you use to support and clarify your ideas in a speech?
2. How do you choose which ones to use?
3. As a listener, what kinds of supporting materials best seem to get your attention?

Using Statistics: Some Tips

GUIDELINES

1. Make sure your statistics come from reliable, neutral sources.
2. Use statistics sparingly.
3. Take the time to explain the statistics to your listeners.
4. Display statistics visually whenever possible. This saves explanation time.

Summary

A key to effective speaking is the quality and currency of material you gather to support and clarify your ideas. Listeners appreciate worthwhile information that is presented so that they can remember the main ideas. Just as communication begins with you, an effective speech begins with you, your views, and experiences. You can also find a wide variety of useful information in the library. The reference section has a broad range of materials that can be helpful. In addition, there are numerous electronic databases (Lexis-Nexis, ERIC, etc.) where you can find up-to-date information on most topics. Interviews provide expert opinion, and the World Wide Web is an easily accessed source. Be sure to evaluate the information gained on the Web even more carefully than that from other, more traditional, sources, however, because Web-based material has not always undergone the same rigorous evaluation process. When you use Web-based materials, you should follow the assessment guidelines provided.

The research process can be both interesting and entertaining if you begin the process early, know what you need to look for, take careful notes, and write down all necessary information about your sources, including specific URLs, so that you and others can find the information later.

A good speaker knows that effective research that supports and clarifies main points can make the difference between a good and a poor speech. Testimony, examples, definitions, and statistics are the four basic types of supporting and clarifying materials. The materials you use will vary greatly depending on the topic and purpose. Your goal should always be to clarify your ideas so that your listeners will remember and even make use of it at some time, either now or in the future.

DISCUSSION STARTERS

1. What do you need to know about a topic before you consult with others or use the library?
2. When is an interview a particularly appropriate method?
3. What does one need to know and do to be an effective interviewer?
4. Your speech topic is "date rape." When you go to the library to do research, where should you begin?
5. Why is the reference section a good place to gather materials for a speech?
6. What role do supporting and clarifying materials play?
7. On what basis should you judge the effectiveness of a source of information in supporting a particular point of view?
8. As a listener, how do you feel when you hear someone using statistics in a speech?
9. When should we use electronic sources to find information?
10. How and why should we evaluate web sources?

NOTES

1. "Helping Teens Cope with Alzheimer's Disease," *Advances: The Alzheimer's Association Newsletter* (Spring 2001), 3.
2. Adapted from a speech by Samantha Burt, Oral Communication, University of Northern Iowa, October 2002. Used by permission.
3. M. C. Redmond, "Malignant Hyperthermia: Perianesthesia Recognition, Treatment and Care," *Journal of PeriAnesthesia Nursing 16,* 4 (August 2001): 259–270.
4. D. Corcoran, "Talking Numbers with Edward R. Tufte: Campaigning for the Charts That Teach," *New York Times,* February 6, 2000, C4.

5. Adapted from remarks made in an oral defense of an unpublished M.A. thesis by Anna Levina, entitled "Recent Jewish Immigrants' Communciation In Postville, Iowa: A Case Study," University of Northern Iowa, June 3, 2003.
6. From "I Have a Dream" by Martin Luther King Jr., Copyright 1967, Martin Luther King Jr., copyright renewed 1995, Coretta Scott King. Reprinted by arrangement with the Estate of Martin Luther King Jr., c/o Writers House as agent for the proprietor, New York, NY.
7. "Calculus," World Book Multimedia Encyclopedia, Mac OS X Edition, Version 6.0.2, 2001.
8. M. Szegedy-Maszak, "Tyranny of Mind," *U.S. News & World Report* (May 12, 2003), 48.
9. "Should You Be Screened for Lung Cancer?" *Women's Health Reporter,* 3(11) (2002): 1.
10. "Sun," World Book Multimedia Encyclopedia, Mac OS X Edition, Version 6.0.2, 2001.
11. "Washington Monument," World Book Multimedia Encyclopedia, Mac OS X Edition, Version 6.0.2, 2001.

"Nothing is as necessary for success as the single-minded pursuit of an objective."
—Fred Smith

CHAPTER 9 Organizing and Outlining Your Speech

THIS CHAPTER WILL HELP YOU:

- Identify the purposes of the three main parts of speech.
- Identify suitable content for the three main parts of a speech.
- Name the main points of a speech.
- Assess the organizational patterns described and choose the best one for your speeches.
- Use transitions, signposts, internal previews, and internal summaries when you organize your speeches.
- Complete preliminary and presentational outlines for your speeches.
- Use websites to find examples of outlines.

CASE STUDY

We have all experienced something such as this: There are two really smart people in class, both get great grades on exams, and each of them talks a lot in class. One is easy to follow when she talks and seems to make perfect sense all the time. You know where she's going and what she means. The other person is hard to follow and never makes sense at all. You always have questions about what she said and wonder how anyone that smart could sound so disorganized. What is the difference in their speaking? One is organized and knows where she's going and helps others know that, too, while the other doesn't seem to have her act totally together. Before you read the rest of the chapter, think about what it takes to help you, as a listener, stay with the speaker.

Questions to think about

1. Do you know what it takes?
2. Are there strategies that work?
3. Does the speaker need to tell you where s/he's going?
4. What do you personally do to try to help others see where you're going when you speak?

One of the toughest things we do after choosing a topic and gathering information is to organize the material into some sequence that others will understand. Organizing ideas might seem as if it were natural, but it is not. It is a skill we learn, and one of the best places to learn and to apply our organizational skills is in the preparation of a speech. Although there are no prescriptions for success, there are guidelines that can be helpful. Most of your professors, especially communication professors, do not want you to have a cookie-cutter speech, but we do offer suggestions that are helpful in organizing your speeches. It is up to you, the speaker, to use some creative touches to help you get your points across to your listeners. Just as a construction worker building a house must start with the footings and the foundation and work up to the roof, there are steps in the organizational process that will help you to construct an organized speech.

Organizing your speech involves arranging its parts into a systematic and meaningful whole. Once you have thoroughly researched your topic, you can simplify your writing task by carefully organizing your material. All speeches are organized into three main parts: introduction, body, and conclusion. By this point, you have determined your speech's general and specific purposes and have begun to think about your thesis statement. This should help guide you in the organizing process. Because the body is the main part of any speech, containing most of its content, we recommend that students begin by working on the body and only later write the introduction and conclusion. Thus we examine the body first.

Organize the Body of Your Speech

The **body** of a speech presents the main content, and organizing it will help you formulate your thesis statement. To ensure that the body of your speech is well organized, your content must be divided into main points that are thoughtfully selected and stated; limited in number; and carefully ordered, connected, and supported.

Develop the Main Points

Well-developed **main points,** the principal subdivisions of a speech, are critical to defining your thesis statement. Assume that the specific purpose of your speech is to inform your audience about cardiopulmonary resuscitation. To determine the main points and help finalize your thesis, ask yourself two questions:

1. What is cardiopulmonary resuscitation?
2. How does it work?

By asking these questions, *if* you have thoroughly researched your subject, you can determine the main points of your speech. The following is an example:

Main Points

I. Cardiopulmonary resuscitation (CPR), is an emergency first-aid procedure used to sustain life in a person whose breathing and heartbeat have stopped.

II. CPR should be administered by someone who has been trained in the procedure.

organizing
Arranging of ideas and elements into a systematic and meaningful whole.

body
The main content of a speech that develops the speaker's general and specific purposes.

main points
The principal subdivisions of a speech.

The thought and time you put into finding the most effective organization for your presentation will result in a speech that is interesting and makes sense to your audience.

The structure of the body of the speech will take shape around these two main points. The main points are derived from research on CPR. If the research or the topic you have chosen indicates that there are more than two main factors to CPR, each significant point would then be an additional main point.

Remember that every piece of information you have gathered does not constitute a main point. Main points are broad, overarching statements that help to organize the many particulars you have found through research. Statements such as "After two years people should retake a CPR course to learn any changes in the procedure" and "You can take CPR courses at either the Red Cross or the American Heart Association office" are not main points.

Relate Main Points, Specific Purpose, and Thesis. The main points serve as the basis for the thesis statement. Together, the specific purpose and the thesis will

Making Connections

Purpose Statements and the Thesis

Suppose your instructor gives you an assignment to present a ten-minute speech to inform your audience about some medical or technological advance. She says the advance you discuss should be something you find important and relevant. She also suggests that you choose a topic on something of importance that affects you or your family. If you cannot think of anything personal, you may choose something from the list she provides. As a practice, choose one of the following topics, and write a general purpose, a specific purpose, and a thesis statement. Be prepared to share and justify your statements with your instructor and classmates.

1. Laser surgery to improve eyesight
2. Reduction surgery for the morbidly obese
3. High-tech wristwatches (that deliver weather, stock quotes, instant messages)
4. On-Star or other global positioning systems
5. A topic of your own choice

determine the direction of the speech. Here is the thesis resulting from the main points noted earlier:

> *Specific purpose:* To inform my audience what cardiopulmonary resuscitation (CPR) is and how it works.
>
> *Thesis:* Cardiopulmonary resuscitation (CPR) can save lives when someone trained in the procedure administers it.

Here is another example of developing purpose, thesis, and main points. Let us say your specific purpose is to inform your listeners about the West Nile virus and how to get rid of the mosquitoes that spread the disease. Your thesis statement might then be something such as "We need to be aware of the causes, the symptoms, and how to combat the West Nile virus, a sometimes deadly mosquito-borne disease." This thesis statement establishes three main points: the causes of the West Nile virus, the symptoms of the disease, and the best ways to combat the mosquitoes that pass the disease along to humans. You will then develop these three points to create the body of your speech.

Or perhaps you are assigned to present a persuasive speech that will persuade your audience to act in some specific way. From your research on nutrition and healthy lifestyles, you know that breakfast is the most important meal of the day, so you decide to persuade your listeners to eat a good breakfast daily. There are numerous approaches you can take, but remember, you ultimately want your listeners to either continue to eat a healthy breakfast or begin doing so. In this speech, you are not just reporting facts; you want your listeners to *do* something. You must make a compelling argument that will make them listen and act.

As you begin your research, you need to think about the general purpose: to persuade my listeners to begin eating or continue to eat breakfast. Then you need to ask yourself, "Why should my listeners eat breakfast?" As you generate answers, the main points of your speech will emerge. Eventually, you determine that a healthy breakfast gives the human body adequate fuel to energize one for the entire day, that "breaking the fast" will cause one's metabolism to kick in, and that when everything works smoothly, the body will burn calories more efficiently, which helps one to avoid midday slumps that lead to junk foods and unhealthy snacking. At this point, you are ready to refine your specific purpose and state your thesis and main points.

> *Specific purpose:* To persuade my audience that eating breakfast can benefit them in three particular ways.
>
> *Thesis:* Eating breakfast gives our bodies energy to begin and maintain our daily tasks, causes our metabolic processes to work efficiently, and provides enough energy to make it through the day without snacking.
>
> *Main points:* (I) Breakfast is the meal that fuels our bodies so that we have the energy to complete our daily tasks. (II) Breakfast is the meal that makes our metabolic process begin its work. (III) Breakfast is the meal that helps our bodies function efficiently throughout the day.

Present the Main Points. Main points, like the specific purpose and thesis, should be carefully developed and written. They should also be specific, vivid, relevant, and parallel in structure. (We use Roman numerals to designate main points because, as you will see later, they eventually become the main elements in the speech outline.)

Be Specific. The more specific the main points, the less confusion they will create and the more meaningful they will be to an audience. It can be easy to misunderstand a speaker who makes vague, overgeneralized statements. Each main point in a speech should also be independent of the others and simple to understand. Compare the following:

Ineffective Main Point

I. Volunteering is a worthwhile activity because it allows you to help others and it accomplishes things that might not otherwise be accomplished, and besides, it makes you feel good about something you have done.

Effective Main Points

I. Volunteering is a worthwhile activity that allows you to help others.

II. Volunteering is a worthwhile activity that allows you to accomplish something that might not otherwise be accomplished.

III. Volunteering is a worthwhile activity that makes you feel good because you have done something to help someone else.

As you can see, the first example contains three ideas in one point, which makes it too complicated. The second example divides the three ideas into three separate points, thus making each one easier to understand.

Use Vivid Language. In Chapter 4, we discussed the importance of language choice. When you listen to or present speeches, you become aware of language. The more vivid the main points, the more likely they are to create interest. Main points should be thought-provoking, attention-grabbing ideas that stand out from the supporting materials. It is more vivid to say "College student Brandi Russell says the proposed federal law requiring parental notification for birth control use would create a ludicrous situation for college students under age eighteen who are on their own" than to say "The proposed federal regulation requiring family planning clinics that receive federal funds to notify parents of anyone under the age of eighteen who wishes to use birth control devices would have a devastating effect on teenagers."

Vivid phrasing should not, however, become overblown or exaggerated. Such language may hurt the speaker's credibility. The limits of good taste and ethical considerations should be taken into account.

Show Relevance. Main points that are relevant to the audience's immediate interests encourage greater involvement and empathy. For instance, instead of saying, "Air pollution has reached high levels," say, "Air pollution in our city has reached high levels." Using direct references to the audience, whenever possible, increases the link between you, what you are saying, and your audience. Audience members like to know how the speaker's subject relates to them and why they should listen.

Create Parallel Structure. Main points should be expressed in parallel structure, that is, using similar grammatical patterns and wording, when possible.

Not Parallel

I. There is a health care crisis in our nation.

II. People now spend inordinately high amounts of money for health care.

II. The current economic situation causes many people to be uninsured.

Parallel

I. Health care in the United States is in a state of crisis.
II. Health care in the United States now costs everyone more money than in the past.
III. Health care in the United States is available only to those who have good insurance or enough money to cover their health care needs.

Parallel structure of the main points makes material easier to develop and to remember. Audiences usually have only one opportunity to hear a speech; therefore anything you can do to make the main points stand out from the rest of the content is to your benefit. In addition, the speaker strengthens the bond with the audience by consistently using the phrase "health care in the United States" in each of the three main points.

Limit the Number of Main Points. The number of main points in your speech will depend on at least three considerations:

1. The time available to deliver the speech
2. The content to be covered in the speech, especially the amount and complexity of the supporting materials required for each point
3. The amount of information that the audience can reasonably comprehend and remember

The time available for most classroom speeches is limited by practical considerations. As a result, most classroom speeches have no more than five main points, and the majority have two or three.

Try to balance the amount of time that you devote to each main point. For example, if you are assigned a five- to seven-minute speech, plan to allow about two minutes for the introduction and conclusion, distributing the remaining time equally among the main points. Of course, this is only a guideline. It isn't always possible to balance the main points exactly, nor should you. The nature of some speech topics requires that some main points be emphasized more than others.

An audience should be able to sort out and recall each main point. This recall is impossible if there are too many points. Common sense tells us that three points are easier to remember than five. Therefore, as a speaker, you must set reasonable expectations for both you and your listeners. If you have too many main points and a limited amount of time, you will be unable to develop each point thoroughly enough to make it clear, convincing, and memorable. Instructors are not arbitrary and capricious in their demand that you stay within the time limits for your assignments; they realize that all presentations inside and outside the classroom have time limits. You need to carefully consider and adhere to the time limits for classroom speeches, because most presentations you give in the workplace, in organizations of which you are a member, and in groups in your place of worship will have time limits.

Order the Main Points

Once you have identified your main points, you must decide the order in which to present them. This takes serious analysis, because the order determines your speech's structure and strategy. The most effective order of presentation depends on the topic, the purpose, and the audience. Several basic patterns of presentation have been recommended and used over the years: time sequence, spatial, topical, problem–solution, cause–effect (or effect–cause), and motivated sequence. Other cultures and co-cultures, however, use alternative organizational patterns that are very effective. Many Native Americans, African Americans, and women, for example, use narrative or storytelling as a way of organizing their presentations. Many speakers effectively use a combination of one or more organizational patterns in a given speech. Until you're confident in your ability to organize your thoughts, you may wish to use one primary organizational pattern in any given speech.

Whatever organizational pattern you choose, you can make that pattern work for you by making your speech compelling. We have talked about telling a story in your presentation. You can use any of the organizational patterns we discuss here and still tell your listeners a story. You don't have to use a storytelling form to generate interest in your speech. You tell a story by making the speech memorable. Think about a speech or lecture you have heard and enjoyed. What did the speaker do to make it enjoyable? I remember a philosophy professor who made the religions of the world come to life every day in class because he told us the story of each of the religions. It wasn't just dry, boring facts. It was a compelling story that I wanted to listen to each day.

The Time-Sequence Pattern. In the **time-sequence pattern,** or chronological pattern, the presentation begins at a particular point in time and continues either forward or backward. The key is to follow a natural time sequence and avoid jumping haphazardly from one date to another. This pattern is especially useful for tracing the steps in a process, the relationships within a series of events, or the development of ideas. Topics such as the history of photographic technology, the steps in setting up an advertising display, and the development of the computer in today's society lend themselves to the time sequence. Here is an example of a time sequence that moves forward from a specific period of time.

Main Points

I. To create the perfect speech, your first step is to choose a topic.

II. To create the perfect speech, your second step is to gather information.

III. To create the perfect speech, your third step is to organize the information.

IV. To create the perfect speech, your fourth step is to prepare and practice.

A reverse-order sequence begins at a specific time period and works chronologically backward. For example, a speech discussing U.S. citizens' concerns, organized in reverse-order time sequence, could be as follows:

I. In the twenty-first century, many U.S. citizens are concerned about environmental issues.

II. In the late twentieth century, many U.S. citizens were concerned about the economy.

III. In the early twentieth century, many U.S. citizens were concerned about the role of the United States in the world.

The time-sequence pattern can also be used to explain a process. Topics such as the development of a small business, how to create silhouette portraits, and how to administer the Heimlich maneuver all have specific steps that you must complete in the correct sequence if the result is to be successful.

Learning Connections

1. What do effective main points contain that ineffective ones do not?
2. Why should we use parallel structure when stating main points?
3. How do we decide how many main points to have?

time-sequence (chronological) pattern
An order of presentation that begins at a particular point in time and continues either forward or backward.

Lance Armstrong, cancer survivor and five-time Tour de France winner, speaks on behalf of his foundation's Tour of Hope. Persuasive speakers of this type often use problem–solution, cause–effect, or the motivated sequence to organize their speeches.

The Spatial Pattern. In a **spatial pattern** of presentation, the content of a speech is organized according to relationships in space. This method is especially appropriate for presentations describing distances, directions, or physical surroundings. For example, a spatial pattern might be used to describe how plants in each area of a garden can create a quiet retreat, the floor plan for an extended deck area on a house, or how to move from one area to another in an art gallery to get maximum effect of the different genre of art represented. A spatial pattern describes the relationships between all the main points. Here is an example of main points organized according to a spatial pattern:

Main Points

I. The master bedroom is on the southeast wing of the house.

II. The guest bedroom is on the southwest wing of the house

III. The children's bedrooms are on the northwest wing of the house.

Both time-sequence and spatial patterns are well suited to informative speeches.

The Topical Pattern. According to the **topical pattern,** the main topic is divided into a series of related subtopics. Each subtopic becomes a main point in the speech, and all main points are joined to form a coherent whole. In this way, the topical pattern is a unifying structure.

The topical pattern is most likely to be used when none of the other patterns of organization can be applied to the topic or purpose of a speech. Topics such as the health benefits of therapeutic massage, the advantages of taking a noncredit writing improvement course, or the guidelines for choosing language for your papers and speeches can easily utilize the topical pattern. Here is how the topical pattern could be used to organize the main points of a speech about the language-based barriers to communication, as follows:

Main Points

I. Language can be misunderstood because of bypassing.

II. Language can be misunderstood because of indiscrimination.

III. Language can be misunderstood because of polarization.

When the topical pattern is used correctly, each main point is parallel in structure and related to the others. Because the topical pattern is versatile, it can be adapted to most speech purposes and can effectively present material related to a variety of topics.

The Problem–Solution Pattern. A speech that follows the **problem–solution pattern** usually has two main points: the problem and the suggested solution. The problem is defined as a need, doubt, uncertainty, or difficulty, and the suggested solution remedies or eliminates the problem without creating other problems. A

spatial pattern
An order of presentation in which the content of a speech is organized according to relationships in space.

topical pattern
An order of presentation in which the main topic is divided into a series of related subtopics.

problem–solution pattern
Order of presentation that first discusses a problem and then suggests solutions.

problem–solution approach could be used to address topics such as the lack of daycare facilities in the workplace, the increased number of students per class because of the budget crisis, and the increased incidence of binge drinking on this campus.

The problem–solution pattern, correctly used, should do more than state a problem and a solution; it should help the audience understand both the problem and the solution and why the solution will work. For example, a speech advocating change in the university's policies toward on-campus drinking might follow this problem–solution pattern:

Making Connections

Presentations in Other Classes

Your humanities professor assigns an oral report designed to increase your knowledge of one of the cultures you have covered in class. All oral reports are due in two weeks.

1. How will you approach this report? What will you do first?
2. How will you choose the organizational strategy for your report?

Problem

I. Each year, we hear about the significant increase in student binge drinking

Solution

II. Students must be taught about the dangers of binge drinking and taught to drink safely.

The problem–solution pattern usually includes three to five of the following:

1. *A definition and description of the problem,* including its symptoms and size
2. *A critical analysis of the problem,* including causes, current actions, and requirements for a solution
3. *Suggestions of possible solutions,* including a description of each solution's strengths and weaknesses
4. *A recommendation of the best solution,* including a thorough justification of its superiority over other proposed solutions
5. *A discussion of the best solution put into operation,* including a description of how the plan can be implemented

The Cause–Effect Pattern. In the **cause–effect pattern,** the speaker explains the causes of an event, problem, or issue and discusses its consequences. Causes and effects may be presented in two different sequences. A speaker may either describe certain forces or factors and then show the results that follow from them or describe conditions or events and then point out the forces or factors that caused them.

Consider this example of using the cause–effect pattern to discuss the effects of computers on students' job placement. A speaker might begin by recounting recent developments in computer procedures that have led to a more accurate analysis of students' skills, and then show that, as a result, the number of students who have obtained first jobs in their chosen fields has increased dramatically. Or the speaker might reverse the process and first point out that the number of jobs that students are landing in their chosen fields is the result of more accurate computer analysis of their skills.

cause–effect pattern
An order of presentation in which the speaker first explains the causes of an event, problem, or issue and then discusses its consequences.

Regardless of the exact sequence, a speech organized by cause and effect has two main points: a description of the factors that are the *cause* and a prediction of identification of the subsequent *effect,* or vice versa. Topics such as eating disorders in young adults, television violence, heart disease, and new approaches to improving memory all lend themselves to the use of the cause–effect pattern.

Using the cause–effect pattern, a speech on the current budget crisis in our nation might be arranged in either of the following ways.

Cause

I. Government officials at all levels failed to account for reduced consumer spending.

Effect

II. This failure to account for the public's attitude has resulted in massive budget shortfalls in each state across the nation.

or

Effect

I. Unless we can raise funds quickly, state governments will have to reduce even more services.

Cause

II. Failure to notice and account for reduced consumer spending caused state governments to continue to spend as if the funds were plentiful.

Because the cause–effect pattern can be used in a variety of ways, it is a useful format for either informative or persuasive speeches. As long as the cause can be directly related to the effect that you are trying to prove, this pattern is an excellent choice for many different topics and a beneficial means of reaching your listeners.

The Motivated Sequence Pattern. A widely used pattern of organization for the persuasive speech is the **motivated sequence,** developed by Professor Alan H. Monroe of Purdue University in the 1930s.[1] This pattern is specifically designed to help the speaker combine sound logic and practical psychology and is briefly mentioned again in Chapter 12. (We cover the idea in this chapter because it is an organizational strategy, but you may wish to refer back to this section as you read Chapter 12.) The motivated sequence is particularly effective because it follows the human thinking process and motivates listeners to take action. The sequence has five steps: attention, need, satisfaction, visualization, and action.

motivated sequence
A pattern of organization specifically developed for persuasive speaking that combines logic and practical psychology. Five steps are involved: attention, need, satisfaction, visualization, and action.

1. *Attention.* In the first step, the persuader attempts to create an interest in the topic so that the audience will want to listen. This step takes place in the introduction and follows the guidelines for an effective presentation. The speaker is subtly saying, "Please pay attention. This is important to you."
2. *Need.* In the second step, the persuader focuses on the problem by analyzing the things that are wrong and relating them to the audience's interests, wants, or desires. At this point the speaker is saying, "This is wrong, and we must do something about it."
3. *Satisfaction.* In the third step, the persuader provides a solution or plan of action that will eliminate the problem and thus satisfy the audience's interests, wants, and desires. The speaker is saying, "What I have to offer is the way to solve the problem."
4. *Visualization.* In the fourth step, the persuader explains in detail how the solution will meet the audience's need. The speaker's message now becomes, "This is how

my plan will work to solve the problem, and if you accept my solution, things will be much better."

5. *Action.* In the fifth and final step, the persuader asks the audience for a commitment to put the proposed solution to work. The speaker basically concludes by saying, "Take action!"

The following is an example of a motivated sequence outline:

To persuade my audience to act now to prevent skin cancer	Specific purpose
Introduction	
I. Approximately 700,000 new cases of skin cancer are diagnosed every year.	Attention
Body	
II. Prevention schemes are most important in dealing with skin cancer because treatment often requires painful, long-term follow-up.	Need
III. Frequent skin inspections and avoiding overexposure to the sun are two surefire ways to reduce the risk of skin cancer.	Satisfaction
IV. It is vital to do frequent (once every three months) self-exams on preexisting skin markings to detect any changes. Also, one must avoid the dangerous ultraviolet rays (UVR) from the sun and artificial devices such as tanning booths.	Visualization
V. Minimize your exposure to the sun, avoid tanning salons, inspect your skin frequently, and use fresh, proper sunscreens to prevent skin cancer from claiming your life!	Action

The motivated sequence is most often used in persuasion. It is also commonly used by advertisers because it sells ideas.

Choosing the Best Pattern. We have emphasized the importance of matching the pattern of organization to your topic, specific purpose, and thesis. You must also consider another key factor: your audience. The wise speaker anticipates responses from the audience. Therefore if your audience analysis indicates that important questions or objections are likely to be raised, you should arrange your main points to meet those objections. For example, if you advocate that a statewide recycling effort be mandated and are certain that someone in your audience will object to mandates of any kind, you might structure your presentation as follows:

Main Points

I. Recycling is an easy way to create more space in our state.

II. Recycling is a good way to reduce and reuse many products.

III. Recycling is cost-efficient.

No matter what pattern you select, as a beginning speaker you should probably use only that pattern when sequencing your main points. As you become more proficient, you might wish to combine patterns.

Connect the Main Points

A conversation can move from one unrelated topic to another without losing meaning or impact, but for a speaker to communicate effectively with an audience, the thoughts in the speech must be systematically connected. The four most common connecting devices that speakers use, singly or in combination, are transitions, signposts, internal previews, and internal summaries.

Transitions. Phrases and words used to link ideas are called **transitions.** They form a bridge between what has already been presented and what will be presented next. Transitions are typically used between the introduction and the body of a speech, between main ideas, between supporting materials and visual aids, and between the body and the conclusion. A transition can review information that has already been presented, preview information to come, or summarize key thoughts. Here are some typical transition statements that might be made in a speech:

Let me move on to my next point.

Now that I have discussed the history of the Internet, I would like to talk about its uses.

Turning now to . . .

The final point I would like to make is . . .

Another example might be . . .

Keeping in mind these four items I discussed, we arrive at the following conclusion.

Signposts. Just as a traffic sign warns drivers about travel conditions, **signposts** are words, phrases, and short statements that let the audience know what is ahead. Here are some typical signposts:

Let me first illustrate . . .

My second point is . . .

To recap . . .

As you look at my chart . . .

Next . . .

Finally . . .

Questions can also be used as signposts:

How powerful is language?

What happens next?

How many people are affected by this plan?

How can we responsibly respond to this issue?

Such questions draw the audience's attention to a forthcoming answer.

A signpost not only prepares an audience for what to expect next but also alerts the audience that the upcoming information is important. Some examples are as follows:

The most essential aspect of this is . . .

Let's look at possible solutions to . . .

The only thing you need to know is . . .

transition
A phrase or word used to link ideas.

signpost
A word, phrase, or short statement that indicates to an audience the direction a speaker will take next.

Internal Previews. Short statements called **internal previews** give advance warning, or a preview, of the point(s) to be covered. Here is an example, "Next we'll look at possible solutions to the problem of budget shortfalls."

Internal Summaries. An **internal summary** is a short review statement given at the end of a main point. For example

> Let me briefly summarize what I have said so far. In a time of fewer dollars from the legislature, and rising costs, finances become very tight. For every percentage point of budget shortfall, we must raise tuition by 4 percent. We must convince the governor and the legislature to provide more funding for the university.

Support the Main Points

Main points by themselves are nothing more than assertions. An audience needs supporting and clarifying material in order to accept what a speaker says. It is crucial that each main point be supported and that the support be relevant and logically organized. When supporting materials are included, the body of a speech expands to outline form, in which the main points are followed by subpoints, which in turn may be broken into further supporting points.

Learning Connections

1. When might you use a topical pattern for organizing your speech?
2. When should we use a time sequence pattern?
3. What strategies help us connect ideas within the speech?

I. Body language can help you make a positive impression on prospective employers.
   A. There are twelve tips to help you make your best impression.
      1. According to June 2003 *Communication Briefings,*[2] if you lean toward people when you listen, the speaker will have a more positive view of you.
      2. Let your smile convey the warm, friendly person you are.
      3. Pay extra attention to your good posture to communicate your confidence.

- Main point
- Support and clarifying material

Supporting materials should be clearly related to the specific purpose, thesis, and main points of the speech.

Organize the Introduction of Your Speech

Experienced speakers often develop their introductions after, not before, the body of the speech. An **introduction** includes opening statements that serve two important functions: motivating the audience to listen and orienting them to the subject. Therefore your introduction should prepare your audience for the main ideas of your speech by setting the stage for the topic.

Your introduction should be based on the information you gathered in your audience analysis. If your analysis was accurate and thorough, you should have a pretty

internal preview
Short statements that give advance warning, or preview, of the point(s) to be covered.

internal summary
A short review statement given at the end of a main point.

introduction
Opening statements that orient the audience to the subject and motivate them to listen.

Nobel prize–winning author Toni Morrison is a world-renowned novelist who has many resources she can call on to arouse the interest of an audience. She might refer to the subject or occasion, tell stories, use personal and biographical information, present a startling statement, use humor, read passages from her work, or ask rhetorical questions to get her audience's attention.

good understanding of your audience's frame of reference and how it might differ from your own. Your introduction should meet these three goals:

1. Orient the audience to the topic
2. Motivate the audience to listen
3. Forecast (preview) the main points

Orient the Audience to the Topic

Decide how much background information to provide based on what your audience knows or does not know about your subject. This is the appropriate time to gain attention, state your specific purpose and thesis statement, and define terms, if necessary, that are essential to understanding the speech.

Several approaches can be used to gain attention and arouse the interest of your audience, including referring to the subject or occasion, using personal references or narratives, asking rhetorical questions, presenting a startling statement, using humor, or using quotations. You should choose these devices carefully to fit the audience, occasion, and context. None is always effective, and each has limitations. For example, using humor to focus your listeners' attention on a serious topic such as disease would not be effective. Consider the overall speech as you choose your approach, because all parts of the speech must fit together well to achieve your desired purpose.

Refer to the Subject or Occasion. You may be asked to speak on a special occasion such as a holiday, founders' day, graduation, or an anniversary. Here is a sample attention-getter related to an occasion:

> It is truly a privilege to speak at this convocation. I am honored to be a part of the celebration honoring you for completing all of the requirements leading up to your admission into the teacher education program.

Use Personal References or Narratives. Whenever you can relate your own experience to a speech, do so. Personal experiences make your speech more meaningful to your audience and show them that you know your subject. Here is how a speaker used a personal experience to introduce a speech on why she didn't drink milk:

> As a child, I was always forced to drink milk. I never wanted to drink it, and I never asked for milk at meals or for snacks. A few years ago I learned why I "didn't like milk"—I have a lactose intolerance. And people who have a lactose intolerance probably should not drink milk, unless it's soy or rice milk, instead of a dairy product.

Ask Rhetorical Questions. A rhetorical question is a question for which no answer is expected. Asking rhetorical questions in an introduction usually encourages an audience to become intellectually involved. (Asking real questions is also an effective way to get your audience interested in and involved in the speech, but it is important to let the audience know that you intend to get answers from them when asking this type of question.) Such questions can also be used to create suspense. Here is one example of rhetorical questions used to involve the audience.

> Does dining on prepared low-cal, low-fat fare help weight loss? What would you say if I told you that the Weight Watchers frozen dinners you've been nuking to help you maintain a lower calorie level may not be the right choice? Kathy K. Isoldi, MS, RD, coordinator of nutritional services at the Cornell Comprehensive Weight Control Center, points out that skimping on calories and protein can backfire, leaving you hungry in an hour or two and tempted to reach for less healthful snacks.[3]

Present a Startling Statement. A startling statement can be used when you want to shock or surprise your audience. Startling statements are extremely effective at getting attention, as shown by this example, "The harsh reality is this: Party time is over!" Startling stories can also be used to get your audience's attention:

> There may be a time bomb within your body. Really. It may be ticking away unmercifully, and unless you recognize the symptoms and change your lifestyle, that time bomb may cause you to have serious health problems and even affect the length of your life. The time bomb within is stress. "We're all under stress," according to Drs. Bruce McEwen and George Chrousos. And, when we're stressed, our bodies react with a "fight-or-flight" response. The body pumps out adrenaline, increasing heart rate and blood pressure (and readying us to fight), and sending more blood to our muscles (so we can flee).[4]

Use Humor. A funny story or relevant joke not only gains the attention of your audience but also relaxes them. Stories and jokes must be tied to the content of the speech and not offered simply for the sake of humor. One speaker began his talk as follows:

> The last time I gave a speech to this large a group, an audience member raised his hand in the back row and shouted, "I can't hear you." Immediately, a hand went up in the front row, and the person asked, "Can I move back there?" Now I know all of you want to hear me, so I'll try to speak loud enough so that you can understand what I have to say about becoming familiar with the room in which your speech will be made so that you know how to present your ideas.

The class was quietly doing its lesson when Russell, suffering from problems at home, prepared to employ an attention-getting device.

Use Quotations. Sometimes a quotation can grab your audience's attention, and if cited accurately, it can also add to the believability of your speech. A student talking about the future started her speech as follows.

> Lee Iacocca once said, "It's important to talk to people in their own language. If you do it well, they'll say, 'God, he said exactly what I was thinking.' And when they begin to respect you, they'll follow you to the death."[5] Today I want to talk with you about the power of language and how you can use it to help you be a competent communicator.

Whatever you choose to gain attention and maintain interest in your introduction, it should be relevant and orient the audience to the topic.

State the Specific Purpose and Thesis. After getting your audience's attention, you need to state the specific purpose and thesis statement of your speech. Both the specific purpose and thesis statement were discussed in detail earlier in this chapter. Sometimes the specific purpose and thesis statement are best stated together; sometimes it is appropriate to state the specific purpose at the beginning and the thesis toward the end of the introduction, where it serves as a preview of the speech. By stating the specific purpose and thesis, you are orienting your topic to the audience and giving them a clear indication of where you are headed with your speech. Also, this preview is essential in helping your audience recall what you said, because they have only one opportunity to hear your message.

Motivate the Audience to Listen

Design your introductory comments to gain the attention and interest of your audience. You must hold their interest and attention throughout the entire presentation, but that task will be easier if you can capture them by making the topic significant and important to them and by establishing your credibility.

A standard way of making your topic relevant is simply to point out the reasons for presenting your speech. It is important that the audience find a reason to listen to the speech as early in the speech as possible. You should also consider whether it is necessary to establish your credibility in speaking on the topic you have selected.

credibility
A speaker's believability, based on the audience's evaluation of the speaker's competence, experience, character, and charisma.

Credibility refers to a speaker's believability based on the audience's evaluation of the speaker's competence, experience, and character. If, for example, Madonna, who is a singer, entertainer, and actor, were to speak on health care or violence in our society, she would have to establish her credibility on the subject by relating the subject to herself and by indicating how she became an expert on the topic.

Forecast the Main Points

Before you finish introducing your speech, let the audience know what you will cover in the speech itself. This is known as *forecasting,* and it affords listeners a "road map" so that they know where you will take them in the remainder of your speech. Forecasting helps your audience be better listeners.

Let's look at some sample introductions. The following portions show you how to orient and motivate your listeners and forecast the main points of your speech:

> "A Pentagon project to develop a digital super diary that records heartbeats, travel, Internet chats—everything a person does—also could provide private companies with powerful software to analyze behavior. . . . Known as LifeLog, the project aims to capture and analyze a multimedia record of everywhere a subject goes and everything he or she sees, hears, reads, says, and touches." This amazing statement from an AP wire service article on the front page of our newspaper details how the Defense Advanced Research Projects Agency, or DARPA, plans to have the digital diary in place in the next two years.
>
> Now I don't know about you, but I'm very concerned that the same military agency that brought us the Internet and the global positioning satellite system has bids out on a project that violates our privacy in this invasive manner. "Big Brother" will not only be watching us, but also *recording* everything we do! This is not even an antiterrorism tool. Instead, the agency calls LifeLog a tool to capture "one person's experience in and interactions with the world."[6]
>
> Although DARPA claims that this is a tool people will choose, we should be concerned about its potential uses. In my speech, I will explain how LifeLog operates and the applications DARPA envisions for its use.

- Orienting material
- Motivating material
- Forecasting of main point

Can you label the specific parts of the previous introduction? Now look at the following example. The specific parts are labeled for you.

> Selena was walking toward the garden when she collapsed. She was rushed to the hospital and admitted for observation. After two days of testing, Selena was told that she was suffering from acute chronic stress and needed to change her lifestyle or she could face serious health problems. Now you might think, "This only happens to older people," but Selena is only 20 and is a full-time college student who works forty hours per week. Her stress is the kind of stress any of us could experience.
>
> Stress is a part of our daily lives. Some of us even believe that it's what holds us together! And a certain amount of stress is actually good for you—it helps you focus and get things accomplished.
>
> But chronic stress can cause depression and anxiety and even suppress the immune system.[7]

- Orienting material (attention-getter)
- Motivating material (significance of topic)
- (effects)

The next introduction accomplishes several functions at one time: It gets attention, it relates the topic directly to the audience and to the speaker, it establishes the speaker's credibility on the topic, and it also notes the main points of the speech.

What do you fear most? Surveys conducted over the past twenty years suggest that Americans' greatest fears were death, accidents, and heights. Most, however, identify fear of public speaking as their absolute greatest fear. Most of us in this room would probably agree with this finding. Speaking is never easy, but the experiences I have had in the business world and in this class have made me more confident and a better speaker. Today I'd like to define speech anxiety, identify its causes and effects, and share ideas about how to control or reduce anxiety.

- Rhetorical question
- Citing research to establish credibility
- Relating topic to audience
- Establishing credibility
- Thesis and forecasting of main points

The following introduction incorporates background and an attention-getter; it provides listeners with a reason to listen, points up the significance of the topic, lets the listener know "what's in it for me," and states the specific purpose and thesis:

A Sample Introduction

Six weeks ago, my friend purchased a prairie dog. Today my friend is covered with a rash and ugly pockmarks on his face, neck, trunk, hands, and arms. He's had severe fever and chills, and he's wishing he had never even seen a prairie dog. My friend contracted monkeypox, the latest example of how animals are making us sick.

- Background and attention-getter

Robert G. Webster, a leading virologist at the St. Jude Children's Research Hospital in Memphis, says, "There are probably hundreds if not thousands—maybe even millions of viruses out there . . . we don't even know they're there until we disturb them. SARS is probably just a gentle breeze of what one of these big ones is going to do someday."[8] Scientists agree that animals are transmitting viruses, bacteria, and parasites to humans more rapidly than ever before, spawning ailments known as zoonotic diseases.[9] Why do you need to know this? Because, according to Stephen S. Morse of Columbia University, "There are a multitude of factors that allow people to come in contact with what may once have been infections that were buried deeply into the ecology. With the global traffic of people and goods . . . there are many more pathways, or highways, for what I called some years ago, 'viral traffic.' "[10]

- Reason to listen
- Significance of topic
- Relevance

After hearing my speech, I hope you will have a better understanding of zoonotic disease. We'll first look at what zoonotic diseases are, how they develop and spread, and how best to avoid zoonotic disease.

- Specific purpose and thesis

Making Connections

Effective Introductions

The introduction is critical to effective speaking. Researchers and business people say that speakers must get the listeners' attention in the first fifteen seconds or risk losing them. Communication scholar David Zarefsky suggests that "The introduction to a speech powerfully affects the audience's first impression of a speaker."[11] With that in mind, evaluate the following introduction:

According to the World Book Encyclopedia Dictionary, zoonotic diseases are those passed on to people through contact with animals.[12] *Zoonotic diseases are increasing at an alarming rate. Today we'll talk about zoonotic diseases.*

1. What is missing from this introduction?
2. What would you do to improve it? Why?

GUIDELINES

Develop Your Introduction

1. Keep the introduction relatively brief, making up only 5 to 10 percent of the speech's total content.
2. Allow plenty of time to prepare the introduction carefully. Because it is critical to the success of your speech, it should not be rushed or written at the last minute.
3. Make the introduction creative and interesting. To accomplish this, think of several possible introductions, and choose the most effective one.
4. As you research your speech, watch for material to use in the introduction. Keep a notebook or file of interesting quotations, stories, humorous statements, and other items that might give your opening some dazzle. But remember: A successful introduction *must* be relevant to the speech topic.
5. Develop the introduction after you have completed the main part of your speech. Relevant introductions are easier to create after you have determined the content and direction of the body.
6. Write out the introduction, word for word. This section of the speech is too important to improvise or leave to chance. In addition, knowing exactly what you will say at the beginning of your speech will give you confidence and help you get off to a strong start. Then, practice delivering the introduction until you can present it conversationally, but flawlessly.

Organize the Conclusion of Your Speech

Your **conclusion** should focus your audience's thoughts on the specific purpose of your speech and bring your most important points together in a condensed and uniform way. Your conclusion should relate to your introduction, helping your audience make the connections between the various parts and points of the message. In persuasive speeches, you may also use your conclusion to spell out the action or policies you recommend to solve a problem. In every case, your conclusion should reinforce what you want your audience to remember.

conclusion
Closing statements that focus the audience's thoughts on the specific purpose of a speech and bring the most important points together in a condensed and uniform way.

Because your conclusion is as important as any other part of your presentation, you should give it the same amount of attention. Be especially careful to avoid adding new information in this part of the speech. Also, remember that you, as a speaker, have only one chance to get your message across to your audience. Repetition is an important strategy for helping listeners recall the important information you have presented. Your conclusion should

1. Let your listeners know that you are finishing the speech.
2. Make your thesis clear to your listeners.
3. Reinforce your purpose by reviewing your main points.
4. Leave your listeners with a memorable thought.
5. Tie everything together.

Show That You Are Finishing the Speech

You need to prepare your listeners for the end of your speech; otherwise, they are left hanging and uncomfortable, sensing that something is missing. You should not bluntly state that you are finishing or even say, "In conclusion,. . . ." Instead, you should carefully and creatively indicate that the speech is winding down. An example might be, "As you have seen in this speech, there are ways we can become better listeners."

Make Your Thesis Clear

Repetition is important when you have only one chance for the listeners to hear your message. Be sure you creatively remind your listeners of your central idea, "As I stated early in my speech, effective listening is a highly valued skill that can be learned."

Review the Main Points

Repeating the main points of a speech is particularly helpful any time you want your audience to remember your main points. For example, the speaker who informed her audience about barriers to effective listening concluded her speech as follows:

> Let me review the barriers that have the most impact on our listening. They are language, factual, mental, and physical distractions. If you remember these and how they affect listening, you will be a more effective listener.

In addition to helping the audience remember your content, reviewing the speech reinforces both your purpose and the thesis statement.

End with a Memorable Thought

A memorable thought may include referring back to an attention-getting device, citing a quotation, or issuing a challenge or appeal. Citing a memorable quotation can be a good way to leave a lasting impression on your audience. When it is relevant and reinforces your thesis statement, a quotation can give your speech additional authority and help to increase your credibility. It is crucial that you always cite the source of all quoted information or any information that is not your own. (The importance of citing sources and the responsibilities of a speaker to cite sources are discussed in Chapter 10.) A speech on zoonotic diseases might conclude as follows:

Monkeypox is just one of the numerous viral diseases carried by animals and is one of the least dangerous. Lassa fever is another that sparks epidemics in West Africa that kill as many as half of its victims and it is spread by a cute little rat. "Someone could decide to make cute pocket pets out of those critters," said Peter Jahrling, a senior scientific adviser to the U.S. Army Medical Research Institute of Infectious Diseases. "Then we'd have an outbreak of Lassa fever here to worry about."[13] We need to be aware of the dangers involved in keeping exotic pets if we value our lives and our health.

If your purpose is to persuade, the conclusion may also include a challenge or appeal to action. The following conclusion recaps the main points and asks the listeners to take action:

> Sleep researchers are just beginning to understand what we have lost when we lose sleep. Our bodies change drastically when we're sleep deprived and there are many health risks. Our hormone levels change to the point that our energy levels are very low when we awaken and are actually comparable to the low morning levels usually associated with the elderly. Furthermore, sleep deprivation may lead to obesity, a decline in immune function, fuzzy thinking, and even to cancer risks. You need to change your schedules! You need at least eight hours of sleep. Plan your work so that you can always get a good night's rest. If you do get behind, take a nap! A short nap works best—about forty-five minutes can improve your health, your attitude, and your thinking. I urge you to take charge of your life. Get some sleep![14]

Making Connections

Writing Conclusions

The conclusion of the speech is important to you, the speaker, and to your listeners. A conclusion leaves your listeners with something to remember—it should summarize and synthesize the material you've covered. Analyze the following conclusion and answer the questions following.

> *Today I've talked with you about zoonotic diseases and how they are spread. In conclusion, let me emphasize the fact that not all animals will spread zoonotic diseases, but they could. Thank you.*

1. What's wrong with this conclusion?
2. What would you do to improve it? Why?

Develop Your Conclusion

GUIDELINES

1. The conclusion should be brief and should end with a definite summarizing statement. The conclusion should account for between 5 and 15 percent of the content of the speech.
2. The conclusion should not contain information that was *not* already mentioned in either the introduction or the body of your speech.
3. The preparation of the conclusion should not be rushed. Allow plenty of time to develop it, and write it carefully.
4. Leave your audience with an impact that will make your speech memorable. Think of several possible endings, and choose the one that best serves the purpose of your speech.
5. Write out the conclusion word for word. Then learn it well so that you can end your speech smoothly, conversationally, and confidently.

Signal your audience that your speech is nearing its end by using phrases such as "Today, we have examined . . . ," "In the past minutes, we have examined . . . ,"

Learning Connections

1. What should you include in the introduction?
2. How do you tie the introduction, the body, and the conclusion together?
3. Why should you not say, "So, in conclusion, . . ."?

"Finally, let me say. . . ." Each prepares your audience for your concluding remarks. The following conclusion lets listeners know that the speech is nearly finished and it summarizes and synthesizes the major points covered. There is an appeal for action, and listeners are left with a memorable thought.

Today I have shared with you some important points about skin cancer.	Signal of speech's end
It is important to understand the three types of skin cancer including risk factors and recognition of the tumors. Even though Americans love to get a nice tan, it is one of the most dangerous things that you can do in relation to getting skin cancer.	Summary of main points
There are some very specific things you can do in order to prevent skin cancer. First, you must minimize sun exposure by avoiding tanning salons and using fresh sunscreen appropriate for your skin type and the length of time you're in the sun. You must also be able to recognize the changes in the skin that may indicate skin cancer when you conduct self-exams every three months. With early detection most skin cancers are very curable.	Appeal for action
With a little knowledge and a little effort you can prevent skin cancer from claiming your life!	Memorable final thought

Outline Your Speech

Outlining is one of the most difficult (and, therefore, mistakenly avoided) steps in preparing a speech. Outlining and organizing are similar terms. **Outlining** involves arranging the entire contents of a speech in a logical sequence and writing that sequence in a standardized form. The outline is often referred to as the blueprint or skeleton of a speech. Organizing is arranging ideas or elements in a systematic and meaningful way. To organize your speech, select one of the patterns of organization discussed earlier in the chapter. Both organizing and outlining involve arranging information to form a meaningful sequence, but outlining is a more rigorous written process. David Zarefsky, communication scholar and the author of a public speaking textbook says, "Speakers depend on outlines at two stages: when they put the speech together and when they deliver it. Each stage requires a different kind of outline."[15]

Outlining is more detailed than organizing and helps to unify and clarify thinking, makes relationships clear, and provides the proper balance and emphasis for each point as it relates to the specific purpose of a speech or written paper. Outlining also helps to ensure that information is both accurate and relevant.

As you prepare your outline, you will gain an overview of your entire presentation. Developing an outline should help you gauge the amount of support you have for each of your main points and identify any points that need further development. The actual process of outlining usually requires three steps:

outlining
Arranging materials in a logical sequence, often referred to as the blueprint or skeleton of a speech, and writing out that sequence in a standardized form.

1. Create a preliminary outline that identifies the topic and the main points to be covered in the speech.
2. Expand the preliminary outline into a full-sentence outline that clearly and fully develops the speech's content.
3. Condense the full-sentence outline into a presentational outline to aid delivery.

Making Connections

Ordering Ideas in an Outline

For a speech entitled "Making Reading Your Hobby," rearrange the following sentences in proper outline form for the body. Make sure to arrange the content in a logical sequence. Place the number of each sentence in the proper place in the outline. (See page 248 to verify your answers.)

1. Low-cost rental libraries are numerous.
2. Reading is enjoyable.
3. It may lead to advancement in one's job.
4. Books contain exciting tales of love and adventure.
5. Many paperback books cost only $7.95 to $10.95.
6. People who read books are most successful socially.
7. Reading is profitable.
8. One meets many interesting characters in books.
9. Reading is inexpensive.

I. ______________________
   A. ______________________
   B. ______________________
II. ______________________
   A. ______________________
   B. ______________________
III. ______________________
   A. ______________________
   B. ______________________

The Preliminary Outline

A **preliminary outline** is a list of all the points that may be used in a speech. Suppose you are preparing a four- to six-minute informative speech on the development, uses, and benefits of femtosecond technology.[16] Because of the limited amount of time, you know you cannot possibly cover everything related to the topic. And because your general purpose is to inform, you need to focus the content of your speech in that direction. So recalling what you have already read about topic selection, audience analysis, gathering information, and using supporting and clarifying materials, you determine your specific purpose: To inform my audience about femtosecond technology, its development, its uses, and its benefits. On the basis of this specific purpose, you can prepare a preliminary outline of possible main points, as shown in the following sample preliminary outline. Once your possible main points are arranged in this way, you will find it easier to analyze your thoughts. You can then decide exactly which main thoughts to include in your speech and

preliminary outline
A list of all the main points that may be used in a speech.

choose the best order for presenting them. Here is what your preliminary outline might look like:

A Sample Preliminary Outline

Femtosecond technology — Topic

To inform — General purpose

To inform my audience about the development of femtosecond technology and its uses and benefits — Specific purpose

Possible main points:

I. Sven Airinhouse hypothesized that there were many complex levels in a chemical reaction.

II. Professor Ahmed Zewail determined that science would have to create a faster way to measure time.

III. Zewail's research resulted in two types of machines: one capable of taking snapshots every femtosecond and a laser that can cut at a femtosecond pace.

IV. Femtosecond cutting is sharp, even, and smooth.

V. Femtosecond technology can be applied to medical and technical fields.

VI. Femtosecond technology can be used in dentistry.

VII. Femtosecond pulse laser procedure can be used to repair heart damage.

VIII. Data transmission will be enhanced by femtosecond technology.

IX. Obstacles need to be overcome.

full-sentence outline
An outline that expands on the ideas you have decided to include in your speech. It identifies the main points and subpoints you will cover, written as full sentences.

The Full-Sentence Outline

A **full-sentence outline** expands on the ideas you have decided to include in your speech. The preliminary outline identified possible topics. The full-sentence outline identifies the main points and subpoints you will cover, written as full sentences. Although you will not have every single word you'll utter included in a full-sentence outline, you will have a fairly detailed view of the speech. The full-sentence outline is one I require of my students as a final outline, turned in with their evaluation sheet prior to speaking. A good outline helps the speaker to stay on task and provides reminders of what comes next. The full-sentence outline should conclude with a bibliography or list of references identifying all sources you have used in your speech and helps you create a presentational outline that we will discuss in succeeding pages.

GUIDELINES Outlining

1. The preliminary outline should list the possible topics you might cover in the speech.
2. A good outline should identify the importance of the ideas you will present.

3. The outline should provide an overview of your content.
4. The outline should help you clarify your thinking; it gives you the ordering of ideas and the amount of supporting material you have for those ideas.
5. It is helpful to write out the entire introduction and conclusion in your outline so that you can make sure you have included everything you need.

Making Connections

Comparing Outlines—The Text and the Web

In this chapter we have suggested that organizing and outlining are essential in the speech process. Here is a web-based activity to give you practice in analyzing and evaluating others' outlines and speeches.

1. Access the Web.
2. Set your browser to Ask Jeeves at www.ask.com.
3. Ask the question "How should I outline my speech?"
4. Check five of the responses. Do not include anything like "sample term paper outlines."
5. What kinds of information did you find? What are the similarities between the web responses and what we have talked about in this chapter? Differences? Who created the sites? What are their qualifications?
6. Check the "Related Searches" in the right column. Are there more specific examples?
7. If there is a "Sample Outline of Informative Speech," click on that response.
8. Read the outline and evaluate its content with the guidelines we have provided in this chapter. How does this sample compare with our guidelines in the text and in the boxes?
9. Evaluate the speech and explain your rationale to a classmate or to the class in general.

A Sample Full-Sentence Outline

Development and Uses of Femtosecond Technology—A New Science to Give Us Time — Title

Femtosecond technology — Topic

To inform — General purpose

To inform my audience about femtosecond technology, its development, its uses, and its benefits — Specific purpose

Scientists have created technology that is faster, better, and cooler and that will revolutionize everything from computers to advanced telecommunications to dentistry. — Thesis

Introduction — Attention-getting

In today's world, animation is big business. We have interactive CD-ROMs, DVDs, the Internet, and whatever story the people at Disney's historic revisionist department decides to debase this week! Back in earlier times, however, animation was much simpler. Each sheet of paper was a picture; moved rapidly, the pictures become an animation. Even the Disney blockbusters of today all boil down to this concept: a simple chain — Explanation reaction of moving pictures. As early as the nineteenth century, scientists functioned under the same construct as animators, with all of chemistry boiled down to a series of simple chain reactions. The problem was that they could see only the individual molecules and the end product; there was no science capable of watching the reaction take place, like being unable to watch the pages turn. But, according to the February 6, 1998, *Science* magazine, researchers have finally been able to catch up with chemical reactions, literally. This new science is called femtosecond technology and is built around a new increment of time, equivalent to one quadrillionth, or 0.000000000000001, of a second, a femtosecond.

● Significance of topic

So why should this take time out of your day? Well, because the January 26, 1999, *Asia Pulse* magazine points out that femtosecond technology is promising to revolutionize everything from ultra-high-speed computers to advanced telecommunications to a trip to the dentist's office. So follow me to "Femtoland," where we'll first understand what a femtosecond is and how it is used; second, we'll examine femtosecond technology's applications; and finally, we'll look ahead to an everyday life that is so used to this technology it's as normal as a Disney cartoon.

● Thesis

● Forecasting of main points

Body

I. Sven Airinhouse hypothesized that there were many complex levels to chemical reactions.

● Main point

   A. With nothing faster than a microscope, Sven could not prove it.

● Background

   B. It would take another 10 years for the femtosecond to herald a scientific breakthrough.

   C. To understand its origins, we must look at two specific areas: how femtosecond technology came to be and how scientists have harnessed its power.

● Transition

II. Professor Ahmed Zewail of the California Institute of Technology looked for reasons some chemical reactions that look possible on paper do work and others do not.

● Second main point

   A. Zewail became convinced that the reason this discrepancy existed was simply because it was impossible to look at every stage of a reaction, making it unpredictable.

● Explanation

   B. For the next seven years, Zewail dedicated himself to finding a way to see every stage of a reaction.

   C. Using the most modern high-tech forms of scientific photography, Zewail could watch chemical reactions happening as quickly as a picosecond, one trillionth of a second.

      1. This was still not fast enough to see every step.

      2. I am now about three minutes into my speech; about 180 quadrillion femtoseconds have already passed.

● Relevant supporting materials

III. Zewail's research resulted in two types of machines: one, a camera capable of taking snapshots of a chemical reaction every femtosecond and the other, a laser that can cut at a femtosecond pace.

● Third main point

A. The machine looks like a tiny car wash. — Explanation

1. A group of molecules is placed at one end and put through the first stage, getting zapped by lasers, causing chemical reactions.

a. At the other end, the molecules are completely different.

b. A choice of scents is provided.

c. A laser-powered camera snaps pictures at a femtosecond pace, creating a sort of animated film of how molecules interact and change.

2. The same machine setup also works to cut at femtosecond pace.

a. The laser slices through materials so rapidly there is no fray.

b. The result is a smooth, even edge.

B. Researchers created femtosecond technology to be able to know how chemicals react and, more important, to be able to control the reactions. — Significance

C. When examining the current applications of this new science, it is important to look at them in two realms: medical and technical. — Transition

IV. Femtosecond technology can be beneficially used in dentistry and medical applications. — Fourth main point

A. Slow lasers that move at a nanosecond can cause teeth to crack or create random-shaped holes. — Supporting materials

1. Femtosecond lasers move so quickly they cause no damage to the tooth.

2. This means fewer chances for infection, cavities, or later tooth loss.

B. Femtosecond lasers aid in vision correction, therapeutic eye surgery, and minor forms of heart surgery. — Supporting materials

1. Femtosecond pulse procedure allows drilling clean, small holes.

2. Femtosecond procedures create fewer complications, faster healing, less pain, no infection, and no side effects.

V. Modern technology is all about speed. — Fifth main point

A. Computers and data transmission benefit from femtosecond technology. — Supporting materials

1. Computers and telecommunications instruments can now go three times faster.

2. Optical disks will make floppies obsolete because they store more information more efficiently.

B. Femtosecond technology is comparable to stepping on the moon for the first time. — Information relevance

C. Heart implants are currently metal.
    1. The human body often rejects metal parts.
    2. Femtosecond lasers are using different materials, including organic ones, to make transplants less painful and more successful.

D. Laboratory researchers are experimenting with femtosecond technology for DNA exploration and repair.

Scientific researchers are hoping that future development in the femtosecond laser pulse will help bring a clearer picture to this subatomic film strip, and become so commonplace that it is no longer expensive or experimental.

Conclusion

Richard Johnson, noted chemist, wrote in the *Houston Chronicle,* "Dr. Zewail has given birth to a new era of chemistry." Although that may not seem important to those of us who couldn't care less about chemistry, the applications resulting from this new era will provide us with the ability to live better and longer lives. From the beginning of time, science has been measured in a series of steps. One scientist theorizes what is possible, and years later, the theories are proved true. By examining the origins of femtosecond technology, its current uses, and the applications of the future, it is clear that this was indeed the culmination of years of building from one idea to the next. Animators started out with stick figures and ended up with the seamless beauty of modern animation work. The femtosecond started with an observation and has ended up with the promise of faster, better, and just plain cooler technology. It didn't happen in a femtosecond, or even in the blink of an eye, but for scientists, that's okay. With this measurement, they have all the time in the world.

- Supporting materials
- Internal summary
- Supporting materials
- Significance of topic
- Summary
- Synthesis

Bibliography

Asia Pulse, January 26, 1999.

Femtosecond Laser Pulses. 1999.

Houston Chronicle, May 6, 1997.

Houston Chronicle, October 27, 1998.

Laser Focus World, September 1, 1998.

London Independent, October 11, 1998.

Photochemistry and Photobiology, March, 1999.

Physics World, January 1, 1999.

PR Newswire, January 7, 1999.

Science, February 6, 1998.

Science, October 30, 1999.

The Presentational Outline

A **presentational outline** is a full-sentence outline in which detail is minimized and key words and phrases replace full sentences. This is the outline you will work from when you present your speech. The advantages of the presentational outline as a delivery aid are that it is concise, requires little space, and is comprehensible at a glance.

Your presentational outline should include your main points and sufficient clarifying and supporting material to aid you in making your presentation. The outline may also include your complete introduction and conclusion, although the choice is up to you. Key words and phrases are important to use in a presentational outline because they will remind you of the points you want to make. Some speakers use codes, symbols, or even colors to remind them of key points, vocal pauses, changes in speaking rate, and so on. But remember, if your presentational outline is too long, complex, or detailed, you can easily get too involved in your notes and lose contact with your audience. The following example on femtosecond technology shows a concise, condensed outline.

presentational outline
A full-sentence outline in which detail is minimized and key words and phrases replace full sentences.

A Sample Presentational Outline

Development and Uses of Femtosecond Technology: A New Science to Give Us Time
(Topic)

To inform
(General purpose)

To inform my audience about femtosecond technology, its development, its uses, and its benefits
(Specific purpose)

Scientists have created technology that is faster, better, and cooler and that will revolutionize everything from computers to advanced telecommunications to dentistry.
(Thesis)

SHARE! DON'T READ—TAKE A BREATH!

SMILE AT AUDIENCE.
(Reminders about delivery)

Introduction

I. Animation part of everyday lives

A. How animation works

B. Chemistry very much like animation

C. Rapid chemical reactions now seen with femtosecond technology

BRIEF PAUSE—TAKE A BREATH

MOVE SLIGHTLY, NATURALLY—SMILE!
(Reminders about delivery)

II. New science, femtosecond technology, built around new increment of time, one quadrillionth, or (VA #1) 0.000000000000001, of a second

SHOW VISUAL AID #1—POINT TO NUMBERS

A. The January 26, 1999, *Asia Pulse*—femtosecond technology promising to revolutionize everything—ultra-high-speed computers to advanced telecommunications to a trip to the dentist's office
(Thesis (source))
(Help speaker remember)

B. What a femtosecond is and how it is used, current applications, look ahead

PAUSE—TAKE A BREATH—MOVE SLIGHTLY

Forecasting of main points of body

Body

I. Sven Airinhouse's hypothesis—many complex levels

A. Sven could not prove

B. One hundred and ten years for the femtosecond to herald a scientific breakthrough

C. Two specific areas: how femtosecond technology came to be and how scientists have used it

Transition

PAUSE BRIEFLY

II. Professor Ahmed Zewail of the California Institute of Technology—account for discrepancies.

A. Impossible to look at every stage of a reaction

B. Find way to see every stage

C. High-tech scientific photography—watch chemical reactions—picosecond, one trillionth of a second

1. Still not fast enough

2. Already spent 180 quadrillion femtoseconds

PAUSE—MOVE SLIGHTLY—LET AUDIENCE KNOW CHANGE

III. Zewail's research resulted in two types of machines: camera and laser.

A. Machine like tiny car wash

1. First stage

a. Molecules completely different

b. Choice of scents provided

c. Laser-powered camera

2. Same machine setup—cuts at femtosecond pace

a. Slices cleanly

b. Leaves smooth, even edge

B. Researchers seeking reactions and to control

C. Current applications: medical and technical

Transition

PAUSE

IV. Uses in dentistry and medicine

GET VISUAL AIDS READY

A. Slow lasers move at nanosecond—damage teeth

SHOW VISUAL AID #2—POINT TO THE PICTURE

1. Femtosecond lasers—move quickly, no damage
2. Fewer chances for infection, cavities, or later tooth loss

SHOW VISUAL AID #3—POINT TO IT

B. Femtosecond lasers—vision correction, therapeutic eye surgery, and minor heart surgery

SHOW VISUAL AID #4—POINT OUT WHILE SPEAKING

1. Allows drilling clean, small holes
2. Creates fewer problems

SHOW VISUAL AID #5—POINT TO JAGGED HOLES

SLOW DOWN

V. Modern technology-speed

A. Computers and data transmission benefit

1. Computers and telecommunications three times faster
2. Floppies obsolete—more information more efficiently

B. Comparable to first time on the moon

C. Heart implants currently metal

1. Body rejects
2. Different materials for less pain, greater success

D. Experiments with femtosecond for DNA exploration and repair

Scientific researchers and the future: clearer views, less expense, commonplace, not experimental

PAUSE—LOOK AT ENTIRE AUDIENCE—SMILE.

Conclusion

I. Richard Johnson, noted chemist, wrote in the *Houston Chronicle,* "Dr. Zewail has given birth to a new era of chemistry."

A. The resulting applications will allow us to live better and longer lives.

B. Scientists theorize and prove.

1. Uses and applications promise a better future.
2. Scientists now have "all the time in the world!"

- Supporting materials
- Supporting materials
- Fifth main point
- Supporting materials
- Information relevance
- Supporting materials
- Internal summary
- Delivery suggestions
- Supporting materials
- Significance of topic
- Summary
- Synthesis

Making Connections

Citing Web Sources

Just as you can find information on the Web and find ways to critically evaluate websites, you can also find some excellent websites to help you create your reference pages. The Modern Language Association and the American Psychological Association provide excellent print sources for this purpose. There are many websites, too, to help you create your bibliographies or reference pages. One superb source, a very complete listing of how to cite all types of sources, can be found at the Duke University Libraries.[17] We have provided information on organizing and outlining; your instructor will explain the specific type of reference page you'll need to include with your outlines. This activity will help you learn more about the ways we cite sources from journals, books, newspaper articles, government documents, websites, and articles from electronic databases. Here's what you need to do:

1. Access the Web.
2. Go to www.lib.duke.edu/libguide/citing.htm.
3. Determine how to cite two different kinds of print sources.
4. Then determine how to cite two different web sources.
5. Look again and see whether you can learn how to cite an email interview. If that site does not include personal or email interviews or conversations, search for another site to determine how to cite interviews.
6. Bookmark these sites or print them so that you have a handy reference to citing sources.

The presentational outline can be easily transferred onto note cards. Some speakers prefer to use note cards, and in many classroom situations students are required to use them. Figure 9.1 illustrates note cards that might be used in presenting your speech. The number of note cards and their use should be kept to a minimum. Classroom assignments sometimes specify that you use only one side of two or three cards. When this is the case, you need to adjust the amount and type of information that you include to aid you in remembering key information. The advantage of using note cards is that they are easier to handle than full sheets of paper and usually require only one hand, thus freeing the hands for gestures.

GUIDELINES Using Presentational Note Cards

1. Use only a few note cards (they are a help but cannot capture the whole speech).
2. Always number the note cards so that if they get out of order, you can reorder them quickly.
3. Write on only one side of the card.
4. Use abbreviations as much as possible.
5. Do not write out your speech—use an outline format.
6. If you prefer, write out the introduction and conclusion in their entirety.
7. List only the main points and subpoints on the cards.
8. If necessary, write out quotations, statistical data, and other information that must be cited accurately (see Figure 9.1 for sample note cards).

FIGURE 9.1

Sample Presentational Note Cards Note cards should be easy to read. They help the speaker recall information and serve as a reminder of the speech's key ideas.

WHY SHOULD YOU AVOID DAIRY PRODUCTS? 1

Get prepared—look at entire audience, take a deep breath

As a child, I never really liked milk or even ice cream. And, in fact, when either was offered, I often refused. No, I'm not crazy, and not abnormal, but I do have a lactose intolerance.

Lactose intolerance, according to the National Digestive Diseases Information Clearinghouse, is the inability to digest significant amounts of lactose, the predominant sugar of milk.

Lactose intolerance affects many people who are unaware that they have it. To enlighten you about its effects, I will share what lactose intolerance is, how it is diagnosed, how it is treated, and how to have a nutritionally balanced diet without dairy products.

Pause-slow

I. What is lactose intolerance and how is it diagnosed?
  A. Shortage of enzyme lactose 2
    1. Distressing results (*show Visual I*)
    2. Common symptoms
  B. Causes of lactose intolerance
    1. Born with LI
    2. Develops over time (*slow chart*)
      a. 30–50 million Americans have LI
      b. nearly 75% of African Americans and Native Americans have LI [*NDDIC*]
      c. 90% of Asian Americans are LI
II. Treatment
  A. Children
  B. Adults

III. What to avoid, how to balance nutrition

[look at audience, get A-V materials ready to show]

  A. Avoid or limit these foods [*show poster*] 3
  B. Include these calcium-rich foods [*show chart*]
  C. Calcium needed [*show calcium table*]

[*be sure to show visuals AND talk about them*]
[*Put American Dietetic Association (ADA) and International Foundation for Functional Gastrointestinal Disorders (IFFGD) addresses on overhead*]

All information in the note cards came from National Digestive Diseases Information (NDDK), National Institutes of Health, www.niddk.nih.gov/health/digest/pubs/lactose.htm, "Lactose Intolerance," accessed June 16, 2003.

Summary

Effective organization can help you present a speech that your audience will be able to follow, understand, and appreciate. There is an old anecdote that is often used by speech teachers and business consultants: If you want to get your audience to listen to you, you must tell them what you're going to tell them, tell them, and tell them what you just told them. In other words, you have to have an introduction, a body, and a conclusion. Good speech organization is a skill that carries over into writing papers, giving directions, and other school- and work-related tasks. The body of the speech is where you tell your audience about your topic. There are main points and subpoints, all of which should be constructed in such a way as to tell a logical, coherent, interesting "story." You'll want to make sure you have adequate research material to support and clarify your points.

You can utilize one of seven different patterns of organization in the body of the speech. The choice you make depends on your general and specific purposes and on how you wish to present your ideas. You will need to connect the main points and subpoints in your speech with special organizing strategies. And you need to be sure that you say everything you need to say about the topic in the time you have.

The introduction helps you orient your listeners to your speech content and provides them with reasons to listen. The conclusion summarizes and synthesizes your speech so that listeners remember it.

DISCUSSION STARTERS

1. How can organization help a speaker?
2. How does organization or the lack of it affect listeners?
3. How can you make your ideas more meaningful to your listeners?
4. Why should you learn about different patterns of organization?
5. What does the introduction accomplish?
6. Why is the conclusion every bit as important as the rest of the speech?
7. What do outlines of your speech accomplish?

ANSWERS AND EXPLANATIONS

Making Connections: Ordering Ideas in an Outline (page 237)

One set of possible answers: I. (2), A. (4), B. (8), II. (9), A. (1), B. (5), III. (7), A. (3), B. (6).

NOTES

1. B. E. Gronbeck, R. E. McKerrow, D. Ehninger, and A. H. Monroe, *Principles and Types of Speech Communication,* 14th ed. (Glenview, Ill.: Scott, Foresman/Little, Brown Higher Education, 1999), 180–203.
2. "A New Look at Body Language Cues," *Communication Briefings* (Alexandria, Va.: Communication Briefings, 2003).
3. "Frozen 'Diet' Dinners," *Women's Health Reporter* 4(6) (2003), 1, 7.
4. M. Terletsky, "Strike Back at Stress," *Women's Health Reporter* 4(6) (2003), 4.
5. Lee Iacocca, cited in Glenn Van Ekeren, *Speaker's Sourcebook II* (Englewood Cliffs, NJ: Prentice Hall, 1994), 73.

6. "'Super Diary' Project Could Record Person's Every Move," from the AP Wire Service in (Waterloo-Cedar Falls) *Courier,* 3 June 2003, A1, A5.
7. M. Terletsky, op. cit.
8. "Infections More Widespread as Animals Pass Them On," from *The Washington Post,* in the (Waterloo-Cedar Falls) *Courier,* 16 June 2003, A5.
9. Ibid.
10. Ibid.
11. D. Zarefsky, *Public Speaking Strategies for Success* (Boston: Allyn and Bacon, 2002), 212.
12. Zoonotic, *World Book Dictionary,* Mac OS X Edition Media CD, Version 6.0.2, 2002. Chicago: World Book, Inc.
13. "Infections More Widespread as Animals Pass Them On," op. cit.
14. S. Brink, "Sleepless Society," *U.S. News and World Report,* October 16, 2000, 62.
15. Zarefsky, 240.
16. These outline examples are based on "Development and Uses of Femtosecond Technology: A New Science to Give Us Time," a speech by Brian S. Davis, four-time public speaking champion and University of Northern Iowa graduate student. Used by permission.
17. Kelley A. Lawton and Laura Cousineau, Duke University Libraries, and Van E. Hillard, The University Writing Program, Guide to Library Research, www.lib.duke.edu/libguide/citing.htm (accessed June 16, 2003).

"Through communication competence, individuals are able to integrate themselves with the reality and the reality with themselves."
—Young Yun Kim

CHAPTER 10

Managing Anxiety and Delivering Your Speech

THIS CHAPTER WILL HELP YOU:

- Describe the preparation process for creating effective speeches.
- Explain the importance of ethics in speech preparation.
- Identify vocal and physical factors that contribute to effective delivery.
- Explain the four methods of speech delivery and provide a rationale for how and when each might be used.
- Describe how presentational aids can be used to create an effective speech.
- Demonstrate self-confidence in your presentations.

CASE STUDY

At the beginning of the semester, I ask my students to tell me something they think I really ought to know about them. At least 75 percent indicate that they are very anxious about getting up in front of the class to "give a speech." As the title of this chapter indicates, we learn to *manage* our anxieties not eliminate them. To manage your anxiety, you need to reflect a bit about why you are anxious.

Questions to think about

1. When do you feel anxious?
2. What causes your anxiety?
3. Are there things other than getting up in front of your classmates that make you anxious?
4. What have you done to survive this anxiety in the past?

Presenting speeches is fun. You might not believe that now, but if you have carefully completed all your work up to this point, you, too, may enjoy presenting your thoughts in front of the class. You have researched, organized, and arranged your ideas. Now you can focus on the delivery.

Every speaker should prepare for the speech presentation. If you can, rehearse in the classroom. If not, find a room comparable to the one where you'll give your speech, and practice out loud. If possible, get someone to listen to you and provide you with feedback about both content and delivery. What does this do for you? First, it allows you to know what the speech sounds like. The written word and the spoken word are not always the same and do not have the same effect. Practice helps you hear that. Second, practicing in front of someone provides you with listener response, and you need that to help you make the right choices and to feel more confident about the speech.

Qualities of Effective Speakers

By cultivating certain personal qualities, you can enhance the likelihood that your listeners will accept your message. The most effective speakers are ethical, knowledgeable, prepared, and self-confident.

Ethics

Ethics, an individual's system of moral principles, plays a key role in communication. As speakers, we are responsible for what we tell others. We should always hold the highest ethical standards. We must communicate with honesty, sincerity, and integrity. In addition, a responsible, ethical speaker presents worthwhile and accurate information in a fair manner. Communication scholar David Zarefsky says, "Speech has tremendous power and the person who wields it bears great responsibility . . . both speakers and listeners should seek high standards of ethical conduct.[1]

Ethical speakers do not distort or falsify evidence to misrepresent information, do not make unsupported attacks on opponents in order to discredit them, do not deceive an audience about their intention or objective in an attempt to persuade or take advantage, do not use irrelevant emotional appeals to sensationalize the message and divert attention from the facts, and do not pose as an authority when they are not.[2]

Ethical speakers always cite the sources of their information. Any time you use information and ideas that are not your own, you are obligated to cite the originator or source. The use of another person's information, language, or ideas without citing the originator or author, thus making it appear that you are the originator, is referred to as plagiarism. For example, it is unethical to use statistical data, direct quotations, or any information that you did not originate without giving credit to the originator. Most speeches, unless otherwise specified, require that you as the speaker be the originator of the speech's content. Of course, it is perfectly legitimate to use a reasonable amount of information and ideas from others, as long as you give them credit and cite your sources within the speech.

Avoiding Plagiarism

GUIDELINES

1. Do not rely on a single article as the only source of information for a speech.
2. Avoid using other people's language and ideas.
3. Get information and ideas from a variety of sources, and integrate them into your own thoughts.
4. Cite sources prior to quoting such material—"Dr. Wilson, in her 2003 article on healthy living, stated 'The best. . . .' "
5. Always identify your sources—"*Newsweek* last week indicated that President Bush's tax plan is . . . " or "According to Robert Jones, a leading economist, in the May 29, 2003, *Wall Street Journal,* 'Our economy is. . . .' "
6. Give credit to the originator of the ideas you use—"Fred Keller, an educational psychologist, created the instructional program that we now use in. . . ."

Similarly, listeners are also responsible for determining the truth. We expect speakers to be ethical, but as listeners we must be willing to verify the information we receive to ensure that it is accurate and valid. Zarefsky states, "Above all, listeners have the responsibility to think critically about the speech. . . . Do not reject or refuse to consider the speaker's message simply because it differs from what you already believe. Assess the speech carefully to decide whether it merits your support."[3] (See Chapter 6 for a discussion of the responsibilities of the listener.)

Knowledge

Knowledge is a speaker's greatest asset. Knowing your subject is essential if you plan to "reach" your listeners. Noted speakers are almost always avid readers. To enhance your understanding of events, people, and values, you must read and observe things around you. From experience, you know that it is easier to talk about things you are familiar with than those you are not. Many colleges, universities, and businesses have identified the characteristics of an "educated person." As an educated person, you should not only know about past international, national, regional, and local events, but also keep abreast of current events. You should read all kinds of books, at least one trade (professional) magazine, and one daily newspaper, in addition to listening to news broadcasts and documentaries.

In Chapter 8, we explained the importance of completing adequate research. You might have considerable knowledge about a topic, but you still need to complete careful research to add to that information base. Most instructors have minimum requirements for sources, both numbers and types. Sometimes students think they don't have to do much research. From many years of

Making Connections

The Ethics of Speaking

June presented an interesting speech about acupuncture as a healing process. June has never had acupuncture treatments, nor has she actually interviewed an acupuncturist. Her major source of information is the website of a person who practices acupuncture. June has not learned anything about the person's training or background. She did find a brief description and explanation from the latest online Encyclopedia Britannica.

1. Is June in violation of the ethics of public speaking? If so, how?
2. What does June need to do to make sure she is ethical in this speech?
3. Where can she get additional information to create an effective, ethical speech?

Know Your Scholar

David Zarefsky *Northwestern University*

David Zarefsky is Owen L. Coon Professor of Argumentation and Debate and Professor of Communication Studies at Northwestern University, where he served as Dean of the School of Speech from 1988 through June 2000.

Zarefsky's research and teaching are in the areas of rhetorical history and criticism, argumentation and debate, and forensics. He is the author, co-author, or editor of eight books and the author of over fifty articles in professional journals. Two of his books have won the Winans-Wichelns Award for Distinguished Scholarship in Rhetoric and Public Address, an award of the National Communication Association: *President Johnson's War on Poverty: Rhetoric and History* (University of Alabama Press, 1986) and *Lincoln, Douglas, and Slavery: In the Crucible of Public Debate* (University of Chicago Press, 1990). He is one of only three individuals to have won this award twice. In 1994, he was named to the ranks of NCA Distinguished Scholars. He also has twice won the Best Article Award from the Southern States Communication Association.

At Northwestern, Zarefsky has taught courses in the study of American public discourse, with a special focus on the pre–Civil War years and on the 1960s. He also has taught courses in argumentation theory, persuasion, and public speaking. On thirteen different occasions, he was named to the student government's honor roll for distinguished teaching. Zarefsky also has two videocourses, "Abraham Lincoln: In His Own Words" and "Argumentation: The Study of Effective Reasoning," marketed by The Teaching Company.

In 1993, Zarefsky was President of the National Communication Association, and in 2001, he received its Distinguished Service Award. He held the presidency of the Central States Communication Association in 1986–87. He has held numerous other positions in both those organizations and in the American Forensic Association, whose journal he edited from 1977 to 1980. From 1984 to 1989, he was the Director of the National Debate Tournament. He is currently the NCA delegate to the American Council of Learned Societies and a member of the Board of Directors of the Rhetoric Society of America. From 1997 to 2001, he was on the National Advisory Council and the Steering Committee for the Center for Presidential Studies in the George Bush School of Government and Public Service at Texas A&M University.

listening to speeches and receiving class members' responses, I can tell you that more research is always required! The more you do, the better your speech will be. Speeches require the same kind of diligent preparation as exams. If you want to establish yourself as a knowledgeable person, you will gather more information than you could possibly use in your speech. Why? So that you have a solid foundation for your speech and so that you can answer questions your listeners might ask. Effective speakers do not limit their research, nor do they present superficial speeches. Competent communicators make sure they have a strong knowledge base for all presentations.

Preparation

People rarely make speeches without at least some preparation, and the most successful speakers are very well prepared. Poet Maya Angelou often makes speeches and gives poetry readings at colleges, universities, and other venues across the country. Angelou visited our respective campuses during September 2000. In her speech, she discussed her preparation for the presentation. Her remarks included references to planning and practicing the entire presentation well in advance of her scheduled ap-

Making Connections

Citing Your Sources

Dussadee had to give a speech about communication similarities or differences in the United States and her own culture, Thailand. She was concerned that many of the ideas she was sharing were not quotations from other sources, and she would not have very many oral footnotes. Her teacher told her that personal experience speeches do not require as many outside sources because the information should come from the students' own lives. When should we seek out other sources? Where do we look for good sources? What kinds of experiences might go into a personal experience speech? How does a speaker let the listeners know that these are personal experiences?

pearances. She indicated that the prior preparation and practice allowed her to respond to the situation and the listeners much more freely than if she had not prepared in advance.

A successful speech is somewhat like a successful business meeting or athletic event—all require planning, preparation, and work. Preparation means more than practicing the speech ahead of time. It also means that speakers will think through the situation and possible snags or problems. In the example in the previous paragraph, we mentioned that Maya Angelou carefully prepared herself before her presentations. Her preparation included not only practice but also a process of thinking through all possible audience responses so that she could effectively handle questions.

Wil Linkugel, a retired professor of speech communication at the University of Kansas, told this story, which illustrates the importance of practice:

> A student athlete was delivering a speech to the class. The student, speaking in a monotone voice, kept reading from a prepared script. Finally, Professor Linkugel interrupted the student.
>
> *Professor:* Why don't you put down your notes and just tell us what your notes say?
>
> *Student:* I can't do that. I'll never get it right.
>
> *Professor:* Let's see what you can do.
>
> The student tried speaking without his notes, but the result, although greatly improved, left much to be desired.
>
> *Student:* I'll never do this right!
>
> *Professor:* In football practice, if you were running a pass pattern and you didn't do it right, what would your coach make you do?
>
> *Student:* We'd run it over again.
>
> *Professor:* How many times would you run it over?
>
> *Student:* As many times as it would take to get it right.

What message was Professor Linkugel trying to get across to the student? Is there a message in the story for you? Whether playing football or delivering a speech, for the beginner as well as the experienced speaker, preparation, practice, and knowledge of the fundamentals are important. Remember, however, that you don't want to practice so much that your speech sounds memorized or "canned." Effective speakers should

A good speech depends on good delivery, and good delivery almost always depends on practice. After organizing and writing a speech, present the speech out loud to a friend in an informal setting or in front of a mirror. Make changes, if necessary, to make the speech more effective.

sound conversational, not mechanical. Too much practice can make you lose the spark of spontaneity and reduce your effectiveness.

Self-Confidence

Self-confidence, or the belief in oneself, is so essential to becoming an effective speaker that much of this book's content is aimed at helping you strengthen this quality. Refer back to the information in Chapter 3 to make the associations between self-image, self-concept, self-confidence, and a variety of communication situations. Because self-confidence is so strongly influenced by anxiety, we discuss this problem in detail.

Managing Speech Anxiety

The *World Book Encyclopedia/Dictionary* defines *anxiety* as "uneasy thoughts or fears about what may happen; troubled, worried, or uneasy feeling."[4] If you experience the fear of speaking before an audience—a condition known as **speech anxiety,** or stage fright—it might help to know that you are not alone. It is perfectly normal to encounter some anxiety before, during, and sometimes even after a speech. In fact, even the most experienced speakers confess to having some anxiety about speaking before a group. What should you know about stage fright? This question, for some teachers of public speaking, is controversial. If the subject is presented, will the mere mention of anxiety create unnecessary anxiety in the speaker? That is, will the discussion of stage fright bring out more anxiety in speakers than they would experience if it had never been mentioned at all? There is no evidence to suggest that discussing stage fright increases or decreases it, but it is commonly accepted that the more we know about stage fright and how to cope with it, the better able we are to *control* it.

speech anxiety
Fear of speaking before an audience.

Communication apprehension and speech anxiety are two of the most researched areas in communication. One of the reasons is that speaking in front of others is identified as people's greatest fear.[5] You should keep in mind that anxiety is normal. Most of us have some degree of anxiety when we speak in front of others. Anxiety is only a problem when we cannot control it or when we choose not to communicate because of it.

Communication Apprehension

Communication apprehension, the most severe form of speech anxiety, was defined in Chapter 3 as anxiety syndrome associated with either real or anticipated communication with another person or persons.[6] Communication apprehension can be seen in individuals who either consciously or subconsciously have decided to remain silent. They perceive that their silence offers them greater advantages than speaking out, or that the disadvantages of communicating outweigh any potential gains they might receive. Communication apprehensive individuals fear speaking in all contexts, including one-on-one communication and small-group discussions. Among the fears of those with communication apprehension is that of speaking before a group. However, not everyone who fears speaking before a group necessarily suffers from communication apprehension. That term refers to the much deeper problem of virtually cutting oneself off from most, if not all, communication with others.

Symptoms of Speech Anxiety

Speech anxiety refers more specifically to the fear of speaking before a group. Anxiety is a condition during which our bodies secrete hormones and adrenaline that eventually overload our physical and emotional responses. These chemical reactions are the same as those you might experience when you are waiting to see a friend you haven't seen in years or going to your first job interview. Your heart begins to beat faster, and your blood pressure begins to rise. More sugar is pumped into your system, and your stomach might begin to churn. When you experience these reactions, you may feel as if your body is operating in high gear and that little or nothing can be done about it. You have to realize that some of these feelings are perfectly normal and, for most us, will not interfere with our speech performance.

Speakers who experience speech anxiety often display the visible signs listed in Table 10.1. These behaviors can occur separately or in any combination, depending on the degree of anxiety the speaker is experiencing.

Speakers who experience speech anxiety may also make telling statements. For example, they may offer self-critical excuses or apologies such as "I'm not any good at

> **Making Connections**
>
> **Communication Apprehension**
>
> What happens to you when you have to give a speech or are expected to contribute in a group discussion? Do you look forward to it, or are you afraid to make your presentation or even to speak up? When you give a speech, do you forget things? Do you feel tense and nervous? James McCroskey has extensively researched communication apprehension. Those who teach special speech anxiety sections suggest that the first step in learning to manage your anxiety is to recognize it. Then try some deep abdominal breathing before speaking or contributing in a group. If you breathe deeply and concentrate on your breathing, you are unable to think about your nervousness, and that nervousness tends to subside.[7] Check the Notes section for a specific source that can provide helpful strategies.[8]

TABLE 10.1

Behaviors Associated with Speech Anxiety

Voice	Quivering, too soft, monotonous, too fast, nonemphatic
Fluency	Stammering, halting, awkward pauses, hunting for words, speech blocks
Mouth and throat	Breathing heavily, clearing throat often, swallowing repeatedly
Facial expressions	No eye contact, rolling eyes, tense facial muscles, grimaces, twitches
Arms and hands	Rigid and tense, fidgeting, waving hands
Body movement	Swaying, pacing, shuffling feet, weight shifts
Nonvisible Symptoms	Feeling too warm, too much saliva, dry mouth, butterflies in the stomach

Adapted from A. Mulac and A. R. Sherman, "Behavior Assessment of Speech Anxiety," *Quarterly Journal of Speech* 60, 2 (April 1974): 138.

this anyway," "I didn't really prepare for this because I didn't have enough time," or "I never was able to say this correctly." Instead of improving the situation, these comments tend to draw more attention to speakers' nervousness and thus magnify the problem.

Speakers who have speech anxiety often overestimate how much the audience notices about their behavior. The audience, for their part, tends to underestimate a speaker's anxiety. For example, audiences cannot detect a speaker who is experiencing butterflies unless the butterflies cause an observable reaction or the speaker's voice sounds nervous.

Causes of Speech Anxiety

Just as physicians can better treat an illness if they know its cause, people can better reduce and control speech anxiety if they can determine the underlying problem. Many people with speech anxiety treat only the symptoms and tend to ignore the causes, but trying to remove the symptoms without understanding the causes is usually a losing battle.

Severe speech anxiety begins at an early age as a result of negative feedback in the home. For example, children who are not encouraged to communicate or are punished for doing so are likely to learn that communicating is undesirable and that silence is beneficial. As these children avoid communicating, others may unknowingly contribute further to their fear by asking questions such as "Cat got your tongue?" or "You're afraid to talk, aren't you?" Such words can make the anxious children feel inadequate and thus perpetuate the fear and anxiety associated with communicating.

People may also develop speech anxiety if they constantly hear that speaking in front of others can be a terrible experience. Being told immediately before giving a speech, "Don't worry about it—you'll do fine," reinforces the notion that something can go wrong. If speakers believe that something can go wrong and that they might make fools of themselves, they are apt to lose confidence and develop speech anxiety.

In our society, success, winning, and "being number one" are too often considered all-important. When we can't be the most successful, we sometimes consider ourselves failures. No one likes to fail. Therefore we are apt to feel that success brings rewards and failure brings punishment. If you are a winner, you are praised; if you are a loser, you are ridiculed. As a result, we place tremendous pressure on ourselves and others to be successful.

When we haven't been successful at something, we are often told to try again. But if the consequences of the failure are dramatic and the payoff for success doesn't seem worth the effort, we may prefer to avoid the situation. Avoidance may result in punishment, but we may perceive that as better than trying to do something and failing. Sometimes society is more lenient. For example, in a competition we assume that there will be a winner and a loser. No one likes to lose, but playing your best and losing is often acceptable. When someone makes a mistake in a speech, however, we may be more critical. Rather than acknowledging that the person is making an honest effort, we might perceive him or her as inadequate or unskilled. Consequently, the stress created by fear of making mistakes in front of others can be so great that it produces anxiety and sometimes complete avoidance of speaking situations. Among the other most common causes of speech anxiety are the following:

Fear of physical unattractiveness
Fear of social inadequacy
Fear of criticism
Fear of the unknown
Fear of speech anxiety
Conflicting emotions
Excitement from anticipation[9]

We learn to respond in specific ways when facing something that creates anxiety because we have become conditioned to do so. Each of these common reactions to a speech-making situation is *learned.* Because speech anxiety is a learned behavior, the only solution for its sufferers is to examine the potential reasons for the anxiety and learn how to use this knowledge to manage the discomfort.

Speech Anxiety and Other Cultures

Every year, increasing numbers of international students and Americans whose first language is not English enter higher education in the United States. In spite of their differences, most of these students do not ask to be treated any differently than anyone else. But because of the language and cultural differences these students have experienced, they do deserve understanding and patience as they communicate with U.S. students. In a study of Asian students, Ester Yook and Bill Seiler found that most were anxious about presenting speeches. They were concerned about whether they would be understood by their audience because of their accent, tone, and pronunciation.[10] They were also concerned that if they were unable to "think in English," they might not be able to find the right word or expression needed on the spot, resulting in a humiliating experience.

Another source of anxiety for Asian students, according to Yook and Seiler, occurs because they sometimes have difficulty understanding the speech assignment fully. The potential for misunderstanding the assignment and their perceived lack of English fluency lead many Asian students to memorize their speeches. The memorization, however, prevents many Asian students from being conversational in style and adds to their perceived ineffectiveness and anxiety as communicators. Communicating in front of others creates some anxiety for most of us, but being from a different culture and speaking English as a second language can create additional stress.

Native Americans represent another group who have more anxiety when speaking because of cultural differences. In the Native American culture, eye contact is limited. In speaking situations in the dominant culture, eye contact is expected. Native American students explain that they feel even more uncomfortable when they are reminded that eye contact is critical. Those from different cultural and language backgrounds want their situations to be understood.

Treating Speech Anxiety

Although speaking before a group can produce stress and anxiety, few people allow their nervousness to prevent them from trying and succeeding.[11] In fact, as mentioned earlier, even well-known speakers feel some nervousness before giving a speech, but they have learned to *control* it. The key to successful control of your anxiety is the desire to control it. To cope with speech anxiety, we must realize that the potential for failure always exists, but that we can't let it stop us from trying. If we allowed the possibility of failure to overwhelm us, we probably would never do or learn anything. A child beginning to walk is a prime example of how most of our learning occurs. At first, the child wobbles, takes a small step, and falls. But when the child falls, someone is usually there to offer help, support, and encouragement to continue. In addition, the child usually is determined to walk regardless of the difficulties. Speech making, like learning to walk, involves many of the same processes. Help, support, and encouragement are important, but the essential ingredient is determination to succeed.

Most successful people will tell you that before they were successful, they had some failures and moments of embarrassment. Their drive and self-confidence pushed them to try again. Some of our first speeches were not very good, and we were quite nervous about speaking in front of our classmates. However, it didn't take us long to realize that even the best speakers in the class felt the same way. The only difference was that they weren't afraid to make a mistake.

Many of us are too hard on ourselves. Some students, after giving a speech, will say that they were extremely nervous, though the audience detected no signs of nervousness. To the audience, the speaker appeared relaxed and in control.

There are no cures for speech anxiety—only ways to reduce, manage, or control it so that it does not interfere with your presentation. Experts suggest several guidelines to help you reduce your anxieties:

1. *Select a topic you enjoy and know.* The more you know about a subject, the easier it will be for you to talk about it. According to one research study, people who are highly anxious tend to be more negative in their assessments of themselves and more concerned with what others think of them. In addition, they tend to choose unfamiliar speech topics, which compounds their problem.[12] Sometimes, however, it is not possible to choose your own topic. In business settings, for example, we are often required to report information for specific situations in which the topic is selected by the circumstances. In this case, the speaker must work harder to have adequate information and to focus on accomplishing what is necessary for that situation.

2. *Be prepared.* Because anxious people are more negative in their self-assessments, they tend to spend less time preparing, convinced they are not going to succeed no matter what they do. Thus, they set themselves up for failure, which perpetuates the cycle of anxiety and failure. Preparation can break the cycle. Know your audience and become familiar with the physical surroundings in which you are going to speak (such as the room size, lighting, placement of microphone, and audiovisual equipment). This will help create confidence by reducing the unknown. In Chapter 9, we advised you that carefully organizing your speech will help you be more effective. The work you put into research, organization, and practice will also help you be more confident.

3. *Be confident.* Confidence plays a key role in controlling anxiety. We are often amazed at how many students sell themselves short. We have heard many student speakers over the years, and each of them had the ability and potential skill to be an effective speaker. Students who didn't believe that they could be successful seemed to have the most difficulty giving speeches. We have also had students who were extremely quiet in class, but when it came to speaking, they were exceptional. One student who seldom talked in class was asked how she felt after her speech, and she indicated that she was surprised at how good she felt. The first minute or so, she was nervous, she said, but once she realized that she knew what she was talking about and the audience appeared to be listening, she completely forgot about her nervousness and concentrated on informing her audience. You only have to try. Even if you do not do as well as you would like, the instructor is there to help you and your classmates and wants you to do well.

4. *Think positively.* Visualize yourself giving a successful speech. Some students tell us it is easy to think positively but it doesn't help them give a successful speech. We disagree. Positive thought does work. There is ample proof to suggest that those who think positively and visualize themselves doing well often surpass their own expectations. Thinking that you are going to do poorly, however, is a sure path to failure.

5. *Practice.* The better you know the content of your speech and your delivery plan, the more comfortable you will feel about your presentation. Few things are done well without some practice. For example, the quarterback who executes a perfect touchdown pass, the gymnast who scores a 10 in floor exercise, the actor who presents a flawless performance, the student who draws beautiful pictures, the person who passes the road test for a driver's license, and the person who gives a polished and interesting speech have spent hours—and sometimes years—in practice. Knowing that you don't have weeks, months, or years to practice your speech, you must practice as much as you can with the realization that you may not perfect all aspects of your speech. Remember that almost all speakers are somewhat nervous before a speech and that nervousness is perfectly normal.

Giving a speech and completing a pass play in a football game are not the same thing, but both require similar preparation. The successful pass play requires research, organization, learning, observation, practice, willingness to work hard, ability to perform, confidence, knowing your opponent's defenses (or knowing your audience), and timing. A successful speech presentation requires all of the aforementioned factors in addition to selecting an appropriate topic.

GUIDELINES Controlling Speech Anxiety

1. Realize that almost everyone has some anxiety about presenting a speech. You are not alone.
2. Select a topic that you are familiar with and that you enjoy, if possible.
3. Know your audience and the surroundings in which your presentation will take place.
4. Think positively. Prepare yourself mentally for success. Believe that you are going to be successful, and you probably will be.
5. Practice, practice, and then practice more!
6. Ask your instructor for additional advice and other possible treatment programs that may be available.
7. Don't give up. Others want you to succeed, and you can if that is what you want.

If none of the strategies in the accompanying Guidelines feature help to reduce your anxiety, then you should probably seek professional help. Individuals who suffer from abnormal levels of speech anxiety should know that the negative feelings associated with communicating in front of others do not simply occur; they develop over a long period of time. Therefore these negative feelings do not always disappear easily. But speech anxiety is a problem that we can do something about with help. Most university settings have psychologists or counselors who are trained to reduce the fear of speaking in public. Some colleges offer special sections of the beginning communication course for those who are anxious about speaking in front of others.

Systematic desensitization is a relaxation technique designed to reduce the tenseness associated with anxiety.[13] The goal is to help you develop a new, relaxed response to the anxiety-provoking event. Try this. Imagine yourself standing in front of this class, ready to give your speech. Visualize the wonderful speech you will give. You confidently place your notes on the lectern, look at the audience, smile, take a deep breath, and begin speaking. Your audience smiles and nods throughout the speech, and you become more and more relaxed as you speak. When you finish, they applaud loudly. Someone says, "That was a wonderful speech!" Remember how if felt to be so relaxed. Go through this visualization process, and think about how relaxed you are. This kind of mental rehearsal helps you change negative thoughts to positive ones.

Overcoming anxiety in public speaking situations is not easy, but you must remember that some anxiety can be helpful and is a normal reaction to speaking in public. When we asked students how they dealt with their fear of speaking, they suggested the following:

systematic desensitization
A relaxation technique designed to reduce the tenseness associated with anxiety.

1. Practice, and have your introduction, main points, and conclusion clear in your mind. Students believe that once they know their introductions, main points, and conclusions, it is a lot easier to remember the details.
2. Walk confidently to the speaking area. Students believe that this helps create confidence. If you're confident, it is likely you will feel relaxed. In other words, positive behavior results in positive outcomes.

Making Connections

Anxiety and You

Your nervousness does not have to control you. You can control it. But you must learn to control your thoughts about anxiety. One of our students (Scott Gordon) wrote a poem, "Ode to Nervousness," to share with his classmates. In the poem, Scott says that he is very anxious about presenting his speech. His heart is beating rapidly, he is shaking, and his palms are sweating. By the end of the speech, however, he feels good about himself and his speech.

1. Have you ever had that kind of experience?
2. What caused your feelings to change?

3. Do not start your speech until you are ready. The students suggest that having everything under control before you start to speak makes it easier to relax and concentrate on the speech, rather than on yourself.
4. Look at your audience, and focus most of the time on friendly faces. Students believe that concentrating on those who are likely to give positive feedback will help to promote a good feeling about speaking.

These suggestions are probably not new, and they are not surprising, but they will help in your quest to become a successful speaker. The best thing you can do is continue to give speeches in class and take more classes that will afford opportunities to speak under the supervision of a trained instructor. You can reduce and control your fear of speaking, but you must make that happen by acting on the guidelines we have provided here.

Learning Connections

1. What do you do to overcome your anxiety in other situations (exams, athletic competitions, concerts, reading aloud in your religious worship services)?
2. Why are you anxious?
3. How can you learn to think about something other than your anxieties?

Methods of Delivery

An effective delivery conveys the speaker's purpose and ideas clearly and interestingly so that the audience attends to and retains what was said as it was intended by the speaker. The effectiveness of a speech therefore depends both on what is said and how it is conveyed. No two speakers are alike. For example, it is unlikely that anyone could deliver the "I Have a Dream" speech as effectively as Martin Luther King, Jr., did. This speech, widely regarded as a masterpiece, was delivered on August 28, 1963, to more than 200,000 people gathered in Washington, D.C., to participate in a peaceful demonstration furthering the cause of equal rights for African Americans. If you have heard a recording of this speech, you know how King's delivery affected his audience. He had a rich baritone voice modulated by the cadences of a Southern Baptist preacher and the fervor of a crusader. Although the words of the speech can be repeated and King's style can be imitated, the setting, timing, and circumstances cannot be reconstructed. Therefore the effect that King had on that day can never be repeated.

A poorly written speech can be improved by effective delivery, and a well-written speech can be ruined by ineffective delivery. No set of rules will guarantee an effective delivery in every situation. The only consistent rule is that you must be yourself! Of course, as a beginning speaker, you probably have many questions about how to deliver a speech: How many notes should I use? Will I need a microphone? Where and how should I stand? Where or at whom should I look? How many and what kinds of gestures should I use? How and when should I use my visual aids? How loudly should I speak? How fast or slow should my speaking be?

Such questions are valid, but the answers will vary from person to person and from situation to situation. In the end, effective delivery comes from practice under the direction of a competent instructor. An awareness of self and knowledge of effective delivery also help to improve delivery. Although a speech may be delivered in many different ways, the four most common methods of delivery are impromptu, manuscript, memorized, and extemporaneous (see Table 10.2).

TABLE 10.2

Methods of Delivery: Advantages and Disadvantages

	ADVANTAGES	DISADVANTAGES
Impromptu	Spontaneous Flexible Conversational	No time for preparation Can be inaccurate Difficult to organize Can be stressful
Manuscript	Good for material that is technical or detailed or that requires complete preciseness High accuracy Can be timed to the second Prepared	No flexibility Great amount of preparation time Difficult to adapt to audience response May sound mechanical Lack of eye contact
Memorized	Good for short speeches Speaker can concentrate on delivery Easier to maintain eye contact Prepared	Inflexible Requires practice and repetition Speaker can forget or lose place Difficult to adapt to audience response May sound mechanical
Extemporaneous	Organized Flexible Conversational Prepared Great amount of eye contact	May be intimidating to inexperienced speakers

Impromptu Delivery

The delivery of a speech with little or no formal planning or preparation (no research, no organization) is called **impromptu delivery.** You have used this method many times, perhaps without even realizing it. Whenever you speak without prior preparation, whether in response to a question in class, to a sudden request at a business meeting, or to a comment made by a friend, you are using the impromptu method of delivery. The more formal or demanding the situation, the more most speakers prefer to avoid this approach. At times, however, you have no choice. In such cases, muster your self-control, relax, and concentrate on what you wish to say. The lack of preparation time distinguishes the impromptu method from other methods of delivery and forces speakers to depend solely on their ability to think on their feet.

Manuscript Delivery

Reading the speech word for word is known as **manuscript delivery.** Speakers who use this method are never at a loss for words. A speaker should use a manuscript for situations in which every word, phrase, and sentence must be stated precisely. Using a manuscript is not uncommon for politicians, clergy, teachers, and others who need to present information completely and accurately or who are likely to be quoted after their presentations. But in learning how to give a speech, manuscript delivery is often discouraged, because it invites the speaker to concentrate more on the script than the audience and reduces eye contact with the audience. Also, speakers who work from manuscripts are less able to adapt to the reactions of the audience and thus may sound mechanical. They are so busy concentrating on reading the speech that they may be unable to respond to their listeners.

impromptu delivery
A delivery style in which a speaker delivers a speech with little or no planning or preparation.

manuscript delivery
A delivery style in which a speaker writes the speech in its entirety and then reads it word for word.

Manuscript Delivery

GUIDELINES

1. *Write your manuscript for the ear.* There is a difference between content written to be read silently and that to be read aloud. The silent reader can go back to a previous sentence for reference and can reread a passage if it is unclear the first time, but a person listening to a speech cannot. Be listener oriented.
2. *Prepare your manuscript in an easy-to-read format.* Type it triple-spaced. Use special marks and comments to point out areas you plan to emphasize.
3. *Think about what you are saying.* The presence of a manuscript often tempts a speaker to read words instead of thoughts. Try to sound spontaneous and give meaning to the manuscript.
4. *Read with expression and vocal emphasis.* Remember that your voice can add meaning to the words. Thus the expressive use of your voice becomes an added dimension to the reading of the words.
5. *Practice reading out loud,* preferably with a tape recorder. The key to success is to sound as if the thoughts you are reading are fresh. The manuscript should be presented with enthusiasm, vigor, and interest.[14]

memorized delivery
A delivery style in which a speaker memorizes a speech in its entirety from a word-for-word script.

Memorized Delivery

Memorized delivery requires that you memorize your speech in its entirety, usually from a word-for-word script. This kind of delivery is used for short presentations, such as toasts, acceptance speeches, and introductions, and is also commonly used by speakers in contests and on lecture circuits. Speakers frequently memorize certain parts of their speeches, including examples, short stories, statistics, quotations, and other materials that they can call up at the appropriate time. Politicians, salespeople, tour guides, and others often have a memorized pitch, or speech, to fit their needs.

Memorization has one advantage. You can concentrate less on what you have to say and focus more on your delivery. Of course, this is true only if you are extremely confident and have memorized your speech so completely that you don't need to think about each word. One disadvantage of memorized delivery is its lack of flexibility; it doesn't allow for much, if any, adaptation to your audience. Beginning speakers face another disadvantage: They might forget what they want to say and become embarrassed. In addition, it is difficult to deliver a memorized speech without sounding mechanical. Effective presentation of a memorized address requires a great deal of practice and confidence. The Guidelines feature about manuscript delivery applies equally to memorized delivery.

Extemporaneous Delivery

In **extemporaneous delivery,** the speaker uses a carefully prepared and researched speech but delivers it from notes, with a high degree of spontaneity. Extemporaneous delivery is the method that is most commonly used in speech classrooms and in other public communication situations. When you give a report at work, for example, you will probably be expected to present your remarks extemporaneously. If you are a member of a problem-solving group at your place of worship and you have been selected to present the group's deliberations, you will also be expected to deliver your remarks in an extemporaneous manner. Instructors often require extemporaneous delivery in the communication classroom because it is the best style for most instances of public speaking.

Extemporaneous delivery is situated somewhere between memorized or manuscript delivery and impromptu delivery. Speakers depend on a brief presentational outline or notes and choose the actual wording of the speech at the time of delivery. (See Chapter 9 for a discussion of presentational outlines.) Speakers sometimes prefer to use a key word outline, which simply outlines the points and subpoints of the speech using key words. This helps keep the speaker organized and on track but does not allow the speaker to become too reliant on the outline or notes.

Learning Connections

1. Why do your instructors require extemporaneous delivery?
2. What are the advantages? Disadvantages?
3. How can extemporaneous delivery help the speaker and the listeners?

An extemporaneous speech might at first seem as difficult as an impromptu speech, but, in fact, it is much easier. Because it eliminates memorization and manuscript writing, it leaves more time for preparation and practice. Thus once you have prepared your outline, you can begin to practice your delivery. The goal of the extemporaneous method is a conversational and spontaneous quality. Conversationality and spontaneity are two hallmarks of speech delivery that listeners find appealing. It is much easier to listen to and attend to speakers who are conversational, lively, and spontaneous. Each time you practice your speech, the wording should be somewhat different, although the content remains the same. Your objective should always be to use delivery to help you share meaningful ideas with your audience.

extemporaneous delivery
A delivery style in which the speaker carefully prepares the speech in advance but delivers it using only a few notes and with a high degree of spontaneity.

These are the advantages of extemporaneous delivery: It gives you better control of your presentation than the impromptu method, it allows more spontaneity and directness than the memorized and manuscript methods of delivery, and it is more

The speaker here is using an extemporaneous delivery, a carefully prepared and researched speech, but delivers it from notes with a high degree of spontaneity.

adaptable to a variety of speaking situations than the other methods. Most teachers, as well as professional speakers, prefer to use the extemporaneous method because it allows them to adjust to the situation moment by moment. Extemporaneous delivery also allows audience members to become more involved in listening to the message.

Vocal and Physical Aspects of Delivery

Without solid content and valid sources, nothing is worth communicating; but without effective delivery, even the most compelling information cannot be clearly and vividly presented. Because the audience is the ultimate judge of effectiveness, you must deliver your speech well to involve them in your speech. Each audience member likes to feel as if he or she is being addressed personally. Try to think of your presentation as a conversation and your audience as your partners in dialogue. Then use your voice and body to create this impression.

Vocal Aspects

Many beginning speakers overlook the important role that voice plays in delivery. As you speak, your voice should be pleasant to listen to, relate easily and clearly to your thoughts, and express a range of emotions. Your voice should convey the meaning to your listeners that you wish to convey. The more natural, spontaneous, and effortless you appear to be, regardless of how hard you are working, the more your listener can focus on what you are saying rather than how you are saying it. Three aspects of voice that determine the effectiveness of delivery are vocal quality, intelligibility, and vocal variety.

vocal quality The overall impression a speaker's voice makes on his or her listeners.

Vocal Quality. The overall impression a speaker's voice makes on listeners is referred to as **vocal quality.** Voices may be harsh, nasal, thin, mellow, resonant, or full-bodied. Attitude can affect the quality of the voice and reveal to listeners whether the speaker is happy, confident, angry, fearful, or sad. Think about those times when you were extremely tired: How does your voice sound? Can you hide your tiredness from people listening to you? Probably not. Think about times when you were really excited about a topic. How do you think you sounded to your listeners? Generally, when we're really involved and interested in something, the voice carries energy and excitement that draws others into the conversation. Vocal quality is a highly accurate indicator of the presenter's sincerity. Also, listeners tend to believe speakers whose vocal delivery is interesting and easy to listen to are more credible speakers and will probably be more willing to listen to speakers who use their voices effectively.

Intelligibility. A speaker's **intelligibility,** the degree to which an audience can hear and understand words, is determined by vocal volume; distinctiveness of sound; accuracy of pronunciation; articulation; and stress placed on syllables, words, and phrases. The keys to high intelligibility are self-awareness and consideration for listeners.

To determine the proper volume, consider the size of the room, and observe listeners' reactions. Do listeners look as if they're straining to hear you? Or is your voice too loud or booming for the size of the room?

We have all been known to mispronounce words. For example, a common word like *February* is often mispronounced as *Feb-u-ary.* Sometimes we mispronounce words out of habit, incorrect learning, or a regionalism. For example, many people pronounce *realtor* as *re-la-tor* instead of *real-tor.* When we mispronounce words, we lower our intelligibility and also run the risk of lowering our credibility. Speakers often drop off word endings, which makes it difficult to understand what is being said; the dropping of the *g* from words ending in *ing,* for example, makes it difficult for persons from other cultures to understand the words. Saying "I'm gonna tell you about . . . " instead of "I'm going to tell you about . . . " also may result in a loss of credibility. Effective speakers need to make sure that the words they use are clearly spoken, correctly used, and understandable. Always check a pronunciation dictionary for the most accurate pronunciations.

Grammatical correctness is an important consideration. Not only is the classroom teacher bothered by incorrect grammar and inappropriate use of words, but also in the world outside the classroom, we are judged by the way we present our ideas. This suggests that before we present a speech, we should practice it before a friend or colleague who might detect our errors, dropped sounds, grammatically incorrect words, and mispronunciations.

There is a difference, however, between mispronounced words and regional and ethnic dialects that affect pronunciation. The effect dialect has on an audience depends a great deal on the makeup of the audience and whether or not they understand the difference between dialect usage and standard pronunciation of words. Speakers should always strive to learn similarities and differences between their own dialects and those of others and adapt their messages to the situation. An African American student who uses Ebonics when speaking with friends, for example, needs to adjust language in the classroom and the workplace so that he or she can be easily understood by listeners.

intelligibility
Speaker's vocal volume, distinctiveness of sound, clarity of pronunciation, articulation, and stress placed on syllables, words, and phrases.

Good articulation involves producing and saying words clearly and distinctly. Physical problems, such as cleft palate, difficulty in controlling the tongue, or a misaligned jaw, can create articulation problems that require specialized help, but most articulation problems result from laziness. We sometimes chop, slur, or mumble words because we do not take the time to learn the words correctly. People say "gonna" instead of "going to," "didja" instead of "did you," or "dunno" instead of "don't know." Such articulation errors often result from habit and sloppiness rather than ignorance of what is correct.

Unfortunately, many people don't realize that their articulation is sloppy or incorrect unless someone tells them. Listen to what you say and how you sound. Concentrate on identifying and eliminating your most common articulation errors. Correcting articulation errors can be well worth the effort; you will sound more intelligent and more professional, and you will further establish your credibility as an educated person.

We need to make two more points about intelligibility. Avoid fillers and vocal pauses, which clutter speeches. Fillers such as "um," "uh," "ah," "and uh," "like," and, "you know" can become both distracting and irritating to your listeners. Most communication instructors will note (and probably reduce your grade) when your speech has too many vocal fillers. The second point refers to the use of appropriate language. Adjust your language to suit the formal presentation. Just as you would not speak to your grandmother or a religious leader in the same way you speak with a group of your friends, you need to acknowledge the formality of the speaking situation by using appropriate language. Do not use slang terms or profanity, and do not use language and sentence structure that reduce your credibility. If you're not sure about what is and is not appropriate, check with your instructor.

Making Connections

Speaking Well

Have you ever really listened to a radio or television personality? How do they sound? We have a friend who spent twenty-seven years as an on-air radio announcer. When he speaks, he is very clear, he does not drop end sounds, and his voice is naturally animated. He is an interesting conversationalist. And you never hear fillers such as "um," or "uh," or "like," or "you know" when he speaks. In your next class session, listen to your classmates.

1. What effect do those fillers have on you?
2. Is there someone who uses "like" often?
3. Are you distracted by that? If so, why?

Making Connections

Use of Pauses

Read the following (aloud) without a pause.

Adam said that he had a fear of public speaking and he said getting up in front of people is much more frightening than the thought of death or even taxes and he hoped he would be able to avoid giving speeches even though he had to take an oral communication class.

Now read the same sentences and pause appropriately with periods and commas.

Adam said that he had a fear of public speaking. He said, "Getting up in front of people is much more frightening than the thought of death, or even taxes." And he hoped he would be able to avoid giving speeches, even though he had to take an oral communication class.

1. What difference do the pauses make in what you hear?
2. How did the use of verbal punctuation—your pauses—help to convey the meaning?

Vocal Variety. The combination of rate, force, and pitch variations that add to a speaker's overall vocal quality is called **vocal variety.** Such variety gives feeling to your delivery and adds emphasis to what you say. Your voice allows listeners to perceive subtle differences in the intent of your messages by altering rate, force, and pitch, promoting a genuine understanding between you and your audience.

Rate is the speed at which a speaker speaks—usually between 120 and 150 words per minute. Speaking at the appropriate rate requires self-awareness. A rate that is too fast, is too slow, or never changes can detract from the impact of your message.

vocal variety
Variations in rate, force, and pitch.

rate
Speed at which a speaker speaks, normally between 120 words and 150 words per minute.

Making Connections

Your Voice and Your Message

Read the following poem from William Wordsworth aloud in a monotone—with no variety in force, rate, or pitch.

My apprehensions come in crowds;
I dread the rustling of the grass;
The very shadows of the clouds
Have power to shake me as they pass;
I question things and do not find
One that will answer to my mind;
And all the world appears unkind.[15]

Now read the poem as conversationally as you can. Use vocal variety in force, rate, and pitch. Use the semicolons and the period to create pauses.

1. What was the difference between the two readings?
2. How can you use this exercise to help you remember to be conversational?

Sometimes when we're nervous, our speaking rate increases so much that we are practically unintelligible to our listeners. We must learn to control this rapid rate by breathing deeply before we begin speaking and by purposely using pauses to help us slow down and concentrate on the message.

Pauses are important. A pause can be an effective means of gaining attention, adding emphasis to an important point, and enabling listeners to follow shifts in ideas. Pauses punctuate and emphasize thoughts. Beginning speakers need to realize the important contribution of both rate and pauses to the overall effect of their presentations. Listen carefully to accomplished speakers. Notice how an effective speaker varies rate and uses pauses to set off ideas, to prepare for the next point, and to provide silent emphasis for ideas. Again, accomplished speakers tend to do this within the context of a conversational style.

Force is the intensity and volume of the voice. You must choose a volume level that is comfortable for your audience. However, you can use force to communicate your ideas with confidence and vigor, to emphasize an important point, and to regain lagging interest. By learning how to use force, you can greatly increase your effectiveness as a speaker.

Pitch refers to how low or high the voice is on a tonal scale. Variety in pitch can eliminate monotony and add emphasis to key words. Variety in pitch contributes to greater conversationality and, thus, makes it easy for the listener to maintain interest in and attention to the speaker and message.

Obviously, any change in rate, force, or pitch makes a word, phrase, or sentence stand out. The greater the amount of change or the more sudden the change is, the more emphatic the word or statement will be. You can use such contrasts to make selected ideas seem more important than the material delivered without such variations.

Physical Aspects

In Chapter 5, we discussed nonverbal communication in depth. You are encouraged to review that chapter, because much of the information about nonverbal communication will aid you in your speaking performances. Among the physical factors that can affect delivery are personal appearance, body movement, gestures, facial expressions, and eye contact. Each of these must be well coordinated and relevant to the purpose of your speech.

force
The intensity and volume level of the voice.

pitch
How low or high the voice is on a tonal scale.

Personal Appearance. Personal appearance—what a speaker looks like and the way a speaker dresses, grooms, and presents himself or herself to others—is an extremely important consideration. Typical "student attire" is not always acceptable. As a general rule, you should use common sense in dressing for the occasion. For example,

Making Connections

Nonverbal Behavior and Effective Presentation of Information

Physical and vocal factors can play an important role in the effect of your presentation on your listeners. Your messages and your delivery can be enhanced or damaged by the way you present ideas. In an effort to analyze the behaviors of others in presenting information, take the next few days to observe professors, classmates, and others as they present information. Consider the messages (words, ideas) and the manner of presentation (physical and vocal factors of delivery). Take notes about the presenter and the presentation, and then answer these questions:

1. How did the speakers use their voices to communicate ideas?
2. How did speakers vary their rates? What was the effect?
3. How were pauses used? When? To what effect?
4. What positive factors of physical and vocal delivery did you observe? What effect did these positive aspects have on you, the listener?
5. What negative factors of physical and vocal delivery did you observe? What effect did these negatives have on you as the listener?
6. What will you remember about presentations from this activity?

large, dangly earrings, "busy" printed T-shirts, and caps may distract your audience from what you are saying (and have a negative effect on the people evaluating your presentation). Most instructors frown on speakers wearing caps for a variety of other reasons as well: It is in questionable taste, and caps hide your facial expressions. First impressions are based mainly on appearance. Your audience may form quick and hard-to-change opinions about your attitude toward them and yourself. In this way, appearance can affect your credibility.

Research in nonverbal and relational communication suggests that personal appearance plays a role in communication. Appearance can have an impact on a speaker's self-image and thus affect how the speaker communicates with others.[16] Dress for a special occasion when you present your speech. When you look good, you feel good, and that positively affects your performance.

Body Movement. Body movement is closely related to personal appearance. It includes posture, which should be relaxed and natural; avoid slouching. Because an audience's attention instinctively follows moving objects, your motions should be easy and purposeful. The use of movement—stepping to the side, forward, or backward—can hold attention and help to communicate ideas. Movement can also serve as a nonverbal transition between points. Purposeful movement, along with posture, can indicate confidence and convey a positive self-image. Too much movement, or unmotivated, nervous movement, however, can distract your audience, make them think you are not poised and confident, and detract from your credibility.

Gestures. You can use **gestures**—movements of the head, arms, and hands—to help illustrate, emphasize, or clarify a point. Gestures should be spontaneous, not forced. For example, when you are talking to acquaintances about something you have strong feelings about, your gestures come naturally. If you are sad, angry, or happy, you automatically make gestures that express your emotions. To obtain equally natural gestures when giving a speech, you need to be equally involved in what you are

gesture A movement of the head, arms, or hands that helps to illustrate, emphasize, or clarify an idea.

Making Connections

Technology and Speech Delivery

Technology has influenced every aspect of our lives, including the way teachers teach, students learn, and businesspeople make presentations. One of our communication colleagues, Dr. Lynn Disbrow of Sinclair Community College in Ohio, suggests that technology forces us all to be learners and that we all have to learn differently because of technology. How has technology affected the way speakers deliver their speeches? Let's Ask Jeeves.

1. Access your web browser.
2. Key in www.ask.com.
3. When you get Jeeves, phrase a question such as "How has technology affected speech delivery?"
4. Quickly look through the first few responses. Do they look like helpful answers? If so, read the responses. If not, ask another, similar question.
5. Read and compare the first ten new responses.
6. Answer the question, "How has technology affected speech delivery?"

saying. If you concentrate on getting your message across rather than on your gestures, you will find yourself moving more freely and naturally.

When you are first learning how to give a speech, using gestures might seem a bit uncomfortable, but not using gestures might also seem uncomfortable. To overcome this problem, practice the use of gestures in front of others who are willing to offer positive suggestions to help you improve. Be assured that as you give more and more speeches, you will find that gesturing becomes more natural and easier to do. Soon, without even thinking, you'll be using strong and smooth-flowing gestures that help to hold your audience's attention and add meaning to your message.

Facial Expressions. As defined in Chapter 5, facial expressions are configurations of the face that can reflect, augment, contradict, or be unrelated to a speaker's vocal delivery. They account for much of the emotional impact of a speaker's message. Your face is a very expressive part of your body. Facial expressions quickly and accurately tell your audience a lot about you. For example, whether you are serious, happy, worried, or angry, the audience will be able to "read" your face. Because your audience will infer a great deal from your facial expression, it is important to look warm and friendly. Such an expression will inform your listeners that you are interested in them and in what you are saying. Of course, your topic, your purpose, the situation, and your audience will all determine exactly what facial expressions are appropriate as you progress through your speech.

Eye Contact. The extent to which a speaker looks *directly* at audience members, making **eye contact,** is associated with facial expression. Facial expressions indicate a speaker's feelings about the message, while eye contact seems more related to a speaker's feelings about the listeners. Eye contact is the most important physical aspect of delivery, as it indicates interest and concern for others and implies self-confidence. Most speech communication teachers recommend that you look at your audience while you are speaking, not over their heads or at a spot on the wall.

eye contact
The extent to which a speaker looks directly at audience members.

Looking at members of the audience establishes a communicative bond between your listeners and you. Failure to make eye contact is the quickest way to lose listeners. Speakers who ignore their audiences are often perceived as tentative, ill at ease, insincere, or dishonest.

Eye contact with your audience should be pleasant and personal. Give your listeners the feeling that you are talking to them as individuals in a casual conversation. When speaking to a small audience (five to thirty people), try to look at each individual for a few seconds at a time. To avoid looking shifty, move your eyes gradually and smoothly from one person to another. For larger groups, it is best to scan the audience and occasionally talk to a specific member or members. Do not look over people's heads, and avoid staring, which can give the impression that you're angry or hostile. Try not to make your listeners uncomfortable. We have students serve as peer listeners and evaluate speakers. They often comment on failure to establish eye contact and note when a speaker looks at a few and not the entire audience. If you look at only one or two people, others will feel left out, and those whom you "stared at" will feel uncomfortable.

Your eyes should convey that you are confident, sincere, and speaking with conviction. The message your audience should get from your eye contact is that you care about them and about what you are saying. At first, establishing eye contact with an audience may make you uncomfortable, but as you gain experience, you will begin to feel more at ease. You will soon find that making eye contact puts you in control of the situation and helps you to answer these questions: Can they hear me? Do they understand? Are they listening?

Working to strengthen your use of positive vocal and physical behaviors and to reduce negative ones will greatly improve your delivery of a speech. Table 10.3 lists several behaviors that can detract from a speech's effectiveness. Observing yourself in

TABLE 10.3

Distracting Speaker Behaviors

General Delivery	*Eyes*	*Body*
Rapid speech	Rolling eyes	Tense, rigid
Speaking too slowly	Looking at the floor or ceiling	Sloppy posture
Sighing	Staring	Swaying
Nervous laughter or smiles	Lack of sustained eye contact	Dancing
Choppiness	*Voice*	Hunched shoulders
Awkward pauses	Monotone	Leaning on lectern
Face	Singsong patterns	*Feet*
Scowls	Nasal voice	Shuffling
Listless look	Mumbling	Weight shifts
Hands	Too soft	Crossing legs
Waving	Too loud	Leg/foot shakes
Playing with hair or object (such as notecards or a pen)		
Hands in pocket		

front of a mirror or asking a supportive friend for feedback during a practice session will help you avoid these problems.

Presentational Aids

Speeches and presentations can often be strengthened by the addition of materials to help audience members focus on and remember the topic. **Presentational aids,** also referred to as visual aids or audiovisual aids, are materials and equipment, such as diagrams, models, real objects, photographs, tables, charts, graphs, and computer-generated materials, that speakers may use to enhance the content of the speech as well as the delivery. Students often think that the only time they will be required to use presentational aids is in classroom speech assignments. In reality, speeches using visual materials are presented frequently, and many speeches depend on them. Imagine an architect explaining the floor plans for a new high-rise office building without a drawing, model, or photograph; a company executive explaining this year's annual profits and losses compared to last year's without a chart or graph; a coach explaining a play without a diagram; a teacher telling the class where Mauritius is located without a map or globe; or a salesperson selling a product without showing it.

Our world has become extremely information oriented. Because people are constantly bombarded with information from a variety of sources, it is important to present information in a way that captures the interest and attention of listeners. This is difficult when the audience is already experiencing information overload. Good aids can help.

Such presentational aids offer many advantages. If "a picture is worth a thousand words," then presentational aids are an excellent way to strengthen and reinforce the development and proof of a point. Such aids are a special form of supporting and clarifying materials, because they combine both verbal and visual modes of presentation. When carefully designed and used, presentational aids can help a speaker do the following:

Save time

Gain attention and hold interest

Clarify and support main points

Reinforce or emphasize main points

Improve retention of information

Research has shown that audiences remember information longer when it is accompanied by visual or presentational aids.[17] In many of today's businesses, employees are required to make presentations and to use the computer to enhance their presentations. Some company managers believe that unless the presenter uses the computer for audio, visual, or audiovisual aids, the speaker is not really performing well. Although classroom teachers do not always require the use of computer-generated or computer-assisted presentational materials, it is important to realize that they are common in the workplace. More and more, educators are required to make computer-aided presentations. Even medical doctors and dentists are creating multimedia presentational aids to help explain procedures, illnesses, and treatments to their patients. We'll next look at types of presentational aids and the methods of presenting them in speeches.

presentational aids Materials and equipment, such as diagrams, models, real objects, photographs, tables, charts, and graphs, that speakers may use to enhance the speech's content as well as their delivery.

Choosing and Using Presentational Aids

When planning to use presentational aids, keep the following guidelines in mind:

1. *Presentational aids should serve a need.* They should never be used just for the sake of using them. In some cases, visual aids are not appropriate, but in others, they can get a point across better than words alone. For example, it is easier to show an audience how to create PowerPoint slides than it is to tell them. Furthermore, it is easier to tell *and* to show them.

2. *Presentational aids should be planned and adapted to the audience and the situation.* For example, the size of the visual aid and the distance between you and your audience should be considered. The visual material should be kept simple and free from too much detail.

3. *Presentational aids should not dominate or take over a speaker's job.* They should supplement, but never replace, the speaker. Do not rely too heavily on visual aids; instead, use them to help elaborate or explain a point or idea or to create interest. In a speech, visual aids always require explanation by the speaker in order to make them meaningful.

4. *Presentational aids should look as professionally prepared as possible.* Accurate and neat materials will create a positive impression on the audience and reflect favorably on the competence of the speaker. Aids should be free from factual and spelling errors. They should also be bright, attractive, and easy to read from any spot in the audience. Audience members ought to be able to see, read, and understand the presentational aid once the speaker has carefully explained it.

5. *Presentational aids should be practical—easy to prepare, use, and transport.* Aids should not interfere with the speaker and presentation, and they should not call undue attention to themselves.

6. *Presentational aids that are not original or that contain information that is not yours require documentation.* Cite your source either directly on the aid where your audience can see it or in the context of your speech.

7. *Visuals should contain only one idea—one graph per poster, and so on.* Remember that presentational aids you provide are meant to clarify and strengthen your message. You want to limit yourself to one idea per poster, slide, chart, graph, or computerated screen so that your listeners can focus on that one idea at the time you are talking about that point or concept. Too much information distracts your listeners.

Using aids during a presentation requires planning and coordination. They should not distract the audience or interrupt the flow of the speech. See the Guidelines feature on page 279 for ideas on using these aids.

Kinds of Presentational Aids

There are many different kinds of visual aids. Those most frequently used include posters, real objects, models, photographs, diagrams, tables, and graphs. A special discussion of computer-generated graphics, scanned pictures, digitized pictures, and digitized video clips is included in a later section.

Real Objects. A real object is any article related to the speech topic that a speaker displays or demonstrates, such as a musical instrument, piece of sporting equipment, or kind of food. Using a real object can make your topic more immediate and interesting, but it can also create problems if the object is too large, too small, or too impractical to show. Pets, for example, are often unpredictable and can be distracting before, during, and after a speech.

Models. When displaying the actual article is not practical because of size or cost, a model should be considered. A model—or representation of a real object—allows a speaker to enlarge or shrink an object to a convenient size for display. It would be impractical to show the actual circuitry of a computer microchip, which is no larger than a pinhead, or the inside of an actual space shuttle, which is enormous (not to mention inaccessible). Models are appropriate in such circumstances.

Models can also be life-size. Cardiopulmonary resuscitation (CPR) is a popular and important subject. To demonstrate this procedure, speakers often use life-size dummies of humans.

Photographs and Prints. When models are neither available nor practical, a photograph may be used. A photograph is an excellent device for explaining details and surroundings. One student, speaking on artistic style, brought prints of several paintings to illustrate their differences. A student who spoke on the construction of the Egyptian pyramids showed photos that she had taken on a vacation trip. She realized that the original photos were too small, so she had them enlarged for effective use in the classroom. The typical photograph is usually too small to be seen clearly unless the speaker moves through the audience or passes it around or scans it into a computer presentation. In both instances, the advantage of using photos is somewhat diminished because the audience tends to pay more attention to the pictures than to what is being said.

A large-scale model, here a model sea horse, allows the speaker to clearly point the salient features to the audience.

Drawings, Sketches, and Diagrams. When photographs or prints are unavailable, are too small, or lack adequate detail, a drawing, sketch, or diagram may be used. Don't worry if you're not artistic, because most drawings used in classroom speeches are relatively simple. For example, Figure 10.1 is a line drawing used to describe a laboratory design. The diagram simply shows the division of the room for various functions and makes a professor's explanation of a seating arrangement much easier for students to comprehend.

Similarly, a speaker might use an architect's blueprint, a chart illustrating a company's organizational structure, a sketch of the basic positions of waterskiing, or a map of various segments of land. Virtually anything can be diagrammed or sketched.

FIGURE 10.1

Example of a Simple Line Drawing Line drawings do not need to be elaborate or complex. In fact, line drawings, sketches, and diagrams can be rather simple.

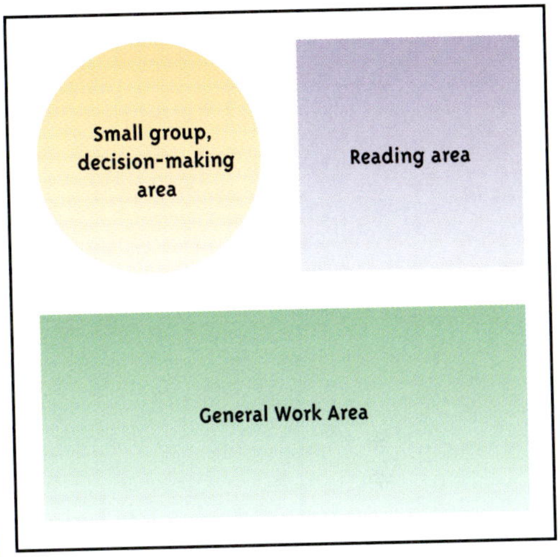

Tables and Graphs. Tables and graphs are used mainly to display statistics. A table is an orderly arrangement of data in columns to highlight similarities and differences, as shown in Figure 10.2.

Tables conveniently display large amounts of data in a relatively small space, but remember that a complex or lengthy (and perhaps boring) table will require an equally complex and lengthy explanation. As with any visual aid you decide to use, a table must be concise, simple, and clear so that the important information is easy to spot. Complex data are often better illustrated by a graph.

FIGURE 10.2

Example of Data Presented as a Table Tables display large amounts of data in a relatively small space. The more complex the data, the more explanation is required to make the table meaningful to your listeners.

Tax Relief Gained by Jobs and Growth Tax Relief Reconciliation Act of 2003

MARITAL STATUS	INCOME	NUMBER OF CHILDREN	ANNUAL TAX SAVINGS
Single	$41,000	0	$211
Single	$63,000	0	$551
Married	$41,000	2	$1,208
Married	$63,000	2	$1,100

Calculations by Jon Ford, Certified Financial Planner. Adapted from Waterloo-Cedar Falls Courier, *June 8, 2003, p. C1.*

Make sure the table title actually reflects content of the table.

Column heads should be simple, brief, and accurately identify the information in the table body.

Items in each column of the table should be parallel in structure.

If the table does not reflect your own data, be sure to give a complete source.

FIGURE 10.3

Example of Data Presented as a Line Graph Line graphs are particularly helpful in clarifying comparative data over time.

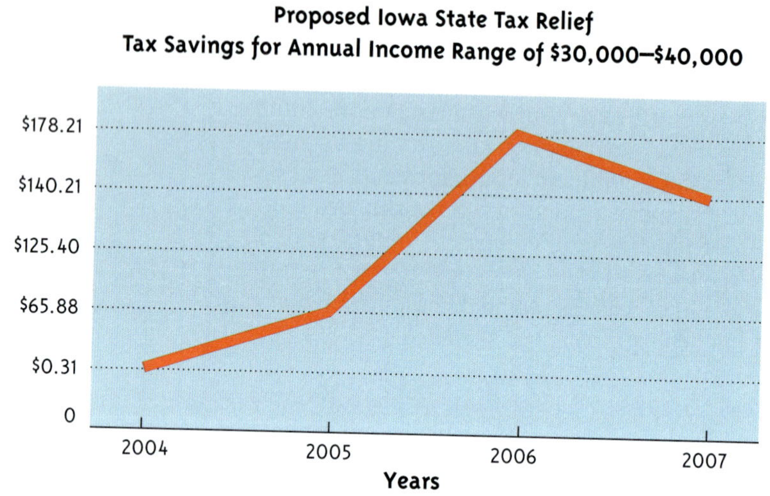

Adapted from Republican Staff Analysis (Iowa State Legislature), "Tax Cut Favors Richest Iowans," Waterloo-Cedar Falls *Courier,* June 8, 2003, pp. A1, A7.

Graphs help to make statistical data vivid and illustrate relationships in ways that are easy for the audience to grasp. Line graphs, as illustrated in Figure 10.3, are particularly helpful for clarifying comparative data over time. Such graphs can help trace trends and show increases and decreases over a span of days, months, or years. Note in Figure 10.3 the projected sharp increase from $65.88 in 2005 to $178.21 in 2006 and a drop back to $140.21 in 2007.

FIGURE 10.4

Example of Data Presented as a Bar Graph Bar graphs present comparative data much more clearly and vividly than does, for example, a table.

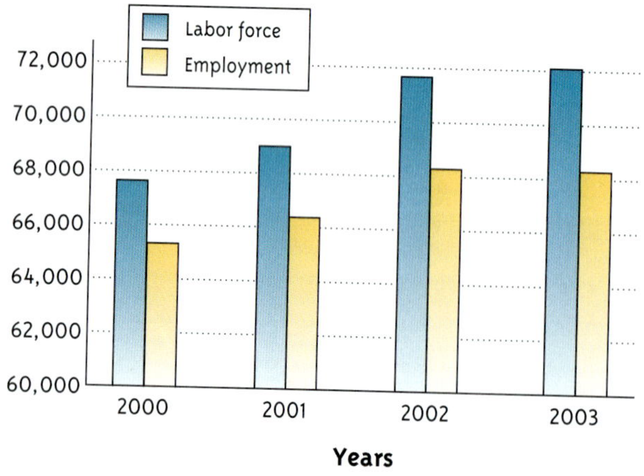

Adapted from Waterloo-Cedar Falls *Courier,* June 8, 2003, p. C1.

Bar graphs are another simple way to show comparisons. Note how much easier it is to compare the data depicted in the bar graph in Figure 10.4 than the data arranged in table form in Figure 10.2. Whenever possible, your visual aids should present only one or two basic relationships, so that your audience can quickly grasp your point.

Pie graphs are used to illustrate proportional divisions of a whole set of data. Each wedge of the pie represents a percentage of the whole. Pie graphs are often used to show distribution patterns and to illustrate national, state, or local budgets. Note in Figure 10.5 that the pie graph starts with a radius drawn vertically from the center to the

FIGURE 10.5

Example of Data Presented as a Pie Graph A pie graph illustrates proportions of a whole set of data. Each wedge represents a percentage of the whole.

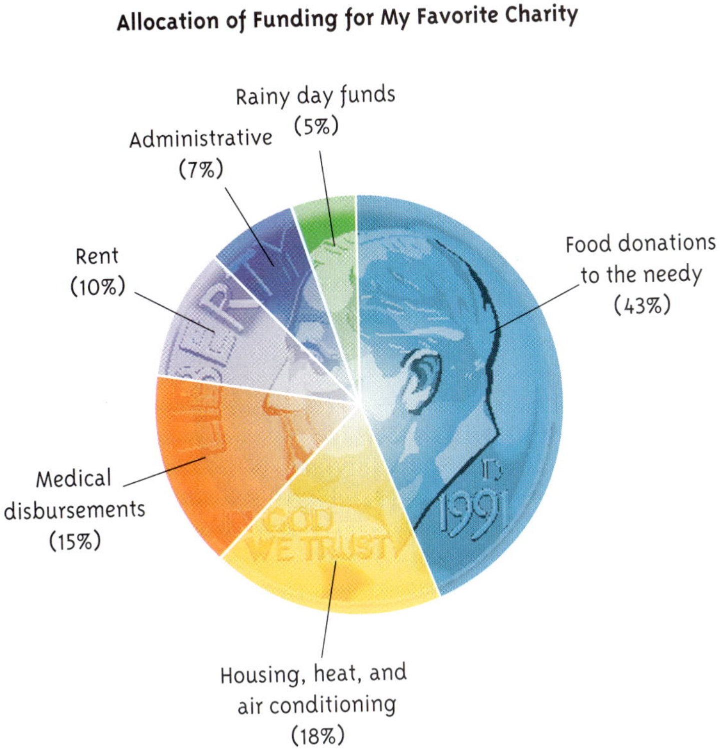

twelve o'clock position. Each segment is then drawn in clockwise, beginning with the largest and continuing down to the smallest.

Using Presentational Aids

GUIDELINES

1. Display visual materials only while you are using them. Do not distract your audience by showing your aids too early or by leaving them on display after you've finished talking about them. Even with a PowerPoint presentation, you can create a black, blank, or white screen in order not to distract your listeners.
2. Keep your presentational aids on display long enough to give everyone ample opportunity to absorb the information. Find the happy medium between "too long" and "not long enough."
3. Ensure that everyone can see your aids by making them neat, simple, large, bright, and readable. If you're using computer-generated text, the same guidelines apply. Depending on the size of the room, however, your font size should rarely be less than 36 points. For larger rooms, a 48-point or a 60-point font is desirable. The same thing applies to the television screen if you're in a distance learning classroom. Size, background, and color of text all become critical issues. For televised

presentations, a blue background with either a white or yellow text color is preferable. The opposite is true for yellow or white on overhead transparencies and many posters, charts, or graphs. Light colors fade and are virtually invisible on acetate and paper products. Red and black text work better for noncomputer presentational aids and often work better for computerized aids. Practice in the room with the equipment you'll use, well ahead of time.

4. Do not talk to your displayed objects or to the chalkboard. Discuss the content while maintaining eye contact with your audience.
5. Do not stand in front of your presentational aids. Determine where you will place or show your aids, and use a pointer or a laser to avoid blocking your audience's view.
6. Practice using your presentational aids until you feel comfortable with them. It becomes quite obvious to your listeners if you're uncomfortable and unfamiliar with the aids you've selected.

Methods of Presentation

The most frequently used methods of presentation are chalkboards, posters, projected visuals, and handouts.

Chalkboard. Although the chalkboard is the most readily available method of presenting visual aids, at least in most classrooms, some instructors will not allow you to use it. If you are unsure, check with your instructor. If it is allowed, here are several things to consider when you are planning to use a chalkboard:

1. *When to put information on the board.* Preferences vary from speaker to speaker and from instructor to instructor. Some speakers write on the board before they speak. If putting the information on the board before you speak will not interfere with other presentations and if you can cover what you have written (so as not to distract from other presentations), preparing the board in advance can simplify your delivery. To be safe, ask your instructor about his or her preference.

2. *How to write on the board.* This, of course, depends on the size of the room and your writing skills. Your writing should always be large enough and neat enough for everyone in the room to read. The appearance of your writing on the board communicates a message about you and your speech. Therefore you want what you write to create a positive impression.

3. *How to use the board when delivering your speech.* Even when reading from the board, you should always try to face your audience. Use a pointer, a ruler, or your outstretched arm to help guide listeners to the information on which you want them to focus. Whether writing on the board or reading from it, avoid talking to the chalkboard rather than your audience.

The chalkboard is a convenient visual device, but do not be fooled by its convenience. If it is not used properly, it can be more of a distraction than an aid. Practice writing on the board before your speech. This will give you an idea of how it feels to write on the board. You will also be able to determine how large to write so that those sitting in the back row can see the information.

Posters. Posters are another commonly used method of presenting information visually. The greatest advantage of posters is that they can be prepared in advance, which makes the speaker seem more efficient and professional. Many of the guidelines for writing on the chalkboard also apply to using posters. Here are three specific suggestions for using posters:

1. If an easel is not available, check to see whether there are clips on the board for hanging posters or whether you will need to use masking tape. If you must use masking tape, make large loops of tape and place them on the back of the poster in advance. Then, when you are ready to display the poster, merely place it on the board, pressing firmly on the tape loops to secure it. If you have more than one poster, you can place several of them on the board at once, or you can display each individually as you need it.
2. Make sure the poster is made of firm cardboard so that it will support itself if you have to stand it on a chalk tray or a table.
3. Posters should be displayed only when they are referred to in the speech. The rest of the time they should be turned over or covered so they don't distract the audience.

Projected Visuals. The most common projected materials are slides, movies, overhead transparencies, and videotapes. The projection of such visuals requires planning and familiarity with the mechanical equipment. Each form has advantages and disadvantages, so knowing what each can and cannot do is vital. For example, showing slides and movies requires a darkened room, and the projectors may be noisy. Yet both enable you to show places and things that you could not show any other way. Films and videos add motion, color, and sound. But they can be costly and often tend to dominate a presentation by replacing the speaker for a period of time.

The most popular projected visual is the overhead transparency. These materials can be prepared in advance or created during a presentation, and whether prepared by the speaker or a professional, they are relatively inexpensive. In addition, overhead projectors are easy to use and do not require a darkened room.

When using an Elmo or overhead projector, consider the following:

1. Make sure the projector is focused correctly so that everyone in the room can read what is on the transparency.
2. Cover information on the transparency until it is needed.
3. Use a pointer (pencil or pen) to direct the audience's attention to what is being discussed.
4. Practice using the overhead. Check it beforehand to make sure it is working correctly.

Mechanical devices, because of their potential for breakdown, require a backup method. It is a good idea to carry a spare bulb in case one burns out and to bring copies of visual aids in handout form.

Handouts. Handouts can be a useful means of presenting information to your audience. If you are presenting a speech on organ donation, for example, you may want to hand out a copy of the form many states ask potential donors to carry. Or if your speech mentions helpful persons or related organizations, a handout may list these, together with addresses or websites, so that audience members may obtain additional information. Handouts are particularly helpful if you are unable to use any other method. Among their advantages are that they can be prepared in advance and that each audience member gets a personal copy. Their main disadvantage is that they can become a distraction. Passing them out can interrupt the flow of your presentation, and audience members may pay more attention to the handouts than to the speech itself. As a result, you should use handouts only when you have no other alternatives or when you have a creative reason for doing so. In addition, you should wait until the end of the presentation to use them, if possible.

Computer-Generated Presentational Aids

As a presentational tool, the computer has gained ever-increasing acceptance in both education and business. Many colleges and universities now require the use of computer-generated materials in a variety of presentations throughout a student's academic career. This class may be a good place to get a head start on preparing and using computer presentations. When you enter the workplace, you will be prepared to use the computer for your presentations.

Several excellent presentational software programs are available in college and university computer laboratories. Among the most popular is Microsoft's PowerPoint, which allows the presenter to select or create backgrounds, formats, layouts, colors, and tools to make a professional presentation (see Figure 10.6). Images and text can be animated to fade, dissolve, or move in from the top, the bottom, or either side of the slide. The presenter can scan in pictures, text, or other visuals (such as a brochure, a poster,

FIGURE 10.6

Example of a Computer-Generated Visual Aid Clip art from a presentational software program such as PowerPoint can enhance your presentations.

Veterinary medicine is one of the fastest growing majors in the Midwest, as can be seen in this chart:

Number of veterinary medicine majors (midwestern universities)	700	850	1000	1670
Year	1973	1983	1993	2003

a photograph), use a digital still camera, use a digital movie camera, use digitized clips from movies or other videos, and so on. The possibilities are almost endless. The kinds of materials we can create using the computer are limited only by the time, money, resources, and creativity at our disposal. The guidelines for use of other audiovisual aids apply to use of computer presentational materials, as well. There are, however, some additional suggestions you should consider if you are planning to use the computer to enhance your presentations. These are listed in the accompanying Guidelines feature.

Using Computer-Generated Aids

GUIDELINES

1. Do not overdo it! Just as you can have too many points in a speech and too many materials for traditional visual aids, you can present too much material on the computer. As a general rule, use a visual to support only 25 percent of your presentation. Select the materials carefully. Too many pictures, graphs, words, images, and animations can result in overload.
2. Make sure that the font size you use in your presentation is appropriate. Use nothing less than a 40-point font for a regular classroom. In a large lecture hall, use 60 points for headings and topics, and no less than 48 points for subpoints, quotations, and explanations.
3. Don't put too much on any given screen. It's easy to overdo it. If you put too many words or images on the "slides," people will not listen to what you have to say.
4. Remember that the computer visual is like any other visual: It is there to enhance the presentation, not to take the place of the speaker's words and ideas.
5. Practice using your computer visuals in the room in which you will present the speech, if possible, because what you see on the screen of your monitor and what people see on the screen in the presentation room may not be the same. Colors do not always enhance the material as well as they appear to on the small monitor screen. Sometimes the lighting can make a tremendous difference, and if you cannot dim the lights, you may want to change the background so that the materials are visible, clear, and easy to read anywhere in the audience. Check to see whether lighting and reflections will cause problems and whether there are decreased sight lines at certain angles in the room. Also, practice to make sure you do not lose eye contact with your audience while presenting these aids. Using the computer should not distract you from staying in touch with your audience.

Developing Presentational Aids

Today, many computer programs and technologies can help you develop presentational aids. If your university or college has a media center, and most do, check with the center or your instructor to learn about the most modern and easiest methods available for developing visuals. Certain programs and techniques will allow you to make graphics, charts, custom-made diagrams, and many other types of visual aids. Making professional-looking visual aids, whether computer-generated or traditional, is often quite simple and may require only that you become familiar with your school's offerings. Remember, too, that not every speech requires a high-tech application. In fact, many experts believe that we've gone

Learning Connections

1. When might you use a presentational aid?
2. What criteria will you use in choosing the aid?
3. What are the advantages of each type discussed in this chapter?

too far in our use of graphics and images. Fewer images of higher quality, with more information, are preferable.

Your Delivery

The best way to ensure effective delivery is to practice, practice, practice. Practice early and often until you feel comfortable with your speech content. Exactly how much practice you will need depends on a number of considerations, including how much experience you have had speaking before audiences, how familiar you are with your subject, and how long your speech is. There is no magic amount of time that will make your delivery perfect.

If your speech is not to be memorized, make sure to use slightly different wording in each run-through. When you memorize a speech, it is possible to master the words without mastering the content. Your goal should be to learn your speech, which will mean that you have mastered its ideas.

In practicing your delivery, it is important to start with small segments. For example, practice the introduction, then one main point at a time, and then the conclusion. After you have rehearsed each small segment several times in isolation, practice the entire speech until you have mastered the content and the ideas flow smoothly.

If possible, practice in the same room in which you will speak or under similar conditions. This helps you see how things look from the front of the class and to plan where you should place your visual aids. Your last practice session should leave you with a sense of confidence and a desire to present your speech.

Finally, concentrate on what you are saying and to whom you are saying it. Above all, be yourself.

Summary

Competent communicators are prepared, knowledgeable, confident speakers who are ethical. Ethical speakers always provide oral footnotes within the speech and, they provide fair and accurate information.

Speakers who suffer from too much anxiety will have trouble giving speeches and keeping the audience's attention. The best way to overcome your anxiety is to understand it, control it, and be so well prepared that you are ready to share your ideas and know that you will do well. Students from other cultures and co-cultures have added anxiety because of language concerns. If you are seriously anxious about communicating with others, you might have communication apprehension that will take special strategies to help you manage your fears.

Most communication professors say that an extemporaneous delivery is best. This means that you are fully prepared but present your speech in a conversational manner, using note cards to help you stay organized and on track.

Vocal and physical delivery should enhance your message. Although a speech is a formal presentation, you should not be rigid or mechanical, either vocally or physically. Instead, you should look and sound as if you really want to share your ideas with your listeners and you care about what they think. Effective speakers are listener oriented. They think about the content and the delivery well in advance and practice many times so that they can maintain eye contact with their listeners.

Presentational aids can help to make your content memorable. You can choose actual objects or some kind of medium such as posters or drawings. Because many employers require use of PowerPoint or other computer-generated presentations, it is good to incorporate technology whenever it helps you make your points better.

DISCUSSION STARTERS

1. Why should we consider ethical behavior when we create and deliver speeches?
2. How does preparation help speakers?
3. Why do you think people have anxieties about giving speeches?
4. How can listeners help speakers to overcome their nervousness?
5. Why is vocal variety important?
6. What factors of physical delivery have made an impact on you as an audience member?
7. Think about an effective presentation. What vocal factors helped make that presentation effective?
8. Why do communication instructors recommend or require extemporaneous delivery?
9. Why should speakers be listener oriented?
10. What do presentational aids do for the audience?
11. When and how should presentational aids be used?

NOTES

1. D. Zarefsky, *Public Speaking Strategies for Success,* 2nd ed. (Boston: Allyn and Bacon, 2002), 25.
2. R. L. Johannesen, *Ethics in Human Communication* (Prospects Heights, Ill.: Waveland Press, 2002).
3. Zarefsky, p. 25.
4. "Anxiety," *World Book Encyclopedia/Dictionary*, Mac OS X Edition, Version 6.0.2 multimedia edition, 2001.
5. A variety of sources identify fear of public speaking as "Americans' greatest fear." *The Book of Lists,* Volume 4, by Amy Wallace and David Walleshensky identifies "fear of public speaking" ahead of even death. And business and training consultants write articles, make presentations, and even give workshops on fear of public speaking. One such consultant, T. S. Eggleston, has an article on his website, www.the-eggman.com/writings/fearspk1.htm, accessed June 9, 2003.
6. J. C. McCroskey, "The Communication Apprehension Perspective," in *Avoiding Communication: Shyness, Reticence, and Communication Apprehension,* eds. J. A. Daly and J. C. McCroskey (Beverly Hills, Calif.: Sage, 1984), 13.
7. K. K. Dwyer, *Conquer Your Speechfright* (New York: Harcourt, 1998).
8. If your school does not have a systematic desensitization program you can write to the National Communication Association, 5105 Backlick Rd., Building E, Annandale, VA 22003, for information on how to reduce stage fright. Also, see J. Ayres and T. Hoft, *Coping with Speech Anxiety* (Norwood, N.J.: Ablex, 1994).
9. E. C. Buehler and W. Linkugel, *Speech: A First Course* (New York: HarperCollins, 1962).
10. E. Yook and W. J. Seiler, "An Investigation into the Communication Needs and Concerns of Asian Students in Speech Communication Performance Classes," *Basic Communication Course Annual* 2 (November 1990): 47–75.
11. D. W. Stacks and J. D. Stone, "An Examination of the Effect of Basic Speech Courses, Self-Concept, and Self-Disclosure on Communication Apprehension," *Communication Education* 33 (1984): 317–32; and R. S. Littlefield and T. L. Sellnow, "The Use of Self-Disclosure as a Means for Reducing Stage Fright in Beginning Speakers," *Communication Education* 36 (1987): 62–64.
12. J. A. Daly, A. L. Vangelisti, H. L. Neel, and P. D. Cavanaugh, "Pre-Performance Concerns Associated with Public Speaking Anxiety," *Communication Quarterly* 37 (1989): 39–53.
13. Dwyer, pp. 73–83.
14. J. C. Humes, "Read a Speech Like a Pro," in *Talk Your Way to the Top* (New York: McGraw-Hill, 1980), 125–35; and J. Venlenti, *Speak Up with Confidence: How to Prepare, Learn, and Deliver Effective Speeches* (New York: Morrow, 1982), 23–26.
15. W. Wordsworth, "The Affliction of Margaret," in *The Complete Poetical Works of William Wordsworth* (London: Macmillan, 1888).
16. S. Chaiken, "Communicator Physical Attractiveness and Persuasion," *Journal of Personality and Social Psychology* 37 (1979): 1387–97.
17. E. P. Zayas-Baya, "Instructional Media in the Total Language Picture," *International Journal of Instructional Media* 5 (1977–78): 145–50.

"Humans experience life as a series of ongoing narratives, as conflicts, characters, beginnings, middles, and ends."

—Walter Fisher

CHAPTER 11 Informative Speaking

THIS CHAPTER WILL HELP YOU:

- Explain the power of information.
- Choose an appropriate topic for your assignments.
- Create a need to hear the information in your listeners.
- Demonstrate how to increase your listeners' knowledge of your topic through your organization and language.
- Deliver an informative speech that meets specific criteria.
- Use evaluation criteria to assess your own speeches prior to classroom presentation.

CASE STUDY

You settle into your seat only to hear the instructor say, "Your first formal speaking assignment for the week of October 6 is an informative speech on a communication concept from the list of topics I am now handing out. There will be no repeats, so when you choose your topic, be sure to mark your name on the appropriate line on the master list."

In this situation, you have fewer choices than usual, but you do have choices.

Questions to think about

1. What might you consider as a communication concept that you want to know more about? Why?
2. How do you feel about having your choices limited to a specific set of concepts?
3. Would you rather have complete freedom? Why or why not?

In the opening case study, the instructor gave an assignment for an informative speech. Why do *you* think the informative speech is one of the first that is assigned? Much of what we do in our lives involves information; someone asks for information, and another provides it. **Information,** according to the 2002 World Book Dictionary CD-ROM, is "knowledge given or received of some fact or circumstance."[1] That sounds pretty simple, right? Think about telling someone who is unfamiliar with computers how to add memory. Is that simple? Or is it simple to tell how to save a person's life using the Heimlich maneuver? If you have ever tried some fairly complex explanations, you know that it takes time and careful choice of language and demonstrations to accomplish your goal.

Teachers inform on a daily basis. So do people in many other jobs. If you lack the skills to carefully explain, both you and your listeners may be frustrated. To help you with this process, we discuss all aspects of the informative speech in this chapter, from choosing a topic to delivering the speech. Informative speaking is one of the most common types of speeches we present in all aspects of our lives. Learning what you need to know and be able to do in informative speaking will help you in your personal, career, home, and family life. We believe that the informative speech provides the basis for every speaking situation we face; thus if you learn the fundamentals of informative speaking, you will be able to apply those concepts to all other presentations.

Information and Power

Being informed helps to reduce uncertainty. Thus the person who possesses and controls information has power. When people need information concerning something about which they know little, they tend to turn to those who can provide the necessary information. The greater your desire to have important information, the more valuable that information is to you. Thus people who have the information you want,

Making Connections

Presenting Information to Others

Every professor has a favored way to present information. Some like linear thoughts and straight presentation of the material. Others like to tell stories or provide personal examples. Each style may be effective or not, depending on many different factors. For the next week, carefully observe your professors and take notes on what they do well and what they need to improve as they present information. Be prepared to discuss answers to the following questions after a week of observing and note taking:

1. What do effective instructors do that makes them effective?
2. Think about those effective behaviors. How might you use some of those effective qualities in delivering your informative speech? Why do you think you could use them?
3. What must a speaker do to successfully get *you* and your classmates to listen?

information
Knowledge given or received about some fact or circumstance.

The informative speech is meant to increase knowledge, whereas the purpose of the persuasive speech is to alter attitudes and behavior. Often there is a fine distinction between informative and persuasive speeches because there are elements of persuasion in an informative speech and there is information in a persuasive speech.

in a sense, gain control over you because of their power to give or withhold the knowledge you seek.

The ability to communicate information is essential in our society and will play an increasingly important role in the future. Over the years, we have moved from an economy based on agriculture and heavy industries, such as steel, machinery, and automobile manufacturing, to an economy based on knowledge industries, such as research, health services, banking, training, and communications. During the 1950s, only about 17 percent of our labor force held information-related jobs. This figure has now increased to more than 75 percent. This demand puts even more emphasis on workers' needs for greater skills in producing, storing, and delivering information. Much of the information we send and receive is written, but most is spoken. For example, teachers, trainers, consultants, media specialists, salespeople, technicians, mechanics, artists, doctors, nurses, lawyers, elected officials, and managers all depend on oral communication to succeed in their work.

Making Connections

Freedom Forum Online

The Freedom Forum Online provides resources on current news related to free speech, free expression, and journalism. Stories are grouped by subject (e.g., First Amendment, free press, technology, professional journalism), with the top story in each section featured on the main page. Freedom Forum Online is a nonpartisan, international foundation dedicated to "free press, free speech, and free spirit for all people."

1. Access Freedom Forum Online at www.freedomforum.org.
2. Click on one of the top stories on the main page and read the whole story.
3. Share the story you read with others and find out what they learned.

Distinctions between Informative and Persuasive Speaking

The general goal of informative speakers is to increase their listeners' knowledge. There is a fine distinction between informing and persuading. The informative speech is meant to increase knowledge, whereas the persuasive speech is meant to alter attitudes and behavior. Information can be presented without any attempt at persuasion, but persuasion cannot be accomplished without attempting to inform.

Two examples will illustrate the difference between information and persuasion. You go into an electronics store to look at a computer. The salesperson wants to sell one, so she will do her best to persuade you to buy a computer. She will share all kinds of information about the computer: its speed, its memory, its flexibility, the ease of maintenance, the modem, the firewall, an explanation of all features, the warranty, and the help available to you. She will provide you with ample information and then make comparisons with other computers or, at the very least, give you compelling reasons to buy that computer from her. She may give you knowledge and understanding (information) about the computer, and she tries to persuade you, but you do not purchase the computer. She still made a persuasive speech even though you did not buy, because her goal was persuasive: She wanted you to buy the computer.

Your humanities professor explains deductive and inductive reasoning. He wants students to understand how these two types of reasoning can be used to help solve problems. He does not want to persuade you how things should be done; instead, he wants to help you gain knowledge and understanding so that you can solve the problem on your own. He moves to persuasion only if he tries to convince you that one method is better than another for solving problems.

The key to understanding the difference between information and persuasion lies in recognizing that *although information may contain some elements of persuasion, all persuasion must provide information.* What separates an informative speech from a persuasive one is the goal of the speaker. Persuasion is discussed in more detail in the next chapter.

Topics for Informative Speeches

Surprisingly, some students believe that they have little information to share with others. In actuality, most students have a wealth of information and a vast list of potential topics based on what they have learned from classes, readings, and other experiences. For example, your wellness class probably gives you all kinds of useful, relevant, health and wellness information. Think about topics mentioned or covered in other classes, such as agriculture, industrial technology, technology in the workplace, computers in the workplace, the Internet, working from home, biological discoveries to create better living, computers and agriculture, computers and mechanics, computers and art, changes in education, graphic design, photography, medical advances, alternative health care, global terrorism, gender issues in the twenty-first century, the impact of an elderly population on our governmental agencies, the need for philanthropy, new jobs in the music industry, spirituality and religion, and multiculturalism. The list is endless, and the potential for informative topics is almost limitless.

There are some guidelines (suggested in Chapter 7) for selecting a speech topic. They are as follows:

1. Choose a topic that will allow you to convey an important thought or action to your audience.
2. Choose a topic that is familiar and interesting to you.
3. Choose a topic that is important to you.
4. Choose a topic that will be or can be made interesting to your audience.
5. Choose a topic that can be well developed within the speech's time limit.

Communicating with others is easier when they see value in and uses for the information presented. Most audiences want the information they receive to be important and useful to them. Select a topic that is potentially useful to your listeners. Some topics speak for themselves, such as "Eat Right to Live Healthy" or "The Career Center and Your Job Search." These topics suggest that a typical college audience might find them useful or beneficial if not at the moment, then in the near future. Topics with less evident value, such as "Biotechnology and World Hunger," might seem less interesting, so you will have to clearly identify incentives to your audience to encourage them to listen. Remember, if you are passionately interested in something, chances are that you can get your listeners interested. Although you might doubt that you have a worthwhile topic, if you think about your own special interests, past experiences, and special knowledge, you will discover that you, too, have a great deal to share.

Successful speakers next consider their audiences. They communicate information accurately and clearly, but most important, they make the information they

Making Connections

Web Searches for Informative Topics

We have stated that the topics for informative speeches are virtually limitless. The Web can be an excellent source of ideas and even some information for your speeches. Be sure to find additional information from a variety of sources, however, to meet your instructor's requirements. Here are some excellent sources for interesting informative possibilities:

1. The Public Broadcasting System has a superb website highlighting various up-to-date programs at www.pbs.org. Bookmark this site so that you can come back to get more ideas or to find additional information. To get a taste of what is available, once you are on the home page, click on "Explore" and then click on "Arts." Once you are there, scroll through the list and note any topics of specific interest to you and read one of the interesting ones.
2. Great American Speeches, at www.pbs.org/greatspeeches, is a PBS site that offers a collection of more than ninety speeches from many of the nation's most influential speakers. Some of the speeches include background and audio or video clips.
3. The Invisible Web (billed as the "search engine of search engines"), at http://invisibleweb.com, indexes more than 10,000 databases, archives, and search engines and offers links to targeted search sources. Users can search by key word, ask for an advanced search, or browse a list of eighteen categories in the InvisibleWeb or twenty-four categories in the "Hot List."
4. Bartleby.com, www.bartleby.com, is a source for free online literature, verse, and reference books. Electronic versions of thirty-five reference works are available, including *The Columbia Encyclopedia*, the *American Heritage Dictionary*, *Roget's II: The New Thesaurus*, *Simpson's Contemporary Quotations*, *World Orations*, *The New Dictionary of Cultural Literacy*, and the *American Heritage Book of English Usage*.

present meaningful and interesting to their audience by providing new information or correcting misinformation.

Informative speech topics can be classified in many different ways. One scheme divides them into speeches about objects, processes, events, and concepts.[2]

Objects

Speeches about objects examine concrete subjects, such as people, animals, structures, and places. Here are some possible object topics:

Reality television
Crisis hotlines
Celebrity biographies
Biomedical advances
Artistic techniques
The commonalities of music
Medical benefits from rain forests
J. R. R. Tolkien and the *Lord of the Rings*
Volunteerism and college students
Mental health practices
The arts
The Discovery Channel
Hillary Rodham Clinton
Laura Bush
Harry Potter mania
J. K. Rowling
MP3 technology updates
The theater

These topics are general and must be narrowed in order to meet the guidelines of most classroom speaking situations.

Here are some specific purpose statements for informative speeches about concrete subjects, following the guidelines suggested in Chapter 7:

- To inform the audience about the latest innovations in MP3 technology
- To inform the audience about J. K. Rowling's contributions to literature
- To share the increasing role of crisis hotlines in community mental health care
- To inform my listeners about the many medical products that come from tropical rain forests

Each of these purpose statements is appropriate for an informative speech.

Processes

A process topic usually focuses on a demonstration in which the speaker explains how something is done or how it takes place. Here are a few sample specific purpose statements for informative speeches about processes:

- To inform my listeners how to use an automated external defibrillator if someone's heart stops
- To explain how to create a portfolio that will get you the best job
- To inform my audience about the process of developing negatives
- To inform my audience about creating a healthy lifestyle by beginning with what they eat

Speeches about processes generally serve two purposes: to increase understanding and to teach someone *how to do something.* This could involve anything from how to do CPR to how to buy the right car.

Process speeches are usually organized in time-sequence (chronological) order, meaning that they proceed step by step from the beginning of the process to its end. For example, if you were to explain to your audience how to skydive, you would take them through all the necessary steps and procedures so that they would understand exactly what a skydiver does.

The demonstration of a process usually benefits from the use of a visual aid. Some processes may require an actual demonstration in order to be understood. For example, to inform listeners about how to fold napkins might require that you do the folding during the speech presentation.

Events

Informative speeches about events discuss happenings or occasions. The many possible topics include the following:

Animal cloning since Dolly
Liberia and U.S. troop deployment
The popularity of regional theaters
Developing countries and their impact
The effects of medical malpractice
Saving Venice from the water
Stem cell research
The Boston Marathon
The war on terrorism
Nature, nurture, and you
The truth behind *The Mercury 13*
Election 2004

Appropriate specific purposes for some of these topics might include the following:

- To inform the audience about the latest animal cloning experiments
- To inform the audience about the thirteen women who were rejected by NASA's 1961 space program despite equal or superior abilities
- To share information about medical malpractice suits and their effect on you
- To share the reasons for the increasing popularity of regional theaters

Concepts

Speeches about concepts deal with abstract topics such as beliefs, theories, ideas, and principles. The challenge is to make the subject matter concrete so that the audience can easily understand it. Concept-based topics include the following:

Communication anxiety
Problem solving
Reading as entertainment
Intercultural communication
Relational dialectics
Freedom
Interpersonal needs
Philosophy

These topics are too vague to be meaningful. If you were to ask a dozen people what each term or phrase means, you would probably receive a dozen different answers. The speaker is responsible for narrowing and focusing the subject so that the audience understands the intended meaning. Here are specific purpose statements based on some of the general, abstract topics:

- To inform my listeners about the symptoms and effects of communication anxiety

- To share information about relational dialectics so that they can understand why people in relationships have problems
- To help my listeners understand the steps in the problem-solving process so that they can use the process in their own lives
- To help my listeners learn the differences between reading for classes and reading for entertainment

Speeches about concepts take extra time and effort to develop because of their abstract nature. These topics require the use of concrete examples, definitions, and clear language.

Whether a speech is about an object, a process, an event, or a concept is not always clear because a subject may overlap these categories. Often the specific purpose that the speaker chooses to emphasize determines the category. It is important to decide your approach to the subject and then develop your speech accordingly. If you are unsure of which approach to take, review Chapter 7 for more specific information about topic selection and how to determine which topics may be best suited for you and your audience (see the appendix at the end of this chapter for more topics).

Learning Connections

1. What is the difference between informative speeches and persuasive speeches?
2. What topics are suitable for informative speeches?
3. Where can you find information for the informative speech?

GUIDELINES Preparing the Informative Speech

1. When preparing to present an informative speech, you should begin with yourself. What are your interests? What are you passionately concerned about?
2. Informative speeches should appeal to the audience and provide them with knowledge of something potentially useful or beneficial.
3. Your audience will listen to you if you make the speech compelling.

Making Connections

Planning Your Speech

As you can see, there is a lot to do to get ready for a speech. Here is an exercise designed to help you make the connections required as you use the information in this public communication unit.

1. Select one of the purpose statements from each of the categories of information presented on the previous pages.
2. For that purpose statement, indicate an organizational pattern you think would work and explain why it is appropriate.
3. What presentational aids might be useful and why?
4. What forms of support do you think would help make your listeners attend and remember this information?

The Dalai Lama successfully speaks about abstract concepts, such as peace, humanity, and human dignity, by using concrete examples that his listeners can relate to.

Preparing and Developing an Informative Speech

The previous chapters on public communication relate directly to the principles and skills of informative speaking. All aspects of topic selection; audience analysis; information gathering; preparation of supporting and clarifying materials; and organizing, outlining, and delivering a speech are crucial to the effectiveness and eventual success of your informative presentation. In addition, you should be familiar with strategies for competing with distractions and noises, such as students arriving late, an airplane flying overhead, a lawn mower outside the window, and whispering in the audience. Such interferences cannot be ignored if you want to be successful in transmitting information to others. To achieve your main goal of increasing the audience's knowledge, you must strive to attain two subgoals: gain their attention and increase their understanding.

Gain and Maintain Audience Attention

Motivating the audience to pay attention is critical to the success of any speech (see Chapter 9 for more on motivating your audience to listen). To accomplish this, you should follow a strategy that will work well for your audience.

Generate a Need for the Information. A student gave a speech on the benefits of seat belt use. After reading his peer evaluations and reflecting on his videotaped speech, he emailed to ask if we knew why people did not like the speech. When he was asked whether he had determined how many people in his class do not use seat belts, he did not have an answer. When asked if he knew what the Iowa average of seat belt use was, he did not have those statistics either. When we told him the latest statistics from the Highway Patrol and the Department of Transportation suggest that 82 percent of Iowans use seat belts, he was surprised. That should tell you two reasons his listeners did not seem to like his speech: Most of them already knew the benefits of seat belt use and use them regularly; and he had not done enough research to go beyond what his listeners already knew. As a result, his audience did not feel motivated to listen. How could he have avoided choosing a topic his audience wasn't interested in? He might have done a survey to find out what they knew, or he might have looked carefully at Iowa statistics. Or he could have found a way to make the speech more relevant to his listeners in this way:

> I realize most of you already wear seat belts when you drive or ride in a vehicle, but did you know that even in Iowa, where seat belt usage is said to be at 90 percent, injuries resulting because a seat belt was not in use account for more than 25 percent of all traffic deaths? That means that six of us in this class could have life-threatening injuries if we were involved in an automobile accident and were not wearing a seat belt.

This opening acknowledges the high percentage of people in the state who use seat belts, and it also piques interest because it asks a rhetorical question to make the listener aware of the consequences of that failure (Notice that the speaker also makes the percentages memorable by identifying the number of class members who could be affected.)

Let's look at other examples of rhetorical questions used to begin a speech:

- The Harry Potter books have created quite a following. Did you know that thousands of copies of the latest one were sold in advance?
- Despite the bad economy, charitable giving increased in 2002. Do you know why?
- Why would I make an outrageous claim such as "People drink too much milk, because milk is not really good for you"?
- Do you know why so many U.S. drivers are involved in accidents?

Speakers can also use questions meant to generate responses from the audience as a strategy to gain and maintain audience interest and attention.

Create Information Relevance. People are much more likely to pay attention when they believe a speech relates directly to them. A speaker who gives an audience a reason to listen by relating the topic to their needs and interests creates **information relevance.** Ask yourself whether the information you intend to present is relevant to your listeners. If it is not, think about how you might make it so. One student presented a speech on wind energy. It was apparent that she had done a lot of research because she cited numerous sources and had interesting visuals. The problem was that she talked only about wind energy in California and Denmark and never mentioned that it is a viable source of energy in her own state. Her listeners needed to know how this could affect them at home, not somewhere thousands of miles away.

Another speaker talked about the contributions of space technology to our everyday lives. She held up several items of clothing with Velcro fasteners and pointed out how Velcro is familiar to us now but was originally developed for the space program. The audience recognized the relevance of her topic and paid closer attention.

information relevance
Making information relevant to an audience to give them a reason to listen.

Provide a Fresh Perspective. Information that is perceived as *new* also attracts the attention of an audience. But whenever this statement is mentioned in class, someone responds, "But there isn't anything new to present." Actually, discussing something new does not necessarily mean that you have to present something about which the audience has never heard. It does mean that you need to devise a new view or angle. There are subjects that we have heard discussed many times, such as AIDS, pollution, smoking, drugs, safe sex, and recycling. A speaker who provides a fresh perspective on a familiar topic makes it more interesting and thus increases the chances of holding the audience's attention. One speaker informed the audience about illegal drugs that are medically helpful in treating certain diseases. She began her speech in the following manner:

> You have read and heard so much about cocaine, crack, heroin, and other illegal drugs that you are probably sick of the subject, but these drugs are not all bad. You might at first think that I am too liberal, but my mother is on drugs and I am glad of it. You see, my mother is suffering from cancer, and the only relief she can get is from the small doses of heroin she receives each day to ease the pain. Today, I am going to inform you about illegal drugs that actually aid our sick and dying.

This approach is not necessarily new, but it is different. Rather than taking a stand either for or against the banning of illegal drugs, the speaker focused on certain instances in which the use of illegal drugs can be beneficial. This also helped her to stay within the guidelines of the informative speech.

Focus on the Unusual. Sometimes focusing on an unusual aspect of a topic helps a speaker maintain the attention of the audience. A speaker might begin his speech like this:

> You're all aware, I'm sure, that Thomas Jefferson is the acknowledged author of the Declaration of Independence. Did you know, however, that Jefferson had a very fine editor who made the words immortal?
>
> The Continental Congress of 1776 appointed a committee to draft a declaration of independence from Great Britain that explained the decision. The committee comprised Thomas Jefferson, Benjamin Franklin, John Adams, Roger Sherman, and Robert Livingston. Jefferson was the committee chair and the one who wrote the first draft. Jefferson and Franklin held similar views on what was needed in the document, but their writing styles were quite different. Jefferson was much more poetic and philosophical than Franklin. Jefferson was also acknowledged to be the person who should create this important rationale for the colonies to revolt from an unjust system. A new book, *Benjamin Franklin: An American Life* by Walter Isaacson (2003), suggests that "Jefferson . . . borrowed freely from the phrasings of others, including the resounding Declaration of Rights in the new Virginia Constitution that had just been drafted by his fellow planter George Mason, in a manner that today might subject him to questions of plagiarism but back then was considered not only proper but learned."[3]
>
> According to Isaacson, Jefferson finished his draft and made some changes suggested by others and then asked, "Will Doctor Franklin be so good as to peruse it?"[4] Franklin made only a few changes, but one is particularly compelling. Jefferson wrote, "We hold these truths to be sacred and undeniable," and Franklin changed that phrase to "We hold these truths to be self-evident." What a difference word choice makes! Isaacson says that Jefferson's words implied that the principle in question—the equality of people and their endowment by their creator with inalienable rights—was an assertion of religion. Franklin's edit turned it instead to an assertion of rationality.[5]
>
> Later, the Congress formed into a committee of the whole to consider Jefferson's draft. Massive changes were made, but Franklin's immortal phrase "We hold these truths to be self-evident" has gained immortality.
>
> So what were the other contributions of Benjamin Franklin to the United States of America? They were significant. Let me share with you today Franklin's contributions to foreign diplomacy as an ambassador to France and his other contributions to U.S. government as we now know it.

Gaining and maintaining the attention of the audience is extremely important in presenting information. Audience members must believe they will benefit from receiving the information, believe it is relevant to their lives, and find it interesting enough to want to listen. Achieving this can be quite challenging to the beginning speaker, but by making your audience the central focus of the speech and using a little creativity, you can easily gain and hold their attention.

Increase Understanding of the Topic

Once you have gained your listeners' attention, you have created the opportunity to increase their understanding. Understanding is the ability to interpret, grasp, or assign meaning to an idea. You can increase your audience's understanding by organizing your presentation systematically, choosing appropriate language, and providing clear definitions.

Organize Your Presentation. In a well-organized speech, ideas are managed in a clear and orderly sequence that makes the material easy to follow and understand. Effective organization helps increase the speaker's credibility and improves the audience's comprehension and retention of information. See Chapter 9 and review the two organizational techniques that aid listeners' understanding: planned repetition and advance organizers.

Plan for Repetition. **Planned repetition** is the deliberate restating of a thought to increase the likelihood that the audience will understand and remember it. The repetition of information generally helps us remember things more completely. For example, if you called directory assistance to get a phone number and have nothing to write the number on until you call, you probably say the number over and over so that you can remember it long enough to dial it.

The power of repetition is so great that it is the guiding principle behind most television commercials. Although we might find it bothersome, the constant repetition of the same commercial reminds us of the product and thus increases the chances of our purchasing it. You can use this same principle in an informative speech to get your audience to remember key ideas. For example, you might say the following:

> A high-context culture is one where the location and the activities make a difference. In a high-context culture, the meaning of the communication act is inferred from the location. If you go to dinner in a high-context culture, you will not talk business, because in high-context cultures, a social setting is for social communication; a business setting is for business communication.
>
> The combination to the safe is 37–45–72–6. That's 37–45–72–6.

planned repetition The deliberate restating of a thought to increase the likelihood that the audience will understand and remember it.

advance organizer A statement that warns the listener that significant information is coming.

You could also show the safe's combination on a computer slide presentation, put it on a poster, or write it on the board for additional repetition and emphasis. Internal summaries and previews may also include repetition to help the listener remember the points you've already made and to help them stay focused on what is to come in the speech.

Use Advance Organizers. **Advance organizers** are similar to signposts in that they signal what is coming, but they also warn that the information coming is significant. They signal the listener to pay attention.

Two points are critical here.

You will need to know this in order to be able to complete the task.

The following information is essential.

These warnings get the attention of your audience and emphasize that the forthcoming information is both necessary and important. Teachers use advance organizers to make sure that students know what is essential. Examples include the following:

You'll see this again.

The next exam will require you to demonstrate your knowledge of this concept.

If you understand these two points, you will be able to solve the problem.

Advance organizers also serve as previews of main points. Using advance organizers in an informative speech introduction helps your audience concentrate and focus on what is coming in the speech. For example, one speaker used the following statement in her introduction to let the audience know what was coming and what was important to meet her specific purpose:

> To see how all of this fits together, I will first provide an operational definition of anger management; then we'll talk about the steps involved in learning to manage our anger; and finally, we'll learn three strategies to help us calm down and think.

Choose Language Carefully. It is extremely important to match your level of language to the knowledge your audience already has about your topic. If you are speaking with experts or with people who are familiar with your topic, you are free to use technical terms without explaining them, but if your audience is unfamiliar with your subject, you will need to choose your words carefully and define any special terms. In some cases, you should avoid technical terms altogether. This may be necessary when such terms would only confuse your audience or when your audience lacks the ability or background to understand them. Sometimes a speaker's use of too many technical terms will turn an audience off or even create hostility. A speaker should choose language carefully to avoid creating unnecessary problems. When possible, choose words that are concrete rather than words that are abstract, and use descriptions to make your points clearer.

Secretary of State Colin Powell is known for his use of clear and understandable language when he informs others.

Use Concrete Words. To increase your audience's understanding, try to use as many concrete words as possible. In Chapter 4, we said that concrete words are symbols for specific things one can experience through the senses. Concrete words stand for specific people, places, things, or acts: Marilyn Shaw, Boston, iMac, taking notes in Oral Communication class. Familiar, concrete language allows your listeners to form mental images similar to yours. If you say that something is the size of

Making Connections

Choose Concrete Language

In Chapter 4, we stated that concrete language is more meaningful and more easily understandable to listeners than is abstract language. Rewrite the following sentences to make them more concrete:

1. The computer is a huge benefit for students and workers.
2. The bridge was constructed of masses of steel that ran for a great distance.
3. The university provides access to all students, regardless of background or origin.
4. Sex on campus has declined dramatically for quite some time.
5. Alcohol consumption in America is dangerous.

Discuss your changes in class.

a quarter, your listeners should form a fairly accurate picture of what you have in mind. Concrete words leave less room for misinterpretation and misunderstanding.

Abstract words refer to ideas, qualities, or relationships: truth, liberty, the pursuit of happiness, friendship. The meaning of these words relies on the experiences and intentions of the people who express them. If a speaker says, "The mass transit system is good," we don't know whether he means that it is cost effective, on time, or beneficial for riders. Abstract language is imprecise and often leaves listeners confused about the speaker's intent.

If a speaker says, "The grading system at this college is unfair," listeners might have so many questions that they fail to listen to the rest of the speech. A more precise statement would be "The grading system in this college is unfair for two reasons: First, grading here is heavily reliant on exams, and second, the scale is arbitrary because anything below a 70 percent is failing and it takes a 94 percent or higher to get an A." The second effort is much clearer and more forceful than the first and leaves no doubt in the listener's mind about the speaker's intent.

Use Description. To make something more concrete, a speaker might describe its size, quantity, shape, weight, composition, texture, color, age, strength, or fit. Words used to describe something are called **descriptors.** The more descriptors a speaker uses that relate to the listeners' experiences, the greater is the likelihood that the message will be understood. Andrea used descriptors in talking about constructing a sturdy deck that meets the building codes in her city:

> First you have to have poured concrete pads or bases for the deck supports. The City Building Codes office will provide you with the specific numbers. Our deck is ten feet wide, forty feet long, and ten feet high. That means that we had to dig fourteen inch in diameter holes that were three feet deep and spaced at four-foot intervals. In our case, that meant we needed ten support pads on both the front and back sides of the deck. The city inspector inspected and approved those foundation pads before we could pour the concrete. The concrete must be a special mixture of eight bags of cement, forty-five gallons of water, and one cubic yard of aggregate. The concrete plant will add limestone, sand, and gravel to the cement and water mixture. The concrete is delivered in a truck that mixes the ingredients from the plant to the destination and during the pour. The concrete comes out of the truck's chute and slides into your carefully prepared holes. It is gray in color and the consistency of cake batter; it almost looks like lava from a volcano as it slides down the chute. When dry, these concrete pads are very hard and will hold the equivalent of 200 pounds per square inch.

descriptors
Words used to describe something.

Andrea's explanations provide size (height, length, and width as well as depth and diameter of the pads), quantities, color, texture, and strength. Her personal experience helped to make the description more meaningful.

Use Definitions. One way to ensure your audience's understanding is to define all potentially unfamiliar and complex words. Consider the importance of definitions in the following cases: Julia had been involved in computer programming and in her speech discussed flow sheets and GIGO; Daya spoke on communication apprehension, Sally on the squeal rule, and Jacques on the problem of ethnocentrism. In each situation, many in the audience may not have understood the speaker's subject unless the basic terms were explained. For example, Julia defined *flow sheets* as written instructions that programmers use to set up step-by-step operations to be performed by the computer and *GIGO* as computer jargon meaning "garbage in, garbage out," or you get out of the computer what you put into it. Daya defined *communication apprehension* as the fear of communicating with others. Sally, in her speech, explained that a doctor uses the *squeal rule* when he or she tells the parents of a teenage girl that she is using birth control pills. *Ethnocentrism* was defined in Jacques's speech as the belief in the inherent superiority of one's own group and culture over another.

Making Connections

Give Ideas Life!

The words we use are very important. Language choices should help speakers to communicate effectively. The following phrases are rather boring.

Hip-hop music
A favorite off-campus gathering place
The basketball arena
The student union
The Internet café
Campus food locations

1. Create lively language by using concrete words, descriptors, and definitions of the six phrases.
2. Compare the original phrases with your creations. What differences do you find?
3. Compare your changes with those of your classmates. What are the similarities and differences?

The most common form of definition used by speakers, the logical definition, usually contains two parts: the dictionary definition and the characteristics that distinguish the term from other members of the same category. An operational definition explains how an object or concept works, and a definition by example explains a term or a concept by using examples, either verbal or actual, to illustrate a point. In addition, there are four other methods of clearly defining a term for your listeners: using contrast, synonyms, antonyms, and etymologies.

Show Contrasts. A **contrast definition** is used to show or emphasize differences. This type of definition is helpful when you want to distinguish between similar terms. For example, a speaker discussing communication apprehension and speech anxiety differentiated one term from the other by stating that communication apprehension is a trait or global anxiety, whereas speech anxiety is a state or situational anxiety. A person suffering from communication apprehension might also have speech anxiety, but a person with speech anxiety will not necessarily have communication apprehension. A contrast definition might also point out differences in causes and effects. Thus the speaker might point out that people with communication apprehension actively avoid all interaction with others, whereas people with speech anxiety merely feel a bit of controllable discomfort when addressing an audience.

contrast definition
A definition that shows or emphasizes differences.

synonym
A word, term, or concept that is the same or nearly the same in meaning as another word, term, or concept.

Use Synonyms. The use of synonyms can also help clarify the meaning of a word. A **synonym** is a word, phrase, or concept that has exactly the same or nearly the same meaning as another word, term, or concept. In describing a communicative extrovert, a speaker used the phrases "willingness to talk openly," "uninhibited speech," and "ability to speak in any situation without reservation." Each phrase describes the behavior that might be exhibited by a person who is a communicative extrovert.

Use Antonyms. In contrast, an **antonym** is a word, phrase, or concept that has the opposite meaning of another word, phrase, or concept. For example, a communicative extravert is the opposite of someone with communication apprehension. Such a person is not shy, reserved, unwilling to talk, or afraid to speak. The person greatly enjoys talking with others. Using an antonym helps the audience to compare differences and leaves the audience with a memorable definition of an unfamiliar term.

Use Etymologies. An **etymology** is a form of definition that traces the origin and development of a word. One student used etymology to explain how the Olympic Games got their name. In the Greek system of telling time, an Olympiad was the period of four years that elapsed between two successive celebrations of the Olympian. This method of figuring time became common in about 300 B.C., and all events were dated from 776 B.C., the beginning of the first known Olympic Games. Such a definition provides the audience with a novel way to remember key information. The *Oxford English Dictionary* or the *Etymological Dictionary of Modern English* are excellent sources of word etymologies.

Whenever there is any possibility that your audience may not understand a term or concept, select the kind of definition that will provide the clearest explanation. In some instances, more than one kind of definition might be necessary. To err by overdefining is better than providing an inadequate definition that leaves your audience wondering what you are talking about.

Learning Connections

1. Why should we use concrete words?
2. How do descriptors help to make content meaningful?
3. How often do your professors use definitions in their lectures and discussions?

Hints for Effective Informative Speaking

Almost everything we have covered in the text up to this point is relevant to informative speaking and audience participation. Adhering to the following two additional guidelines should be particularly helpful in ensuring your success: Avoid assumptions, and personalize information.

Avoid Assumptions. A student began speaking on CPR by emphasizing how important it is in saving lives. However, she failed to explain that the acronym CPR stands for *cardiovascular pulmonary resuscitation;* she assumed that everyone already knew that. Most of the audience did understand, but a number of people did not. In addition, some knew what the acronym meant but did not know how the technique worked. Because at least half of the class was unfamiliar with the technique, they found the speaker's presentation confusing and frustrating. One mistaken assumption undercut all the work she had put into her speech. Follow these guidelines to avoid making assumptions:

1. Ask yourself whether your listeners already know what you are talking about. Audience analysis may be appropriate. If you are addressing your class, randomly select some of your classmates and ask them what they know about your topic and its related terminology.

antonym
A word, phrase, or concept that is opposite in meaning to another word, phrase, or concept.

etymology
A form of definition that traces the origin and development of a word.

2. If you believe that even one audience member might not understand, take the time to define and explain your topic.

3. If you believe that a majority of your audience already knows what you mean, say something like, "Many of you probably know what euthanasia is, but for those who don't, ..." In this way, you acknowledge those who already know and help those who do not.

4. Do not make the assumption that your audience needs introductory information, especially if you have any doubts about what they know. You can always move through your basic definitions and explanations quickly if your audience seems to understand, but it is difficult to regain their interest and attention once you start talking over their heads.

Personalize Information. When you relate your topic to your listeners so that they can see its relevance for them, you are personalizing information. Judy presented a speech about nutrition and the eating habits of people in the United States. It was an interesting speech, but the practice audience didn't understand what it had to do with them. In revising her speech, Judy surveyed students in her residence hall and class about their eating habits. Then she personalized the information for her audience as follows:

> Bad eating habits can cause problems that you may not be aware of. In a survey I took, I found that many college students like you fail to eat a variety of foods from the necessary basic food groups every day. In fact, my data indicate that 61 percent of you—that is more than half of you—do not eat balanced meals. Furthermore, I found that 50 percent of you skip breakfast at least five times a week.
>
> What does this mean to you? According to nutrition experts, people who eat balanced meals are more motivated and less tired than people who don't eat balanced meals. In fact, those of you who drink a can of pop and eat a candy bar for breakfast—and you know who you are—are more likely to have high blood pressure, lack ambition, feel highly stressed, and be vulnerable to chronic diseases later in life.

Information that is personalized not only holds attention, but also attracts interest. For example, think of your most effective instructors. Chances are that they take ordinary material and personalize it into meaningful, interesting knowledge. Listening to a string of facts can be frustrating, but a speech comes to life when it contains personal illustrations.

Most of us are interested in others. If we were not, there would be no *People* magazine, no *National Enquirer,* no *Late Show with David Letterman,* no *Survivor,* no *Joe Millionaire,* and no *Oprah.* Stories are much more likely to affect listeners than are statistics. Whenever possible, personalize your information and dramatize it in human terms.

One student began an informative speech about the Heimlich maneuver, a technique used to clear the throat of someone who is choking, by relating the story of

Making Connections

Your Informative Speech

Soon you will present an informative speech in front of your classmates. Think about and answer these questions (plan to share your responses in class).

1. How will you choose a topic?
2. How will you begin your preparations?
3. What are the unique characteristics of an informative speech?
4. How will you get your classmates to listen to you?
5. How long do you think it will take to put this speech together? What makes you think that?

a four-year-old boy who saved his three-year-old friend. The boy, who had watched a television show in which the maneuver was used to save the life of one of the main characters, simply reenacted what he saw. By using this dramatic, real-life episode, the student was able to grab his audience's attention and prepare them for his discussion of who developed the technique, how it works, and how many lives it has saved.

GUIDELINES Personalizing Information in Your Speeches

1. Use examples and information that specifically relate to your audience.
2. Draw conclusions that your audience can identify with, and explain what the conclusions may mean for them.
3. Refer to people who are similar to your audience members, for example, single parents, nontraditional students, minority students, international students, computer science majors, commuters who must drive to campus.
4. Refer to topics and events that affect your listeners, such as campus activities, elections, state and local laws, social events, tax cuts or increases, cultural programs, and career decisions.

GUIDELINES Developing and Preparing an Informative Speech

1. Select a topic that is appropriate for an informative speech. (Because the audience is a critical component, you might want to do an audience analysis, item 3 below, before you select a topic, or at least consider the audience during the topic selection process.)
2. Research the topic in which you are interested.
3. Analyze the audience: Narrow the topic so that it will allow you to inform your audience about something they do not already know.
4. Decide whether you will be able to cover your topic adequately in the given time limit.
5. Determine your specific purpose: Word it to ensure that it meets the objective of the informative speech.
6. Organize the speech: Select and word your main points so that they are clear and meet your specific purpose.
7. Develop clarifying and supporting materials to ensure that your audience will understand everything about which you are talking.
8. Check the organization of your speech against the guidelines of effective organization specified in Chapter 9.
9. Avoid assumptions.
10. Personalize information to your listeners as much as possible.
11. Practice the delivery.
12. After delivering your speech, analyze the effectiveness of it.

The successful informative speech always considers the listeners. The speaker carefully thinks about the following questions: What do I want my listeners to learn from my speech? What will be the best way to deliver my speech so my listeners will understand and retain the information? How will I know if I was successful in accomplishing my purpose?

Evaluating the Informative Speech

Every instructor uses specific criteria to evaluate a speaker's competence in creating and delivering a speech. The following are some common criteria used by instructors all across the nation. Keep them in mind as you prepare your speech.

We have also included a speaker's self-evaluation form and a listener evaluation form (Figures 11.1 and 11.2) so that both speakers and audience members will be aware of their responsibilities to each other.

Topic

The selection of a topic should meet the following criteria:

- The topic should merit your audience's attention.
- The treatment of the topic should take into account the audience's level of knowledge of it.
- The audience should be able to see the relationship between the topic and the speaker and between the topic and themselves.

FIGURE 11.1

Speaker's Self-Evaluation Form After you have completed an informative speech, take a few moments to think about your preparation and presentation. Complete the phrases on this form by stating what you would do similarly or differently, and why, if you were to give this same speech again.

Title of speech: ________________________________.

Date and place given: ________________________________.

My topic was ________________________________.

My research could be improved by ________________________________.

The organizational pattern I chose was ________________________________.

The introduction was ________________________________.

The body of the speech needed ________________________________.

My conclusion seemed to be ________________________________.

My explanation of ideas should ________________________________.

The support I provided for my ideas was ________________________________.

My use of language might ________________________________.

My visual delivery was ________________________________.

My vocal delivery needed ________________________________.

The ways I adapted my topic, ideas, and language to this audience were ________________________________

________________________________.

Things I would change are ________________________________,

because ________________________________.

Things I would retain are ________________________________,

because ________________________________.

FIGURE 11.2

Listener's Evaluation Form This form can be used to evaluate speeches given by your classmates. Follow your instructor's directions for providing such feedback.

Speaker ____________________ Topic ____________________
Date ____________________
The appropriateness of the topic for this class, assignment, and context was ____________________.
One new or different perspective I gained was ____________________.
The organization of the speech was ____________________.
The reasons for my comments on organization are ____________________.
I identified the speaker's purpose as ____________________.
The speaker needed to explain ____________________.
The types of supporting materials used ____________________.
Presentational aids, if used, were ____________________.
The speaker's language should have ____________________.
The speaker could improve the physical aspects of delivery by ____________________.
The one comment I wish to make about vocal delivery is ____________________.
One aspect I especially liked was ____________________.
One area that needs improvement in the future is ____________________.

- The topic of the speech should be adequately covered in the time available. The topic should be narrow enough to be fully developed.

General Requirements

These general requirements hold for all informative speech presentations:

- The speech's purpose should be clearly to inform and should be stated as such.
- The speech should meet the time requirements set by the assignment.
- The speaker should cite sources of information other than the speaker's own.
- The speech's purpose should be relevant to the assignment and relate to the audience.
- The speech should show evidence of careful preparation.

Audience Analysis

The speaker must shape the speech to suit the audience, which often requires research (for example, determining the listeners' past experiences, beliefs, attitudes, values). The choices the speaker makes regarding content and the development of ideas should be customized for the listeners' benefit.

A speaker explains to an interested group how to become a movie extra. As he tells them what they must do, he keeps in mind the objectives of being an extra, techniques in speech delivery to reinforce key points, and how to determine whether his speech is accomplishing his objectives.

- The speech should reflect appropriate audience analysis.
- The speech should show the audience why the topic is important to them.
- At several points the speaker should make contact with the listeners by using familiar examples or showing knowledge of their preferences or experiences.

Supporting Materials

Supporting materials supply documented evidence that the information conveyed in the speech is accurate and credible.

- The speech should be well documented.
- The sources should be cited completely and accurately.
- The research should be up to date.
- The speaker should use adequate and sufficient clarifying materials.
- Visual aids, if used, should be appropriate, add to the audience's understanding of the speech's content, and follow the guidelines established by the assignment.

Organization

When judging the organization, the evaluator looks for a carefully planned, well-developed informative speech that takes a unified approach to the material being presented.

- The introduction should be properly developed.
    - It should orient the audience to the topic, gaining attention and arousing interest.
    - It should include a specific purpose and thesis statement.

    - It should define terms (if necessary).
    - It should be relevant.
    - It should establish credibility.
- The organization of the body should be clear and easy to follow.
    - The main points should be clear and parallel in structure.
    - The main points should be related to the purpose of the speech.
    - Transitions should provide appropriate links between ideas.
    - The organizational pattern should be appropriate.
- The conclusion should be properly developed.
    - It should reinforce the purpose by reviewing the main points.
    - It should end with a memorable thought.

Delivery

The delivery techniques provide evidence that the speaker is aware of what the audience is interested in hearing, is involved in and enthusiastic about the topic, and is interested in sharing the material with the listeners.

- The speaker's stance and posture should be appropriate.
- The speaker's eye contact with the audience should be appropriate.
- The speaker should follow the assignment in method of delivery (use of notes and number of note cards).
- The speaker's facial expressions should help to convey and clarify thoughts.
- The speaker's body movements should be appropriate and effective.
- The speaker's vocal delivery should enhance the speech with appropriate volume and rate, conversational quality, enthusiastic tone, clear enunciation, appropriate pauses, and appropriate vocal variety.

Language Choice

Language choice can enhance and clarify ideas considerably.

- Language choice should be appropriate to the assignment and audience.
- Word choice should be appropriate for the college level.
- Grammar should be appropriate and show college-level competence.
- Word pronunciations should be correct.

Speakers should always analyze their presentations. We are often called on to make reports or provide information in the workplace, in the groups of which we are members, and in classrooms (ours and others). Because speaking is so prevalent, it is important that the speaker step back and carefully and critically reflect on the speech, the situation, the audience, and the performance. If we hope to become effective communicators in public settings, we need to use reflective thinking to objectively analyze what happened and how successful we were. Figure 11.1 (on page 305) shows a sample speaker's self-evaluation form to facilitate this reflection process.

We spend a great deal more time listening to speeches than we do making speeches, and though the focus of this book may seem to be on making effective speeches, it is also important for each of us to be a critical consumer of speeches and other presentations. Figure 11.2 (on page 306) provides a sample listener evaluation form to help the listener directly respond to the speaker, in writing. It is helpful for the speaker to obtain listeners' perspectives on a speech. Honest and tactful feedback can be invaluable. But it is also a good idea to closely evaluate presentations for yourself, even when you will not be passing your comments on to the speaker. Listeners are encouraged to use Figure 11.2 as a basis for creating their own evaluations and applying their own criteria to presentations.

A Sample Informative Speech with Commentary

The following speech (with our commentary) is an informative speech written and delivered by Samantha Burt, a student at the University of Northern Iowa. Samantha creatively used many of the strategies discussed in this chapter.

Down Syndrome Informative Speech

Samantha Burt, UNI[6]

Introduction

Raising a child with a disability can be a rewarding, yet challenging task. I know this firsthand because my son was diagnosed with Down syndrome at birth. There are many prenatal tests than can detect Down syndrome and other disabilities. The National Institute of Child Health and Development published some shocking results on their website this year regarding those tests. According to their figures, 94 percent of parents who receive a diagnosis of Down syndrome choose to abort that child. I am here to tell you that those parents have no idea what they are missing out on.

- Samantha begins her speech with her thesis statement. She then offers her own personal experience. This personalization gives her credibility, but it also increases interest for the audience.
- She immediately brings in some compelling statistics that provide information she responds to that gets listeners' attention.

Many expecting parents feel anxious about the health of their developing child. If you ask them if they want a boy or girl, many times the answer will simply be, "just a healthy baby." But what if that baby is not the "typical" child? What if that child has a mental or physical handicap? *Today I hope to dispel some of the fears you may have of having a child with a disability.* I would like to tell you what it feels like to receive this type of diagnosis for your child, some of the different emotions parents go through, and finally the advantages that you experience as a parent.

- Samantha brings in common knowledge with words her listeners might often have heard or even expressed. Rhetorical questions make the audience think about the topic, followed by the specific purpose, and then forecasting of the three points she will cover in her speech.

Body

What does it feel like to find out your child is very different than what you expected? It is very hard to put into words, but Emily Pert Kingsley, a writer from *Sesame Street* and mother of a child with Down syndrome, put it into words very eloquently. I would like to share what she has written with you.

- Again, she uses a rhetorical question to orient her listeners to her position and keep them involved. She quickly brings in another source to show her research and to provide additional support.

Welcome to Holland

I am often asked to describe the experience of raising a child with a disability—to try to help people who have not shared that unique experience to understand it, to imagine how it would feel. It's like this . . . When you're going to have a baby, it's like planning a fabulous vacation trip—to Italy. You buy a bunch of guide books and make your wonderful plans. The Coliseum. The Michelangelo David. The gondolas in Venice. You may learn some handy phrases in Italian. It's all very exciting. After months of eager anticipation, the day finally arrives. You pack your bags and off you go. Several hours later, the plane lands. The stewardess comes in and says, "Welcome to Holland." *"Holland?!?"* you say, "What do you mean Holland?? I signed up for Italy! I'm supposed to be in Italy. All my life I've dreamed of going to Italy." But there's been a change in the flight plan. They've landed in Holland and there you must stay. The important thing is that they haven't taken you to a horrible, disgusting, filthy place, full of pestilence, famine, and disease. It's just a different place.

So you must go out and buy new guide books. And you must learn a whole new language. And you will meet a whole group of people you would never have met.

It's just a *different* place. It's slower-paced than Italy, less flashy than Italy. But after you have been there for a while and catch your breath, you look around . . . and you begin to notice that Holland has windmills. . . . Holland has tulips. Holland even has Rembrandts.

But everyone you know is busy coming and going from Italy . . . and they are all bragging about what a wonderful time they had there. And for the rest of your life, you will say, "Yes, that's where I was supposed to go. That's what I had planned."

And the pain of that will never, ever, ever, ever go away . . . because the loss of that dream is a very, very significant loss.

But . . . if you spend your life mourning that fact that you didn't get to Italy, you may never be free to enjoy the very special, the very lovely things . . . about Holland.

● The use of Kingsley's story (an extended metaphor) allows Samantha to make comparisons throughout the speech.

The day arrived for us to go home from the hospital with our new son. The Hospital to Home Focus Group published a pamphlet which they sent home with us. This pamphlet goes through all the different emotions that we, as parents of a child with a disability, were likely to face. The first emotion is shock. We were definitely shocked when we received Tanner's diagnosis. The second stage is denial. We went through that also.

Although the doctors were sure beyond a shadow of a doubt that Tanner had Down syndrome, we did not believe it until we had blood tests to prove it. The next step is grief. This may sound strange, but you literally grieve for the child that you thought you were going to have. I was brought back to reality from this grieving stage when my mother asked me if I would rather be planning a funeral as another couple in the hospital was doing for their baby who had died. However, this led to the next stage, guilt. Of course you are going to feel guilty. You are grieving as if you had lost a child when in reality your child is right before your eyes.

● At this point, Samantha moves back to her own story and weaves her experiences in with information from another source. Her first major point, the parents' feelings blends right into the second major point about the emotions of parents who have a Down syndrome baby. She does not signal us that this is happening with a transition, but it seems to flow well from one point to to the next. She also skillfully uses her own experiences as she cites information from one of her sources.

Many parents feel angry or embarrassed. Some want to place blame. Often parents try to bargain with God. "God if you will cure my child, I promise I will never do this or that again!" Finally, you experience the final stage when you learn to adapt and get down to the business of raising your precious child.

We went home from the hospital with a huge stack of books, all on the subject of Down syndrome. We intended to get educated on Down syndrome since our knowledge of it was little to nothing. We found out that we were very fortunate that Tanner was so healthy. Many children born with Down syndrome have heart defects or intestinal blockage. Book after book explained the many other health problems we needed to watch for, such as thyroid dysfunction, leukemia, or vision or hearing impairments. The books told us that he was much more prone to respiratory infections and as an adult he had a higher risk than normal of developing Alzheimer's. Finally, we put the books away with the most important lesson we learned from them being, that our child was a baby like any other baby. He required sleep, diaper changes, milk, and most of all, our love.

So, maybe you are asking yourself, okay he needs to be treated like a regular baby but what happens when he grows up? You may be wondering what his limitations are and what will be the quality of his life? Well, that depends on how you define quality of life. If you define it as an impressive career, expensive car, fancy house, star of the football team, or the class math genius, then, no, most likely he will not have or be those things. But I would define quality of life as a person's ability to have meaningful relationships with other human beings. Tanner is certainly capable of this. When I came home from the hospital I was actually superficial enough to think about how other people would view Tanner. Would others think that my baby was cute? I brought some pictures along to share with you. (Show picture on overhead) This is when Tanner was just a baby. You can see that he did look a little different, but I was so wrong about how other people would react to him. It was unbelievable the way people were drawn to Tanner. I had people everywhere I went talking to him, playing with him, and telling me what a cutie I had. In fact, I think I had more positive comments about Tanner than both of my other children put together. (Present second picture of Tanner.) He has an incredible bond with people. Many others I've talked to who know someone with Down syndrome have had similar comments about them. (Show last picture.)

● More rhetorical questions serve as a way to interact with the listeners and keep them involved. They also serve as a transition. She brings in definitions to make her case.

● (Personal definition)

● (Presentational aid)

● (Second presentational aid)

● (Third presentational aid)

As sweet as he is, I'm not going to tell you that raising Tanner is easy because it is far from easy. Tanner is now four years old and is not yet toilet trained. He talks constantly but unfortunately we understand very little of it. He is fiercely stubborn and gets frustrated at times with his own limitations. Many times I feel pressure from well-meaning family members to hurry up and toilet train him among other things.

● Samantha relies heavily on her own personal experiences, but she uses specific events and behaviors and relates them to her other sources. In this case, Samantha's personal experiences and her story make the speech more compelling.

In spite of the challenges, there are also advantages to having a child like Tanner. First of all, that love that he shows everyone he meets he lavishes on me tenfold. He is definitely a mommy's boy. I've had the opportunity

● Samantha does not include a transition as she moves into her third main point. Again, her own story is her way of reaching her to meet a lot of really kind people through clinics, hospitals, and family support groups. Area Education Agency 7 (AEA 7) does a lot to meet the needs of people in the area with disabilities, and I've met a number of wonderful people through this agency. Also, I didn't know what I wanted to be when I "grew up." Now I am back here at UNI studying to be a special education teacher, so that I can help educate other children with disabilities.

listeners. Her references to people and places who provide help allows us to understand more about the situation and that there are sources of support for families. Her own experience helped her make a career choice.

Conclusion

If down the road someday you have a child and find out that this child is disabled in some way, don't be afraid. Many of us have been down this road before you. Whether it is Down syndrome or some other disability, there is a ton of support out there. Today, I have shared with you the emotions, challenges, and rewards that I have experienced as a parent. Yes, I planned a trip to Italy and ended up in Holland, but remember Holland is a wonderful, unique place to visit.

● Samantha quickly moves to a conclusion, where she makes a summary statement and leaves us with something to remember and recaps her main points. While her words are not always specific, they are clear and descriptive.

References

Donald, Jane. *Therapeutic Counseling for Parents.* 1996. Seattle, WA: Hospital-to-Home Focus Group.

http://www.nichd.nih.gov/publications/pubs/downsyndrome/down.htm. *Facts About Down Syndrome.* 2002. National Institute of Child Health and Development.

Kingsley, Emily Perl. *Welcome to Holland.* Date and publisher unknown.

Personal experiences from four and one half years of living with and loving Tanner.

Pueschel, Siegfried M. *A Parent's Guide to Down Syndrome.* 1990. Baltimore, MD: Paul H. Brookes Publishing Company.

Analysis and Evaluation

Samantha Burt had more than the average amount of information for her speech. Her personal experiences make her topic choice more compelling for her (she was passionate about the topic and could include her own story) and for her audience. Those personal experiences also increase her credibility with her audience, and the story makes the speech even more interesting for her listeners. Samantha is very conversational in her approach and in her language choices. She begins her speech with the thesis statement, establishes her credibility in the second sentence, and cites her first source in the fourth sentence. This, along with her own personal experience, is an indication of Samantha's expertise in the subject. She makes her listeners aware of her own views. In the second paragraph, still a part of the introduction, Samantha relates to expectant parents and their desire for a healthy child. She uses two rhetorical questions to make her listeners think about a child who is not "healthy." She then states the specific purpose, "Today I hope to dispel some of the fears you may have of having a child with a disability," and goes on to forecast the three main points of her speech: what it feels like to receive this type of diagnosis, the different emotions parents experience, and the advantages a parent experiences.

In the body of the speech, Samantha follows through on the three points she forecast at the end of her longer introduction. Again she uses other sources to back up what she is saying and to provide another perspective. The "Welcome to Holland" story is an extended metaphor that Samantha uses to make the point that although a Down syndrome child is a different "trip" than what was planned or expected, there are benefits just the same. The remainder of her speech reinforces the idea that there are benefits despite the surprise. Samantha reminds us throughout the speech that she and her husband had much to learn about having a child with Down syndrome and that they are still learning about the condition but that they also realize that their son is just that: a son who deserves to be loved and cherished.

Samantha relates the topic back to questions the listeners might be asking, and then she answers those questions. She provides definitions and explanations as well as her own definition of *quality of life* as "a person's ability to have meaningful relationships with other human beings." This spin on the definition demonstrates that her son Tanner has that ability and thus has a quality of life that transcends what we usually think of as "necessary" or "important."

There are no transitions between point one, the way it feels to get a diagnosis of Down syndrome for your newborn, and point two, the different emotions parents feel, but we can follow her thinking and make sense of it. It just takes a moment to adjust to the fact that she moves from the feelings about diagnosis to the gamut of emotions experienced. A transition to separate and yet link the two would be helpful. You might think that it doesn't make a difference, but if you are a listener, it does indeed throw you off at least momentarily. Sometimes, that means that a listener just tunes out. In this case, Samantha might have lost some of us at points, but her passion about her story brought us back in to be with her for most of the speech. And although she did refer to specific sources, we did not get complete citations so we would have a hard time using only her speech to allow us to find her sources so we could seek additional information.

Samantha spent a majority of her time in developing the first two main points. The part of her speech about the third point, the benefits of having a Down syndrome child, was shorter and seemed rushed because of that. Although she makes it clear in the discussion of points one and two that there are benefits, they really are not a part of that third major point. Despite that, this is a speech we can remember. The strength of the story, her passion for sharing the story, and the difference it has made in her life are compelling features. She did not use all the organizing strategies we talked about (advance organizers, internal previews, internal summaries, signposts, and transitions). She did, however, put together a speech based on her own experiences and created with the listeners in mind. Sometimes a speech can make the audience sit up and take notice even if some of the elements are missing. This is not to say that we should plan it that way, but sometimes our organizational strategies are forgotten because we are in front of a group. Despite that, we can sometimes still have an impact on the audience as Samantha did. Reread the speech. What would you do to improve Samantha's speech? Why?

Summary

The ability to present and receive information is vital in an information-oriented society. People who possess information and communicate it effectively possess power and command respect.

We are often asked to give informative speeches. The goal of an informative speech is to increase understanding. The goal of persuasive speaking is to change (alter) attitudes and/or behaviors. Information can be presented without attempting to persuade, but persuasion cannot be attempted without information.

Topics for informative speeches are almost limitless. You should choose something that interests you, that you already have some knowledge about, and that you can find additional information on through your research. Your topic should also be of interest and potentially useful for your listeners. Your specific purpose and the type of topic you choose will determine how you present the speech.

To increase your listeners' knowledge of the topic, you must gain their attention and increase their understanding of the topic. Listeners pay more attention to something that is meaningful to them and obviously important to the speaker. Listeners want novel ideas and want to know "what's in it for me?" The audience will listen if you give them reasons to listen.

Language choice and organization are both critical to audience understanding. The speaker must carefully plan the presentation. Language choice, as we discussed in Chapter 4, is very important in getting your message across and in helping listeners remember. Think about the ways your professors present information. Some of them are more interesting than others. What do the ones you label as "interesting" do that others do not? Did the chapter suggest some of the successful strategies you've noticed? Can you incorporate some of these effective strategies into your speeches?

The evaluation criteria should make you aware of the characteristics of an effective informative speech and speaker. Competent communicators analyze their listeners so they know their choices will work. They find ample sources from a variety of references, and they work to show their listeners the importance of the topic.

DISCUSSION STARTERS

1. What is the role of information in our lives?
2. Explain the concept "Information gives one power."
3. What are some examples of one who has the information holding the power?
4. What advice would you give someone about selecting a topic for an informative speech?
5. Where can we go to get information for our speeches?
6. Identify three topics that will work for an informative speech, and explain how you can make them interesting to and relevant for your audience.
7. What does it take to be an effective informative speaker?
8. Which of the criteria identified in the chapter mean the most to you as a listener?

NOTES

1. "Information," 2002 World Book Dictionary Media CD, Version 6.0.2, Mac OS X Edition.
2. This section is based on S. E. Lucas, *The Art of Public Speaking,* 6th ed. (Boston: McGraw-Hill, 1998), 343–52. The categories as cited in Lucas were described first by J. H. Bryns, *Speak for Yourself: An Introduction to Public Speaking* (New York: Random House, 1981), Chaps. 10–15.
3. W. Isaacson, *Benjamin Franklin: An American Life* (New York: Simon & Schuster, Inc, 2003).
4. Ibid.
5. Ibid.
6. Samantha Burt, University of Northern Iowa student, speech presented in Oral Communication, October 2002. Used with student speaker's permission.

CHAPTER 11 Appendix

Informative Speech Topics

Here are some possible topics for informative speeches. The items listed are not titles of specific speeches and need to be narrowed to fit specific purposes, time limits, or other requirements set by your instructor.

Graphic design and you
Bioengineering: Bane or benefit?
Tattoos, body piercing, and tongue forking
Slang and communication
Save your hearing!
PETA and your pets
Binge drinking on the college campus
Christian terrorism
Comparing the forms of music: Classical to contemporary
Presidential campaigns: Too long?
Martha Stewart's legal battles
Is pool a family sport?
Advanced video games
Changes in voting after 2000
Laser technology
Road rage
Migraine medications
Anger management
Biomedical engineering
Identity fraud
Caffeine and you
Muslim terrorism
Increased global warming
New treatments for multiple sclerosis
Peace Corps opportunities
Baseball's cork bats
The plastic footware fad
The Mars space exploration
Healthier Food: Organic
Hard drive retrieval
Ethics and business practices
International adoptions

"Persuasion is a central feature of every sphere of human communication."
—Robert H. Gass and John S. Seiter

CHAPTER 12 Persuasive Speaking

THIS CHAPTER WILL HELP YOU:

- Identify the goals of persuasion.
- Describe the way you approach a topic suitable for a persuasive speech.
- Demonstrate your credibility as a speaker.
- Apply evaluation criteria to your own speeches prior to presentation so you can make changes prior to the speech.
- Recognize errors in your own thinking so that you can correct them.
- Present a speech that demonstrates your ability to construct and support your persuasive goal.

CASE STUDY

In this class and in many other instances in your personal life, you will need to convince your listeners to think and act in specific ways. When you are asked to make a presentation to convince your colleagues that an addition needs to be added to your place of worship, you will try to be very persuasive. If you ask your banker for a loan to purchase a new vehicle, you must appear to be credible and creditworthy and may also employ persuasive strategies.

Questions to think about

1. How have you tried to persuade someone to do something in the last week?
2. Were you successful? Why or why not?
3. What did you do to sound more credible?
4. What would you do differently in a similar situation?

Most of us must convince or persuade others or be persuaded by others each day. If you are not trying to persuade someone, someone is trying to persuade you. Each time you ask your professor to excuse your absence from a class or to allow you to turn in a late paper, you are attempting to persuade. When someone recommends a specific book or video or asks you to vote for a specific candidate, you are a consumer of persuasion.

Because persuasion is so much a part of our everyday activities, it is important to understand it thoroughly. In this chapter, we discuss how to select a persuasive speech topic, how to establish credibility, and how to prepare and develop a persuasive speech. We also provide guidelines for persuading others effectively and for being effective consumers of persuasion.

The Goal of Persuasive Speaking

Persuasion is a communication process, involving both verbal and nonverbal messages, that attempts to reinforce or change listeners' attitudes, beliefs, values, or behaviors. David Zarefsky, for example, says that "persuasive strategies aim not only to provide information but also to affect audience members' attitudes and behavior. They ask for a greater degree of commitment from listeners than informative strategies do."[1] Is it possible to change people's attitudes, beliefs, or values without changing their behaviors? The answer is yes. You might, for example, present your friend with reasons for attending one concert rather than another. Your friend might agree and still not buy a ticket. Were you persuasive? You might have been able to convince your friend that your ideas are valid but not to alter her behavior. Which is more important?

The ultimate goal of all persuasion is action or change. Successful persuasion reinforces existing beliefs, attitudes, or behaviors; changes existing beliefs, attitudes, or behaviors; or leads to new beliefs, attitudes, or behaviors. When you want to convince someone not to change, you try to reinforce the existing belief, attitude, or behavior. At other times, you may want a person to do something different. When a speaker's main goal is to achieve change or action, the speaker will pursue one of four subgoals: adoption, discontinuance, deterrence, or continuance of a particular behavior.[2]

persuasion
A communication process, involving both verbal and nonverbal messages, that attempts to reinforce or change listeners' attitudes, beliefs, values, or behavior.

adoption
An action subgoal that asks listeners to demonstrate their acceptance of attitudes, beliefs, or values by performing the behavior suggested by the speaker.

Persuasion is usually not a one-shot deal; often, persuasion occurs over time, and the effect of a persuasive message on a listener is not apparent until some time after it has been received. In other words, the listener might think about the message for a long time and, with additional experiences, messages, and information, decide that a speaker was right. The listener might then decide to follow through on the speaker's request for action or change.

Adoption is an action subgoal that asks listeners to demonstrate their acceptance of an attitude, belief, or value by performing the behavior suggested by the speaker. One of your classmates might give a speech on becoming a Big Brother or Big Sister in your college community. If you had not previously even considered spending time with a young person but decide to do so after the speech and you become a Big Brother or Sister, you have displayed adoption. Your classmate has persuaded you. This adoption of the persuasive message might be only temporary, and you might not stay with the program throughout your college career, but you have responded positively to your classmate's initial persuasive message: to adopt a behavior.

Not all persuasion leads to change. People may be persuaded by an argument in theory and still not want to take action. Most skateboarders know that wearing helmets, kneepads, and wrist and hand protectors is important for safety, but some choose not to use these protective devices.

Discontinuance is the opposite of adoption. **Discontinuance** is an action subgoal that asks listeners to demonstrate their acceptance of an attitude, belief, or value by avoiding certain behaviors. If your action subgoal is discontinuance, you want your listeners to stop doing something—going without breakfast, paying high rent, or parking illegally. In these instances, you are trying to get your listeners to discontinue doing something negative.

Deterrence is an action subgoal that asks listeners to demonstrate their acceptance of an attitude, belief, or value by avoiding certain behaviors. Sample deterrent messages would be if you don't avoid breakfast, don't start avoiding it now; if you don't use illegal drugs, don't start now; if you are registered to vote, don't stop going to the polls. This action subgoal is similar to discontinuance in that you do not want a negative behavior to occur; but in deterrence, you are trying to *prevent* its occurrence rather than *end* its occurrence.

Making Connections

Persuasion in Your Life

How often do you attempt to persuade someone? How often are you a consumer of persuasive messages? Try this. Choose two days in the coming week to keep track of persuasion in your life.

1. Record the specific instances when you try to convince or persuade someone to do something or when another tries to persuade you to do something.
2. Reflect on the efficacy of those persuasion attempts.
3. What specific strategies were present when the persuasive attempt achieved the desired results?

discontinuance
An action subgoal that asks listeners to demonstrate their alteration of an attitude, belief, or value by stopping certain behaviors.

deterrence
An action subgoal that asks listeners to demonstrate their acceptance of an attitude, belief, or value by avoiding certain behavior.

Making Connections

Search the Web for Persuasive Examples

The following sites contain interesting speeches. Check them out, and see if you can determine which speeches are persuasive, and evaluate the reasons you think they are effective or ineffective.

1. If you are interested in political communication, you will find the televised presidential debates at www.museum.tv/debateweb/html/history/1976/video/htm. This website is divided into four sections: the Great Debate; Televised Debate History: 1960 to 1996; Television: The Great Equalizer?; and Curriculum Resources.
2. The Gifts of Speech site at http://gos.sbc.edu/browse.html offers speeches of influential women from around the world.
3. The top 100 speeches of the twentieth century can be found at http://gos.sbc.edu/top100.html.
4. The Nobel Lectures by women can be found at http://gos.sbc.edu/notel.html.
5. You will find a list of persuasive topics and questions at www.valencia.cc.fl.us/lrcwest/kaysmith.html.

Continuance is an action subgoal that asks listeners to demonstrate their acceptance of an attitude, belief, or value by continuing to perform the behavior suggested by the speaker. For example, if you eat breakfast, don't stop; continue to volunteer as a Big Brother or Big Sister; purchase and consume more organic foods. This action subgoal is similar to adoption because you want a positive behavior to occur; but with continuance, you are trying to *keep* an existing behavior rather than *begin* a new behavior.

Note that the first two action subgoals, adoption and discontinuance, ask people to *change* their behavior, whereas the last two, deterrence and continuance, ask people *not to change,* but to continue doing what they are already doing or not change to something new.

Getting others to change or not to change their behaviors is not always easy. A speaker might have to settle for a change in attitudes, beliefs, or values, such as accepting the idea of wearing seat belts, is part of the persuasive process and must almost always occur before a change in behavior can take place. Not all persuasive speaking will lead to action, nor should persuasive speakers consider themselves failures if they do not obtain behavior change. Sometimes listeners will not immediately accept another's views, but after time and thought, the listener might decide that the persuasive message heard weeks ago was accurate and be influenced enough to change a belief, an attitude, or even a behavior. Persuasion usually occurs over time; and therefore the speaker might not always be aware of whether the message was truly persuasive. Often, listeners are persuaded only after they have heard similar messages from a variety of people, over a period of time. Especially as a beginner at persuasive speaking, you should not always expect to obtain a change in attitude, action, or behavior, but you should be able to get others to listen to what you have to say and to consider your point of view.

continuance
An action goal that asks listeners to demonstrate their acceptance of an attitude, belief, or value by continuing to perform the behavior suggested by the speaker.

Topics for Persuasive Speeches

Some topics and themes lend themselves more readily to persuasive speaking than others do. Especially adaptable are current and controversial subjects. The list of topics in the appendix at the end of this chapter shows how varied the possibilities are. You will increase your likelihood of success if you follow these suggestions:

1. Whenever possible, select a topic that you are interested in, know something about, want to speak about, need to speak about, or are personally concerned about. Remember, it is not always possible to choose your own topic; sometimes someone else chooses it for you. For example, a nursing supervisor might tell one of the nurses that he has to speak to a group of visitors about the importance of using sunblock to prevent skin cancer. Certainly, that might not be the first topic of choice for the nurse, but he does meet some of the other criteria for speaking on the subject: knowledge of the topic, awareness of the need, and a personal and professional concern about the topic.
2. Select a subject that is worthwhile and of potential concern to your audience.
3. Select a topic with a goal for influence or action. For example, the notion that exercise and eating well are good for your health might be a good persuasive theme, but if everyone in your audience is healthy and physically in good shape, could you find a strong persuasive strategy?
4. Select an issue that is current, but avoid one that is common knowledge or that has been discussed widely unless you plan to add a new perspective to it (see Chapter 7 on selecting a topic and the appendix at the end of this chapter for a list of persuasive topics).

Persuasive speeches are often, but not always, given on topics for which two or more opposing viewpoints exist and in situations in which the speaker's point of view differs from that of the audience. For example, the speaker might want the audience to support higher tuition because it will lead to more quality instruction, but most of the audience may believe that tuition is already too high. Especially when a speaker's goal is adoption or discontinuance, there must be some difference between the speaker's view and that of the audience, or there is no need for persuasion. However, when the speaker's goal is deterrence or avoidance, the speaker's and the audience's points of view might be more closely united. In such cases the speaker's goal is to reinforce beliefs, attitudes, or behaviors that are similar to those proposed in the speech.

Sometimes speakers want their listeners to think about something from a new perspective, and they try to influence the listeners to accept a specific point of view. The speaker's goal is to persuade the listeners that one point of view is sound, valid, or worthwhile, and the speaker wants to influence the listeners to accept that specific perspective. Such speeches typically address questions of fact, questions of value, questions of policy, or any combination of the three types of questions.

Questions of Fact

A **question of fact** asks what is true and what is false. Consider these questions: Which building is the tallest in the world? Who is the richest person in the world? Which basketball player scored the most points last season? Which university was the first to be established? Who first developed the computer and for what uses? These questions can be answered with a fact that can be verified in reference books. Because they are so cut and dried, there can be little debate about them, thus making them weak topics for a persuasive speech.

question of fact
A question that asks what is true and what is false.

In contrast, persuasive speeches may be built on predictions of future events that will eventually become matters of fact. Consider these: Who will be the next president of the United States? Which college football team will win the national championship next year? Will computers replace textbooks? Although none of these questions can be answered with certainty, a persuasive speaker could build an effective case predicting the answer to each.

Persuasive speeches can also be based on complicated answers to questions of fact or justifications for answers that are unclear. Why did so many tragic air disasters occur during the past decade? Was it because of drugs? Poorly trained air traffic controllers? Overworked controllers? Outdated equipment? Insufficient rules for the use of airspace near airports? Although no one answer covers the entire situation, a speaker could build a strong argument to show that one of these factors is the primary cause of air accidents.

Finally, some persuasive speeches may attempt to answer questions of fact that are not completely verifiable: Do unidentified flying objects really exist? Can hypnotism enable a person to relive past lives? Is there intelligent life in outer space? A speech on the benefits of a credit union account might be planned this way:

To persuade my listeners that credit unions are better than banks — *Specific purpose*

You have many banking choices, but a credit union account provides the greatest benefits in terms of efficiency and convenience. — *Thesis*

Main points

I. A credit union account is the most cost efficient.
   A. Only a low minimum balance is required for interest-bearing accounts.
   B. There are low or no fees for these accounts.
II. A credit union account is the most convenient.
   A. There are longer hours at a credit union.
   B. There are locations close to campus.

On the surface, questions of fact may appear more appropriate for an informative speech than for a persuasive one, but if you consider the difficulty of persuading an audience that college athletics are big business, that a major fire will destroy much of Southern California, or that the pyramids of Egypt were designed by an intelligence far superior to ours today, you can see that questions of fact can offer rich possibilities for persuasion.

Questions of Value

A **question of value** asks whether something is good or bad, desirable or undesirable. Value was defined in Chapter 3 as a general, relatively long-lasting ideal that guides behavior. A value requires a more judgmental response than a fact. Here are some typical questions of value: Who was the best president of this country? Who was the most influential world leader? Are international students better students? The answers to these questions are not based solely on fact, but on what each individual considers to be right or wrong, ethical or unethical, acceptable or unacceptable.

question of value
A question that asks whether something is good or bad, desirable or undesirable.

The answers to questions of value may seem to be based solely on personal opinion and subjectivity rather than on objective evidence, but this is not the case.

Effective persuasive speakers will have evidence to support their positions and will be able to justify their opinions. For example, suppose a speaker says that bars should not target college students with their drink specials. He might plan his speech as follows:

● Specific purpose

To persuade my listeners to support legislation banning alcohol specials such as two-fers or dollar draws

● Thesis

Bar owners target college students with their specials, thus encouraging underage drinking and excessive drinking.

● Main points

I. Bar owners' advertised drink specials encourage underage college students drinking.
   A. Underage college students interviewed by the campus newspaper stated that bar advertisements made them feel they needed to go there to drink.
   B. Underage college students are quoted as saying that the advertisements enticed them.

II. College students attribute bar specials as a cause of excessive drinking.
   A. Bar specials mean that cash-strapped students can get more drinks for their money.
   B. Once college students get to the bars and imbibe the specials, they forget to think about the dangers of excessive drinking.

Values vary dramatically from one person to the next. Person A might think that rap music is bad for society, and Person B might think that it is good for society; Person A might think that alcohol should be illegal on campus, and Person B might think it should be legal. When it comes to questions of value, one person's judgment is no better or worse than another's. People's values are usually complicated because they are rooted in emotion rather than reason. It is often extremely difficult to get people to change their values. A speaker's position on a question of value might be difficult to defend. You will need to gather a great deal of research and evidence and build a strong case to support one value over another—even though you know your values are right—because your listeners also believe that their values are right.

Values are complicated. The cartoon illustrates the point that values are often based on emotion and personal views and, thus, are difficult to change.

Questions of Policy

A **question of policy** goes beyond seeking judgmental responses to seeking courses of action. Whereas a question of value asks whether something is right or wrong, a question of policy asks whether something should or should not be done. Should student parking on campus be more accessible? Should universities provide birth control to students? Should all students be tested for drugs before entering college? Should the government provide basic health care for every U.S. citizen? Should everyone working in jobs that involve the safety of others be tested for drugs? Questions of policy involve both facts and values and are therefore never simple. And the answers to questions of policy are not agreed on by everyone in the same way.

Persuasive speakers can defend an existing policy, suggest modifications of an existing policy, suggest a new policy to replace an old one, or create a policy where none exists. If you defend an existing policy, you must persuade your listeners that what exists is best for the situation. If you want to modify or replace an existing policy, you must persuade your listeners that the old policy does not work and that your new one will. If you hope to create a new policy, you must persuade your audience that a policy is needed and that yours is the right one for the situation.

question of policy A question that asks what actions should be taken.

Learning Connections

1. How are informative and persuasive speeches similar? How are they different?
2. What are the differences between questions of fact, value, and policy?
3. Why should we be concerned about questions of fact, value, and policy?

When discussing questions of policy, persuasive speakers usually focus on three considerations: need, plan, and suitability. If you believe that things are not fine as they are, then you must argue that there is a *need* for change. When you advocate change, you must provide a *plan,* or a solution. The plan tells the audience what you think should be done. Finally, you must defend your plan by explaining its *suitability* for the situation. Study the use of need, plan, and suitability in the following:

To persuade my listeners that embryonic stem cell research should be unrestricted and have full government funding — Specific purpose

Embryonic stem cell research is a new research area that has the potential for numerous treatments and cures for many disabling and terminal diseases and conditions. — Thesis

I. According to the National Institutes of Health, there are 128 million people in the United States living with incurable or untreatable diseases or conditions. — Need
   A. Stem cell research is most promising in treating these conditions.
   B. Stem cell research is already helping people with Parkinson's disease and Alzheimer's disease.

II. We must lobby Congress and our state legislatures to provide funding for embryonic stem cell research. — Plan
   A. The first step is to educate policymakers on the benefits of embryonic stem cell research.
   B. The second step is to lobby for the repeal of laws against stem cell research.

III. Educational lobbying campaigns can help both the public and our policymakers learn about the true nature of embryonic stem cell research.
  A. Educational lobbying campaigns can educate people about the benefits of this research.
  B. Once policymakers and the public are aware of the benefits, restrictions can be lifted to promote additional research.[3]

● Suitability

Persuasive Claims

When attempting to answer questions of fact, value, and policy, we cannot always develop a formal logical answer that will irrefutably counter the objections of others. Formal rules of argument do not always determine who is right and who is wrong. Even when you supply compelling evidence to support your view, most evidence is not 100 percent clear-cut and may be interpreted in different ways. These factors make persuasive speaking especially challenging.

Stephen Toulmin, a British philosopher, developed a model to help understand everyday persuasive arguments.[4] Although not everyone uses Toulmin's model for understanding and presenting arguments, a brief discussion of the model may be helpful, to both listeners and speakers, as a means of evaluating arguments. Toulmin's approach to supporting a persuasive position or argument involves three basic parts: claim, data, and warrant. The *claim* is what the persuader wants or hopes will be believed, accepted, or done (or, in terms of what we discussed in the previous section, whether it is a fact, a value, or a policy). Claims, however, require evidence, or what Toulmin refers to as *data.* Data are the supporting materials or evidence that should influence the listener to accept the claim as stated. Unfortunately, there is not always a clear or irrefutable relationship between the claim and the data. Thus the persuader must explain the relationship between the claim and

Making Connections

Persuasion in the Classroom

You will soon be choosing topics, completing research, organizing your information, and presenting a persuasive speech for class. As with every aspect of the communication process, you must begin with yourself. Think about and answer these questions to help you begin the persuasive speaking process.

1. What are some topics, issues, or concepts about which you have very strong feelings?
2. What are some controversial topics about which you already have some knowledge?
3. About which of those topics are you willing to find additional information?
4. Which of those topics seem likely to have some appeal for your classmates?

the data. Toulmin refers to this as the *warrant.* Here is a possible application of Toulmin's model:

Claim: Emergency room physicians are ill prepared to treat patients.

Data: According to Dr. Emily Greene of the National Institutes of Health, almost one in every nine patients (of the more than nine million emergency room patients each year) are mistreated by inadequately trained emergency room physicians.

Warrant: Because these physicians are not certified in emergency medicine, they cause inestimable harm to the millions who seek help in our nation's emergency rooms. Furthermore, they attach additional costs to patients' bills.

According to Toulmin's model, listeners can usually respond to the claims in three ways.

1. They can accept the claim at face value. This usually occurs when it is common knowledge that the claim is probably true. For example, the statement that U.S. educational programs need improvement is generally acceptable at face value.

2. They can reject the claim outright at face value. This usually happens when the claim is clearly false, such as the claim there is no pollution in U.S. lakes and streams. It also occurs when listeners are biased against the claim or see no relationship between the claim and themselves. For example, if a claim that U.S. forests are not being depleted is made to a group trying to preserve the environment, it is unlikely they would accept this claim because of their biased views.

3. They can accept or reject the claim according to their evaluation of data and warrant. The person making the claim must provide evidence to support the claim or demonstrate that it is true.

When speakers provide evidence to support their claims, it is still up to listeners to accept the claim based on the evidence presented. Listeners essentially have three options:

1. They can accept the claim as supported by evidence.
2. They can reject the claim as not supported by the evidence.
3. They can request that the speaker provide more evidence to support the claim.

Competent speakers must develop arguments strong enough to make the claim and the supporting evidence stand on their own merits. They realize that not everyone will interpret the evidence in the same way they do, nor will everyone be convinced, even though the evidence they present may be, in their opinion, the best there is.

Establishing Credibility

The most valuable tool that you, as a persuasive speaker, can possess is credibility or believability based on the audience's evaluation of you as a speaker. At various points in this book, we have referrred to the speaker's credibility. Listeners will assess your

An audience will judge your competence by the amount of knowledge, degree of involvement, and extent of experience you display. The more expertise you show in your subject, the more likely it is that your audience will accept what you have to say.

competence, knowledge, and experience; your charisma and energy; and your character. The audience is the ultimate judge of credibility, but there is much you can do to influence their opinion. The key is to establish yourself as worthy of the listeners' attention right from the beginning of your speech.

Competence

An audience will judge your competence by the amount of knowledge, degree of involvement, and extent of experience you display. The more expertise you show in your subject, the more likely it is that your audience will accept what you have to say. You can establish your expertise in several ways:

1. *Demonstrate involvement.* One student, in urging action to avoid the chemical pollution of water, described her mother's death as a result of drinking contaminated water. Although her firsthand experiences did not in themselves make her an expert environmentalist, they clearly established her involvement in the issue.

2. *Relate experience.* One student chose to speak on the value of internships. Because he had participated in the internship program, his audience accepted him as knowledgeable and committed.

3. *Cite research.* Quoting information from written sources and interviews with experts can add weight and objectivity to your arguments. Mentioning sources that are respected by your listeners adds to your credibility and indicates that you are well read. Let's say you want to persuade your listeners that they can overcome communication apprehension. The following research may enhance your credibility on this topic:

> According to James McCroskey, the communication professor who created the concept of communication apprehension, thousands of people in the United States alone suffer from

some degree of communication apprehension. McCroskey has published hundreds of articles on the symptoms and effects of communication. McCroskey's website identifies him as the author, co-author, or editor of forty-four books and two hundred journal articles. *The Quiet Ones: Communication Apprehension and Shyness*, deals with communication apprehension. You can visit his website at www.jamesmccroskey.com.[5]

Character

An audience's judgment of your character is based on their perceptions of your trustworthiness and ethics. The best way to establish your character is to be honest and fair.

Trustworthiness. A speaker's **trustworthiness** is the audience's perception of the speaker's reliability and dependability. Others attribute trustworthiness to us based on their past experiences with us. For example, instructors may judge our reliability according to whether we come to class every time it meets. Friends may evaluate our dependability according to how we have followed through on our promises. People who have had positive experiences with us are more apt to believe we are trustworthy.

Ethics. In Chapter 1, we defined ethics as an individual's system of moral principles and stated that ethics play a key role in communication. Though this is certainly true in communication in general, it is especially true in persuasion. Persuasive speakers who are known to be unethical or dishonest are less likely to succeed in achieving their persuasive purpose than are people recognized as ethical and honest. You must earn your reputation as an ethical person through your actions. The best way to establish yourself as an ethical speaker is to do the following:

1. *Cite sources when information is not your own, and cite them accurately.* As you develop your speech, be sure you give credit to sources of information and to ideas that are not your own. If you do not mention the sources of your information, you are guilty of plagiarism. Provide the audience with an **oral footnote,** such as "the following was taken from . . . " or "the following is a quotation from. . . . " Be specific about from whom and where your information came.

2. *Do not falsify or distort information in order to make your point.* Never make up information, attribute information to a source who is not responsible for it, take quotations out of context, or distort information to meet your purpose.

3. *Show respect for your audience.* When audience members perceive that you are being respectful, even though they may not agree with your point of view, they are more likely to listen. And when they listen, you at least have a chance of persuading them. Do not try to trick audience members into accepting your point of view or to ridicule them for not agreeing with you.

trustworthiness
The audience's perception of a speaker's reliability and dependability.

oral footnote
Providing within the speech the source that particular information comes from, such as "According to *Time* magazine of September 20, 1998. . . ."

charisma
The appeal or attractiveness that the audience perceives in the speaker, contributing to the speaker's credibility.

Charisma

As we stated earlier, other factors influence the way the audience perceives you. Among those is **charisma,** or the appeal or attractiveness that the audience perceives in the speaker contributing to the speaker's credibility. We often associate charisma with leaders who have special appeal for large numbers of people. Charismatic speakers seem to be sincerely interested in their listeners, speak with energy and enthusiasm,

Making Connections

Credible Speakers

We constantly hear someone speaking on a variety of topics in a variety of situations. Some speakers seem more believable than others.

1. What characteristics or behaviors make someone credible in your view?
2. What do credible speakers do that you could emulate?
3. Check with your friends, family, or classmates, and compare people you each label as credible speakers. Why were there similarities and differences in your views?

and generally seem attractive and likable. A credible speaker will take command of the speaking situation and engage the listeners so that they know that the message is honest, well prepared, and relevant. Charismatic speakers are able to get the audience involved in their messages.

Your audience's evaluation of your credibility will ultimately determine whether they accept or reject your persuasive goals. You should remember that credibility is earned, that it depends on others' perceptions, and that it is not permanent. Credibility changes from topic to topic, from situation to situation, and from audience to audience, and so you must establish your credibility each time you speak.

Becoming Effective Consumers of Persuasion

We spend a great deal of our lives listening to persuasive messages of one kind or another. It is important to think about what it means to be an effective consumer of those messages. (Refer to Chapter 6 to review the role of the listener in the persuasive process.)

As listeners, we have both the right and the responsibility to get accurate, reliable, and worthwhile information. Listen carefully to the message, and ask these questions:

How knowledgeable is the speaker?

What sources has the speaker used to gain additional information?

Are these sources reliable and unbiased?

Are there real advantages to accepting this position?

Is the evidence presented in the argument worthwhile?

Can I believe the evidence?

Where can I get additional information?

Does the argument seem logical?

It pays to closely analyze and evaluate the information presented, whether you are listening to an advertisement, a telemarketer, a political candidate, a religious leader, or a financial planner. Use questions like these to evaluate information:

Is this *really* good information?

Making Connections

Persuasion on the Web

Students sometimes have trouble finding sources for statistics and general information to help them organize and develop their persuasive speeches. The following sites may prove helpful.

1. Pub List is an archive of some 150,000 periodicals. The listings contain publisher information as well as information about the periodicals themselves: www. publist.com.
2. A website for statistical data in the areas of agriculture, crime, demographics, economics, education, energy, environment, health, income, labor, natural resources, safety, and transportation is found at www.fedstats.gov.
3. Government websites may be found at www.firstgov.com. This URL links the user to 20,000 government websites in a streamlined search-by-topic search engine.
4. Findarticles.com offers free access to full-text articles published in more than 350 magazines and journals dating from 1998. You can search the database by key word or subject category at www.findarticles.com/PI/index.jhtml.
5. OnlineNewspapers.com is a metasite that indexes 10,000 online newspapers from around the world. These are offered by country, province, or state with links to the newspapers' home pages: www.onlinenewspapers.com.

Is the information really relevant to me?

How can I learn more about this?

What additional questions should I ask to make sure that I get accurate and reliable information and sources?

Does the information really support the argument, or is it interesting but not essentially related?

Is there sufficient support for the claims and arguments?

Are there errors in the reasoning or the evidence?

Does the message basically make sense—and why or why not?

Learning Connections

1. How does credibility affect the listener?
2. Why should we be concerned with credibility?
3. What can you do to enhance your credibility during your persuasive speech?

Also pay attention to the person delivering the message:

Is the speaker ethical and trustworthy? What is the evidence?

Is the speaker competent and knowledgeable? What is the evidence?

Preparing and Developing a Persuasive Speech

In a classroom situation, you typically will have only one opportunity to coax your audience to accept your persuasive purpose. Therefore it is important to set realistic persuasive goals and to give some special thought to what is covered in Chapters 7, 8, and

9 about researching, organizing, and gathering support for your speech. Review those chapters for a complete perspective. Much of this section reinforces these earlier chapters.

Researching the Topic

Research for a persuasive speech must be especially thorough. You will need to gather as much information as possible about your topic, because the more you know, the better equipped you will be to support your position. When doing your research, look primarily for evidence that supports and clarifies your views. If, in the process, you discover information that contradicts your stand, make note of it and look for material that you can use to refute such information. Anticipating possible objections is especially helpful when your position is controversial and when your audience's opinions are likely to be split. If you know the arguments that could be used against you, you will be better able to support and defend your position.

Organizing the Speech

A persuasive speech requires making several special decisions that will affect its organization. Here are decisions especially related to persuasive speaking:

1. *Should you present one side or both sides of an issue?* The answer to this question depends on your audience. If your listeners basically support your position, then presenting one side may be sufficient. If their views are divided or opposed to your position, it may be more effective to present both sides. This decision also depends on your audience's knowledge of the topic and their evaluation of your credibility. If audience members are well informed and educated, presenting both sides of an argument helps minimize the effect that counterarguments can have on your audience.

2. *When should you present your strongest arguments?* Presenting your strongest arguments at either the beginning or the end of your speech is more effective than presenting them in the middle. A good strategy is to state your strongest arguments early and then repeat them toward the end. Because audience attention is most likely to wander in the middle of a speech, that is a good time to present personal examples supporting your position.

3. *What is the best way to organize your persuasive speech?* The most effective sequence of presentation depends on your topic, specific purpose, and audience. Among the patterns of organization that work well for persuasive speeches are problem–solution, cause–effect, and Monroe's motivated sequence, which were discussed in Chapter 9.

Supporting Materials

In persuasive speeches, speakers try to influence audience members through the impressiveness of their supporting materials. They choose their supporting materials carefully to build the kind of appeal that is most likely to sway their listeners. Based on the topic and their audience analysis, persuasive speakers try to appeal to their listeners' needs, to logic, or to emotions.

Appeals to Needs. **Appeals to needs** attempt to move people to action by calling on physical and psychological requirements and desires. Of course, different people have different needs, but most of us want to protect or enhance factors that affect our physical, safety, social, and self-esteem needs according to psychologist Abraham Maslow. According to Maslow's hierarchy of individual needs, our lower-order needs must be satisfied before higher-order needs.[6]

Physical needs are our most basic physiological requirements, such as food, water, sleep, sex, and other physical comforts. *Safety needs* pertain to our desires for stability, order, protection from violence, freedom from stress and disease, security, and structure. *Social needs* relate to our hopes to be loved and to belong, and our needs for affection from family and friends, for membership in groups, and for the acceptance and approval of others. *Self-esteem needs* reflect our desires for recognition, respect from others, and self-respect.

Speakers can appeal to any of these needs to motivate listeners to take action. For example, a speaker trying to sell individual retirement accounts would aim his appeal at our needs for security and stability; a speaker who hoped to persuade us to lose weight would call on our needs for physical comfort, acceptance by others, and self-esteem. Our readiness to accept ideas or to take action depends heavily on the speaker's ability to relate a message to our needs.

Logical Appeals. Attempts to move people to action through the use of evidence and proof are called **logical appeals.** When speakers lead their listeners to think "Yes, that's logical" or "That makes sense," they are building a case by calling on their audience's ability to reason. To accomplish this, competent persuasive speakers use evidence such as statistics, examples, testimony, and any other supporting materials that will sway their listeners.

A logical appeal requires an ability to argue for your point of view. When you argue in persuasive speaking, you usually make a claim or state an argument or *proposition,* which is what you want your listeners to believe after you have completed your speech. A claim or proposition usually assumes that there is more than one way to do things. For example, abortion should be illegal or abortion should be legal, the electoral process should or should not be changed. Speakers usually try to justify such a position with reason and evidence. The *justification,* or data, involves the use of all the supporting materials you can find to support your claim or proposition, including statistics, facts, examples, testimony, pictures, objects, and so on.

appeal to needs
An attempt to move people to action by calling on their physical and psychological requirements and desires.

logical appeal
An attempt to move people to action through the use of evidence and proof.

deductive reasoning
A sequence of thought that moves from general information to a specific conclusion; it consists of a general premise, a minor premise, and a conclusion.

In presenting their evidence, persuasive speakers guide their listeners through a carefully planned sequence of thought that clearly leads to the desired conclusion. This train of logic may fall into one of four categories: deductive reasoning, inductive reasoning, causal reasoning, or reasoning by analogy.

Deductive reasoning is a sequence of thought that moves from general information to a specific conclusion. It presents a general premise (a generalization) and a minor premise (a specific instance) that leads to a precise deduction (a conclusion about the instance). One student set up his argument as follows:

General Premise:	Heart disease is a major health concern in the Midwest.
Minor Premise:	Iowa is a part of the Midwest.
Conclusion:	Therefore heart disease is a major health concern in Iowa.

Great care must be taken to ensure that the premises are accurate because faulty premises can lead only to a faulty conclusion. For example:

General Premise: All college professors are liberal.
Minor Premise: Dr. Smith is a college professor.
Conclusion: Therefore Dr. Smith is liberal in her views.

The general premise must be both accurate and defensible before deductive reasoning can be used effectively as evidence to support a position.

Inductive reasoning is the opposite of deductive reasoning; it is a sequence of thought that moves from the specific to the general. An argument based on inductive reasoning usually progresses from a series of related facts or situations to a general conclusion. A student discussing university teaching evaluations wants her listeners to agree that speech professors at her university are excellent teachers. She therefore leads them through the following sequence of inductive reasoning:

Facts:

1. My speech communication professor is an excellent classroom teacher.
2. The speech professor I had last semester was also an excellent classroom teacher.
3. My roommate's speech professor is an excellent classroom teacher.
4. My roommate has a friend whose speech professor is an excellent classroom teacher.

Conclusion: Speech professors at this university are, in general, excellent classroom teachers.

When your facts can be verified, when there are a sufficient number of facts, and when there are sufficient links between the facts and the conclusion, inductive reasoning can be an excellent way to persuade an audience of the validity of your argument.

Of course, inductive reasoning can also be misused. For example, how often have you heard general statements such as these: All athletes take easy majors; all politicians are liars; all religiously devout people are dangerous. Each of these generalizations is usually based on some past experience, but the problem is that such experiences are not always sufficient to support the conclusion.

To avoid problems when using inductive reasoning, make sure your facts are accurate and that they support your conclusion. Also, make sure your conclusion does not extend beyond the facts you have presented. You will undermine your own case if your conclusion is so general that someone can easily point out exceptions to it.

Causal reasoning is a sequence of thought that links causes with effects. Thus it always implies or includes the word *because*: The earth's temperature is rising *because* the ozone layer is thinning. As in any form of reasoning, it is necessary to support the conclusion with evidence. In the example in this paragraph, the speaker would go on to cite scientific evidence linking thinning ozone to rising temperatures. The more verifiable and valid the evidence, the more defensible is the conclusion about the cause-and-effect relationship between ozone and temperature. Even though other factors may also be causes of the earth's warming, the speaker's argument can be considered reasonable if it is based on scientific evidence that supports the speaker's point of view.

Reasoning by analogy is a sequence of thoughts that compares similar things or circumstances in order to draw a conclusion. It says, in effect, that what holds true in one case will also hold true in a similar case. In arguing that American auto

inductive reasoning
A sequence of thought that moves from specific facts to a general conclusion.

causal reasoning
A sequence of thought that links causes with effects; it either implies or explicitly states the word *because*.

reasoning by analogy
A sequence of thought that compares similar things or circumstances in order to draw a conclusion.

manufacturers should change their approach to production, you might use the following reasoning:

General Premise:	U.S. automobile production must improve.
Minor Premise:	The Japanese method of auto production has been extremely successful.
Conclusion:	U.S. auto manufacturers should adopt the Japanese method if they wish to be successful.

Analogies can be useful reasoning tools when they are used wisely and with appropriate support for the conclusion. The relationship in the analogy must be valid, and the conclusion should be based on the assumption that all other factors are equal. For instance, our example is based on the assumption that the Japanese method is a good way to manufacture cars and that U.S. manufacturers could be just as successful as the Japanese. However, if the argument implied that the Japanese method's success could be traced to the workers' pride, dedication, and involvement in the production process, then similar factors would have to be applied to the U.S. workforce. Thus to avoid problems in drawing analogies, it is crucial to consider any dissimilarities that may refute your point.

You might wish to base your speech on a single form of reasoning, or you might prefer a combination of types of reasoning. Whatever your choice, you must remember that your argument is only as good as the evidence you use to support it.

Emotional Appeals. Attempts to move people to action by playing on their feelings—for example, by making them feel guilty, unhappy, afraid, happy, proud, sympathetic, or nostalgic—are known as **emotional appeals.** Because emotions are extremely strong motivators, this form of appeal can be highly effective. Note how the following introduction to a persuasive speech appeals to the emotions:

> My grandfather is a wonderful, caring person. He was always the person who would listen to me and lend me a shoulder to cry on. He is also one of the most intelligent people I've ever known. When I was growing up, Grandpa gave me suggestions to help me solve all kinds of problems, everything from completing my homework, to discussing why my

Making Connections

Persuasion in Everyday Life

We are constantly bombarded by attempts at persuasion. A telemarketer wants you to take advantage of a "free" vacation, someone else wants you to change your long-distance service, and still another wants you to donate money to a worthy cause. For the next two days, keep track of the number of times you are presented with persuasive messages.

1. What were people attempting to persuade you to do?
2. What strategies did they use to try to persuade you?
3. How successful were their attempts?
4. Why did some succeed and others did not?
5. How ethical were the speakers?

emotional appeal
An attempt to move people to action by playing on their feelings.

friends were not friendly, to helping me find a summer job. Today, however, my grandfather doesn't know who I am, let alone my name, and he often doesn't even realize that I'm in the room with him. You see, Grandpa suffers from Alzheimer's disease. There is no cure, and we still don't know very much about it. What we do know, however, is that it takes the real person and their minds and leaves a hollow shell.

Emotional appeals can be so powerful that they sway people to do things that might not be logical. A student's cheating on an exam, for example, can by no means be justified through logical thought, but the student may believe that she is justified from an emotional viewpoint because of parental pressure to get good grades. In fact, persuasive speakers often mix both logical and emotional appeals to achieve the strongest effect. Persuasive speakers need to be aware of the issue of ethics discussed throughout this text. A speaker must present valid, reliable information in a way that will appeal to the listeners but will not violate their rights or their responsibilities. The speaker should be fair, accurate in presenting views, careful in presenting information, and attentive to the strategies used. An ethical speaker uses emotional appeals carefully and truthfully.

Speakers need to use persuasive strategies to win over their listeners. The speaker is aware that listeners expect a strong, clear message to which the speaker is committed and in which the speaker believes. Here, Bono calls on President Bush and Congress to keep their promise to help Africa combat AIDS.

Persuasive Strategies

Speakers need to use persuasive strategies to win over their listeners. First, the speaker needs to demonstrate *rhetorical sensitivity,* that is, the speaker needs to be aware of the audience and their needs, the situation, the time limits, and what listeners want and are willing to hear. The speaker is aware that listeners expect a strong, clear message to which the speaker is committed and in which the speaker believes. The speaker will also carefully adapt the message so that the listeners know that it is relevant and important to them. The audience expects the speaker to motivate them or make them want to hear the speech and learn more about the argument. The audience expects to understand the speaker's point. The audience expects the speaker to repeat and reinforce the message so that they are influenced to, at the very least, accept that the speaker has a point worth considering. All in all, the persuasive speaker will always keep the listener in mind while reinforcing the argument.

Fallacies in Argument Development

As both creators and consumers of persuasive messages, all of us must be able to analyze and evaluate others' as well as our own use of reasoning to support persuasive messages (see Chapter 6). It is especially important to avoid causing listeners to question your credibility by presenting flawed arguments. Arguments that are flawed because they do not follow the rules of logic and, therefore, are not believable are called

fallacies. Flawed reasoning occurs all the time, and often people do not realize that they have used flawed arguments. As a critical thinker, however, it is important that you understand what fallacies are, how to recognize them, and why you should not use them or let others use them in their communication.

Many different types of fallacies are used in communication, but only the commonly used or major errors are presented here. Let's look at basic fallacies in reasoning and evidence.

Fallacies of Reason

Questionable Cause. **Questionable cause** is a common fallacy that occurs when a speaker alleges something that does not relate to or produce the outcome claimed in the argument. Wanting to know what has caused certain events to occur is part of our nature. If cheating on campus is increasing, people want to know why; if our taxes are increasing or decreasing, we want to know why; if parking spaces at work or on campus are to be eliminated, we want to know why. In our desire to know the cause of certain events or behaviors, we sometimes attribute what has happened to something that is not even related to the situation. For example, the claim that the drinking of alcohol on campus has increased this year because there is nothing else to do is a questionable cause, especially if the same number of activities exists on campus as in past years.

Ad Hominem. When someone attacks a person rather than an argument, he or she is resorting to a fallacy called an **ad hominem.** This is also referred to as *name-calling.* When you call someone a geek, a nerd, or a jerk in response to an argument being made, in order to diminish the relevance or significance of the argument, you are using name-calling as a means to refute the argument. What is wrong with this? Such an approach is a smoke screen; it shows your inability to provide good counterarguments or evidence to challenge what the other person is claiming. Sidestepping an issue by name-calling, ridiculing, or otherwise personally attacking another person can successfully diffuse an argument, but doing so usually results in a fallacious argument.

Fallacies of Evidence

Fact versus Opinion. A major misuse of information involves the presentation of facts and opinions. Speakers who state opinions as if they are facts can be misleading and may be presenting a fallacious argument. For example, "our university's policy on drinking is too stringent" and "our university is short 250 parking spaces" are both statements of information. Which is fact, and which is opinion? The first statement is opinion, and the second is fact. How can you tell which is which? Facts can be verified; the lack of parking spaces can be verified, whereas the university's policy on drinking may be stringent or not, which is a matter of opinion.

Giving opinions can be helpful in persuasive speeches or arguments, but to treat an opinion as if it were fact or a fact as though it were an opinion is an error in critical thinking. In either case, you will appear to claim too little or too much and raise questions about your competence and ethics.

Red Herring. Another misuse or avoidance of facts is the use of irrelevant information to divert attention from the real issue. This occurs when a speaker wishes to draw attention away from an issue that is being questioned or challenged. For example, have you ever questioned someone about something he or she did wrong, and the response

fallacy
An argument that is flawed because it does not follow the rules of logic.

questionable cause
A fallacy that occurs when a speaker alleges something that does not relate to or produce the outcome claimed in the argument.

ad hominem
A fallacy that attacks a person rather than the argument itself. This is also referred to as *name-calling.*

you got didn't relate to the event to which you were referring? In fact, the person may change the subject or even attack your credibility to avoid discussing the issue. Irrelevant information used to divert attention away from the real issue is referred to as a **red herring** fallacy.

Hasty Generalization. As a common critical thinking fallacy, the **hasty generalization** occurs when a speaker doesn't have sufficient data and therefore argues or reasons from a specific example. Conclusions are drawn from insufficient data or cases. It is not uncommon to find people making generalizations based on only one or only a few examples. For instance, to argue that male students think date rape is not a problem on their campus, a speaker might cite the opinions of two or three close friends. The speaker then states the following conclusion: "In surveying people I know, I have found that most students do not believe that date rape is a problem on our campus." The argument that date rape is not a problem might sound impressive, but it does not represent a large or representative sample of students; therefore the claim is unjustified. The argument can be refuted as a hasty generalization.

Making Connections

Thinking about Persuasive Speaking

Think about the insights and skills you have gained about public speaking so far. As you prepare to present a persuasive speech, consider information presented in previous chapters of this book and by your instructor in class, and address the following issues:

1. Identify four appropriate topics for your persuasive speech, and explain why these topics are appropriate for you, your audience, and the situation.
2. How might you use questions of fact, value, and policy as the basis of your speech?
3. Determine how you will establish your credibility.
4. What kinds of appeals will you make to reach the audience of your classmates?

red herring
A fallacy that uses irrelevant information to divert attention away from the real issue.

hasty generalization
A fallacy that occurs when a speaker does not have sufficient data and therefore argues or reasons from a specific example.

When you develop or encounter arguments or reasoning that do not fit any of the fallacies described in the text but you doubt the argument's validity, put the argument to the following test: Can the argument be outlined? Do the data support the claim? Is there a solid relationship between the data and the claim? It is not important to know the name of a specific type of fallacy but to analyze how arguments are developed and used in order to determine whether they are valid.

Making Effective Persuasive Speeches

GUIDELINES

1. Be realistic in setting your persuasive goal and determining what you expect to achieve.
2. Conduct a thorough audience analysis to help you choose the most appropriate strategy for accomplishing your persuasive goal.
3. Clearly identify a need so that the audience recognizes that something should be done.
4. Be sure your solution is consistent with the audience's beliefs, attitudes, values, ethical standards, and experiences.
5. Make sure your solution is workable and practical so that your listeners can actually do or accept what you are asking of them.
6. Point out the advantages of what you offer and how those advantages will benefit your listeners. Remember that people are unlikely to accept your persuasive goal unless they see something in it for themselves.

7. Build your argument so any possible objections to your proposal by the audience will be clearly outweighed by the benefits the audience members will gain if they accept your proposal.
8. Use only valid and reliable evidence to support your persuasive goal.
9. Be ethical and fair in both content and tactics.
10. Practice until you are able to present your speech without having to read it word for word.
11. Deliver your speech with enthusiasm, sincerity, and confidence.

Evaluating the Persuasive Speech

Here are some of the criteria used to evaluate the competence of the speaker and the effectiveness of a persuasive speech. Your instructor may consider these areas when evaluating your speech. You should be aware of them while preparing a persuasive speech presentation.

Topic

The selection of topic should meet the following criteria:

- The topic should merit the audience's attention.
- The audience should be able to see the relationship between the topic and speaker and between the topic and themselves.
- The topic should be able to be adequately covered in the time available. The topic should have been narrowed enough to be fully developed.

General Requirements

The following represent general requirements of most persuasive speech presentations:

- The speech's purpose should be clearly to persuade and stated as such.
- The speech should meet the time requirements set by the assignment.
- The speaker should cite sources of information that are not his or her own.
- The speech purpose should be relevant to the assignment and related to the audience.
- The speech should show evidence of careful preparation.

Audience Analysis

The speaker must shape the speech to suit the audience. This often requires research into the listeners' past experiences, beliefs, attitudes, and values. The choices the speaker makes regarding content and development of ideas should be tailored to the audience. (Chapter 7 provides details on audience analysis.)

- The speech should reflect appropriate audience analysis.

- The speaker should relate to and refer to audience members to get them involved and interested in the topic.
- The speech should include a goal, that is, the audience should be asked to think something, believe something, or take action.
- The speech should show the audience why the topic is important and relevant to them.

Supporting Materials

Supporting materials supply documented evidence that the information conveyed in the speech is accurate and credible.

- The supporting materials help the audience to believe the information.
- The supporting materials should appeal to the audience's needs, logic, and emotions.
- The supporting materials should include a variety of factual statements, statistical data, personal experiences, analogies, contrasts, examples and illustrations, expert testimony, value appeals, and eyewitness accounts.
- Visual aids should be used where appropriate and helpful; they should follow guidelines established by the assignment.
- The supporting materials should be documented, cited correctly, and up to date.
- The supporting materials help the speaker to establish and maintain credibility.

Organization

When judging the organization, the evaluator looks for a carefully planned, well-developed persuasive speech that takes a unified approach to the material being presented.

- The introduction should be properly developed.
  - It should orient the audience to the topic.
  - It should gain the audience's attention and arouse interest.
  - It should include a specific purpose and thesis statement.
  - It should define terms (if necessary).
  - It should motivate the audience to listen.
  - It should be relevant.
  - It should establish credibility.
- The organization of the body should be clear and easy to follow.
  - The main points should be clear and parallel in structure.
  - The main points should be related to the purpose of the speech.
  - Transitions should provide appropriate links between ideas.
  - The organizational pattern should be appropriate.
- The conclusion should be properly developed.
  - It should reinforce the purpose by reviewing the main points.
  - It should end with a memorable thought.
  - The audience should know what action is expected of them in response to the speech.

Poet and best-selling author Maya Angelou speaks with high energy and enthusiasm to an audience on the University of Northern Iowa's campus. She is able to get her audience involved in and enthusiastic about her topic, and the enthusiasm on both sides is infectious.

Delivery

The delivery techniques provide evidence that the speaker is aware of what the audience is interested in hearing, is involved in and enthusiastic about the topic, and is interested in sharing the material with the listeners.

- The speaker should be enthusiastic.
- The speaker should convey a persuasive attitude through focus, energy, and appropriate vocal variety.
- Nonverbal communication (gestures, movements, eye contact, posture, facial expression) should enhance and clarify the verbal delivery.
- The speaker should be aware of the audience's presence and reactions and should adjust his or her delivery accordingly.
- The speaker should be confident and poised.
- The speaker should convey a sense of the topic's relevance and importance.
- The speaker's vocal delivery should enhance the speech with appropriate volume, appropriate rate, conversational quality, enthusiastic tone, clear enunciation, appropriate pauses, and appropriate vocal variety.

Language Choice

As we discussed at length in Chapter 4, effective use of language is critical to communication. It is especially essential to use language carefully when crafting a persuasive message. Clear, vivid, specific, and acceptable language should be used to enhance and clarify ideas.

- The language choice should be appropriate to the assignment and audience.
- The language should be compelling.

- The word choice should be appropriate for the speaker, topic, situation, and audience.
- Grammar should be appropriate and show both competence and an awareness of the "formal" speaking situation.
- Word pronunciations should be correct.

Speakers should evaluate their own speeches and those of others. The forms in Figures 12.1 and 12.2 can help you analyze and reflect on the speeches you give and those to which you listen.

FIGURE 12.1

Speaker's Self-Evaluation Form On completing your persuasive speech, take a few moments to reflect on and think about all its elements. Using this form can help. Put yourself in the place of your listeners, and be specific in your comments on each aspect of the speech.

Title of speech: ______

Date and place given: ______

Topic selection ______

Research ______

Appropriateness *(to you, the classroom, the situation, the audience, the time limits)*

______

Organization ______

The introduction ______

The body ______

The conclusion ______

Explanation and clarity of ideas ______

Soundness of the claims or arguments presented ______

Support for ideas *(Valid, worthwhile, ethical, sufficient number, clear?)*

______

Use of language ______

Visual delivery *(movement, gestures, eye contact, posture)* ______

______

Vocal delivery *(conversationality, sincerity, variety, ease of listening)*

______

The ways I adapted this speech to this audience: ______

______

If you made this speech again, what would you change? Why? ______

______

What would you retain? Why? ______

______

FIGURE 12.2

Sample Listener Evaluation Form for Persuasive Speeches Listeners are often called on to evaluate speakers. Some instructors have listeners complete an evaluation similar to this one. It provides the speaker with invaluable information. It is also a good critical thinking exercise for the listener.

Speaker________________ Topic ________________ Date __________

1. What was the speaker's specific purpose? ________________
2. What was the speaker's thesis? ________________
3. Which arguments did you believe? Which arguments did you have a hard time believing? Were you convinced about the claim or argument the speaker presented? Why or why not? ________________
4. What would it take to make you change your beliefs, attitudes, or behaviors about this topic? Do you think you might be influenced by this speaker and the stand taken in this speech? ________________
5. Did you hear any faulty reasoning in this speech? What kind? How could the reasoning be improved? ________________
6. Did the speaker provide support for arguments, statements, and claims? What types of evidence and support were provided? ________________
7. Was the speaker believable? Why or why not? What could the speaker do to be more believable? ________________
8. Was the speaker ethical? Fair? Accurate? ________________
9. What kinds of appeals were used? ________________
10. Was the speaker easy to follow? Was the organization clear? ________________

GUIDELINES Tips for Persuasive Speakers

1. Establish yourself as an ethical communicator by employing good research, oral footnotes, and careful use of language and information.
2. Use repetition and restatement to help your listeners remember your speech.
3. Use appropriate organizational patterns.
4. Select appropriate supporting materials.
5. Use sound reasoning. Think about Toulmin's model and make your claim, support your claim with evidence (data), and show how the claim and date connect (warrant).

A Sample Persuasive Speech with Commentary

The following transcript was inspired by a November 2002 speech by Tim Schmidt, a student in an Oral Communication class at the University of Northern Iowa. I am indebted to Tim for making me think about the topic of stem cell research. This speech is not Tim's speech, but the idea for it came from his in-class speech. This speech was created to help readers see how strategies discussed in this textbook can be used. You, the reader, can undoubtedly create an even better speech than this.

Supporting Embryonic Stem Cell Research

To persuade my audience to support embryonic stem cell research to continue without government restrictions

- Purpose

Embryonic stem cell research is relatively new, since research on stem cells began about twenty years ago and embryonic stem cell research began in 1998. The government has placed restrictions on the research that will delay the research and increase the time until we have possible treatments and cures for many disabling and terminal diseases and conditions.

Introduction

- Logical and emotional appeals are used to get listeners' attention.
- Opposing views are identified.
- The speaker's position is reinforced.
- Thesis
- Preview

According to the National Institutes of Health, there are 128 million people in the United States living with a disease or condition that is untreatable or incurable. Stem cell research is the most promising research today that can lead to effective treatment and cures of such diseases as Alzheimer's and Parkinson's. Although there are pros and cons, especially a concern for the moral or ethical issues, it should be noted that the potential for providing cures is considerably greater from stem cell research than from any other single form of research to date. We all need to support this form of research to save our parents, our grandparents, and possibly even ourselves from debilitating and currently incurable diseases. Let me share with you the facts about stem cell research and what is involved. Then we'll discuss how the research is used and what it does. Finally, we will discuss the restrictions and problems faced by those who conduct stem cell research.

Body

- The speech begins with the argument people have used against stem cell research. Identification of where stem cells are used and the sources.
- Explanation

Most people misunderstand embryonic stem cell research. The embryonic stem cells are not harvested from aborted fetuses. Instead, couples who visit fertility clinics donate their unneeded embryonic cells to medical researchers seeking cures to such horrific diseases as muscular dystrophy, multiple sclerosis, and other muscular, spinal, brain, heart, and lung diseases or injuries. The embryos used in research are no longer needed and have been donated to research because they must be discarded after five years. Another source for embryonic stem cells are the umbilical cords of newborns, and they offer much potential as a source of stem cells. In addition, current researchers use adult stem cells. What are embryonic stem cells? They are cells in a young embryo that will differentiate to become organs or tissues and have a high replication rate. The National Institutes of Health, or NIH, define embryonic stem cells as "primitive or undifferentiated cells from an embryo that have the potential to become a wide variety of specialized cell types." These cells are capable of replicating; that is, they multiply quickly. In research labs, NIH says that these stem cells go through a process by which they can take on the features of a specialized cell such as heart, liver, or muscle. Because of this, stem cells have the potential to be used to treat many different illnesses. It should be noted that adults also have stem cells and can be the source of cells for research and medical treatments. Adult stem cells do not grow rapidly and cannot differentiate into other tissues than the tissue in which they reside. Adult stem cells give researchers little data in studying the development of tissues and organs, and they can only be used in specific areas. If brain cells are used, they can be used only for brain cell treatments. Now that we know something about the process, let's look at how the research can be used.

A major benefit of stem cell research is the knowledge it contributes to medicine. The study of the development of tissues and organs gives researchers a better understanding of how diseases such as cancer and birth defects develop. This knowledge leads to new treatments because the stem cells can be grown to create new tissue for the heart, muscles, bone marrow, and nerves. Researchers can, for example, grow new brain cells to replace faulty cells in the brains of people suffering from brain injuries, Parkinson's, or Alzheimer's. According to Dr. Stephen Minger, King's College, London, new stem cell research shows a promise for curing type 1 diabetes and Parkinson's disease. The NIH identifies stem cells as a potential cure or treatment for serious heart disease, even for those who have suffered severe heart attack damage. Stem cell researchers can also grow specific and particular cells for testing. In fact, researchers at the NIH and at medical schools throughout the world say that stem cell research holds great promise for finding treatment and possibly cures for deafness, blindness, lung disease, liver damage, muscular diseases, and brain and spinal injuries.

- Transition
- Benefits identified
- The need for research is established.
- Solution

What the research suggests is that stem cells can bring major medical benefits. To create those beneficial treatments and cures, however, there must be funding and permission for medical schools to conduct the research. In Congressional hearings from 1999 through 2001, NIH doctors testified that stem cell research has many benefits and only one major "fault." There is a mistaken belief on the part of government officials and some members of the public that this research violates the sanctity of life. Actually, these NIH doctors suggest that the embryos used in research will be discarded if not used. They suggest that adult stem cell research is also blocked with lack of funding and the too-rigid restrictions placed on researchers at NIH and in the medical schools throughout the world. Dr. Arthur Caplan, Director, Center for Bioethics, University of Pennsylvania, says that we need to pursue stem cell research in order to benefit the millions of people who now have or may have incurable diseases. Because of this mistaken belief that stem cell research does not recognize the sanctity of life of the embryo, funding is very low. Last year, the NIH budget for this type of research was only about $8 million, and that provides funding for only sixty lines of research. In addition, that low figure does not allow for the purchase or maintenance of equipment to conduct the research.

- Transition
- Preview of next point
- Restrictions are identified.

I encourage you to contact our U.S. senators and representatives as well as members of the Iowa legislature. We must increase both federal and state funding if we are to find cures for horrific disease. I have a petition for both Senator Harkin and Congressperson Grassley that I will pass around. If you support this kind of research, and I hope you do, please sign the petition, and I will mail them. A second petition will go to our local legislators, urging them to provide more state funding and fewer research restrictions.

- Call for action

If a member of your family were suffering from any of the hundreds of diseases that might be cured because of stem cell research, I'm sure you would vote for the research that promises to find cures or treatment for us and our loved ones. Please sign both petitions. Support full research for more than sixty people. Support funding to purchase and replace much-needed equipment to continue the search for answers, cures, and help for millions.

- Conclusion
- Emotional and logical appeals reinforced

References

"Do No Harm: The Coalition of Americans for Scientific Research and Health Care Which Does No Harm to Human Life, Including Embryos," www.stemcellresearch.org. Accessed September 15, 2003.

National Institutes of Health, " Stem Cell Information," Stem Cell Information Home Page, NIH, Bethesda, Maryland, 20892, and Department of Health and Human Services, http://stemcells.nih.gov/stemcell/whatAreStemCells.asp. Last updated March 17, 2003. Accessed September 15, 2003.

"Stem Cell Progress on Parkinson's," BBC news, UK edition, http://news.bbc.uk/1/hi/sci/tech. Last updated September 15, 2003. Accessed September 15, 2003.

"Stem Cell Research and Information," American Association for the Advancement of Science and Institute for Civil Society, www.aaas.org/spp/sfrl/Projects/stem/main.htm.

"Stem Cells Shown to Regenerate Damaged Lung Tissues for First Time," Stem Cell Research Foundation, September 2003, www.stemcellresearchfoundation.org.

"UK Human Embryonic Stem Cell First," BBC UK edition, news.bbc.co.uk/l/hi/sci/tech/3144925.stm. Last updated August 13, 2003. Accessed September 15, 2003.

Evaluation and Analysis

This speech makes use of a controversial topic about which the speaker feels strongly and presents a speech encouraging the listeners to take action. In fact, the speaker would actually bring petitions in for the listeners to sign, and the speaker states that she will mail them to the appropriate legislative offices. This speech was purposely created to demonstrate how a controversial topic can use both logical and emotional appeals to create a need and offer a viable solution. Because this speech is limited to a seven- to ten-minute time frame, the speaker cannot cover everything but must make choices about how much of the opposing views may be presented to ensure that the listeners understand that there are many perspectives on the subject and the speaker knows this but wants the listeners to act and think in a specific way for specific reasons.

If you were presenting this speech, what would you change? How would you change it? Why? What did the author leave out that you think would make the speech better? What, if anything, did she include that caused you to think about the topic in a different way?

Summary

We need to be aware that persuasion affects us every day in almost every aspect of our lives. We attempt to persuade others just as others attempt to persuade us. Persuasion is an active, goal-oriented process. The subgoals of persuasion involve persuasive strategies to get people to act or believe in specific ways.

When you are assigned to present a persuasive speech in class or to a work group or for an organization of which you are a member, you need to think about your own interest in a topic and its value to your listeners. You should also consider whether or not it is a suitable action goal. You will answer questions of fact, values, or policies in your persuasive attempts. The Toulmin model can help you make clear arguments so that your listeners understand the claims, data, and warrants inherent within your persuasive attempt.

If you want your audience to listen to you and accept your views, you need to be perceived as a credible speaker who knows what she or he is talking about. Citing sources and providing oral footnotes can enhance your appeal to your listeners.

Effective persuasive speakers pay careful attention to research, organization, and supporting materials. Effective consumers of persuasion are concerned with good, reliable, relevant information from ethical sources and should carefully listen to, analyze, and evaluate all persuasive messages. Good speakers will avoid the fallacies of arguments and consider the criteria and strategies included in this chapter in order to be more persuasive.

DISCUSSION STARTERS

1. How does persuasion affect you?
2. What factors influence your view of an effective persuasive speaker?
3. Why do we suggest that behavioral change is the ultimate goal of persuasion?
4. What characteristics enhance your own evaluation of a speaker?
5. If speakers do not appear to be credible in your eyes, what can they do to gain or regain credibility?
6. What are the major differences between informative and persuasive speeches?
7. Are supporting materials used differently in a persuasive speech than they are in an informative speech? Explain your views.
8. How do you know whether a speaker is effective?
9. What factors are essential in an effective persuasive speech?

NOTES

1. D. Zarefsky, *Public Speaking Strategies for Success,* 3rd ed. (Boston: Allyn and Bacon, 2002), 388.
2. Adapted from W. Fotheringham, *Perspectives on Persuasion* (Boston: Allyn and Bacon, 1966), 33.
3. Adapted from a speech by Tim Schmidt, Oral Communication, University of Northern Iowa, Fall 2003, and used with permission.
4. S. Toulmin, *The Uses of Argument* (Cambridge: Cambridge University Press, 1969), 94–145.
5. J. McCroskey website, www.jamesmccroskey.com. Accessed September 15, 2003.
6. A. H. Maslow, *Motivation and Personality,* 2nd ed. (New York: Harper & Row, 1970). Maslow, in this edition, includes two additional desires or needs—the need to know and understand and an aesthetic desire—as higher stages of his hierarchy. These are often associated with subcategories of self-actualization, which is not included here.
7. This speech was created for this text. The author acknowledges Tim Schmidt, a student in Oral Communication at the University of Northern Iowa, who gave a speech, "Embryonic Stem Cell Research," in November 2002. Tim did give us permission to use his speech, but we instead chose to include more than just embryonic stem cell research and used different sources for the speech. Special thanks to Pastor Tom Ogilvie for sharing his view of the ethical perspective.

CHAPTER 12 Appendix

Persuasive Speech Topics

Here are some possible topics for persuasive speeches. The items listed are not necessarily titles of specific speeches and might need to be narrowed to fit specific purposes, time limits, or other requirements set by your instructor.

Increasing stem cell research
Legalizing stem cell research
The benefits of massage therapy
Raising environmental awareness
Put a stop to homelessness!
Shelter for the homeless
How you can help stop elder abuse
Recognizing child/partner abuse
Dangers on the Internet
Stop Internet censorship
Global warming and the environment
Avoid ultraviolet rays and save your life
How to avoid war and conflict in the world
Say no to diets; say yes to a healthy lifestyle!
Funding stem cell research
Choosing chiropractic medicine
Alternative health care practices
Donate to environmental groups
Reorganize U.S. education
Funding spousal abuse centers
Choosing your spring break location
Get rid of the electoral college!
Preparing for future employment
The Internet must be censored!
Keep politicians honest!
Limit terms of elected office

PART THREE
Connecting in Relational Contexts

"You can make more friends in two months by becoming interested in other people than you can in two years by trying to get other people interested in you."
—Dale Carnegie

CHAPTER 13 Interpersonal Communication

THIS CHAPTER WILL HELP YOU:

- Improve your interpersonal communication.
- Analyze the motivation of others and how it relates to interacting with others.
- Know the connection and differences between online and face-to-face interaction.
- Improve your small talk when attempting to initiate relationships.
- Become more competent in your use of self-disclosure.

CASE STUDY

The following is taken from an essay entitled "The Donut Shop Experiment," written by Jonathan Butler, a high school history teacher in Riverside, California. According to Mr. Butler, he and a group of his friends and relatives wanted to do something different on a Saturday night. They were tired of board games and television. So about ten of them, some under age thirty and some over—brothers, a sister, a friend, in-laws, and parents—struck on the idea that the group of them would infiltrate a little café in twos and threes, at different times, until all were seated around the counter. They would arrange themselves as couples chatting, an old man sitting alone, or three friends in row. Their plan was to interrelate—"get acquainted" as total strangers appearing to get to know one another. They wanted to see how the others in the café would react.

They chose a doughnut shop with a truck-stop atmosphere that lacked any promise socially. Then one of them asked the cashier, "Say, do you use bleached flour in these doughnuts?" From that one question, conversation sprang, and relationships began to form.

Butler writes, "the conversation ranged from food to politics to music to how strangers never talk in strange places like a café." The people in the café, according to Butler, reflected on what they were doing and laughed, realizing that an improbable conglomerate of people had formed some kind of community.

The group of ten left the café and arrived back at Butler's home dazed by the experience. Butler ends the story with "How thin the walls that divide us from one another at ballparks and grocery stores and restaurants. How paper-thin."[1]

CASE STUDY *(continued)*

Questions to think about

1. What does Butler's last statement mean to you?
2. Why is it so easy for some people to start relationships in computer chatrooms but totally ignore someone who might be standing or sitting right next to them?
3. Are there lessons to be learned from this case study about communication? About relationships? If so, what are the lessons?
4. Try a similar experiment of your own, and report your findings to class.

You often see job announcements, job descriptions, or help wanted ads stating, "Wanted: person with excellent interpersonal communication skills." What does it mean to possess excellent interpersonal communication skills? It is our purpose in this chapter and the following chapters in this section to provide you with an answer to this question and more.

Interpersonal Communication and Relationships

Whether in a doughnut shop, chatroom, classroom, workplace, airport, library, student union, dorm, bus stop, athletic event, wedding, meeting, airplane, or anyplace where people interact verbally or nonverbally, they are most likely using interpersonal communication. In Chapter 1, we defined interpersonal communication as the informal exchange of information between two or more people. This definition implies that interpersonal communication occurs between two or more people, is casual, considered private, and reveals personal information. Dyadic communication and small-group communication were also defined in Chapter 1 as forms of interpersonal communication.

We know that not all of our interpersonal communication is personal or private. Casual conversation or small talk is often very impersonal and can be very public. Interviewing, which is a form of interpersonal communication, is dyadic by definition and may include casual or small talk but is usually more formal, more highly structured, and more likely private.

Most communication scholars believe that for communication to be interpersonal, the people involved must treat each other as unique individuals, regardless of the context or form of the interaction. Of course, we must also recognize that when interacting with others, our interactions are affected by the relationship we have with the other person or people.

Interpersonal communication is often thought of as interaction that occurs among those with whom we have close relationships. This, of course, is not always true; for example, there are people who will disclose the most personal information about family or themselves to complete strangers while seated on an airplane but not communicate that same information to a loved one. Thus interpersonal communication occurs in a variety of contexts; can be impersonal/superficial or personal/intimate, private or public, unstructured or highly structured; and occurs at all stages of relationship development.

Making Connections

Communicating with People with Disabilities

At times, we avoid communicating with certain individuals because we are uncomfortable, feel awkward, or aren't sure how to approach them. No matter our own level of physical ability, when encountering people who have a physical disability, some of us are uncertain about what to say or how to behave. Often, rather than attempting to reduce our uncertainty or fear, we might go out of our way to sidestep any interaction at all.

Most people who have physical disabilities will tell you that they don't want special treatment—most prefer to be treated like any other person, as a "person first." It is a shame that our fear of the unknown can prevent us from interacting and developing a relationship with someone.

1. Why do we enter into conversations with some individuals and not with others, especially others who might be different from us?
2. How do you feel and behave when you encounter someone with a disability?
3. What advice would you give to help reduce people's fear or uncertainty about communicating with individuals who have a disability?
4. Create a set of guidelines that you believe will facilitate more free communication among people of different physical abilities.

If you need more information about communicating with people with disabilities, ask your instructor or go to your library to obtain the *Handbook of Communication and People with Disabilities: Research and Application,* edited by Dawn O. Braithwaite and Teresa L. Thompson (Mahwah, N.J.: Erlbaum, 2000). It is an outstanding resource that covers a wide variety of communication research and applications related to people with disabilities. You can also visit the website of the AXIS Center for Public Awareness of People with Disabilities, www.axiscenter.org. Or stop by your college's Accommodation Resource Center or call your community's branch of the League of Human Dignity for guidelines for communicating with persons with disabilities. Another resource is the home page of the ADA Information Center's Americans with Disabilities Act, www.ada.org. It would be worthwhile to discuss in class any guidelines you obtain.

Learning Connections

1. What aspects of your interpersonal communication skills do you wish to improve?
2. What is the appropriate etiquette in meeting someone who is of a higher status than yourself? An older person than yourself? A person from a different culture?

A **relationship** is an association between at least two people. It can be new or old, momentary or long lasting, superficial or involved, casual or intimate, friendly or unfriendly, relaxed or tense, hateful or loving, important or unimportant, good or bad, happy or unhappy, and so on. Relationships can also be described in terms of the level of intimacy or kinship, for example, girlfriend, boyfriend, lover, wife, husband, mother, father, child, uncle, cousin, stepparent, or stepchild. Sometimes relationships can be described on the basis of the roles people have in the relationship, for example, roommates, Internet friends, neighbors, boss and employee, coworkers, classmates, doctor and patient, ex-spouses, and so on. Relationships can be described in terms of time spent together, for example, "I knew her in high school" or "They just met him the other day." Relationships may be based on shared activities or participation in events, for example, "We play volleyball together," "We go to the same yoga classes," "He is in my class," "She works with me," or "We both are from the same hometown."[2] Relationships are sometimes described in terms of situation or happenstance, for example, "We met on the plane," "We sat at the same dinner table on the cruise ship," "We met at a bus stop," "We sat next to each other at the game," "We

relationship
An association between at least two people, which may be described in terms of intimacy or kinship.

Most people who have physical disabilities will tell you that they don't want special treatment. Most prefer to be treated like any other person—as a person first.

met over spring break in Florida," or "She takes her kids to the same daycare." However we describe them, we all have a need to form relationships with others.

Motivation and Need to Form Relationships

Most of us want to develop relationships to give our lives meaning and to fulfill a variety of social and psychological needs we have as human beings. Our motivations for staying in relationships are certainly varied and not always completely understood, as when people who have choices remain in abusive relationships. In this section, we discuss four different but related theories that help to explain why we have such a strong desire to interact, to form and keep relationships with others: uncertainty reduction theory, predicted outcome value theory, social exchange theory, and fundamental interpersonal relations orientation theory.

Uncertainty Reduction Theory

In the opening case study, the motivation of the group in the doughnut shop was to find out how others would react to their behavior. The desire to know about others and to understand how and why they behave as they do can be partially explained by uncertainty reduction theory.[3] **Uncertainty reduction theory,** developed by communication scholars Charles Berger and Richard Calabrese, suggests that when we meet others to whom we are attracted, our need to know about them tends to make us draw inferences initially from the physical data that we observe. An urge or desire to reduce our uncertainty about those individuals motivates our desire for further communication with them. The theory's core assumption is that when strangers meet, they seek to reduce uncertainty about each other. The more attracted we are to the other person, the stronger is the desire to know more about that person.

According to the theory, reducing uncertainty is necessary in relationship development, so as we increase our desire to develop a relationship with others, we utilize more uncertainty reduction behavior. There are three stages of initial interaction. During the *entry phase,* we learn information that is easily observed, for example physical appearance cues such as sex, age, height, skin color, physical attractiveness, and economic or social status. We can easily supplement these observations with additional information, which we can obtain either from others or via conversation during this phase of relationship development. When we first meet someone, however, our communication is usually controlled by social rules and norms. That is, it is usually considered improper in the entry phase to ask intimate personal questions of the other person. When people begin to share attitudes, beliefs and values, and more personal information, they have entered the *personal phase* of the relationship. During this phase, the communication is less constrained, and there is more openness to freely

uncertainty reduction theory
A theory suggesting that when we meet others to whom we are attracted, our need to know about them tends to make us draw inferences from observable physical data.

Making Connections

It's Me That Counts

Brad and Paige have been dating for more than six months. They agree that they have a very close relationship. After a romantic dinner at their favorite restaurant, Brad and Paige go back to Paige's apartment and are in the middle of some serious kissing when Paige says, "Brad, I want you to stop. I don't want to go any further." Brad says, "Are you kidding me? Don't you love me? I mean, it's not like we haven't been going out for six months." Paige does not respond immediately; she seems to have been caught off guard. Finally, she says, "Brad, I do know how you feel about me, and I do trust you, but going all the way just isn't right for me. I also don't want to end up having a kid before we are married." Brad quickly says, "But I thought you really cared about me. You know, Paige, I love you!" Paige replies, "I know, but I am not ready for sex, and I really don't want to until I am married—you have to understand that."

1. Do you think Brad's communication is motivated more out of self-interest than interest in Paige? Explain.
2. How would you describe Brad and Paige's relationship based on their interaction with each other?
3. Describe the relationship in terms of social exchange theory.

communicate. The third phase of initial interaction is the *exit phase.* It is in this phase that the future of the relationship is decided. Effective interpersonal communication is often the critical difference between termination or continuation of the relationship.

Predicted Outcome Value Theory

Michael Sunnafrank, a communication scholar, developed the predicted outcome value theory,[4] which provides another explanation for why people seek to interact and to learn more about those whom they meet. **Predicted outcome value theory** suggests that people connect with others not so much to reduce uncertainty but because they believe that rewards or positive outcomes will result.

Predicted outcome value theory offers a number of possibilities for how we predict certain outcomes in developing relationships. The theory further implies that people who predict greater positive outcomes will be more successful in developing and establishing relationships than will those who predict greater negative outcomes. In other words, those who predict a positive outcome from a relationship will communicate or guide conversations to ensure that the relationship will have a better chance of succeeding. Those who predict negative outcomes from a relationship communicate in ways that block relational development. Do you agree with the theory that we initiate or continue interaction with others only because of the potential rewards that we might gain from them? The issue of rewards and costs are further explained in social exchange theory, which we discuss next.

predicted outcome value theory
A theory that suggests that people connect with others because they believe that rewards or positive outcomes will result.

Social Exchange Theory

Social psychologists John W. Thibaut and Harold H. Kelley originated the **social exchange theory,** which is based on the assumption that people consciously and deliberately weigh the costs and rewards associated with a relationship or interaction and

social exchange theory
A theory based on the assumption that people consciously and deliberately weigh the costs and rewards associated with a relationship or interaction.

will seek out relationships that reward them and avoid those that are costly.[5] Thibaut and Kelley believe that we are motivated to develop and maintain relationships in terms of the exchange of rewards and costs. A **reward** is anything that we perceive as beneficial to our self-interest. It refers to things or relationships that bring us pleasure, satisfaction, or gratification. For example, outcomes such as good feelings, prestige, economic gain, and fulfillment of emotional needs are considered rewards. **Costs** are things that we perceive to be not beneficial to our self-interest. They refer to outcomes such as time, energy, and anxiety that we do not want to incur.

According to the theory, we are motivated out of self-interest to act or behave in certain ways. For example, if the rewards we gain are higher than any potential costs we incur, then we regard the relationship or interaction as pleasant and satisfying. But if our reward gain (rewards minus costs) falls below a certain level, then we find the relationship unsatisfactory or unpleasant. The ratio between rewards and costs varies from person to person and from situation to situation. Thus what is a desirable ratio of rewards and costs for one person may be much different for another person. If a relationship is healthy and satisfying, there is probably a good balance most of the time between rewards and costs, with rewards outweighing costs. Most relationships begin and prosper because the people involved benefit in some way from it.

Fundamental Interpersonal Relations Orientation Theory

Interpersonal communication literature consistently discusses the premise that each of us needs to include others in our activities and to be included in theirs, to exert control over others and have them control us, and to give affection to others as well as receive it from others. Will Schutz, a psychologist and one of the most respected leaders in the field of human relations, developed **fundamental interpersonal relations orientation theory,** which provides insight into our communication behaviors. Schutz's theory consists of three needs: affection, inclusion, and control.[6] Although many other needs exist, according to Schutz, most of our interpersonal behavior and motivation can be directly related to our need for affection, inclusion, and control. Although needs differ from person to person, from situation to situation, and from culture to culture, knowing and understanding our interpersonal needs should help us understand how they influence our interactions with others.

For most of us, our interpersonal needs do not remain static; desire and importance vary with circumstances. For instance, giving and receiving affection might be far more important in a relationship, especially as the relationship intensifies and moves toward bonding, whereas inclusion might be more significant when a relationship is coming apart. Awareness of personal needs and the needs of others also varies depending on the depth of a relationship, the timing, the context, and so forth. Let's look more carefully at each of the interpersonal needs and how they influence our interpersonal interactions.

reward
Anything that we perceive as beneficial to our self-interest.

costs
Negative rewards, things that we perceive to be not beneficial to our self-interests.

fundamental interpersonal relations orientation theory
A theory that provides insight into our motivation to communicate. This theory consists of three needs: affection, inclusion, and control.

The Need for Affection. The need for affection is the need to feel likable or lovable. Every day we see people striving to fulfill this need; for example, people who join social groups or dating services are seeking to fulfill their need for belonging and love. According to Schutz's theory, a person who seems to be liked by many and therefore has adequately fulfilled this need is referred to as *personal.* Someone who is unable to fulfill this need is labeled either *underpersonal* or *overpersonal.*

Underpersonal people avoid emotional commitments or involvement with others. If we examine these individuals, we often find that they are hiding their true selves

Making Connections

Joe Millionaire: Reality or Not?

The popular TV show *Joe Millionaire,* in which twenty single women were whisked off to France for a chance to compete for a handsome man who they were told had recently inherited fifty million dollars. In fact, the man, Evan Marriott, was a construction worker who had about $19,000 in his savings account. The premise of the show was that the women would try to capture his attention through various activities and conversations and he would eliminate them one by one until he got to the final one. The finalist was then told that he was just a "regular Joe" with a construction worker's bank account. She then had to decide whether he was still the man of her dreams.

1. Which of the four theories we just described illustrates what took place on the show? Explain.
2. What does this type of show tell about how we view relationships in our society?
3. Why do you think shows like this are so popular?
4. What ethical issues does the show raise?

because they fear that others will not like them as they are. These people, like all other human beings, have a need for affection, but they have learned to cover it by not letting others get close to them. Do you know someone who seems to fit this category? Why do you think this person is unwilling to get close to others?

Overpersonal individuals are the opposite of underpersonals. They need affection so badly that they often go to extremes to ensure acceptance by others. They frequently seek approval by being extremely intimate in what they communicate. These individuals may be possessive and get jealous when others talk to their friends.

Personal people tend to be poised, confident, mature, and able to deal with almost everyone with whom they come in contact. Personals want to be liked, but they do not consider being liked by everyone essential for happiness. They are easy to talk with and are at ease with themselves.

The Need for Inclusion. The interpersonal need for inclusion encompasses our needs to feel significant and worthwhile. Schutz describes individuals in terms of this need as *social, undersocial,* or *oversocial.* Undersocial people do not like being around other people because, like underpersonal individuals, they find communicating with others threatening. They tend to be shy and find initiating conversations with others difficult. Typically, undersocials find it difficult to speak out and generally avoid saying anything for fear of drawing attention to themselves.

Oversocial people cannot stop themselves from getting involved and communicating with others. They attempt to dominate conversations, often speak out of turn, and find it hard to keep quiet. They prefer situations in which they can take over relationships by dominating the flow of communication. The oversocial person fears being ignored by others. Can you think of people who have the tendency to be oversocial? How do you react to them?

Social people have satisfied their needs for inclusion. They are capable of handling situations with or without others, and few, if any, situations make them feel uncomfortable. They have confidence in themselves and are assertive enough to speak when they feel it is necessary to do so.

The Need for Control. Schutz's third need is for control, which is derived from responsibility and leadership. Almost all of us have some need to control others and our surroundings. However, some individuals wish to be controlled by others. The strength of this need and the way we manifest it determine whether we are *abdicrats, autocrats,* or *democrats,* according to Schutz.

Abdicrats are extremely submissive to others. They have little or no self-confidence, often perceive themselves as incompetent, take few risks, rarely make decisions on their own, and need much reinforcement to believe they are useful and capable.

Autocrats never have enough control. In a group, they are always willing to make the decisions or at least voice strong opinions about what decision ought to be made. Because autocrats have a strong need for power, they might not care whom they hurt in their search for control. And they show little, if any, respect for others.

Democrats have their control needs essentially satisfied. They are comfortable as either leaders or followers, do not exaggerate either the leader's or the follower's role, and are open minded and willing to accept others' suggestions for the good of the group. They like to get things done but not at the expense of someone else.

Schutz's theory of needs clearly illustrates the reasons that motivate us to communicate with others. We develop relationships with others for many reasons. The social needs we have discussed explain a great deal about our motivation to form relationships, but there are other reasons to develop relationships: to avoid or lessen feelings of loneliness, to learn more about ourselves, and to share our lives with others.

Learning Connections

1. What recommendations do you have for interacting with a person who has a disability?
2. Which of the four theories is the most useful for explaining why we form relationships?
3. Which theory best illustrates that some of us are in relationships because of the benefits we gain from the relationship? Explain why.

Relationships: Getting to Know Others and Ourselves

One of the most interesting aspects of being a human being is the way we react to other people—making acquaintances, becoming friends with a few of those acquaintances, and sometimes actively disliking others. Each of us tends to evaluate others in positive and negative terms, and they, of course, evaluate us in return.[7]

Some very specific and generally predictable factors determine whom we will get to know and how well we will get to know them. Relationships can be based on love or hate or any of the possibilities in between. Of the more than five billion people living, any one of us will come into contact with only a few. Of this small percentage, there remain hundreds of potential friends, enemies, and lovers. We, however, tend to form meaningful relationships with a small number of individuals at any given time. Researchers have often asked how we decide which relationships will become meaningful and lasting. How would you answer this question?

Learning about Others through Face-to-Face Relationships

Whether we get to know others might have little or nothing to do with their specific characteristics or ours. Usually, the likelihood of two people becoming acquainted has to do with contact through physical proximity and a positive rather than a negative experience at the time of the face-to-face contact. Often, the contact is not planned but occurs because of circumstances. For example, contact may take place with a person sitting next to you in an airplane, with a neighbor, a classmate, a co-worker, a member of your religious organization, a person standing next to you in line in the cafeteria, a player on your softball team, and so on. After you encounter a person several times and easily recognize him or her, you will likely become comfortable interacting with the person or at least making small talk.

Small talk is casual conversation that is often impersonal and superficial, including an exchange of hellos or comments about the weather, newsworthy events, or trivia. Most relationships begin with small talk and often depend on small talk to continue. Small talk provides an avenue for getting to know another person by talking about nonthreatening, impersonal subjects. Some people, however, believe that small talk is a waste of their time, because it is based on trivial, unimportant information. Most communication scholars, however, believe that relationships develop through the exchange of small talk.

Small talk or casual conversation is important in the development of social skills and relating to people. Casual conversation, one on one, is also a good way to learn how to establish the basis for communicating and responding.

In meeting people for the first time, opening lines play a crucial role in establishing relationships. Many prescriptions for good and bad opening lines are provided by the media, friends and acquaintances, and other sources. However, most do not identify the importance of the relationship of those communicating, the context, and the nonverbal cues of the communicators.[8] For example, people meeting in a professional business setting usually shake hands and introduce themselves, whereas meeting people on an airplane is much more informal and introductions often do not occur even though the conversation might become more than simply small talk.

Making Connections

Greeting Etiquette: Rules of Engagement

Discuss in class the appropriate ways to greet others:

1. Greeting your peers
2. Greetings others older or of higher status than yourself
3. Greeting others from a different culture while in your own surroundings
4. Greeting others from a different culture while in their surroundings

There are many communicative situations that require a specific type of etiquette, for example, dinner table etiquette or, email etiquette, that you might wish to discuss in your class as well. You can do an Internet search using the key word *etiquette* to find other areas that interest you.

small talk
Casual conversation that is often impersonal and superficial, including greetings, comments about the weather, newsworthy events, or trivia.

Making Connections

The Importance of Small Talk

The following is paraphrased from an analysis of a survey of married couples, which reveals the importance of small talk:

According to a Chicago *Tribune* article, two social scientists at the University of California, Berkeley, after surveying thirty-one married couples (average age, early forties, averaging twenty years of marriage) found that small talk might save marriages. According to the survey results, the communication that was valued the most was not long sessions of hashing out a couple's differences, but easygoing, pleasant conversations related to everyday happenings.

Wives, in particular, felt that this kind of open, casual chatting was an indication of mutual affection. Husbands, on the other hand, valued emphatic listening by their wives more than discussions; this they interpreted as a sign of affection from their wives.

1. Why do you think men and women take these two different perspectives on the type of communication they exchange?
2. Are there any assumptions that should be considered in interpreting the findings of the survey?
3. What role does small talk play in building and maintaining your relationships? Explain.

"A Survey of Married Couples Point to Importance of Small Talk," *Chicago Tribune Newspaper,* February 26, 1987.

Besides opening lines, small talk serves many functions and is a way of maintaining a sense of community or fellowship with others. We often use small talk to satisfy our need for inclusion because it requires individuals to communicate with one another. Small talk generally does not create disagreement or conflict. It does create supportiveness and affirmation, which are indispensable for people to form relationships. It generally serves as a proving ground for both new and established relationships. In this sense, it becomes an "audition for new relationships." A research study examining types of conversations people engage in found that nearly half of all the conversations with acquaintances, friends, romantic partners, family members, and others consist of relatively informal, superficial talk.[9]

Small talk is a safe way for us to let others know something about us and at the same time let us begin to learn something about them. It is a way of vying for time to determine what we wish to share with others. If something we share about ourselves isn't working, we can shift to something else about ourselves very quickly. Small talk allows us to reduce uncertainties about another person without revealing too much about ourselves. If everything seems to click in the small talk conversations,

Opening lines do create first impressions and play a crucial role in establishing or initiating relationships. It is usually safer to use innocuous lines—you're more likely to get a positive response.

it is more likely that conversations will move from superficial to more self-revealing communication.

Small talk is also important because it can serve as an interpersonal buffer. Because it is usually nonthreatening, small talk can serve as a release, escape valve, or diversion from more serious talk that requires more conscious thought and effort.[10]

Suggestions for More Effective Small Talk

GUIDELINES

1. *Use the other person's name as much as possible as you talk with him or her.* Have the person restate it or spell it for you if necessary. Knowing and recalling a person's name creates the impression that the person matters to you and helps make small talk more comfortable.
2. *Look at the other person, but strive for balance and comfort in eye contact.* When you look at the other person, you are indicating that you are paying attention and are interested in him or her.
3. *Be careful in your use of eye contact with people of different cultural or ethnic backgrounds than your own.* For example, Hispanic and Japanese cultures believe that staring at someone or looking into someone's eyes is disrespectful. When communicating with people from these cultures, you might focus on the face in general but not directly on their eyes.
4. *Get the other person to talk about himself or herself.* People generally like to talk about themselves. It can be a strong motivator for continuing the conversation. Listen carefully, and ask questions such as "Tell me about your hometown," "What do you do?," "What do you like to do in your spare time?," "Tell me about yourself." Use follow-up questions to keep the person talking if necessary.
5. *Keep small talk casual, light, and positive.* Moving too quickly to disclose personal information can be threatening and a real conversation stopper. Also, no one likes negative people or whiners. If you come across as one, your likelihood of future interaction is reduced dramatically.
6. *Use small talk to help reduce the uncertainty between yourself and others.* By doing so, you will increase your chances of initiating and developing a more lasting relationship.[11]

Learning about Others through Online Relationships

As you know, with only a few clicks of a computer mouse, we can interact with someone, any subject, at any time, and in any place in the world. Face-to-face interactions usually allow us to form impressions much more quickly than we can by using computer-mediate communication. The likelihood of connecting to others and interacting with strangers, however, increases dramatically online.

The computer has indeed changed our way of interacting and connecting to others. For example, in our local newspaper, the following was featured in the Life section: "Chatroom brought them together." In the article, it explains how Shelly Zoz and Brian Davis met for the first time. In her first message to Brian, Shelly wrote, "Is it true?" He responded, "Is what true?" Before the evening was over, according to the article, they had exchanged telephone numbers. Brian said, "It was amazing. Everything just clicked between us." Shelly was quoted in the article as saying, "A lot

Making Connections

Interpersonal Success and Failure

Take a clean sheet of paper and fold it in half lengthwise. You now have two columns. Label the column on your left "Person A: Likely to experience interpersonal failure," and label the column on your right "Person B: Likely to experience interpersonal success." In their respective columns, list the characteristics, behaviors, and strategies that you believe characterize Person A and Person B in a situation in which each approaches someone of the same sex for the first time. Then answer the following questions in class:

1. Which characteristics, behaviors, and strategies would be the same or different if Person A and Person B were meeting someone of a different sex? Why?
2. Which characteristics, behaviors, and strategies would be the same or different if Person A and Person B were meeting someone from a sexual orientation or an ethnic or cultural background that differed from their own?
3. How might Person A and Person B approach others over the Internet? What behaviors and strategies might succeed or fail in this communication context?
4. What did you learn from this exercise about interpersonal communication?

of people in these chat rooms will feed you full of stuff and expect you to believe it, but he seemed honest." She went on, "We talked and talked about our feelings, and we were really on the same wavelength." Their first online encounter was in March 1999; by May, they had decided to meet in person. Brian drove the 1,500 miles to Lincoln, Nebraska, to meet Shelly. They met and liked what they saw, and they plan to marry. "A lot of people think meeting someone through a chatroom is totally nuts," Shelly said, "People are shocked that it worked out."[12]

Although many online connections that occur between individuals and groups of individuals are limited because of the lack of proximity of the individuals involved, it is more and more common for these types of interactions to result in relationships. Malcolm Parks and Kory Floyd, communication scholars, surveyed twenty-four newsgroups and asked a random sample of the users whether they had formed new acquaintances, friendships, or other personal relationships as result of their interaction online. Almost two-thirds of those responding to the survey said that a personal relationship resulted from someone they had met on the Internet.[13]

Women, it seems, are more likely to form relationships on the Internet than men are. Research has found that 72 percent of women and 55 percent of men surveyed who interact on the Internet have formed personal online relationships. Not surprisingly, the more time you spend online, the more likely you are to form more online relationships.[14]

Making Connections

Relationships: What's on the Internet?

Select one of the popular search engines, such as AltaVista, Yahoo, Google, Snap, Excite, and HotBot, and do a search on the words *relationships* and *Internet dangers.*

1. What do you find?
2. What does your search tell you about relationships? About dangers?
3. Select a site that interests you and determine what the site has to offer and how it might help you understand relationships and interpersonal communication.
4. Prepare a brief report about the site you selected in item 3. Present or discuss your findings in class.

The Internet chat room has made it possible for us to interact with people anywhere in the world with just a few clicks of the mouse and strokes of the keyboard. But do you think an online relationship is as satisfying as a face-to-face relationship?

Cell phones and PDAs (personal digital assistants such as Handsprings and Palm Pilots) are also changing the way people flirt and connect with others. With its roots in emailing and instant messaging, text messaging via cell phones or PDAs has become another extremely popular way to communicate because people are willing to write things they might not normally say over the phone or in person. Many people are wired today, and almost anyone can be reached at any given time, so the lines of communication are more open than ever. This can create a new set of problems.[15]

Although chatrooms, email communication, text messaging, and Internet dating services are expedient ways to initiate conversations with strangers, they might not be the best way to develop relationships with others. In fact, they can be outright dangerous.

Kevin Koelling, a psychotherapist, says, "I've seen everything from marriages breaking down to people using the Internet as an escape from the problems they need to deal with in their marriage."[16] Deb Hope, a psychology professor at the University of Nebraska, said, "Chat rooms can be dangerous to people who may not have the best judgment about relationships anyway. You can end up getting involved with someone—maybe even agreeing to meet them—and really not know who they are at all."[17] People have been exploited, taken advantage of, or even victimized by someone they meet via the Internet.[18] Communication is the overriding factor that will determine the kind of relationship that develops, if any at all, and how long it will last.

There are advantages and disadvantages to interacting with people online. The advantages are that you can remain anonymous, it is generally safe because physical contact is possible only if you allow it to occur, and you can choose the time and place of that contact. On the Internet, you share personality or inner qualities only through the words you transmit, and this can be an advantage as well as a disadvantage. We know that a person's voice and appearance provide a lot of information about that

Learning Connections

1. Why are your first interactions with others so important in developing relationships even if only temporary?
2. When you engage in small talk with people from other cultures or people with disabilities, are there any considerations you should take into account?
3. What advice would you give to a person who would like to meet someone online?

person. Without hearing the other person's voice, without seeing the other person, and without being able to touch him or her (e.g., a handshake, a hug, a kiss), the relationship will remain a mediated relationship that allows two people to communicate, but nothing more. Of course, through technology, we can hear and see images of the other person via telephone, microphones, pictures, and minivideo cameras without ever having actual face-to-face contact. It is our belief, however, that interaction via technology can never replace face-to-face interaction or fulfill interpersonal needs. In Chapter 14, we discuss more about relationship development over the Internet.

self-disclosure Voluntary sharing of information about the self that another person is not likely to know.

Johari Window A graphic model describing human interaction that is useful because it depicts four different levels of knowledge that exists in our relationships with others.

Self-Disclosure in Relationships

Relationships are built on interaction. The more sincere, honest, and open the interactions, the stronger and more lasting the relationship will be. Much of our interpersonal communication, however, is small talk. Such light conversation might not provide a means for us to learn who we are, to fulfill our interpersonal needs, or to grow in our relationships. Nonetheless, it does maintain an important opening to further interaction. Self-disclosure is one type of interaction that changes as a relationship becomes closer.

To reduce uncertainty as suggested by uncertainty reduction theory or predicted outcome value theory and to meet our physical and emotional needs, we must communicate who we are; we must disclose information about ourselves. **Self-disclosure,** or the voluntary sharing of information about ourselves that another person is not likely to know, can be as simple and nonthreatening as telling our name or as complex and threatening as revealing deep feelings.

When self-disclosure occurs in caring relationships, it usually results in greater self-understanding and self-improvement. The principal benefit of self-disclosure should be personal growth. In addition, our self-disclosure to others encourages them to reciprocate and creates an atmosphere that fosters interpersonal communication and meaningful relationships.

Making Connections

Just Friends

The following excerpt is from an article by Patty Beutler, "Just Friends: Having a Pal of the Opposite Sex Has Many Advantages."

When Holly Pace played matchmaker last year for her girlfriend, she ended up with a best friend—her girlfriend's boyfriend. Tyler Fritz no longer goes out with that girl, but he's remained Holly's best buddy. "I love her to death," he said without reservation. He's not talking about the sort of love that makes his palms sweat or his heart pump wildly. Instead, it's a comfortable, say-anything relationship.

1. What are the advantages to having a best friend (not a romantic relationship) of the opposite sex?
2. What are the disadvantages to having a best friend (not a romantic relationship) of the opposite sex?
3. How do your answers to these questions relate to what you have learned so far in this chapter?

Self-Disclosure: The Process

Our use of self-disclosure is not static, and it can move back and forth from expressing our social self-identity (including our roles as students, parents, friends, or sports fans) to very personal, intimate information

To reduce uncertainty and to meet our physical and emotional needs, we must communicate who we are; we must disclose information about ourselves. When self-disclosure occurs in caring relationships, it usually results in greater self-understanding and self-improvement.

about our private lives. Generally, we express our social selves in relationships or in relatively formal settings. In any relationship, there is always tension between the need for privacy and the need for intimacy or more personal disclosure. According to communication scholar William Rawlins and others, the dynamic between the need for privacy and the need for intimacy creates movement in relationships.[19] When we express our personal selves with another or others, the communication moves toward the intimate end of the continuum. When we wish to maintain our privacy by expressing only our social selves, the communication moves toward the social end of the continuum. To benefit from disclosure, we must realize that it is an ongoing process that is incorporated into our daily interaction with others. The process of self-disclosure is best illustrated via the Johari Window and the social penetration model.

FIGURE 13.1

The Johari Window The Johari Window illustrates four kinds of information: the open area, the blind area, the hidden area, and the unknown area. In a relationship, certain areas of information are available to and hidden from each person. What we know about others is gained primarily through self-disclosure and interpersonal communication.

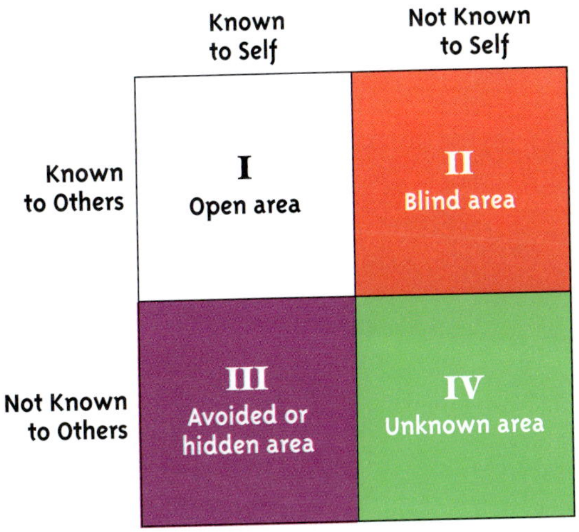

J. Luft, *Group Processes: An Introduction to Group Dynamics,* Palo Alto, Calif.: National Press, 1970. Reprinted by permission.

Johari Window Model

One way to visualize and understand the dynamics of the self-disclosure process is to examine the **Johari Window** (see Figure 13.1), named after the first names of its creators, Joseph Luft and Harry Ingham.[20] It is one the most useful models describing human interaction because it depicts four different levels of knowledge that exist in our relationships with others. The lines dividing

FIGURE 13.2

Variation on the Johari Window As self-disclosure increases in relationships, the *open area* becomes larger. The open area represents what is known about the self and others in a relationship.

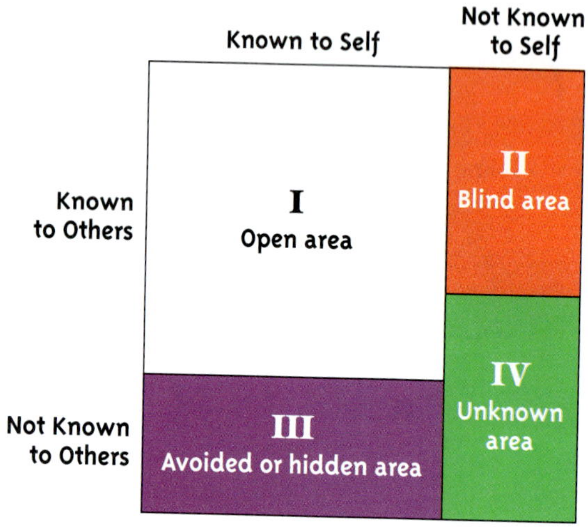

J. Luft, *Group Processes: An Introduction to Group Dynamics*, Palo Alto, Calif.: National Press, 1970. Reprinted by permission.

the four panes are like shades, which can move as interaction progresses and the relationship develops.

Area I: The Open Area. The open area contains information that is known both to the self and to others, because it is readily available through observation or willingness to share. For example, when people meet for the first time, they undoubtedly note each other's height, weight, skin color, and sex. They may freely share their names, hometowns, career fields, schools, majors, and courses they are taking.

During the first meeting, individuals usually disclose minimal information about themselves. At this point the open area is relatively small. But as people get to know each other through additional interactions, this area becomes much larger, as shown in Figure 13.2.

Area II: The Blind Area. The blind area includes information that others perceive about us but that we do not recognize or acknowledge about ourselves. For example, instructors who show favoritism to certain students may not realize that their behavior is being interpreted in that way. In fact, when confronted with student evaluations that point out the problem, teachers often deny such behavior and argue that they treat everyone equally.

Area III: The Hidden Area. The hidden area includes personal and private information about ourselves that we choose not to disclose to others. Others cannot know personal information unless we choose to disclose it, and we are particularly selective about disclosing such private information. As a relationship grows, more and more private information is typically shared and the hidden area shrinks, but it is never completely eliminated.

Area IV: The Unknown Area. The fourth window is the unknown area, which contains information that is not known to us or to others. Simply because we are human, we may submerge or repress certain information in the subconscious—perhaps a difficult part of our personality, a sexual preference, or the harm a drug is having on us physically or mentally. We may remain ignorant of these factors throughout life, or they may emerge through therapy, or through hypnosis or other consciousness-altering experiences. Another example of material in the unknown area might be an event that we seem to recall but cannot verify with certainty. Finally, we don't know about certain aspects of ourselves because they haven't had the opportunity to surface. For example, can you be sure that you can successfully give artificial respiration to someone if you have never done it? You might think you can, but you won't really know until you actually have the occasion to try it.

Generally, the more guarded, or defensive you tend to be, the more likely you are to withhold information about yourself from others. Therefore in your relationships, the open area will tend to be smaller. The more willing you are to communicate and to encourage feedback, the larger your open area will be.

The Johari Window provides a helpful model of how the information we share with others shapes the overall relationship. It doesn't, however, explain why some people tend to disclose more than others. Researchers have found that women are more likely to disclose personal information than men are, although that is not true in all situations. For example, one research study suggests that women are likely to disclose more about themselves to intimate friends, whereas men are more likely than women to disclose personal information to strangers or casual acquaintances.[21] The choice of who will receive the disclosure is just as significant as the content of the disclosure. The site www.knowmegame.com/Johari_Window/johari_window.html provides some additional insight related to the Johari Window that you might find interesting and fun.

FIGURE 13.3

Social Penetration Model The social penetration model portrays relationship development as starting with factual information and small talk. But as the relationship develops, conversations become more personal, including feelings about self and values.

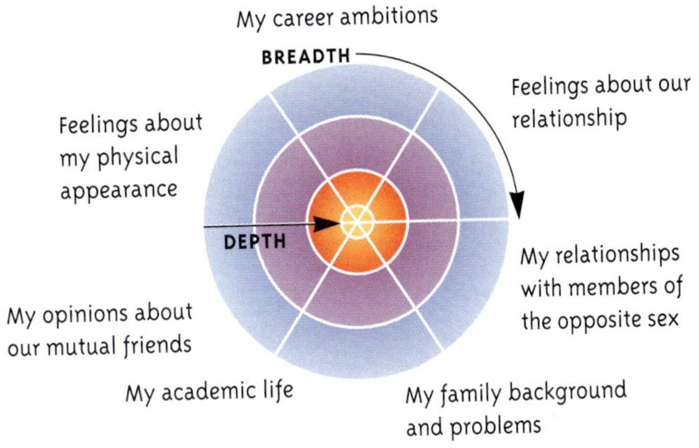

From *Social Penetration: The Development of Interpersonal Relationships.* Copyright © 1973 by Irwin Altman and Dalmas Taylor.

Social Penetration Model

Social penetration model, which was developed by social psychologists Irwin Altman and Dalmas Taylor, provides another view of how people enter relationships and how their communication moves from superficial levels to more intimate and self-revealing talk. **Social penetration,** according to Altman and Taylor, is the process of increasing disclosure and intimacy in a relationship.[22] Figure 13.3 illustrates this view. According to this model, self-disclosure increases gradually as the relationship develops. The figure resembles a dartboard, with the outer ring representing superficial communication and the innermost circle, or bull's-eye, representing the intimacy and depth of a close relationship. As we begin new relationships, we tend to provide information such as "Hi, I'm Bill, and I love to watch basketball." As relationships develop from casual acquaintances into friendship, conversations lend themselves to more intimate topics. When you first meet someone, the information exchanged mostly consists of biographical facts, such as your name and interests. The first levels of a casual interaction are characterized by a breadth of information that doesn't run too deep. But as the relationship becomes more intimate, it will involve more depth of personal information. The depth is represented on the model as penetration from external factual information (the outer ring) to inner feelings (the center of the circle), revealing more about self-concept and values.

The model shows the degrees of intimacy in interpersonal communication. For example, the statements "My name is Bill" and "I love you with all my heart" express two very different levels of exchange in the development of a relationship. One is factual and the other involves a sharing of emotions and personal feelings. Once deeper

social penetration The process of increasing disclosure and intimacy in a relationship.

levels are reached, the participants increasingly share more breadth *and* depth of personal information. Giving a person sensitive information about oneself is, in a sense, giving him or her power. Judgment is needed to determine whether the person is worthy of trust. Yet even in the best circumstances, when both parties are sincere in their wish to deepen the relationship, doing so can be challenging.

Why Do We Self-Disclose?

Self-disclosure is essential to forming and maintaining relationships. The types of relationships we have with others are often determined by the level and depth of what we disclose about ourselves to each other. We self-disclose to others for many reasons in addition to helping us develop long-term relationships. We will discuss three explanations as to why we self-disclose to others: self-presentation, relationship building, and catharsis.

Self-Presentation. **Self-presentation** is an intentional self-disclosure tactic that we use to reveal certain aspects about ourselves for specific reasons. An example of self-presentation is the employment interview. When you are asked to talk about yourself in an employment interview, you are often asked to discuss your background, experiences, and accomplishments. The information you provide is given with the idea that you are going to emphasize points that would make you suited for the job. Sometimes we self-disclose to save face. For example, some politicians who know that something negative about themselves is going to be revealed in the media will often break the news before the media does in an attempt to soften the negative impact and to preserve their reputations as much as possible.

Relationship Building. We self-disclose to start or maintain relationships. Self-disclosure via small talk or social conversation is one way we enter into relationships with others. The level of self-disclosure at some point can move to more intimate and self-revealing talk as the relationship develops. There are, of course, exceptions to this progression, and the depth and number of interactions can vary dramatically from one relationship to another. Also, moving from light social talk to more intimate and revealing talk does not necessarily imply that the relationship will automatically be a quality relationship.[23]

A relationship's location on the continuum between casual acquaintance and intimate confidant is determined by how people interact with each other and their specific communication behaviors. The way we communicate with another person reflects the nature and type of the relationship.

Catharsis. Self-disclosing communication can be a form of communicative release or catharsis. This is especially true when we want to rid ourselves of information that is causing tension or guilt. Catharsis provides a way of getting something off our chest to reduce stress. Although this type of self-disclosure can have positive effects on our health, the primary motivation is personal gratification.[24] One benefit of this type of disclosure is that it makes us better relationship partners.

self-presentation
An intentional self-disclosure tactic that we use to reveal certain aspects about ourselves for specific reasons.

When Shouldn't We Self-Disclose Too Much?

Although full disclosure can be cleansing, it can also be harmful, risky, unwise, or insensitive as well as detrimental to a relationship. At one time or another, most of us

Making Connections

Self-Disclosure on the Internet

Now you can send Instant Messages back and forth with the people you want—It's hassle-free no matter how you are connected on the Internet! Private conversations and Instant Communication—to sign up today—click here.

Hundreds of chatrooms and online services offer you the ability to interact with people around the world. Think about this mode of communication as you answer the following questions:

1. Are chatrooms and email really private?
2. What precautions should be taken when sending personal information over the Internet?
3. Why is it sometimes easier to reveal personal information about yourself to someone whom you have never met in person?
4. Has the Internet become an escape from "real" relationships? In what ways?
5. Do you believe that online communication will bring about the demise of face-to-face communication?

have chosen not to say what was on our minds or not to tell others something about ourselves, themselves, or others because it might be hurtful. There are many reasons for withholding information, but it is usually to protect others, to avoid a potentially negative reaction, or to avoid hurting others or ourselves. Self-disclosure therefore is not always wise or appropriate.

The open and honest sharing of our feelings, thoughts, concerns, and secrets with others is at the heart of self-disclosure. This openness and honesty would be ideal, but it is not always practical or wise. Ultimately, self-disclosure must be based on personal judgment rather than rigid rules. The key should always be concern for both self and others.

Self-Disclosure, Privacy, and Gender

How much is too much self-disclosure and when does it begin to invade or affect our privacy? **Privacy** is "the claim of individuals, groups, or institutions to determine for themselves when, how, and to what extent information about themselves is communicated to others."[25] These are not easy questions to answer because what might be appropriate for one situation may not be for another. Thus an important task for people in relationships is the negotiation of privacy boundaries.[26] Privacy boundaries work in a way very similar to personal space boundaries as discussed in Chapter 5. Just as we control and protect access to our physical self, for example, how close we allow others to come to us, in the same way we control and protect our privacy boundaries. Sandra Petronio, a communication scholar and expert in the area of privacy and how we manage our privacy boundaries, states

> Revealing private information is risky because there is a potential vulnerability when revealing aspects of the self. Receiving private information from another may also

privacy
The claim of individuals, groups, or institutions to determine for themselves when, how, and to what extent information about themselves is communicated to others.

> result in the need for protecting oneself. In order to manage disclosing and receiving privacy information, individuals erect a metaphoric boundary to reduce the possibility of losing face and as a means of protection. Also, people use a set of rules or criteria to control the boundary and regulate the flow of private information to and from others.[27]

The process of sharing more and more personal information about one's self with another person encourages further intrusion into one's privacy whether wanted or unwanted. It would seem to be common sense, but privacy boundaries are not always clear to either party in a relationship. For example, a man and a woman have been dating for several years and had been sexually intimate, but they are not married. The couple might try to control the privacy of their relationship, because revealing relational secrets could be embarrassing, or they could be fully open about their relationship. The determination of what should be kept private from each other and what should be kept private from others is usually negotiated by the mutual consent of the parties involved in the relationship. According to Petronio,

> There is a time when disclosure of some information is weighted more heavily than keeping it private. Likewise, privacy might be more heavily weighted than disclosure or secrecy. Some measure of secrecy may be considered proportionately more important than privacy and disclosure in a particular situation.[28]

When or if the boundaries of a relationship are violated or crossed, tensions may result, creating an imbalance in the relationship. Thus, negotiations between relationship partners often involve what can and should be shared and what is or should be off limits. Boundaries are erected to protect, control the flow of information,

Know Your Scholar

Sandra Petronio *Indiana University-Purdue University*

Sandra Petronio (Ph.D., University of Michigan) is professor of interpersonal, family and health communication at Indiana University-Purdue University in Indianapolis, Indiana. She was the 2002 recipient of the National Communication Association's (NCA) Bernard Brommel Award for Distinguished Scholarship and Service in Family Communication. The Brommel Award is the field's highest honor, bestowed by NCA, the nation's foremost academic and professional communication association in family communication.

Petronio developed one of the nation's first university courses in family communication twenty-two years ago and has built a long history of research in the field. Her book *Boundaries of Privacy: Dialectics of Disclosure* was recently published by State University of New York Press. This book represents twenty years of research on how people manage their privacy and offers a practical theory about why people make decisions about revealing and concealing private information. Her work examines the everyday problems in our personal relationships, our health concerns, and our work, to investigate the way we manage our private lives. Petronio argues that in addition to owning our private information, we also should take responsibility for guarding the privacy of others who have put their trust in us. If not, it could lead to betrayal, errors in judgment, deception, gossip, and privacy dilemmas. Her book serves as guide to understanding why certain decisions about privacy succeed while others fail.

and regulate vulnerability. When one partner violates the privacy of the other, for example, attempts are made to reconstruct the privacy boundary by changing the topic or by avoiding the situation.

As we learned in Chapter 2, using the terms *women* and *men* as identifiers to describe or distinguish communication between the sexes is troublesome. The terms imply sameness across all women and all men that might or might not be true. For example, to say "Women disclose their feelings more often than men do" is probably true, but it may not be true for all women or all men. Some men disclose more feelings than some women do, and vice versa. Thus, we must be careful to avoid stereotyping solely based on biological sex differences.[29]

Some research and some authors support the notion that men and women do communicate using different sets of rules and meanings. Deborah Tannen, who was mentioned earlier in the book, has reviewed many research studies and has taken the position that women's verbal and nonverbal behaviors are different from men's. For example, she has found that men talk less personally or inclusively when compared to women and that women tend to make more validating and confirming statements than men do.[30]

Women are more likely to talk about their relationships and disclose a deeper level of intimacy, but men often do not center their talk on relational closeness.[31] Concerning relationships, many men take the attitude that "If it ain't broke, why fix it?" Women may be more likely to express the attitude "If it's going well, how can we make it go better?"

In his study of 200 male and female college students, communication scholar Lawrence Rosenfeld found that males avoid self-disclosure in order to maintain control of a relationship and to avoid having to face things about themselves. Females, according to Rosenfeld, refrain from self-disclosure in order to avoid personal hurt and problems with their relationships.[32] All of us should have someone with whom we can share our feelings and thoughts, because it is generally good for our well-being and personal satisfaction. Self-disclosure is the most sensitive and beautiful form of communication that we can engage in, but it must be done with care. Some scholars suggest that revealing personal information requires rhetorical sensitivity.

It also appears that men and women differ in the defensive and protective strategies they use to reduce embarrassment and maintain privacy boundaries. Men's defensive strategies include blaming the incident on something else, laughing at their own behavior, or retreating from the situation, whereas women's defensive strategies often include blaming others and criticizing themselves. No matter how privacy is defined or explained, the means by which people regulate the release of private information is through disclosure.[33]

Cultural Issues in Self-Disclosure

In general, people from different cultural backgrounds tend to follow similar patterns of self-disclosure. For example, people from various cultures are likely to begin relationships with small talk and progress to more intimate levels of interaction as the relationship continues. Of course, there are differences, especially in the initial contact stage, in some cultures; but in general, as people become friends, those differences seem to diminish.

Think about some of the characteristics that describe your cultural background, however, and how they might or might not influence your communication. Do you see yourself simply as an American, or identified with some other ethnic or racial group: African American, Filipino American, Latino, Vietnamese, Korean, German or white? Do others view you the same way? How does your ethnicity affect your communication and with whom you choose to communicate? Do you use certain expressions that are understood only by members of your ethnic group? When you interact with people from a different ethnic group, how difficult is it for you to communicate? Thinking about the answers to these questions will help you to understand cultural differences and why interacting with people from diverse backgrounds is much more complex than simply exchanging information. It requires thought, a recognition of differences, and some adjustments for communication to be meaningful to both parties. Not everyone thinks and communicates in exactly the same way. This may be especially important to remember when we interact with people from cultures different than our own.

There are individual differences in the way people from various cultures disclose personal information. These differences often form fairly stable ethnic communication patterns that have been identified by research. For example, members of some cultures are more direct than indirect, more elaborate than succinct, more personal than contextual, and more functional than emotional.

Rhetorical Sensitivity

According to communication scholars Roderick Hart and Don Burks, **rhetorical sensitivity** is an alternative form of communication that can be applied to situations in which wide-open self-disclosure could be harmful. It represents a cautious approach to exchanging information while developing a relationship.[34] Rhetorically sensitive people can balance their self-interest with the interests of others. They can adjust their communication to take into account the beliefs, values, and mood of the other person. Considering the other person's views or feelings does not mean changing your own view or position, but it does mean finding an effective way to communicate your thoughts without offending or hurting the other person. Honest self-disclosure can be harmful if it is stated in a way that damages the relationship. Rhetorically sensitive individuals generally display the following attributes:

1. They accept personal complexity; they understand that every person is made up of many selves. For example, one person may be a mother, a daughter, a Republican, an Asian American, an abuse victim, a student, and a consumer.
2. They are flexible and avoid rigidity in communicating with others.
3. They do not change their own values, but they can communicate them in a variety of ways to avoid offending others.
4. They sense when it is appropriate to communicate something and when it is not.[35] Rhetorically sensitive people understand self-disclosure and know how to adapt their messages to a particular audience and situation.
5. They are aware of the language they choose, such as gender-inclusive nonsexist language; they do not use homophobic or racist language or inappropriate jokes that offend others.

rhetorical sensitivity A cautious approach to self-disclosure in which the situation and factors about the other person are considered before communication begins.

General Conclusions about Self-Disclosure

Research findings support these general conclusions about self-disclosure, whatever the interaction level obtained in a relationship:

1. Disclosure increases with increased relational intimacy.
2. Disclosure increases when rewarded—the reward outweighs the risk of disclosing.
3. Disclosure increases with the need to reduce uncertainty in a relationship.
4. Disclosure tends to be reciprocal—when one person in a relationship increases self-disclosure, the other person will typically follow suit.
5. Women tend to disclose personal information more often than men do.
6. Women seem to disclose more with those to whom they are close, whereas men seem to disclose more with those whom they trust.
7. Disclosure is culturally regulated by norms of appropriateness.
8. People will disclose themselves to people they like.
9. People will overestimate the amount of self-disclosure they actually permit.
10. Self-disclosure does not automatically indicate attraction and, if inappropriate, can cause negative reactions.
11. Liking someone and wanting a relationship to continue can, in fact, discourage self-disclosure, because of the risk that self-disclosure might damage the relationship.[36]

The open and honest sharing of our feelings, concerns, and secrets with others is at the heart of self-disclosure. This does not mean, however, that we must disclose everything or that we cannot withhold information if it is likely to hurt us or someone else. The goal is to match the amount and kind of self-disclosure to the situation.

Ultimately, self-disclosure must be based on personal judgment rather than rigid rules. The key should always be concern for both self and others. Self-disclosure is the most sensitive and beautiful form of communication that we can engage in as we develop and maintain lasting relationships. There are many reasons we sometimes find it difficult to open ourselves to others. However, when based on mutual feelings and genuine communication, relationships cannot help but grow and mature.

Learning Connections

1. What role does self-disclosure have in relationship development?
2. What are the similarities and differences between the Johari Window and the social penetration model?
3. Does self-disclosure mean the same thing in different cultures? Explain.
4. What does ensuring privacy mean to you?
5. Describe what it means to be rhetorically sensitive.

Appropriate Self-Disclosure

GUIDELINES

1. *Use reasoned self-disclosure.* Although open and honest relationships are desirable, it is important to recognize situational constraints. For example, as a youngster, you might have been caught shoplifting from a local store. You shoplifted only that one time. However, you are now running for public office, and you

must decide whether to disclose the fact that you stole from a local store. To do so would more than likely hurt your chances of winning the election. Therefore, you choose not to bring up the issue. This does not mean that you are being dishonest. In some situations and with certain individuals, not revealing a specific past behavior might be reasonable—particularly if it has little to do with the situation at hand.

2. *Make self-disclosure a two-way process.* Relationships built on one-sided exchanges are generally not very enduring, meaningful, or healthy. People are more likely to disclose information when they feel safe and when their open communication is positively received. It therefore follows that each party will feel safer if both are involved in the self-disclosure process. Once a mutual give-and-take is established, if one person increases self-disclosure, the other person will usually follow suit. Trust increases, self-disclosure continues, and the relationship grows in a healthy way.
3. *Make self-disclosure appropriate to the situation and the person.* When we disclose personal information about ourselves, we run the risk of being rejected. We can somewhat minimize this risk if we carefully match the disclosure to the person and the situation. Self-disclosure should be a slow process; rushing it can increase vulnerability unnecessarily. In addition, it is safest to disclose only to truly caring people and to be sensitive to both their verbal and nonverbal cues. Disclosing too much too soon or disclosing to the wrong person can lead to embarrassment and pain—and sometimes serious harm.
4. *Consider diversity.* The appropriateness and the level of self-disclosure vary by culture, group, and individual. The Japanese culture, for example, does not foster self-expression in the same way that U.S. or Korean cultures do. Consider these differences as you decide how to disclose personal information.
5. *Avoid indiscriminate self-disclosure.* Once you disclose something, you cannot take it back, though you may try to qualify what you have said.
6. *Be positive.* You should avoid being overly negative about people and issues, particularly in newly forming relationships. Negative self-disclosure can be a real turnoff as well as a tremendous drag on any relationship.

Summary

Interpersonal communication is the informal exchange of information between two or more people. It is interpersonal communication that allows relationships to become established and to grow, satisfying our social needs. Because we have social needs and the desire to know others, uncertainty reduction theory and predicted outcome value theory are discussed as motivators for interpersonal communication.

Many of the needs that we have as humans can be satisfied through communication. Two approaches that attempt to explain needs are Thibaut and Kelley's social exchange theory and Schutz's fundamental interpersonal relations orientation theory. Schutz's theory implies that we have three needs: the need for affection, the need for inclusion, and the need for control. Thibaut and Kelley's theory is based on the assumption that people consciously and deliberately consider the costs and rewards associated with a relationship or interaction and that they will seek out relationships that are rewarding and avoid those that are costly.

If we encounter people more than once and they become recognizable, we are more likely to be comfortable interacting with them or at least making small talk with them. Competent communicators know the importance of small talk as a social skill.

We develop relationships to avoid or reduce loneliness, to learn about ourselves, and to share. Lasting relationships are open, a feature that allows for relatively free self-disclosure. The more information we reveal about ourselves, the more likely we are to have relationships that will grow and mature into healthy and satisfying experiences.

The Johari Window is a graphic model that depicts four areas of information about each of us: the open area, the blind area, the hidden area, and the unknown area. These four areas expand and contract in relationships over time and from situation to situation.

The social penetration model is an example of how people enter relationships and how their communication moves from superficial levels of small talk to more intimate and self-revealing talk. We disclose information about ourselves because we recognize possible advantages that we gain from doing so. This approach of becoming known to others is called self-presentation. Privacy is our way of controlling what others know about us, and it should be up to us to determine when, how, and to what extent we provide information about ourselves to others. Rhetorical sensitivity is an alternative form of communication that competent communicators use when they know that too much self-disclosure could be harmful to those involved. Because frankness creates vulnerability, each participant must consider situational constraints when deciding what should or should not be disclosed.

DISCUSSION STARTERS

1. In your opinion which of the four theories discussed in this chapter best explains our motivation in our need to know others and form relationships?
2. How do our interpersonal needs influence our communication with others?
3. Many older people believe that young people today have no manners when communicating? Do you agree or disagree? Why?
4. Explain the rules or guidelines for proper or polite communication with others.
5. What are the advantages and disadvantages of interacting with people online?
6. Has politically correct communication gone too far?
7. What does it mean to be rhetorically sensitive?
8. Is honesty always the best policy when self-disclosing? Explain.
9. If you were to develop a set of rules for effective self-disclosure, what would they be?
10. Why do you think people stay in abusive relationships?

NOTES

1. Adapted from an article written by Jonathan Butler entitled "The Donut Shop Experiment" in *The Front Porch Where People Share Life* published by The Front Porch, LLC, © 2002.
2. M. L. Knapp and A. L. Vangelisti, *Interpersonal Communication and Human Relationships,* 4th ed. (Boston: Allyn and Bacon, 2000), 34.
3. C. R. Berger and R. J. Calabrese, "Some Explorations in Initial Interactions and Beyond: Toward a Developmental Theory of Interpersonal Communication," *Human Communication Research* 1 (1975): 98–112; and C. R. Berger, "Response—Uncertain Outcome Values in Predicted Relationships: Uncertainty Reduction Theory Then and Now," *Human Communication Research* 13 (1986): 34–38.
4. M. Sunnafrank, "Predicted Outcome Value During Initial Interactions: A Reformulation of Uncertainty Reduction Theory," *Human Communication Research* 13 (1986): 3–33; K. Kellermann and R. Reynolds, "When Ignorance Is Bliss: The Role of Motivation to Reduce Uncertainty in Uncertainty Reduction Theory," *Human Communication Research* 17 (1990): 5–75; and M. Sunnafrank, "Predicted Outcome Value and Uncertainty Reduction Theories: A Test of Competing Perspectives," *Human Communication Theory* 17 (1990): 76–103.
5. J. W. Thibaut and H. H. Kelley, *The Social Psychology of Groups,* 2nd ed. (New Brunswick, N.J.: Transaction Books, 1986), 9–30; and E. Griffin, *A First Look at Communication Theory,* 5th ed. (New York: McGraw-Hill, 2003), 136–139.
6. W. C. Schutz, *The Interpersonal Underworld* (Palo Alto, Calif.: Science and Behavior Books, 1966), 13–20.
7. B. Park and C. Flink, "A Social Relations Analysis of Agreement in Liking Judgments," *Journal of Personality and Social Psychology* 56 (1989): 506–51.
8. M. Moore, "Nonverbal Courtship Patterns in Women! Context and Consequences," *Ethology and Sociobiology* 6 (1985): 237–47.
9. D. J. Goldsmith and L. A. Baxter, "Constituting Relationship Talk: A Taxonomy of Speech Events in Social and Personal Relationships," *Human Communication Research* 18 (1996): 87–114.
10. J. Levin and A. Arluke, *Gossip: The Inside Scoop* (New York: Plenum, 1987), 28–29.
11. J. S. Caputo, H. C. Hazel, and C. McMahon, *Interpersonal Communication: Competency Through Critical Thinking* (Boston: Allyn and Bacon, 1994), 98–99.
12. B. Reeves, "Chat Room Brought Them Together," *Lincoln Journal Star,* 25 June 2000, sec. J, 1.
13. M. R. Parks and K. Floyd, "Making Friends in Cyberspace," *Journal of Communication* 46 (1996): 85.
14. M. Irvine, "Wireless Gadgets: Flirt-Friendly," *Lincoln Journal Star,* September 22, 2002, 9A.
15. Ibid.
16. B. Reeves, "Caught in the Net: Proceed with Caution, *Lincoln Journal Star,* 25 June 2000, sec. J, 1.
17. Ibid.
18. Ibid.
19. W. Rawlins, "Negotiating Close Friendships. The Dialectic of Conjunctive Freedoms," *Human Communication Research* 9 (1983): 255–66; and L. Baxter and B. Montgomery, *Relating: Dialogue and Dialects* (New York: Guilford, 1996), 133–39.
20. J. Luft, *Group Processes: An Introduction to Group Dynamics* (Palo Alto, Calif.: National Press, 1970), 11–14.
21. J. Stokes, A. Fuehrer, and L. Childs, "Gender Differences in Self-Disclosure to Various Target Persons," *Journal of Counseling Psychology* 27 (1980): 192–98.
22. I. Altman and D. Taylor, *Social Penetration: The Development of Interpersonal Relationships* (New York: Holt, Rinehart & Winston, 1973); and Knapp and Vangelisti, 14–20.
23. A. L. Sillars and M. D. Scott, "Interpersonal Perception Between Intimates: An Integrative Review," *Human Communication Research* 10 (1983): 153–76.
24. J. W. Pennebaker, *Opening Up: The Healing Power of Expressing Emotions* (New York: Guilford, 1990).
25. V. J. Derlega, S. Metts, S. Petronio, and S. T. Margulis, *Self-Disclosure* (Newbury Park, Calif.: Sage, 1993), 74.
26. S. Petronio, "The Boundries of Privacy: Praxis of Everyday Life," in *Balancing the Secrets of Private Disclosures,* ed. S. Petronio (Hillsdale, N.J.: Erlbaum, 2000), 9–15.
27. S. Petronio, "Communication Boundary Management: A Theoretical Model of Managing Disclosure of Private Information Between Marital Couples," *Communication Theory* 1 (1991): 311.
28. S. Petronio (2000), 14.
29. J. T. Wood, *Gendered Lives: Communication, Gender, and Culture,* 3rd ed. (Belmont, Calif: Wadsworth, 1999), 21–22; and J. T. Wood, *Gendered Lives: Communication, Gender and Culture,* 5th ed. (Belmont, Calif.: Thomson Wadsworth, 2003), 186–193.
30. D. Tannen, *You Just Don't Understand: Women and Men in Conversation* (New York: Morrow, 1990).
31. C. K. Riessman, *Divorce Talk: Women and Men Make Sense of Personal Relationships* (New Brunswick, N.J.: Rutgers University Press, 1990).
32. L. B. Rosenfeld, "Self-Disclosure Avoidance: Why I Am Afraid to Tell You Who I Am," *Communication Monographs* 46 (1979): 63–74.

33. S. Petronio, "Communication Strategies to Reduce Embarrassment Differences Between Men and Women," *The Western Journal of Speech Communication* 48 (1984): 28–38.
34. R. P. Hart and D. M. Burks, "Rhetorical Sensitivity and Social Interaction," *Speech Monographs* 39 (1972): 75–91.
35. S. W. Littlejohn, *Theories of Human Communication,* 6th ed. (Belmont, Calif.: Wadsworth, 1999), 103–4.
36. A. P. Bochner, "The Functions of Human Communicating in Interpersonal Bonding," in *Handbook of Rhetorical and Communication Theory,* eds. C. C. Arnold and J. W. Bowers (Boston: Allyn and Bacon, 1984), 554–621.

13A Culture in Interpersonal Communication

Crouching Tiger, Hidden Dragon (2000)

No culture can live, if it attempts to be exclusive.

—Mahatma Gandhi

The fantasy story of two lovers, Mu Bai and Shu Lien, who cannot express their love because of cultural prohibitions, is vividly portrayed in Ang Lee's Crouching Tiger, Hidden Dragon. *Although the film takes place in ancient China, it clearly illustrates the ever-present influence of culture on a wide variety of behaviors. In this chapter we look at culture and its influence on interpersonal communication, some of the ways in which cultures differ, and the nature of intercultural communication, especially ways you can increase your own intercultural communication effectiveness.*

CULTURE AND INTERPERSONAL COMMUNICATION

A walk through any large city and many small towns, through the schools and colleges, and into the business and manufacturing centers will convince you that the United States is largely a collection of many different cultures. These cultures coexist somewhat separately but also with each influencing each other. This coexistence has led some researchers to refer to these cultures as cocultures (Schuter, 1990; Samovar & Porter, 1991; Jandt, 2001). Consider these facts (*The New York Times Almanac,* 2002; *The World Almanac and Book of Facts*, 2002):

The foreign-born population of the United States is increasing dramatically. In 1980 the foreign-born population was 14 million (about 6.2 percent of the total population), in 1990 it was 19.8 million (7.9 percent), and in 2000 it was 28.4 million (10.4 percent). Increasingly frequent communication in a multicultural context is inevitable.

In your more immediate environment consider the number of foreign students who come to the United States to continue their education. For the years 2000-2001, China leads the list with 59,939 students. India is next with 54,664. Other countries with large numbers of students in the United States are Japan (46,497), South Korea (46,000), Taiwan (28,566), Canada (25,279), Indonesia (11,625), Thailand (11,187), Turkey (10,983), and Mexico (10,670) (*New York Times,* Education Life, Section 4A, January 13, 2002). Frequent intercultural communication is simply a part of college life today.

Also, corporations in the United States are becoming more and more intercultural. Large and small corporations commonly announce that future growth will depend on expansion into foreign countries. United States manufacturing, media, information technology, and farming interests depend on foreign purchase. Business opportunities, therefore, have an increasingly international dimension, making cultural awareness and intercultural communication competence essential skills for professional success.

The Nature of Culture

Culture refers to the relatively specialized lifestyle of a group of people—consisting of their values, beliefs, artifacts, ways of behaving, and ways of communicating. Included in culture would be all that members of a social group have produced and developed—their language, modes of thinking, art, laws, and religion.

Culture is not synonymous with race or nationality. However, members of a particular race or country are often taught similar beliefs, attitudes, and values. This similarity makes it possible to speak of "Hispanic culture" or "African American culture." But, lest we be guilty of stereotyping, recognize that within any large culture—especially a culture based on race or nationality—there will be enormous differences. The Kansas farmer and the Wall Street executive may both be, say, German American, but they may differ widely in their attitudes and beliefs and in their general lifestyles. In some ways the Kansas farmer may be closer in attitudes and values to the Chinese farmer than to the Philadelphia lawyer.

Gender—although transmitted genetically and not by communication—is considered a cultural variable largely because cultures teach boys and girls different attitudes, beliefs, values, and ways of communicating and relating to one another (Payne, 2001). So, you act like a man or a woman in part because of what your culture has taught you about how men and women should act. Further, you can view male–female communication as cross-cultural because of the numerous differences in the way men and women speak and listen (Eckstein & Goldman, 2001). This does not deny that biological differences also play a role in the differences between male and female behavior. In fact, recent research continues to uncover biological roots of behaviors we once thought were entirely learned, like happiness and shyness, for example (McCroskey, 1997).

Culture is passed on from one generation to the next through communication, not through genes. Thus, culture does not refer to color of skin or shape of eyes. Culture does refer to beliefs in a supreme being, to attitudes toward success and happiness, and to the values placed on friendship, love, family, or money, since these are transmitted through communication.

Culture is transmitted from one generation to another through **enculturation,** a process by which you learn the culture into which you're born (your native culture). Parents, peer groups, schools, religious institutions, and government agencies are the main teachers of culture. One relatively new instrument for spreading culture is the Internet. Because the Internet, although worldwide, is so dominated by the United States and by the English language and idiom, the culture of the Internet is dominated by the culture of the United States. "Some countries," notes one media watcher, "already unhappy with the encroachment of American culture—from jeans to Mickey Mouse to movies and TV programs—are worried that their cultures will be further eroded by an American dominance in cyberspace" (Pollack, 1995, D1).

Through enculturation you develop an ethnic identity, a commitment to the beliefs and philosophy of your culture (Chung & Ting-Toomey, 1999). The degree to which you identify with your cultural group can be measured by your responses to questions such as these (from Ting-Toomey, 1981).

Using a 5-point scale with "1" meaning strongly disagree and "5" meaning strongly agree, indicate how true of you the following statements are.

1. I am increasing my involvement in activities with my ethnic group.
2. I involve myself in causes that will help members of my ethnic group.
3. It feels natural being part of my ethnic group.
4. I have spent time trying to find out more about my own ethnic group.
5. I am happy to be a member of my ethnic group.
6. I have a strong sense of belonging to my ethnic group.
7. I often talk to other members of my group to learn more about my ethnic culture.

High scores (say 4s and 5s) indicate a strong commitment to your culture's values and beliefs; low numbers (1s and 2s) indicate a relatively weak commitment.

A different process of learning culture is **acculturation,** the process by which you learn the rules and norms of a culture different from your native culture. Through acculturation, your original or native culture is modified by direct contact with (or exposure to) a new and different culture. For example, when immigrants settle in the United States, the host country, their own culture becomes influenced by the host culture.

Gradually, the values, ways of behaving, and beliefs of the host culture become more and more a part of the immigrants' culture. At the same time, the host culture changes, too, as it interacts with the immigrants' culture. Generally, however, the culture of the immigrant changes more. The reasons for this are that the host country's members far outnumber the immigrant group, and the media are largely dominated by and reflect the values and customs of the host culture.

Before exploring further the role of culture in communication, consider your own cultural values and beliefs by taking the accompanying self-test. This test will suggest how your own cultural values and beliefs might influence the messages you send and the messages you listen to in your interpersonal communication.

TEST YOURSELF *What Are Your Cultural Beliefs and Values?*

The extremes of 10 cultural differences are identified below. For each characteristic indicate your own values: If your values are *very* similar to the extremes, select 1 or 7. If your values are *quite* similar to the extremes, select 2 or 6. If your values are *fairly* similar to the extremes, select 3 or 5. If you're in the middle, select 4.

Men and women are equal and are entitled to equality in all areas.	**Gender Equality** 1 2 3 4 5 6 7	Men and women should stick to their specific and different cultural roles.
"Success" is measured by your contribution to the group.	**Group and Individual Orientation** 1 2 3 4 5 6 7	"Success" is measured by how far you outperform others.
You should enjoy yourself as much as possible.	**Pleasure Orientation/ Hedonism** 1 2 3 4 5 6 7	You should work as much as possible.
Religion is the final arbiter of what is right and wrong; your obligation is to abide by your religion's rules.	**Religion** 1 2 3 4 5 6 7	Religion is like any other social institution; it's not inherently moral or right just because it's a religion.
Your first obligation is to your family; each person is responsible for the welfare of her or his family.	**Family** 1 2 3 4 5 6 7	Your first obligation is to yourself; each person is responsible for her- or himself.
Work hard now for a better future.	**Time Orientation** 1 2 3 4 5 6 7	Live in the present; the future may never come.
Marriage, once made, is forever.	**Marriage** 1 2 3 4 5 6 7	Marriage should be maintained as long as it's rewarding and dissolved when it's not.
People should express their emotions openly and freely.	**Emotional Expression** 1 2 3 4 5 6 7	People should not reveal their emotions, especially negative ones.
Money should be a major consideration in just about any decision you make.	**Money** 1 2 3 4 5 6 7	Money should not enter into life's really important decisions such as what relationship to enter or what career to pursue.

The world is just; bad things happen to bad people and good things happen to good people.	**Belief in a Just World** 1 2 3 4 5 6 7	The world is random; bad and good things happen to people without reference to whether they're good or bad.

How did you do? As demonstrated throughout this text and as research shows, your cultural values and beliefs influence your interpersonal communications as well as your decision making, assessments of coworkers, teamwork, trust in others, the importance you place on diversity in the workplace, and your attitudes toward the role of women in the workplace (Stephens & Greer, 1995; Bochner & Hesketh; 1994). For example, your beliefs and values about gender equality will influence the way in which you communicate with and about the opposite sex. Your group and individual orientation will influence how you perform in work teams and how you deal with your peers at school and at work. Your degree of hedonism will influence the kinds of interactions you engage in, the books you read, the television programs you watch.

What will you do? So, there are no right or wrong answers to this test. What makes this particular test of value for our purposes is that it asks you to examine your own cultural values and beliefs and hopefully stimulates you to go the next step and ask yourself how these values and beliefs influence your interpersonal communication. As you review the 10 characteristics, try to identify at least one specific way in which your attitudes on each of these characteristics in the self-test influence your communication.

ETHICS in Interpersonal Communication

Culture and Ethics

One of the most shocking revelations to come to world attention from the events of September 11, 2001, was the way in which women were treated under Taliban rule in Afghanistan; they could not be educated or even go out in public without a male relative escort, and when in public had to wear garments that covered their entire body.

Throughout history, of course, there have been numerous cultural practices that today would be judged unethical and even illegal. Sacrificing virgins to the gods, burning people who held different religious beliefs, and sending children to fight wars are obvious examples. But, even today, there are practices woven deep into the fabric of different cultures that many people would find unethical, for example:

- bronco riding, a practice where a bull's testicles are tied so that it experiences so much pain that it bucks and tries to throw off the rider
- clitoridectomy, whereby part or all of a young girl's clitoris is surgically removed so that she can never experience sexual intercourse without extreme pain, a practice designed to keep her a virgin until marriage
- the belief and practice that a woman must be subservient to her husband's will
- the practice of wearing fur—in some cases necessitating the killing of wild animals and in others raising animals so they can be killed when their pelts are worth the most money

What would you do? *Imagine that you're on a television talk show on cultural diversity. During the discussion each of the above-mentioned practices is discussed with approval by different members of the panel who argue that each culture has a right to its own practices and beliefs and that no one has the right to object to these practices. Given your own beliefs about these issues and about cultural diversity in general, what ethical obligations do you have as a member of this panel?*

The Relevance of Culture

There are lots of reasons for the cultural emphasis you'll find in this book. Most obvious, perhaps, are the vast demographic changes taking place throughout the United States. Whereas at one time the United States was a country largely populated by Europeans, it's now a country greatly influenced by the enormous number of new citizens from Latin and South America, Africa, and Asia. Along with the aforementioned demographic shift so noticeable on college campuses, these changes have brought different interpersonal customs and the need to understand and adapt to new ways of looking at communication.

As a people we've become increasingly sensitive to cultural differences. American society has moved from an assimilationist perspective (people should leave their native culture behind and adapt to their new culture) to one that values cultural diversity (people should retain their native cultural ways). With some notable exceptions—hate speech, racism, sexism, homophobia, and classism come quickly to mind—we are more concerned with saying the right thing and ultimately with developing a society where all cultures can coexist and enrich each other. The ability to interact effectively with members of other cultures often translates into financial gain and increased employment opportunities and advancement prospects as well.

Today, most countries are economically dependent on each other. Our economic lives depend on our ability to communicate effectively across different cultures. Similarly, our political well-being depends in great part on that of other cultures. Political unrest in any part of the world—South Africa, Eastern Europe, Asia, and the Middle East, to take a few examples—affects our own security. Intercultural communication and understanding seem more crucial now than ever.

The rapid spread of technology has made intercultural communication as easy as it is inevitable. News from foreign countries is commonplace. You see nightly—in vivid detail—what is going on in remote countries just as you see what's happening in your own city and state. Of course, the Internet has made intercultural communication as easy as writing a note on your computer. You can now just as easily communicate by e-mail with someone in Asia or Europe, for example, as you can with someone in another U.S. city or state.

Still another reason culture is so important is that interpersonal competence is culture-specific; what proves effective in one culture may prove ineffective in another. For example, in the United States corporate executives get down to business during the first several minutes of a meeting. In Japan, business executives interact socially for an extended period and try to find out something about each other. Thus, the communication principle influenced by U.S. culture would advise participants to get down to the meeting's agenda during the first five minutes. The principle influenced by Japanese culture would advise participants to avoid dealing with business until everyone has socialized sufficiently and feels well enough acquainted to begin negotiations. Giving a birthday gift to a close friend would be appreciated by many, but among Jehovah's Witnesses, for example, this act would be frowned upon since they don't celebrate birthdays (Dresser, 1996). Neither principle is right, and neither is wrong. Each is effective within its own culture and ineffective outside its own culture.

The Aim of a Cultural Perspective

Because culture permeates all forms of communication, it's necessary to understand its influences if you're to understand how communication works and master its skills. As illustrated throughout this text, culture influences communications of all types

INTER MEDIA

Cultural Imperialism

Cultural imperialism refers to a process whereby business and political practices, but especially media products, are exported to other cultures and come to extend the influence of the exporting culture over that of the importing culture. The theory argues that the media from developed countries such as the United States and Western Europe have come to dominate the cultures of countries importing such media and at the same time to denigrate the customs and values of the local, less technologically sophisticated cultures (Folkerts & Lacy, 2001).

Media products from the United States are likely to emphasize its dominant attitudes and values, for example, the preference for competition, the importance of individuality, and the advantages of capitalism and democracy. When these media products—movies, television programs, and music, for example—are consumed by other cultures, the values and attitudes embedded in these products can quickly become the values and attitudes of these other cultures.

Television programs, films, and music from the United States and Western Europe are so popular and so in demand in developing countries that they may actually inhibit the growth of the indigenous culture's own talent. To combat this trend, some countries (Canada, France, Taiwan, and South Korea among them) have imposed restrictions on the amount of United States television programming that can be imported (Rodman, 2001).

From another perspective, however, you might argue that much as people in the United States profit as new cultures exert their influence, developing cultures profit as United States media introduce new perspectives on government and politics, foods, educational technologies, and health, for example.

Follow Up What do you think of the influence the media from the United States and Western Europe is having on cultures throughout the world? How do you evaluate it? Do you see advantages? Disadvantages?

(Moon, 1996). It influences what you say to yourself and how you talk with friends, lovers, and family in everyday conversation (for example, Shibazaki & Brennan, 1998). It influences how you interact in groups and how much importance you place on the group versus the individual. It influences the topics you talk about and the strategies you use in communicating information or in persuading. It influences how you use the media and the credibility you attribute to them.

A cultural emphasis helps distinguish what is universal (true for all people) from what is relative (true for people in one culture and not true for people in other cultures) (Matsumoto, 1994). The principles for communicating information and for changing listeners' attitudes, for example, will vary from one culture to another. If you're to understand communication, then you need to know how its principles vary and how the principles must be qualified and adjusted on the basis of cultural differences.

A good example is that of age. If you were raised in the United States, you probably grew up with a youth bias (young is good, old is not so good)—an attitude the media reinforces daily—and may well have assumed that this preference for youth is universal across all cultures. But it isn't and if you assume it is, you may be in for intercultural difficulties. A good example is the case of the American journalist in China who remarked that the government official he was talking with was probably too young to remember a particular event, a comment that would be taken as a compliment by most youth-oriented Americans. But to the Chinese it would be perceived as an insult, as a suggestion that the official was too young to deserve respect (Smith, 2002).

This cultural understanding is needed to communicate effectively in the wide variety of intercultural situations. Success in interpersonal communication—at your job and in

View point Social Darwinism, or cultural evolution, holds that much as the human species evolved from lower life forms to Homo sapiens, cultures also evolve. Consequently, some cultures may be considered advanced and others primitive. Cultural relativism, on the other hand, holds that all cultures are different but that no culture is superior or inferior to any other (Berry, Poortinga, Segall, & Dasen, 1992). What argument can you advance in support of or against each position?

your social and personal life—will depend in great part on your understanding of and your ability to communicate effectively with persons who are culturally different from yourself. Daily the media bombard you with evidence of racial tensions, religious disagreements, sexual bias, and in general, the problems caused when intercultural communication fails.

This emphasis on culture does not imply that you should accept all cultural practices or that all cultural practices are equal (Hatfield & Rapson, 1996). Consider this case in point (*Time*, 2 December 1993, 61). Assume you're a judge and the following case is presented to you: A Chinese immigrant killed his wife in New York because he suspected her of cheating. A "cultural defense" was offered, essentially claiming that infidelity so shames a man that he is uncontrollable in his anger. Would this cultural defense have influenced your judgment? In the actual case, influenced by an anthropologist's testimony that infidelity is so serious in Chinese culture that it pushed the defendant to commit the crime, the judge sentenced the defendant to five years' probation.

Further, a cultural emphasis does not imply that you have to accept or follow all of the practices of your own culture. For example, even if the majority in your culture find cockfighting acceptable, you need not agree with or follow the practice. Nor need you consider this practice equal to a cultural practice in which animals are treated kindly. You can reject capitalism or communism or socialism regardless of the culture in which you were raised. Of course, going against your culture's traditions and values is often very difficult. But it's important to realize that culture influences, it does not determine, your values or behavior. Often personality factors (your degree of assertiveness, extroversion, or optimism, for example) will prove more influential than culture (Hatfield & Rapson, 1996).

As demonstrated throughout this text, cultural differences exist throughout the interpersonal communication spectrum—from the way you use eye contact to the way you develop or dissolve a relationship (Chang & Holt, 1996). But these should not blind you to the great number of similarities existing among even the most widely separated cultures. When discussing differences, remember that these are usually questions of degree rather than all-or-none. For example, most cultures value honesty, but some cultures give it greater emphasis than others. The advances in media and technology and the widespread use of the Internet, for example, are influencing cultures and cultural change and are perhaps homogenizing the different cultures, lessening the differences and increasing the similarities.

You'll see the cultural emphasis in this text in two ways. First, this chapter focuses on the role of culture in interpersonal communication, the ways cultures differ, and intercultural communication—especially the principles for increasing intercultural communication effectiveness. Second, cultural issues are integrated throughout the text as they relate to the topic being discussed. For example, when discussing self-disclosure or the meanings of nonverbal gestures, we also consider how different cultures view these forms of communication.

HOW CULTURES DIFFER

Cultures, of course, differ in a wide variety of ways and, for purposes of communication, the difference that probably comes to mind first is that of languages. And certainly, cultures do differ in the languages spoken and understood. In fact, one of the most popular theories in intercultural communication, the language relativity hypothesis, argued that the language you speak influences your thoughts and behaviors and since cultures differ so widely in their languages, they will also differ in their ways of thinking and behaving.

Subsequent research and theory, however, did not support the extreme claims made by linguistic relativity researchers (Pinker, 1994). A more modified hypothesis is currently supported: The language you speak helps to *highlight* what you see and how you talk about it. For example, if you speak a language that is rich in color terms (English is a good example), you would find it easier to highlight and talk about nuances of color than would someone from a culture that has fewer color terms (some cultures distinguish only two or three or four parts of the color spectrum). This does not mean, however, that people *see* the world differently; only that their language helps (or doesn't help) them to focus on certain variations in nature and makes it easier (or more difficult) to talk about them. Nor does it mean that people speaking widely differing languages are doomed to misunderstanding each other. Translation enables us to understand a great deal of the meaning in a foreign-language message. We also have a ready arsenal of communication skills, which you'll encounter throughout this course, that can help bridge the communication gap between members of different cultures.

Language differences are not the only differences between cultures that will influence intercultural communication. Let's take a look at five such differences: power distances, masculine and feminine orientation, collectivism and individualism, high and low context, and time orientations (Gudykunst, 1991; Hall & Hall, 1987; Hofstede, 1997). As you review these differences, recognize that they are matters of degree. Characteristics aren't necessarily present in one culture and absent in the other; rather they're present in both but to different degrees. And that's what this discussion focuses on: degrees of differences, not absolute differences.

Power Distances

In some cultures power is concentrated in the hands of a few, and there is a great difference in the power held by these people and that held by the ordinary citizen. These are called high-power-distance cultures; examples are Mexico, Brazil, India, and the Philippines (Hofstede, 1983, 1997). In low-power-distance cultures, power is more

WEB EXPLORATION
To learn more about power distances, go to www.ablongman.com/devito.

ASK the *Researcher*

Confronting Family Prejudice

My family, I'm embarrassed to say, is really prejudiced against other races and religions. They can't see any value in the contributions of other cultures or the wisdom in other religions. How can I insert a note of reason into their discussions and get them to be less prejudiced?

Deep-seated and strong prejudices are very resistant. They may be based on fear or dislike of any sort of difference—feelings the person may not even admit to himself or herself. Typically, these feelings have been supported by peer groups for a long time and so the prejudiced person sees these opinions as reasonable and natural.

The most realistic goal may be to get them to respect your own feelings. Tell them that you're upset by this type of talk and you don't wish to be around it. Be assertive and consistent. Make it clear that you're upset and that you're asking them to stop telling those types of jokes, using that kind of language, etc. It's your right. If they don't stop, leave the room.

Reducing their prejudice may take a very long time. You can try showing them that the same type of thinking can apply to their own group. You also can try to have them meet members of the group that disconfirm their stereotypes.

For further information see M. L. Hecht, ed. (1998). *Communicating prejudice.* Newbury Park, CA: Sage, and B. Lott and D. Maluso, eds. (1995). *The social psychology of interpersonal discrimination.* New York: Guilford.

Michael L. Hecht (Ph.D., University of Illinois) is professor and head of the Department of Communication Arts and Science at Penn State University where he teaches courses and conducts research in interethnic relationships, identity, culture and drug prevention, and interpersonal relationships. He's recently developed a successful culturally appropriate drug prevention program for middle school students and is involved in an international project to improve intergroup relationships. mhecht@psu.edu (Reprinted by permission of Dr. Michael L. Hecht.)

evenly distributed throughout the citizenry; examples include Denmark, New Zealand, Sweden, and to a lesser extent the United States. These differences affect interpersonal communication and relationships in a variety of ways.

Friendship and dating relationships will be influenced by the power distance between groups (Andersen, 1991). For example, in India (high power distance), friendships and romantic relationships are expected to take place within your cultural class; in Sweden (low power distance), a person is expected to select friends and romantic partners not on the basis of class or culture, but on individual factors such as personality, appearance, and the like.

In low-power-distance cultures there is a general feeling of equality that is consistent with acting assertively, and so you're expected to confront a friend, partner, or supervisor assertively (Borden, 1991). In high-power-distance cultures, direct confrontation and assertiveness may be viewed negatively, especially if directed at a superior.

In high-power-distance cultures you're taught to have great respect for authority; people in these cultures see authority as desirable and beneficial, and challenges to authority are generally not welcomed (Westwood, Tang, & Kirkbride, 1992; Bochner & Hesketh, 1994). In low-power-distance cultures, there's a certain distrust for authority; it's seen as a kind of necessary evil that should be limited as much as possible. This difference in attitudes toward authority can be seen right in the classroom. In high-power-distance cultures there's a great power distance between students and teachers; students are expected to be modest, polite, and totally respectful. In low-power-distance cultures students are expected to demonstrate their knowledge and command of the subject matter, participate in discussions with the teacher, and even challenge the teacher, something many high-power-distance culture members wouldn't even think of doing. The same differences can be seen in patient–doctor communication. Patients from high-power-distance cultures are less likely to challenge their doctors or admit that they don't understand the medical terminology than would patients in low-power-distance cultures.

High-power-distance cultures rely more on symbols of power. For example, titles (Dr., Professor, Chef, Inspector) are more important in high-power-distance cultures. Failure to include these in forms of address is a serious breach of etiquette. Low-power-distance cultures rely less on symbols of power, and less of a problem is created if you fail to use a respectful title (Victor, 1992). But even in low-power-distance cultures you may create problems if, for example, you call a medical doctor, police captain, military officer, or professor Ms. or Mr.

In the United States, two people quickly move from Title plus Last Name (Mr. or Ms. Smith) to First Name (Pat). In low-power-distance cultures less of a problem is created if you're too informal or if you presume to exchange first names before sufficient interaction has taken place. In high-power-distance cultures too great an informality—especially between those differing greatly in power—would be a serious breach of etiquette. Again, in even the lowest power distance culture, you may still create problems if you call your English professor Pat.

Masculine and Feminine Cultures

A popular classification of cultures is in terms of their masculinity and femininity (Hofstede, 1997, 1998). In a highly "masculine" culture men are viewed as assertive, oriented to material success, and strong; women on the other hand are viewed as modest, focused on the quality of life, and tender. In a highly "feminine" culture, both men and women are encouraged to be modest, oriented to maintaining the quality of life, and tender. The ten countries with the highest masculinity score (beginning with the highest) are Japan, Austria, Venezuela, Italy, Switzerland, Mexico, Ireland, Jamaica, Great Britain, and Germany. The ten countries with the highest femininity score (beginning with the highest) are Sweden, Norway, Netherlands, Denmark, Costa Rica, Yugoslavia, Finland, Chile, Portugal, and Thailand. Out of 53 countries ranked, the United States ranks 15th most masculine (Hofstede, 1997).

Masculine cultures emphasize success and socialize their people to be assertive, ambitious, and competitive. Members of masculine cultures are thus more likely to confront conflicts directly and to competitively fight out any differences; they're more likely to emphasize win–lose conflict strategies. **Feminine cultures** emphasize the quality of life and socialize their people to be modest and to emphasize close interpersonal relationships. Members of feminine cultures are thus more likely to emphasize compromise and negotiation in resolving conflicts; they're more likely to seek win–win solutions.

Organizations can also be viewed in terms of masculinity or femininity. Masculine organizations emphasize competitiveness and aggressiveness. They focus on the bottom line and reward their workers on the basis of their contribution to the organization. Feminine organizations are less competitive and less aggressive. They're more likely to emphasize worker satisfaction and reward their workers on the basis of need; those who have large families, for example, may get better raises than the single people, even if the singles have contributed more to the organization.

Individual and Collective Orientation

Cultures differ in the extent to which they promote individual values (for example, power, achievement, hedonism, and stimulation) versus collectivist values (for example, benevolence, tradition, and conformity). The countries with the highest individualist orientation (beginning with the highest) are the United States, Australia, Great

WEB EXPLORATION
To learn more about individual and collectivist orientation, go to www.ablongman.com/devito.

Britain, Canada, Netherlands, New Zealand, Italy, Belgium, Denmark, Sweden, France, and Ireland. Countries with the highest collectivist orientation (beginning with the highest) are Guatemala, Ecuador, Panama, Venezuela, Colombia, Indonesia, Pakistan, Costa Rica, Peru, Taiwan, and South Korea (Hofstede, 1983, 1997; Hatfield & Rapson, 1996; Kapoor, Wolfe, & Blue, 1995). With a few notable exceptions, the individualist countries are wealthy and the collectivist countries are poor. For example, Japan and Hong Kong—which score in the middle—are wealthier than many of the most individualist countries. The following self-test will help you examine your own orientation toward individualism or collectivism.

TEST YOURSELF *Are You an Individualist or a Collectivist?*

Respond to each of the following statements in terms of how true they are of your behavior and thinking: 1 = almost always true, 2 = more often true than false, 3 = true about half the time and false about half the time, 4 = more often false than true, and 5 = almost always false.

______ 1. My own goals, rather than the goals of my group (for example, my extended family, my organization), are more important.

______ 2. I feel responsible for myself and to my own conscience rather than for the entire group and to the group's values and rules.

______ 3. Success to me depends on my contribution to the group effort and the group's success rather than to my own individual success or to surpassing others.

______ 4. I make a clear distinction between who is the leader and who are the followers and similarly make a clear distinction between members of my own cultural group and outsiders.

______ 5. In business transactions personal relationships are extremely important, so I would spend considerable time getting to know people with whom I do business.

______ 6. In my communications I prefer a direct and explicit communication style; I believe in "telling it like it is," even if it hurts.

How did you do? To compute your individualist–collectivist score, follow these steps:

1. Reverse the scores for items 3 and 5 (if your response was 1 reverse it to a 5, if your response was 2 reverse it to a 4, if your response was 3 keep it as 3, if your response was 4 reverse it to a 2, if your response was 5 reverse it to a 1).
2. Add your scores for all 6 items, being sure to use the reverse scores for items 3 and 5 in your calculations. Your score should be between 6 (indicating a highly individualist orientation) and 30 (indicating a highly collectivist orientation).
3. Position your score on the following scale:

6 ______________________________ 15 ______________________________ 30

highly individualist — about equally individualist and collectivist — highly collectivist

What will you do? Does this scale and score accurately measure the way in which you see yourself on this dimension? Is this orientation going to help you achieve your personal and professional goals? Might it hinder you?

One of the major differences between these two orientations is in the extent to which an individual's goals or the group's goals are given precedence. Individual and collective tendencies are, of course, not mutually exclusive; this is not an all-or-none orientation but rather one of emphasis. You probably have both tendencies. Thus, you may, for example, compete with other members of your basketball team for most baskets or most valuable player award (and thus emphasize individual goals). At the same time, however, you will—in a game—act in a way that will benefit the entire team (and thus emphasize group goals). In actual practice both individual and collective tendencies will help you and your team each achieve your goals. Yet most people and most cultures have a dominant orientation; they're more individually oriented (they see themselves as independent) or more collectively oriented (they see themselves as interdependent) in most situations, most of the time (cf., Singelis, 1994).

In some instances, however, these tendencies may come into conflict. For example, do you shoot for the basket and try to raise your own individual score or do you pass the ball to another player who is better positioned to score and thus benefit the team as a whole? You make this distinction in popular talk when you call someone a team player (collectivist orientation) or an individual player (individualist orientation).

In an **individualist culture** members are responsible for themselves and perhaps their immediate family. In a **collectivist culture** members are responsible for the entire group.

In an individualist culture success is measured by the extent to which you surpass other members of your group; you would take pride in standing out from the crowd.

View point In 1995, the Emma Lazarus poem inscribed on the Statute of Liberty was changed. The original last five lines of the poem, "The New Colossus," are as follows [the words in brackets were deleted]:

> Give me your tired, your poor,
> Your huddled masses yearning to breathe free,
> [the wretched refuse of your teeming shore]
> Send these, the homeless, tempest-tost to me
> I lift my lamp beside the golden door.

The late Harvard zoologist Stephen Jay Gould, commenting on this change, notes that it no longer represents what Lazarus wrote (Gould, 1995). "The language police triumph," Gould laments, "and integrity bleeds." On the other hand, it can be argued that calling immigrants "wretched refuse" is insulting and that if Lazarus were writing today, she wouldn't have used that phrase. Would you have supported deleting this line?

Your heroes—in the media, for example—are likely to be those who are unique and who stand apart. In a collectivist culture success is measured by your contribution to the achievements of the group as a whole; you would take pride in your similarity to other members of your group. Your heroes, in contrast, are more likely to be team players who do not stand out from the rest of the group's members. Not surprisingly, advertisements in individualist cultures emphasize individual preferences and benefits, independence, and personal success; advertisements in collectivist cultures emphasize group benefits, family integrity, and group harmony (Han & Shavitt, 1994).

In an individualist culture you're responsible to your own conscience, and responsibility is largely an individual matter; in a collectivistic culture you're responsible to the rules of the social group, and responsibility for an accomplishment or a failure is shared by all members. Competition is fostered in individualist cultures while cooperation is promoted in collectivist cultures.

In an individualist culture you might compete for leadership in a small group setting, and there would likely be a very clear distinction between leaders and members. In a collectivist culture leadership would be shared and rotated; there is likely to be little distinction between leader and members. These orientations will also influence the kinds of communication members consider appropriate in an organizational context. For example, individualist members will favor clarity and directness while collectivists will favor "face-saving" and the avoidance of hurting others or arousing negative evaluations (Kim & Sharkey, 1995).

Distinctions between in-group members and out-group members are extremely important in collectivist cultures. In individualist cultures, where the person's individuality is prized, the distinction is likely to be less important.

High- and Low-Context Cultures

Cultures also differ in the extent to which information is made explicit or is assumed to be in the context or in the persons communicating. A **high-context culture** is one in which much of the information in communication is in the context or in the person—for example, information that was shared through previous communications, through assumptions about each other, and through shared experiences. The information is thus known by all participants but isn't explicitly stated in the verbal messages. A **low-context culture** is one in which most of the information is explicitly stated in the verbal message. In formal transactions it would be stated in written (or contract) form.

To further appreciate the distinction between high and low context, consider giving directions ("Where's the voter registration center?") to someone who knows the neighborhood and to a newcomer to your city. With someone who knows the neighborhood (a high-context situation), you can assume that she or he knows the local landmarks. So you can give directions such as "next to the laundromat on Main Street" or "the corner of Albany and Elm." With the newcomer (a low-context situation), you can't assume that she or he shares any information with you. So you would have to use only those directions that a stranger would understand, for example, "make a left at the next stop sign" or "go two blocks and then turn right."

High-context cultures are also collectivist cultures (Gudykunst, Ting-Toomey, & Chua, 1988; Gudykunst & Kim, 1992). These cultures (Japanese, Arabic, Latin American, Thai, Korean, Apache, and Mexican are examples) place great emphasis on personal relationships and oral agreements (Victor, 1992). Low-context cultures are also individualist cultures. These cultures (German, Swedish, Norwegian, and American are examples) place less emphasis on personal relationships and more emphasis on verbalized, explicit explanation, and on written contracts in business transactions. The

Table 2.1 **Differences in Individual (Low-Context) and Collective (High-Context) Cultures**

In every culture there will be variations in each of these characteristics. View these, therefore, as general tendencies rather than absolutes. Further, increased mobility, changing immigration patterns, and exposure to media from different parts of the world will gradually decrease the differences between these two orientations. This table is based on the work of Hall (1983) and Hall & Hall (1987) and the interpretations by Gudykunst (1991) and Victor (1992).

Individual (Low-Context) Cultures	*Collective (High-Context) Cultures*
Your own goals are most important	The group's goals are most important
You're responsible for yourself and to your own conscience	You're responsible for the entire group and to the group's values and rules
Success depends on your surpassing others	Success depends on your contribution to the group
Competition is emphasized	Cooperation is emphasized
Clear distinction is made between leaders and members	Little distinction is made between leaders and members; leadership would normally be shared
In-group versus out-group distinctions are of little importance	In-group versus out-group distinctions are of great importance
Information is made explicit; little is left unsaid	Information is often left implicit and much goes unsaid
Personal relationships are less important; hence, little time is spent getting to know each other in meetings and conferences	Personal relationships are extremely important; hence, much time is spent getting to know each other in meetings and conferences
Directness is valued; face-saving is seldom thought of	Indirectness is valued and face-saving is a major consideration

characteristics of individual–collective and high- and low-context cultures discussed here are summarized in Table 2.1.

Members of high-context cultures spend lots of time getting to know each other interpersonally and socially before any important transactions take place. Because of this prior personal knowledge, a great deal of information is shared by the members and therefore does not have to be explicitly stated. Members of low-context cultures spend much less time getting to know each other and hence don't have that shared knowledge. As a result everything has to be stated explicitly.

This difference between high- and low-context orientation is partly responsible for the differences observed in Japanese and American business groups (alluded to in Chapter 1). The Japanese spend lots of time getting to know each other before conducting actual business, whereas Americans get down to business very quickly. The Japanese (and other high-context cultures) want to get to know each other because important information isn't made explicit. They have to know you so they can read your nonverbals, for example (Sanders, Wiseman, & Matz, 1991). Americans can get right down to business because all important information will be stated explicitly.

To high-context cultural members, what is omitted or assumed is a vital part of the communication transaction. Silence, for example, is highly valued (Basso, 1972). To low-context cultural members, what is omitted creates ambiguity, but this ambiguity is simply something that will be eliminated by explicit and direct communication. To high-context cultural members, ambiguity is something to be avoided; it's a sign that the interpersonal and social interactions have not proved sufficient to establish a shared base of information (Gudykunst, 1983).

When this simple difference isn't understood, intercultural misunderstandings can easily result. For example, the directness characteristic of the low-context culture may seem insulting, insensitive, or unnecessary to the high-context cultural member. Conversely, to the low-context member, the high-context cultural member may appear vague, underhanded, or dishonest in his or her reluctance to be explicit or engage in communication that a low-context member would consider open and direct.

Another frequent source of intercultural misunderstanding that can be traced to the differences in high and low context can be seen in face-saving (Hall & Hall, 1987). High-context cultures place much more emphasis on face-saving. For example, they're more likely to avoid argument for fear of causing others to lose face; on the other hand, low-context members (with their individualistic orientation) will use argument to win a point. Similarly, in high-context cultures criticism should only take place in private. Low-context cultures may not make this public–private distinction. Low-context managers who criticize high-context workers in public will find that their criticism causes interpersonal problems and does little to resolve the original difficulty (Victor, 1992).

Members of high-context cultures are reluctant to say no for fear of offending and causing the person to lose face. Thus, it's necessary to be able to read when the Japanese executive's "yes" means yes and when it means no. The difference isn't in the words used but in the way in which they're used.

Time Orientations

TRY IT!
Apply your insights on time orientations; go to www.ablongman.com/devito.

Cultures differ greatly in the way they view time. One important distinction is between displaced and diffused time orientations (Hall, 1959). In a **displaced time orientation,** time is viewed exactly. Persons with this orientation will be exactly on time. In a **diffused time orientation,** time is seen as approximate rather than exact. People with this orientation are usually late for appointments because they understand, for example, a scheduled time of 8:00 P.M. as meaning anywhere from 7:45 to 8:15 or 8:30.

Even the accuracy of clocks varies in different cultures and probably reflects each culture's time orientation. In one study, clocks in Japan were found to be the most accurate, while clocks in Indonesia were least accurate. Clocks in England, Italy, Taiwan, and the United States fell between these two extremes in accuracy. Not surprisingly, when the speed of pedestrians in these countries was measured, the Japanese were found to walk the fastest and the Indonesians the slowest. Such differences reflect the different ways in which cultures treat time and their general attitude toward the importance of time in everyday life (LeVine & Bartlett, 1984).

Another important distinction is that between monochronic and polychronic time orientations (Hall, 1959, 1976; Hall & Hall, 1987). Consider your own time behavior by asking yourself the following questions.

Do you

1. (a) Do one thing at a time or (b) do several things at one time?
2. (a) Treat time schedules and plans very seriously and only break them for the most serious of reasons or (b) treat time schedules and plans as useful but not sacred and break them for any of a variety of reasons?

3. (a) Consider your job the most important part of your life, ahead of even family or (b) consider the family and interpersonal relationships more important than the job?
4. (a) Consider privacy extremely important, seldom borrow or lend to others, and work independently or (b) involve yourself actively with others and work in the presence of and with lots of people at the same time?

If you selected the (a) responses, you're more likely a monochronic person. If you selected the (b) responses, you're more likely a polychronic person. Monochronic people or cultures (the United States, Germany, Scandinavia, and Switzerland are good examples) schedule one thing at a time. Time is compartmentalized; there is a time for everything, and everything has its own time. Polychronic people or cultures (Latin Americans, Mediterranean people, and Arabs are good examples), on the other hand, schedule a number of things at the same time. Eating, conducting business with several different people, and taking care of family matters may all be conducted at the same time. No culture is entirely monochronic or polychronic; rather, these are general tendencies that are found across a large part of the culture. Some cultures combine both time orientations; Japanese culture and parts of American culture are examples where both orientations are found.

INTERCULTURAL COMMUNICATION

Understanding the role of culture in communication is an essential foundation for understanding intercultural communication as it occurs in an interpersonal context. As a preface to this discussion you may want to take the accompanying self-test to explore your own openness to intercultural communication.

TEST YOURSELF *How Open Are You Interculturally?*

Select a specific culture (national, racial, or religious) different from your own, and substitute this culture for the phrase "interculturally different" in each question below. Indicate how open you would be to communicating in each of these situations, using the following scale: 5 = very open and willing, 4 = open and willing, 3 = neutral, 2 = closed and unwilling, and 1 = very closed and unwilling.

_______ 1. Talk with an interculturally different person while alone waiting for a bus.

_______ 2. Talk with an interculturally different person in the presence of those who are interculturally similar to you.

_______ 3. Have a close friendship with an interculturally different person.

_______ 4. Have a long-term romantic relationship with an interculturally different person.

_______ 5. Participate in a problem-solving group that is composed predominantly of interculturally different people.

_______ 6. Openly and fairly observe an information-sharing group consisting predominantly of interculturally different people.

_______ 7. Lead a group of interculturally different people through a problem-solving or information-sharing situation.

_______ 8. Participate in a consciousness-raising group that is composed of one half interculturally different people.

_______ 9. Listen openly and fairly to a conversation by an interculturally different person.

_______ 10. Ascribe a level of credibility for an interculturally different person identical to that ascribed to an interculturally similar person—all other things being equal.

How did you do? To calculate your total score, simply add your scores for all 10 questions. High scores (say, above 35) indicate considerable openness; low scores (say, below 20) indicate a lack of openness. Not surprisingly, research finds that people who are more willing to communicate interculturally have more friends from foreign countries than do those with less willingness (Kassing, 1997).

What will you do? Use these numbers for purposes of thinking critically about your intercultural openness rather than to indicate any absolute level of openness or closedness. For example, did you select the "interculturally different" group on the basis of how positively or negatively you felt about them? With what group would you be most open to interacting? Least open? Are there specific types of interpersonal communication you'd be less likely to be open to than others? For example, did you indicate a greater level of openness in Question 1 than Question 10? Why?

The Nature of Intercultural Communication

Intercultural communication refers to communication between persons who have different cultural beliefs, values, or ways of behaving. The model in Figure 2.1 illustrates this concept. The larger circles represent the culture of the individual communicator. The inner circles identify the communicators (the sources/receivers). In this model each communicator is a member of a different culture. In some instances the cultural differences are relatively slight—say, between persons from Toronto and New York. In other instances the cultural differences are great—say, between persons from Borneo and Germany, or between persons from rural Nigeria and industrialized England.

All messages originate from a specific and unique cultural context, and that context influences their content and form. You communicate as you do largely as a result of your culture. Culture (along with the processes of enculturation and acculturation) influences every aspect of your communication experience.

Principles for Improving Intercultural Communication

Murphy's Law ("Anything that can go wrong will go wrong") is especially applicable to intercultural communication. Intercultural communication is, of course, subject to all

Figure 2.1

A Model of Intercultural Communication

This model of intercultural communication illustrates that culture is a part of every communication act. More specifically, it illustrates that the messages you send and the messages you receive will be influenced by your cultural beliefs, values, and attitudes.

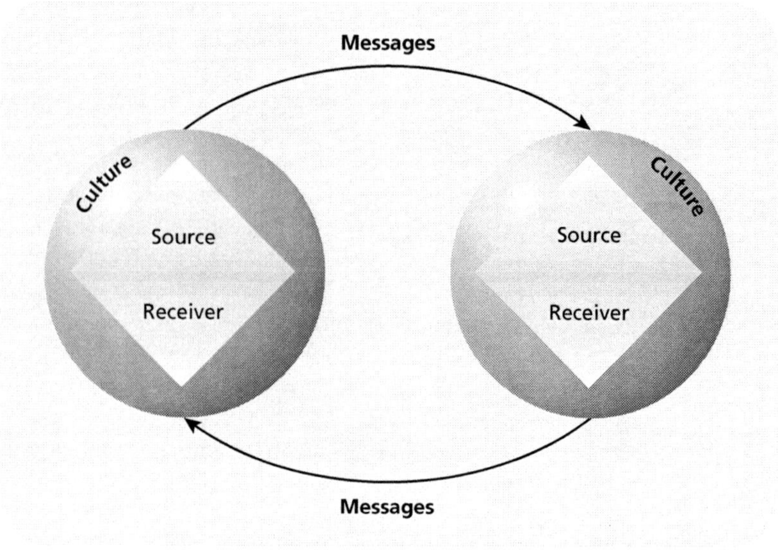

Increasing Interpersonal Effectiveness

Cultural Sensitivity

Cultural sensitivity is an attitude and way of behaving in which you're aware of and acknowledge cultural differences; it's crucial for global issues such as world peace and economic growth as well as for effective interpersonal communication and for general success (Franklin & Mizell, 1995). Without cultural sensitivity there can be no effective interpersonal communication between people who differ in gender, race, nationality, or affective orientation. So, be mindful of the cultural differences between yourself and the other person. Remember that the techniques of interpersonal communication that work well with European Americans may not work well with Asian Americans; what proves effective in Japan may not in Mexico. The close physical distance that is normal in Arab cultures may prove too familiar or too intrusive in much of the United States and Northern Europe. The empathy that most Americans welcome may be discomforting for the average Korean (Yun, 1976).

Increasing Cultural Sensitivity In this chapter we identified several guidelines for more effective intercultural communication; these suggestions are the best advice to follow in achieving cultural sensitivity:

- Prepare yourself. Read about and listen carefully for culturally influenced behaviors.
- Recognize and face fears of acting inappropriately toward members of different cultures.
- Recognize differences between yourself and people from other cultures.
- Recognize that there are often enormous differences within cultural groups.
- Recognize differences in meaning; words rarely mean the same thing to members of different cultures.
- Become conscious of the cultural rules and customs of others.

the same barriers and problems as are the other forms of communication discussed throughout this text. Drawing on a number of intercultural researchers, we cover here the principles designed to counteract the barriers that are unique to intercultural communication (Barna, 1991; Ruben, 1985; Spitzberg, 1991).

Prepare Yourself There's no better preparation for intercultural communication than learning about the other culture. Fortunately, there are numerous sources to draw on. View a documentary or movie that presents a realistic view of the culture. Read material about the culture by persons from that culture as well as by "outsiders." Scan magazines and websites from that culture. Talk with members of that culture. Chat on international IRC channels. Read materials addressed to people who need to communicate with those from other cultures. For example, recent titles include: *Do's and Taboos of Hosting International Visitors* (Axtell, 1990), *Mind Your Manners: Managing Business Cultures in Europe* (Mole, 1998), *Do's and Taboos around the World* (Axtell, 1994), *The Executive Guide to Asia-Pacific Communications* (James, 1995), *How to Negotiate Anything with Anyone Anywhere around the World* (Acuff, 1993), and *Internationally Yours: Writing and Communication Successfully in Today's Global Marketplace* (DeVries, 1994), *International Business Etiquette in Europe: What You Need to Know to Conduct Business Abroad with Charm and Savvy* (Sabath, 1999), and *Global Etiquette Guide to Mexico and Latin America* (Foster, 2002).

Another part of this preparation is to recognize and face your own fears that may stand in the way of effective intercultural communication (Gudykunst, 1994; Stephan & Stephan, 1985). For example, you may fear for your self-esteem. You may become anxious about your ability to control the intercultural situation or you may worry about your own level of discomfort. You may fear saying something that will be considered politically incorrect or culturally insensitive and thereby losing face.

You may fear that you'll be taken advantage of by the member of this other culture. Depending on your own stereotypes you may fear being lied to, financially duped, or made fun of. You may fear that members of this other group will react to you negatively. You may fear, for example, that they will not like you or may disapprove of your attitudes or beliefs or perhaps even reject you as a person. Conversely, you may fear negative reactions from members of your own group. They might, for example, disapprove of your socializing with the culturally different.

Some fears, of course, are reasonable. In many cases, however, they're groundless. Either way, they need to be assessed logically and their consequences weighed carefully. Then you'll be able to make informed choices about your communications.

Reduce Uncertainty All communication interactions involve uncertainty and ambiguity. Not surprisingly, this uncertainty and ambiguity is greater when there are large cultural differences (Berger & Bradac, 1982; Gudykunst, 1989, 1993). Because of this greater uncertainty in intercultural communication, more time and effort are required to reduce it and thus to communicate meaningfully. Reducing your uncertainty about another person will not only make your communication more effective, but will also increase your liking for the person (Douglas, 1994). In situations of great uncertainty the techniques of effective communication (for example, active listening, perception checking, being specific, and seeking feedback) take on special importance.

View point In 1995, the United States Department of Education issued recommendations covering the types of religious communications public schools may permit (*New York Times,* August 26, 1995, pp. 1, 8). Among the permitted activities are: student prayer, student-initiated discussions of religion, saying grace, proselytizing that would not be considered harassment, and the wearing of religious symbols and clothing. Among the forbidden activities: prayer endorsed by teachers or administrators, invitations to prayer that could constitute harassment, teaching of a particular religion (rather than about religion), and encouraging either religious or antireligious activity. How do you feel about these recommendations and, more generally, about the appropriate role, if any, of religion in public schools?

Active listening (Chapter 5) and perception checking techniques (Chapter 4), for example, help you to verify the accuracy of your perceptions and allow you to revise and amend any incorrect perceptions. Being specific reduces ambiguity and the chances of misunderstandings. Misunderstanding is a lot more likely when talking about "neglect" (a highly abstract concept) than when talking about "forgetting your last birthday" (a specific event).

Seeking feedback helps you to correct any possible misconceptions almost immediately. Seek feedback on whether you're making yourself clear ("Does that make sense?" "Do you see where to put the widget?"). Similarly, seek feedback to make sure you understand what the other person is saying ("Do you mean that you'll never speak with them again? Do you mean that literally?").

Although you're always in danger of misperceiving and misevaluating another person, you're in special danger in intercultural situations. Therefore, try to resist your natural tendency to judge others quickly and permanently. A judgment made early is likely to be based on too little information. Because of this, flexibility and a willingness to revise opinions are essential intercultural skills.

Recognize Differences To communicate interculturally you need to recognize the differences between yourself and people from other cultures, the differences within the other cultural group, and the numerous differences in meaning.

Differences between Yourself and the Culturally Different A common barrier to intercultural communication occurs when you assume that similarities exist and that differences do not. This is especially true of values, attitudes, and beliefs. You might easily accept different hairstyles, clothing, and foods. In basic values and beliefs, however, you may assume that deep down everyone is really alike. They aren't. When you assume similarities and ignore differences, you'll fail to notice important distinctions and when communicating will convey to others that your ways are the right ways and that their ways are not important to you. Consider this example. An American invites a Filipino coworker to dinner. The Filipino politely refuses. The American is hurt and feels that the Filipino does not want to be friendly. The Filipino is hurt and concludes that the invitation was not extended sincerely. Here, it seems, both the American and the Filipino assume that their customs for inviting people to dinner are the same when, in fact, they aren't. A Filipino expects to be invited several times before accepting a dinner invitation. When an invitation is given only once it's viewed as insincere.

Here's another example. An American college student hears the news that her favorite uncle has died. She bites her lip, pulls herself up, and politely excuses herself from the group of foreign students with whom she is having dinner. The Russian thinks: "How unfriendly." The Italian thinks: "How insincere." The Brazilian thinks: "How unconcerned." To many Americans, it's a sign of bravery to endure pain (physical or emotional) in silence and without any outward show of emotion. To members of other groups, such silence is often interpreted negatively to mean that the individual does not consider them friends who can share such sorrow. In other cultures, people are expected to reveal to friends how they feel.

Differences within the Culturally Different Group Within every cultural group there are vast and important differences. As all Americans are not alike, neither are all Indonesians, Greeks, Mexicans, and so on. When you ignore these differences, when you assume that all persons covered by the same label (in this case a national or racial label) are the same, you're guilty of stereotyping. A good example of this is seen in the use of the term "African American." The term stresses the unity of Africa and those who are of African descent and is analogous to "Asian American" or "European American." At the same time, it ignores the great diversity within the African continent when, for example, it's used as analogous to "German American" or "Japanese American." A more analogous comparison would be "Nigerian American" or "Ethiopian American." Within each culture there are smaller cultures that differ greatly from each other and from the larger culture.

Differences in Meaning Meaning exists not in words but in people (a principle returned to in Chapter 6). Consider, for example, the differences in meaning for words such as *woman* to an American and a Muslim, *religion* to a born-again Christian and an atheist, and *lunch* to a Chinese rice farmer and a Madison Avenue advertising executive. Even though the same word is used, its meanings will vary greatly depending on the listeners' cultural definitions.

A left-handed American who eats with the left hand may be seen by a Muslim as obscene. To the Muslim, the left hand isn't used for eating or for shaking hands but to clean oneself after excretory functions. So, using the left hand to eat or to shake hands is considered insulting and obscene.

Adjust Your Communication Intercultural communication (in fact, all interpersonal communication) takes place only to the extent that you and the person you're trying to communicate with share the same system of symbols. Your communication will be hindered to the extent that your language and nonverbal systems differ. This **adjustment** principle takes on particular relevance when you realize that no two persons share identical symbol systems. Parents and children, for example, not only have different vocabularies but also, even more important, have different meanings for some of the terms they have in common. People in close relationships—either as intimate friends or as romantic partners—realize that learning the other person's signals takes a long time and, often, great patience. If you want to understand what another person means—by smiling, by saying "I love you," by arguing about trivial matters, by self-deprecating comments—you have to learn their system of signals.

This principle is especially important in intercultural communication largely because people from different cultures use different signals and sometimes the same signals to signify quite different things. Focused eye contact means honesty and openness in much of the United States. But that same behavior may signify arrogance or disrespect in Japan and in many Hispanic cultures if it occurs between a youngster and someone significantly older.

Part of the art of intercultural communication is learning the other person's signals, how they're used, and what they mean. Furthermore, you have to share your own system of signals with others so that they can better understand you. Although some people may know what you mean by your silence or by your avoidance of eye contact, others may not. You cannot expect others to decode your behaviors accurately without help.

An interesting theory largely revolving around adjustment is communication accommodation theory. This theory holds that speakers will adjust to or accommodate the speaking style of their listeners to gain, for example, social approval and greater communication efficiency (Giles, Mulac, Bradac, & Johnson, 1987). For example, when two people have a similar speech rate, they're more attracted to each other than to those with dissimilar rates (Buller, LePoire, Aune, & Eloy, 1992). Also, the speaker who uses

ASK the Researcher

Accommodating for Effectiveness

I find your theory of communication accommodation really interesting, but I'm a really practical type of person and I'm taking this course to make myself a more effective communicator. So what I really want to know is how can I use this theory to make myself more effective socially and professionally, especially when talking with people who are culturally different from me?

Being seen to put effort after accommodating culturally dissimilar others is usually appreciated by them, leading to liking, respect, etc.,—but the trick is to get it just "right." Don't underaccommodate and be seen as uncaring or culturally insensitive, yet don't overdo it either (e.g., overaccommodating with an exaggerated accent to be "ethnically cool" or affiliative)—as that might be patronizing, invasive, or even ridiculing. Also, avoid accommodating to some stereotype of what you believe someone *should* sound like (given inferences about their ethnicity) but, rather, attune to how they actually do communicate. Finally, be wary of misattributing (and then getting upset at) their apparent divergence(s) from you as, necessarily, intended disrespect. Their nonaligning to your "language" and/or nonverbals may be more a statement of how they value and sustain their own distinctive heritage than any lack of interest in you as a person. Managing the converging–diverging balancing act is a critical element of communicative competence, be it between ethnicities, generations, genders, sexual orientations or whatever other cultural groupings.

For further information see Giles, H. & Noels, K. *Communication accommodation in intercultural encounters.* In J. Martin, T. Nakayama, & L. Flores (eds.), (2001). *Readings in cultural contexts* (2nd ed.) Mountain View: Mayfield, pp. 139–149.

Howard Giles (Ph.D., D.Sc., University of Bristol) is a professor of communication at the University of California, Santa Barbara, and teaches courses in intercultural, intergroup, and intergenerational communication. Giles is also a reserve sergeant with the Santa Barbara Police Department. HowieGiles@aol.com (Reprinted by permission of Dr. Howard Giles.)

language intensity similar to that of listeners is judged to have greater credibility than the speaker who uses intensity different from that of listeners (Aune & Kikuchi, 1993). Still another study found that roommates who were similar in communication competence and low in verbal aggressiveness were highest in roommate liking and satisfaction (Martin & Anderson, 1995).

As you adjust your communications, recognize that each culture has its own rules and customs for communicating (Barna, 1991; Ruben, 1985; Spitzberg, 1991). These rules identify what is appropriate and what is inappropriate. Thus, for example, in American culture you would call a person you wish to date three or four days in advance. In certain Asian cultures, you might call the person's parents weeks or even months in advance. In American culture you say, as a general friendly gesture and not as a specific invitation, "come over and pay us a visit." To members of other cultures, this comment is sufficient for the listeners to actually visit at their convenience. In some cultures, people show respect by avoiding direct eye contact with the person to whom they're speaking. In other cultures, this same eye avoidance would signal disinterest. If a young American girl is talking with an older Indonesian man, for example, she's expected to avoid direct eye contact. To an Indonesian, direct eye contact in this situation would be considered disrespectful. In some southern European cultures men walk arm in arm. In American culture this is considered inappropriate.

A good example of a series of rules for an extremely large and important culture appears in Table 2.2 on page 58, "Interpersonal Communication Tips between People with and without Disabilities."

Table 2.2 Interpersonal Communication Tips
Between people with and without disabilities

Other "Tips" tables focus on visual impairment (Chapter 1), hearing loss (Chapter 5), and speech and language disorders (Chapter 9); here we look at communication between those with general disabilities, for example, people in wheelchairs or with, say, cerebral palsy and those who have no such disability. The suggestions offered here are considered appropriate in the United States but not necessarily in other cultures. For example, although most people in the United States accept the phrase "person with mental retardation," it's considered offensive to many in the United Kingdom (Fernald, 1995).

If you're the one without such a disability:

1. Avoid negative terms and terms that define the person as disabled such as "the disabled" or "the handicapped." Instead say "person with a disability," always putting the person and not the disability first. Avoid terms that describe the person with a disability as abnormal; for example when you define the person without a disability as normal, you in effect say that the person with a disability isn't normal. Similarly, say "seizure" instead of "fit," "person with cerebral palsy," instead of "cerebral palsy victim," "wheelchair user" instead of "wheelchair bound."
2. Treat assistive devices such as wheelchairs, canes, walkers, or crutches as the personal property of the user; be careful not to move these out of your way since they're for the convenience of the person with the disability. Avoid leaning on a person's wheelchair, for example; it's similar to leaning on a person.
3. If you shake hands with others in a group, also shake hands with the person with the disability. Don't avoid shaking hands because the individual's hand is paralyzed, say.
4. Avoid talking about the person with a disability in the third person. For example, avoid saying, "Doesn't he get around beautifully with those new crutches." Always direct your comments directly to the individual.
5. Don't assume that people who have a disability (for example, if their speech is slurred as it may be with people who have cerebral palsy or cleft palate) are intellectually impaired; they definitely are not. So be especially careful not to talk down to such people, as research shows many people do (Unger, 2001). Similarly, use the same level of formality with people who have disabilities as you do with people who do not have such disabilities. Often, for example, people will be more informal and will, say, use a person's first name or even a diminutive ("Bobby" or "Katie") when addressing a person with disabilities when they will use a title plus last name to others.
6. If you're not sure how to act—for example, whether or not to offer walking assistance—ask: "Would you like me to help you into the dining room?" And, more important, accept the person's response. If he or she says "no," then that means no; don't insist.
7. If the person is in a wheelchair, it might be helpful for you to sit down or kneel down to get on the same eye level.

If you're the one with a disability:

1. Let the other person know if he or she can do anything to assist you in communicating. For example, if you want someone to speak in a louder voice, ask. If you want to relax and have someone push your wheelchair, say so.
2. Be patient and understanding with those who may not know how to act or what to say. Put them at ease as best you can.
3. If you detect discomfort in the other person, you might talk a bit about your disability to show that you're not uncomfortable and that you understand that others may not know how you feel. But, of course, you are under no obligation to educate the public so don't feel this is something you should or have to do. If it makes you more comfortable, then do it; otherwise, don't.

These suggestions are based on a number of sources, for example, http://www.empowermentzone.com/etiquet.txt (the website for the National Center for Access Unlimited), http://www.dol.gov/dol/odep/public/media/reports/fact/comucate.htm, http://www.dissvcs.uga.edu/com-peodis.html, and http://www.ucpa.org/ucp_generaldoc.cfm (all accessed 4/5/02).

Recognize Culture Shock **Culture shock** refers to the psychological reaction you experience when you're in a culture very different from your own (Furnham & Bochner, 1986). Culture shock is normal; most people experience it when entering a new and different culture. Nevertheless, it can be unpleasant and frustrating. Part of this results from feelings of alienation, conspicuousness, and difference from everyone else. When you lack knowledge of the rules and customs of the new society, you cannot communicate effectively. You're apt to blunder frequently and seriously. In your culture shock you may not know basic things:

- how to ask someone for a favor or pay someone a compliment
- how to extend or accept an invitation for dinner
- how early or how late to arrive for an appointment
- how long you should stay when visiting someone
- how to distinguish seriousness from playfulness and politeness from indifference
- how to dress for an informal, formal, or business function
- how to order a meal in a restaurant or how to summon a waiter

TRY IT!
Apply your understanding of culture shock; go to www.ablongman.com/devito.

Anthropologist Kalervo Oberg (1960), who first used the term culture shock, notes that it occurs in stages. These stages are useful for examining many encounters with the new and the different. Going away to college, moving in together, or joining the military, for example, can also result in culture shock. In explaining culture shock, we use the example of moving away from home into your own apartment to illustrate its four stages.

Stage One: The Honeymoon At first you experience fascination, even enchantment, with the new culture and its people. You finally have your own apartment. You're your own boss. Finally, on your own! When in groups of people who are culturally different, this stage is characterized by cordiality and friendship in these early and superficial relationships. Many tourists remain at this stage because their stay in foreign countries is so brief.

Stage Two: The Crisis Here, the differences between your own culture and the new one create problems. No longer do you find dinner ready for you unless you do it yourself. Your clothes are not washed or ironed unless you do them yourself. Feelings of frustration and inadequacy come to the fore. This is the stage at which you experience the actual shock of the new culture. One study of foreign students coming from over 100 different countries and studying in 11 different countries found that 25 percent of the students experienced depression (Klineberg & Hull, 1979).

Stage Three: The Recovery During this period you gain the skills necessary to function effectively. You learn how to shop, cook, and plan a meal. You find a local laundry and figure you'll learn how to iron later. You learn the language and ways of the new culture. Your feelings of inadequacy subside.

Stage Four: The Adjustment At this final stage, you adjust to and come to enjoy the new culture and the new experiences. You may still experience periodic difficulties and strains, but on a whole, the experience is pleasant. Actually, you're now a pretty decent cook. You're even coming to enjoy it. You're making a good salary so why learn to iron?

People may also experience culture shock when they return to their original culture after living in a foreign culture, a kind of reverse culture shock (Jandt, 1999). Consider, for example, the Peace Corps volunteers who work in a rural and economically deprived area. Upon returning to Las Vegas or Beverly Hills, they too may experience culture shock. A sailor who serves long periods aboard ship and then returns to an isolated farming community might also experience culture shock. In these cases, however, the recovery period is shorter and the sense of inadequacy and frustration is less.

REVIEWING Key Terms and Concepts in Culture in Interpersonal Communication

This unit explored the nature of culture and identified some key concepts and principles that explain the role of culture in interpersonal communication.

Nature of Culture and Interpersonal Communication

What is culture and how is it transmitted?

- **Culture:** The relatively specialized lifestyle of a group of people (values, beliefs, artifacts, ways of behaving) that are passed from one generation to the next by means of communication (not genes).
- **Enculturation:** The process through which you learn the culture into which you're born.
- **Acculturation:** The process by which you learn the rules and norms of a culture that is different from your native culture and that modifies your original or native culture.

How Cultures Differ

How do cultures differ from each other? How do these differences affect interpersonal communication?

- In high-power-distance cultures, power is concentrated in the hands of a few and there is a great difference between those with and those without power. In low-power-distance cultures, the power is more equally shared throughout the citizenry.
- In highly masculine cultures, men are viewed as strong, assertive, and focused on being successful, whereas women are viewed as modest, tender, and focused on the quality of life. In highly feminine cultures, men and women are viewed more similarly.
- A collectivist culture emphasizes the group and subordinates the individual's goals to those of the group. An individualist culture emphasizes the individual and subordinates the group's goals to the individual's.
- In high-context cultures, much of the information is in the context; in low-context cultures, information is explicitly stated in the verbal message.
- Different cultures view time very differently.
    - Displaced and diffused time orientations identify how accurately and specifically time is viewed and defined.
    - Monochronic people do one thing at a time; polychronic people do several things at the same time.

Intercultural Communication

What is intercultural communication and what are its central principles?

- Intercultural communication refers to communication between people who have different cultures, beliefs, values, and ways of behaving.
- Some intercultural communication principles include: prepare yourself, reduce uncertainty, recognize differences (between yourself and others, within the culturally different group, and in meanings), adjust your communication, and recognize culture shock.

APPLYING Key Terms and Concepts in Culture in Interpersonal Communication

1. In this age of multiculturalism, how do you feel about Article II, Section 1 of the United States Constitution? The relevant section reads: "No person except a natural born citizen, or a citizen of the United States, at the time of the adoption of this Constitution, shall be eligible to the office of President."
2. It's been argued that in the United States women are more likely to view themselves as interdependents, having a more collectivist orientation, while men are more likely to view themselves as independents, having a more individualist orientation (Cross & Madson, 1997). Does your experience support this?
3. Visit one of the numerous travel websites (for example, http://www.globalpassage.com/netstop, http://travel.epicurious.com/travel/g_cnt/home.html, http://www.travelchannel.com/, and http://www.lonelyplanet.com/). What can you learn about intercultural communication from such sources?
4. Informal time terms (for example, soon, right away, early, in a while, as soon as possible) seem to create communication problems because they're ambiguous; different people will often give the terms different meanings. How might you go about reducing or eliminating the ambiguity created by these terms?
5. Visit one of the online news organizations (for example, www.pbs.org/, www.npr.org, www.c/net.com, www.reu-tershealth.com, or www.cnnfn.com) for a recent item on culture. Of what value might such information be to someone engaging in intercultural communication?
6. Has anyone ever assumed something about you because you were a member of a particular culture that was not true? Did you find this disturbing?
7. International students commonly experience culture shock. If you're an international student, describe your culture shock experiences. If you're not an international student, describe the culture shock you might experience if you were to study in another culture.
8. Do teachers and students or lawyers and witnesses or doctors and patients accommodate each other's communication style? In what direction is there likely to be greater accommodation? For example, is the teacher or the student more likely to accommodate the other?
9. Are the media and the Internet—because of their dominance by the United States—fostering an Americanization of different cultures? Do you see this as a loss of valuable

diversity? Or do you see it as the result of a democratic process whereby people select the values and customs they wish to adopt? Somewhere in between?

10. In a small group, with the class as a whole, or in a brief paper, discuss how your beliefs, attitudes, and values were influenced by the culture in which you were raised. Were you taught that penalties are incurred for going against these beliefs, attitudes, and values?

EXPERIENCING Key Terms and Concepts in Culture in Interpersonal Communication

Go to www.ablongman.com/devito.

These exercises enable you to explore a wide variety of cultural issues and their relationships to interpersonal communication.

(1) **Random Pairs** sets up specific intercultural dyads and asks you to consider how these dyads might influence communication. (2) **Cultural Beliefs** asks you to examine some of your own cultural beliefs. (3) **From Culture to Gender** explores the relationship of culture to gender beliefs. (4) **Cultural Identities** allows for the exploration of the strengths in the cultures represented by class members and others. (5) **The Sources of Your Cultural Beliefs** explores the origin of your own beliefs about a wide variety of issues. (6) **Confronting Intercultural Obstacles** presents situations that can cause intercultural conflict and asks you how you'd head off the potential conflict or resolve it.

ResearchNavigator.com

RESEARCHING with Research Navigator Key Terms and Concepts in Culture in Interpersonal Communication

Go to http://www.researchnavigator.com.

Reading an article.

Read a popular or scholarly article on the nature of culture, cultural differences, or intercultural communication. On the basis of this article, what can you add to the discussion presented in this chapter?

Investigating key terms.

Investigate one of the key terms discussed in this chapter (for example, culture, power distances, masculine and feminine cultures, individual and collective orientation, high- and low-context cultures, language relativity, uncertainty reduction, culture shock, intercultural communication, cultural imperialism, and cultural sensitivity). What additional insights can you provide?

Finding answers.

Try finding answers to one of the following questions or design a research study to answer it.

- How does culture affect interpersonal communication?
- How do cultures differ in their ways of communicating?
- What are some of the culturally influenced communication differences between men and women?
- Why is intercultural communication often more difficult than communicating with members of your own culture?
- Are persons with greater education more likely to enter intercultural relationships than less educated persons?

"Some people come into our lives and quickly go. Some people move our souls to dance. They awaken us to understanding with the passing whisper of their wisdom. Some people make the sky more beautiful to gaze upon. They stay in our lives for awhile, leave footprints on our hearts."
—Anonymous

CHAPTER 14 Developing Relationships

THIS CHAPTER WILL HELP YOU:

- Understand the stages of relationship development and deterioration.
- Know how dialectical tensions push and pull on relationships.
- Explain what interpersonal conflict is and how to resolve it.
- Determine when a relationship is in trouble and how to use relational repair strategies.
- Improve your interpersonal communication skills and competencies in personal and professional relationships.

CASE STUDY

At some time in your life, you probably moved into a new neighborhood, apartment complex, or dorm where you didn't know a soul. During the first days, however, some people you passed on the sidewalk, in the hallways, or elsewhere began to seem familiar. You most likely didn't know them yet, but at least you recognized them. Eventually, you probably became acquainted with some of these former strangers. Why? It is interesting to think about why some of those individuals became acquaintances while others remained strangers.

You can probably think of a day when you really felt great about yourself and your accomplishments and then had nothing but good experiences the rest of the day. Try to remember how you felt about the people you encountered that morning, afternoon, and evening. You might also think of your worst day, when everything went wrong.

Questions to think about

1. What is the lesson to be learned in the beginning of the case study, as it relates to interacting with others?
2. What is the lesson to be learned in the bottom half of the case study as it relates to our communication with others?
3. In what ways do our emotional states of mind affect our perceptions of others? Their perception of us?
4. Describe in your own words what happens to communication during the various stages of relationship develoment, moving from being an acquaintance to being a close friend.
5. Describe what happens to communication when a relationship is in the stages of coming apart or breaking up.

It is a human tendency to evaluate almost everything and everyone and to form attitudes about the people, objects, and events in our lives. As we encounter other individuals at school, work, or in our neighborhoods, we develop attitudes about each of them. These interpersonal evaluations fall along a dimension ranging from like to dislike and also help to determine the type of relationship that may be formed—for example, friend, close acquaintance, superficial acquaintance, annoying acquaintance, or undesirable.

In Chapter 13, we stated that relationships have the potential to form any time two people make contact with each other, whether face to face or via some other medium such as the phone or the computer. Most contacts are made accidentally, depending on factors like those described in the opening case study; they can also occur via classes you chose to take, seating arrangement in those classes, who happens to be in a chat room when you enter it, or the physical arrangements of a workplace, all of which increase the odds that you will come into repeated contact with people, while at the same time decreasing the odds that such contact will occur with others. As a result, although this might not seem all that surprising, physical proximity and timing are very often how people meet and begin relationships with each other.

The opening case study in Chapter 13 and the one in this chapter illustrate some ways in which relationships are formed. Whether a relationship evolves into any kind of ongoing or lasting one depends on many factors, such as attraction, motivation, and need—all of which were discussed in Chapter 13. Communication, however, is the overriding factor that determines and affects the type and depth of relationships that are formed and how long they last.

Making Connections

Interpersonal Communication Competencies

Three questions we should ask ourselves are (1) "What are the interpersonal communication skills needed to initiate and maintain a conversation with others?" (2) "Do we have those skills?" and (3) "How effective are we at using those skills?"

1. With your classmates as a whole, in small groups, or on your own, create a list of interpersonal communication skills that are needed to initiate a conversation with a person whom you have just met, to maintain the conversation, and to leave a good impression.
2. With your classmates as a whole, in small groups, or on your own, create a list of interpersonal behaviors that irritate or turn you off to others to the point that you don't want to have to interaction with the other person again.
3. With your classmates as a whole, in small groups, or on your own, describe the interpersonal communication skills needed and/or social etiquette required to be effective in the following situations: a job interview, a class discussion, talking to the president of your school, talking to your best friend's parents, talking to your doctor, talking with a person from a foreign country, and others—your choice!

Forming and Dissolving Relationships

How we progress as individuals, survive, develop intimacy, and make sense of our world depends on how we relate to others. The depth and quality of our relationships, as explained in Chapter 13, depend on the kind, amount, and effectiveness of the communication that takes place. This chapter explores why some people are interpersonally attracted to others and the stages of growth and deterioration that most relationships go through, which are best exemplified by Mark Knapp's theory of relationship stages and Steve Duck's theory of dissolution stages. The chapter also discusses interpersonal conflict, conflict management, and how to improve interpersonal communication competency.

Interpersonal Attraction

Most of us develop relationships quite routinely, although the process is easier for some people than it is for others. Every day, we are enormously influenced by first impressions. **Interpersonal attraction** is the desire to interact with someone based on a variety of factors, including physical attractiveness, personality, rewards, proximity, or similarities. Although these are perhaps obvious referents, interpersonal attraction is a very complex phenomenon. Communication scholars James McCroskey and Thomas McCain identified three types of attraction: (1) social attraction ("He would fit into my circle of friends"), (2) physical attraction ("I think she's quite pretty"), and (3) task attraction ("My confidence in her ability to get the job done makes me want to work with her").[1] In other words, interpersonal attraction has a lot to do with evaluating other people. What factors make people socially attractive to you such that you would wish to connect with them to form relationships?

Any given person (including you) is liked by some people, disliked by some, and seen as indifferent by many others. Why? This question is not easily answered, but, to some extent, differences in attraction depend on the person who is making the evaluation. Attraction also depends in part on the similarities and differences between the evaluator and the person being evaluated. As acquaintances evolve from first encounters to more engaged relationships, two additional factors come into play: the need to associate with someone and reactions to observable physical attributes.

What leads to attraction and eventual friendship? There are at least six billion people on our planet, and several thousand of them could conceivably become your friends. That is exceedingly unlikely to happen, however. Any one of us is likely to become aware of, interact with, and get to know only a small fraction of these individuals. Of those in this relatively small subgroup, only a few will become acquaintances, fewer still will become friends, and most will remain strangers. What determines awareness, interaction, and differential attraction?

Once two people come into contact and experience relatively positive affects, they begin a transition, the initiating stages of a possible relationship. They may simply remain superficial acquaintances who exchange friendly greetings whenever they happen to encounter one another but never interact otherwise. Or they may begin to talk, learn each other's names, and exchange bits and pieces of information. At this point, they might be described as close acquaintances. Which of these two outcomes occurs depends on (1) the extent to which each person is motivated by the need to associate or the need for inclusion (discussed in Chapter 13) and (2) the way each person reacts to the observable physical attributes of the other.

interpersonal attraction
The desire to interact with someone based on a variety of factors, including physical attractiveness, personality, rewards, proximity, or similarities.

Making Connections

Finding the Right One

A promotion advertising "the world's largest and most successful introduction service" states, "Too many people let precious time slip by . . . just hoping that somehow that special someone will magically appear." The promotional letter goes on

> *If it hasn't happened for you yet as you go about your daily life—at home, work, and play—now is the time to* stop waiting *and* start looking beyond your own circle of friends and activities for that special person.
>
> *The Right One® can help you find that person. We can introduce you to many successful, intelligent and compatible singles—people who share your interestes, your goals and your values—*people who are already out there looking for you. *Since The Right One® reaches millions of people each month, we provide a continuous stream of new singles for our members to meet. Visit our Web Site www.therightone.com. (Advertisement sent to rural route boxholder)*

Meeting Place

> Seeking country gentleman, *honest, intelligent, sensitive, shy DWF, blue/blonde, N/S, attractive, petite, enjoys dancing, walking, movies, rodeos, C&W music, reading, animals (have dog, miniature donkey). Seeking compatible male, emotionally, financially secure, for LTR.*
>
> Is love to give, . . . *to a special lady. DWM, 32, affectionate, carpenter. Seeking S/DCF with good self-esteem, for friendship first, healthy relationship, possible romantic marriage.*

1. Why are matching services and personal ads such as these so popular in our society?
2. Write your own ad for the Meeting Place. You may wish to share your ad in a discussion.
3. Go to the home page of The Right One® (www.therightone.com). Look over the various links on the site. Which links did you find of interest and how does the site relate to what you have read so far?

Physical Attributes

When we like—or dislike—some people at first sight, it is an indication that we have observed something about them that appears to provide information. For example, if a stranger reminds you of someone you know and like, your positive response to the person you already know is extended by association to the person you don't know at all.[2] You tend to like the stranger simply on the basis of a superficial resemblance to someone else. In other instances, the cue might not be related to a specific person in your past but to a subgroup of people to whom you respond positively—the stranger has a Wisconsin accent, for example, and you have a fondness for people from your home state. In a similar way, resemblance to a specific person you know and dislike or to a subgroup of people you dislike can cause you instantly to dislike or avoid a stranger. As we discussed in Chapters 2 and 5, stereotypes are poor predictors of behavior, but, nevertheless, we find ourselves reacting to other people on the basis of superficial characteristics.

Most of us have learned that "beauty is only skin deep," and we know that reacting to stereotypes on the basis of appearance is meaningless. However, people do in fact respond positively to those who are very attractive and negatively to those who are very unattractive.[3] This is especially true in the early stages of interpersonal contact with strangers. In U.S. society, we commonly accept or reject people on the basis of observable characteristics such as skin color, sexual orientation, height, weight, accent, and hair color. Physical attractiveness is a very powerful message and influences many types of interpersonal evaluations, but appearance is especially crucial with respect to attraction to members of the opposite sex.[4]

Culture and Attraction. In U.S. culture, both males and females are strongly influenced by attractiveness. People, in general, do respond strongly to physical attractiveness—the aesthetically appealing outward appearance—of others. This is especially true when a person judges someone's desirability as a date. It appears that attractiveness can sometimes outweigh other considerations in interacting with others. For example, in an experiment, undergraduate males were in general very eager to be accepted by an attractive female stranger—so much so that they would ingratiate themselves by expressing false attitudes in order to win the approval of attractive women. In response to unattractive women, they did the opposite and expressed false disagreements in order to avoid further interaction. Overall, males are generally more responsive to attractiveness in females than females are responsive to male attractiveness.[5]

Research shows that people in general tend to have high levels of agreement about who is or is not attractive, even across racial and ethnic lines. In most cultures, at any given time, general agreement exists as to what constitutes attractiveness and what does not. For example, most of us would find it difficult to express what attractiveness is. However, most of us "know it when we see it."[6]

Communication and Attraction. How does attractiveness affect relationships and interpersonal communication? Most people, according to one research study, are afraid of being rejected by those who are more attractive than they are. Many people tend to reject others who are far less attractive than they believe themselves to be; in other words, they are saying, "I can do better than that." As a result, people tend to pair off, especially in romantic relationships, by selecting individuals whom they consider similar in attractiveness. "Mismatches" do occur, such as portrayed in the characters of Catherine (an attractive woman) and Vincent (unattractive disfigured man) in the story of "Beauty and the Beast." Why do these exceptions occur, and what explains them? If one person in a relationship is more attractive than another, for example, people tend to infer that the less attractive person in the relationship has an attribute that "balances" the mismatch, such as wealth, power, intelligence, sex appeal, or fame. For example, in "Beauty and the Beast" Vincent's appearance is unattractive, but his kindness, gentleness, and bravery make Catherine's love for him believable. Whether we wish to accept it or not, physical appearance does play a role in determining relationships. Although this attractiveness might not always predict the outcome of a relationship, research has shown that physical attractiveness is important as an attention getter.[7]

Influence and Attraction. Most of us are aware that sometimes our first impressions and reasons for being attracted to another are not completely rational. Sudden lust, love at first sight, or the intense dislike of someone with whom we have had no previous contact can seem inexplicable. Many social psychologists suggest that relationship development has a lot to do with the "chemistry" between the individuals in the relationship. Either the chemistry is right and the relationship develops, or it's a mismatch and the relationship never seems to move beyond the initial stages. The chemistry explanation probably holds some truth, but many other variables influence the development of a relationship.

We are most often attracted to individuals who support us and have similar interests, attitudes, likes, and dislikes. In fact, when asked to characterize their ideal friend,

The fairy tale "Beauty and the Beast" is an ancient story that continues to hold meaning. Its theme raises an interesting question: What is the basis of attraction between people? People usually select partners whom they perceive to be similarly physically attractive or more attractive than themselves. In what cases might there be an exception to this rule?

people often describe someone who is similar to their perceptions of themselves. For example, those who are religious tend to seek other religious people, those who like sports tend to seek other sports fans, and those who like children tend to seek others who like children. Of course, opposites sometimes do attract, but relationships in which there are significant differences in important attitudes or behaviors are often strained and more likely to deteriorate than are those that have no significant disparities.

Gender and Attraction. Another gender difference is exhibited in the personal ads placed by males and females who are seeking a romantic partner. It was generally found that women stress their appearance and men stress their material resources.[8] It could be, of course, that those who write ads are simply echoing widespread cultural beliefs about what people assume is most appealing to the opposite sex. One research study investigated the number of replies that certain types of ad messages received.[9] In other words, do some factors in the ads attract more potential mates than others? Several interesting gender differences were found. For women, age as stated in their ads was negatively related to the number of replies; that is the older a woman was, the fewer replies. For men, the opposite was true; the older a man was, the more replies he received. Also, the higher men's stated income and educational level, the more replies. For women, in contrast, these factors were unrelated to how many responses the ad generated. Thus a personal ad placed by a man was most effective if it indicated a mature, rich, educated individual. In ads placed by a woman, the only relevant ad content related to its effectiveness was age—the younger, the better. Interestingly, ads placed by gay men indicated a preference for younger males, and ads placed by heterosexual men indicated a preference for younger female partners. Whatever the reason, for both genders and for both heterosexuals and homosexuals, attractiveness is a positive characteristic, and numerous stereotypes are consistently associated with appearance.[10]

Meeting on the Internet

In Chapter 13, we discussed how initial interaction on the Internet could result in relationships and the fact that the growth of those relationships is often limited for a variety of reasons. According to Malcolm Parks and Kory Floyd, two communication scholars whose research on Internet interaction was mentioned in Chapter 13, there are conflicting theories on interpersonal communication and relationship development. Because Internet interaction is limited by fewer social cues (i.e., nonverbal communication) and potential feedback delays can lead to uncertainty (and difficulty in reducing uncertainty about the other person), the development of personal relationships might be prevented, or at least retarded.[11]

Online interactions are generally assumed to lack many of the typical characteristics of face-to-face discussions that can aid in relationship development. An important question that researchers are asking is "Are the conditions that exist in face-to-face interactions necessary for a relationship to develop into something that is ongoing or lasting?" Predicted outcome value theory and social exchange theory, discussed in Chapter 13, assert that the motivation to form relationships is the forecast of a positive reward–cost ratio. In uncertainty theory, also discussed in Chapter 13, the driving force is the reduction in uncertainty about the other person and the relationship itself. None of these theories require physical contact or frequent interaction as necessary conditions for a relationship to develop. Thus proximity and other conditions that occur in face-to-face interactions may be helpful, but they are not required for a relationship to be rewarding or fulfilling; they are not necessary for interactants to develop feelings for each other and do not affect how cyberpartners treat each other.[12]

Parks and Floyd, in addition to finding that women are more likely to form relationships on the Internet than men are, also found that age and marital status were not related to the likelihood of developing a personal relationship online. People who were married and divorced, according to the survey results, were equally likely to form personal relationships over the Internet. In fact, of the 176 people Parks and Floyd surveyed, about 30 percent developed personal relationships. The more in depth and personal an Internet relationship becomes, the more likely it is that communication will move beyond cyberspace to more private and direct channels such as the telephone, letters, or face-to-face communication.[13] As with all relationships, Internet relationships also go through stages of coming together and coming apart.

Knapp's Stages of Coming Together

Theorists and communication scholars such as Mark Knapp[14] believe that for relationships to develop into something more than a brief encounter, they must go through different stages of growth. Knapp indicates that these stages do little to explain the multitude of personal and societal expectations that illustrate his model. He explains that in each case, the type of relationship that develops will depend on mutual and ongoing expectations: What is the relationship? What will it lead to? What should it lead to? What behavior is expected?

Although the relationship stages in Knapp's theory are generally described as romantic in nature, he does not preclude or suggest that only romantic relationships or mixed-gender relationships are included in the model. In fact, Knapp's latest textbook, *Interpersonal Communication and Human Relationships,* co-authored with Anita Vangelisti,[15] suggests that any and all kinds of relationships, including same-sex partners, can reach the highest level of commitment. David McWhirter and Andrew Mattison, research psychologists, found that when same-sex intimate relationships form, the same patterns or stages of development occur as with mixed-sex pairs.[16] Knapp and Vangelisti further suggest that their approach is more heavily oriented toward mixed-gender pairs but that it is not intended to exclude relationships between same-sex pairs. Not all relationships go through the stages at the same rate, in the same way, or sequentially, and many move in and out of the stages. The coming-together sequence, however, often progresses from initiating to experimenting, intensifying, integrating, and ultimately bonding.[17]

Initiating. Initiating is the stage during which individuals meet and interact for the first time. The initial interaction might consist of a brief exchange of words, either electronically or in person, or of eye contact during which the two individuals recognize each other's existence and potential interest to meet and converse. If conversation does not begin, the initiating stage may end, and the potential relationship might not progress any further. Whether the interaction continues depends on various assessments that the individuals make—for example, whether the other person is attractive or unattractive, approachable or unapproachable. A connection must be made to motivate one or both of the individuals to continue the interaction if a relationship is to develop. The decision to pursue the relationship also depends on whether the other person is open for the encounter. Is she or he in a hurry, too busy, or too involved with others?

During the initiating stage, we mentally process many impressions that lead to a key decision: "Yes, I do want to meet you" or "No, I am not interested in you." It might take less than fifteen seconds to determine whether a relationship will progress. At this stage, most of us feel extreme vulnerability and caution, even though there is considerable variance in people's initiating behaviors. The Internet seemingly is playing a larger and larger role in how people from all over the world meet and interact. People of all ages are using cyberspace to develop friendships as well as romantic relationships.

Experimenting. Experimenting is the stage of coming together that requires risk taking because little is known as yet about the other person. You attempt to answer the question "Who is this person?" This stage can be extremely awkward, consisting mainly of small talk: "What's your name?" "Where are you from?" "What's your major?" "Do you know so-and-so?" Such conversation serves several important functions in the development of a relationship: (1) It uncovers similarities and interests that might lead to deeper conversation, (2) it serves as an audition for the potential friend, (3) it lets the other person know who you are and provides clues as to how he or she can get to know you better, and (4) it establishes the common ground you share with the other person.

The experimenting stage, although involving some risk, is usually pleasant, relaxed, and uncritical. Involvement and commitment are limited—and often remain that way through the duration of the relationship. Most relationships do not progress beyond this stage, but this does not imply that these relationships are meaningless or useless. Relationships that remain at the experimental level can become satisfying friendships.

Intensifying. The intensifying stage marks an increase in the participants' commitment and involvement in the relationship. Simply put, the two people become close friends. The commitment is typified by an increased sharing of more personal and private information, or self-disclosure (see Chapter 13), about oneself and one's family. For example, at this stage, it would not be unusual to share confidences such as "My mother and father are affectionate people," "I love you," "I am a sensitive person," "I once cheated

Making Connections

The Virtual Relationship

Use the Internet to develop a cyber relationship with someone. You may use email, join a Yahoo group, or enter a chatroom discussion either with existing contacts or new ones. Keep a log of all messages that you send and receive from the initial contact to help you retrace the steps in the relationship's development. It might take you several tries to find someone who is willing to interact with you over time. Answer the following questions after you have had at least eight to ten different interactions.

1. What principles from this and the previous chapter can you apply to this type of interaction?
2. What difficulties, if any, did you encounter while developing an electronically mediated relationship? How did it differ from face-to-face relationship development?
3. What did you learn about relationship development in general by using the Internet?

on an exam," "My father is having another relationship," "I was promoted," "I drink too heavily," and "I don't use drugs."

Although the relationship deepens at this stage, there is still a sense of caution and testing to gain approval before continuing. In typical romantic relationships, we see much testing of commitment—sitting close, for instance, may occur before holding hands, hugging, or kissing. Each behavior in the relationship is engaged in order to seek approval. The relationship is beginning to mature, and the participants become more sensitive to each other's needs. During this phase, many things happen verbally:

1. Forms of address become informal—a first name, nickname, or a term of endearment is used.
2. Use of the first-person plural becomes more common—"We should do this" or "Let's do this."
3. Private symbols begin to develop—special slang or jargon or conventional language forms with mutually understood, private meanings.
4. Verbal shortcuts built on a backlog of accumulated and shared assumptions, knowledge, and experiences appear. For instance, your friend needs to be told that he or she is loved; you say that the person is important to you but never say that you love him or her.
5. More direct expressions of commitment may appear—"We really have a good thing going" or "I don't know who I'd talk to if you weren't around." Sometimes such expressions receive an echo—"I really like you a lot" or "I really like you, too, Dion."
6. Each partner acts increasingly as a helper in the other's daily process of understanding what he or she is all about—"In other words, you mean you're . . . " or "But yesterday you said you were. . . . "

The integrating stage of relationship development conveys a sense of togetherness. The two people have established a deep commitment, and the relationship has become extremely important to them.

Integrating. When integrating occurs, the relationship has a sense of togetherness. Others expect to see the individuals together, and when they do not, they often ask about the other person. The two people have established a deep commitment, and the relationship has become extremely important to them. Many assumptions take place between the individuals. For example, sharing is expected, and borrowing from the other person usually needs no formal request because it is assumed to be all right.

Although a strong mutual commitment characterizes this stage of a relationship, it does not mean a total giving of oneself to the other. The verbal and nonverbal expressions of the integrating stage take many forms. For example, some individuals believe their relationship is something special or unique. Some share rings, pins, pictures, and other artifacts to illustrate to themselves and others their commitment to each other. The two may begin to behave in similar ways. Still others indicate their sense of togetherness through word choice—*our* account, *our* apartment, *our* stereo, *our* car.

Bonding. The final stage in a relationship's development and growth is bonding, the public announcement of the commitment—as when a couple announces that they are engaged or getting married. Bonding involves the understanding that the commitment has progressed from private knowledge to public knowledge, thus making a breakup of the relationship more difficult.

The relationship at this stage is contractual in nature, even though a formal contract, such as a marriage license, is not required. Both parties must understand, however, that a relationship exists, which entails explicit and implicit agreements to hold it together. The commitment implies that the relationship is "for better or for worse" and is defined according to established norms, policies, or laws of the culture and society in which it exists.

Knapp's Stages of Coming Apart

In U.S. culture, there are no guarantees that a commitment will create a lasting relationship. When a relationship stops growing and differences begin to emerge, the coming-apart process begins. Some relationships go through some or all of the stages in this process and emerge stronger than before, but when the forces that pull a relationship apart are stronger than the forces that hold it together, the alliance will end. Like the coming-together process, Knapp's coming-apart stages do not flow necessarily in a sequential order, and it is likely that relationships often move into and out of the stages. The coming-apart process has five stages: differentiating, circumscribing, stagnating, avoiding, and terminating.[18]

Differentiating. In differentiating, the first stage of coming apart, the differences between the individuals are highlighted and become forces that slow or limit the growth of the relationship. The pair's communication tends to focus on how each differs from the other, and there is less tolerance of these differences. Indeed, differences that were once overlooked or negotiated now become the center of attention, putting stress on the relationship and its existence. Typically, things that were once described as "ours" now become "mine": "This is my apartment," "These are my books," and "They are my friends."

Conversations often move from mild disagreement to heated anger: "Do I have to do all the work around here? You don't do a darn thing." "Why is it that your so-called friends never clean up after themselves?" "I pay the phone bill, but you're the one who uses it the most." Conflict begins to overshadow the more positive aspects of the relationship and might lead to abuse of one or both parties in the relationship.

Circumscribing. In the circumscribing stage, information exchange is reduced, and some areas of difference are completely avoided because conversation would only lead to a deepening of the conflict. Comments during this stage might include the following: "I don't want to talk about it." "Can't you see that I'm busy?" "Why do you keep bringing up the past?" "Let's just be friends and forget it." Communication loses some of its personal qualities, is less spontaneous, and becomes increasingly superficial as the relationship becomes more strained. Interactions, in their amount and depth of disclosure, resemble those of the initiating and experimenting stages of coming together: "Have you eaten?" "Did I get any calls today?" "I saw Joe, and he said to say hi."

People in the circumscribing stage often conceal their faltering relationship in public. For example, driving to a party, a couple might sit in cold silence, staring stonily into space. But once they arrive at their destination, they put on their party personalities—smiling, telling jokes, and not disagreeing with one another. When they return to the privacy of their car, they resume their cold behavior.

> **Making Connections**
>
> **Just Want to Be Friends!**
>
> Knapp's stages of relational coming together and apart seems to apply best to traditional romantic relationships. This, according to some critics, leaves out a variety of other same-sex or mixed-sex relationships that are equally important in our lives. What do you think?
>
> 1. How well do Knapp's stages explain other types of relationships besides romantic? For example, you could test the model with good or best friends, parent and child, grandparent and grandchild, co-workers, and others.
> 2. What changes do you think need to be made to make Knapp's stages more in line with what you described above? Create your own stages if you wish.

Stagnating. The relationship reaches a standstill at the stagnating stage. The participants avoid interaction and take care to sidestep controversy. Some people that believe this is the "boring" stage of a relationship, yet they do not do anything about it. Little hope remains for the relationship once it has deteriorated to this stage, yet one of the participants might still want it to be revived.

During stagnation, both verbal and nonverbal communication tend to be thoroughly thought out, and the partners plan what to say, making interactions stylized and cold. Both parties are apt to reflect unhappiness and to act as if each is a stranger to the other.

Often the stagnation stage is relatively brief, but sometimes it is extended because of complications. For example, some people are seriously distressed by the loss of their relationship even though they know that parting is the right decision. Other people may count on the survival of the relationship, such as children, making the breakup more difficult. Others may prolong the situation in fear of experiencing additional pain and in hope of getting the relationship back on track or in an attempt to punish the other person.

Avoiding. Up to this point, the participants in the relationship are still seeing each other or sharing the same living quarters. But the fourth stage, the avoiding stage, is marked by physical distancing and eventual separation. The basic message is "I am not interested in being with you anymore." As far as the participants are concerned, the relationship is over, and they have no interest in reestablishing it.

At times, the interaction in this stage is brief, direct, unfriendly, and even antagonistic: "I really don't care to see you." "Don't call me—we have nothing to discuss." "I'm busy tonight. For that matter, I'm going to be busy for quite some time."

Terminating. The last stage in the breaking up of a relationship occurs when the individuals take the necessary steps to end it. Termination can be early, that is, when the relationship has barely begun, or it can occur after many years. For relationships that break up in the early stages of development, such as initiating or experimenting, the feelings of parting are usually not complex or lasting.

The interaction during this stage is self-centered and seeks to justify the termination: "I need to do something for myself—I've always put more into the relationship than I've gotten out of it." "We just have too many differences that I didn't know existed until now." "I found out that we just weren't meant for each other." When both individuals know that the relationship is ending, they say good-bye to each other in three ways: in a summary statement, in behaviors signaling the termination or limited contact, and in comments about what the relationship will be like in the future, if there is to be any relationship at all.[19]

Summary statements review the relationship and provide a rationale for its termination: "Although our love used to be very special, we both have changed over the years. We are not the same couple that we were when we first met." Ending behaviors reflect new rules of contact: "It would be good for both of us not to see so much of each other." "I wish you would stop coming over all the time." Finally, when the relationship is over, the participants state their preferences for dealing with each other in the future: "I don't want to see you anymore." "We can get together once in a while, but I only want us to be friends and nothing more." See Table 14.1 for dialogue that represents each stage of relationship development.

The Process of Coming Together and Coming Apart. The stages of coming together and coming apart are complex and continuous as we move into, through, and out of

TABLE 14.1

Knapp's Stages of Relationship Development

PROCESS	STAGE	REPRESENTATIVE DIALOGUE
Coming together	Initiating	"Hi, how ya doin' "? "Fine. You?"
	Experimenting	"Oh, so you like to ski . . . so do I." "You do? Great. Where do you go?"
	Intensifying	"I . . . I think I love you." "I love you too."
	Integrating	"I feel so much a part of you." "Yeah, we are like one person." "What happens to you happens to me."
	Bonding	"I want to be with you always." "Let's get married."
Coming apart	Differentiating	"I just don't like big social gatherings." "Sometimes I don't understand you. This is one area where I'm certainly not like you at all."
	Circumscribing	"Did you have a good time on your trip?" "What time will dinner be ready?"
	Stagnating	"What's there to talk about?" "Right. I know what you're going to say, and you know what I'm going to say."
	Avoiding	"I'm so busy, I don't know when I'll be able to see you." "If I'm not around, you'll understand."
	Terminating	"I'm leaving you . . . and don't bother trying to contact me." "Don't worry."

From Mark L. Knapp and Anita L. Vengelisti, *Interpersonal Communication and Human Relationships,* 4e. Published by Allyn and Bacon, Boston, MA.

Making Connections

Retracing a Relationship's Progress

Clearly, no two relationships are alike, nor do they all evolve in the same way. Consider a relationship that is important to you, and then complete the following steps:

1. Record the significant developments in the relationship, from the time of the first meeting to the present. Label these developments according to Knapp's stages.
2. After you have completed the labeling, imagine that your relationship is a book, and each stage or period in the relationship's history is a chapter. Create a title for each chapter, capturing that essence of the relationship during that period. You can have as many chapters as you find necessary to describe the relationship.
3. After you have titled each chapter, write a brief synopsis of what each title means. Do the chapters follow any particular pattern of development?
4. What are the similarities and differences between the stages of your relationship and Knapp's stages?

Adapted from Leslie A. Baxter, "Dialectical Contradictions in Relationships Development," *Journal of Social and Personal Relationships* (1990) 7: 69–88. Reprinted in *Contemporary Perspectives on Interpersonal Communication,* eds. Sandra Petronio, Jess K. Alberts, Michael L. Hecht, and Jerry Buley (Dubuque, Iowa: Brown & Benchmark, 1993), 92–93.

relationships. Knapp and Vangelisti acknowledge that not all relationships move through each of the escalating and deescalating stages at the same pace or always in sequential order, but they state that most relationships do go through the interaction stages systematically and sequentially. They also suggest that it is possible for people to skip steps during both the growth process of a relationship and the deterioration of a relationship. You might have had or heard of relationships that go from the initiating stage—"Hi, my name is"—to "Let's go to your place so that we can get to know each other better." These relationships move from the initiating step right to the intensifying step. Termination may occur suddenly and without warning in this situation, thus violating or skipping all the steps of coming apart. For example, in *Runaway Bride,* a popular movie in the late 1990s, Julia Roberts portrays a character who fell in love with several different men, but in each case, she left them standing at the altar because she did not believe the relationship was right.

Knapp and Vangelisti also suggest that relationships can move forward and backward from one stage to the next. The direction a relationship takes depends on how one evaluates the various rewards and costs (social exchange theory—see Chapter 13) and whether the rewards outweigh the costs or vice versa, thus moving the relationship either forward or backward. According to Knapp and Vangelisti, the possibility of stability at a given stage may occur for a period of time in which the relationship remains the same. However, relationships are not static for very long; therefore it is natural for all relationships, including the most stable, to experience periods of instability. Each stage can also create its own movement, and like most things, the stages themselves have a beginning, middle, and end.

There are at least three reasons, according to Knapp, why relationships move through the stages sequentially: (1) Each stage provides information that allows movement to the next, (2) each stage enables the participants to predict what might or might not occur in the next stage, and (3) skipping a stage creates risk and uncertainty in the relationship.[20] Relationships that are happy and satisfying last because the participants have learned to satisfy each other through their communication.

Duck's Phases of Dissolution

Communication scholar Steve Duck theorizes that dissolving relationships go through a rather complex decision-making process that does not always follow a specific order of stages, in contrast to the model of Knapp's coming-apart stages. According to Duck, relationship breakups often occur sporadically, inconsistently, and with uncertainty over a period of time, but in deciding what to do about a potential breakup, a person proceeds through the following four phases: intrapyschic, dyadic, social, and grave-dressing. The termination of the relationship is strongly affected by the partners' social networks, and the influence of others outside the relationship is often reflected in any or all of the phases of a breakup. The uncertainty, or "on again, off again" approach that some relationships take as they dissolve defines the phases of Duck's approach.[21]

The Intrapsychic Phase. During the intrapsychic phase, people begin to internally assess their dissatisfaction with a relationship. This phase involves perception, assessments, and decision making about what to do about the relationship. In this phase, communication may actually decrease at times, and each of the partners might seek comfort from others outside the relationship. The intrapsychic phase is similar in some respects to Knapp's differentiating stage in which differences between the individuals become noticeable to at least one of the individuals in the relationship. Communication may decrease or become more self-centered and thus lead to more conflict and argument rather than negotiation.

The Dyadic Phase. In the dyadic phase, the people in the relationship discuss the status of their relationship. The interactions vary from cooperative to uncooperative in discussing the partners' unsatisfying traits or behaviors and whether to solve the problem or to separate. There is much negotiation, persuasion, and argument during this period; each person is trying to get the other person to comply or change in some fashion. Sometimes the dyadic phase ends with an agreement to repair the relationship, but if it doesn't, the relationship may eventually move on to the next phase. The dyadic phase would be consistent with what may occur as a relationship moves through Knapp's differentiating stage to the circumscribing stage. In this phase, it is likely that there is more conflict and less negotiation; the partners might also avoid subjects that may inflame the interaction. Thus when interaction occurs during this phase in the relationship breakup, it moves toward more impersonal or formalized conversations as illustrated in Knapp's circumscribing stage.

The Social Phase. In the social phase, the relationship difficulties become more public within the context of family, friends, co-workers, or other acquaintances. Most relationships that break up, except possibly secret love affairs, do not stand completely alone and usually have an impact on others outside the dissolving relationship. For example, there is usually an effect on the children if parents separate. During this phase, the opinions and feelings of others often have an impact on what a couple eventually does. For example, children of a married couple might influence the couple to stay together in spite of their differences. The concern might become, "What kind of relationship should be continued, if any? How should it be presented to others?"

Other issues include where to place blame, how to save face, how to explain what has happened, and who should be sought out for support or to provide approval for the decision.

The social phase includes most aspects of the remaining three stages of Knapp's coming-apart process: stagnating, avoiding, and termination. It is clear that the relationship has reached what appears to be an impasse, and therefore continuing it is most unlikely. However, the major difference between the theories of Duck and Knapp is that Duck emphasized the impact the breakup of the relationship will have on others as well as the influence others will have on the relationship. Knapp's stages do not address this issue directly. According to Duck, the individuals will seek out the approval of others, whereas Knapp is more concerned with how the individuals justify the breakup to themselves.

The Grave-Dressing Phase. Duck names the final phase *grave-dressing* because after the breakup, each partner gives an account of why the relationship ended. This phase includes some similarities to Knapp's termination stage, because it is in this stage, according to Knapp, that individuals begin to justify to others why the relationship had to end. These explanations aid in the healing process, in coping, and in the recovery from the breakup itself. It is not unusual for one or both individuals in the relationship to explain to others why the relationship dissolved. For example, if the relationship ended on friendly terms, you might hear statements such as "It just didn't work—we were too different" or "We needed time to grow, so we decided not to see each other for a while." If the relationship ended on unfriendly terms, however, you might hear explanations such as "He always wanted things for himself—he was selfish" or "She never seemed to be satisfied with what I'd do for her." Men and women handle relationship failures differently. Women, for example, tend to confide in their friends, whereas men tend to start a new relationship as quickly as possible.[22]

Not all relationships, however, end with mutual agreement that the relationship should be terminated. You are probably aware of situations in which one partner did not want to lose the other, but the person ending the relationship simply saw no reason to continue it. In such a case, the grave-dressing phase is usually one-sided; the person ending the relationship might say, "It just wasn't working" or "I have found someone new." Meanwhile, the person who does not want the relationship to end looks for a way to keep it going and cannot face the fact it is over. The person tries to justify to himself or herself and others that the termination is only temporary and that the other person will come to his or her senses and return.

Each phase poses certain communication challenges that Duck refers to as "social management problems." For example, in the intrapsychic phase, one must have the ability to discuss the perceived differences with one's partner. In the social phase, one must be able to discuss the breakup with others outside of the relationship. Clearly, as relationships move into and out of various phases, communication plays a significant role.

The research of Leslie Baxter, a communication scholar, supports some of Duck's explanations regarding dissolving relationships. Baxter believes that disengagement often involves repeated attempts to limit or end relationships. They are cyclical in nature and involve different communication strategies. Moreover, the communication strategies used during the breakup of relationships involve varying degrees of directness and concern for the other person.[23] The direct strategies are explicit statements describing the desire to end the relationship, whereas the indirect strategies are more subtle in design. For example, an indirect strategy for breaking up might involve using excuses such as "I have too much work to do," implying "I cannot see you now."

Someone with concern for the other person is more likely to use the indirect approach; the direct approach is much more expedient and may show little or no concern for hurting the other person. Baxter implies that strategies used in ending a relationship depend greatly on whether the breakup is one-sided or agreed on by both parties. As suggested earlier, agreed-on breakups usually involve some negotiation and face saving on behalf of both parties involved. All relationships, however, move through various stages and often move between various levels of tension or conflict.

To put it simply, relationships can be messy at times. This is true for even the best and most stable relationships because of the tensions that all relationships encounter from time to time. In fact, most romantic partners converse with each other less than a few hours a day, rarely self-disclose, often fight, on occasion become verbally and even physically violent, are rude to each other, and are more concerned with themselves than with sharing intimacies.[24] It is therefore not unusual that relationships don't measure up to the ideal, because most relationships—whether romantic, family, close friendship, or work-related—encounter difficult contradictions almost every day. These tensions and the conflicts that emerge from them are discussed in the following section.

Learning Connections

1. Does the information about forming and dissolving relationships presented here reflect your experiences? Explain or discuss the differences.
2. What does it mean to be interpersonally attracted to someone?
3. Do you agree or disagree with what the text says about physical attributes and their importance in relationships? Explain your position.
4. Compare and contrast Knapp's stages of coming apart and Duck's phases of dissolution? Which do you think explains the breakup of a relation more accurately? Why?

Dialectical Theory: Push and Pull

Relationships contain many contradictions or tensions, which push and pull in many different directions at the same time. For example, you might want your best friend to spend more time with you, but when your friend does, you decide that you want more time to yourself. This might lead to your friend saying, "I thought you wanted to spend more time together, and now that we can, you're never around. So what do you want?" This illustrates the contradictory impulses or **dialectic** that push and pull us in conflicting directions with others. By contradictory impulses, we mean that each person is having two opposing and interacting desires, which push and pull the relationship in different directions. There are three commonly identified dialectical tensions described in the research: connected–autonomy, openness–closedness, and novelty–predictability (see Table 14.2).[25]

Connection–Autonomy. Relationships require both the desire to connect to another person and the desire to retain autonomy as an individual. We want to connect to others, such as partners, friends, parents, siblings, or co-workers, but we also want to retain some control and independence or autonomy over our lives. There is a desire for our close relationships to be defined as "us," but this does not mean that we want to sacrifice our individuality or control over who we are.

dialectic Contradictory impulses that push and pull us in conflicting directions with others.

When there is too much emphasis on connection or integration in a relationship, it can lead to the feeling of being smothered or consumed by a partner, friend, parent, or co-worker, such that we feel entrapped and controlled by the relationship, thus leaving us with no life of our own. Intimacy at its highest level does require a bonding that connects us with another person emotionally, intellectually, and physically, but it does not mean or require a complete loss of self. In healthy relationships, there is a reasonable balance of being connected and maintaining autonomy. Relationships that move too far in one direction or the other in terms of control versus autonomy are usually relationships that are extremely unstable and potentially destructive.

TABLE 14.2
Dialectical Theory: Push and Pull

TENSIONS	PUSH	PULL
Connection–autonomy	Dependent	Independent
	Together	Alone
Openness–closedness	Reveal	Conceal
	Public	Private
Novelty–predictability	Ambivalence	Certainty
	Different	Same

Openness–Closedness. The second dialectic tension is the desire to be open and expressive on the one hand and closed and private on the other. In U.S. culture, we are encouraged to be open and honest with others because we are a society that admires those who are open and truthful. But even at the beginning of new relationships, when we are seeking as much information as we can about the other person, there is a counterforce that cautions against revealing too much too soon about ourselves. This tension between self-disclosing and keeping our privacy continues throughout the various stages of relationship development. We know that open expression is a necessary prerequisite in order for us to reach intimacy and bonding with another person. We also know that when we reveal ourselves to another individual, we make our relationship and ourselves more vulnerable. As discussed in Chapter 13, privacy is important for a relationship to survive. All of us therefore face the dilemma of how much self-disclosure or honesty we should allow there to be with friends, relatives, and romantic partners and how much will be too much. Too much self-disclosure, as you learned in Chapter 13, can lead to strains on a relationship and is a sign of not being a competent, or, at the very least, a thoughtful, communicator. Relationships grow on the strength of the trust that is established between partners. When the trust that exists between partners is violated by revealing private information or by telling a partner something he or she is not prepared to hear, the relationship is at risk for deterioration or termination.

Making Connections

Temptation: Cheating to Trade Up

The reality television show *Temptation Island* tries to provoke committed but unmarried couples into promiscuous behavior by cheating on their partners. This show is a knock-off of the popular *Survivor*. The basic assumption of *Temptation Island* is that participants should be ready to trade in a current partner if a more attractive one comes along. The theme is "just go with the flow."

1. Is resisting deliberate temptation by another attractive person an effective way to prove that a relationship is strong? Explain.
2. How might we use dialectical theory to explain this show's impact on participants' relationships? On viewers' relationships?
3. What is this show communicating about relationships?
4. Discuss the ethical implications of this show and how they might affect communication in a relationship.

Novelty–Predictability. To develop and build healthy relationships, a certain amount of predictability is needed. Without some stability or constancy, there is too much potential for uncertainty and ambivalence for a long-term relationship to survive. Therefore we need relationships in which we know that we can count on a certain amount of predictability. Families are a central stabilizing force in most people's lives and provide an anchor for security in a very unpredictable world. Predictability is a comfort to most of us because we know what to expect. Too much predictability in some aspects of a relationship, however, may make the relationship routine and boring, thus requiring a call for something unique or different. The drive for wanting things to be consistent and predictable and the desire for novelty and difference creates a dialectical tension that requires competent communication in a relationship in order to relieve tension and prevent a destructive conflict from occurring. Pushes and pulls, or dialectic tensions, will always be part of every relationship in which we are involved, and how competently we communicate will determine whether a relationship grows, stagnates, or terminates.

Managing Relational Tensions

How we deal with the tensions in our lives create some interesting communication challenges for each of us. It is also important to understand that relationships have both private and public dimensions and that relationships do not exist in vacuum. There are many tensions or pushes and pulls from outside of a relationship as well as inside that can directly or indirectly effect how the parties in a relationship deal with or manage their dialectical tensions. Communication scholars Leslie Baxter and Barbara Montgomery suggest a number of approaches to enable us to manage our dialectical tensions.[26] The least helpful in dealing with tensions is *denial* that tension exits. How many times have you heard someone who is facing stress or tension say, "Everything is fine—there's no problem." The denial strategy is avoidance or cover-up, which often leads to lying or deception, if not to yourself, then most certainly to others. The dialectical tension does not disappear by denying its existence; it must be dealt with through communication.

Baxter, in a 1990 study, suggests that most people utilize a variety of strategies to manage their dialectical tensions.[27] The most often chosen are selection, segmentation, reframing, moderation, and reaffirmation. The strategy of *selection* is a strategy in which one end of the dialectical tension is chosen over the other. For example, a married couple finding themselves in a dilemma with their in-laws might choose to go along with the in-laws rather than do what they want to do so as not to create hardships or more distancing between themselves and the in-laws. In other words, they are choosing predictability over novelty.

The strategy of *segmentation* is a tactic in which a couple compartmentalizes different aspects of their relationship. For example, a couple might manage the tension between being open and being closed with each other by deciding to share information about their mutual friends but not to discuss their past romantic encounters with each other because that might be too hurtful or to insensitive. Thus some things are agreed to be open for discussion, and others are closed.

Reframing is a strategy that allows tensions to be redefined so as to dilute the tension, make it less obvious, or even make it disappear. Couples who have long-distance relationships, for example, might say that being apart has brought more intimacy and closeness to their relationship. Even though there is a great deal of stress in the relationship due to their physical separation, the couple have reframed it to mean that distance allows for great intimacy and closeness—but does it?

The strategy of *moderation* is characterized by compromises in which deals are struck to help reduce tensions. For example, a parent wants to know everything about your private life and is constantly asking you questions about personal things that you really do not want to share. You choose to answer some of the less private questions but ignore the most personal ones, thus reducing some of the tension created by the questions.

Reaffirmation is the strategy in which individuals recognize that dialectical tensions will always be present and therefore we should accept them and even embrace the challenges they produce. We should not ignore them or deny them, but we should consider dialectical tension as part of being human. Relationships are always going through pushes and pulls, and to grow and obtain a lasting relationship, the parties must manage and control the tensions through communication. The result of not managing and controlling tensions will likely be conflict.

Interpersonal Conflict

Conflict, like dialectic tensions in relationships, can occur for a variety of reasons, most of which are actions taken to block or interfere with others' interests because of perceptions of incompatible interests.

Conflict, according to William Wilmot and Joyce Hocker, "is an expressed struggle between at least two interdependent parties who perceive incompatible goals, scarce resources, and interference from others in achieving their goals."[28] The key terms in the definition are *expressed struggle, interdependent parties, incompatible goals, scarce resources,* and *interference from others.* For example, suppose you want to go to a dance on Friday evening and your friend wants to go to a movie. Both of you explain your desire about what you would like to do (expressed struggle), neither of you wants to go out alone on Friday evening (interdependent parties), you cannot go to both the dance and the movie in the same evening (incompatible goals), neither of you can afford to do both because of time and money (scarce resources), and your friend will not consider going to the dance (interference). You have incompatible goals, and one person must lose for the other to win.

The word *conflict* almost automatically brings to mind such things as fight, abuse, aggressiveness, violence, mistreatment, argument, disagreement, quarrel, clash, and differences. Not one of these words has a positive tone or gives us any reason to believe anything good can come from conflict. Wilmot and Hocker suggest that words such as exiting, strengthening, helpful, clarifying, growth producing, creative, courageous, enriching, intimate, opportune, and energizing could also be associated with conflict but most likely are not.[29] Why?

It seems that we sometimes exert a lot of energy to avoid conflict when in fact disagreements and differences of opinion can lead ultimately to compromise and solutions that might be far better for everyone. Conflict plays such a major role in U.S. culture that we need to understand its causes, why it is often destructive, and how we can better manage it or at least control it.

conflict
An expressed struggle between at least two independent parties who perceive incompatible goals, scarce resources, and interference from others in achieving their goals.

What Causes Conflict?

Suppose you asked a large number of people to describe the major factor that contributes to conflict in interpersonal relationships. How do you think they would answer? The number one answer you would likely receive is poor or inadequate communication.

Know Your Scholar

Bill Wilmot *The Collaboration Institute*

Bill Wilmot has focused on personal relationships, interpersonal conflict, and mediation during his academic career. His teaching and research have always focused on application, trying to make sure the academic work has some practical benefit. Of his numerous books, the best-known are *Dyadic Communication* and *Interpersonal Conflict,* which is now in its sixth edition.

As a result of fusing academic and applied work, Bill serves as professional mediator and has entered into over 300 disputes. He now specializes in workplace disputes, ranging from supervisor–employee concerns to upper management problems. He also often works with entire work teams that have become stalled on projects. All of his applied work is driven by his passion for making a difference in people's lives.

Bill is director of the Collaboration Institute (www.collaborationinstitute.com), a consortium of communication professionals dedicated to helping others. He has received awards for teaching and a few years ago was recognized by the Western State Communication Association with its highest honor, the Distinguished Service Award. He is a Professor Emeritus at the University of Montana, and when he is not traveling, he resides at his mountaintop home in Montana with his wife Melanie Trost and Rosie, "the best dog in all of America."

However, if you asked the same people what is the best way to resolve or eliminate conflict, they would more than likely also say communication. Isn't it interesting that communication is cited as both a cause of conflict and solution for resolving it? What does this tell you? It should tell you that we often attribute the causes for and the resolution of conflict to "communication" and not ourselves. In other words, we don't take responsibility for conflict, but rather blame communication. If we use communication effectively and carefully, we can reduce or at least manage conflict more readily.

Our definition of conflict emphasizes the existence as well as the recognition of incompatible goals. Indeed, incompatible interests are the defining features of conflict. Yet conflicts can fail to develop, even though there are incompatible interests; in other situations, conflicts may occur when opposing interests do not exist but are believed to exist.[30] Clearly, then, conflict involves much more than opposing views of interest. In fact, a growing body of research suggests that social factors play a role that is as strong as, or even stronger than, incompatible interests in initiating conflicts; these social factors include faulty communication, faulty attributions, faulty perceptions, including stereotypes or prejudices, and personal traits or characteristics.

Faulty communication is a social factor that can lead to conflict. This is evident by the fact that individuals communicate in ways that anger or annoy others even though it might not be the communicator's intention to do so. Have you ever been harshly criticized in a way that you believed was unjustified, insensitive, unfair, and not the least bit helpful? If you have, you know that this type of perceived criticism leaves you feeling upset, angry, and ready to attack, thus setting the stage for conflict even though the criticism might not have been a result of incompatible goals.

Faulty attributions, such as errors concerning the causes behind others' behaviors, is one social factor that may lead to conflict.[31] When individuals believe that their goals or interests have been thwarted, they generally try to determine why. Was it poor planning on their part? Was it simply a case of bad luck? Was it a lack of the appro-

Faulty communication is a social factor that may lead to conflict. This is evident when people communicate in ways that anger or annoy each other.

priate resources to reach the goal? Or was it because of someone's intentional interference? If it is concluded that the latter is the reason, then the seeds for conflict may be planted, even if the other person actually had nothing to do with the situation. Thus erroneous attributions concerning the causes of negative outcomes can and often do play an important role in instigating conflicts and sometimes result in conflicts when they readily could have been avoided.

Another cause of conflict is faulty perceptions and our tendency to perceive our own views as objective and reflecting reality but to perceive others' views as biased or lacking in reality. As a result, stereotyping or prejudices create conflicting views by magnifying differences between our views and those of others, especially others whom we believe are different from us. Differences may be magnified for many of us when we confront cultures different than our own.

Finally, personal traits or characteristics can lead to conflict. This is especially true of Type A individuals: those who are highly competitive, like to win, are always in a hurry, and are relatively irritable when others interfere with the reaching of goals. Type A individuals, because of their nature, are more likely to get into conflicts than Type B individuals, who are calmer and less irritable about events around them.

So what causes conflict? Conflict does not stem solely from incompatible goals. On the contrary, conflict often results from social factors such as long-standing grudges or resentment, the desire for revenge, inaccurate social perceptions, ineffective communication, and similar factors. Although the major cause of conflict may be incompatible goals, the social and cognitive causes of conflict are also factors to consider.

Does Conflict Have to Be Destructive?

Conflict does *not* have to be destructive. It becomes so when the parties involved are unwilling to negotiate their differences and instead engage in tactics that are harmful and hurtful—a win-at-any-cost approach. Here are some ways in which conflict can be destructive:

- When the resolution of the conflict ends with a winner and a loser
- When the individuals involved act too aggressively, when they withdraw from each other, when they withhold their feelings from each other, or when they accuse each other of causing their problems
- When it prevents us from doing our work or feeling good about ourselves
- When it forces us to do things that we do not want to do
- When the outcome is more important than the relationship

Of course not all relationship breakups are the result of conflict, nor are all relationship breakups necessarily destructive or harmful. However, when conflict results in the termination of relationships and leaves one or both of the parties feeling foolish, inadequate, or angry, it is usually destructive.

When Is Conflict Beneficial?

There is little doubt that most of us see more destructiveness than benefits in conflict. However, not all conflict is that way. Many societies see conflict, including our own, as contradictory in that it can be sometimes good and sometimes bad. When is it appropriate to engage in conflict? The answer to this is confusing to most of us because of the contradictions as to when engaging in conflict can be helpful and when it should be avoided. For example, it is okay to have conflicts over ideas, but to attack someone personally for his or her ideas is not okay. In other words, it is good to have disagreements or conflicting views about ideas, but it is not good to attack individuals' for their ideas because that is what becomes destructive.

Here are some benefits of conflict:

- It can bring out problems that need to be solved.
- It can bring people together to clarify their goals and to look for new ways to do things.
- It can eliminate resentments and help people to understand each other.
- It can bring out creativity in solving our differences.
- It can produce acceptable solutions that allow people to live more in harmony with each other.
- It can help people pay attention to other points of view.
- It can bring new life into a relationship and strengthen it.

Constructive conflict is characterized by a we-orientation, cooperation, and flexibility.[32] When and if possible, it is good to reach a solution that is agreeable to all. This does not mean that we have to feel warm and fuzzy while the differences are worked out, but it does mean that conflicting parties must be willing to negotiate, respect the other party's differences, and cooperate to resolve differences. Constructive conflict can be frustrating and difficult as well as contentious, and it does require competent communicators who are knowledgeable, skillful, sensitive, committed, and ethical in resolving their differences.

What Are Useful Strategies for Conflict Management or Resolution in Interpersonal Relationships?

Because most interpersonal conflicts can be costly in terms of time, stress, energy, and other resources, people who are experiencing conflict generally choose to resolve their differences as quickly as possible especially if they are able to do so. Of course, there are situations in which conflicts are not confronted, and there are also times when conflicts go on for an indefinite period of time, but generally speaking, these are not beneficial to a relationship's growth. Therefore we need to learn how to deal with conflict in ways that will benefit our relationships and us. How we deal with disagreements or conflict can either strengthen a relationship or split it apart. In other words, conflict can be managed well, or it can be managed poorly.

There are many different ways to resolve conflicts. The conflict literature refers mainly to five options: withdrawing, accommodating, forcing, negotiating, and collaboration.[33] Each strategy involves a different outcome, which can be either positive, negative, or both in its effect on relationships that are involved in conflict.

Withdrawing. When we choose to avoid further conflict by either psychologically or physically removing ourselves from the situation, we are withdrawing. Withdrawing can be done in a number of ways, such as changing the topic, cracking jokes, ignoring, or leaving the situation altogether. Usually, when a withdrawal strategy is used, the conflict is temporarily avoided, but it really doesn't go away. Withdrawal is a temporary escape from the conflict, but both parties know that it has not been resolved.

Stonewalling is a powerful form of avoiding conflict.[34] When people exhibit stony silence, refuse to discuss problems, or physically remove themselves from another person who is complaining, disagreeing, or attacking, they are said to be stonewalling. Consider the following discussion:

Melissa: We need to discuss your unwillingness to set a budget. Your use of the credit card is going to bankrupt your father and me.

Tiff: It isn't a problem, and there is nothing to talk about.

Melissa: We have got to talk about it because you are ruining our credit.

Tiff: Get a life, I am not ruining anything. I'll pay you back. [leaves the house]

Tiff is stonewalling by withdrawing from the conflict and claiming that she has everything under control. She believes that to discuss her use of the credit card will only make the conflict between her and her mother worse. Her mother is likely becoming frustrated with Tiff's stonewalling about the use of the credit card. Stonewalling by Tiff can also communicate her disapproval, self-righteousness, indifference, and defensiveness toward her mother.

Research indicates that avoidance is a frequently used way to manage conflict. Most of us want to avoid conflict whenever we can. For example, one research study found that 50 percent of the time, college students used avoiding or withdrawing strategies to keep conflict from escalating.[35] Other research studies have found that when facing conflict men use stonewalling more often than women do because of their fear that they won't be able to control themselves.[36]

The only real advantage to withdrawal is that it gives time for one or both individuals involved in the conflict to think about it and to calm down before again trying to deal with the conflict. The disadvantage is that it can create more hostility and ultimately make dealing with the conflict more difficult in the long run. So withdrawal can be a useful strategy, but it is also limited in its ability to resolve the conflict itself.

Accommodating. A person who uses accommodating as a means for managing or resolving conflicts does not assert his or her own needs but rather prefers to go along to get along. This form of conflict management requires that one person yields or gives in to another person's needs and desires. The accommodator is setting aside his or her concerns in favor of pleasing the other person because holding the relationship together is more important than continuing the conflict. In most situations, when someone accommodates to another to resolve a conflict, the accommodating person gives up and loses, and the other person wins. However, the accommodating person might simply decide that the conflict just isn't worth the stress and the destruction of the relationship, so in a sense it is a win–win situation. Of course, if one person is always accommodating another in a committed relationship, then there is winning and losing.

Accommodation tactics according to Alan Silars and Bill Wilmot, communication scholars, include giving up or giving in, disengagement, denial of needs, or a desire to get along.[37] When a person *gives up or gives in* to the other person, he or she is basically saying, "Have it your way," "I don't want to fight about this," or "Whatever." If the person *disengages,* he or she is saying, "I don't care," "I don't want any part of it," or "I don't have the time to fight about this." If the person *denies* his or her own needs, the person is saying, "I am okay, you go without me" or "I can take care of it, even if I have to stay longer." Finally, if the person is motivated by *desire to get along,* he or she is saying, "It's more important to work together than it is for me to what I want" or "I am unhappy and miserable when we fight. Let's let this go and start over again. I don't even know what we are fighting about."

From an individual satisfaction standpoint, the accommodating strategy requires one person to give up something, whereas the other person achieves something. Although the strategy is appropriate in certain conflict situations, such as whether to go to a basketball game or to the theater, it should be used sparingly because it can have negative effects both on the individuals and on the relationship itself. This is especially true if one side always tends to accommodate the other side to avoid or reduce conflict. When this happens, it is a clear sign that there is a power imbalance in the relationship, which means that the other person is saying, "I have little or no choice." When this occurs, it is a sign of an unhealthy relationship or a relationship that is one-sided.

Forcing. Forcing is a strategy in which one person has power and dominance over another person. It can result in aggression that could include threats, criticisms, hostile remarks and jokes, ridicule, sarcasm, intimidation, fault finding, coercion, or manipulation. Extreme cases of forcing include date rape, child abuse, and sexual harassment. This is a win–lose situation. The person with the power can claim the victory, and the other person loses. However, in this situation, the competition is unfair because one individual has more control and power over the other, which ensures a victory regardless of the virtue of the other person's position.

Consider a relationship in which one person has power or control over the other. It is a relationship that is unequal and can lead to abuse. Of course, there are times when the dominance of one person could serve the relationship, such as in an emergency situation in which a decision has to be made quickly. The essence of force is to pressure others to agree with something so that we get what we want. The more force we use to get others to do what we want or to agree with us, the more likely it is that resentment will increase, leading to more destructive types of conflicts.

Negotiating. Negotiating usually involves a give-and-take process and leads to each party having some satisfaction and some dissatisfaction with the outcome. In other words, "Give a little and get a little." Some people interpret this to be a lose–lose style of conflict management.

In U.S. culture, many of us are led to believe that compromise or negotiation is a good way for both parties in a conflict to resolve their differences. We are told that it is fair for both because it means that both parties win something and both lose something. Thus compromise appears on the surface to be a reasonable approach to conflict and is extremely popular among many individuals, although there are potential problems with it. The most obvious problem is that the quality of the solution might be reduced. This is especially true if one of the parties in the conflict actually had a better solution that had to be compromised in order to reach agreement. Compromise can become an easy way out and might prevent creative new solutions from emerging. In addition, the compromise approach is often not the first choice in personal relationships because it often requires that one or both parties have to give in or give up on what they want.

Despite the negative aspects of negotiating or compromising, it might be the only possible way to approach a conflict. This is most likely true when the parties involved have equal power, if no other alternative is available, if the outcome is not critical, if essential values are not undermined, or if the settlement is only a temporary one until a better solution can be found.

Collaboration. Collaboration is a strategy of conflict management that requires cooperation and mutual respect. It usually involves a problem-solving approach that addresses all the concerns of both parties to arrive at a solution that is mutually satisfying. It is a "we" rather than a "me" approach to negotiation. It might require extra effort by both parties because more resources and considerations of new options that meet the approval of both parties might be needed.

For collaboration to work as a strategy, both parties must recognize that there is a conflict, and they must want to find creative ways to resolve their differences. When both parties recognize that a conflict exists, they usually engage in some sort of confrontation, which is the opposite of avoidance. There are different degrees of confrontation, ranging from the very violent (often depicted in the media) to the respectful. For collaboration to be successful, both parties must be willing to resolve their differences, treat each other as equals, be honest and open in their differences, be empathetic toward each other, and be willing to listen to each other's points of view.

The collaboration strategy is considered a win–win situation for both sides in the conflict. Both sides believe that they have accomplished or gained something from the solution because of their willingness to listen to each other concerning the issues. In addition, when both parties believe that

Making Connections

Conflict Online

Conflict can occur just as easily online as it does in face-to-face communication. Some people believe that there is a tendency to communicate more forcefully and directly via the computer than in face-to-face interactions. Thus, rather than resolving conflicts or differences, the conflicts tend to escalate more readily over the computer.

1. Why do you think conflict occurs so easily online?
2. What can you do to reduce online conflicts?
3. Create a guide to improving online communication etiquette. What advice would you give in your guide to others to reduce or prevent online conflicts?

For help, do an Internet search using the key words "online etiquette."

Making Connections

Deception in a Relationship

I (Darin) have always been a little concerned about Oliva—she is such a charmer. She told me that she was through with Aaron, her old boyfriend. We began sleeping together, spending a couple of nights plus weekends together at each other's places. Then a friend of mine told me that she saw Oliva with her "ex," and it didn't look as if they had parted ways. My friend also said that Oliva and her "ex" appeared to be intensely involved with each other. I saw Oliva today, and she didn't act differently. In fact, she acted as if everything was the same.

1. What do you think you would do in this situation?
2. What would you tell Darin to do?
3. What does a situation like this one do to a relationship?
4. Is there anything that Oliva can do to explain her behavior to Darin?
5. Are there any considerations that Darin should take into account before he jumps to conclusions?

Learning Connections

1. Explain the three commonly identified dialectical tensions, and provide examples for each from your own experiences.
2. Which strategy for managing relational tensions would you most likely use? Why?
3. Define *conflict* in your own words.
4. What are the positive effects of conflict on relationships? Explain.
5. Describe in your own words the best way to resolve conflict in personal relationships.

they have had the opportunity to voice their opinions and they have agreed in good faith to settle the dispute, it truly is a win–win situation. The collaboration strategy to manage conflict is the best strategy for a relationship, because it shows that each party cares about the other's well-being and interests. According to Wilmot and Hocker, collaborating, as a conflict management style, produces consistently positive outcomes that leave the participants satisfied with their decisions, the process, and the growth that occurs in their interpersonal relationship.[38]

Many scholars agree that conflict is inevitable in all relationships and that conflict need not be destructive. Conflict often produces stronger and more durable relationships. Conflict in itself should be considered not negative or destructive but a natural part of any relationship.

Signs That Show a Relationship Is in Trouble

Before we concede that a relationship is over, certain warning signs as well as some possible repair strategies might help to prevent its dissolution.

Aggressive Behavior. A preliminary warning sign that a relationship is heading toward trouble is when one of the parties becomes a little too aggressive by aiming hurtful communication at the other party. All of us, at one time or another, say something that we wished we hadn't said to someone about whom we care. However, whether intentionally or not, when people communicate hurtful statements to one another with increasing frequency, it is a possible sign that their relationship is in trouble.

Lies. Another warning sign that a relationship is in trouble is when one person deceives another by lying about something. Whether the lie is significant or trivial, it weakens the relationship's foundation, which is trust. Most of the time acts of deception have consequences that people don't fully consider when justifying their reasons for lying. You can probably think of many such consequences not only for the person being deceived but also for the deceiver. A relationship built on deceit is not likely to succeed for very long.

Betrayal. Another warning sign that a relationship is in trouble is betrayal. Betrayal can happen when someone trusts another person and, in one way or another, that trust is broken. For example, if you tell a friend a personal secret and especially ask for complete confidentiality and the friend then spreads the story to others, you have been betrayed. Deception and betrayal are similar; in fact, they are almost synonymous. The difference is that betrayal violates a confidence and an agreed-on expectation. Some common examples of betrayal include extramarital affairs, gossip, and harmful criticism behind someone's back.

Relationships that are injured by deception and betrayal are often not repairable because of the amount of hurt such breaches of trust cause. However, situations such as arguments that have gotten out of hand or misunderstandings can often be corrected or resolved. In these cases, competent communication can help repair and possibly save the relationship.

Relational Repair Strategies

For situations in which both parties want to preserve the relationship, Duck has suggested the following repair tactics:

- Engage in more open and honest communication, and exhibit a willingness to listen to the other person with an open mind.
- Be willing to bring out the other person's positive side.
- Evaluate the potential rewards and costs for keeping the relationship together versus the rewards and costs for changing or ending it.
- Seek out the support of others to help keep the relationship together.
- Both parties must be willing to focus on the positive aspects of their relationship.
- Both parties must be willing to reinterpret the other's behaviors as positive and well intentioned.
- Both parties have to be willing to reduce negativity and try to keep a balanced perspective.[39]

Repairing relationships requires cooperation and mutual agreement; both parties must want to keep the relationship together in order to solve their differences. It also requires effective interpersonal communication.

Improving Communication Competence in Relationships

The goal of this book is to encourage readers to become competent communicators. Communication scholars Brent Burleson and Wendy Samter describe the following interpersonal skills as important in developing and maintaining relationships:

conversational skill (the ability to initiate, maintain, and terminate enjoyable casual conversations), *referential skill* (the ability to convey information clearly and unambiguously), *ego supportive skill* (the ability to make another person feel good about himself or herself), *comforting skill* (the ability to make others feel better when depressed, sad, or upset), *persuasive skill* (the ability to get people to modify their thoughts and behaviors), *narrative skill* (the ability to entertain through jokes, gossip, stories, etc.), and *regulations* (the ability to help someone who has violated a norm to fix the mistake effectively).[40] How would you rate yourself on each of the above communication skills? Most of us would likely rate ourselves as pretty good at using most of skills, but we would also likely say that we could be better at each of them.

In the remainder of this chapter, we are going to provide you with some suggestions that should help you to become a more competent communicator. By this point, you probably agree that effective communicators share the following characteristics:

1. Effective communicators address issues clearly and try to avoid ambiguous or abstract statements.
2. Effective communicators are likely to treat others with respect and therefore would not deliberately yell abuses or throw temper tantrums.
3. Effective communicators know that the use of praise, making the other person feel special, and telling them what they want to hear will most likely produce desired responses.[41]

At first glance, these statements make a lot of sense. However, each of us can probably think of times when being a little abstract or ambiguous was better than being too clear or direct in our communication. In certain situations, getting angry or throwing a tantrum might be appropriate to get across a point. It sometimes boils down to the difference between being honest and being brutally frank—being brutal never facilitates communication. Finally, you can probably also think of situations in which too much praise or too much agreement can lead to mistrust. Interpersonal situations often require a variety of communication strategies, some of which may violate expected norms. Although we are not endorsing unethical behaviors, disrespect, or rudeness, some situations demand unusual strategies.

The following section offers a variety of behaviors and actions that can improve interpersonal communication.

Establish Supportive and Caring Relationships

Establishing supportive and caring relationships is important to our well-being, and this process is generally easier when communication is both positive and supportive.[42] In other words, as the old cliché goes, "If you can't say something nice, don't say anything at all." One research study discusses romantic actions and verbal and nonverbal assurances that may affect commitment and satisfaction in relationships.[43] Positive strategies for romantic exchanges include the following:

1. Act cheerful and positive when talking to the other.
2. Do favors for the other, or help with tasks.
3. Initiate celebrations of special events from your shared past, such as the first time you met.

4. Do things to surprise the other person.
5. Suggest that you go out to eat together at a favorite or special restaurant.
6. Create a romantic environment, perhaps with candlelight and flowers.
7. Give the other person items of sentimental value, such as gifts or cards.
8. Suggest ways to spend time doing things together.

Assurances include the following verbal and nonverbal actions:

1. Physically display affection through kisses and hugs.
2. Express aloud to the other person what it would be like without him or her.
3. Reminisce aloud with the other about good times you have had together in the past.
4. Say "I love you."
5. Express long-term commitment to the relationship.
6. Act in playful ways toward the other person.

The research findings suggest that engaging in behaviors such as these do increase relationship commitment and satisfaction. However, it is interesting that females were more likely than males to report use of assurance and romance strategies, which suggests that females tend to undertake more relationship maintenance activity than their male partners do.

Nurture a Supportive Environment

Positive and supportive communication occurs in environments that are caring, open, flexible, warm, animated, and receptive. In such environments, communication is constructive and centers on the individuals and their relationship. Here are some descriptions of how people feel when constructive communication is at the center of their relationship.[44]

I feel that I can talk and that there is someone who will listen to me.
I feel accepted and supported.
I feel there is a willingness to see my point of view.
I don't feel a need or pressure to change—I am accepted for who I am.
I don't feel that I am constantly being judged or evaluated.
I feel that I am trusted.
I feel that I am treated with respect as a person.
I feel that I am treated fairly.
I feel good about myself and about us.
I feel like a responsible person.
I feel that I have control over myself.
I feel that someone is interested in me and cares about me.
I don't feel as if I have to justify everything that I do.

One of the most effective and constructive means of demonstrating care and support for someone is to invite more communication.

Invite More Communication

Many of us listen to others express their feelings and then immediately express our own. This gives the impression that we do not even acknowledge the other person's existence, let alone what he or she has said. In contrast, skilled and caring communicators usually do not respond immediately with ideas, judgments, or feelings that express their own views. Instead, they invite others to express more of their thoughts by responding with noncommittal responses such as these:

Interesting.
Uh-huh.
You did, huh.
I see.
Oh.
Really?

Or they might be more direct in asking the other person to continue, saying, for example,

That's interesting. Go on.
Tell me about it.
Let's discuss it.
Tell me everything.
I understand. What else happened?

Such invitations to talk can contribute much to the development of a meaningful relationship. The willingness to listen and reserve judgment creates a positive and supportive environment that, in effect, tells people they are valuable, they are loved, and they have control over their own behavior.

Learning Connections

1. How would you describe deception and its effects on a relationship?
2. A good friend has come to you because the relationship that he is in has been falling apart. Your friend, however, does not want to end the relationship with the other person. What action steps would you recommend to help your friend repair the relationship?
3. What does a supporting and caring relationship mean to you?

Summary

In our everyday lives, we are enormously influenced by first impressions and often tend to make snap judgments about people and form instant likes and dislikes. Interpersonal attraction, which includes physical attractiveness, personality, rewards, proximity, and similarities all play a significant role in our desire to interact with others. Relationships, whether existing for a moment or for a lifetime, go through a series of stages of development and deterioration. There are five stages of coming together and five stages of coming apart. All relationships move through at least some of these stages but might not move through them in the same order or with the same intensity.

There are three reasons for the complex and continuous process of coming together and coming apart: Each stage provides information for the next, each stage helps to predict what might or might not occur in the next stage, and skipping a stage can create risk and uncertainty in a relationship. The phases of dissolving a relationship involve a complex decision-making process that does not always follow a specific series of stages. Breakups often occur sporadically, inconsistently, and with uncertainty over a period of time.

Relationships are often messy, and even the most stable seem to go through various pushes and pulls, which can create tensions between partners. There are three dialectical tensions commonly mentioned in the research that describes the pushes and pulls: connection–autonomy, openness–closedness, and novelty–predictability.

Conflict is inevitable in all relationships. It is an expressed struggle between incompatible goals, scarce resources, and interference from others in achieving goals. Conflict is also caused by social factors that include faulty attributions and faulty communication. Managing conflict is not easy; in fact, resolving conflicts requires the use of a variety of strategies, including withdrawing, accommodating, forcing, negotiating, and collaboration.

There are signs that show a relationship is in trouble. They include aggressive behavior, deception, and betrayal. To help repair and possibly save relationships, competent communicators know how to use repair strategies and effective interpersonal communication. In a positive and supportive environment, communication between individuals usually reflects caring, openness, flexibility, warmth, animation, and receptivity. The best way to develop and maintain relationships is to invite more communication.

DISCUSSION STARTERS

1. In your opinion, what elements play the strongest role in the development of relationships? Explain.
2. What did you agree with and disagree with in the explanation of the stages of relationship development?
3. Compare and contrast Knapp's coming-apart stages with Duck's dissolution stages.
4. Describe what it takes to have a lasting relationship.
5. What happens when a relationship begins to come apart?
6. In what ways can conflict be constructive? Destructive?
7. What advice would you give to someone who wanted to improve his or her interpersonal communication?
8. What does it mean to be a competent interpersonal communicator?

NOTES

1. J. C. McCroskey and T. A. McCain, "The Measurement of Interpersonal Attraction," *Speech Monographs* 41 (1974): 261–66.
2. S. M. Andersen and A. Baum, "Transference in Interpersonal Relations: Influences and Affect Based on Significant Representations," *Journal of Personality* 62 (1994): 459–97.
3. M. A. Collins and L. A. Zebrowitz, "The Contributions of Appearance to Occupational Outcomes in Civilian and Military Settings," *Journal of Applied Social Psychology* 25 (1995): 129–63.
4. S. Sprecher and S. W. Duck, "Sweet Talk: The Importance of Perceived Communication for Romantic and Friendship Attraction Experienced during a

Get-Acquainted Date," *Personality and Social Psychology Bulletin* 20 (1994): 391–400.
5. T. F. Cash and R. N. Kicullen, "The Aye of the Beholder: Susceptibility to Sexism and Beautyism in the Evaluation of Managerial Applicants," *Journal of Applied Social Psychology* 15 (1985): 591–605; V. S. Folkes, "Forming Relationships and the Matching Hypothesis," *Journal of Personality and Social Psychology* 8 (1982): 631–36; E. Hatfield and S. Sprecher, *Mirror, Mirror... The Importance of Looks in Everyday Life* (Albany, N.Y.: SUNY Press, 1986); Collins and Zebrowitz; Sprecher and Duck; D. Plesser-Storr, "Self-Presentation by Men to Attractive and Unattractive Women: Tactics of Ingratiation, Blasting, and Basking" (Ph.D. diss., State University of New York at Albany, 1995); and A. Feingold, "Good-Looking People Are Not What We Think: An Integration of the Experimental Literature on Physical Attractiveness Stereotyping with the Literature on Correlates of Physical Attractiveness" (unpublished manuscript, Yale University, New Haven, Conn., 1990).
6. M. R. Cunningham, A. R. Roberts, C. H. Wu, A. P. Barbee, and P. B. Druen, " 'Their Ideas of Beauty Are, on the Whole, the Same as Ours': Consistency and Variability in the Cross-Cultural Perception of Female Attractiveness," *Journal of Personality and Social Psychology* 68 (1995): 261–79; and L. Banner, *American Beauty* (New York: Knopf, 1983).
7. W. M. Bernstein, B. O. Stephenson, M. L. Snyder, and R. A. Wicklund, "Causal Ambiguity and Heterosexual Affiliation," *Journal of Experimental Social Psychology* 19 (1983): 78–92; K. H. Price and S. G. Vandenberg, "Matching for Physical Attractiveness in Married Couples," *Personality and Social Psychology* 5 (1979): 398–400; and M. Lea, "Factors Underlying Friendship: An Analysis of Responses on the Acquaintance Description Form in Relation to Wright's Friendship Model," *Journal of Social and Personal Relationships* 6 (1989): 275–92.
8. K. Deaux and R. Hanna, "Courtship in the Personal Column: The Influence of Gender and Sexual Orientation," *Sex Roles* 11 (1984): 363–75.
9. H. R. Baize Jr. and J. E. Schroeder, "Personality and Mate Selection in Personal Ads: Evolutionary Preferences in a Public Mate Selection Process," *Journal of Social Behavior and Personality* 10 (1995): 517–36.
10. L. Mealey, "Bulking Up: The Roles of Sex and Sexual Orientation on Attempts to Manipulate Physical Attractiveness," *Journal of Sex Research* 34 (1997): 223–28.
11. M. R. Parks and K. Floyd, "Making Friends in Cyberspace," *Journal of Communication* 45 (1996): 84.
12. Ibid.
13. Ibid., 85.
14. M. Knapp, *Social Intercourse: From Greeting to Good-Bye* (Boston: Allyn and Bacon, 1978), 3–28.
15. M. L. Knapp and A. L. Vangelisti, *Interpersonal Communication and Human Relationship,* 4th ed. (Boston: Allyn and Bacon, 2000), 38.
16. D. P. McWhirter and A. M. Mattison, *The Male Couple* (Englewood Cliffs, N.J.: Prentice-Hall, 1984).
17. Knapp and Vangelisti, 39–44.
18. Ibid., 40–45.
19. M. L. Knapp, R. P. Hart, G. W. Friedrich, and G. M. Shulman, "The Rhetoric of Goodbye: Verbal and Nonverbal Correlates of Human Leave-Taking," *Speech Monographs* 40 (1973): 182–98.
20. Knapp and Vangelisti, 58–62.
21. S. W. Duck, ed., *Personal Relationships 4: Dissolving Personal Relationships* (London: Academic Press, 1982); L. A. Baxter, "Accomplishing Relationship Disengagement," in *Understanding Personal Relationships: An Interdisciplinary Approach,* eds. S. W. Duck and D. Perlman (Beverly Hills, Calif.: Sage, 1985), 243–66; S. W. Duck, *Human Relationships: An Introduction to Social Psychology* (Beverly Hills, Calif.: Sage, 1986); and S. Duck, "A Topography of Relationships Disengagement and Dissolution," in *Personal Relationships,* ed. S. Duck (London: Academic Press, 1982), 1–30.
22. K. A. Sorenson, S. M. Russel, D. J. Harkness, and J. H. Harvey, "Account-Making, Confiding, and Coping with the Ending of a Close Relationship," *Journal of Social Behavior and Personality* 8 (1993): 73–86.
23. L. A. Baxter, "Trajectories of Relationships Disengagement," *Journal of Social and Personal Relationship* 1 (1984): 29–48; and L. A. Baxter, "Strategies for Ending Relationship: Two Studies," *Western Journal of Speech Communication* 46 (1982): 223–41.
24. L. A. Baxter and B. Montgomery, *Relation: Dialogues and Dialect* (New York: Guilford, 1996).
25. J. T. Wood, "Dilectical Theory," in *Making Connections: Readings in Relational Communication,* 2nd ed., eds. Kathleen M. Galvin and Pamela J. Cooper (Los Angeles, Calif.: Roxbury, 2000), 132–38; L. A. Baxter, "Dialectical Contradictions in Relationship Development," *Journal of Social and Personal Relationships* 7 (1990): 69–88; and L. A. Baxter, "Thinking Dialogically About Communication in Interpersonal Relationships," in *Structure in Human Communication,* ed. R. Conville (Westport, Conn.: Greenwood, 1994).
26. Baxter and Montgomery, 185–206.
27. L. A. Baxter, "Dialectical Contradictions in Relationship Development," *Journal of Social and Personal Relationships* 7 (1990): 69–88.
28. W. Wilmot and J. Hocker, *Interpersonal Conflict,* 6th ed. (New York: McGraw-Hill, 2001), 41.

29. Ibid., 14.
30. C. K. W. DeDreu and P. A. M. Van Lang, "Impact of Social Value Orientation on Negotiator Cognition and Behavior," *Personality and Social Psychology Bulletin* 21 (1995): 1178–88; and D. Tjosvold and C. DeDreu, "Managing Conflict in Dutch Organizations: A Test of the Relevance of Deutsch's Co-operation Theory," *Journal of Applied Social Psychology* 27 (1997): 2213–27.
31. R. A. Baron, "Attributions and Organizational Conflict," in *Attribution Theory: Applications to Achievement, Mental Health, and Interpersonal Conflict,* eds. S. Graha and V. Folkes (Hillsdale, N.J.: Erlbaum, 1990), 185–204; and R. Cropanzano, ed., *Justice in the Workplace* (Hillsdale, N.J.: Erlbaum, 1993), 79–103.
32. W. Wilmot and J. Hocker (2001), 94, 173–76.
33. A. C. Filley, *Interpersonal Conflict Resolution* (Glenview, Il.: Scott, Foresman, 1975); D. D. Cahn, "Intimate in Conflict: A Research Review," in *Intimates in Conflict: A Communication Perspective,* ed. D. D. Cahn (Hillsdale, N.J.: Erlbaum, 1990), 1–24; W. W. Cupach and D. J. Canary, *Competence in Interpersonal Conflict* (New York: McGraw-Hill, 1997); and R. Blake and J. Mouton, *The Managerial Grid* (Houston: Gulf Publishing, 1964).
34. A. L. Sillars, S. G. Coletti, D. Parry, and M. A. Rogers, "Coding Verbal Conflict Tactics: Nonverbal and Perceptual Correlates of the 'Avoidance–Distributive–Integrative' Distinction," *Human Communication Research* 9 (1982): 83–95.
35. J. Gottman and S. Carrere, "Why Can't Men and Women Get Along? Developmental Notes and Marital Inequities," in *Communication Relational Maintenance,* eds. D. Canary and L. Stafford (New York: Academic Press, 1994).
36. J. Gottman, *Why Marriages Succeed and Fail: And How You Can Make Yours Last* (New York: Simon and Schuster, 1994); and J. Gottman, *The Marriage Clinic: A Scientifically Based Marital Therapy* (New York: Norton, 1999).
37. A. L. Sillars and W. W. Wilmot, "Communication Strategies in Conflict and Mediation," in *Communicating Strategically: Strategies in Interpersonal Communication,* eds. J. Wiemann and J. A. Daly (Hillsdale, N.J.: Erlbaum, 1994), 163–190.
38. W. Wilmot and J. Hocker (2001), 237.
39. S. W. Duck, "A Perspective on the Repair of Personal Relationships: Repair of What, When?" in *Personal Relationships 5: Repairing Personal Relationships,* ed. S. W. Duck (New York: Macmillan, 1984).
40. B. R. Burleson and W. Samter, "Effects of Cognitive Complexity on the Perceived Importance of Communication Skills in Friends," *Communication Research* 17 (1990): 165–82; W. Samter and B. R. Burleson, "Evaluations of Communication Skills as Predictors of Peer Acceptance in a Group Living Situation," *Communication Studies* 41 (1990): 311–26; B. R. Burleson, J. G. Delia, and J. L. Applegate, "The Socialization of Person-Centered Communication: Parent's Contributions to Their Children's' Social-Cognitive and Communication Skills," in *Explaining Family Interactions,* eds. M. A. Fitzpatrick and A. L. Vangelisti (Thousand Oaks, Calif.: Sage, 1995), 34–76.
41. Knapp and Vangelisti, (2000), 400.
42. J. M. Reisman, "Friendliness and Its Correlates," *Journal of Social and Clinical Psychology* 2 (1984): 143–55.
43. E. P. Simon and L. A. Baxter, "Attachment-Style Differences in Relationship Maintenance Strategies," *Western Journal of Communication* 57 (fall 1993): 416–30.
44. Ideas for this section are derived from a Parent Effectiveness Training workshop and from T. Gordon, *Parent Effectiveness Training* (New York: Wyden, 1970).

"Never doubt that a small group of thoughtful, committed citizens can change the world; indeed, it's the only thing that ever does."

—Margaret Mead

CHAPTER 15

Group and Team Communication

THIS CHAPTER WILL HELP YOU:

- Make the connection between group communication and other types of communication discussed in previous chapters.
- Explain what a group is and what it is not and understand the importance of groups in our lives.
- Distinguish between primary and secondary groups and their purposes.
- Learn to perform more effectively in special types of groups, such as project teams, work teams, and focus groups.
- Avoid the disadvantages and limitations of group communication.
- Ensure that members of groups that you participate in are ethical.
- Utilize technology to communicate effectively in groups.

CASE STUDY

The class assignment is over, and group X has accomplished its goal. Each member is satisfied not only with his or her contributions but also with the group's accomplishments. Group X's meetings ran smoothly, and little if any time was wasted in reaching the goal.

Group Y obtained the same goal as group X, but no one is satisfied with what was achieved or with the group experience itself. In fact, group Y's members feel that the assignment was a complete waste of their time. Group Y's members disliked the assignment and indicated that they learned little or nothing about group communication.

Questions to think about

1. What do you think might have caused the differences in the outcomes of the two groups?
2. What communication skills and behaviors are necessary for effective groups?
3. On a 1 to 7 scale, with 1 being inadequate and 7 being excellent, assess your group communication skills. Assess your leadership skills. What are your strengths and what are the areas in which you need to improve?
4. What is it that effective group members do that ineffective group members do not?
5. What is it that effective group leaders do that ineffective group leaders do not?

The answers to the above questions illustrate that many variables contribute to a group's success or failure. No two groups will produce identical results, because no two groups are identical in makeup. Furthermore, prior success cannot guarantee that a group will produce similarly successful results. Nonetheless, understanding key principles and factors along with improving your competencies as a group member or group leader can increase the chances for achieving personal satisfaction and group success.

This chapter explains how group members communicate, what a small group is, the different purposes that groups can serve, the characteristics that are common to small groups, the disadvantages of groups, how gender differences affect group communication, the importance of ethical behavior in groups, and how groups can use technology effectively. Chapter 16 explores leadership, member participation, problem solving and decision making, conflict management, and group performance evaluation.

Small-Group Communication: Making the Connection

Effective communication is one of the major factors that influence whether a group experience is successful and satisfying. Small-group communication does differ from other types of communication in that it requires a variety of communication skills and must include at least three interacting people. By contrast, interviewing and interpersonal communication usually involve only two people interacting, whereas public speaking involves one person speaking and many listeners. However, interviewing, interpersonal communication, and presentational skills are all necessary for effective group communication to occur, whatever the size of the group. For example, the ability to ask effective questions, deal with interpersonal relationships, resolve conflicts, and present one's ideas as well as listening skills are important in communicating with groups. In addition, constructive group communication requires that the group members respect one another, speak clearly, provide credible information, support each other, foster a positive climate, challenge each others' ideas and positions, persuade each other, resolve conflicts, listen effectively, and hold high ethical standards.

Making Connections

Group Satisfaction

The case study at the beginning of the chapter describes two groups—group X and group Y—and the members' levels of satisfaction with their respective groups.

1. What do you think groups should do to ensure member satisfaction?
2. What did you learn from the case study about group communication?
3. Discuss in class your most recent group experience. What did you like about it? What didn't you like about it?

If each of us would stop to list the times we have participated in groups during the past month, we would have evidence of how common our group participation is in our lives. The family is probably the predominant small group. However, if you are like most, you have participated in many groups, some small and some large, during the past month alone. When we associate with other people and discuss common issues or problems, we are involved in group communication.

Small-group communication involves the exchange of information among a relatively small number of people, ideally five to seven, who share a common purpose, such as solving a problem, making a decision, or sharing information. Effective group communication requires a communication style that is honest, flexible, assertive, enthusiastic, and tolerant of others. Effective group members recognize the importance of all group members' input and want to ensure that everyone has an opportunity to participate. They are not only willing to listen to others, but also are willing to discuss ideas and issues whether they agree or disagree with them. Our primary focus in this chapter and the next is small groups, so we will not include much information about large public discussion group presentations such as symposiums, which are not discussions but a series of brief speeches related to a central topic, or panels, which are discussions involving specialists or well-informed people who share their views on a common topic for the benefit of an audience. Nor will we include the comprehensive study of group dynamics.

What Is a Group?

A group is not simply a collection of people gathered in the same place. To qualify as a group, the people must be related in six ways:

1. *Perceptions:* Do the members make an impression on one another?
2. *Motivation:* Are there rewards for being together?
3. *Goals:* Do the members have a common purpose?
4. *Organization:* Does each person have some role or task?
5. *Interdependence:* Must each person depend on the others for his or her efforts to be successful?
6. *Interaction:* Is the number of persons small enough so that each person can communicate with every other person?[1]

The crew team is a specialized group characterized by close-knit, interdependent relationships and made up of people with different complementary abilities and a strong sense of group identity.

For our purposes, we define a **group** as a collection of individuals who influence one another, have a common purpose, take on roles, are interdependent, and interact together. If any element is not included, what exists is a collection of independent people, not a group. People standing at a corner waiting for a bus, for example, meet some of the criteria of a group. They have a common purpose (transportation), they may interact, and they may make an impression on one another. But they do not constitute a group according to our definition because they are not interdependent, and they do not take on roles. They do share certain basic goals, such as getting to a destination safely. But they don't expect to interact in the future and usually don't perceive themselves as part of a group—unless some type of emergency occurred, which would change their status radically. Deciding whether a collection of persons constitutes a true group is a complex matter.

Group Formation: Why Do People Join Groups?

Take a moment to think about all the groups to which you belong: student organizations, clubs, religious groups, social groups, work groups, informal groups of friends. Why did you join them in the first place? It doesn't take a scholar to tell you that people join groups for many reasons, and your reasons are probably similar to those that motivate others to join groups. Paul Paulus, a social psychologist, suggests that at least five common reasons explain why people join groups:

1. Groups help to satisfy important psychological and social needs, such as the need for attention and affection or the need to belong. Imagine what it would be like to be absolutely alone, in total isolation from others. Very few of us find such a prospect appealing.
2. Group membership helps people achieve goals that otherwise might not be accomplished. Groups make it easier to perform certain tasks, solve difficult problems, and make complex decisions that might overwhelm one individual.
3. Group membership can provide multiple sources of information and knowledge that might not be available to one individual.
4. Groups can help to meet the need for security. The old saying that there is safety in numbers rings true in many situations; belonging to groups can provide protection and security against common enemies. For example, people join neighborhood watch groups to protect themselves from criminal activity.
5. Group membership can also contribute to an individual's positive social identity—it becomes part of a person's self-concept (see Chapter 3). Of course, the more prestigious and restrictive the groups are to which a person is admitted, the more the self-concept is bolstered.[2]

group
A collection of individuals who influence one another, have a common purpose, take on roles, are interdependent, and interact together.

Cultural factors such as individualistic or collective orientations can have a profound effect on how people perceive groups and group activities. All cultures vary in the degree to which they emphasize individualism and collectivism. If you hold an individualistic orientation, you tend to stress self or personal goals and achievements over group goals and achievements.[3] Individualist cultures have an "I" consciousness and a tendency to focus on individual accomplishments.[4] That is, they are more likely

Know Your Scholar

Carolyn Calloway-Thomas *Indiana University*

Carolyn Calloway-Thomas is Associate Professor of Communication and Culture at Indiana University. A former Ford Fellow and Fulbright and Carnegie Scholar, she is co-author of *Intercultural Communication: Roots and Routes* and co-editor of *Martin Luther King, Jr. and the Sermonic Power of Public Discourse.* In 2000, she was the recipient of the National Communication Association's Robert J. Kibler Award. The Kibler Award recognizes individuals for their dedication to excellence and commitment to the profession.

Calloway-Thomas's work explores dimensions of African American rhetoric and intercultural communication. In her research on African American communication, Calloway-Thomas examines the space between the rhetorical practices of African Americans and the landscape of African American orality. She is keen to understand the rhetorical features of an African American oral tradition and how such features can serve as means for understanding traditional forms of rhetorical discourse. Drawing on the speeches and writings of Martin Luther King, Jr., W. E. B. DuBois, T. Thomas Fortune, and others, her research helps us to understand some of the basic assumptions that African Americans have about their culture.

to depend on themselves and have less commitment to group membership. For example, most North Americans value self-help, self-sufficiency, self-actualization, and personal achievements. According to Carolyn Calloway-Thomas, Pamela Cooper, and Cecil Blake, the United States, Canada, Australia, the Netherlands, and New Zealand are nations that tend to foster and celebrate individual accomplishments.[5] Generally, people who have individualistic perspectives find working in groups more challenging and often frustrating.

If you hold a collectivistic orientation, which is more predominant in Asian and Latin American countries such as Japan, China, Taiwan, Pakistan, Colombia, Guatemala, and Panama, you are more likely to put aside your individual goals for the well-being of the group.[6] Collectivist cultures have a "we" consciousness and a tendency to focus on group or team accomplishments. They also have a propensity toward working in groups and find group work to be very rewarding and satisfying. No culture, however, is entirely individualist or collectivist. All cultures comprise a mix of individualism and collectivism, but usually one or the other dominates.[7]

How you contribute to a group may depend on whether you have an individualistic or collectivistic orientation. These two perspectives have implications for group formation and collaboration. See Table 15.1 for a comparison of individualistic and collectivistic approaches to joining and working in groups or teams.

Another force that brings people together to form groups is a *common goal.* Examples of common goals include protesting a change in dormitory visitation rules, fighting a road expansion into a neighborhood, lobbying for a safer community, supporting a charity, or working for equal campus access for physically impaired students. The goal itself draws people into a group, even though their approaches to the goal may differ.

Learning Connections

1. Describe a competent group participant.
2. What is the difference between a group and a collection of people?
3. Why do people join groups?
4. Compare the ways in which people from individualistic and collectivist cultures approach working in groups.

TABLE 15.1

Individualist and Collectivist Orientations: A Comparison of Small Groups

INDIVIDUALIST ASSUMPTIONS	COLLECTIVISTIC ASSUMPTIONS
Individuals make better decisions than groups do.	The group's decision should supersede individual decisions.
Leaders and not the group members should do the planning.	The group should do the planning.
Individuals should be rewarded for their performance.	Reward and recognition should be shared among group members.
Competition among individual group members is good.	Teamwork is more important than competition.
The best way to get things done is to work with individuals as opposed to an entire group.	The group is the best way to accomplish goals.
Groups or teams are often perceived as a waste of time.	The commitment to the group is strongest when the group reaches consensus.

Adapted from S. A. Beebe and J. M. Masterson, *Communicating in Small Groups,* 7th ed. (Boston: Allyn and Bacon, 2003), 20; and J. Mole, *Mind Your Manner: Managing Business Cultures in Europe* (London: Nicholas Brealey Publishing Limited, 1995).

People also avoid joining groups at times. Groups are sometimes perceived as ineffective and time-consuming; they require much work yet accomplish little. The most frequent complaint from students regarding groups is that groups are a waste of time. It is our hope that this chapter and the next will reduce the effect of negative experiences you might have had in the past and encourage you to participate actively in future group situations.

Types and Purposes of Small Groups

So far, you have read about what a group is and is not and why people join groups, as well as the role communication plays in groups. It is also important to understand the types of groups and why they are formed. There are two major categories of small groups: *primary* and *secondary.* Each serves different human needs, but characteristics of each are found in almost every group in which we participate.

Primary Groups

primary group
A group that focuses on social and interpersonal relationships.

Primary groups focus on social or interpersonal relationships among members and exist primarily to satisfy what are labeled primary needs such as those we discussed in Chapter 13: the need for inclusion (belonging) and affection (esteem, likeability, love). Primary groups are usually long-term and include family, roommates, friends who meet to socialize, co-workers sharing time off together, and other groups of friends who might share vacations, card games, and so on. The groups might at times make decisions, solve problems, or take on a particular task, but their main purpose is to socialize, support one another, chat about a variety of topics, let off steam, and enjoy each other's company.

Communication scholars Robert Harnack, Thorrel Fest, and Barbara Jones have identified two main categories of social reasons for participating in primary groups outside of the family group: socialization and catharsis.[8]

Socialization. We often engage in small-group communication when socializing with others, such as at parties or at any event where people share time and conversation. When we gather in small groups for social purposes, our goals are to strengthen our interpersonal relationships and to promote our own well-being. Such groups fulfill our interpersonal needs for inclusion and affection.

Catharsis. Small-group communication allows us to vent our emotions, including frustrations, fears, and gripes, as well as hopes and desires. When we have a chance to let others know how we feel about something, we often experience catharsis, or a release from tension. This purpose is usually accomplished in the supportive atmosphere of bull sessions or family discussions, where self-disclosure is appropriate. Cathartic group communication tends to focus on personal problems rather than on interpersonal needs.

The main purpose of the primary group is member enjoyment and one another's companionship and support. Primary groups are not the main focus of this and the next chapter; typically, primary groups are studied in sociology, psychology, and interpersonal communication courses. Primary groups are at the heart of interpersonal communication, and they are important to understanding small-group communication in general.[9]

Secondary Groups

Secondary groups, which will be the main focus of this and the next chapter, exist to accomplish tasks or achieve goals. They are formed for the purpose of doing work such as a class assignment, solving a problem, or making a decision. Members join together to enable themselves to exert power over their situation and others. The main reason for secondary groups is to get something done, but they can also help members achieve their primary needs for socialization and affection. Secondary groups include a variety of types of groups: decision making, problem solving, committees, learning and information sharing, and therapy or personal growth (see Table 15.2).[10]

Decision Making. People come together in groups to make decisions on issues such as deciding which spring vacation trip to take, where to hold a dance, which play to stage, or which computer is the most practical for their needs. It is not unusual for groups to vote on such issues to determine the group's decision. Voting is done especially when there is no clear agreement as to which decision is most acceptable to the group members. When voting, groups usually accept the majority's position. Discussing alternatives with others helps people to decide which choice is the best not only for themselves but for the group as a whole. In addition, when everyone in the group participates in the decision-making process, all are more likely to accept the

secondary group
A group that exists to accomplish tasks or achieve goals.

TABLE 15.2

Types and Purposes of Small Groups

GROUP TYPE	GROUP PURPOSE	EXAMPLES
Primary	To fill basic needs of inclusion and affection with others	Family Close friends Co-workers Neighbors
Secondary	To accomplish a task or achieve a goal	Decision making Problem solving Committee Learning group Therapy group

final outcome and to help carry it out. Most of us resent being told what to do; we are more tolerant of a decision if we helped to shape it.

A classic research study demonstrated the value of group decision making. The study focused on a garment factory where managers had always made decisions without seeking input from their workers. The managers decided to update some of their production techniques, but the workers were resisting the changes. To analyze the problem, an experiment was set up in which workers were divided into groups using three different procedures: (1) a no-participation procedure, which reflected the way things had always been done—employees had no voice in planning and change; (2) a participation-through-representation procedure, in which a few employees were involved in the decision-making process; and (3) a total-participation procedure, in which all the employees were involved. In each case, whether the workers contributed or not, the final decision belonged to management. The results revealed that

1. The no-participation group continued to resist changes.
2. Both the participation groups relearned their jobs significantly faster and surpassed the previous average production levels much sooner.
3. The total-participation group performed slightly better than the participation-through-representation group.[11]

What conclusion can you draw from these results regarding decision making in groups?

Problem Solving. Small groups can also excel at solving problems. People form problem-solving groups in almost every imaginable context: in the workplace, in government, in school, and at home. The problems they attempt to solve include how to improve health care, how to make a better product, how to perform a task more effectively or efficiently, how to stop violence, how to resolve the parking problem on campus, and how to improve a faltering relationship.

As you can see, groups can serve a variety of purposes and often serve multiple purposes at the same time. For example, a group can solve problems while at the same time serving as a learning, social, cathartic, or therapeutic outlet for its members. It was customary in the early and middle years of the twentieth century for most people to work relatively independently of one another. Even in large organizations, people had individual responsibilities and coordinated with others only when it was necessary to do so. Recently, the value of having people work in groups has been recognized, and a group approach has been implemented in many settings, including the workplace and the classroom. This trend has taken hold not only in the United States, but also throughout the world. Just think of the many types of groups we hear about in our personal lives and in the news: cooperative learning groups, project or work teams, personal growth groups, committees, quality control groups, activity groups, and so on.

Committees. Committees are groups that are either appointed or elected and have been assigned a specific task by a larger group or person with authority, such as a teacher, supervisor, or leader. Committees are usually formed to solve problems, make decisions, or gather information for another group or larger group so that it can make decisions or solve problems. Committee work is often seen as time consuming, and many people react negatively to committee work. This is unfortunate and is more likely due to the people in the committee or the lack of defined goals assigned to the committee. If properly assigned and led, committees can investigate and report findings; recommend a course of action; formulate policies, principles, or guidelines for carrying out actions; and much more.

Learning and Information Sharing. The most common reason why people join small groups is to share information and to learn from one another. The sharing of information occurs in all kinds of group settings; the most familiar ones are corporations, schools, religious organizations, families, and service or social clubs. The underlying purpose of learning or information-sharing groups is to educate, inform, or improve understanding related to specific issues or areas of concern.

Therapy or Personal Growth. Therapeutic group sessions primarily help people alter their attitudes, feelings, or behaviors about some aspect of their personal life. For example, a therapeutic group might include people who have drinking, drug, or other problems, such as coping with the loss of a loved one. Usually, the therapeutic group is led by a professional who is trained in group psychotherapy or counseling.

As with most communication contexts, groups are not purely primary or secondary. Small groups that you will be involved in are likely to include elements of all the groups described: social, task, decision making, problem solving, personal growth, and learning. Throughout this book, especially in the remainder of this chapter and the next, we hope to provide you with the necessary communication skills to become a competent group participant.

Learning Connections

1. Distinguish between primary and secondary groups.
2. How can understanding the different group purposes make you a more effective group member? A more effective group leader?
3. In which types of groups are you most likely to participate during your career?

Project or Work Teams

Because they are so common in our society and in the classroom, we have chosen to discuss groups known as project teams or work teams. Many scholars who study

The work team is ideally suited for solving workplace problems. Each person brings his or her own special expertise to the table and coordinates efforts with others on a common solution.

groups believe that there is a distinction between group involvement and team involvement.[12] A **team** is a special form of group, characterized by close-knit relationships among people with different and complementary abilities and by a strong sense of identity. Similar to groups, teams involve interaction, interdependence, common goals, personality, commitment, cohesiveness, and rules. Teams do differ from groups, however, in three ways:

1. Teams are more likely to consist of people with diverse abilities. For example, a surgical team performing an operation might include several surgeons, an anesthetist, and several nurses, each contributing a different skill or perspective to the task at hand. A group consists of several people, each contributing to the common goal of the group, whereas a team consists of people who have a specialization in and different perspectives on a common situation.

2. Teams usually develop more interdependence. A sports team, for example, usually cannot succeed unless all the players believe they are part of a unit.

3. Members of teams have a high degree of group identity and are more likely to identify themselves as team members than as individuals who happen to be on a team.[13]

team
A special form of group that is characterized by a close-knit relationship among people with different and complementary abilities and by a strong sense of identity.

project team
Individuals representing different specialties who are assigned to coordinate the successful completion of an assigned task.

Thus all teams consist of groups, but not all groups are teams.

Project or work teams have existed for years in almost every type of organization. Typically, project or work teams consist of a variety of individuals who get together to solve problems or make decisions. In a **project team,** these individuals are usually specialists assigned to coordinate the successful completion of an assigned task (such as finding adequate and accessible parking for all who need it). Project teams in general work quickly to determine what needs to be done, and then they do it. They also often possess little history, usually work under a deadline, and may have difficulty establishing mutually agreed-on relationships.

Making Connections

Lessons from Geese

Each of the following facts about geese contains a lesson about working in groups. Read each fact and note what its particular lesson might be. The first one has been completed for you.

Fact 1: As each goose flaps its wings, it creates an "uplift" for the birds that follow. By flying in a V formation, the whole flock adds 71 percent greater flying range than could be achieved if each bird flew alone.

Lesson: People who share a common direction and a sense of the group's goal can usually accomplish it more quickly and easily. Mutual support makes everyone more efficient.

Fact 2: When a goose falls out of formation, it suddenly feels the drag and resistance of flying alone. It quickly moves back into formation to take advantage of the lifting power of the bird immediately in front of it.

Lesson: ______________________________

____

Fact 3: When the goose tires, it rotates back into formation, and another goose flies to the front position.

Lesson: ______________________________

____

Fact 4: The geese flying in formation honk to encourage those up front to keep up their speed.

Lesson: ______________________________

____

Fact 5: When a goose gets sick or wounded or is shot down, two geese drop out of the formation and follow it down to help and protect it. They stay with it until it dies or is able to fly again. Then they launch out with another formation or catch up with the flock.

Lesson: ______________________________

____

The "Lessons from Geese" facts were obtained at a religious retreat. The source was listed as Anonymous.

work team
A group of people responsible for an entire work process or a segment of the process that delivers a product or service to an internal or external customer.

A **work team** is a group of people responsible for an entire work process or segment of the process that delivers a product or service to an internal or external customer. For example, a university department would be considered a work team. Their goal is to deliver instruction in a certain subject area to students as effectively and efficiently as possible. Usually university departments have a history, they entail mutually agreed-on relationships, and the members work as a group to serve its own and the university's missions. Work teams often are subdivisions of a larger organization and can exist for an indefinite period of time or until a specific project is completed. Work teams also serve many purposes, including solving problems, making decisions, socializing, and learning.

The **focus group,** a special form of work team, tries to find out what its members think about specific ideas, issues, or people. A focus group usually consists of a manageable number of participants and a facilitator or leader. The facilitator runs the meeting, typically using a prepared list of questions and probes to encourage participants to contribute their ideas, beliefs, feelings, and perceptions related to the assigned topic.[14] The facilitator does not offer personal opinions or judgments but guides group members as they express themselves. The information that is gathered in the focus group sessions is analyzed and then used in decision making.

Following are sample questions that might be asked of a focus group: What do college students think of binge drinking? How do nontraditional students feel about returning to the classroom? Is the government responding to the needs of Native Americans? Focus groups have been used by advertising agencies to determine which ads might appeal to certain markets and by political campaign planners to determine what issues are important for candidates to address in speeches.

Learning Connections

1. Explain how a team differs from a special group?
2. In what ways have focus groups been used in the United States?

Characteristics of Small Groups

Small groups have a number of characteristics in common, including interdependence, commitment, cohesiveness, group size, norms, and group culture, that make each group unique. These characteristics also determine who will join the group, how well the group will function and achieve its goals, and how the members will interact.

Interdependence

Probably the most essential characteristic of a small group is **interdependence**—the fact that group members are mutually dependent. Interdependence is reflected in all the other group characteristics, for without it there would be no group. Interdependence is built on each member's willingness to subordinate his or her individual desires and goals in order to accomplish the group's goal.

Groups function best and are most satisfying for their members when each individual recognizes and respects the crucial role that interdependence plays in group processes. A group's success is indeed based on each member's cooperation and willingness to work toward a common goal.

focus group
A special form of work team that ascertains what its members think about specific ideas, issues, or people.

interdependence
Mutual dependence of group members on one another.

commitment
The desire of group members to work together to complete a task to the satisfaction of the entire group.

Commitment

Another important characteristic of a group is commitment—to the task, to the group, and to the other individuals in the group. **Commitment** is the desire of group members to work together to complete their task to the satisfaction of the entire group. Members' commitment stems from interpersonal attraction; commonality of attitudes, beliefs, and values; the fulfillment of interpersonal needs; and the rewards that the group can offer.

Commitment is important to a group's effectiveness and ultimate success. For example, how often have you been in a group in which one or two members did the work and the others did little or nothing? Those who do little or nothing lack commitment and ultimately affect the group's cohesiveness and effectiveness. Working to accomplish a difficult task even when other group members slack off reflects commitment. For a group to be truly effective, all of its members must be committed to the group, its members, and the successful completion of its task. Commitment shows that the members' desire to remain in the group is greater than the desire to leave it.

Cohesiveness

As an extension of commitment, **cohesiveness** refers to the attraction that group members feel for one another and their willingness to stick together. Consider two groups. In the first, members like one another very much, strongly desire the goals the group is seeking, and believe that they could not find another group that would better satisfy their needs. In the second, the opposite is true: Members don't care for one another, they do not share common goals, and they are actively seeking other groups to join that might offer them more rewards. Which group would exert a stronger pull on its members? The answer should be obvious: the first. The rewards for being in the first group outweigh those of leaving the group. Cohesiveness is based on each member's need to remain in the group and the group's ability to provide members with rewards, making it worthwhile to give time and energy to the group. In a sense, cohesiveness is a form of loyalty or commitment. However, cohesiveness in a group does not automatically ensure success, and when there is too much cohesiveness, it can lead to problems.

Although cohesiveness is an important characteristic of every group, it should not lead to conformity or an unwillingness to change an unsuccessful decision or policy. Cohesiveness is a positive force when it attracts members of the group toward one another and increases effective group interaction, but it can become a negative influence if group members "go along simply to get along" or lose the ability to question group decisions.

Group Size

Group size relates to the number of participants involved in a given small group and has important ramifications for the group's effectiveness. Although there is no perfect number of members for a group, groups of certain sizes seem appropriate for certain kinds of tasks. For example, five-member groups are the most effective for dealing with intellectual tasks; coordinating, analyzing, and evaluating information; and making administrative decisions. Many small-group experts recommend that groups have no fewer than three and no more than nine members. It is also recommended that for some decision-making and problem-solving groups, an odd number of participants, for example five, seven, or nine, helps to ensure that there are fewer stalemates because in voting on issues, it is likely there will be a tie unless someone abstains or doesn't vote. Others believe that the ideal size is five to seven members.

A group that is too small can limit the information and ideas generated, whereas a group that is too large can limit the contribution that each person can make. As a group increases in size, the number of possible interactions increases dramatically (see

cohesiveness
The attraction that group members feel for each other and willingness to stick together; a form of loyalty.

TABLE 15.3

Group Size and Potential Interactions

NUMBER IN GROUP	POSSIBLE INTERACTIONS
2	2
3	9
4	28
5	75
6	186
7	411
8	1,056

Table 15.3). They include all the possible interactions between individual members and combinations of members. For example, in a three-person group, person A could interact with B and C separately or with B and C simultaneously. Both B and C have similar interaction possibilities, thus resulting in nine possible interactions.[15]

An important consideration in deciding on group size is that the larger the group is, the greater is the variety of skills and information that will be possessed by its members. However, the advantages gained when a group has more than seven members seem to be outweighed by potential disadvantages. For example, in a certain sense, ten opinions are superior to five and twenty opinions are superior to ten. But having twice as many opinions can create twice as much potential for conflict and make consensus at least twice as difficult to reach.

In addition, some consideration should be given to the number of men and women in the group. As was indicated earlier, stereotypical differences between men and women do exist in our society: Therefore, when possible, it is best to form groups with an equal number of men and women or groups in which women form the majority. These two combinations tend to reduce stereotypical behavior and create a more balanced group perspective. When deciding on the most effective size for a group, remember the following points:

1. Large groups reduce the time and amount of individual interaction.
2. Large groups provide a greater opportunity for aggressive members to assert their dominance. As a result, less assertive members might feel isolated and might withdraw from the group altogether.
3. Large groups make it difficult to follow a set agenda. It is easy for someone in a large group to switch topics or introduce subjects that are not related to the group's original priorities.

Group Norms

The expected and shared ways in which group members behave are called **norms.** Both informal and formal guidelines determine which behaviors are acceptable and which are not. In most group situations, the norms are informal and unwritten. In your communication class, for example, certain behaviors are expected of you. At a minimum, it is assumed that you will read your assignments, respect others' rights to speak, do your own work, and be on time for class. However, there may also be formal written rules, such as specific dates for the completion of assignments, attendance requirements, and guidelines for achieving specific grades.

For a group to function effectively, its members must agree on how things are to be done. Therefore no matter what their size or task, groups establish norms. This is done for a variety of reasons; the strongest one is that shared ways of behaving enable members to attain group goals and to satisfy interpersonal needs. Without guidelines for behavior, most groups would be ineffective and disorganized.

norms
Expected and shared ways in which group members behave.

Norms also help to give structure to a group. If members know what is expected of them, they are more likely to act accordingly and function more efficiently. Norms can be as simple as getting the task done or as involved as participating in complex rituals and ceremonies that must be respected if a member is to remain in the group.

In more formal situations, to increase efficiency and order, many groups use preestablished rules to guide their interaction. *Robert's Rules of Order* is the most widely used authority on conducting social, business, and government meetings. Such formal rules specify the roles of members, how meetings are to be conducted, and how topics for discussion are to be introduced, discussed, and accepted or rejected by the group's members. When it is important to maintain formal order, a group may appoint a parliamentarian to ensure that rules are correctly interpreted and followed.

Group culture is created by many factors, including the interaction patterns of the group's members, the roles members are assigned, the group's purpose, the mixture of people included in the group, members' behaviors, and norms and rules that the group follows.

Group Culture

Just like societies, organizations, and other large groups, small groups develop unique cultures. **Group culture,** according to communication scholars John Brilhart and Gloria Galanes, is "the pattern of values, beliefs, norms, and behaviors that are shared by group members and that shape a group's individual 'personality.' "[16] Group culture is created by many factors, including the interaction patterns of group members, the roles members are assigned, the purpose for the group, the mixture of people included in the group, members' behaviors, and norms and rules that the group follows.

The group's culture underlies all of its actions and behaviors. The culture of a group is not static; it is constantly changing and developing as it adapts to each new

Making Connections

Rules, Rules, Rules

You have been participating in small groups and have decided that in general they are a waste of your time because nothing ever seems to get accomplished, or when it does, it seems to take forever. People talk out of turn, interrupt each other, don't listen, come unprepared, and so on. Agreed-on rules can solve this problem.

1. Write a one-page paper explaining why rules are necessary to effective, efficient group interaction.
2. Develop a written list of rules for communicating in small groups, and discuss them with your classmates.

group culture
The pattern of values, beliefs, norms, and behaviors that is shared by group members and that shapes a group's individual personality.

Learning Connections

1. Which characteristic of a group helps group members to feel that their contributions are important?
2. Explain the value of group cohesiveness.
3. When should size be a factor in determining a group?
4. What norms are important for establishing a quality group culture?
5. Explain the advantages of group decision making or problem solving.

situation or event it confronts and to the needs of the group and its members. A group's culture is expressed in behaviors such as how its members organize it, who begins the interactions, how much interaction is allowed by any one member, who interacts with whom, how formally or informally people behave, how much or how little conflict is allowed, how much or how little socializing takes place, and how much or how little tolerance the group allows for ambiguity. These factors, as well as others, weave together to create each group's unique culture.

Gender Differences in Group Communication

The differences between the way men and women communicate in groups are not clear, and the results of research are not always accurate or fair to one gender or the other. We could probably agree that most men are physically stronger than most women, but some women are stronger than some men. To say that men on average are physically stronger than women is a reasonable statement. But to say that all men are stronger than all women is not accurate, and it is not fair. Much of the research examining women and men is done by comparing averages. Thus specific individual behaviors are usually not accounted for, leaving only averages for our consideration.

Research shows that groups consisting of both men and women are more likely to be dominated by men talking than by women talking. Men tend to demonstrate more task-related behavior than do women; that is, men tend to be more goal oriented than women and can be more impatient about moving on to the next issue or problem. Women tend to offer positive responses to others' comments and, in general, tend to express their subjective opinions more readily than men. Men tend to be more objective in their comments than women.[17]

Because of stereotypical beliefs that exist in U.S. culture, women are sometimes perceived to be less competent than men in solving problems or making decisions. However, little if any difference has been found by researchers between men and women in their problem-solving abilities. The research does suggest that men appear to be better at certain kinds of problem-solving tasks than women, but that difference is reduced or eliminated when men and women work together and when all are highly motivated to solve the problem.[18]

When groups compete, it appears that, on average, women are more cooperative with their opponents than men are. Women are more likely to share resources with their opponents and are interested in fairness more than in winning. Men, on average, are more willing to engage in aggressive behavior and gain advantage through deception and deceit than women are. Also, men are more likely to be antisocial, using revenge, verbal aggression, and even physical violence, whereas women are more likely to use socially acceptable behavior such as reasoning and understanding to solve conflict.[19]

When groups are small, women prefer to work with other women, whereas men don't seem to have a gender preference. It is much more difficult for men to achieve cohesiveness in all-male groups than in mixed-sex groups. As U.S. culture continues to evolve, our stereotypes of men and women will change, together with the roles they play in groups. When comparing the research on men and women based on gender rather than biological sex, we are beginning to find that differences are based less on biological sex than on masculine and feminine traits. That is, individuals who have masculine traits, whether they are male or female, are more likely to be competitive and attempt to dominate and control interactions. More feminine individuals—of either sex—are less likely to display those behaviors.[20] It is important that both men and women understand the stereotypes that exist and make sure that each person who participates in a group is provided equal opportunities to participate.

Ethical Behavior in Group Communication

For groups to perform effectively, leaders and members must be ethical. There are behavioral assumptions that all people in civilized societies are expected to follow—laws, rules, standards, or agreed-on norms of a general culture. Individualism is a belief in the dignity and sacredness of the individual over the community or group. Cultures that stress individualism emphasize that people should think, make decisions, and speak for themselves and live on their own, whereas collectivist societies make clear distinctions between in-groups and out-groups and place more value on the other than on the self. Collectivist societies place a greater value on community, groupness, harmony, and maintaining face.[21]

It is important to realize that groups, by their very nature, take on a collectivist value in that the group must be more important than the individual if the group is to succeed. This can raise ethical considerations as to the commitment one has toward other group members and the group's goal. This does not mean that individuals should condone unethical behaviors, but it does mean that the success of individuals can be accomplished only through the success of the group as a whole. These expectations apply especially to behaviors within groups and raise some special ethical concerns that all groups and group members should consider when participating in group-related activities.

1. *All group members should have the right to state an opinion or a unique perspective.* No one should be prevented from speaking openly, even when expressing unpopular views. Of course, group members must also be sensitive and responsible in making sure that their honest statements do not violate someone else's civil rights. Similarly it is inappropriate to ridicule or belittle members of the group in private or public, because they may disagree with a certain point of view. There is nothing wrong with disagreeing with another person's ideas; it is wrong, however, to attack the person instead of the idea.

2. *Group members should be willing to share all legitimate information that might benefit the group in reaching its goal.* Deliberately withholding information that might benefit the group is a violation of the group's trust and is unethical. Yes, there might be times when withholding information to protect the group or specific group members is appropriate. If a group member or members have a vested interest outside of the group that results in introducing false, faulty, or misleading information or in withholding information, however, it is the obligation of that member or members to notify the group or excuse themselves from the group.

3. *All group members should conduct themselves with honesty and integrity.* Members of a group should not deliberately deceive or present information that is false or untruthful. It is unacceptable to present inaccurate information in an attempt to persuade others to accept a particular viewpoint. The same principle would hold for the group itself: It would be wrong for the group to present to others results based on misrepresentation of facts. It is deceitful to persuade others to accept conclusions that are supported by misinformation. Integrity of group members individually and together as a group include other dimensions. For example, when a group makes a decision based on fair and ethical procedures, everyone should support the decision. Individual members should be willing to place the good of the group ahead of their own individual goals. The bottom line is that group members should ultimately do everything they can to benefit the group's goals.

4. *Confidential information shared in the group should remain confidential.* It is extremely unethical to share information outside of the group that members agree to keep private.

5. *Group members must use information ethically.* Members should give credit to the source of the information, should not falsify data or information, and should present all relevant information and all points of view to prevent bias. Ethical use of information helps produce effective, sound results, whatever the task.

GUIDELINES Ethical Behavior in Groups

1. All members should have the right to state an opinion or a unique perspective.
2. Group members should be willing to share all legitimate information that may benefit the group in reaching its goal.
3. All group members should conduct themselves with honesty and integrity.
4. Confidential information shared in the group should remain confidential.
5. Group members must use information ethically.

Technology and Groups

Have you ever had a problem or question that you couldn't answer or one about which you were unsure of the best answer? Did you think there must be others who know the answer or who are interested in the same issues that interest you? If so, the Internet could be your answer. A quick web search allows you to find groups of people who are interested in discussing almost any issue. If the topic that you are interested in isn't already on the Internet, then you can easily create your own website. One type of groups that are formed to discuss a particular topic on the Internet are referred to as newsgroups. A **newsgroup** is an online bulletin board where people can read and post messages about the topics of their choice. Once you post a message to a newsgroup, everyone who visits that newsgroup can read your comments and respond if they wish to do so. Newsgroups provide a vehicle whereby email messages are systematically made available to large groups of people.

newsgroup An online bulletin board where people can read and post messages about topics of their choice.

The newsgroup, in a sense, resembles a gathering place similar to the local town meeting hall or restaurant where people come together to discuss subjects of mutual

Making Connections

Group Success

Go back to the chapter's opening scenario, describing the experiences of group X and group Y. Group X members were very satisfied with their work and with one another, whereas group Y members were unsatisfied.

1. What do you think group X members did differently from group Y? What made them successful?
2. What recommendations would you give to group Y members to help them improve their group's experience?
3. How could technology be used by either group's members to improve their communication?

interest. With newsgroups, however, the communication occurs over the Internet and is electronically written, not orally discussed, as in the typical face-to-face small group arena. Like small groups, newsgroups revolve around specific topics, such as computers, social issues, literature and science, entertainment, hobbies, or current issues. Newsgroups provide easy access for meeting and communicating with people who share your interests from all over the world without having to leave their computers.

When members of formalized and established groups cannot meet in person, other forms of technology may provide a solution. Because of the cost and inconvenience of bringing people together, more and more organizations are opting to use such technologies as teleconferencing, videoconferencing, or interactive computer conferencing to hold meetings. **Teleconferencing** uses telephones and speakerphones to connect people in different locations. Speakerphones enable people in different locations to interact at one given location. Although extremely cost-effective, teleconferencing is limited because you cannot see those at the other locations. **Videoconferencing** is an extension of teleconferencing that includes picture and sound. It eliminates one limitation of teleconferencing in that it allows people at different locations to see each other via television. Thus a benefit of videoconferencing is the ability of those involved in the discussion to hear and see everyone at all locations. Disadvantages of videoconferencing include its cost and the need for special equipment to allow both picture and sound to be transmitted. Videoconferencing, however, is much more vulnerable to extremely frustrating equipment failures than teleconferencing.

Interactive computer conferencing is similar to videoconferencing except that the interaction occurs via computer. Although interactive computer conferencing requires special equipment and software for both sound and picture, it is far more cost effective than videoconferencing. The advantages of interactive computer conferencing include convenience, in that interaction can occur from almost any location, and the fact that only a computer and connected video camera are required. In addition, interactive computer conferencing usually does not require technicians to operate the equipment once it is installed. Its disadvantages are similar to those of videoconferencing in that equipment failures can occur and getting online is not always easy.

Ultimately, the success of any technology for group sharing depends on two factors: accessibility and use. We use technology to communicate within groups if the technology is readily available and if all members know how to use it effectively.

teleconferencing Use of telephones and speakerphones to connect people in different locations.

videoconferencing An extension of teleconferencing that includes picture and sound.

interactive computer conferencing Similar to videoconferencing except that the interaction occurs via computer.

Learning Connections

1. Compare and contrast the way men and women approach participation in groups.
2. Describe the characteristics of an ethical group participant.
3. Is technology a good thing for group communication?

When technologies are available, group members must agree on which technologies they will use, how often they will use them, and for what purposes.

In addition, if the technologies are to be empowering and useful, group members must agree on mutual expectations and rules that will guide the use of each technology. If an individual fails to check messages regularly, comes poorly prepared to teleconferences, or is not included in the exchanges by the other group members, the group will likely not be very successful. Groups that have used technology to communicate are aware that different types of technologies affect the richness and speed of their communication. Clearly, training and experience in the appropriate application of electronic communication technologies are critical to success.

Disadvantages of Small Groups

Most of what we have said so far about groups has been positive, and it is true that there are many advantages to groups over individuals working alone. But there are also limitations related to groups that can lead to less effective and less satisfying outcomes.

Going Along to Get Along

Too much cohesiveness can lead to conformity and blind loyalty to a group even when it is not in the individual group member's best interest to do so. Groups can become too cohesive or committed, resulting in **groupthink**—a dysfunction in which group members see the harmony of the group as being more important than considering new ideas, critically examining their own assumptions, changing their own flawed decisions, or allowing new members to participate.[22] The following situation illustrates groupthink. Students are asked to choose one of three solutions to a certain social problem. One group is formed for each solution. Each group is asked to defend its solution and to persuade the instructor that its solution is the best. As an incentive for preparing a sound argument, students are told that the instructor will accept only one group solution as the best.

As the groups begin to organize, their members make a modest effort to pull together. Each group selects a representative to present its argument. After hearing each representative, the instructor announces that he or she is undecided as to which group offered the best solution. Therefore all groups have one more chance to develop their arguments. The instructor also announces that students who did not like their group's solution are welcome to join another group. No one switches groups, even though some are tempted to do so after hearing presentations by other group representatives.

groupthink
A dysfunction in which group members value the harmony of the group more than new ideas, fail to critically examine ideas, hesitate to change flawed decisions, or lack willingness to allow new members to participate.

To raise the stakes, the instructor states that the groups with the second- and third-best solutions will be assigned a research project over the weekend, whereas the winning group will be exempt from this assignment. In response, the intensity within each group builds. Members pull their chairs closer together and talk more forcibly about their solution. They support one another's views more openly. The common objective has become clear and compelling: The students are motivated to persuade their instructor in order to avoid the research project. Oddly enough, this particular type of motivation can be hazardous. Groupthink is more likely to occur when a group's cohesiveness and commitment are too high and when the group is under pressure to achieve consensus at the expense of doing the best possible work. Once this collective state of mind develops, it seems that groups become unwilling and perhaps unable to change a decision, even if they realize that it is a poor one.

Research on groupthink indicates that it is a real and pervasive phenomenon that can explain some of the disastrous decisions made by groups.[23] One such outcome of groupthink occurred when a group of IBM executives in 1980 refused to consider the purchase of Microsoft's operating system from Bill Gates. The executives' decision resulted in a loss of revenues worth billions of dollars and, eventually, the emergence of a gargantuan competitor in the computer industry. In this case, the IBM executives were unwilling to consider new information. They simply thought the Microsoft operating system wouldn't work. Not one member of the executive committee was willing to go against the thinking of the group as a whole. We all now know that Bill Gates, the chairman of Microsoft, is one of the richest people in the world.

According to Irving Janis, a specialist in organizational behavior, eight symptoms lead to groupthink. They fall into three categories:

1. Overestimation of the group's power and morality
   - An illusion that the group is invulnerable, which creates excessive optimism and encourages taking extreme risks
   - A belief that the group will not be judged on the basis of the ethical or moral consequences of its decisions
2. Closed-mindedness
   - A tendency to rationalize or discount negative information that might lead members to reconsider their assumptions before making a decision
   - Stereotypical views of other groups as too weak and stupid to warrant genuine attempts to negotiate differences
3. Pressures toward uniformity
   - Individual self-censorship of differences that deviate from the group (That is, members are inclined to minimize their uniqueness and doubt the importance of their individual contributions.)
   - A shared illusion of unanimity that pushes members to conform to the majority view as a result of self-censorship and the assumption that silence means consent
   - Pressure on group members who express arguments that differ from the majority to conform by making it clear that dissent is contrary to what is expected of all loyal members
   - The setting of "mindguards" against threatening information in order to protect the group members from adverse information that might shatter their shared complacency regarding their decisions[24]

Procedures can be used to minimize the possibility of groupthink. Here are some examples:

- Assign one group member to be a "devil's advocate" who intentionally questions and criticizes the group's actions.
- Set a guideline to prevent leaders from expressing their preferences first.
- Ensure that every group member has an opportunity to voice an opinion.

- Encourage individuals to express disagreement without being chastised by the group for doing so.
- Use computer technology to encourage thorough problem solving.
- Invite outside experts to participate or review conclusions to ensure all views have been considered.[25]

Time Consuming

A second disadvantage of groups is that the decision-making or problem-solving process can be time-consuming. It almost always takes longer to accomplish something when a group does it. The more members there are in a group, the more time it takes to accomplish the group's objectives. Individuals can almost always complete a task in a shorter amount of time than a group. For example, if you were to take a math problem-solving test, you would probably read each problem silently to yourself, write notes to yourself on scratch paper, and then attempt to solve the problems. If you were in a group, you would first have to discuss each problem, decide how the problem should be solved, and then work out the solution to the problem. In other words, group work is different than individual work because there must be interaction between and among the members. How can you ensure that groups use their time wisely and effectively?

Varying Communication Styles

A third disadvantage is that in most groups it is not possible for all members to contribute equally. One reason for this is time, but also because each member has a different communication style and comfort level with the group, members contribute unequally. Some members might dominate and overwhelm conversations, whereas other members might not contribute at all. Also, the most verbally aggressive and dominant person in the group might not have the best ideas. In Chapter 16, we discuss in more detail self-centered behaviors of group members and how to control those behaviors that hinder a group's effectiveness. What can be done to ensure that everyone has an equal opportunity to participate and contribute to the group?

Unfair Workloads

A fourth disadvantage of groups is that members believe the workload is unfair in the group. The most frequent complaint we hear from students about working on group projects is that they believe that some group members do not do their fair share of the work. This is referred to as social loafing. **Social loafing** is the tendency for individuals to lower their work effort after they join a group.[26] For example, suppose that you and several people are helping a friend move. To lift the heaviest pieces, you all pitch in. Will all the people helping exert equal effort? Probably not. Some will lift as much as they can, whereas others will simply hang on, perhaps even grunting loudly in order to seem as if they are helping more than they are. Social loafers can also be irresponsible by not showing up on time or not showing up at all because they believe others will do the work for them. Motivation seems to be the central reason for social loafing. Although there is no magical list of procedures or behaviors that will reduce social loafing, here are few suggestions: Make outputs individually identifiable, increase commitment to the task and the sense of task importance, make sure that each person's contribution is unique—not identical—to those of others, and build group cohesiveness. If these suggestions do not work, and if it is possible or reasonable, eliminate noncontributors from the group.

social loafing
Tendency for individuals to lower their work effort after they join a group.

Pressure to Fail

A fifth disadvantage is that sometimes groups may not meet their potential, because the majority of group members place pressure on the most capable members not to excel. The implication is that the weaker group members control the outcome and therefore require others who might want to excel to do only the minimum necessary to get the job done and no more. In fact, members who do not cooperate and do excel beyond other group members might find themselves teased, chastised, or worse for breaking the group's norm. This phenomenon occurs when groups decide to meet the minimum expectations; it is very similar to groupthink. How can this type of situation be avoided?

Making Connections

Effective Groups

Several questions were implied or posed in the section on disadvantages of small groups. Write answers for them and discuss them in class.

1. How can you ensure that the group uses its time wisely and effectively?
2. What can be done to ensure that everyone has an equal opportunity to participate and contribute to the group?
3. Are there other suggestions on how to deal with social loafers that are better than those suggested or that can be added to the list?
4. How can weak group members be kept from lowering the group's productivity?
5. Describe the behaviors of a successful group.

Grouphate Phenomenon

Finally, people who have had only negative experiences with groups or those who do not have the communication skills to be effective in groups dislike group work. This dislike for groups has been termed the **grouphate phenomenon.**[27] For some people, group work is so distasteful that they avoid group situations whenever possible. In our experience, those who hate participating in groups the most are those who have little or no skill or lack training in how to communicate in groups. What can people do to eliminate or reduce their dislike of groups?

People who are not skilled communicators usually find group work overwhelming and unsatisfactory because they don't know how to use communication to benefit them in solving problems, resolving conflicts, or expressing themselves.

Learning Connections

1. When is too much cohesiveness a problem?
2. Which disadvantage is the one that bothers you the most? What suggestions do you have for avoiding it?

Summary

Almost everyone participates in small-group communication on a regular basis either at school, at work, or in some other context. Small-group communication is the exchange of information that occurs among a relatively small number of people, ideally five to seven, who share a common purpose such as doing a job, learning, or solving a problem. Groups are collections of individuals who influence one another, have a common purpose, take on roles, are interdependent, and interact with one another.

People join groups for a variety of reasons. Groups help to meet both psychological and social needs, allow individuals to reach goals that they might not otherwise be able to attain, provide multiple sources of information and ideas, provide security, and can contribute to a positive social identity. Cultural orientation also determines, to some extent, our predisposition to join groups and helps to form our perception of the

grouphate phenomenon
Dislike for groups.

value of groups. Cultures that have individualistic orientations stress the self or personal goals, whereas collectivistic orientations stress putting aside individual goals for the well-being of the group. A major force in bringing people together to form groups is that they have a common goal.

There are primary groups, which focus on social or interpersonal relationships, and secondary groups, which exist to accomplish tasks or achieve goals. There are special forms of groups, such as teams, project teams, work teams, and focus groups. Each type of group or team has various characteristics that make small groups a unique context for communication. They involve interdependence, commitment, cohesiveness, size, and culture. Sometimes group members lose their individual identity and give up the individual right to free thought even when it is not in their best interest to do so. This is referred to as groupthink.

There are many advantages to groups; these include better decisions and solutions to problems, but there are also disadvantages including the feeling that groups take too much time, not everyone contributes equally, some members don't take their responsibilities seriously and do their fair share of the work, referred to as social loafing, and some individuals simply dislike groups because of bad experiences they had with them; this is called the grouphate phenomenon.

Technology is playing a larger and larger role in group interaction. There are online bulletin boards where people discuss popular and controversial issues. One type of such groups are referred to as newsgroups. More and more businesses because of travel expenses and convenience are using methods such as teleconferencing, videoconferencing, and interactive computer conferencing to allow groups of employees to discuss problems and issues and make decisions.

DISCUSSION STARTERS

1. What do you like most about working in groups? What do you like least about working in groups?
2. What causes groups to be inefficient? What can be done to make them more efficient?
3. Which group characteristic (interdependence, commitment, cohesiveness, group size, or group culture) do you think is the most important for a group to succeed? Why?
4. What is it that competent group communicators do that others do not?
5. Discuss two norms that exist in your class that could be applied to a group.
6. Can you think of a recent event in which groupthink came into play? What happened?
7. Explain what you think are the differences that women and men might bring to a group discussion.
8. Explain how technology can help groups to accomplish their goals.
9. What does it mean to you to be an ethical group member?
10. How does a social loafer affect a group's climate, motivation, and productivity?

NOTES

1. M. E. Shaw, *Group Dynamics: The Psychology of Small Group Behavior,* 2nd ed. (New York: McGraw-Hill, 1976), 6–10.
2. P. B. Paulus, ed., *Psychology of Group Influence,* 2nd ed. (Hillsdale, N.J.: Erlbaum, 1989).
3. B. B. Haslett and J. Ruebus, "What Differences Do Individual Differences in Groups Make?" in *The Handbook of Group Theory and Research,* 2nd ed., eds. L. R. Frey, D. S. Gouran, and M. S. Poole (Thousand Oaks, Calif.: Sage, 1999), 115–38; and C. H. Hui and

H. C. Trandis, "Individualism–Collectivism: A Study of Cross-Cultural Research," *Journal of Cross-Cultural Psychology* 17 (1986): 225–48.
4. H. C. Triandis, *Individualism and Collectiveness* (Boulder, Colo.: Westview Press, 1995).
5. C. Calloway-Thomas, P. J. Cooper, and C. Blake, *Intercultural Communication Roots and Routes* (Boston: Allyn and Bacon, 1999), 113–14.
6. Ibid., 114.
7. H. C. Triandis, "Cross-Cultural Studies of Individualism and Collectiveness," in *Cross-Cultural Perspective,* ed. J. Berman (Lincoln: University of Nebraska Press, 1990); and G. Hofstede, *Cultures and Organizations: Software of the Mind* (New York: McGraw-Hill, 1991).
8. R. V. Harnack, T. B. Fest, and B. S. Jones, *Group Discussion Theory and Technique,* 2nd ed. (Englewood Cliffs, N.J.: Prentice-Hall, 1977), 25–28; and J. K. Brilhart and G. J. Galanes, *Effective Group Discussion,* 7th ed. (New York: McGraw-Hill, 1998), 9–15, 133–36.
9. J. K. Brilhart, *Effective Group Communication Theory and Practice,* 10th ed. (New York: McGraw-Hill, 2001), 11.
10. Ibid., 12–14.
11. L. Coch and J. R. P. French Jr., "Overcoming Resistance to Change," in *Group Dynamics: Research and Theory,* 2nd ed., eds. D. Cartwright and A. Zander (Evanston, Ill.: Row Peterson, 1960), 319–41.
12. Brilhart, Galanes, and Adams, 8.
13. G. Lumsden, D. Lumsden, and S. Ketrow, *Communicating in Groups and Teams,* 4th ed. (Belmont, Calif.: Wadsworth, 2004).
14. L. C. Lederman, "Assessing Educational Effectiveness: The Focus Group Interview as a Technique for Data Collection," *Communication Education* 39 (1990): 117–27.
15. R. Bostrum, "Patterns of Communicative Interaction in Small Groups," *Speech Monographs* 37 (1970): 257–63.
16. Brilhart and Galanes, *Effective Group Discussion,* 124.
17. L. P. Stewart, P. J. Cooper, A. D. Stewart, and S. H. Friedley, *Communication and Gender,* 4th ed. (Boston: Allyn and Bacon, 2003), 44–50; D. N. Maltz and R. A. Borker, "A Cultural Approach to Male–Female Miscommunication," in *Language and Social Identity,* ed. J. J. Gumperz (Cambridge: Cambridge University Press, 1982), 195–216; and E. Baird, "Sex Differences in Group Communication: A Review of Relevant Research," *Quarterly Journal of Speech* 62 (1976): 179–92.
18. B. F. Meeker and P. A. Weitzel-O'Neil, "Sex Roles and Interpersonal Behavior in Task-Oriented Groups," *American Sociological Review* 42 (1977): 91–105; R. L. Hoffman and N. K. V. Maier, "Quality and Acceptance of Problem Solutions by Members of Homogeneous and Heterogeneous Groups," *Journal of Abnormal and Social Psychology* 62 (1961): 401–7.
19. J. C. McCroskey, V. P. Richmond, and R. A. Stewart, *One on One: The Foundations of Interpersonal Communication* (Englewood Cliffs, N.J.: Prentice-Hall, 1986), 244–47; M. E. Roloff, "The Impact of Socialization on Sex Differences in Conflict Resolution" (paper presented at the annual convention of the International Communication Association, Acapulco, Mexico, May 1980); E. A. Mabry, "Some Theoretical Implications of Female and Male Interaction in Unstructured Small Groups," *Small Group Behavior* 20 (1989): 536–50; and W. E. Jurma and B. C. Wright, "Follower Reactions to Male and Female Leaders Who Maintain or Lose Reward Power," *Small Group Research* 21 (1990): 97–112.
20. J. Bond and W. Vinacke, "Coalition in Mixed Sex Triads," *Sociometry* 24 (1961): 61–65; B. A. Fisher, "Differential Effects of Sexual Composition Interaction Patterns in Dyads," *Human Communication Research* 9 (1983): 225–38; Jurma and Wright; and D. J. Canary and B. H. Spitzberg, "Appropriateness and Effectiveness Perceptions of Conflict Strategies," *Human Communication Research* 14 (1987): 93–118.
21. C. Calloway-Thomas et al., 113–14.
22. I. L. Janis, *Groupthink: Psychological Studies of Policy Decisions and Fiascoes,* 2nd ed. (Boston: Houghton Mifflin, 1983).
23. P. E. Tetlock, R. S. Peterson, C. McGuire, S. Change, and P. Feld, "Assessing Political Group Dynamics: A Test of the Group Think Model," *Journal of Personality and Social Pyschology* 63 (1992): 403–25.
24. Janis.
25. Brilhart, Galanes, and Adams, 236–238.
26. S. J. Karau and K. D. Williams, "Social Loafing: A Meta-Analytic Review and Theoretical Integration," *Journal of Personality and Social Psychology* 65 (1993): 681–706; B. K. Latané and S. Harkins, "Many Hands Make Light the Work: The Causes and Consequences of Social-Loafing," *Journal of Personality and Social Psychology* 37 (1979): 822–32; and B. G. Schultz, "Improving Group Communication Performance," in *The Handbook of Group Communication Theory and Research,* eds. L. R. Frey, D. S. Gouran, and M. S. Poole (Thousand Oaks, Calif.: Sage, 1999), 371–94.
27. S. Sorensen, "Grouphate" (paper presented at the International Communication Association, Minneapolis, Minn., May 1981).

"The most important quality in a leader is that of being acknowledged as such."
—André Maurois

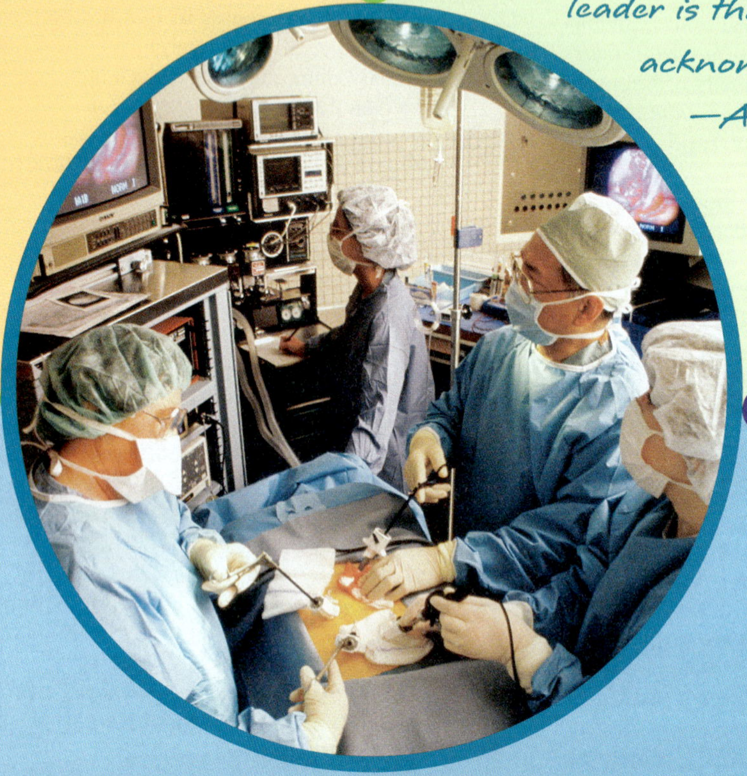

CHAPTER 16

Participating in Groups and Teams

THIS CHAPTER WILL HELP YOU:

- Recognize why team building is important in groups.
- Know the roles and responsibilities of group leaders.
- Explain differences in men's and women's leadership styles.
- Specify the responsibilities of group participants.
- Recognize and understand group task roles, group building and maintenance roles, and self-centered roles.
- Conduct efficient and effective group meetings.
- Use effective problem-solving and decision-making steps.
- Manage and use conflict strategies to ensure positive outcomes.
- Develop and use criteria for evaluating groups.

Here is a riddle: "What is more boring than a droning professor, more tedious than peeling potatoes, and more frustrating than a perpetual busy signal when you need to reach someone by phone?" The answer, according to many business people, is a meeting.

—*Cox News Service, 1990*

CASE STUDY

If you can, do a quick survey of your friends, relatives, or people you work with, and ask them why they think people don't like to have group meetings. You probably have your own list of reasons to avoid meetings—especially those that promise to be dull.

Questions to think about

1. Why do most people have negative feelings toward group meetings?
2. Who is ultimately responsible for ensuring that meetings are not boring, unproductive, and inefficient?
3. Can the benefits of holding group meetings outweigh some of the negative attitudes toward them?
4. In your opinion, what has to happen for a group meeting to be enjoyable?

Meetings and group discussions have been the brunt of many jokes and often have led to frustration, but working in groups can be a wonderful experience and can lead to outcomes that are far better than those individuals can provide by themselves. If you are like most people, you have likely been in meetings in which great interaction took place, time was used wisely, good progress was made toward a particular goal or accomplishing a task, lots of good ideas were shared, respect for each person's contributions was shown even though disagreement and conflict sometimes occurred, differences were resolved by open discussion, and decisions were supported by everyone. People leave such meetings with a real sense of accomplishment.

What is the difference between an effective and an ineffective group meeting? To answer this question, this chapter explores seven crucial aspects of small group communication: team building, leadership, conducting a meeting, member participation, methods of group problem solving and decision making, conflict management, and evaluation.

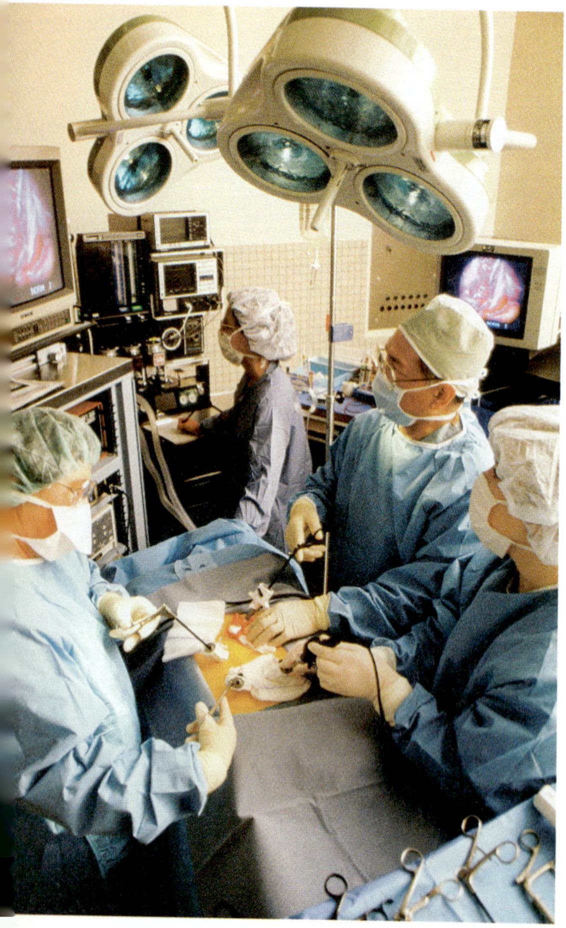

Members of an operating room team have a strong sense of identity with the group, and they cooperate fully because each has a specific role to play. This is a very effective group form.

Team Building

Not all groups will become teams or work as teams, but it is important to understand that the more a group acts or becomes like a team, the more likely it is that the group (as characterized in Chapter 15 as having a close-knit relationship among people with different and complementary abilities and by a strong sense of identity) will be successful. A team is likely to be more successful or effective because when people know they are part of a team, they tend to cooperate more fully; they form a close-knit relationship and a strong sense of identity. As with any group or organization, a team needs a purpose and goals. For groups to establish a team approach, they must first set very clear and specific goals as well as determine roles.

Setting Goals

It is unusual when participating in a group assignment to find that all members participate with the same amount of enthusiasm or motivation. This is especially true when a topic is assigned by an instructor or when the group selects a topic that not all group members see as important. Unfortunately, the level of enthusiasm and motivation differ in most group situations, whether in class or out. One way to avoid this problem is to establish goals that are not only clear and specific, but also challenging and worthwhile for each group member.[1] If group members believe that the goals are trivial and unimportant, they will likely not participate, or if they do participate, it will be with little or no motivation. If the group members understand that their work effort and decisions will result in rewards, be appreciated, and be considered worthwhile, however, they are more likely to take ownership of their actions and behaviors as well as be motivated to accomplish their goals.

Making Connections

What Makes a Leader?

List the characteristics and skills you believe a good leader must possess in order to lead a group. Then rank each characteristic, using 1 as the most important, 2 as the second most important, and so on.

Form small groups (three to seven members) to discuss each person's ranking of characteristics and skills. Together create a new ranked list of characteristics and skills for effective leaders using those generated by each person in the group and any new characteristics as determined by the group. Select one group member to write the group's top five characteristics and skills on the board and to explain why the group made these selections. After all groups have had a turn, follow these steps:

1. In an open class discussion, create a class list of the top five characteristics and skills using the group lists or any additions that may result from the class discussion.
2. How do people acquire the leadership characteristics and skills presented on the class list?
3. List five people whom you believe to be effective leaders—they can be well known or not so well known.
4. Under the names, list the characteristics and skills they possess that qualifies them for your list of effective leaders.
5. Do all these leaders have the same qualities, or are there differences? What qualities are universal among all the leaders mentioned, if any? Discuss your answers, if time permits, in class.
6. Discuss the role of ethics or morals in leadership behavior.

How can a group effectively determine whether its goals are clear and specific? If a group's goal is stated vaguely, the group will likely find it difficult to organize itself and to know when it has arrived at a solution or conclusion. For example, if a group discusses a topic such as "crime on campus is on the rise," this topic provides little or no direction as to what needs to be done. However, if the topic is restated as "What specific actions should be taken by the campus to help reduce the crime rate by the end of the school year?," this tells the group exactly what it needs to accomplish: specific actions for reducing crime on campus. If the group also believes that the specific actions they propose could be actually used to reduce crime on campus, that would even be more of an incentive for the group to accomplish its goal. It would also give them a reason to take ownership of what they discuss.

Determining Roles

Once the group has established and understands its goal, it must determine the roles of its members. Everyone in the group must be responsible for something, and everyone must be held accountable for what they are responsible to provide to the group. For example, a football team requires a head coach (a leader), assistant coaches (a subgroup within the larger group), players who have the talent and desire to fill the positions necessary to play the game, public relations people to promote the team, and so on. Everyone on the team has roles and assigned duties to accomplish. Football players cannot function as a team if there is no structure or if the coaches and players are uncertain of the roles they are

Learning Connections

1. Why is it important for a group to act like a team?
2. What does a group need to do to become a team?
3. When can a team approach be harmful to a group's outcome?

suppose to fulfill. The same is true of any group; if the members are uncertain of their roles and there is no structure, the group will not be able to function effectively.

Leadership

Leadership is an influence process that includes any behavior that helps to clarify a group's purpose or guide a group to achieve its goals. A **leader** is a person who is assigned or selected, or who emerges from a group, to guide or provide direction toward reaching the group's goals. In most cases, only one person has the title of leader, although there are times when the assigned or appointed leader does not show leadership even though he or she has the title of leader. It is also true that sometimes two or more people may emerge and share the leader responsibilities via their leadership behaviors. In other words, a leader is a role or title held in a group, whereas leadership is the behavior that influences or facilitates group members to achieve the group's goal or goals.

Leading a Group

A leader is the person at the center of a group's attention or the person to whom the group members address their messages. For example, in business meetings, the boss is usually the leader, and the employees focus their attention on the boss, addressing their communications to him or her. At times, employees may address messages to other employees, or one employee might hold the attention of the group, but in neither situation does an employee actually become the leader of the meeting.

Another way to identify a leader is by the behaviors that he or she displays in guiding a group to its specific goal. If a person communicates a direction and the group members follow that direction to reach the goal, that person is demonstrating leadership.

Finally, a leader can be identified by his or her position or title, such as student council president, chairperson of a committee, boss, teacher, coach, captain, father, mother, and so on. But this method of identification requires caution. Even though a title signifies that a person is the stated leader, it does not mean that that person has leadership skills.

In most cases, a leader's ability to lead determines the success or failure of a group. Granted, not all successes or failures can be traced directly to the person in charge because the participants, the nature of the task to be accomplished, and the information available for completing the task also contribute to the outcome. The role of the leader in small-group projects is to get the task done. To do this, the leader must be objective enough to determine how the group is functioning and whether it is progressing toward its goal. This requires, at times, the ability to "step back" and examine the group objectively.

Leaders must help address two sets of needs found in all groups. **Task needs** are related to the content of the task and all behaviors that lead to the completion of the task, including defining and assessing the task, gathering information, studying the problem, and solving the problem. **Maintenance needs** are related to organizing and developing a group such that members realize personal satisfaction from working together. Maintenance needs pertain to intangibles such as atmosphere, structure, role responsibility, praise, and social–emotional control. To meet both task and maintenance needs, leaders in small groups must perform a number of functions:

leadership
An influence process that includes any behavior that helps clarify a group's purpose or guides the group to achieve its goals.

leader
A person who is assigned or selected, or who emerges from a group, to guide or provide direction toward reaching the group's goals.

task needs
Need related to the content of a task and all behaviors that lead to the completion of it.

maintenance needs
Needs related to organizing and developing a group so that the members can realize personal satisfaction from working together.

Initiating—preparing members for the discussion

Organizing—keeping members on track

Maintaining effective interaction—encouraging participation

Ensuring member satisfaction—promoting interpersonal relationships

Facilitating understanding—encouraging effective listening

Stimulating creativity and critical thinking—encouraging evaluation and improvement

Leadership Styles and Behavior

All leaders are definitely not alike. They may share certain characteristics to a degree, but they differ greatly in terms of personal, behavioral, or leadership style. Although there are probably as many different styles of leadership as there are leaders, research on leader behavior seems to suggest that most leaders can be placed along a small number of dimensions relating to their overall leadership behaviors. Two such dimensions emerged early on in leadership research and have been repeatedly confirmed. The first is known as **initiating structure** (or task-oriented leaders).[2] These are leaders who focus on getting the job done. They engage in actions such as organizing work, making sure rules are followed, setting goals, and making sure that everyone knows who is in charge. You probably have experienced leaders like this, and in some group situations, this style can get the job done or the problem solved, but this leadership style tends to sacrifice relationship development unless doing so will help to get the task done more quickly. In contrast, leaders who are low on this dimension are less organized, do not establish clear goals, and are not very concerned about their recognition as a leader.

The second dimension is known as **consideration** (or relationship-oriented leaders). These are leaders who focus on establishing good interpersonal relationships and on being liked by group members. They engage in such actions as doing favors for group members, take time to explain things to them, and watch out for their well-being. Leaders who are low in this dimension, by contrast, do not care about the group members or whether they get along with them. (See Figure 16.1 for an overview of these two basic dimensions of leader behavior.)

Is either of these behavior styles superior? Probably not! Both offer a mixed pattern of advantages and disadvantages. What do you think those might be? Leaders who have high concern for people generally have high group morale, but these leaders often avoid telling others what to do, nor do they like to provide group members with negative feedback. This could result in inefficiency and not getting things done in a timely manner. In contrast, when leaders are high on getting the job done, efficiency might be good, but group members might conclude that the leader cares only about getting the job done and not about them. It appears that leaders who are high on both dimensions are likely to have groups that are highly productive and enjoy working together in getting the task done. In other words, leaders who can balance the two dimensions are often considered superior leaders in comparison to those leaders showing other patterns of behavior.

Leadership may also be classified according to how much or how little power the leader assigns to the group members. Researchers have identified three primary styles of leadership: autocratic, democratic, and laissez-faire,[3] each having a very distinctive approach to the communication that occurs within the group (see Table 16.1).

initiating structure
A dimension of leadership that focuses on getting the job done.

consideration
A dimension of leadership that focuses on establishing good interpersonal relationships and on being liked by group members.

FIGURE 16.1

Basic Dimensions of Leader Behavior

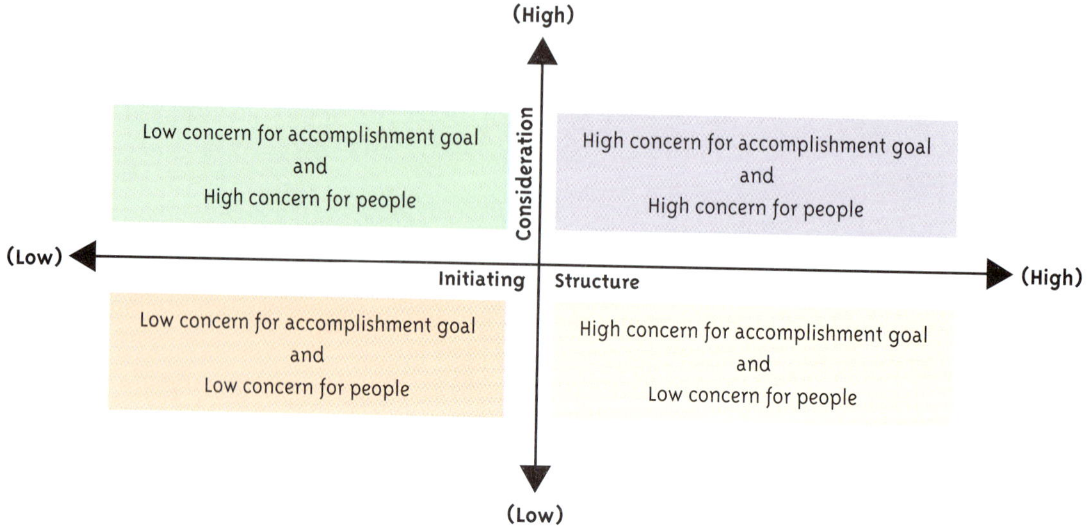

autocratic leader A leader who has complete control.

democratic leader A leader who shares control.

laissez–faire leader A leader who gives up control.

However, many leaders cannot be easily classified in one of the three styles exclusively. Often, effective leaders use a combination of styles or blends of the styles, which may change from one situation to the next.

In theory, the differences among the three styles of leadership are clear. The **autocratic leader** has complete control, the **democratic leader** shares control, and the **laissez-faire leader** gives up control. In practice, though, the three styles are not always so clear-cut. Most leaders do not use the same style all the time but vary their style to match each situation. Certain circumstances, group members, and group purposes call for direct control, whereas others require little or no control. For example, a military leader in combat and a doctor in a medical emergency will undoubtedly be

TABLE 16.1

Leadership Styles: A Comparison

AUTOCRATIC	DEMOCRATIC	LAISSEZ-FAIRE
Keeps complete control	Shares control	Gives up control
Sets policy and makes all decisions for the group	Involves members in setting policy and making decisions; does not make any decisions without consulting group members	Gives total freedom to group members to make policies and decisions; gets involved only when called on
Defines tasks and assigns them to members	May guide task assignment to be sure work is accomplished, but allows members to divide work	Completely avoids participation

Leadership style is classified by how much or how little power the leader assigns to group members. Democratic leaders, for example, guide and direct the group and, though committed to being open to all points of view, they represent only a majority or plurality of points of view of the group.

autocratic leaders. Such situations require immediate action, and putting decisions to a vote could create great problems.

The democratic leadership style is most often used when a leader is elected. For example, the president of the student government and the chair of a committee would probably use a democratic style. This style is most common when the leader is both a representative and a member of the group. The laissez-faire leadership style is often used when group members do not want or need a rigid structure to accomplish their goal, such as a group conducting a study session. If such a group decided that they needed a leader, they would take appropriate action, but in most cases, the group does not desire or require any assistance, and so it remains leaderless.

Making Connections

Choosing a Leadership Style

Tia was elected chairperson of her church's administrative council. She was very pleased that others saw her as a leader, given that she was the youngest person and the only African American who had run for the position.

The committee was made up of seven members and, besides Tia, there was only one other female member. Even though this was only her third year on the church council (most members had served for longer periods), Tia felt ready to take charge but also knew that her assignment was not going to be easy. A tremendous amount of work had to be done in a short time, and controversial issues were involved. Despite having less experience than most members, she was confident and knew that she could do the job.

1. What advice would you give to Tia regarding her choice of leadership style?
2. What other concerns should Tia have, if any?
3. Would these concerns be different if Tia were a male? If so, why?

Leaders are not always free to follow the leadership style they prefer. For example, people who would rather be democratic or laissez-faire leaders might discover that pressures from others, the need to get things done in a certain way, or the desire to save time and energy require them to be more autocratic than they would like to be. On other occasions, when it is important for members to agree with a decision, leaders are more likely to use a democratic style. No single leadership style is perfect in all situations.

Researchers have concluded that skilled leaders have the ability to understand a situation and adapt their behaviors to meet its particular constraints.[4] Leadership entails the ability to determine the most appropriate style and behaviors for given situations. Here are some sample situations to which effective leadership is able to adapt:

- When group members are not committed or are unwilling to accept responsibility for implementing a decision, effective leaders use an autocratic style of leadership. For example, if a group of students has been given a class assignment in which only one student is prepared to do the work and knows what needs to be done, an autocratic style would be appropriate.
- If group members are highly committed and willing to accept responsibility for implementing a decision, effective leaders use a democratic style of leadership. For example, if a group of responsible students is working on a classroom assignment in which all are committed and prepared, a democratic style would be an appropriate situation for a leader to use.
- If group members are highly motivated to complete a task and have the knowledge and expertise to accomplish the task, effective leaders realize that they should delegate the task to the group members and use a laissez-faire style of leadership. For example, if a group of highly talented, independent, and motivated students is working together to complete a class assignment in which each student knows his or her responsibilities, a laissez-faire style would be appropriate.

Effective leaders examine situations, understand the groups they are leading, and determine what actions need to be taken to accomplish a given task. Although it is impossible to say exactly which styles work best in certain situations, common sense indicates that a leader needs to be flexible to promote productivity and satisfaction in a given group.

Research, although not conclusive, suggests that the democratic leadership style is superior to the autocratic style in getting a task done and at the same time satisfies group members.[5] Autocratic leaders are likely to get more done, but member satisfaction is considerably lower. Probably the most significant research finding is that autocratic leaders generate more hostility and aggression among group members, whereas democratic leaders produce more originality, individuality, and independence. Groups with laissez-faire leaders accomplish less, produce work of lower quality, and waste more time.

Leadership and Gender Differences

One factor that may impede the progress of females as leaders involves their own expectations. However, at the present time, it is clear that women can definitely be effective leaders. Women have been elected to major offices (e.g., governors, mayors, and senators), have been appointed to the Supreme Court, hold high ranks in the mil-

Making Connections

Are Women Better Leaders?

According to an article in *U.S. News & World Report* (January 29, 2001), more women are taking on leadership roles in government and business. The article stated that women have a greater tendency to take a holistic, contextual view of issues, whereas men tend to compartmentalize and assess the cause and effect of issues in a linear fashion. On the basis of what this article appears to say, women are therefore better leaders.

1. Defend or refute the article's contention that women are better leaders.
2. What does it mean to be holistic, and why would that make a person a better leader?
3. When considering the traits we generally associate with leadership, are they more likely to be masculine or feminine? Explain.
4. Who do you think is a very effective female leader? A very effective male leader? What do they have in common? What are their differences?

itary, and in a few cases head major corporations. But how do people react to women in positions of authority? Do they hold women to a higher standard than men? Do they hold women in equally high regard as men? The answers to these questions are often mixed, but in general, women are not reacted to as positively or with the same high regard as men. It appears that what subordinates say is much the same toward both female and male leaders. The difference is that they use more negative nonverbal behaviors toward female leaders.[6]

What might be even more disturbing than the negative nonverbal behaviors is that when women serve as leaders, they tend to receive lower evaluations from both male and female subordinates than men do.[7] This is especially true for female leaders who adapt a more masculine style of leadership, such as autocratic or directive, in areas in which men are the most predominant leaders. It is also particularly true when men evaluate women leaders. These findings seem to suggest that in spite of their progress, women continue to face subtle disadvantages even when they do obtain positions of leadership and authority.[8]

It has also been shown that both women and men seem to prefer having men in positions of authority.[9] This might be related to cultural values and how authority is determined and learned in a society. The result is that in most cases, women as well as men seem to feel more comfortable when a man is in charge. Clearly, such attitudes operate against women in many contexts.

Do male leaders and female leaders differ in their style or approach to leadership? What do you think? Marilyn Loden, in her book *Feminine Leadership or How to Succeed in Business Without Being One of the Boys*, contends that the sexes do indeed differ in terms of leadership style.[10] Loden believes that female leaders often adopt a style that emphasizes cooperation and indirect means of management, whereas males tend to exhibit an "I'm in charge," directive strategy. But research on male and female leadership done by social scientists has generally found no consistent or significant difference between the sexes in terms of leadership style. The question is "Who is right?"

Because of the complexity of the subject, finding the answer to this question is not simple. In a review of 150 research studies, Alice Eagly and Blair Johnson found that potential differences between male and female leadership styles had been examined on two dimensions: (1) task accomplishment versus maintenance of interpersonal relationships and (2) participative (democratic) versus directive (autocratic) leadership style.[11] Sex-role stereotypes suggest that female leaders might show more concern for interpersonal relations and tend to be more democratic in their leadership style than male leaders are. Results of Eagly and Johnson's study, however, did not support these stereotypes. Their results suggest that no evidence supports any substantial difference between males and females regarding the first dimension (task accomplishment versus maintenance of interpersonal relationships). There is, however, a significant difference between males and females regarding the second dimension (participative versus directive leadership style). Eagly and Johnson found that females were more democratic, or participative, in style than males were. What do you think accounts for this difference?

According to Eagly and Johnson, the difference in leadership style might exist because, as evidence suggests, women generally possess better interpersonal skills than men do. However, this cause-and-effect connection is only speculative. Much more research must be done before a definitive conclusion can be drawn about gender differences in leadership style and whether (and in what situations) those differences might be to a leader's advantage or disadvantage. It does appear that, in spite of the progress made regarding women in leadership roles, female leaders continue to face disadvantages in many settings. Although their behavior or style differs from that of male leaders in only a few minor aspects, women's leadership skills are still generally judged to be inferior to those of men.[12] Of course, we can only hope that this bias will change as gender stereotypes weaken and as more women gain leadership positions.

Learning Connections

1. Is leadership necessary for a group to succeed? Why or why not?
2. Describe the characteristics or behaviors of an effective leader?
3. Which leadership style makes the best leader?
4. Compare and contrast male and female leaders.

Conducting a Meeting

When a group meets for the first time, the members usually begin by introducing themselves and briefly telling their reasons for joining the group or what they hope to accomplish as members.

After introductions, and depending on the nature of the group and its assigned task, members may appoint or elect a recording secretary. This person keeps a written account of the meeting's discussions that may be consulted later if necessary.

To ensure efficiency, procedures must be established, and meetings must be conducted according to a well-organized plan. The best way to accomplish this is by producing an **agenda,** a list of all topics to be discussed during a meeting. The leader usually determines the agenda, either alone or in consultation with the group members before each meeting. Sometimes, at the end of one meeting, the agenda for the next meeting is established. A typical meeting agenda might look like this:

agenda
A list of all topics to be discussed during a meeting.

1. Call to order
2. Introduction of new members
3. Reading, correction, and approval of minutes from previous meeting
4. Unfinished business
5. New business
6. Announcements
7. Adjournment

Learning Connections

1. What suggestions do you have for planning or setting an agenda in order to ensure that a group's time is used efficiently?
2. What are the advantages and disadvantages of a meeting plan or agenda?

Not all meetings operate in exactly the same way, but having an agenda should make any meeting run smoothly. Classroom groups might not follow a formal structure, but in general, they need a sense of organization and an informal agenda.

Planning and Managing a Meeting

GUIDELINES

1. Identify a purpose, plan an agenda, and distribute the agenda in advance.
2. Invite only people who need to be there (*not* everyone who might have an opinion on the topic).
3. Establish start, break, and stop times, and stick to them.
4. Assign a moderator (leader) to keep the discussion on track.
5. Decide what follow-up actions are needed after the meeting, and set deadlines for their completion.
6. Avoid holding unnecessary meetings.
7. Don't let people drone on, dominate, or avoid participation during discussions.
8. Don't allow conversations to wander off the subject.
9. Follow up to make sure that members act on decisions made at the meeting.

From Harrison Conference Services, Business Schools at the University of Georgia and Georgia State University.

Member Participation

For a group to be successful, all of its members must be actively involved. Just like leaders, members of groups have certain responsibilities. The more members know about their leader's role and each other's roles, the better equipped they will be to perform. Furthermore, leaders change from time to time, so members should be ready to assume greater responsibility if doing so will benefit the group.

Roles of Group Members

Successful group outcomes depend on group members assuming various roles that are constructive and beneficial to the group's outcome. There are many roles that group members can play. Group scholars Kenneth Benne and Paul Sheats developed a comprehensive list of roles that group members can assume.[13] Benne and Sheats classified the roles into three categories: group task, group building and maintenance, and self-centered roles.

Group task roles help the group to accomplish its task or objective. They are behaviors that orient the group to the task, allow for the exchange of ideas and opinions, and motivate the group to complete the task.

Group building and maintenance roles help to define a group's social atmosphere. These roles include behaviors that function to maintain a positive interpersonal climate within the group. A person who tries to maintain a peaceful, harmonious climate by mediating disagreements and resolving conflicts performs a maintenance function.

Individuals may adopt self-centered roles, which are generally counterproductive or destructive to a group, that tend to hinder group progress. In most groups, members are eager to make constructive contributions. From time to time, however, you will encounter individuals whose attitudes are not so positive. For the good of the group, it is important to recognize such people and learn how to cope with them. See Table 16.2 for various roles of group members.

Contributions of Group Members

Recognizing and handling counterproductive contributions are the responsibilities not only of the leader but also of each group member. Sometimes the best approach to these situations is to discuss them openly: "John, you sure have been quiet about this problem. What do you think?" "Sally, your jokes seem to indicate that you don't believe the issue is very serious. Why?" Sometimes conflict needs to be resolved with a vote by the group. This lets members know the position of the majority so that discussion can continue.

Comments That Are Open to Evaluation. One of the greatest anxieties group members face is presenting their ideas for the group's evaluation. Group discussion can lead to the best possible information and the best possible decision, but this will happen only if members offer their comments for evaluation. Criticism should not be ignored or avoided. At the same time, members must remember that evaluations can be constructive only when they focus on the contribution and not on the person who originated it. It is one thing to find fault with specific data; it is quite another thing to find fault with the person who presented the data. Criticism should be based on what is said, not on who said it. To give effective criticism, members should describe and clarify their thoughts on the topic rather than simply finding fault.

Provocative Comments. Comments should be made not only to bring the group closer to its goal, but also to fuel thought for further contributions. This is worthwhile even if it makes for a somewhat longer meeting. If an idea has not been fully discussed and evaluated, appropriate decisions cannot be made. Asking questions (even ones that seem trivial), challenging assumptions, presenting bold new ideas (even if they seem unusual), and disagreeing can be valuable as long as they are focused on making the final group product the best one possible.

Group participants need to study the meeting's agenda in advance so that they will be prepared to contribute. Meaningful input often calls for research, so each participant should be willing to spend time and energy on advanced preparation. Probably one of the greatest weaknesses of

Learning Connections

1. If you could choose group members to help you solve a problem or make an important decision, what would you want them to be like?
2. Explain how you would approach group members who exhibited self-centered behaviors?
3. What advice would you give to someone who wants to be a team player in a group?

TABLE 16.2

Roles Group Members Can Play

GROUP TASK ROLES	BEHAVIORS
Initiator–contributor	Provides direction and guidance, proposes new ideas, suggests solutions, or approaches to the problem
Information seeker	Sees the need for more information, asks for clarification of ideas and relevance
Information giver	Provides information, including facts, examples, statistics, and other evidence
Opinion seeker	Asks about people's feelings and views related to the task
Opinion giver	Provides personal beliefs, opinions, or judgments about ideas being considered by the group
Elaborator	Extends information and clarifies viewpoints, ideas, and solutions
Coordinator	Clarifies and notes relationships among ideas, viewpoints, and suggestions
Orienter	Attempts to summarize what has occurred
Evaluator/critic	Makes an effort to evaluate the evidence and conclusions
Energizer	Tries to motivate to the group to take action
Recorder	Records the discussion for future reference
Tester of agreements	Determines how close the group is to reaching agreement
GROUP BUILDING AND MAINTENANCE ROLES	**BEHAVIORS**
Encourager	Offers praise by recognizing others' contributions
Harmonizer	Mediates disagreements, attempts to maintain positive interpersonal climate
Compromiser	Attempts to resolve conflicts by trying to find acceptable solutions to disagreements
Gatekeeper	Manages and directs the flow of communication
Standard setter	Articulates standards and goals that the group is to achieve
Follower	Goes along with the ideas and views of other group members
Feeling expresser	Highlights for the group its feelings, emotions, and attitudes
SELF-CENTERED ROLES	**BEHAVIORS**
Aggressor	Deflates the status of others to make themselves look better
Blocker	Resists, disagrees with, and opposes issues beyond reasonableness
Recognition seeker	Must be the center of attention, otherwise dissatisfied
Self-confessor	Contributes irrelevant information about self
Buffoon	Constantly jokes or engages in other kinds of horseplay
Dominator	Wants to be in charge of everything (autocrat)
Help seeker	Joins groups to satisfy personal needs
Withdrawer	Prefers not to participate at all

Adapted from K. D. Benne and P. Sheats, "Functional Roles of Group Members," *Journal of Social Issues* 4 (1948): 41–49.

Making Connections

The Buffoon

Jessica has always been fun to be around. She loves to kid and play practical jokes. The group has been fairly tolerant of her antics and at times has really had a good laugh, actually helping to reduce the group's stress level. But her recent behavior has really gotten out of control. In fact, her jokes are no longer appreciated, cause disruption, and show insensitivity to other members of the group.

No one has been willing to say anything to Jessica because they don't want to hurt her feelings. Besides, her other contributions have been excellent, and she has indispensable information regarding the problem the group is trying to solve. The situation is even more delicate because she is very sensitive and somewhat of a hothead. Members fear that if someone tells her to stop her unproductive behavior, she will leave the group.

You believe that Jessica doesn't think much of you as a leader. However, the group's morale has been steadily declining because of her, and if you don't say something to Jessica, other members might leave the group.

1. What should you do about this situation?
2. Are any ethical considerations involved in handling this problem?

beginning group participants is their tendency to arrive at meetings unprepared. The group must then either spend time helping them catch up or do without their contributions. Either way, valuable time, effort, and input are lost. Also, successful group outcomes depend on group-centered attitudes and behaviors, which enhance participation and member satisfaction; they include open-mindedness, a positive attitude, the ability to listen, a willingness to contribute, and preparation.

Problem Solving and Decision Making

Although the goal of some discussions, such as those in classrooms, is to share information, the goal of most discussions is to solve problems and make decisions: How can we raise more money for new computers? Who should be held responsible for date rape? What can be done to eliminate violence in our organization? How can we streamline production? How can we get the Hollywood media to reduce sex and violence in films and TV programs?

When solving problems and making decisions, groups must consider the alternatives and arrive at joint conclusions. To do this most effectively, they must take an organized and thorough approach to determine the exact nature of the problem and discuss its many aspects and potential solutions.

Determining the Problem

Groups are usually formed because a task needs to be accomplished. As groups are being formed, members already have an idea of their purposes and goals. In the classroom, groups are often formed to discuss particular topics in order to learn something. In communication classrooms, for example, small groups sometimes discuss subjects related to communication and sometimes simply allow students to learn about small-group communication by experiencing it.

Unless your instructor assigns a topic, the first step of your group effort is to select a problem or topic. This is not always easy; after all, the topic has to be both important and interesting to everyone in the group to ensure a good discussion. A starting place might be areas that need improvement on your campus: What should be the role of athletics on the campus? Should better protection be provided for students who attend evening classes? The surrounding community is also a source for discussion topics: What can be done about public parking in the downtown area? What can the business community do to help college students get better jobs?

State, regional, and national issues can provide a broader base for topics: Can the state provide sufficient funding to the university? What should be the role of the federal government in providing loans to students? Selecting from thousands of topics and problems takes time. However, if the group does its homework, picking a topic that is agreeable to all members should not be difficult.

After a topic or problem is selected, it should be stated in the form of a question. There are four types of discussion questions: questions of fact, interpretation, value, and policy. A question of fact asks whether something is true or false; its answer can be verified: What is the current cost of tuition? How many students are enrolled in each of the various colleges on campus? A **question of interpretation** asks for the meaning or explanation of something: How does the economy of the state affect tuition? How can athletics contribute to a better education? A question of value asks whether something is good or bad, desirable or undesirable: Which college offers the best education for its students? Do coeducational dormitories provide satisfactory living conditions? A question of policy asks what actions should be taken: What restrictions should be placed on alcohol consumption on campus? What role should students have in evaluating instruction on campus?

Questions of fact leave little room for discussion. The answer can usually be found through research, and unless there are discrepancies in the data, no discussion is required. In contrast, questions of interpretation, value, and policy are not easily answered and thus make for good discussions. When phrasing discussion questions, whether for a classroom learning experience or another context, keep the following guidelines in mind:

1. The wording should reflect the discussion purpose or task at hand.
2. The wording should focus attention on the real problem.
3. The wording should specify whose behavior is subject to change.
4. The wording should not suggest possible solutions.
5. The wording should avoid emotional language.[14]

Discussing the Problem

In group situations, whether in the classroom or another context, it is important to determine a plan for carrying out the task or assignment. The agenda for discussing a problem, for example, usually includes the following five specific steps developed by the philosopher John Dewey: definition of the problem, analysis of the problem, suggestions of possible solutions, selection of the best solution, and putting the best solution into operation.[15] The steps developed by Dewey are referred to as "reflective thinking" steps because they provide a logical, rational, way of structuring group interaction. Here is an outline of a typical problem-solving discussion:

question of interpretation
A question that asks for the meaning or explanation of something.

I. Definition of the problem
   A. *Symptoms.* How does the problem show itself, or what are the difficulties?
   B. *Size.* How large is the problem? Is it increasing or decreasing? What results can be expected if the problem is not solved?
   C. *Goal.* What general state of affairs is desired (in contrast to the present unsatisfactory one)?

II. Analysis of the problem
   A. *Causes of the problem.* What causes or conditions underlie the difficulties?
   B. *Present efforts to solve the problem.* What is being done now to deal with the problem? In what ways are these efforts unsuccessful? What hints do they provide for further attacks on the problem?
   C. *Requirements of a solution*
      1. *Direction.* Where shall we attack the problem?
         a. Would an attack on some outstanding symptom be the most fruitful approach?
         b. Is there a cause that would be worthwhile to attack? It would need these two essential characteristics:
            (1) Would its removal substantially eliminate or greatly modify the problem?
            (2) Could its removal be accomplished with facilities—personnel, equipment, finances—that are (or can be made) available?
      2. *Boundaries.* What other values—social customs, laws, institutions—must not be harmed in attempting to solve this problem?

III. Suggestions of possible solutions
   A. *One possible solution*
      1. *Nature.* What, specifically, is the plan?
      2. *Strengths.* In what ways would this plan effectively fulfill the requirements or criteria of a solution, that is, make notable progress in the direction and stay satisfactorily within the boundaries of a solution?
      3. *Weaknesses.* In what ways would this plan fall short of effectively fulfilling these requirements or criteria?
   B. *Another possible solution*
   C. *Another possible solution*
   D. *Another possible solution*

IV. Selection of the best solution
   A. *Best solution (or solution with modifications).* How is this solution better than the others?
   B. *Part of problem unsolved.* If the solution leaves any part unsolved, why is it still considered the best?

V. Putting the best solution into operation
   A. *Major difficulties to be faced*
   B. *Possible ways of overcoming difficulties*
   C. *Best way to overcome difficulties*

Applying Reflective Thinking to Problem Solving and Decision Making

In solving problems and making decisions, it is always wise to incorporate a reflective thinking process that follows a plan such as the one suggested by John Dewey. The Dewey reflective thinking steps should be used as a guide to decision making, not an exact formula in approaching every problem that needs to be solved. Randy Hirokawa, a communication scholar, concluded that a systematic approach to group problem solving and decision making is better than no organized approach at all.[16] We also believe that organization and direction are important in group problem-solving interaction, but inflexible, lock-step organizations can stifle or reduce a group's ability to arrive at the best solutions.

Applying Reflective Thinking to Problem Solving

GUIDELINES

1. *Clearly identify the problem you are trying to solve.* The discussion of a topic can be a good exercise, but if the discussion is not focused clearly or goals are not clearly defined as suggested earlier in the chapter, the discussion might wander without direction. For example, a group that decides to discuss the quality of public education but does not define what its purpose is for discussing the topic will likely not come to any conclusion. The group should focus on a clearly identified issue or problem, such as "How can public education be improved with limited resources?"
2. *Phrase the problem as a question to help guide the discussion.* Stating the problem or issue in the form of a question helps the group focus and direct the discussion more easily. See the list of suggestions on page 451 for the best way to phrase a question.
3. *Do not start suggesting solutions until you have fully analyzed the problem.* Most group scholars generally agree that problems should be thoroughly researched to arrive at the best solutions. This will help you avoid thinking of solutions prematurely or before you have a complete understanding of the causes, effects, and symptoms of the problem under discussion.
4. *In the definition and analysis steps of reflective thinking, do not confuse the causes of the problem with its symptoms.* Perspiration is a symptom that a person is warm or nervous. The cause for the perspiration, however, might be a stressful situation such as having to give a speech, not dressing appropriately for weather conditions, or any number of other reasons. The key to successful problem solving is reflective thinking that examines the symptoms in search of the causes.
5. *Appoint at least one member of the group to remind others to follow the reflective thinking steps.* Although the reflective thinking steps were designed sequentially and should be followed as such, it is not unusual for groups to deviate from the order. Thus it is a good idea to assign some members to monitor the procedures to ensure that the group does not deviate too far from its structure.

From S. A. Beebe and J. T. Masterson, *Communicating in Small Groups,* 7th ed. (Boston: Allyn & Bacon, 2003), 231–232.

Roger Firestein, a small-group scholar, recommends that all members, whether leaders or participants, should help to keep the group on track and periodically ask the following questions:[17]

1. Do we have sufficient evidence to support our solution?
2. Have we examined a reasonable number of alternatives?
3. Did we reexamine discarded solutions to ensure they should be discarded?

4. Have we come to closure too quickly?
5. Were we open-minded in our thinking?

Brainstorming

Sometimes groups find themselves unable to generate new ideas or to be creative in solving a particular aspect of a problem. In such cases, they may find brainstorming (also discussed in Chapter 7) helpful. Brainstorming, a technique used to generate as many ideas as possible within a limited amount of time, can be used during any phase of the group discussion process to produce topics, information, or solutions to problems. During the brainstorming session, group members suggest as many ideas as possible pertaining to the topic, no matter how far-fetched they might seem. One person records the ideas for later analysis. The leader lets the comments flow freely and may prompt the group by suggesting extensions of ideas that have been generated.

GUIDELINES Productive Brainstorming

1. Don't criticize any idea, either verbally or nonverbally.
2. No idea is too wild—encourage creativity.
3. Quantity is important—the more ideas, the better.
4. Seize opportunities to improve on or to add to ideas suggested by others.
5. Record all ideas generated by the group.
6. At the end of a specified time, evaluate ideas and determine which is the best.
7. Don't set too short a time limit.
8. Make brainstorming part of the group's strategy.

From A. Osborn, *Applied Imagination: Principles and Procedures of Creative Thinking* (New York: Scribner, 1953), 300–301.

The leader of a brainstorming group should create an open atmosphere that encourages creativity and spontaneity. Therefore it is important that the leader be a person of high energy who responds enthusiastically to new ideas. The leader should provide reinforcement and support to all members and encourage the members to keep contributing if they hit a dry spell. For example, the leader can use prompts such as these: "Let's generate at least two more ideas." "We've done great up to now—let's try one more time to generate some really far-out ideas."

Group members, as well as the leader, must not express disapproval (communicated by comments or looks) of any items until all ideas have been generated. Once the group has run out of ideas or time, the results should be evaluated. During this stage, members should work together to appraise each and every idea. The goal is to determine which idea or ideas merit more attention. It is appropriate to discard ideas that are unfeasible or weak, to improve undeveloped ideas, to consolidate related ideas, and to discuss further the most promising ones.

Brainstorming via Technology

In Chapter 15, we discussed ways newsgroups allow groups of individuals to communicate with each other over the Internet to share and obtain information on a variety

Making Connections

Stormin' with the Brain

To begin this activity, the instructor should divide the class into groups of four to six students each. Each group should select one of the following four topics:

Ways to increase diversity on campus

Incorporating technology into the classroom

Ideas to reduce alcohol consumption by students

An exciting, interesting spring break destination

Before the group discusses the agreed-on topic, each individual group member should create a list of ideas. Then the group as a whole should spend approximately ten minutes generating a list of ideas on the same topic. Make sure the group adheres to the accompanying guidelines for productive brainstorming.

1. After the group has finished the brainstorming session, discuss the value of brainstorming.
2. What did you learn about brainstorming?

of subjects. Similarly, groups can use electronic brainstorming, in which a group generates ideas, solutions, or strategies and inputs their thoughts onto the computer, displaying them either via a liquid crystal display (LCD) projector on a large screen to the entire group or to individual computer screens in a lab, in separate rooms, or at another location. This high-tech approach uses the same principles that face-to-face brainstorming uses except all the ideas are input on a computer instead of being written on a chalkboard or notepad. Advantages of this method include the speed of recording and the ability for group members to send their ideas simultaneously.

Another advantage according to the research is that electronic brainstorming generates more ideas than traditional brainstorming approaches.[18] It has been speculated that the increase in ideas and contributions by group members is because of the anonymity of the person who is generating the idea.[19] Group members feel less pressure and less embarrassment about ideas that are later rejected. The ideas that are generated are considered not on the basis of who suggested them but solely on their merit and quality. Like traditional brainstorming, electronic brainstorming encourages group interaction by allowing individual group members to build on the ideas of others.

Reaching Group Consensus

The goal of most groups is to arrive at decisions or solutions that are agreed on and acceptable to at least most of the group members, if not all them. The process of reaching consensus assumes that all group members have been able to express how they feel and think about the alternatives and have been given equitable opportunities to influence the outcome. However, it is important that consensus should not come too quickly; if it does, the group is likely a victim of groupthink. Consensus on controversial issues usually does not come easily. It requires a certain amount of patience and a willingness to look for areas of agreement. This, of course, can be very time consuming.

Learning Connections

1. What would be your strategy or plan for guiding a group in solving a problem? In making a decision?
2. What does it mean to obtain group consensus?
3. Explain what you might do to overcome obstacles in obtaining group consensus.

Is the time it takes to reach consensus worth the effort? It has been proven time after time that groups that use effective group discussion methods, such as open communication, come prepared to discuss, are willing to challenge ideas and evidence, and almost always arrive at better-quality decisions than individuals alone.[20] It has also been shown that groups that reach agreement regardless of the time it takes are more likely to take ownership of their decisions and maintain their agreement longer.[21]

Communication scholars Steven Beebe and John Masterson provide three recommendations for reaching consensus in groups:

1. Groups have a tendency to change topics and to get off track, so members should try to keep themselves oriented toward the group's goal. The reason groups often don't reach consensus is because they engage in discussing issues that are irrelevant to their goal.
2. Members should be other-oriented and sensitive to all ideas. Listen and do not constantly interrupt one another. Make a good faith effort to set aside your views and seek to understand others.
3. Promote group member interaction and dialogue. It is important that everyone feel that his or her voice is heard and that no one is withholding their views even when they disagree with others.[22]

Managing Group Conflict

When you hear the word *conflict,* what comes to mind? For most people, it conjures up terms such as *argument, dislike, fight, stress, hate, competition, disagreement, hostility, discord, friction, disunity,* and so on. All of these words do relate to conflict. However, they illustrate only the negative side of the concept. After all, in U.S. society, most people value and stress the importance of agreement and getting along with others. However, our society also loves competition. Sayings such as "All's fair in love and war" or "Stick to your guns" are often cited as the American way. We as a people are competitors, and we love to win. But the desires to get along with others yet to beat them in competition as well contradict each other. The idea that if one person wins, another must lose is implanted in almost every American's mind early in life.

On the one hand, we would like to avoid conflict and preserve unity. On the other hand, we cannot experience the thrill of winning unless we enter into conflict. Is there any middle ground between these two polarities? Can conflict be resolved only by forcing someone to lose? Must conflict always hurt someone?

Whenever people come together to communicate, there is bound to be conflict. But conflict does not always have to be harmful. In fact, it can be productive and, if properly managed, can result in better decisions and solutions to problems.

Conflict and Group Communication

Communication scholars William Wilmot and Joyce Hocker suggest that communication and conflict are related in the following ways: Communication behavior often *creates* conflict, communication behavior *reflects* conflict, and communication is the

Making Connections

Jerk or Hero?

Hector is always challenging Reynaldo's and Venita's ideas. He always seems to be disagreeing and asking for more explanation and evidence from Reynaldo and Venita to support what they are saying. It seems that they argue and bicker a lot whenever they are together. Reynaldo is fed up with Hector's attitude and wants to tell Hector to get off his case. Venita, on the other hand, appreciates Hector's way of challenging their ideas, because she recognizes that the best ideas can stand up to criticism.

This is Reynaldo's perception: "Hector is a jerk. What makes him think he can do any better!"

This is Venita's perception: "Hector is difficult but makes me think of ways to improve my ideas. I really appreciate his pushing me to come up with the best ideas."

You have just been asked to join Hector, Reynaldo, and Venita to make a difficult decision that will significantly affect the local economy.

1. What approach should Hector take when he wishes to challenge others' ideas? How will you influence him to use this approach?
2. Will Hector be a benefit or a liability to the group's discussions and decisions? Explain your response.
3. Explain why conflict might sometimes be a good thing in group communication.

vehicle for the productive or destructive management of conflict.[23] *Conflict* was defined by Wilmot and Hocker in Chapter 14 as "an expressed struggle between at least two interdependent parties who perceive incompatible goals, scarce resources, and interference from others in achieving their goals."[24]

Effective group decision making and problem solving often depend on conflict and open disagreement. Of course, too much conflict can create unmanageable tension and heighten disagreement, resulting in personal attacks on individual group members. If personal attacks come to dominate meetings, they produce no benefits and usually lead to hurt feelings, withdrawal, and eventually the disbanding of the group.

The benefits of group conflict, when it is understood and controlled, include a better understanding of group members and issues, better involvement and increased motivation, better decisions, and greater group cohesiveness. These benefits are more likely to occur when groups accept collaboration and compromise.

In collaboration, negotiating and problem solving are used to find a solution that fully meets the needs of all parties involved in a group conflict. In other words, each party achieves its desired results. For example, suppose you are serving on a college curriculum committee in which the student members think that the general education course should be practical, whereas the faculty believes it should be theoretical. There is much discussion, but both sides eventually see the benefits of each view and agree that all the general education courses should include both practice and theory. The result is an ideal solution in which both students and faculty members win. The collaboration between the students and faculty generated by the conflict has resulted in a superior, integrated general education curriculum.

Compromise is a shared outcome. Compromise means that conflicting parties are willing to give up part of their position to arrive at an alternative that includes parts of both parties' original positions. Compromise implies giving up something to gain something more important, so both parties involved gain from the compromise. For

Know Your Scholar

Randy Y. Hirokawa *University of Iowa*

Randy Y. Hirokawa is a Professor and Chair of Communication Studies at the University of Iowa. Dr. Hirokawa's research is related to decision-making groups, which he says are functional necessities in our democratic society. He is the co-editor of two scholarly books and is the author of numerous research articles related to small-group communication. He believes that whenever we face important decisions, we almost automatically turn to groups for help. But he also believes that groups are not magic bullets; groups can make dreadfully bad decisions as easily as they can make wonderfully good ones. Much of the work he has done related to good and bad decisions by groups has contributed to the development and testing of a theoretical framework called the functional perspective. This framework accounts for group decision-making performances in terms of the communication that occurs among group members as they attempt to reach a group decision. He is continuously working on refining and improving this theoretical perspective.

Other work that he has been doing in recent years has focused more narrowly on the relationship between communication and human errors, especially as it pertains to health care decisions.

example, a grading appeals committee made up of two students and four faculty members has been presented with an appeal. A student believes that he should have received an A, and the professor of the course insists that the student got what he earned—a C. After hearing both sides, one student and two faculty members on the committee believe that the student appealing should have received an A, whereas the other student and the other two faculty members believe that the C was appropriate. A deadlock must be resolved. Through compromise, the conflicting parties agree that the student should receive a B. Neither party got exactly what it wanted, but both can agree to the compromise. The positive outcomes of conflict, according to John Brilhart and Gloria Galanes, are as follows:

1. Conflict can produce better understanding of both issues and people.
2. Conflict can increase member motivation.
3. Conflict can produce better decisions.
4. Conflict can produce greater cohesiveness among group members.[25]

Managing Conflict

principled negotiation A procedure that helps group members negotiate consensus by collaboration through the expression of each differing need and a search for alternatives to meet those needs.

For groups to be successful, conflict must be perceived as beneficial. It should not be avoided. In fact, we suggest that it be encouraged as long as it is created in order to produce better group decisions. Avoiding conflict, according to Brilhart and Galanes, "circumvents the very reason for engaging in group discussion."[26]

One of the primary reasons for having small groups in the first place is the notion that two heads are better than one. We also know that when people get together to discuss issues, there is bound to be conflict. If conflict is inevitable and we know that it can be beneficial as well as harmful, how can we ensure that it will facilitate rather than inhibit? The answer is the use of conflict management strategies.

Principled negotiation is a procedure that helps group members negotiate consensus by collaboration through the expression of each differing need and a search for alternatives to meet those needs.[27] It is referred to as "principled" because the procedure is based on ethical principles that encourage participants to be respectful and civilized toward one another. In other words, exchanging information by asking questions instead of making demands or taking a rigid position on differences will aid in producing an agreed-on outcome. Participants must take into account other participants' views and consider them in the way they'd like their own views to be considered. Of course, not every disagreement can be resolved, and at times other approaches might have to be taken. To resolve conflict, participants must be willing to communicate about their differences and must want to find a resolution to their differences.

A legislative committee confers on a bill in a conference setting. To gain agreement on a bill, members who are not in agreement negotiate for consensus by identifying different needs and searching for alternatives to meet those needs.

Ethical Behavior and Conflict

Brilhart and Galanes suggest that using ethical behaviors during a conflict situation creates a better understanding of the issues and increased cohesiveness while at the same time minimizing destructive outcomes, such as hurt feelings and personal attacks.[28] They have listed a number of helpful suggestions to aid individuals on how to behave ethically during conflicts:

1. Express disagreements openly and honestly. It is important to get disagreements on the table for discussion.
2. Stick to the issues. Be direct, and get to the point.
3. Use rhetorical sensitivity when presenting your disagreements. Don't simply put down others' ideas or views.
4. Criticize the idea and not the person.
5. Base disagreements on solid evidence and good reasoning, not on rumor, emotions, or unsubstantiated information.
6. Be receptive to disagreements. Don't become defensive simply because someone disagrees with you. Keep an open mind and listen carefully.
7. Always remain calm even if someone attacks you. Take a reasoned approach, and do not take the attack personally.
8. Look for ways to integrate ideas and to negotiate differences whenever possible.

Learning Connections

1. What are the benefits of conflict in a group?
2. How should conflicts be resolved?
3. What does negotiate mean to you?
4. Which of the eight suggestions for behaving ethically is the most beneficial in preventing conflicts in the first place? Explain.

Evaluating Small-Group Performance

It is important that groups and group members understand that they are responsible for their successes and their failures. It is the responsibility of the group to fix its own problems or at least attempt to fix them. Of course, when a group cannot resolve a problem or if there is a split in the group, sometimes an outside negotiator is necessary, but that should occur only after all other efforts have failed.

To ensure success, every group must periodically evaluate its effectiveness. The evaluation can take place at any time or at the end of one task and before another begins.

Evaluation is also important in classroom exercises. As students learn about group communication, they need their instructor's feedback and also to evaluate themselves. Such self-evaluation should consider the following questions:

1. Are we using our time efficiently? If not, why not?
2. Does everyone have an opportunity to participate?
3. Are some people dominating the discussion?
4. Are people listening to what others are saying?
5. Is each person bringing adequate information and research to the discussion?
6. Is the atmosphere free from personal conflict?
7. Does the group communication stay within the agenda?
8. Are the members happy about what is taking place in the discussion? If not, why not?
9. Do we set realistic goals for our meetings?
10. Do we get things accomplished? If not, why not?

For an evaluation to produce results, its findings must be made known to all members of the group. A crucial requirement for such sharing is a nonthreatening atmosphere. The leader and all the members must be willing to examine the situation without becoming defensive. The group's success is related to each member's willingness to work and cooperate with the others. If the group is not getting its job done, or if its members are unhappy, corrective steps must be taken. Otherwise, people will lose interest in the group, and it may disintegrate or become unproductive and dysfunctional.

Summary

Leadership is the process of influencing behavior that clarifies a group's purpose or guides a group to achieve its goals. A person who is assigned or selected or who emerges from a group to guide or provide direction toward reaching a group's goal is a leader. Leaders are responsible for getting the group to accomplish its task and to ensure that group members find personal satisfaction in working together.

Successful groups depend on group members performing a variety of roles, for example, group task roles such as initiator–contributor, information seeker, information giver, opinion seeker, opinion giver, elaborator, coordinator, orienter, evaluator/critic, energizer, recorder, and tester of agreements. Group building and maintenance roles help to develop a group's social atmosphere and include encouragers, harmonizers, compromisers, gatekeepers, standard setters, followers, and feeling expressers. Sometimes, group members display self-centered roles such as aggressors, blockers, recognition seekers, self-confessors, buffoons, dominators, help seekers, and withdrawers, all of which can be counterproductive and destructive behaviors.

The process of planning and conducting meetings is an important step in reaching a successful outcome for any group. Most groups should use an agenda or list of topics to be discussed to ensure order and to save time. The first step in the process of decision making is to determine the problem or topic, which then should be stated in one of four types of questions: question of fact, question of interpretation, question of value, or question of policy.

When a group hits a snag or becomes bogged down, it might try brainstorming, which is a technique that if used correctly can help the group to generate new ideas and produce creative approaches that they might not ordinarily produce. Groups can create conflicts, as is true any time two or more people come together. However, groups that are competently trained know how to use principled negotiation, a procedure that helps group members negotiate consensus by collaboration in order to look for alternatives to meet differing needs. To ensure continuous success and progress, groups should do a periodic self-analysis and look for areas in which to improve.

DISCUSSION STARTERS

1. Describe a competent leader.
2. Who make better leaders: men or women? Explain.
3. Describe a competent group member.
4. How would you handle a group member who was acting the role of a buffoon?
5. How would you get withdrawn group members back into a discussion without embarrassing them?
6. Set up your organizational strategy for solving the following problem: What should be the role and responsibility of the university in monitoring cultural discrimination?
7. Describe a situation in which use of brainstorming would be appropriate.
8. Determine the criteria that you think would effectively evaluate a group's behavior.

NOTES

1. C. Larson and M. LaFasto, *Teamwork: What Must Go Right, What Can Go Wrong* (Newbury Park, Calif.: Sage, 1989).
2. F. E. Fiedler, *A Theory of Leadership Effectiveness* (New York: McGraw-Hill, 1967); and P. Weissenberg and M. H. Kavanagh, "The Independence of Initiating Structure and Consideration: A Review of the Evidence," *Personnel Psychology* 25 (1972): 119–30.
3. R. K. White and R. Lippitt, *Autocracy and Democracy: An Experimental Inquiry* (New York: Harper & Row, 1960), 26–27.
4. L. G. Bolman and T. E. Deal, *Reframing Organizations: Artistry, Choice, and Leadership,* 2nd ed. (San Francisco: Jossey-Bass, 1997); and G. Morgan, *Images of Organization,* 2nd ed. (Thousand Oaks, Calif.: Sage, 1997).
5. R. K. White and R. Lippitt, "Leader Behavior and Member Reaction in Three 'Social Climates,' " in *Group Dynamics: Research and Theory,* 2nd ed., eds. Dorwin Cartwright and Alvin Zander (New York: Harper & Row, 1960), 527–53; L. P. Bradford and R. Lippitt, "Building a Democratic Work Group," *Personnel* 22 (1945): 142–52; and W. M. Fox, "Group Reaction to Two Types of Conference Leadership," *Human Relations* 10 (1957): 279–89.
6. D. Butler and F. L. Geis, "Nonverbal Affect Response to Male and Female Leaders: Implications for Leadership Evaluations," *Journal of Personal Relationships* 58 (1990): 48–59.
7. Ibid.
8. R. L. Kent and S. E. Moss, "Effects of Sex and Gender Role on Leader Emergence," *Academy of Management Journal* 37 (1994), 1335–46.
9. L. A. Rudman and S. E. Kilianski, "Implicit and Explicit Attitudes toward Female Authority," *Personality and Social Psychology Bulletin* 26 (2000): 1315–29.
10. M. Loden, *Feminine Leadership or How to Succeed in Business Without Being One of the Boys* (New York: Times Books, 1985).

11. A. H. Eagly and B. T. Johnson, "Gender and Leadership Style: A Meta-Analysis," *Psychological Bulletin* 108 (1990): 233–56.
12. D. Forsyth, M. Heiney, and S. Wright, "Biases in Appraisal of Women Leaders," *Group Dynamics: Theory, Research, and Practices* 1 (1997): 98–103; S. Shackelford, W. Wood, and S. Worchel, "Behavioral Styles and the Influence of Women in Mixed-Sex Groups," *Social Psychology* 59 (1996): 284–93; and A. Eagly, S. Karau, M. Makhijani, "Gender and the Effectiveness of Leaders: A Meta-Analysis," *Journal of Personality and Social Psychology* 117 (1995): 125–45.
13. K. D. Benne and P. Sheats, "Functional Roles of Group Members," *Journal of Social Issues* 4 (1948): 41–49.
14. R. V. Harnack, T. B. Fest, and B. S. Jones, *Group Discussion: Theory and Technique,* 2nd ed. (Englewood Cliffs, N.J.: Prentice-Hall, 1997), 153–54.
15. J. Dewey, *How We Think* (Lexington, Mass.: Heath, 1933).
16. R. Y. Hirokawa, "Consensus Group Decision-Making, Quality of Decision and Group Satisfaction: An Attempt to Sort 'Fact' from 'Fiction,' " *Central States Speech Journal* 33 (1982): 407–15; and "Why Informed Groups Make Faulty Decisions: An Investigation of Possible Interaction-Based Explanation," *Small Group Behavior* 18 (1987): 3–29.
17. R. L. Firestein, "Effects of Creative Problem-Solving Training on Communication Behavior in Small Groups," *Small Group Research* 21 (November, 1990): 507–21.
18. M. C. Roy, S. Gauvin, and M. Limayem, "Electronic Group Brainstorming: The Role of Feedback on Productivity," *Small Group Research* 27 (1996): 215–47.
19. J. J. Sosik, B. J. Avolio, and S. S. Kahai, "Inspiring Group Creativity: Comparing Anonymous and Identified Electronic Brainstorming," *Small Group Research* 29 (1998) 3–31; and W. H. Cooper, R. B. Gallupe, S. Pollard, and J. Cadsby, "Some Liberating Effects of Anonymous Electronic Brainstorming," *Small Group Research* 29 (1998): 147–77.
20. R. Y. Hirokawa, 407–15.
21. R. S. DeStephen and R. Y. Hirokawa, "Small Group Consensus: Stability of Group Support of the Decision, Task Process, and Group Relationships," *Small Group Behavior* 19 (1988): 227–39.
22. S. A. Beebe and J. T. Masterson, *Communicating in Small Groups,* 7th ed. (Boston: Allyn and Bacon, 2003), 281.
23. W. Wilmot and J. Hocker, *Interpersonal Conflict,* 6th ed. (New York: McGraw-Hill, 2001), 41.
24. Ibid., p. 43.
25. J. K. Brilhart, G. J. Galanes, and K. Adams, *Effective Group Communication Theory and Practice,* 10th ed. (New York: McGraw-Hill, 2001), 308–10.
26. Ibid., 315.
27. R. Fisher and W. Ury, *Getting to Yes: Negotiating Agreement without Giving In* (Boston: Houghton Mifflin, 1981).
28. J. K. Brilhart and G. J. Galanes, 318–20.

"You never get a second chance to make a first impression."[1]

Appendix

Employment Interviewing: Preparing for Your Future

THIS APPENDIX WILL HELP YOU:

- Know what you should be doing to prepare before the employment interview.
- Use the Internet to locate jobs, send your résumé, research organizations, provide yourself with interview advice, locate job openings, and get a job.
- Describe the qualities that you possess that employers seek in applicants.
- Develop a résumé that will highlight or illustrate your competencies and experiences for prospective employers.
- Interview effectively and competently to ensure that you convey to potential employers your talents and skills and why they should hire you.

CASE STUDY

Rachelle, a mother of two children, started college before having children, but she and her husband decided that she should put her college education on hold in order to raise their children. The children are now in junior and senior high school, and Rachelle has gone back to college and is about to complete her degree in communication studies. Because she doesn't know about all the job opportunities that are available for communication majors, she turns to the Internet for help.

Bill, who is graduating in May, is looking for a public relations position with a major corporation. He has called Mr. Muller, the personnel director of S & S Enterprises, to discuss his chances of being hired by that firm.

Liz is looking for an internship in marketing in order to get some experience before she begins the real job hunt. She has contacted several different marketing firms through her university internship office and is ready to be interviewed.

Sam needs to earn a few dollars in order to make it through college. He decides to get a part-time job and is scheduled to interview with a local clothing store.

Questions to think about

1. Which of the individuals above comes closest to representing you and your employment future?
2. When should you start preparing for your career? Now? In your junior year? In your senior year?
3. What is the value in doing an internship?

The students in the above examples will participate in interviews that will affect the rest of their lives. It is never too early to prepare for your future, whether you are a first-year student or a senior who is about to graduate. The important part of preparing for your future is getting started, and those who start thinking and preparing for their future early will likely be the best prepared. In this appendix, we examine what you need to do to prepare for the employment interview—what you can expect to encounter and how you can make the best impression in the interview.[1]

Preparing for Your Career

The purpose of this book is to help you with the following skills: speaking, organizing, critical thinking, researching, persuading, informing, listening, discussing, making decisions, solving problems, and using nonverbal and verbal communication. Another purpose is to help you develop your leadership and interpersonal skills. After you have completed this course, it will then be up to you to continue developing each skill throughout your education and your lifetime. Because employment interviews are among the most important interpersonal communication events of your life, we have devoted this appendix to them.

Most of you taking this course are probably just beginning your college education. Whether you are a recent high school graduate or have returned to school after pursuing other interests like Rachelle, the following pages on employment interviews will give you important information that will aid you in preparing for your future after graduation. Although graduation and hunting for a full-time job may seem far away, your preparation for them should begin now. You can begin by attending your university or community's career day programs. Such programs bring together undergraduates, graduate students, and alumni with employers from government, private enterprise, and nonprofit organizations. It is a time for everyone—even first-year students—to find out what organizations are looking for in potential employees. If you haven't already started to prepare for your career or first interview, you should begin now. Don't wait until your senior year; that could be too late.

Making Connections

Thinking about Your Future

Refer back to the opening case study, and think about what each person must be able to demonstrate in order to land a job. SKILLS! That one word means a lot to your future. The recurring theme among the experts we surveyed is an emphasis on skills and competencies, rather than on completing specific studies.

Your major alone might not make a decisive difference in your future, but the skills you master and the way you communicate them to others can carry you through a lifetime of careers.

1. What is the message in the statements?
2. What advice would you give to Rachelle, Bill, Liz, and Sam as they prepare themselves for their interviews?

J. Meyers, "The Ideal Job Candidate," *Collegiate Employment Institute Letter,* 15 July 1989, 6; and *Ford's Insider: Continuing Series of College Newspaper Supplements* (Knoxville, Tenn.: 13–30 Ford Corporation, 1980), 14.

Career Research on the Internet

One of the most valuable tools available in preparing for the employment interview is the Internet. The Internet will allow you to research every aspect of the employment interview. For example, you can learn how to prepare for the interview, write a résumé, create an electronic résumé, research organizations, find job opportunities, find out what questions are commonly asked in interviews, and even get advice on what to wear to an interview. Most colleges and universities have a career and placement center that you can visit in person or contact through their home page. The career or placement center's home page can be an extremely valuable source of information. The University of Nebraska's (UNL) Career Services, for example, has one of the most up-to-date home pages on the Internet (see Figure A.1). Its Internet address is www.unl.edu/careers, and it provides information pertaining to almost every aspect of careers and the employment interview. You can click any of the boxed items to explore services and resources. For example, the Job Search Preparation area leads to information on how to search for a job on the Internet, job search strategies, résumé tips and a sample résumé, how to write cover letters and sample cover letters, whom to give as references, how to create a portfolio, information

FIGURE A.1

The University of Nebraska's Career Services Web Page

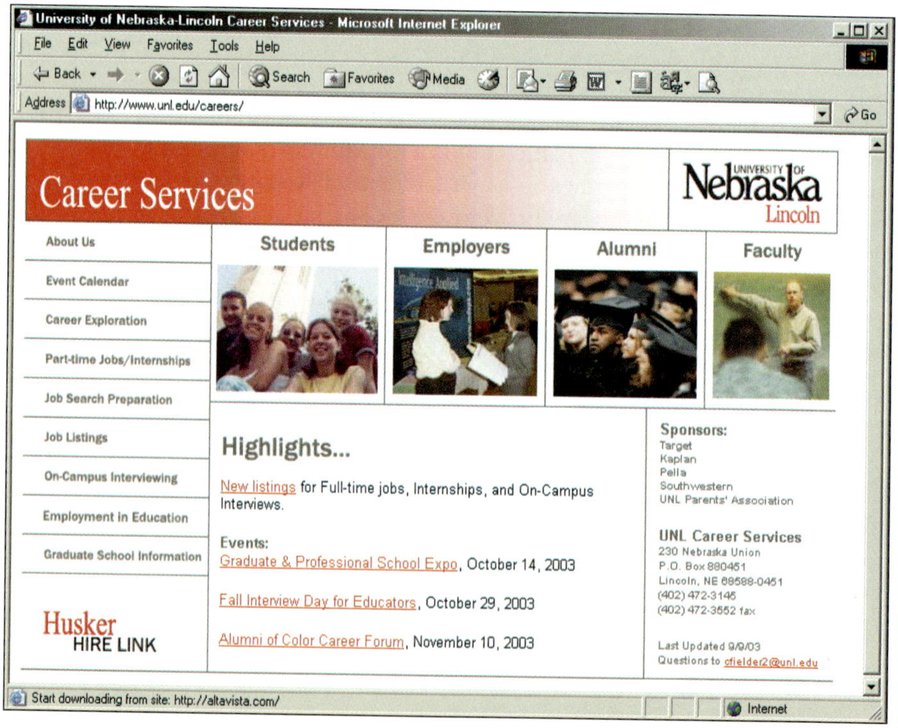

Reprinted by permission. www.unl.edu/careers.

on organizations, and interviewing tips. The Internet is an incredibly valuable tool in preparing for your future career.

You should check with your college or university's career and placement center for its Internet address. You can also access a search engine and type in the word *jobs, career,* or *employment.* With the click of a mouse, you will find a vast array of information about employers, job opportunities, and almost anything else you want to know about getting a job or starting your career.

Choosing a Career

Choosing a career might be the most important decision you will ever make. An estimated 10,000 days of your life are at stake; that's about how much time the average person spends on the job. According to some experts, there are a minimum of 42,000 career options from which college graduates can choose. Every October, *U.S. News & World Report* describes "Best Jobs for the Future." This is a must-see resource for every college student.

Studying the following pages will not guarantee you the perfect job after graduation, but it should help improve your chances of getting it. There are approximately 150 million employment interviews conducted in the United States each year resulting in hundreds of thousands of jobs filled. To compete successfully for available jobs requires planning and preparation. Getting an early start will allow you to take advantage of all the opportunities your college and university provides in the way of extracurricular activities, which will help you develop a strong, diverse background for meeting your career objectives.

Qualities Employers Seek

Demographics of the U.S. workplace are changing more rapidly than ever as we move into the twenty-first century. Cultural diversity is more prevalent for most organizations because we have become a global economy. Women now make up more than 50 percent of the workforce, and there has been rapid growth in the Hispanic and Asian American populations as well. Today, the workforce in many organizations consists of women and men of diverse cultures, languages, and ethnic backgrounds.

During the past few decades, many organizations eliminated millions of middle-management positions. Thus advancement positions in many organizations are limited and difficult to get. In the past, college graduates who started on the ground level of an organization were almost guaranteed that working hard would move them up the organizational ladder to higher management positions. Now the higher management jobs are fewer, and those that are available are very competitive.

Charles Stewart and William Cash, Jr., communication scholars and authors of a top-selling interviewing text, suggest ten universal skills and attitudes that are essential to work in the twenty-first century:

1. You will need to be able to deal comfortably with numbers.
2. You will need to be computer literate.

3. You will need to be customer- and quality-oriented.
4. You will need to have a global and diverse perspective.
5. You will need to speak a second language.
6. You will need strong interpersonal skills.
7. You will need to deal with change and job ambiguity.
8. You will need to nourish a willingness to learn.
9. You will need to take on a team perspective.
10. You will need to be a problem solver.[2]

Dr. Larry Routh (email address: lrouth1@unl.edu), Director of Career Services at the University of Nebraska at Lincoln, suggests that students get as much experience in team building and working in teams as possible.[3] According to Routh, companies are no longer looking exclusively for people with supervisory skills as much as they are looking for individuals who can work with others. One company recruiter asks students the following question: "When you work as a part of a team, what unique role do you play?" Routh said, "Hiring people who are team players is important to many companies who have downsized and have fewer management positions, because they are much more team oriented." For example, one senior student answered the question by indicating that she was the person who brought the group back to task by clarifying and pulling the group ideas to the objective. Dr. Routh suggested that his own strength when working on a team was the ability to brainstorm ideas. Routh's strength is quite different from the senior student's, but both are important to team success. What is your role when working with others? Is it leading, organizing, brainstorming, or something else? You need to know what your strengths are.

Internships are also important. Dr. Routh suggests that students should get involved in internships that are related to the jobs they will seek after graduation. He says that students who can say that they have done the job or similar work will have a better chance at getting a job than those with no experience.

Almost every career requires skills such as writing, speaking, reading, listening, decision making, researching, reasoning, creativity, persuasion, leadership, interpersonal communication, and organization. In addition, a number of characteristics may be important for specific jobs: achievement, aggressiveness, ambition, dependability, discipline, honesty, initiative, motivation, people orientation, persistence, responsibility, self-confidence, sensitivity, sincerity, tenacity, and tough-mindedness.[4] The way you acquire these skills and behaviors is, to a great extent, up to you. Without them, no matter how bright and knowledgeable you might be, landing a job will be extremely difficult if not impossible. The most likely way to obtain these skills and behaviors is through courses, reading, internships, part-time or full-time employment, extracurricular activities, and participation in communication functions. Acquiring most of them requires training and practice under a qualified instructor.

Knowing what an employer is looking for in a potential employee can help an applicant to prepare for an interview. Most employers that we have talked with emphasize the ability to communicate. Can the applicants speak clearly? Can they articulate what kind of person they believe themselves to be? In what kinds of work situations do they perform well? What are their strengths and weaknesses? Employers want to know about the personal qualities of the individual, so they ask questions to draw the applicant out and reveal whether the applicant has a sense of self. They look for an ability to verbalize an idea in clear, simple, understandable language.

They also look for the ability to listen attentively and then the ability to respond to an idea or thought.

They also look for creativity. Is the applicant spontaneous? Some recruiters will ask "off the wall" questions just to see if this "throws" an applicant. How does an applicant respond in these tough situations? Can the applicant be creative with the answers? This is very important to most employers, because in business situations with customers, employees often have to respond to sudden changes and unfamiliar problems. Employers need to know whether an applicant can handle such situations.

What employers look for most are personal qualities: assertiveness, self-motivation, drive, ambition, and a competitive instinct. Applicants should be high achievers and want to work hard. Employers say that they can usually tell about these qualities by how people present themselves and by reviewing the activities in which the applicant has been engaged. Much of this information can be found right on the job application and résumé.

Learning Connections

1. A friend tells you that she doesn't know what career field to go into after graduation. What advice would you give her?
2. If you were to hire someone to work for you, what qualities and skills would you want that person to have?
3. What do you think is the most important quality or characteristic that every employee should possess, regardless of career field?

Preparation for an Interview

Preparation for a job interview takes planning and some thought about what will be expected of you as an applicant. Initial job interviews average only twenty to thirty minutes in length—a short time in comparison to the time you have spent earning a college degree. Yet these are probably the most important minutes you will spend in determining your job future. You would be surprised to learn how many applicants fail to plan adequately. Instead, they enter the interview saying essentially, "Here I am. Now what?" This gives the impression that they are indifferent, an impression that is seldom dispelled in the course of the interview. Ensuring that an impression of indifference isn't left with the employer is up to you. Make sure that you are prepared and that you present a positive picture of yourself.

Writing a Résumé

A **résumé** (sometimes referred to as a vita) is a written document that briefly and accurately describes an individual's personal, educational, and professional qualifications and experiences. A well-written résumé increases a person's chances of making a good impression. A poorly written résumé can seriously jeopardize a person's chances, even though he or she may be well qualified. The résumé should clearly detail the experiences the applicant has had and demonstrate that he or she is an individual who takes action. For example, an assertive person might say, "I can do these things" and "I decided on this course of action," whereas a more passive person might say, "These are the experiences I have had." Employers are looking for people who can demonstrate that they are active and that they can get things done.

résumé A written document that briefly and accurately describes an individual's personal, educational, and professional qualifications and experiences.

Many companies are now requesting that résumés be written so they can be scanned into a computer database. This means that résumés must include key words that describe your competencies and skills. The employer is then able quickly and efficiently to search thousands of résumés for certain key words that describe and

Making Connections

What Every College Student Should Know to Prepare for the Job Interview

To learn firsthand what corporations are looking for today when they hire a college graduate, Seiler interviewed Gary Danek, who recently retired as an account executive with Procter & Gamble (P&G), a Fortune 500 corporation (www.pg.com). Before retiring, Danek had been with P&G for more than thirty-five years and had interviewed hundreds of college students. The Seiler and Danek interview is available on our website at www.ablongman.com/seiler6e.

1. On the basis of what you have read in the interview transcript, what could you do to make yourself a better candidate for a job?
2. If you were to give one piece of advice to someone based on the Danek interview, what would that advice be?
3. If you could ask Mr. Danek a question about what you could do to better prepare yourself for the job interview, what would that question be? Email your question to Bill Seiler (bseiler@unl.edu), and he will forward it to Mr. Danek for his response. Your question will be answered as soon as possible.

narrow down a long list of potentially qualified applicants for a specific job. So that a résumé can be scanned, it must be typed neatly on high-quality white bond paper. You cannot use boldface type, underlining, or bullets if a résumé is to be scanned.

GUIDELINES Emailing Your Résumé to the Employer

1. Always send your résumé to a specific person. Determining whom to send your résumé to might require some research, but the effort of locating a specific individual is well worth it, because you will more likely get a response than if you address it to the company's personnel office or human resources department.
2. Your email memo should introduce yourself and explain what you are seeking and why. The email memo is similar to the typical cover letter that is sent via the post office. It should be brief, usually three or four paragraphs, and never more than one page. It should also be neat, contain no spelling or grammatical errors, be professional in appearance, and be easy to read. Many excellent guides for writing effective cover letters can be found on the Internet. Go to the following websites for help and samples: www.unl.edu/careers/prepare/letters.htm, http://resume.monster.com/archives/coverletter, or do an Internet search using the key words "cover letters." You will find many very helpful sites to guide you in writing an effective cover letter.
3. Attach your résumé to your email document rather than including it after your introductory memo. For a document to be attached to an email message, it must be formatted correctly so that the person receiving the email can open it. If you are uncertain of the best format to use in sending your résumé, send an initial email requesting this information from the employer.

4. If you do not hear back from the person to whom you sent your résumé within a few days, follow with an email message asking whether your message was received.
5. Thank the person for his or her time.

The personal résumé may highlight work experience (see Figure A.2) or skills (see Figure A.3). Many companies also require applicants to complete an application form, which requests personal data (name, address, phone number, social security number, citizenship, and whether you have ever been convicted of a felony), job interests (position desired, data available, and salary desired), educational training (high school, college, or graduate school), references (name, occupation, phone number, and address), employment history (name, address, dates of employment, salary, positions held, and reason for leaving), and possibly voluntary information (sex, race, or ethnic identification; military service record, if you are a veteran or disabled veteran; whether you have a disability).

A résumé is an extremely powerful form of communication. Because it represents an applicant, it must be accurate, complete, and neat. The contents and layouts of résumés vary as widely as the number of individuals who apply for jobs. A general rule, and the safest, is to *keep it simple, limit it to one or two pages, and list items within each section beginning with the most current one.* Employers are busy and do not have time to read lengthy, involved reports.

Most résumés include the following sections: introductory information, career objective, educational training, work experiences, extracurricular activities, and references, which is an optional section. The *introductory information* section should include the applicant's name, address, phone number, and email address. As an applicant, you are not required to provide information that might be used in a discriminatory way. This includes your age, sex, marital status, race, religion, and other data as set forth by the Title VII Equal Employment Opportunity Act of 1972 and other affirmative action laws. The inclusion of such facts in a résumé is up to the applicant, but it is generally advised that they be omitted.

Many employment counselors recommend that a brief *career objective* be stated on the résumé immediately following the introductory information. The objective should be as specific as possible. For example:

> My long-term objective is to become a public relations director in either a major corporation or agency. My immediate goal is to obtain experience in sales, advertising, or marketing related to that long-term objective.

Such a statement can help a potential employer understand the applicant's goals and assess whether those goals relate to a particular job opening or company.

In the *educational training* section of the résumé, the applicant should list colleges and universities attended, degrees conferred, dates of degrees, majors, minors, and special major subjects. Scholarships should be listed, and some statement about grade achievement may be included, although it is not required.

The *work experience* section should include paid and unpaid jobs held, the dates they were held, and their locations. If the applicant has held numerous part-time jobs, only a few of the most important, most recent, and most relevant jobs should be listed. Other job experience can always be discussed at the interview if it is appropriate to do so.

FIGURE A.2

Self-Prepared or Personal Résumé Emphasizing Work Experience This figure illustrates a résumé format that many students use. The résumé layout is fairly standard, but it may vary depending on the work experiences of the individual.

Jo Ann Doe
712 Garfield Street, Apt.2-A
Lincoln, Nebraska 00000
402/555-9797
jdoe@yahoo.com

OBJECTIVE

An administrative assistant position in a federal, state, or city government agency where I can utilize my public relations skills.

EXPERIENCE

Assistant Campaign Manager: Senator Sally Jones, Lincoln, Nebraska (July 1999–November 2000).

Directed and coordinated all public activities.
Arranged and scheduled personal appearances, debates, and media releases.
Purchased, designed, and supervised the development of campaign materials.
Recruited, trained, and supervised community volunteer groups.
Supervised a staff of 16 community volunteers.

Staff Assistant as an Intern: United Volunteer Agency, Lincoln, Nebraska (December 1997–June 1999).

Communicated the scope of Agency programs to Lincoln area businesses and community groups.
Prepared Agency filmstrips, brochures, and news releases.
Conducted public relations information sessions.

Legislative Assistant: Nebraska Legislative Session, Lincoln, Nebraska (June 1996–December 1997).

Collected, compiled, and released information briefs and legislative action profiles to public news media.
Typed and edited legislative bills.

EDUCATION

The University of Nebraska, Lincoln, Nebraska (1997–2001)
Bachelor of Arts Degree. Communication Studies and Journalism.
Grade Point Average: 3.75/4.00.

EDUCATIONAL HIGHLIGHTS

Outstanding Senior Award, Creative Writing Award, Communication Club Secretary, Phi Delta Kappa Vice President.

Related Course Work

Public Relations and Publicity	Survey of Mass Media
Social Political Communication	Interviewing
Public Speaking	Advertising Principles
Federal Grant Development	Public Opinion

Available: Immediately

References: Upon request (This is optional and may or may not be included.)

FIGURE A.3

Self-Prepared or Personal Résumé Emphasizing Skills This figure illustrates a résumé that emphasizes a person's skills. The résumé layout is fairly standard, but it may vary depending on the work experiences and skills of the individual.

Robert L. Smith
1525 East Center Street
Los Angeles, California 00000
213/555-9797
rsmith@hotmail.com

OBJECTIVE	To help a retail company provide high customer satisfaction while managing merchandise efficiently in an entry-level management position.
SKILLS	• Resolved customer problems in retail merchandising • Organized product floor for customer convenience • Successfully dealt with wholesalers • Organized and maintained inventories • Completed college courses in management, personnel, finance, statistics, and marketing
EDUCATION	University of Southern California, Los Angeles, California, Bachelor of Science Degree: Business, May 2000, Management
HONORS	Academic Scholarships, Delta Mu Delta (Business Honorary)
ACTIVITIES and MEMBERSHIPS	President of Delta Mu Delta; Student Senator; Youth Leader of 30 member church youth group.
EXPERIENCE February 98–present	B. C. PRINTING, Los Angeles *Graphic Arts–Delivery Person* • Mastered all aspects of prepress operations • Effectively dealt with and resolved conflicts • Oversaw various camera procedures including working with numerous types of film and preparing press plates
January 97–98	QUALITY PRESS, INC., Los Angeles *Internship Graphic Arts–Delivery Person* • Demonstrated ability to serve and communicate with customers in a diverse office supply operation • Organized and maintained product floor and inventory
Additional Information	Paid 100% of college expenses Worked to support wife and child while attending college Computer training includes Basic, Cobol, Assembler, and Pascal
Available	Immediately
References	Available on request (optional)

In the *extracurricular activities* section, the applicant should list all offices held, all social and professional organizations that he or she was involved in, and any athletic participation. This section demonstrates the applicant's outside interests;

Making Connections

Find Résumé Guidelines on the Internet

The following Internet sites can provide helpful suggestions for preparing a résumé.

www.unl.edu/careers/prepare/resume.htm
Tips and guidelines are provided by the University of Nebraska's Career Services.

www.rileyguide.com/letters.html
The Riley Guide: Resumes and Cover Letters is an extremely helpful guide that discusses the myths about résumés, tells why an Internet résumé is useful, helps you prepare your résumé for the Internet, gives suggestions about posting your résumé, and provides resources for résumé writing.

www.provenresumes.com
This site provides sixty free résumé and job search workshops; it also includes a quiz to rate your résumé.

There are many more Internet sites to help you with your résumé development; all you have to do is search the Internet.

well-roundedness; and social, leadership, and organizational skills. Such information is less important for experienced or older applicants who have demonstrated similar skills in other areas.

The *reference* section is optional and should simply state that the applicant will provide references on request. In preparation, you might make a list of people who are familiar with your work experience and professors in your major field or with whom you have taken several courses. Even though you might not be planning to apply for a job now, it is wise to get to know your professors and to make sure that they get to know you. Find appropriate times (office hours, perhaps) and reasons (discussion of a paper or an assignment) to visit with your professors so they become acquainted with you. Most professors enjoy meeting their students. Use common sense, and don't overstay your visits. Professors will find it easier to write a letter of recommendation for you if they know who you are, and the letter will be more personal and believable.

Never put a person's name on a reference list unless you have his or her permission to do so. When asking individuals to write references for you, be prepared to hand them a copy of your résumé and to tell them what kind of job you are seeking. Contacting people to write letters of recommendation should be done as professionally and efficiently as possible. Remember that you are requesting someone

Making Connections

References

Make a written list of at least three people who could write a letter of recommendation for you. Do not include relatives or friends. After each name on your list, answer the following questions:

1. Why is this person an appropriate reference for me?
2. What does this person know about me, my competencies, and my ability to succeed?

Share your completed list of references and information with your teacher, a career counselor, or a person who could advise you as to the appropriateness of your choices.

to take time to help you. Because most people enjoy helping others, you should never be afraid to ask for a reference.

After you write your résumé, proofread it carefully for errors and omissions. Then ask a counselor in the career and placement office or a professor to suggest improvements. If you follow these simple steps, your completed résumé should be acceptable.

Searching the Job Market

Getting a job requires motivation, energy, hard work, and preparation. Even an applicant with superb qualifications faces tremendous competition for the best positions. According to placement service records, the average applicant spends only about three to ten hours a week searching for employment, but the person who is highly motivated will treat the search as if it were a job itself. The more time a person spends searching, the sooner and more likely he or she will be hired.

Newspaper want ads, professional magazines, placement services, former teachers, and people working in jobs you are interested in can all be good sources of job leads. However, the most productive approach to locating jobs is networking. **Networking** is the systematic contacting of people who can provide information about available jobs or who can offer jobs. Relatives, friends, classmates, colleagues, and people at social and professional gatherings are all potential sources of information. If someone does not know of any job openings himself or herself, ask if he or she knows of anyone who might. Then contact that person. In this way, your network expands from one person to another, and you gain information from each new contact. The more people you know, the better your chances are of being interviewed and the greater your opportunity for employment.

Career fairs have become very popular in recent years as a means for college students and others to learn about jobs and about the companies who are offering them. Most college campuses or the communities in which colleges and universities are located hold career fairs. They are excellent for networking as well as for making contacts with organizations for internships. Contact your career services office at your college or university and ask when the next career fair will be in your area. You should attend as many career fairs as time permits and you should begin going to them as soon as possible. You don't have to wait until your senior year to attend a career fair. By making contact with a company early in your education, you can establish a relationship with that company as well as be in the best position for getting an internship or a job after graduation.

Researching the Company via the Internet

Before arriving for an interview, you should know the full name of the company; background information on the company's history; where its headquarters, plants, offices, or stores are located; what products or services it offers; and what its economic growth has been and how its future prospects look. Such knowledge demonstrates your initiative and interest to the interviewer and can serve as a springboard for discussion. This also shows you have an interest in the company, rather than giving the impression you're settling for whatever job you can find.

It used to be that if you wanted to learn anything about a company, you would have to write to the company for its annual report or for recruiting materials. You could also go to the library and look through publications and special directories for

networking
The systematic contacting of people who can provide information about available jobs or who can offer jobs.

information related to a given company. Today, however, the Internet is the best source of company information, and although you can still go to the library or a career services office and find information, it requires much more work than a few clicks of a mouse. For example, if you wanted to learn about Newell Rubbermaid, all you need to do is search the Internet for "Newell Rubbermaid" and you will find the following address: www.newellco.com. Click on the address and you will find almost anything you'll ever want to know about the company (see Figure A.4). The same search process should get you information on almost any company in the world.

Developing Questions to Ask the Interviewer

In preparation for your meeting, think about possible questions to ask the interviewer. Sometimes an interviewer might choose to say little or to stop talking altogether, in which case it becomes your responsibility to carry the conversation by asking questions and continuing to emphasize your qualifications for the job. Regardless of whether the interviewer stops talking, you should have a list of questions to ask. This does not mean coming to the interview with a written list of questions, but it does mean coming prepared to ask questions such as these: What are the duties and

FIGURE A.4

Newell Rubbermaid's Home Page on the World Wide Web

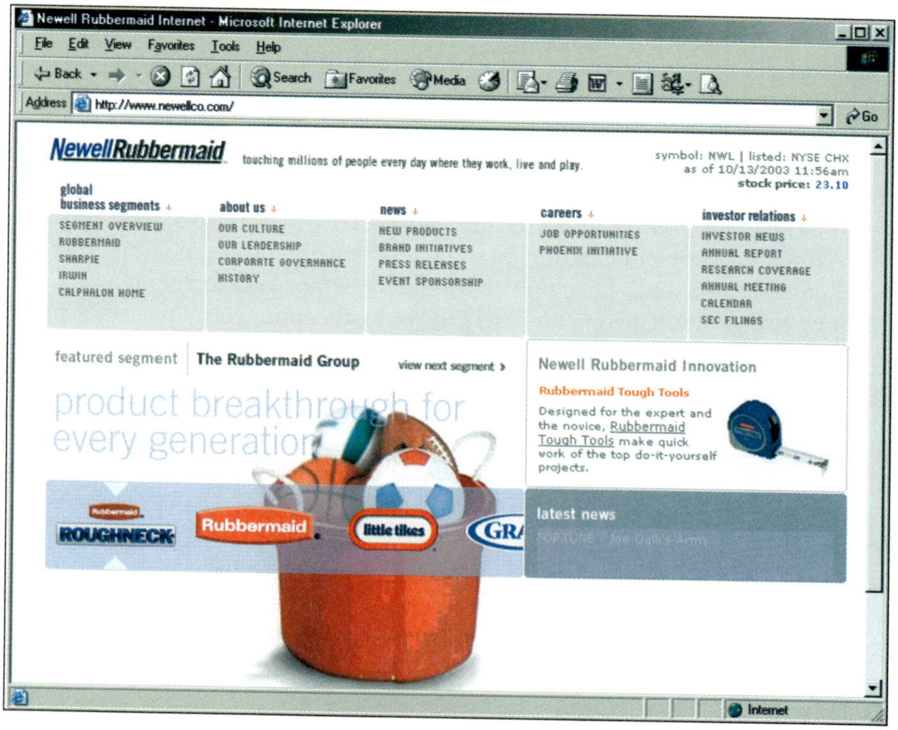

Making Connections

Learning about the Organization

Following are the names of several companies for you to research. For each one, there is a question or questions to which you should be able to find the answers to by doing a search on the Internet. Report your answers to the class if requested to do so.

1. Ford Motor Company—Approximately how many people work for the Ford Motor Company worldwide?
2. Level 3 Communications—Where is its main headquarters?
3. Oracle—When was the company started? Who is its present CEO?
4. Strong Investments Inc.—Approximately what is the amount of assets that Strong manages in billions of dollars? When was the company founded and where?

responsibilities of the job? Does the company provide training programs? How much traveling is involved in the job? What's the next step up from the starting position? Would I be able to continue my education?

How to Dress for an Interview

Your primary goal in dressing for an interview is to feel great about the way you look while projecting an image that matches the requirements of the job and the company. Go for perfection. Wear professionally pressed clothing in natural fabrics. Although casual clothing in many settings is acceptable today, it is still wise to be conservative in what you wear to an interview. This is especially true if you do not know the culture of the organization or business. The interview is usually not the time to make a personal statement of nonconformity or disagreement with society's concept of professional image.[5] There are many excellent websites that address the issue of what is appropriate to wear to a job interview. We suggest that you do a search using the key words "dress for job interview." You will find many sites that provide guidelines for what to wear.

Learning Connections

1. What do you think is the best way to find a job in a tight job market?
2. You are about to begin the interview process. What steps should you take to prepare?
3. You are off to your first interview. In what ways can you influence the perceptions of the interviewer so that you are seen in a favorable way?

The Interview

Much of the responsibility for a successful interview rests with the interviewer, but this doesn't mean that you can merely relax and let things happen. On the contrary, research suggests that most interviewers develop a strong opinion about a job applicant in the first thirty seconds. If you do poorly at the opening, your chances of getting the job are slim, no matter how brilliantly you handle the rest of the interview. It might seem unfair or superficial, but people do judge others on the basis of first impressions, and such impressions can be long-lasting. By all means, be on time for the interview.

GUIDELINES Telephone Interview: Some Tips

Today, it is likely that your preliminary interview will be over the phone. According to Carol Kleiman, many firms screen out candidates who do not demonstrate minimal levels of enthusiasm or communication skills. She cites David Stiefel, consultant with PeopleScout, a Chicago-based firm, who says that about 65 percent of all job candidates are screened out for those reasons. He goes on to suggest that you can successfully obtain an on-site interview on the phone by speaking in a clear, concise voice and by sounding enthusiastic about the job. Here are some specific tips for the phone interview from Connor Cunneen, president of Grow Foodservice Profit, a consulting firm, also cited by Kleiman:

1. Keep yourself motivated.
2. Stand up when taking the call. This will project confidence.
3. Put a mirror in front of you, and check your reflection. By looking positive, you will you sound positive.
4. Dress as if you were actually going to the interview in person.
5. Smile. This might seem like strange advice, but when you smile, you project a positive image that can often be detected even on the phone.[6]

Frequently Asked Questions

One expert states that most applicants make two devastating mistakes when they are being questioned. First, they fail to listen to the question and answer a question that was not asked or give superfluous information. Second, they attempt to answer questions with virtually no preparation. Lack of preparation will reduce the chances of success even for skillful communicators. You should always take a moment to think about your answer before you respond to each question unless it is something that you have already thought through. Here are some of the most common questions interviewers ask and some possible responses to them.

1. *"What can you tell me about yourself?"* This is not an invitation to give your life history. The interviewer is looking for clues about your character, qualifications, ambitions, and motivations. The following is a good example of a positive response. "In high school, I was involved in competitive sports, and I always tried to improve in each sport in which I participated. As a college student, I worked in a clothing store part time and found that I could sell things easily. The sale was important, but for me, it was even more important to make sure that the customer was satisfied. It wasn't long before customers came back to the store and specifically asked for me to help them. I'm very competitive, and it means a lot to me to be the best."

2. *"Why do you want to work for us?"* This is an obvious question, and if you have done research on the company, you should be able to give a good reason. Organize your reasons into several short sentences that clearly spell out your interest. "You are a leader in the field of electronics. Your company is a Fortune 500 company. Your management is very progressive."

3. *"Why should I hire you?"* Once again, you should not be long-winded, but you should provide a summary of your qualifications. Be positive, and show that you are

The employee interview is a key communication event for most people. The applicant should be prepared to discuss goals and skills and be able to clearly answer questions pertaining to why he or she is right for the job.

capable of doing the job. "Based on the internships that I have participated in and the related part-time experiences I have had, I can do the job."

4. *"How do you feel about your progress to date?"* Never apologize for what you have done. "I think I did well in school. In fact, in a number of courses I received the highest exam scores in the class." "As an intern for the X Company, I received some of the highest evaluations that had been given in years." "Considering that I played on the university's volleyball team and worked part time, I think you'll agree that I accomplished quite a bit during my four years in school."

5. *"What would you like to be doing five years from now?"* Know what you can realistically accomplish. You can find out by talking to others about what they accomplished in their first five years with a particular company. "I hope to be the best I can be at my job, and because many in this line of work are promoted to area manager, I am planning on that also."

6. *"What is your greatest weakness?"* You cannot avoid this question by saying that you do not have any; everyone has weaknesses. The best approach is to admit your weakness but show that you are working on it and have a plan to overcome it. If possible, cite a weakness that will work to the company's advantage. "I'm not very good at detail work, but I have been working on it, and I've improved dramatically over the past several years." "I'm such a perfectionist that I won't stop until a report is written just right."

7. *"What is your greatest strength?"* This is a real opportunity to "toot your own horn." Do not brag or get too egotistical, but let the employer know that you believe in yourself and that you know your strengths. "I believe that my strongest asset is my ability to stick to things to get them done. I feel a real sense of accomplishment when I finish a job and it turns out just as I'd planned. I've set some high goals for myself. For example, I want to graduate with highest distinction. And even though I had a slow start in my first year, I made up for it by doing an honor's thesis."

8. *"What goals have you set, and how did you meet them?"* This question examines your ability to plan ahead and meet your plan with specific actions. "Last year, during a magazine drive to raise money for our band trip, I set my goal at raising 20 percent more than I had the year before. I knew the drive was going to begin in September, so I started contacting people in August. I asked each of my customers from last year to give me the name of one or two new people who might also buy a magazine. I not only met my goal but I also was the top salesperson on the drive."

Interviews are now using more questions similar to this last question, based on the premise that the best predictor of future performance is past performance. This type of questioning is referred to as **behavioral-based interview questions,** which are questions that ask directly about a particular skill or trait (to which most interviewees would probably answer "yes"). The interviewer would then follow up by asking for an example of a situation in which the interviewee could demonstrate the skill or trait that would demonstrate and support the "yes" answer they gave to the initial question. For example, to determine whether a person had decision-making skills, an interviewer might ask, "Have you had to make many difficult decisions?" The interviewee would likely respond, "Yes." The follow-up question by the interviewer would attempt to solicit an example of a difficult decision the person had to make by saying something such as "Describe a situation in which you had to make a difficult decision under pressure or when there were time limitations." For more examples of behavioral-based interview questions, go to www.unl.edu/careers/prepare/behavioral.htm.

Here are a few other questions that are commonly asked in the employment interview:

What is your dream job?

What type of supervisors do you do your best work for?

What kind of legacy did you leave in college?

What are the differences between a leader and a manager?

What motivates you to get up in the morning?

Do you consider yourself to be a risk taker?

What was the last risk you took?

What five characteristics would make you a great salesperson?

If an interviewer were to ask you any of the eight most frequently asked questions, do you know how you would answer them? The key is to understand why a question is being asked. Remember, the purpose of the employment interview is to hire the best-qualified person for the job. The more often you can demonstrate through your responses to questions that you are the best qualified, the more likely you will be to get the job offer.

No matter what question you are asked, answer it honestly and succinctly. Most interviewers are looking for positive statements, well-expressed ideas, persuasiveness, and clear thinking under pressure.

behavioral based-interview questions
Questions that ask directly about a particular skill or trait.

If you are asked a question that violates the affirmative action laws, you can decline to answer. You might say, "I'm sorry, but I don't find that question relevant to the position being offered, and it is against affirmative action laws to ask it." You might simply ask the interviewer why he or she is asking you that question. Make sure that you are tactful, but be firm in letting the interviewer know that he or she is doing something illegal.

Other Considerations

As a job applicant, you are expected to show good judgment and common sense about appearance, assertiveness, being on time, and being at the right place. Always maintain eye contact with the interviewer. Show that you are confident by looking straight at the speaker. Eye contact might not get you the job, but lack of eye contact can reduce your chances dramatically.

Most interviewers greet the applicant with a handshake. Make sure that your clasp is firm. Being jittery about the interview can result in cold, clammy hands, which create a negative impression. Therefore try to make sure your hands are warm and dry. If this is not possible, a firm handshake will at least show confidence.

When the interviewer asks you to sit down, if you have a choice, take the chair beside the desk rather than the one in front. This helps to eliminate any barriers between you and the interviewer and also makes you a little more equal, for which the interviewer will unconsciously respect you.

Before leaving, try to find out exactly what action will follow the interview and when it will happen. Shake hands as you say goodbye, and thank the interviewer for spending time with you. If you plan ahead and follow these simple suggestions, you should be able to avoid any serious problems.

Making Connections

Knowing Your Strengths

Call to mind your experiences. If you can respond to the following with good-quality answers, you have a good understanding of who you are and what your strengths are:

1. Describe your greatest accomplishment.
2. Describe a situation in which you influenced a group to support an idea that was important to you.
3. Give an example of a time when you went above and beyond the call of duty to accomplish a task or goal.
4. Describe a situation in which you worked independently on a complex project and achieved good results.
5. Describe a situation in which you were confronted with and solved a difficult problem.
6. Describe a situation in which you took a leadership role in a group.
7. Write a statement that describes you.

Factors Leading to Rejection

Rejection is difficult for all of us to accept, but you should never give up. Being rejected by employers eight or nine times before receiving a job offer is not unusual in the present job market.[7]

Employers from numerous companies were asked, "What negative factors most often lead to the rejection of an applicant?" Here are their responses in order of frequency:

1. Negative personality or poor impression—more specifically, lack of motivation, ambition, maturity, aggressiveness, or enthusiasm
2. Inability to communicate; poor communication skills
3. Lack of competence; inadequate training
4. Low grades; poor grades in major field
5. Lack of specific goals

6. Unrealistic expectations
7. Lack of interest in type of work
8. Unwillingness to travel or relocate
9. Poor preparation for the interview
10. Lack of experience[8]

You must realize that rejection or not receiving a job offer has a lot to do with the number of people seeking jobs and the number of jobs available. You can of course enhance your chances of getting job offers by being prepared and presenting yourself in a positive and energetic way.

Factors Leading to Job Offers

An applicant who is well rounded and has good grades, some relevant work experience, a variety of extracurricular activities, an all-around pleasant personality, and effective written and oral communication skills is more likely to get job offers than are those who do not possess these qualities, according to Jason Meyers of *Collegiate Employment Institute Newsletter.*[9] Meyers says, "Sounds too good to be true? Perhaps it is, but a candidate who strives to attain these qualities and who comes across as a hard-working, mature individual should have a promising career outlook."[10]

A research study cited by Meyers in his article asked recruiters to describe what they believed to be the qualities of a well-rounded individual. They listed maturity, ability to be part of a team, good work ethic, good decision-making skills, superior work habits, and good judgment. Another study cited by Meyers found that the most popular characteristics that recruiters sought in job applicants fit two categories: (1) quantifiable characteristics, such as grade point average, education, and work experience, and (2) interpersonal characteristics, such as communication skills, personality, and career and management skills. The study suggests that a balance of the quantifiable characteristics and interpersonal characteristics is what makes an ideal job candidate.[11]

It seems that those who are well prepared; have effective communication skills; are mature, motivated, hard-working, team players; and can make good decisions will always be in demand. You must ask yourself how you match up to these qualities now and try to improve in those areas in which you are not as strong. You must also be able to demonstrate that you actually possess these qualities through the actions you have taken.

Learning Connections

1. Describe the behavior of someone who is likely to be successful in a job interview and the behavior of someone who is not.
2. What is the most important lesson you learned from this appendix on employment interviewing?

Summary

Choosing a career is one of the most important decisions a person can make, and a successful job interview is a crucial step in achieving that end. Planning and preparation are critical to a successful employment interview. The Internet is one the most valuable tools available in preparing for the employment interview. On the Internet, you can learn how to prepare for the interview, write a résumé, research an organization, find job opportunities, know what questions are most frequently asked, and even what to wear to the interview. Applicants must know their strengths and weaknesses and be able to communicate effectively with the interviewer. Getting a job requires motivation, energy, hard work, and research, plus knowing where to look and whom to contact to obtain the necessary information.

DISCUSSION STARTERS

1. How can the Internet help you prepare for an employment interview?
2. What can you do to increase your chances of getting the best job?
3. If you were an employer, what would you look for in a job applicant?
4. What advice would you give fellow students about writing résumés?
5. Why should personal data such as age, gender, marital status, and religion be omitted from a résumé?
6. How should you go about getting references? Who should you ask?
7. What advice would you give regarding the best methods of doing a job search?
8. What should you know about a company before you are interviewed?
9. Why is it important for an applicant to ask questions of the interviewer?
10. If you were to interview someone for a job with your company, what would be some of the questions that you would ask an applicant? Why?
11. What can someone do to reduce the chances of being rejected?

NOTES

1. K. B. Barbour, F. B. Berg, M. Eannace, J. Greene, M. Hessig, M. Papworth, C. Radin, E. Rezny, and J. Suarez, *The Quest: A Guide to the Job Interview* (Dubuque, Iowa: Kendall/Hunt, 1991), 47.
2. C. J. Stewart and W. B. Cash, Jr., *Interviewing Principles and Practices,* 10th ed. (New York: McGraw-Hill, 2003), 263–64.
3. Interview with Dr. Larry Routh, Director of Career Services (University of Nebraska, Lincoln, September 2000 and March 10, 2003).
4. Stewart and Cash, 181.
5. J. LaFevre, "How You Really Get Hired," *CPC Annual 1990/91,* 34th ed. (Bethlehem, Penn.: College Placement Council).
6. C. Kleiman, "Candidates Making Early Interviews Can Have Lasting Impact," *Lincoln Journal Star,* July 14, 2003, 4A.
7. Routh.
8. *The Endicott Report: Trends in the Employment of College and University Graduates in Business and Industry* (Evanston, Ill.: The Placement Center, Northwestern University, 1980), 8. In the March 2003 interview, Dr. Routh said that the rejection reasons companies give today are not different from what they were in 1980.
9. J. Meyers, "The Ideal Job Candidate," *Collegiate Employment Institute Newsletter,* 15 July, 1989, 6.
10. Ibid.
11. Ibid.

Index

Photo Credits

Page xxxiv, 2, Digital Vision; Page 10, Mike Yamashita/Woodfin Camp & Associates; Page 23, AP/Wide World Photos; Page 25, Dan Bosler/Getty Images; Page 28, 45, Jeff Greenberg/PhotoEdit; Page 31, Michael Smith/Getty Images; Page 39, Thomas Fletcher/Stock Boston; Page 54, 65, Michael Newman/PhotoEdit; Page 59, Kevin Schafer/Getty Images; Page 72, Cassy Cohen/PhotoEdit; Page 78, 102, Paula Bronstein/Getty Images; Page 82, AP/Wide World Photos; Page 90, David Young-Wolff/PhotoEdit; Page 96, Sue Cunningham; Page 108, 124, Lawrence Migdale/Photo Researchers, Inc.; Page 117, Chris Shinn/Getty Images; Page 120 (all), AP/Wide World Photos; Page 122 (left), Inc. G&J Images/Getty Images; Page 122 (middle), Werner Bokelberg/Getty Images; Page 122 (right), Ron Chapple/Getty Images; Page 126, V.C.L./Chris Ryan/Getty Images; Page 138, 146, Syracuse Newspapers/C. W. McKeen/The Image Works; Page 142, Walter Hodges/Getty Images; Page 149, Rachel Epstein/PhotoEdit; Page 157, Dennis MacDonald/PhotoEdit; Page 162, 180, Peter Hvizdak/The Image Works; Page 165, AP/Wide World Photos; Page 166, Barbara Stitzer/PhotoEdit; Page 174, Syracuse Newspapers/Al Campanie/The Image Works; Page 190, 196, Bill Aron/PhotoEdit; Page 193, Michael Newman/PhotoEdit; Page 204, Mike Segar/Reuters/Getty Images; Page 206, Bettmann/CORBIS; Page 214, 216, Richard Pasley/Stock Boston; Page 222, Stan Honda/AFP/CORBIS; Page 228, AP/Wide World Photos; Page 250, 256, Dion Ogust/The Image Works; Page 267, Michael Newman/PhotoEdit; Page 276, Bonnie Kamin/PhotoEdit; Page 286, 299, Alex Wong/Getty Images; Page 289, Chuck Fishman/Woodfin Camp & Associates; Page 295, Stephen Chernin/Getty Images; Page 307, Don Smetzer; Page 316, 327, AP/Wide World Photos; Page 319, Gail Zucker/Stock Boston; Page 335, Wyman Ira/CORBIS Sygma; Page 340, AP/Wide World Photos; Page 348, 352, Bob Daemmrich/Stock Boston; Page 357, David Hanson/Getty Images; Page 361, David Young-Wolff/PhotoEdit; Page 363, Bob Krist; Page 376, 385, Frank Siteman/Stock Boston; Page 382, Walt Disney/Shooting Star; Page 397, Bruce Ayres/Getty Images; Page 410, 413, David W. Hamilton/Getty Images; Page 420, Loren Santow/Getty Images; Page 425, David Young-Wolff/PhotoEdit; Page 436, 438, David Joel/Getty Images; Page 443, Bruce Ayres/Getty Images; Page 459, 479, Bob Daemmrich/Stock Boston.